MEMOIRS

Begun at Twickenham in 1802

LOUIS-PHILIPPE
MEMOIRS
1773-1793

*Translated and
with an Introduction by*
JOHN HARDMAN

*Foreword by
Henri, Comte de Paris*

New York and London
A HELEN AND KURT WOLFF BOOK
HARCOURT BRACE JOVANOVICH

Library of Congress Cataloging in Publication Data

Louis Philippe, King of the French, 1773–1850.
Memoirs.

Translation of Mémoires de Louis Philippe.
"A Helen and Kurt Wolff Book"
Includes index.
1. Louis Philippe, King of the French, 1773–1850.
2. France—Kings and rulers—Biography.
DC268.A3413   944.06'3'0924   [B]   76-44441
ISBN 0-15-158855-4

First edition

B C D E

Contents

Foreword   ix
   by Henri, Comte de Paris

Introduction   xxi
   by John Hardman

Genealogy of the House of France   xxxiv
   936–1850

MEMOIRS   1

Conclusion   419

Index   457

Map of the Battle of Valmy   282

Map of the Battle of Jemappes   335

Illustrations

Between pages 220 and 221

Louis-Philippe in his cradle, his father bent over him
Painting by Nicolas-Bernard Lépicié. Photo, Archives Nationales, Paris.

Louise-Marie-Adélaïde de Bourbon-Penthièvre, Duchesse d'Orléans, mother of Louis-Philippe
Portrait by Mme Vigée-Lebrun. Photo, Archives Nationales, Paris.

Philippe Égalité, his children, and Mme de Genlis
Drawing by F. Stone. Photo, Archives Nationales, Paris.

View of the house at the convent of Belle-Chasse, built by the Duc d'Orléans for the education of his daughters
Photo, Archives Nationales, Paris.

Portrait of Louis XVI by Duplessis (detail)
Musée Carnavalet, Paris. Photo, Bulloz.

Portrait of Marie-Antoinette by Roslin
Versailles. Photo, Bulloz.

Louis XVI inaugurating the first session of the Estates-General, Versailles, May 5, 1789
Photo, Bibliothèque Nationale, Paris.

Louis XVI driving to the Hôtel de Ville, July 17, 1789
Drawing by Prieur. Louvre. Photo, Giraudon.

The inner courtyard and galleries of the Palais Royal, Paris
Musée Carnavalet, Paris. Photo, Bulloz.

Storming of the Bastille and arrest of its governor, July 14, 1789
Engraving by Berthault. Photo, Archives Nationales, Paris.

"To Versailles, to Versailles," October 5, 1789
Contemporary watercolor. Photo, Bibliothèque Nationale, Paris.

Place de Grève, October 6, 1789. The heads of two Bodyguards triumphantly carried on pikes
Photo, Bibliothèque Nationale, Paris.

Louis XVI returning to Paris with his family, October 6, 1789
Drawing by Prieur. Louvre. Photo, Giraudon.

Champs de Mars, preparations for the Feast of the Federation, July 14, 1790
Musée Carnavalet, Paris. Photo, Giraudon.

Louis-Philippe, Duc de Chartres, in 1790
Versailles. Photo, Musées Nationaux–Paris.

Drawing of Louis-Philippe's father, Philippe Égalité, by Angelika Kauffmann
Photo, Bibliothèque Nationale.

Arrest of Louis XVI and his family at Varennes, June 22, 1791
Drawing by Prieur. Louvre. Photo, Giraudon.

Louis XVI accepting the Constitution at the National Assembly, September 14, 1791
Collection Liesville, Ville de Paris. Photo, Bulloz.

Session at the Jacobin Club, January 11, 1792
Photo, Bibliothèque Nationale, Paris.

Robespierre
Lithograph by Fisher. Musée Carnavalet, Paris. Photo, Bulloz.

Marat
Portrait by anonymous artist. Musée Carnavalet, Paris. Photo, Bulloz.

Council of War at Courtray, June 26, 1792. Left to right: Berthier, Lameth, Beurnonville, Biron, Luckner, Louis-Philippe (standing), Valence, Duhoux, d'Aboville, and Lynch
Painting by anonymous artist. Photo, Archives Nationales, Paris.

Proclamation of "La Patrie est en danger," July 22, 1792
Drawing by Prieur. Louvre. Photo, Giraudon.

The people of Paris entering the Tuileries, June 20, 1792
Drawing by Prieur. Louvre. Photo, Giraudon.

Siege and storming of the Tuileries, August 10, 1792
Drawing by Prieur. Louvre. Photo, Giraudon.

Louis-Philippe, Duc de Chartres, in officer's uniform, 1792
Engraving. Photo, Archives Nationales, Paris.

General Dumouriez
Bust by Houdon. Photo, Bulloz.

Danton
Drawing. Musée Carnavalet, Paris. Photo, Bulloz.

Louis the Last and his family on their way to prison in the Temple, August 13, 1792
Contemporary caricature. Bibliothèque Nationale, Paris. Photo, Bulloz.

The first meal of the royal family in the Temple prison
Rothschild Collection, Louvre. Photo, Bulloz.

The Battle of Valmy, September 20, 1792
Watercolor by Théodore Jung. Photo, Archives Nationales, Paris.

The Battle of Jemappes, November 6, 1792
Contemporary etching. Photo, Bibliothèque Nationale, Paris.

Louis XVI as defendant before the Convention, December 1792
Etching after Pelegrini. Photo, Giraudon.

Execution of Louis XVI
Musée Carnavalet, Paris. Photo, Bulloz.

Foreword

When I deposited my family archives in the Archives Nationales, I thought the time had come to publish the memoirs of Louis-Philippe. He began work on them as early as 1802, and they continued to occupy his attention throughout his life, being constantly and meticulously revised. The bicentenary of the birth of my ancestor provides an opportunity for this publication, which, representing, as it does, the author's wishes, cannot be longer deferred. These recollections relate to his childhood, his remarkable education by Mme de Genlis, his response to the succession of events from 1789 to the fall of the monarchy and the first months of the Republic, and also to the part he played in the first campaigns of the armies of the Revolution, from the victory of Valmy to the defeat of Neerwinden, when, as a divisional general of nineteen, a prince without a name, without support or hope, he was forced to expatriate himself to escape the warrant for his arrest issued by the Convention.

Louis-Philippe insists that he is not writing a historical work. His memoirs are, in fact, both more and less than that. They are the evidence of one who, though young, was endowed with rare liveliness of mind and soundness of judgment. He was better placed than anyone to observe and profoundly experience the acts of the tragedy that successively roused Frenchmen to enthusiasm and to horror as the institutions that had regulated the life of the nation for eight centuries collapsed with lightning speed. "The Revolution," Victor Hugo tells us in *Les Misérables,* "had made a very deep impression on him, his memory was like a living image of these great years, minute by minute." The point is that, buffeted as he was from his youth onward by the violence of revolutionary confrontations, fate presented him throughout his life with this dilemma: revolution or counterrevolution. He rejected both from the outset and, with all his powers of reason and of will, tried to avoid them by choosing a third path, that of political and social reform. By so doing he delivered himself up to the spite of the doctrinaire, the hatred of men of party, and the rage of assassins; for on this point our history, from Henri IV to Charles de Gaulle, has repeated itself with devastating logic. Nevertheless, I hope that these reflections of a man who, having suffered the full consequences of refusing to accept inevitable change, speaks from experience will be better heeded and understood in our time.

ix

It is difficult to discuss the French Revolution without treading on a lot of toes, without coming into conflict with opinions which, for all that they have been held for nearly two centuries, have not yet been moderated by the impartiality of History. However, there are so many lessons to be drawn from this crucial stage in the life of France that one ought not to shrink from further research and from presenting, in good faith, one's findings for contemporary readers who are greatly in need of remembering the fatal consequences of a declining society's being blind to its destiny. I consider that the Capetian monarchy's services to my country are so outstanding and so durable that I do not have to hide its faults, especially where these ran counter to its basic mission. I am convinced that the acts of the monarchy remain an example and that the errors it may have committed—under pressure from an aristocracy seduced from its duty by a false conception of honor—shed light on the temptations to which the ruling class today seems to be succumbing, with no motive but self-interest, in a struggle for survival.

The French monarchy was a legitimate authority, to which the rule of succession had been established early and in the simplest, most natural, and imprescriptible way possible. From generation to generation, Frenchmen united under it: it expressed their respect for the past, their desires for the present, and their hopes for the future. Whatever the government, legality alone cannot establish its legitimacy. That is determined equally by its good faith toward the nation and its ability to secure its independence and its unity.

In no other country was the feeling of independence more keenly felt than in France. The origins of the House of Capet are merged with the nation itself. The Most Christian King's desire to be independent from foreign powers took precedence over all other considerations, even religious. He was always able to resist the incursions of the spiritual power, and was sometimes prepared to risk his salvation by braving the threats of theologians wishing to force him to submit the country to imperial supremacy. . . .

The Capetian monarchy stemmed from the feudal fragmentation of the country; its history is a long journey toward the organization of the French nation and the achievement of its unity. To overcome the forces opposed to this tenacious purpose, the Capetian state enlisted and organized successive changes in society; constantly, it relied on new layers of society, enlisting them in turn in the public service. Why was this evolution, in progress for eight hundred years and operating in harmony with human imperatives, no longer able at the end of the eighteenth century to find the means to continue? Why was the Revolution—the product of this deficiency—not the occasion for the monarchy to rediscover itself and take the lead in that "great upsurge of 1789" which began with the cry of "Long live the King!," echoed for a long time by the cheers of the people and of the Assemblies?

It was these questions that Louis-Philippe wished to answer "conscientiously and with scrupulous regard to the truth." I think that the memoirs give a clear and precise account of the first four years of the Revolution, a reliable analysis that makes it possible to get a good grasp of the confused chain of events and to understand the changing and, for the most part, contradictory behavior of the main protagonists.

While a spirit of liberty and a desire for reform spread through the country during the century of the Enlightenment, the reign of Louis XVI was marked from its outset by a tendency toward reaction, which gained ground among the privileged classes. Prelates and parliamentarians attacked authority, resisted measures that made for a less unjust system of taxation, and forced the dismissal of ministers suspected of wanting to put finances on a sound footing. The resurgence of regional and economic particularism alike weakened the authority of the state, already diminished by financial difficulties which it seemed incapable of surmounting. With the arrival of an economic crisis involving unemployment and an increase in the cost of living, the people, reduced to misery, rose up. Then the King saw himself forced to summon the Estates-General.

The Estates-General were convoked, not to propose reforms and, still less, to effect them, but merely to try to put an end to the financial chaos. But already the Revolution had been accomplished in men's minds—so much so that in a few short weeks the three orders were able to denounce or recognize institutions and social structures as outdated; and the King, in turn, had to accept it. The monarchy had lost the initiative and was not to regain it. Thus each party was, in effect, to claim for itself legitimate power: the Court paid lip service to the doctrine but dictated its will to the King by forbidding him to announce a policy, to act, or to carry through his resolutions; the Third Estate, which had wanted "to become something," strove to be everything, though the end result was that it split up and destroyed itself; and the *émigrés,* through an extraordinary aberration, passed beyond the frontiers to create outside France a political and military organization paid for by foreigners but speaking in the name of the King, although they had abandoned him and refused to obey him. As Lamartine wrote in *Histoire des Girondins:* "The King was in the Tuileries, but the monarchy was not there: it was at Coblenz."

As for the people, for the most part all they wanted was a less unjust society and one where they enjoyed more consideration. Seeing themselves deceived by the Court's duplicity, threatened by the *émigrés'* loud talk, and, finally, attacked by foreign armies, they fell prey to fear. In the final analysis, it was fear that came between the French and their monarch. Fear it was that, in a few months, destroyed the mutual trust which had united them for eight centuries.

The King was a prince with astuteness and common sense, but there was a profound conflict between the nature of his education and the monarchical principles that had come down to him. He was a victim of the theological disputes of the preceding century. At the moment when the monarchy reached its apogee, what was, with some exaggeration, called "absolutism" was defined by Bossuet and enshrined in a dogma that no one subsequently could question without passing for an enemy of the monarchy. That is why, in his heart of hearts, Louis XVI was never reconciled to sharing the power that had devolved upon him, even though the morality of Fénelon and the lessons of *Télémaque* haunted his mind. This morality, whose counsel to princes was contained in the words gentleness, humility, a passive will, and repose of the soul in God, was bound to lead a man who would one day find himself confronted with difficult times to martyrdom. And these theories, which preached a return to an idealized form of feudalism, rejected the lessons of the country's greatest public servants, who had destroyed it; they could not but distort the judgment by offending against the past and by offering nothing to present difficulties but absurd solutions. Louis XVI was badly taught, badly served, and badly misunderstood. But this man, who was said to be weak, was able to work out for himself a scrupulous and, later, a heroic application of these moral principles, and his end was nothing short of the sublime and terrible culmination of an ascetic who was not designed to be a king. Thus every man bows before this death, which transcends political mutation, and questions himself anew.

The singular education received by the young Louis-Philippe—who bore at that time the title Duc de Chartres—did not predispose him to such contradictions. By nature a man of action, he was filled with enthusiasm by the first episodes in the Revolution. He joined the Jacobin Club "to learn the tactics of political assemblies and practice speaking in public" and he followed the debates in the National Assembly regularly. Permeated by the new ideas and aflame with patriotism, he nevertheless remained attached to tradition: it was in the army that he dedicated himself to the service of King and country.

The most striking demonstration of France's ambiguous situation in the years 1791 and 1792 is without doubt the state of her army. The old royal troops rubbed shoulders with the national volunteers enrolled after Varennes and again when the country was declared to be in danger. This did not fail to give rise to serious difficulties for a time: differences of outlook, pay, and uniform all helped to keep alive divisions between units. Moreover, the quality of the officers had greatly deteriorated because most of the original officers had abandoned their men to join the emigration.

The presence of Chartres in this imbroglio graphically illustrated the coexistence of royal and revolutionary France, for a moment merged. Here was this seventeen-and-a-half-year-old prince deciding, in June 1791, to take personal command at Vendôme of one of the two regiments he owned, the 14th Dragoons (which had ceased to be called the Chartres). Soon the young colonel found himself there in sole command, with a few officers taken from the ranks, all the rest having preferred to abandon their units rather than take the oath of allegiance to "the nation, the law and the king." Nevertheless, his men made no difficulty about accepting the eldest son of the First Prince of the Blood and were "always happy to have him at their head." Despite his youth, he succeeded admirably in a profession he had to pick up entirely by himself: he was made a *maréchal de camp* "in order of seniority," then gazetted a lieutenant general by the Executive Council, and he obtained commands with the armies on the frontiers as he demanded. His superiors had a high opinion of him and accepted the advice, even the remonstrances, of this greenhorn who was always wanting to advance. This naturally occasioned incidents, often comical, sometimes moving, from which Chartres always came out well, having the art of pleasing, unwavering assurance, and a ready tongue. He was at ease in this atmosphere where tradition and revolution still went hand in hand. He was there when the troops of the line and the volunteers rushed to the fray with one accord, the former shouting "Forever Navarre without fear!" and "Auvergne without blemish!" and the latter "Long live the nation!" For him, it was his "signal good fortune to have exercised a command at the Battle of Valmy," and at Jemappes to have shared the exhilaration of the soldiers, who, after the victory, "were in a manner drunk." As regards Neerwinden, he was proud to be able to say: "I had the consolation that in the sector of my command the battle was not lost." His example demonstrates all that would then still have been possible had the princes and the monarchy's staunchest supporters understood their duty as well and performed it with the same loyalty and courage.

Chartres had resolved to "restrict himself exclusively to carrying out his military duties"—a decision to which Danton's advice was to come as reinforcement. Thus, he held himself aloof from the political struggles and their sanguinary consequences, which horrified him. But with events proceeding speedily, he soon had to look to the situation of his father, who had recently been elected, in company with Robespierre, as a deputy to the Convention for Paris. He did all that was in his power to dissuade him and to prevent him from sitting in judgment on Louis XVI.

Louis-Philippe-Joseph, Duc d'Orléans, was a liberal prince who, in common with many others, admired English political institutions. His disagreement with the Court was public knowledge; he had even gone as far as publicly opposing the King's wishes by protesting against the registration, which he considered illegal, of an edict authorizing the floating cf a 420-million-franc loan to be raised in stages. He demanded equal taxation and the freedom of the individual. As a deputy for the nobility to the Estates-General, he was one of the forty-seven who joined the Third Estate. At this point his popularity was considerable; later he was made "the scapegoat for the Revolution," which he was accused of having financed. There are always people who believe that a government can be overthrown only by the ill will of a few, rather than on account of its own defects.

Louis-Philippe rebuts this accusation with a line of argument that has never been shaken: no proof was given, no serious historian has accepted this ridiculous story. "One can hire a riot, but not a revolution."

Chartres had a deep affection for his father. He speaks of him tenderly and honors his memory. How can one fail to be touched by this boy— so young but so sensible and able to adapt to new pressures, to judge men and affairs with discernment—striving single-handed to save his father from himself, from his friends, and from circumstances to which, in spite of everything, he was ill-suited, this *grand seigneur* from a happier age who too easily persuaded himself that the worst could never come to pass? Nevertheless, the day of the fatal vote arrived for the man whom the Commune of Paris saddled with the name "Égalité." Chartres does not attempt to justify his father's act that broke his heart.

Our age has known similar heartbreaks, so we are in a position to understand how difficult it is to uncover all the reasons and weigh all the responsibilities for some wrongs. If Égalité was a Prince worthy of blame, it should not be forgotten that he was throughout a patriot devoted to his country. He wished to defend it at a time when others were bearing arms against France in the belief that in order to serve the monarchy it was necessary to subjugate the nation.

Nevertheless, after the proclamation of the Republic and the death of the King, Chartres continued to serve in the army, until the day when a vote was passed accusing him of complicity in General Dumouriez's activities and schemes. These would seem of too fanciful a character to have engaged the serious attention of a prudent mind, but it was no time for justifications. Therefore, according to François Burgot, in a speech to the National Convention on December 16, 1792, having "experienced the satisfaction of repaying his debt to the Fatherland by helping to deliver its territory completely from invasion by foreign armies," Chartres saw himself forced to leave the army and soil of his native country, "to support, elsewhere than in the Republic, the misfortune of being born near the throne."

These memoirs contain arresting observations on the dislocation of affairs and men in a period of revolution. Louis-Philippe, who from his youth onward was possessed of an unusually penetrating judgment and whose conduct in these times of confusion was beyond reproach, did not, for all that, tell himself that he had been right and that everyone else had been wrong; he did not throw the first stone at anyone: "all sides made mistakes and all parties," he wrote. That, no doubt, is why, despite the sanguinary madness of the revolutionaries, Chartres remained won over to the side of the Revolution; and, despite the blind perversity of the counterrevolutionaries, he remained loyal to the monarchy. He was the advocate of a policy of balance, between progress and reason, liberty and order, one that recognizes the reality of changes in society and turns to this for support. He was later to characterize this reformist policy—aiming to "improve without destroying"— as that of the *juste milieu*. He derived this opinion from the training of his youth and his experience under the Revolution. He was never to swerve from it and was one day to be in a position to translate it into fact. To be sure, these are not ideas that inflame the imagination of romantics, with little feeling for reality—ideas that stir the people for a moment before subjecting them to other, cruel, consequences. They do not create demigods, or even supermen, but they are capable of molding nations and of causing them to make progress in liberty and peace.

"I have always been a pacific prince": thus Louis-Philippe summed up his life when he fell from power. For Chartres, even then, despite revolutionary fervor, every opportunity for peace seemed worth seizing. In 1791, France was endowed with a constitution that proclaimed Louis XVI "King of the French by the Grace of God and the constitutional law of the State." He saw in this "royal democracy" the promise of a lasting settlement between the nation and the monarchy which would be capable of restoring civil peace. Likewise, the liberation of French territory in 1792 offered, he thought, the possibility of treating with the other Powers, which, after French victories, were disabused of the illusions the *émigrés* had given them. He later believed that a policy of internal and external pacification would have enabled France to avoid "the National Convention with its Committee of Public Safety, the Directory with its Council of Ancients and its Five Hundred and the Emperor Napoleon with his victories and his absolute power." No one, alas, imagined then how prolonged the Revolution would be or foresaw its consequences! Rather than continue the Revolution uselessly and mindlessly, the leaders should have brought it to a conclusion once its declared aims had been achieved, which satisfied nearly all Frenchmen. Unfortunately, no party would agree to cooperate with any of the others; each party thought it was clever enough to carry out a *politique du pire*. This blind intransigence was the cause of the misfortunes that were to cut France off from her past, throw her into chaos, reduce her to dictatorship, and spill oceans of blood for more than twenty years. Robespierre was born of the Royalists' lack of realism, Bonaparte of the Republicans' lack of patriotism.

No one should be indifferent to the activity of the Committee of Public Safety, which saved the country from a foreign yoke by a "sublime surge," coming from the very depths of the national spirit, or to the glorious feats of the Empire, which gave the measure of heroism of which Frenchmen are capable. But the torments of the Terror led to Thermidor; the reign of virtue and reason resulted in insolent contempt for morality and the law. The period that had produced so much heroism and sacrifice went down in tatters: twice France was overrun by the whole of Europe as she had not been for more than three centuries.

France recovered from the greatest crisis in her history with a face that was no longer her own. The relations of Frenchmen with each other and the laws which should have governed them had been arbitrarily established by the imperious will of the man who is persecuted as "the inventor of individualism." Was the nation, then, incapable of organizing itself wisely and in accordance with its own character? Of constructing a régime with balanced powers and of conceiving just and coherent human relationships, where the rights of the individual would not conflict with those of a man in society? Thus organized, would the French nation not have provided other peoples with a compelling example of harmony? Instead of that, it succumbed to imperialism, which Capetian common sense had always resisted, and from a Europe in bondage to Napoleon arose "patriotism engendered by hatred of France," as Edmond Pognon formulates it in *De Gaulle et l'histoire de France*. Laws were taken from other periods and other civilizations which conflicted with French humanist and Christian traditions and which rendered France ungovernable as long as the most unfortunate among the people did not, by their own efforts and as best they could, bring some remedy to the injustices and tyranny of the society imposed upon them. Today we see clearly that, far from being over, this struggle will be fought out to the finish.

When, after disasters and invasion, French Kings had to meet with Frenchmen on principles of government, these were, in fact, basically similar to the Constitution of 1791. Twenty-two years had elapsed without the Monarchy; history had continued without it, and the society it found was no longer one with which it could live in harmony.

Doubtless it is vain to rewrite history; it may also be a waste of time to mine it for information, since everyone today makes it a point of honor to be no one's descendant. After the Revolution of 1848, which deposed him, Louis-Philippe intended to write the history of his life: the present memoirs were to constitute only the first part. Unfortunately, there was not enough time left to him to complete so lengthy a task, and his reign remains ill-defended against absurd disparagements. Let us attempt to throw some light on it.

The July monarchy was a sort of compromise between the Ancien Régime and the Republic. Its internal contradictions were the source of basic misunderstandings which in large part brought about its ruin. They caused a new rupture within the House of France, and this division added still further to the misfortunes that had befallen the principle of legitimacy since 1789. Victor Hugo knew Louis-Philippe well and was conversant with all the circumstances of his having been made king; he relates them as follows: "Louis-Philippe had entered upon royal authority without violence, without any direct action on his part, in virtue of a revolutionary transfer of power . . . he had been born a prince and believed that he had been elected king. He had not at all given himself this mandate; he had not seized it; it had been offered to him and he had accepted in the conviction, albeit mistaken, that the offer had been made according to law and that his acceptance was in accordance with his duty." Louis-Philippe conceived of this duty as a necessary return to the first principles of the Capetian monarchy. In common with his period, he had a taste for and a keen sense of history. After so much drama, he wanted to restore unity to France. "He could sing the Marseillaise with conviction" and at the same time undertake the restoration of the home of the old monarchy, which, without him, would have been doomed to ruin. "He put the statue of Napoleon back on its column, brought his ashes to the Invalides and covered the walls of the palace of Versailles with the living image of his exploits," the Duc d'Aumale informs us.

But History is made of more than symbols: it is comprised of a series of social phenomena, and it is the task of government to facilitate their succession. On the morrow of the Restoration, the bourgeoisie, through force of numbers, ambition, and energy, stood out among the generality of Frenchmen. No other group in society was in a position to provide the framework appropriate to the new society. It alone was equal to the task of effectively developing the wealth of the nation. From the beginnings of the Revolution, the bourgeoisie had recognized its importance and its capacities. When the Restoration collapsed, it saw new prospects opening. But to exploit them, a climate of order and liberty was necessary, and it was Louis-Philippe, the Citizen King, who held the ring while this radical transformation took place. A policy that consists of operating a rise in the social scale of such scope should be recognized as not being entirely without merit.

In taking over the direction of affairs, the bourgeoisie certainly applied the laws of free trade with all the rigor of their logic, but then it submitted to them itself: it reaped the profits but ran the risks. In eighteen years industrial production doubled. The arrival of the bankers to power occurred in 1830 with the formation of a government by the *parti du mouvement*. A system of voting based on property qualifications is imperfect when considered in relation to democracy in the absolute, and naturally shocks people today, accustomed as they are to more sophisticated electorates. Yet one can share Bainville's surprise that Louis-Philippe did not think of introducing universal suffrage, which would perhaps have stabilized the régime. However, such a measure would have been largely a formality, because the new Notables were in a position to ensure a pliant electorate and preclude possible lapses on its part by playing on its fears, for which republican and socialist agitation provided excellent material. It is a formula that has since been constantly exploited, and its success is common knowledge.

To understand this much maligned period one must remember that the policy pursued at a certain point in the Revolutionary period, namely that of aiming at an alliance between the bourgeoisie and the masses, was at that time frankly put aside. This brief experience was remembered only as a reproach to Robespierre for having, by attempting it, "inspired future generations with a horror of rule by the people, a repugnance for the establishment of a republic and doubts about liberty," as Lamartine put it. All periods have their bogeys. Nevertheless, it must be admitted that the policy of the *juste milieu* corresponded exactly to the social and political realities of the period.

It is true that the policy of the *juste milieu*—whose motto was "liberty and public order"—sometimes operated brutally in the repression of disturbances. But as soon as the conflicting classes were able to enter the lists untrammeled by any moderating influence, the result was quite otherwise terrible: four thousand dead, ten thousand arrested, three thousand deported. Such was the balance sheet for the June Days of 1848.

His pacifism was the quality for which the French most reproached Louis-Philippe. On three occasions, alone and acting against the advice of his ministers and popular feeling, he refused to get enmeshed in a situation that would have led to war. On one occasion, having been asked to run the unnecessary risk of war, Louis-Philippe responded: "Let anyone touch Strasbourg—then we shall see!" No one dared risk it while he was in power, for a strong army had been built up again, the King had it firmly in hand, and only the French doubted his patriotism and courage. The fact is that, for a monarch, the highest form of patriotism and courage truly consists in maintaining and strengthening peace if need be, despite his people and at the risk of losing his crown.

The closer understanding between France and England—the first *entente cordiale*—represents one of the most judicious applications of Louis-Philippe's desire for peace. It demonstrates his precise knowledge of the state of Europe and his prescience about the way it would evolve. It was this policy, happily resumed and developed by successive governments, that has twice saved the country from threats that were bearing down on it and that nearly destroyed it forever.

The implacable opposition which assailed the government on all sides in the last part of the reign of Louis-Philippe led it fatally to defend itself by a conservative policy. Was a bolder approach, consisting of rallying the masses, possible at that time? The sequel was to prove the opposite immediately. If Louis-Philippe committed errors, what are they in comparison with the pieces of arrogant folly perpetrated by those who fulminated against him from the heights of their ideology? These dreamers, so ambitious for France and for themselves, of course succeeded in toppling the old King, but then "blind passions" merely gave birth to the most absurd, the most disjointed, and the most ephemeral régime the country had known* and, once more, delivered the nation over to Caesarism, foreign adventures, and defeat.

The monarchy is not a party. The appearance of a royalist party heralds the end of the monarchy. A *majorité dynastique* is contrary to the very nature of the monarchy. It is a mistake for a head of state to base

* That of Napoleon III, nephew of Napoleon Bonaparte.—ED.

his régime on a single political category, because those upon whom he calls to form the government and who provide him with a parliamentary majority are soon in a position to consider authority as their instrument. They are soon possessed by impatience to exercise it themselves. The bourgeois King was no longer enough for the bourgeoisie in 1848: they required the reign of the bourgeoisie.

Be that as it may, it remains true that the institutions as operated under Louis-Philippe and the development of society to which he gave impetus molded the political life of the nation for a long time. The Third Republic, despite the reductions in the powers attributed to the head of state, continued his work by beginning with a significant extension of the social basis of the parliamentary system. But by themselves the Assemblies, whose vicious tendencies the young Duc de Chartres had detected, were incapable of carrying out timely reforms. General de Gaulle, following the example given by the Capetian kings, wished to set France "in harmony with the Age," but social inertia ruined this hope. Nothing would be more paradoxical than to regard this reaction by the Notables as a continuation of the policies of Louis-Philippe, which, quite to the contrary, consisted in removing the constraints of a traditional society in order to allow the free development that corresponded to the requirements of the country. Need one add that such a policy seems today either inadmissible or impracticable, although the sociopolitical problems posed by our times are far more wide-ranging and urgent than those of a century and a half ago?

However exhausted the Citizen King's legacy now seems to many people, there remains, and always will remain, a shining part: "While he was on the throne," attests Victor Hugo, "there was freedom of the press, freedom of parliamentary debate, freedom of conscience and of speech." It is to Louis-Philippe that France owes its freedom. It would be only fair to remember this.

HENRI, COMTE DE PARIS

Introduction

Louis-Philippe d'Orléans, successively Duc de Valois, Duc de Chartres, General Louis Philippe Égalité, exile, Duc d'Orléans, King of the French, and, finally, exile, intended to write memoirs covering the whole of his life and attached great importance to the project. But, although he began it in 1802 and continued to work on it off and on until his death in 1850, he got no further than his precipitate flight from France at the age of nineteen in April 1793, after the Committees of Defense and General Security had ordered his arrest.

It would be well, therefore, to begin with a brief outline of his eventful career. He was born on October 6, 1773, the eldest child of Louis-Philippe-Joseph, Duc de Chartres, and his wife, Louise-Marie-Adélaïde, daughter of the Duc de Bourbon-Penthièvre, and given the title Duc de Valois. His father, called here Philippe, to avoid confusion, inherited the title and position of Duc d'Orléans and First Prince of the Blood on the death of *his* father in 1785. His mother, on the death of her brother, the Prince de Lamballe, in 1768, became the sole heir of her father, the Duc de Penthièvre, the last descendant of Louis XIV's legitimated offspring by Mme de Montespan and the most junior of the Princes of the Blood. Princes of the Blood were distant descendants, in the male line, of former Kings of France. More precisely, the sons and grandsons of the Kings were Children of France and members of the Royal Family, while great-grandsons and their descendants were Princes of the Blood. The line of a Prince of the Blood, then, always began with a King (in the case of the House of Orléans, with Louis XIII) and passed a couple of generations within the confines of the Royal Family before becoming merely princely. The distinction was important in many ways—for example, the King could expect more opposition from a Prince of the Blood than from a member of his family. Suffice it to say here that Louis XV (1715–1774) was disturbed at the prospect of a union between two fabulously wealthy princely families which one day was to make Louis-Philippe by far the richest private individual in France. Louis XV perceived the danger but, as so often, left it at that.

On his grandfather's death in 1785, Louis-Philippe became Duc de Chartres, the title by which he was generally known during the period covered by his memoirs. By this time he had, for three years past, been imbibing liberal ideas from his governess, Mme de Genlis, and the bent of his education, together with his father's pronounced radicalism, meant that when revolution manifested itself, obliquely in 1787 and squarely in 1789, Louis-Philippe embraced the cause enthusiastically. After the fall of the Bastille, Louis XVI's younger brother, the Comte d'Artois, emigrated, as did most of the Princes of the Blood, summoning the French nobility to them and forming them into armed detachments. Philippe, of course, remained, and so did his father-in-law, the Duc de Penthièvre, who in 1792, when France was invaded by foreign and *émigré* armies, remarked: "I have not so far forgotten my old notions as to put up with the Emperor and the King of Prussia sending their armies to Versailles to dictate terms to the King on the pretext of putting him back on the throne."*

In 1790, Louis-Philippe joined the Jacobin Club and took an active part in their proceedings. In June 1791, he went to Vendôme to take personal command of the regiment of Chartres Dragoons, of which he had been colonel in chief since 1785. Sensing that war between France and Austria was inevitable, Louis-Philippe now exerted all his influence to have his regiment moved to what would be the front. Promotion came rapidly; as he writes: "Although I was only eighteen and a half at the time when war was declared, because of the incidence of emigration among those of the rank of staff and senior officers and above I was the most senior colonel in the army on active service: I had been made a colonel because I was a Prince of the Blood, and my commission was dated November 20, 1785."† In the Revolution, promotion was by seniority. Promotion by seniority is an aspect of egalitarianism: For society to work there must be a hierarchy, and this is, doctrinally, the least objectionable way of arriving at it. Thus, paradoxically, the Revolution brought a Prince of the Blood prematurely to the rank of lieutenant general. As his commander in chief, Dumouriez, pointed out, life may have been difficult for a Prince of the Blood in a republic, but to his birth Louis-Philippe owed both the fact that he was a lieutenant general at eighteen and that he was implicitly obeyed by the troops. Obeyed he certainly was, as, for example, at the Battle of Jemappes, when, in command of the center, he rallied the troops, which had fled in disorder, and led them back to take the Austrian positions. So far from being "bourgeois" —a charge often leveled against him—he had a boyish enthusiasm for the noble art of war: "Long live the Chartres Dragoons," he writes in his diary, "there is not a regiment like them in France. . . ."‡ And he was brave, being cited at Valmy and having a horse shot from under him at Neerwinden.

* *Memoirs*, p. 119.
† *Memoirs*, p. 201.
‡ *Un An de la vie de Louis-Philippe 1er ou Journal authentique du Duc de Chartres,* Paris, 1831, p. 83.

However, he was by the autumn of 1792 growing apart from the Revolution as it developed. He was, and always remained, temperamentally a constitutional monarchist. Because Louis XVI was paralyzing the country's defense, he must lose his throne (which he did on August 10), but not his life (which he did on January 21, 1793). The September Massacres, when the people of Paris butchered most of the prison population, disgusted him, and he openly spoke out against them—and was reproved by Danton for his pains. His father accused him of being a Girondin, and that was the group with which he most readily identified. When the war in the Low Countries turned against France, Dumouriez arranged a truce with the Austrians, after the Battle of Neerwinden, and planned to turn his troops against the National Convention. The plan failed when the troops did not respond. Louis-Philippe was heavily implicated and, with Dumouriez and his entire General Staff, escaped behind the Austrian lines, a heavy price on his head.

At this point the memoirs end (though there is a brief section on his wanderings through Europe and the New World), and one may ask why do they end precisely there, when his life had seemingly just begun. Lack of time can scarcely be a sufficient explanation, for during the next forty years he had all too much of that on his hands. A more likely explanation is that the next twenty years (until his return to France in 1814) were not only extremely unpleasant but also, after his brilliant early career, a tremendous anticlimax. For a general who had served both the Revolution and the Republic and who was also the son of a regicide, there was no place in a Europe increasingly receptive to *émigré* doctrines and locked in struggle with the French Republic. For four years he wandered in Europe, remaining in one place only so long as his incognito could be preserved, and traveling as far as Lapland. For eight months he was a geography master at a Swiss boarding school under the assumed name of M. Chabos. In 1796, the Directory, which had succeeded the National Convention, offered to release his younger brothers, Montpensier and Beaujolais, from Fort Saint-Jean in Marseilles provided Louis-Philippe preceded them to America. To this Louis-Philippe readily agreed, but, as he remarks, ". . . the delight of my reunion with my brothers at Philadelphia only added their financial difficulties to my own."* Like many subsequent immigrants from Europe, he found living in the United States very expensive. He was, in fact, entirely dependent on the charity of a few individuals.

By 1800, the political climate of Europe had cooled sufficiently for the brothers to return. They settled in England and took a house at Twickenham. His life there, he tells us, was pleasant; but this we may be permitted to doubt. Born the heir to the richest fortune in France, he was dependent on a modest pension granted to him, as to all the French Princes, by an English government that seemed intent on taking the whole world into

* *Memoirs*, p. 421.

its pay. His father had been taken from Fort Saint-Jean in 1793, tried in Paris, and executed. His brothers had been spared this fate, but in the dungeons had both contracted tuberculosis, from which Montpensier died in 1807 and Beaujolais the year following.

But in 1809 Louis-Philippe married his Bourbon cousin Marie-Amélie, daughter of Ferdinand IV of Naples and a descendant of Louis XIV. Around her he created a second family. She bore him five surviving sons and three daughters. The couple's fertility was in marked contrast to that of the elder branch of the Bourbons.

With the defeat and abdication of Napoleon in 1814, the Bourbons returned to the throne in the person of Louis XVIII, second brother of Louis XVI. Louis XVIII had neither forgotten nor forgiven his cousin's role in the Revolution but, blood being thicker than water, he allowed him to return to his former position.* Louis-Philippe, therefore, returned to France, kissed the bottom step of the Palais Royal, and resumed the sterile career of a Prince of the Blood.

A political role was out of the question, and Louis-Philippe turned his attention to building up a second (and greater) fortune for his family. Much of the Orléans and Penthièvre property was recovered, and when in 1824 compensation (the *milliard* or 1,000,000,000 francs) was granted to *émigrés* who had lost land in the Revolution, Louis-Philippe headed the list. In addition, his fifth son, the Duc d'Aumale, inherited Chantilly, together with the fortune of the last Prince de Bourbon-Condé. Careful management made these assets formidable.

Louis-Philippe's proximity to the throne was greater than his father's had been. Louis XVIII was childless, and of the Comte d'Artois's two sons, the Duc d'Angoulême and the Duc de Berri, neither had children when the latter was assassinated in 1820. At that moment Louis-Philippe must have expected that he or his eldest son would inherit the Crown. In fact, the Duchesse de Berri bore her husband a posthumous child, the Duc de Bordeaux, *l'enfant du miracle.* Nevertheless, the possibility of Louis-Philippe's succeeding to the Crown was still sufficiently real for Louis XVIII to broach the question of a regency, asking whether he could guarantee to protect his great-nephew's interests as well as the Regent Orléans had those of the young Louis XV.† The King received a discouraging, even menacing reply.‡

The natural order of succession was to be anticipated. In July 1830, Charles X, who had succeeded his brother in 1824, fell almost casually,

* Of Louis XVIII's younger brother Artois, the future Charles X, Louis-Philippe notes: "In him . . . the hereditary principle was strong and he sincerely desired that the Orléans branch should not create a gap in the family circle and that it should occupy its place in the order of succession to the throne."
† On the death of the Duc de Bordeaux in 1883, Louis-Philippe's grandson, the Comte de Paris, became the legitimate pretender to the throne.
‡ *Memoirs,* pp. 434–35.

after three days of rioting in Paris (*les trois glorieuses*). Louis-Philippe's role in this is obscure, though this one can say: After his family had waited in the wings for two hundred years, he would not have been human had he declined the Crown. It was offered him by men who wanted to stop the Revolution, to prevent 1792 becoming 1789 once more. Stop the Revolution he did: The franchise was extended from 94,000 to 166,-000 electors, Charles X's constitutional irregularities were formally eschewed—and that was all.

Louis-Philippe was now King of the French, and remained so until February 1848, when he in turn was toppled by a seemingly insignificant armed demonstration. Then once more he took the path of exiles to England, where Queen Victoria put at his disposal Claremont House, in Surrey. There he died shortly afterward, on August 26, 1850.

How one can briefly summarize his reign? It seems to me that his régime was never so firmly established as that of the Bourbon Restoration. Louis XVIII and Charles X possessed the principle of legitimism (a powerful one at the time), and they took over from Napoleon (who had in turn inherited it from the old Kings) the technique of manipulating the provinces through the prefects.* Louis-Philippe did not possess these advantages. The Duc de Berri may have been assassinated, but there were no fewer than seven attempts on Louis-Philippe's life. Louis-Philippe was no less a personal monarch than Charles X had been; in the section of his memoirs analyzing Louis XVI's attitude toward the Constitution, he makes it quite clear that in his view it is perfectly possible for a constitutional monarch to rule as well as reign. His policies were essentially negative ones—peace abroad and the maintenance of the *status quo* at home. In English terms, he was a Whig; in French, a Girondin. But above all, he was an old man—fifty-six in 1830 and seventy-four when he abdicated—and this at the time when a man of forty was considered old. His mind remained alert, but his thinking had been aged by premature experience and the apathy, or lack of receptivity, which this so often engenders. In an old man the natural eye can focus better on distant things than on those close up, but with the inner eye, the positions are reversed. Thus, days before his fall, Louis-Philippe was working through the night on routine trivia. When the July Monarchy consistently refused to contemplate the slightest extension of the franchise, it lost its *raison d'être*. Louis XVIII, one feels, would have seen the necessity and, with his wonted perspicacity and cynicism, would have realized that wide franchises need not return less conservative chambers than narrow ones—and he was the legitimate, anointed descendant of Clovis to boot.

One cannot blame Louis-Philippe for being old. The tragedy of the reign was the accidental death in 1842 of his brilliant (and liberal) heir,

* Stendhal's *Le Rouge et le noir*, published, ironically, in 1830, gives a powerful impression of the régime's solidity—of how thoroughly it had impregnated society with its values.

the Duc d'Orléans. France lamented him as Rome did Germanicus, and it is likely that, had he lived, he would have transformed and perpetuated the monarchy.

Providence, as Louis-Philippe would have put it, had destined him to occupy positions of high responsibility both in extreme youth and in extreme old age. He has left us the record of the former.

As they stand, then, the memoirs primarily consist of an account of Louis-Philippe's singular education at the hands of Mme de Genlis; an examination of, or, rather, an apologia for, his father's conduct during the Revolution and the years preceding; and, finally, of an account of Louis-Philippe's own military career. Essentially they amount to a statement about what it was like to be a Prince of the Blood at the end of the Ancien Régime and the beginning of the Revolution. In addition, as a background to this, there is Louis-Philippe's analysis of events in which he did not directly participate—Louis-Philippe as the historian rather than the diarist. And here he offers a distinctive interpretation of the origins and of the course of the French Revolution.

Before examining these aspects of the memoirs, one thing more needs to be said, about the angle from which they were written. Louis-Philippe did not, unless the need arose, intend to publish his memoirs before his death, and indeed they were not published until 1973. But the bulk of the memoirs was written during his first exile in England (1800–12), when he needed to justify himself to fellow countrymen who had quarreled with the Revolution from the start. They were retouched after 1848, when he had had quite enough of revolutions. This may explain why he is concerned throughout with justifying his conduct to people to the right of him, politically, never to people to the left. Maybe the revolutionary experience had gone sour on him and he had, as suggested earlier, grown more conservative with age, but it is rather disconcerting to find him referring to the Revolution, in which he played such a distinguished role, as "that lamentable occurrence." Paradoxically, he would not, by his actions, disavow the Revolution—for example, by wearing the white cockade or joining Condé's Army—though to have done so would have made life much easier for him. Yet in his memoirs, which no one ever read, he goes some way toward such a disavowal.

Mme de Genlis and the Education of a Prince

The formative influence of Louis-Philippe's boyhood and youth was Stéphanie-Félicité Ducrest de Saint-Aubin, Comtesse de Genlis, novelist, educationalist, who had the rare distinction of being his father's mistress and his mother's confidante. In 1782, she became governor to Philippe's three sons, the Ducs de Valois, Montpensier, and Beaujolais (she was already governess to his daughters). In her memoirs she tells us that her lighthearted suggestion that she should become the children's governor had been taken up by Philippe, who had been complaining to her that their present governor, the Chevalier de Bonnard, was giving them "the manners of a shop-assistant"*—a reason that did nothing to suggest the egalitarian bent their education was to assume. The reason Louis-Philippe gives for his father's unusual decision is that he attributed the general insignificance of Princes of the Blood to the insipid education they received and the flattery with which they were surrounded.

Mme de Genlis's schoolhouse was an annex of the convent of Belle-Chasse, in the Rue Saint-Dominique, and Louis-Philippe was taught there, together with his sister Adélaïde (who was to exert considerable influence on him during his reign), his brothers, and a group of children Mme de Genlis may be said to have collected. The régime was a cross between that favored by Dr. Arnold and that favored by Rousseau: the muscular Christianity that inspired the early nineteenth-century public schools in England coupled with democratic notions derived from Rousseau's educational treatise *Émile*. Accordingly, the pupils ate cheap food off rough plates, slept on palliasses placed on a table,† and performed heavy agricultural labors—no *divertissement champêtre*—for which they wore peasant smocks. For some reason, Philippe did not like to see his children dressed like this, so they had to change when he visited them. On one occasion, Louis-Philippe was working in the fields when he was summoned to Court and had to don Court dress—which gave him pause. He also performed bizarre tasks to develop his body. Thus, although his father was the richest man in France, Louis-Philippe never knew even comfort until he was forty.

As Louis-Philippe observes: "Mme de Genlis turned us into honorable and virtuous republicans, but in her vanity she wanted us to continue to be Princes of the Blood. There was much here that could not be reconciled."‡ This contradiction comes out clearly in an important series of letters she wrote him when he "left home" to join his regiment in 1791, and which, as she put it, "constitutes all the advice which your dear friend can give you."§ After Louis XVI's abortive attempt to escape from Paris, in June 1791, Mme de Genlis sees the possibility of Philippe or his son becoming king. She writes to Louis-Philippe: "You . . . I am perfectly sure, would refuse the throne if it were offered to you *and if you could not ascend it without doing an injustice.*" Her very denial bespeaks ambition! And her pupil is to calculate the effect of everything he does: "Never be alone or unsociable except during the time set aside for study; in all other activities, make sure you are observed—it will be to your advantage. If any chaste, pleasant ladies receive you, be polite to

* Mme de Genlis, *Mémoires*, Paris, 1825, Vol. III, p. 115.
† Even during his reign, Louis-Philippe slept on a hair mattress with a plank underneath.
‡ *Memoirs*, p. 15.
§ *Memoirs*, p. 91; italics mine.

them, attentive, and amiable. In short, overlook nothing that may make you popular. . . ." Earlier, on a visit to Spa in 1787, he has to go to the public well to get water for Mme de Genlis and carry it back to their lodgings "like any water carrier." "Fortunately," he says, "this took place very early in the morning, so we met very few people."* So the fourteen-year-old boy, encountering a world that does not yet share the fancies of Mme de Genlis and J.-J. Rousseau, experiences social embarrassment.

What was the effect of Mme de Genlis on her pupil? What sort of a young man did she turn out? It must be said that by the time Louis-Philippe came to write his memoirs he had drifted apart from Mme de Genlis. The moment of disenchantment may have come in 1793 when Mme de Genlis, in her desire to escape the French armies, attempted to abandon his sister, who had measles, at Saint-Amand: Louis-Philippe lifted his sister bodily from her sickbed and placed her in Mme de Genlis's carriage. In his memoirs, therefore, Louis-Philippe tends to play down the influence of Mme de Genlis. For example, he writes ". . . she never managed to gain for herself the complete ascendancy over my mind to which she aspired. I was too well aware of the poverty of her intellect to submit mine to hers, and she also recognized that the thing was impossible."† Indeed, placed beside the memoirs, the affectionate letters she wrote to him in 1791 seem a little ridiculous. However, a glance at the diary that Louis-Philippe kept at this period leaves one in no doubt that he was deeply in love with her—more so, he was later to confide, than he ever was with any woman. His diary abounds with entries such as "I do not know what will become of me when I am no longer with her," and "Stayed with my friend until 12.30 PM. Nothing in the world is as delectable as she is."‡

By her own account, Mme de Genlis found Louis-Philippe as a little boy who had an abhorrence of dogs and the smell of vinegar and turned him into a man who accepted both of these. He had "an inordinate lack of application" and spent his first lesson with his feet on the table. But she fired his enthusiasm, so that he developed a "stupendous memory," was proficient in English, German, Italian, and Spanish by the age of twelve, while his essays "already heralded that orderliness, judiciousness and right-mindedness on which his character is based."§

Reading the memoirs only, one would come away with the impression that Mme de Genlis rendered Louis-Philippe powerless to resist the revolutionary ideas and that he regretted this. But his memoirs, as noted, seem to have been written to answer criticism only from the right. Also, his acceptance of revolutionary ideas, though enthusiastic, was neither uncriti-

* *Memoirs*, pp. 17–18.
† *Memoirs*, p. 14.
‡ *Journal*, p. 47 and p. 48.
§ Mme de Genlis, *Mémoires*, Vol. III, pp. 122, 123, 131.

cal nor stereotyped. True, he performs certain ritual gestures, such as going around to the house of M. Harny to embrace that playwright after a performance of his *Despotisme renversé*.* But he does not take up Mme de Genlis's suggestion to make "a patriotic little speech" on giving up the insigne of the Order of the Holy Ghost. And, of course, when the time comes, he is able to separate himself from the cause of the Revolution.

One way in which he differs from the typical revolutionary is that, through Mme de Genlis's influence, he remains an orthodox Christian. This is in addition to the normal revolutionary striving after purity. Robespierre would have approved his youthful struggles to remain chaste, though, no doubt, Philippe would have smiled. From his diary one can say, without "side," that he is high-minded and pure. And, in the memoirs, there is a sense of nostalgia for the period of his youth which adds to their vividness. After all, he was to go on to far greater things, but here there is the exhilarating sense of youthful integrity, as yet unaffected by "the world's slow stain," a refusal to compromise or pay court; the sense that his life is important and that he must get the beginning right. Also, there is massive confidence: "I was born under a very lucky star, all the opportunities present themselves and I have only to profit from them"— this he notes on August 3, 1791, after rescuing a man from drowning.†

Of the permanent effects of his education and revolutionary experience, there could be mentioned an unshakable belief in constitutional monarchy (as King of the French he was to exercise considerable personal power, but it was never arbitrary power; Louis XVI often exercised much less power but he was seldom deflected from an action because it would be arbitrary). Also, his assessments of people are invariably based on their own qualities rather than those of their ancestors. I do not think there is a single instance in the memoirs of Louis-Philippe informing us who a man's ancestors were (except his own). The conventional way to introduce a character in the eighteenth century—and Louis-Philippe always remained a man of the eighteenth century—ran roughly as follows: "M. de Lagondie came from an old Breton family which produced a cardinal in the sixteenth century but has since become impoverished." The complete absence of this form is striking. This, however, is not to say that Louis-Philippe was, in any sense, "bourgeois" or that he ever forgot he was a Prince of the Blood. Perhaps indeed in the eighteenth century it was only to those of the Blood Royal—perhaps only to the King—that questions of birth were unimportant. For to deny that the King could dignify whomsoever he pleased implied a limitation of his power.

* *Journal*, p. 49.
† *Journal*, p. 84.

Philippe Égalité and the Predicament of a Prince of the Blood

Philippe's predicament, and that of Louis-Philippe, was merely, in acute form, that of being a Prince of the Blood in France—acute because, of the cadet branches of the ruling house, the Orléans were nearest to the throne. The separate identity of Princes who were but distantly related to the King owed much to the operation of the Salic law in France, whereby the Crown could not be worn by, or inherited through, women. The Salic law doubled the chances of a King's not being succeeded by his offspring, made it necessary to have Princes in reserve, and prevented them from merging into the nobility, as in England. Nor was this merely an academic point. When Henri IV, the first King of the Bourbon branch, succeeded Henri III in 1589, he had not had an ancestor on the throne for three hundred years; when the Comte d'Artois's son the Duc de Berri was assassinated in 1820 before his son was born, it could be expected that Louis-Philippe or his son would one day inherit the throne. The Princes also considered they had the right to a say in the "running" of a crown that they, or their descendants, might one day inherit. This was particularly so during a king's minority (and Louis XIII, Louis XIV, and Louis XV all succeeded as minors), when the Queen Mother Regent was open to the accusation by the Princes that she was frittering away the resources of the Crown. In the Middle Ages, the kings had granted their younger children *apanages,* where they could rule as semi-autonomous potentates, but, as the Crown extended its grip over the provinces, the medieval *apanage* was emasculated, so that, by the eighteenth century, it was a source of wealth but only of the power that wealth confers.

Philippe had sought to find a role for himself by embarking on a naval career. But after the Battle of Ouessant, against England, Louis XVI had ended this career, whether out of fear that his cousin would win renown that would detract from his own or, more likely, because Philippe's father-in-law, the Duc de Penthièvre, was Admiral of France, one of the last great medieval offices, and the prospect of the First Prince of the Blood as successful sailor and admiral alarmed him. That is why, as Louis-Philippe observes, his father would have welcomed the opportunity, held out to him by Louis XVI, of becoming sovereign Duke of Brabant when the Belgians drove out their Austrian rulers. But this came to nothing.

Denied an official role of responsibility, the Princes often led the opposition to the King and assumed the function of the "reversionary interest" performed by the Prince of Wales in England. This was so in the case of the Great Condé, during the minority of Louis XIV, of the Prince de Conti, during Louis XV's struggles with the Parlements, and of Philippe, during the reign of Louis XVI.

Was Philippe's opposition merely factious? Was he merely a rich dabbler in politics who had never suffered oppression under the Ancien

Régime? Louis-Philippe would argue not. His father's opposition was expressed in the traditional form through the Parlement of Paris, of which, as a Prince and peer of France, he enjoyed honorary membership.* He took over the role of "leader of the opposition" from his uncle the Prince de Conti, who, Louis-Philippe tells us, had influenced him considerably. This *parlementaire* opposition reached a climax in November 1787 when, after the King's forced registration of an edict, Philippe declared that the King's action was illegal. For this, the Duc was exiled by *lettre de cachet.*† And, despite his rank, he felt to the full what were considered the despotic tendencies of the Court. The evening after his outburst, he was informed by the Minister for the Maison du Roi (Minister of the Interior) that he must leave Paris before midnight, spend the night at Raincy, and proceed next day to his principal seat, Villers-Cotterêts, where the King forbade him any visitors except members of his family. Despite obligations to the House of Orléans, the Minister did not modify the sentence in any way: If the Ancien Régime was despotic, Philippe was a bona fide martyr.

Louis-Philippe has to spend a good deal of time on the refutation of a charge that is no longer taken seriously, namely, that the French Revolution was an Orléaniste conspiracy. As he observes, "one can hire a riot, but not a revolution." In any case, he suggests, his father's undoubted indebtedness resulted not from the cost of hiring a revolution but from the simple fact that, although his expenditure had not decreased with the Revolution, his income had—largely through the suppression of his *apanage* without his receiving a penny of the compensation voted by the National Assembly.

The picture that finally emerges is not of a great conspirator, but of a man dominated by his weakness. Louis-Philippe breaks off his memoirs before the period of his father's execution, but the picture he gives us of him in the winter of 1792/93 is of a man who has degenerated into a human wreck paralyzed by fear: alone in the vast Palais Royal; deserted by his wife; without any friends save the Duc de Biron and a faithful mistress; without the application of mind to read a book, even a novel, and addicted to a theater whose quality was declining with the advance of revolutionary orthodoxy; an object of contempt to his enemies and embarrassment to his political allies ("friends" he declines to call them); treasuring visits from his children, who yet often reprove him; left, after the fall of the monarchy, without a surname and being forced by the Paris Commune, in order to exercise his right to vote, to choose between Égalité and Publicola—the Second Consul of the Roman Republic who had helped to oust Tarquinius Superbus; forced to adopt Égalité as his surname and yet, to the end, calling his children Chartres, Montpensier, and Beaujolais, even in private; forbidden by the King to serve at the

* For a note on the Parlements, see *Memoirs,* p. 21, note §.
† For a note on *lettres de cachet,* see *Memoirs,* p. 22, note †.

front; constrained by the leaders of the Mountain to stand for election to the National Convention and to be put at the bottom of the poll for the Paris deputies, and, finally, forced to vote for the King's death as a pledge. Here, however, although Philippe's vote caused Louis-Philippe considerable pain, or he says it did, was it really so terrible to vote for the death of a distant cousin with whom he had disagreed all his political life and who had exiled him for five months in 1787–88 and, in effect, banished him to England in October 1789? Inquiring whether he could avoid pronouncing on the King's fate on grounds of kinship, Philippe was told that, at law, he and Louis XVI were not related. Only the Salic law made Philippe's relationship to Louis XVI close, but where was the Salic law in the winter of 1792/93?

One may ask why it is that Louis-Philippe feels it necessary to spend so much time in justifying—*ad nauseum,* it must seem to the reader, and surely beyond the call of filial duty—the conduct of his father. The explanation may lie in the Ancien Régime notion that a man's misdeeds dishonored his descendants. Indeed, Louis-Philippe frequently returns to the hoary allegation that his great-great-grandfather, the Regent, tried to poison his way to the throne by eliminating all of Louis XIV's descendants within reach.

Louis-Philippe's Interpretations of the French Revolution

Because Louis-Philippe was intelligent, because he managed to achieve a remarkable degree of historical detachment, and because of his unusual standpoint as one who had espoused and fought for the cause of the Revolution before detaching himself from it, his interpretation has some original and, in many ways, surprisingly modern themes. He dates the origins of the Revolution from the invention of the printing press and, in particular, to an increased knowledge of the classical democracies of Greece and, especially, Rome. And one would agree that renewed contact with their Latin originals (*libertas, patria, civitas,* et cetera) informed the words that were to make up the distinctive language of the Revolution with a new meaning. Unusually for someone of his period, he discounts the role of personalities in the origins and course of the Revolution, stressing instead that of public opinion, the "real motor," as he puts it. He has, admittedly, a special reason for arguing this point of view, since a substantial part of his memoirs is devoted to demolishing the notion of an Orléaniste conspiracy to bring about a revolution. But in the course of this quest he is driven to analyze in some detail the mechanics of popular politics: the Jacobin Club, with its affiliated clubs in the provinces, and the organization of political activity in the electoral wards or "sections" of Paris. He was one of the first to realize the symbiotic nature of the Revolution and the Counterrevolution: how each fed off and, indeed, could not exist without the other. He realized the mutual attraction of extremes and that tendency of revolutionaries to reserve their wrath less for the enemy than for the comrade who is slightly behindhand in embracing the latest orthodoxy. He notes, ironically, how *émigré* society became democratized as valets and marquises rubbed shoulders in common misfortune. He does not make the elementary mistake of thinking that Louis XVI is in league with the *émigrés* at Coblenz (strong differences of personality and policy divided them), and he realizes how the Emigration weakened the King by depriving him of the only men in whom he was willing to place his trust.

He has some interesting things to say about Louis XVI, and some harsh ones. A constant theme is that a constitutional régime does not, of itself, reduce the power of the monarch, and Louis XVI should have made a go of being such a monarch. Louis, he says, possessed two kinds of power, that deriving, in men's minds, from God and his ancestors—which he did not finally lose until he was shut up in the Temple with no means of communicating with the outside world—and that deriving from the Constitution. He censures Louis for not using the first kind to augment the second and for concentrating on demonstrating the latter's insufficiency. But the really unforgivable sin was to use his power to hinder the country's defense against foreign invasion. Louis, he thought, had no right to consider himself unfettered by promises made after the October Days (when he was forcibly removed from Versailles to Paris) on the grounds that he was a captive. For captivity is relative and the movements of a king must necessarily be more restricted than those of a private citizen: The King of England and the Prince of Wales could not leave the realm without an Act of Parliament.

The memoirs are interspersed with well-turned apothegms. Louis-Philippe is also good at the symbolic anecdote. There is the priest who guides him across the marshes of the Scheldt during his escape from France and asks to be made his almoner when he returns, "for this won't last forever"—curious blend, that, of cynicism and faith. There is the *émigré* officer who, not quite so confident in victory after the Battle of Valmy, asks Louis-Philippe to convey a respectful letter to his father, whom he fears he may have angered by emigrating. There is M. d'Arçon the army engineer who, emigrating in 1792, is told by the Comte d'Artois that he is too late. He replies that "he will not be too late for the other side"—and joins the republican armies.

JOHN HARDMAN

Hugues Capet (936–996)
King of France
m. Adelaïde of Italy

Louis IX (Saint Louis) (1215–1270)
King of France
m. Marguerite de Provence

Henri IV (1553–1610)
King of France
m. Marie de Médicis

Louis XIII (1601–1643)
King of France
m. Anne of Austria

Louis XIV (1638–1715)
King of France
m. Maria Theresa of Austria

Louis of France (1661–1711)
Dauphin of France
m. Marie-Anne of Bavaria

Louis of France (1682–1712)
Duc de Bourgogne, then Dauphin of France
m. Marie-Adélaïde of Savoy

Philippe of France
Duc d'Anjou to 1702,
becomes King Philip V of Spain,
renounces the French Crown for
himself and his descendants.

Louis XV (1710–1774)
King of France
m. Maria Lesczynska

Louis (1726–1763)
Dauphin of France
m. Maria-Josepha of Saxony

Louis XVI (1754–1793)
King of France
m. Marie-Antoinette
of Austria

**Louis, Comte de Provence
(1755–1824)**
King of France as **Louis XVIII**
m. Louise-Marie Josephine of Savoy

**Charles Philippe, Comte d'Artois
(1757–1836)**
King of France as **Charles X**
m. Maria Theresa of Savoy

Louis XVII (1785–1795)
King of France

GENEALOGY OF
THE HOUSE OF FRANCE
936-1850

Philippe of France (1640–1701)
Duc d'Orléans
m. Henrietta of England
m. Charlotte-Elisabeth of Bavaria

Philippe of France (1674–1723)
Duc d'Orléans, Regent
m. Françoise-Marie de Bourbon

Louis d'Orléans (1703–1752)
Duc d'Orléans, First Prince of the Blood
m. Augusta-Maria of Baden

Louis-Philippe d'Orléans (1725–1785)
Duc d'Orléans, First Prince of the Blood
m. Louise-Henriette de Bourbon-Conti

Louis-Philippe Joseph d'Orléans (1747–1793)
Duc d'Orléans, First Prince of the Blood
(Philippe Égalité)
m. Louise-Adélaïde de Bourbon-Penthièvre

Louis-Philippe d'Orléans (1773–1850)
Duc d'Orléans, First Prince of the Blood
King of the French as **Louis-Philippe I**

MEMOIRS

At my age, seventy-six, it is only natural to fear that time will run out for the accomplishment of a work as long as the story of my life; it is therefore with genuine satisfaction that I release here, as a beginning, a faithful if somewhat compressed picture of certain aspects of my political conduct. I may say that I am doing this conscientiously and with a scrupulous regard to the truth.

I KNOW how difficult it is to talk about oneself naturally and how embarrassing it is to do oneself justice without ostentation or false modesty. However, in the age we live in, those who are not ashamed of their conduct must leave behind them an accurate account of the various incidents that make up their lives. I decided years ago to undertake this task, despite its obvious difficulties, and I was merely waiting till I had the time to get down to it. I protest that I am not doing this out of vanity, but I do think it is important to present myself as I am, and as I have been, and to disprove the calumnies that have almost overwhelmed me. I do not want these memoirs to appear during my lifetime, and I do not reckon on publishing them unless I am forced to by future events, which is a distinct possibility! But if I can, I shall save them until I am dead. The death of a man has a decisive influence on his memory; as Shakespeare put it: "Mark the end." For it is only when we are dead that opinions are crystallized and the verdict of history begins to be established. I cannot read the future, but whatever befalls me, it will be a great comfort to have completed this work and deposited it in safe hands. I know that then I shall more easily resign myself to the vicissitudes of fortune. If it is favorable to my memory, all the following details will be avidly sought out; if unfavorable, it will be all the more important for me that they be known. For the rest, whatever degree of importance is attached to my fate and the vicissitudes of my life, it is always worthwhile gathering the observations of contemporaries, as they are doubly precious when they relate to a period such as that in which I have lived, when events present posterity with such striking examples and with lessons that demand a proper understanding.

Other, no less powerful considerations also move me to undertake this task. Several of those whom I mourn, and in particular my unhappy father, are unable to present their conduct in its true colors. It is agreeable for me to fulfill this duty. However, I shall not attempt to justify what cannot be justified, though I will sometimes presume to try to explain what has been thought inexplicable. At all events, I will always be true to myself and never stifle the promptings of my conscience.

I shall go into some details about my education, which was very "democratic," as befitted the times, and which became more so as I got older and the Revolution got nearer. I think it is dangerous to apply mathematical theories to human affairs lest we acquire a taste for perfection that leads us to form chimerical projects that cannot be executed and as a result plunge us into an abyss of disorder and confusion. However, I think we can safely say that the movement toward democracy obeyed the law of gravity and that the further it went, the more force it acquired.

It would be very interesting to discover just when this movement toward democracy first made itself felt, though this, I think, would be impossible. Indeed, it seems to me that we must start with the institutions of Greece and Rome, for we were brought up on the classical authors and learned to regard their institutions as the seedbed of fine actions and qualities and of everything that ennobles man. It is worthy of note that democratic ideas received a stimulus from the Humanists and played a major part in bringing about the Reformation. I make no claim to be a theologian, nor do I want to go into the doctrinal side of that great contest, but it does seem clear that the further the new sects moved from the Church of Rome, the more democratic and egalitarian they became. Thus the great rulers of the period remained loyal to Catholicism, while those of the second rank, such as the petty Princes of Germany and the great nobility in France, adopted the Reformation as a way of counterbalancing those who were stronger than they. Anyone who doubts the truth of this assertion has only to glance at the history of Holland. For in the development of the revolutionary spirit, the help that France gave the Dutch Republic at the time of its struggle for independence from Spanish domination was just as important as that more recently given by Louis XVI to the United States of America against England.

Perhaps the most decisive factor in changing men's way of thinking was the invention of the printing press. Education was made much easier, the existing store of knowledge was passed on intact, and the communication of the scientific discoveries that were being made in all parts of the civilized world was greatly facilitated. It was this great discovery that dealt the most terrible blow to the feudal system and most advanced the leveling of conditions. At first, freedom of the press existed only in Holland and the Free Cities of Germany, spreading then to England and America. But the other governments greatly deluded themselves if they thought they could keep out books that were freely circulating among their neighbors. The discovery of the New World, Vasco da Gama's voyage round the Cape, and improvements in navigation followed in rapid succession and had the fortunate result of increasing the volume of trade. All these causes joined together formed a solid phalanx marching toward the Enlightenment, and its enemies could neither arrest its progress nor dent its armor. A new relationship was called for between the governors and the governed that frankly took into account the increasing strength of the latter and aimed at consolidation through adapting to the new ideas. Alas, this golden rule was but little observed in the reigns that led up to the French Revolution, or during the course of that lamentable

4

occurrence! Queen Elizabeth of England never lost sight of this rule during the forty-four years that she reigned, and so she triumphed over all the tempests that assailed her, leaving behind a memory that is still justly dear to the English, despite her many faults in other directions. If Charles I had not left this path to follow one in the opposite direction, he would probably not have lost his life, England would have been spared the disasters that befell her at this time, and the Stuarts might still be on the throne. God knows what the policies of the Valois Kings in France might have led to if the line had not died out and been providentially replaced by a Henri IV. Henri IV possessed all the advantages that a King could desire. He was fortunate in occupying a middle position between the opposing parties in his kingdom. He was a Protestant in the eyes of the Catholics and a Catholic in the eyes of the Protestants, so that everyone could rally round him, while none felt threatened by him. The only chance for his enemies lay in his death, and that was why the best of our Kings, who brought the most prosperity to France, was so often the target of the assassin's knife.

Under Louis XIII the Protestant side expected persecution from a Prime Minister* who was also a Catholic priest and, as such, hostile to their rights as well as jealous of their success in trade and industry. Therefore, as a protection, they joined forces with the high nobility, who saw in such an alliance a chance to overawe the Court and to increase or maintain their power and influence in the State. The powers of the high nobility were constantly being eroded, so that the people came to regard it as a useless burden that could no longer protect them from the arbitrary power of the Crown. On the other hand, Cardinal Richelieu taught our Kings to fear the high nobility, to humiliate it in every way, and to entrust the exercise of power to men of lower rank, for they were weak enough to believe that they would find more servile agents here who were less able to check the whims of their favorites. This twofold weakening of the high nobility greatly accelerated the triumph of democracy. Since Richelieu's time, our Kings no longer convoked the Estates-General,† and they thought to increase their power by minimizing that of the institutions which stood between them and the people. They forgot that great maxim, "Do as you would be done by," for if the power of the great nobility shielded the people from the arbitrary proceedings of the Crown, it would have rendered the same service for the Kings during the political storms that periodically troubled the State. And once the shields had been destroyed in order that nothing might oppose the encroachments, and

* Cardinal Richelieu.—ED.
† The Estates-General, the nearest equivalent to the English Parliament, did not meet between 1614 and 1789. No conscious decision was taken in 1614 not to summon them again, and they had, in any case, lost the "power of the purse" as early as the fourteenth century. However, their very desuetude made their summoning in 1788 momentous.—ED.

above all the cupidity, of the courtiers, it was no good trying to create new ones in the moment of crisis, no good asking help from groups you had weakened and humiliated. They had no more strength or power left, and because the monarchy had sapped its own foundations, it took only a slight jolt to send it crashing. But why am I so eager to run on ahead with this sad tale? I shall return to what I was saying.

The decline of the great nobility in France could be observed as early as the Fronde,* when the arrest of three judges from the Parlement of Paris caused more stir than that of three Princes of the Blood. Louis XIV learned how to rule from the experience he gained during the Fronde, and because the King knew how to give orders, the Princes of the Blood, the great nobility, and the people learned how to obey. Yet he continued to suppress the Princes and the high nobility throughout his reign even when it was no longer necessary, so that their status at Court was reduced to that of servants with the right of access to the King, and their ambition limited to profiting from this access to gain favors. Louis XIV believed, and his successors have continued in this lamentable policy, that everything that could occasionally obstruct the satisfaction of his good pleasure and hinder his administrative activity should be abolished as tending to undermine his power and diminish the luster of his Crown. So he attracted all the noblemen to his Court in order to lessen their influence on their estates and in provincial affairs. Previously they had tended to live on their estates, but the enticements of the Court and the capital gradually caused them to abandon this practice and establish themselves in Paris. There they ruined themselves, and soon they were seeking to restore their fortunes either by marrying beneath them, which was another step on the road toward equality, or by benefiting from extravagances that were called the King's "generosity," which had the double disadvantage of annoying the public and of making the nobility increasingly unpopular and increasingly dependent on the King. Practically all that remained to the nobles of their former power were some honorific posts and the bulk of army appointments, though even here so many restrictions were successively placed on the commander of an army that the generals came to be scarcely more than the ministers' aides-de-camp. In short, the great nobility retained no more of their former splendor than the luster of names whose fame in history was tarnished by the insignificance of the majority of those who bore them.

England's troubles in the seventeenth century provided another powerful push toward democracy. The mournful spectacle of the proscription of the King and the nobility and the sequestration of property accustomed men to sudden reversals of fortune and thus facilitated their recurrence: *For the deeds of old are like paths to our eyes, o Fingal* (Ossian).

That is what happens in human affairs: The execution of Mary Stuart

* The Fronde, 1648–53, was a desultory civil war during the minority of Louis XIV. —ED.

prepared the way for that of Charles I, which in turn prepared the way for the execution of Louis XVI. Would to God the fatal progression stops there!

The brilliant reign of Louis XIV and the splendors of his Court were succeeded by the Regency of the Duc d'Orléans, my great-great-grandfather, during the minority of Louis XV.

> Happy times noted for their license
> When the fool, jingling his bell,
> Skipped over all of France. —Voltaire*

Open immorality replaced the hypocritical religiosity of Mme de Maintenon. It has rightly been observed that the extremes touch. People found themselves very weary of the ostentation of Louis XIV's Court and began to think that simplicity was much more convenient than magnificence. People gradually wearied of the trappings of their rank; boredom was now the most dreaded misfortune, and amusement the main objective. Rank was easily forgotten in the midst of pleasures, with the result that soon the prestige of the upper classes, which kept the lower classes in a respectful attitude, came to be destroyed. More than ever, everything moved toward equality.

The immorality of Louis XV's reign, the incompetence of his ministers, the disorder in his finances, all seemed to work together to accelerate the development of a democratic philosophy. This attractive yet dangerous philosophy received additional force from the literary mania that broke out at this time and the way in which it was exploited by the *literati,* who began to form an estate within the realm. The Kings and the great nobility thought that literature was the only occupation worthy of them because it was the cheapest way of buying praise. Frederick II—a great man who could easily have dispensed with literary fame—played one of the largest parts in spreading this mania; perhaps he was weak enough to be taken in as much by the success of his verse as by the success of his battles.

I was born on October 6, 1773, shortly before the death of Louis XV.† The first years of my childhood were spent in the same way as all the Princes of the Blood. However, some quirk of the times and the craze for novelty determined that my brothers and I should have a future that was altogether different. The education of the three sons of the first Prince of the Blood was to be supervised by a woman who enjoyed the confidence of both their father and their mother. To explain my father's strange conduct in all this, it is necessary to understand just how much he feared that the normal education given to the Princes of the Blood was respon-

---

* *Temps fortuné marqué par la licence,*
  Où la folie agitant son grelot,
  D'un pied léger, parcourt toute la France.
† Louis XV died on May 10, 1774.—ED.

7

sible for their usual insignificance. He also feared that the Chevalier de Bonnard, who was our subgovernor before we were entrusted to Mme de Genlis, would give us more of a taste for literature than he thought proper. My father never liked men of letters, and in this he stood out against his age. His four-square mind disliked the artificial glitter that often dazzles the bulk of men with little learning, and as he read little or even nothing himself, just about all he knew of literature came from the absurd antics of certain men of letters, their complacency and their abrasive manner, which he always found repellent. I also think that Mme de Genlis, who had a deep knowledge of my father and knew how to get her way with him, gave him to understand that she would bring us up in exactly the way he wished and that she would turn us out just as he wanted. Yet I doubt whether Mme de Genlis would ever have succeeded in supplanting the Chevalier de Bonnard without the ascendancy she acquired over my mother. Such was this ascendancy at the time that I know for certain that my mother strongly urged my father to entrust our education to Mme de Genlis and that she played an important part in his decision to adopt this path.

On January 12, 1782, I was taken to Saint-Cloud together with the Duc de Montpensier who, since his birth, had never been separated from me, and there we were handed over to Mme de Genlis, who was there at that time with one of my two sisters; my elder sister had remained behind in Paris because she had the measles, of which she died a fortnight later.

From our very arrival at Saint-Cloud I noticed a change in our style of life that, although I was very young—eight, in fact—made a very strong impression on me at the time, and looking back in later years seemed even more striking. We had lunch and supper alone at my sister's table, and the only plates were of coarse Delftware with a brown underglaze that contrasted greatly with the silver off which we had always eaten. The food was awful. All of this was supervised by Mme de Genlis's mother, the Baroness d'Andlaw, and she entrusted the cooking to one Gouffi, her domestic, who had to be dismissed after a few months' service.

It seems that at that time neither my father nor my mother wanted us to spend the whole day with Mme de Genlis. We were only with her from five in the afternoon until eight-thirty, when we had supper, having spent most of our time in reading aloud. The rest of the day was taken up with lessons and walks, sometimes with M. Lebrun, who was later made our official subgovernor but at this time was only styled "lector," and sometimes with our tutor, the Abbé Guyot.

In the following month (February 1782) we returned to Paris and went back to living in the Palais Royal, where we had most of our lessons. M. Lebrun and the Abbé Guyot took it in turns to take us to Belle-Chasse at five o'clock in the afternoon and came to collect us at a quarter past eight so that we could have supper in the Palais Royal, but soon we were staying at Belle-Chasse till nine-thirty. We used to go to Saint-Leu for the summer, and Mme de Genlis laid down that all the afternoon lessons should take place in her room, which we could leave only to go for our walk. However, when we returned to Paris, we reverted to the routine of not going to Belle-Chasse till five.

Soon Mme de Genlis was complaining that what we ate at the Palais Royal cost too much, and she had the cook dismissed and replaced by her husband's cook. Our expenditure at the Palais Royal was regulated in a modest and orderly fashion by M. Lebrun. However, this arrangement apparently did not suit Mme de Genlis, who did not care for us to spend so much time at the Palais Royal. Yet it was hard for her to alter it because it had been agreed that our male tutors should give us our lessons there. Still, on Sundays, when there were no lessons, she insisted that we have our lunch at Belle-Chasse and spend the whole day there.

Next she had our dancing master, Vestris, dismissed so that she could replace him with Dossion, who gave us our lessons at Belle-Chasse, and she laid down that we should lunch there three times a week. Poor old Prieur, our head *valet de chambre,* was pensioned off; he was a faithful retainer, attached to my father since his childhood, who had always slept in our room; and Mme de Genlis had allowed him to be at Belle-Chasse whenever we were. Likewise the Abbé Guyot was kept away from Belle-Chasse on the grounds that he had nothing to do there, since he was supposed to give us our lessons at the Palais Royal, and soon he was altogether removed. Finally, after a while our meals at the Palais Royal were discontinued as an unnecessary expense. It was decided that we should arrive at Belle-Chasse at noon every day and that we should stay there until ten o'clock in the evening. These various changes were not all effected till the end of 1786, so that it took Mme de Genlis nearly five years to complete her victory.

I must now try to give a clear picture of this house and those who lived in it. Belle-Chasse was a convent for nuns of the Order of the Holy Sepulcher, within whose walls my father had built a house where his daughters could be educated—though not, surely, his sons, because it was far too small for this. As a result, this house was subject to monastic regulations, but because my father was a Prince of the Blood the rules were slackened to the extent that men could come there during the day, though they kept away from the garden and the convent and left in the evening, so that at night there were only women inside. As soon as you entered this house, you got an idea of its strangeness and realized just how much ideas had changed since it was built. The first thing you noticed was the kitchen; there were servants' rooms, very dark and damp, to the right and left of a long corridor that was just as dark; it was decorated with blue tablets bearing English quotations in gold lettering, but it was so dark in there that I could never read them. This corridor ended in a door with a grille, and two nuns kept the key in a small inner room, again embellished with a tablet bearing English quotations. These two nuns kept up an unremitting vigil at the door. There was a tower to the left, and to the right a parlor, again bristling with inscriptions designed to remind the whole community of the original intention of excluding men from the house as much as possible and living in complete seclusion. My sister and Mme de Genlis took up the first floor; a small room, where Mme de Genlis had the beginnings (never completed) of a natural history collection, served as an antechamber; then came a dining room that was so small it was never used for that purpose after my sister stopped taking her meals alone. The drawing room was very fine. My sister's room was really just a long passage joining the drawing room and Mme de Genlis's room; there were two beds, one for my sister and one for her chambermaid, and the walls were decorated with tapestries of medallions depicting Roman emperors and scenes from Roman history; in the middle was a thick rope hanging from the ceiling, which we were made to climb up like a tree; between the two windows was a kind of recess containing sandbags that we used to haul up to the ceiling by means of a block and tackle, like drawing buckets of water from a well. This was the only room my sister ever had, and it was neither comfortable nor appropriate to her rank, especially when compared to the other rooms. I remember that we gave my sister a little cabin we had fitted out at the Palais Royal so she could have something that locked up; it was six feet long, three feet wide, and three and a half feet high, and it was put in this room.

Mme de Genlis's apartments consisted of a bedroom and two very small closets. Her mother, the Baroness d'Andlaw, and Henriette de Sercey, her niece, lived on the second floor. Mme de Genlis's two daughters, Mme de la Woestine and Mme de Valence, also had a fine suite of rooms on the second floor, and after the marriage of the latter, it was given over in its entirety to Pamela. It consisted of a large bedroom with a rather low ceiling and three very pleasant closets, so that Pamela had the best rooms of anyone. Also on the second floor was a small library that belonged to Mme de Genlis. Above the second floor there were just lofts and attics where the chambermaids lived. There was a very large garden, but after we had been entrusted to Mme de Genlis and my sisters' house had become frequented by men, we stopped going there. The nuns and, I think, the Archbishop of Paris had asked my father that while we were pupils there we should not exercise the rights we had, as Princes, of entering the convent and taking anyone we liked with us. My father gave his consent, thinking that this was fitting for the young boarders now living within the convent.

Step by step, Mme de Genlis removed all the women who had been attached to my sister, cutting her down to one chambermaid* whom she

* Mlle Rime.

made into a sort of subgoverness, since she was present at lessons and made out a report in a sort of diary.

My sister came to Mme de Genlis's room, for lessons on the harp and for readings, only when all the pupils were present. The pupils consisted of my two brothers, my sister and myself, César Ducrest* her nephew, and her niece Mlle de Sercey and Pamela, who were almost the same age.

Pamela was a little girl who had been slipped in among my sisters at Belle-Chasse rather mysteriously. This mystery, and the secrecy surrounding her birth, had aroused curiosity and given rise to a lot of speculation. It was said that she was the fruit of my father's love for Mme de Genlis. This is false: I have my father's authority to deny categorically that she was his daughter, and he charged me to go around saying at every opportunity *that she was not his.* I have carried out this duty all the more scrupulously for being convinced that if my father had the slightest doubt in this respect, he would not have talked to me in the way he did about Pamela. So I know *what she is not,* but not *what she is.* Mme de Genlis had had the idea of giving my sisters a little English girl as a companion so they would get used to speaking English. My father approved of the idea and got in touch with an Englishman called Nathaniel Parker Forth, who did business for my father and for many others in France and England and was said to be a secret agent for both governments. He undertook to find a little English girl such as Mme de Genlis wanted. The parents had to transfer their rights over this child to Mme de Genlis, who wanted to adopt her, and so it was decided to call her Pamela, as an allusion to the novel about Sir C Grandison† that would give this adoption a mysterious and romantic air in accordance with the prevailing fashion.

I believe it was in the year 1780 that Pamela arrived at Belle-Chasse. I have a clear recollection of her arrival; she could only speak English and defied us to pronounce the name of her birthplace (Christchurch). Later on Mme de Genlis forbade her to speak of Christchurch and related romantic tales about her origins; these could have been true, but I doubt it. She always claimed to be afraid that Pamela's mother, or the woman who passed as such, would try to reclaim her. However, in order to persuade this woman to surrender all her rights over Pamela to Mme de Genlis, my father settled a life annuity on her in England, which she continued to receive long after my father's death. Mme de Genlis always referred to her as *an awful woman,* though I never discovered why. Sometimes we were told that she was a chambermaid, sometimes the wife of an English soldier called Syms who had abandoned his wife and child at Fogo in Newfoundland, which could have been true or false, just as it could quite likely have been the case that she was not the mother of

* Son of the Duc d'Orléans's chancellor; Louis-Philippe's aide-de-camp, 1792–93, and companion in exile.—ED.
† I.e., Samuel Richardson's novel *Pamela.*—ED.

Pamela at all, whose origins seem very difficult to ascertain with any exactitude. Be that as it may, the mystery surrounding her birth, the inexplicable favor that Mme de Genlis openly showed her, and her subsequent marriage to a son of the Duke of Leinster, Lord Edward Fitzgerald, all led to conjectures about which I do not claim to be able to give an opinion except, as I have said, that she was not the daughter of my father, because I sincerely do not think she was; for the rest, I do not know. This digression has already taken me too far.

I have already spoken of the way in which my sister was brought up and her education supervised; Pamela fared much worse and learned nothing at all. Luckily for her, she spent all her time with Mlle de Sercey (Henriette), whose education had been very carefully looked after by the Baroness d'Andlaw and who was truly a model pupil: Mme de Genlis did not like Henriette much, and we thought this was because she was jealous of the way in which she outshone Pamela. Henriette was only seventeen when the Baroness died, and though she was then left to her own devices, her application and taste for study made up for the lack of supervision, and there is no doubt that she was often very useful at Belle-Chasse.

César had no supervision either. For a long time he had as his governor a M. Alyon, who had been an apothecary before Mme de Genlis seconded him to help with our education. M. Alyon was the only tutor whom Mme de Genlis allowed to spend the day at Belle-Chasse, but no one recognized his authority, and Mlle Rime, my sister's chambermaid, had more. This lack of supervision resulted in an undesirable laxity in our education, but I must do Mme de Genlis the justice of saying that she watched over me with great vigilance and took much more care over my education than over that of her other pupils. Mme de Genlis kept away anyone who, through character or learning, could outshine her in our eyes or discern and reveal to us her *superficiality*. That is why any of our tutors who had any real merit were relegated to the Palais Royal and scarcely saw us outside the hours from eight in the morning until noon.

The morning, spent in this way at the Palais Royal, was very useful to us. Unfortunately the Comte de Beaujolais,* my youngest brother, did not have the same advantages in this respect as the Duc de Montpensier† and myself. His only teacher was a *valet de chambre* called Barrois, who was doubtless very worthy and certainly too good to be a valet but who could not make up for a total lack of tutors.

Mme de Genlis had had my brother Beaujolais's tutor, the Abbé Mariottini, dismissed by accusing him of being in love with her and of making protestations of love to her. Beaujolais did not have M. Lebrun till after the Revolution, when the damage caused by the negligence of Mme de Genlis was put right, insofar as this was possible. The rest of us spent the whole afternoon in Mme de Genlis's room having lessons in all

* Louis-Charles d'Orléans, 1779–1807.—ED.
† Antoine-Philippe d'Orléans, 1775–1807.—ED.

kinds of subjects—geography, history, chemistry, and several languages. We took our lessons sitting on a large sofa, and Mme de Genlis always had her back to us. She nearly always sat at her desk, or else she painted flowers or made things out of hair or wax, because really she always had to be doing something. Our lessons were interrupted by various kinds of physical exercises, and we had a dancing lesson together in the drawing room. Because Mme de Genlis kept a special eye on me, she wanted me to go to the drawing room as little as possible, for she knew perfectly well that it was not as closely observed as it should have been. I was not particularly keen on going there either, and she ended up stopping my dancing lessons altogether on the pretext that I would always be a bad dancer and that it was a waste of effort giving me lessons. There was something in what she said, and I bear her no grudge. The day ended with various readings given aloud. It would be rather difficult to give an accurate picture of Mme de Genlis's educational system without talking about her ideas, her mode of instruction, and the methods she employed to arrive at her aim. She rarely persevered with any one project, though she always claimed to.

Her ideas were formed by reading and rarely by thinking, so naturally they varied with the books that passed through her hands. She read a lot, but for the most part so quickly that she could only remember what she had read with the help of notes and extracts. The result was that her learning had an artificial and superficial quality about it, though I think this suited her well enough, because her aim was to shine. She had filled her head with names and events and anecdotes in order to appear very learned; she was constantly reading and rereading what she called *disconnected jottings* and collections of quotations. She had prepared for us a lot of chronological abstracts where the histories of the various countries and periods were brought together, but she had not learned anything from them: I think she was incapable of the application that would have been necessary for this. This lack of reflection and application meant that she was incapable of abstract thought. Her mind could never take in at the same time the histories of the different countries in a period and compare them with each other. She read a work of history like a novel or a collection of anecdotes, and it would be true to say that that was how she read all her books. She liked ancient history much more than modern, first because she understood it better and secondly because it accorded with her tastes and emotions. There is no doubt that the Abbé Guyot was the formative influence in our understanding of modern history. It was he who gave us an understanding of how the feudal system succeeded the Roman Empire and how the modern monarchies grew out of feudalism. Mme de Genlis knew nothing of this, and I doubt whether she could have grasped it clearly, for it was very difficult to make her understand extended or complicated relationships. She had a marked predilection for the Age of Chivalry and Gothic times, when she thought that the women,

13

and consequently the passions, reigned supreme. She thought that these knightly sentiments, this enthrallment with the woman of one's dreams, prompted the great acts. She employed every device to stir this ideal in us, though it was the platonic side of love that she wanted to impress upon us. Maybe she had more than one reason for this, and without going into greater detail on this delicate subject, suffice it to say that she realized that a woman's influence is often destroyed by a physical relationship or at least shaken, while platonic love fitted in perfectly with the kind of religious framework she wanted us to adopt. She could exercise an influence only through the passions, and physical passion can never be carried as far as spiritual passion. However, she never managed to gain for herself the complete ascendancy over my mind to which she aspired. I was too well aware of the poverty of her intellect to submit mine to hers, and she also recognized that the thing was impossible. Yet what she realized even more was that emotional men, those who are easily carried away, are most easily dominated by women: The intensity of their feelings and the violence of their passions removes their power of reflection and throws them rapidly into extremes, often indeed diametrically opposite ones, because it is easier to pass from one extreme to the other than to find the golden mean. The Abbé Raynal* has said that of all men, the French most resemble women in character, and this observation has enough truth in it to solve many of the problems connected with the Revolution.

It is true that we are all disposed to let ourselves be guided by our passions and that it is only reflection that can hold us back and show us the right path to follow. It is therefore impossible for someone who is unreflective to be sure how he will act and to follow a consistent course of action. I believe that this is what happened with Mme de Genlis in the course of our education. The plan she started off with was very different from the one that she was following at the end. I thought the first was better because it had less quirks and because it was less influenced than the second by the spirit of the times. The younger one is, the more impressionable; first impressions determine our outlook, and I am glad when I remember that those I received were very sound. Mme de Genlis boasted that her educational system was different from Rousseau's because she wanted to give the impression of starting everything from scratch, but the truth of the matter is that he provided her model and was the only authority that she followed with any consistency. His works all follow the same line, and one can see from them that his philosophy favored the people, that it was republican. I have often heard her talk about Rousseau's refusal to undertake the education of the children of Prince Louis Eugene of Württemberg. I am transcribing the beginning of a letter in which Rousseau gives this Prince some advice about the education of his daughter; I think that this quotation will give a more

* Guillaume Raynal, 1713–96, *philosophe.*—ED.

accurate picture than anything that I could say of the ideas we received from Mme de Genlis and of the way in which she regarded our education herself. Rousseau is speaking:

· Motiers, November 10, 1763

If I had the *misfortune* to be born a Prince, to be *enslaved* by the conventions of my station; if I were *forced* to have a train of servants, that is to say masters, and if *nevertheless* my mind were sufficiently elevated for me to wish to be a man *despite* my rank, to wish to carry out the great responsibilities of being a father, a husband, and a citizen of the Republic of Mankind, I should soon feel the *difficulties of reconciling all of this,* and above all that of bringing up my children in the rank where they had been placed by nature *despite* the one they have among their equals.

So I should begin by saying to myself: We must not wish for incompatible things, we must not wish both to be and not to be. The obstacle I want to overcome is inherent in the nature of things; if that cannot change, the obstacle must remain. I must realize that I cannot have everything that I want, but never mind, no despair: *I will do my best with the available material,* trusting in my zeal and courage. No small part of wisdom is to submit to the yoke of necessity; when the sage does the rest, he has done everything. That is what I would say to myself if I were a Prince. Afterward I should go forward without discouragement and fearing nothing, etc.

It is easy to imagine the number of elaborations and commentaries this text lends itself to; and what a ferment such a leaven must have produced in a passionate woman and in young Princes who were ardent and given to enthusiasm! They were to regard their status as a Prince of the Blood as a burden and to believe that they would be delivered from the heavy *yoke of necessity* if they were relieved of it. They were bound to give a rapturous reception to a great political revolution that unfurled along these lines; and that is what happened to us. We had no doubt that the personal sacrifices we had to make because of the Revolution were a real benefit to humanity, and this opinion led us to take a joyous pride in giving up the things that the Revolution demanded of us. The love of virtue, of morality, and of everything that is good and honorable, sentiments which Mme de Genlis certainly drove home to us at every turn, became themselves in this combination a new stimulus toward democracy and revolution.

I should make it absolutely clear that it was Mme de Genlis's aim to turn me out as a man of honor, and I can say with a good conscience that she succeeded. However, since she was the kind of person who related everything to herself, she used to say that the best reply she could make to her enemies who had tried to blacken her character with calumnies was to give her pupils an austere morality. Now, this quality was very much in accordance with the spirit of the times and the democratic and revolutionary philosophy. Mme de Genlis turned us into honorable and virtuous republicans, but in her vanity she wanted us to continue to be Princes of the Blood. There was much here that could not be reconciled.

15

What she read to us, the lessons she drew from history, and the praise and blame she bestowed on the heroes of Greece and Rome all made the same point, and she constantly strove to make us adopt the moral standards of such men as Epaminondas, Phocion, Cincinnatus, Epictetus, Marcus Aurelius, etc. She made us read and reread the books of the New Testament, whose bent is decidedly democratic and egalitarian. Admittedly, as a matter of form, she made us read through all the books of the Old Testament once, leaving out the risqué bits, but her comments weakened the impression that an unguided reading might have produced. She would exclaim: "What cruelty, what horrors! Still, all this has been changed, all this has been done away with; our Lord came down from Heaven to abolish the old law, and we should only follow it in so far as it accords with the new law which is our guide, it is that we should believe, etc."

She strove to make us very religious and exhorted us to stand our ground against modern views. She strongly advised us to distinguish ourselves from the bulk of our contemporaries by a very strict piety. In short, she turned us into Catholic equivalents of the English Puritans.* It has taken the hard experience of the events I have lived through to knock this *Puritan republicanism*† out of my head and to give me moral principles more in line with my station in life. I confess that I had a painful descent from the illusory world into which Mme de Genlis had launched me to the realities and imperfections of life on earth, and it took a lot of internal struggle before I accepted that in this world perfection is unattainable, that everything here is imperfect and must necessarily be so.

The training of our minds was backed up by a program of physical education that was very good, if a little odd. One of Mme de Genlis's fads was never to do what had been done before, or at least never to do it in the same way, and the effect of this on us, young people given to enthusiasm as it was, was bound to make us become infatuated with all the new ideas of the period. However, I think that the effect of her methods on us was far greater than Mme de Genlis would have wished. A good knowledge of the patient's constitution is essential in estimating the effects of the cure: What may have no effect on a feeble and exhausted person can produce a raging fever in someone who is vigorous and passionate. I owe Mme de Genlis this justice all the more because I have just reproached her with things I would have passed over in silence were I not absolutely convinced of their truth. I shall always try my hardest to be fair, particularly to her. I must say that in the period when we were

* In England the name "Puritan" was given to the strict Presbyterians of Charles I's time and Cromwell's, who himself belonged to this sect. They insisted on maintaining the original simplicity of the Christian religion, as found in the Gospels, *in all its purity*. They wanted the same discipline in politics, to which they applied the democratic principles of the Gospels, which led them to a republican régime.
† Camille Desmoulins refers to Robespierre as "a republican Jansenist."—ED.

educated it was impossible to avoid all the pitfalls and not to err toward one extreme or the other, and one cannot deny Mme de Genlis the credit of having established a liberal education for Princes during the Ancien Régime *and of having always inspired us with sound morals and a good conscience.*

At Saint-Leu we had little kitchen-gardens that we cultivated in earnest and not as a princely amusement, which was right and proper. However, it was rather singular that my sister, Henriette, and Pamela also had gardens which they were *presumed* to be cultivating. So that we could perform these agricultural labors and all our exercises more freely, outside we wore smocks, trousers, and gaiters of coarse cloth, and we wore our *ordinary* clothes only on Sundays and on the days when my father came, because he did not like to see us in rough smocks. Yet he strongly approved of the exercises that could be performed more easily in this outfit, and here he was right. I have reaped many benefits from being hardened to fatigue; if I had not been, I could not have endured the life that was in store for me. Furthermore, what strengthens the body when we are young also strengthens our mind and character.

The outdoor exercises consisted of long walks, riding when we were older, climbing trees, jumping, running, and playing prisoner's base, etc. Actually, we played prisoner's base with all the valets in the house, for without them we would not have had enough people for a game, and it is good exercise. All in all Mme de Genlis's gymnasium was jolly good.

I have already said that though she censured Rousseau, Mme de Genlis followed his principles. So she had to make me *plane wood,* and like Emile* I had to become a *joiner* and *turner* though not a *locksmith,* because she said that this was a dirty trade. I believe she had an additional motive, which was that the late King, Louis XVI, was a rather good locksmith, and because of her passion for being different she preferred us to take up other trades. Moreover, carpentry is a much more pleasant occupation than that of a locksmith, and it is very good exercise, particularly in winter or bad weather when one cannot go out.

Little by little Mme de Genlis included some strange exercises in our education; among others, we had to carry up the baskets containing the day's supply of firewood. This went on all the time at Belle-Chasse. At Saint-Leu we used to go and fill up two pitchers with water from a grotto in the park, carry them back to the château, and deposit them in Mme de Genlis's room. When we went to Spa in 1787, she sent us every morning in the same way to fill the two pitchers from the Pouhon fountain, where those who were taking the mineral waters congregated, and like any water-carriers, she made us carry them across the whole town to the house where we were staying. This public parade through the streets carrying pitchers amazed those who witnessed it; fortunately this took place very

* The title of Rousseau's famous educational treatise.—ED.

17

early in the morning, so we met very few people. As we got older we got stronger, and naturally it was found that our ordinary pitchers were too light, so instead of being filled with water, bags of lead shot were placed inside, and I think that in this way I got up to three hundred pounds.* It was fashionable then to make constant reference to classical times and to revive their practices and their republican institutions, and Mme de Genlis discovered in some book or other a Greek exercise using dumb-bells recommended by Hippocrates for convalescents to tone up the muscles. As soon as she had made this precious discovery, we were ordered to lift up dumbbells twelve times every morning and to use the heaviest weights we could manage. Another exercise was to go up and down the stairs carrying on our backs a basket containing an iron weight. I think I got up to three hundred pounds.

Our food was very frugal. When our education began, we ate alone when we were in the country, and with M. Lebrun and the Abbé Guyot at the Palais Royal. However, at Belle-Chasse Mme de Genlis allowed various people to have lunch with us on the pretext that it was cheaper to maintain just one table. The number of these people increased every year until finally a medley of people, not all of whom were socially desirable, sat around our table. However, this did not happen at Saint-Leu because my father and mother lunched there from time to time, which they never did at Belle-Chasse.

Another peculiarity of our way of life was sleeping on a hard bed. Mme de Genlis had to win us over to this, and there was some delay in putting it into effect. Our beds consisted of a paillasse placed on a table. It is easy to get used to this kind of bed, and it is a good habit for young people to acquire.

There is no need to go into greater detail about my education, and I must now start to recount the events in which I took part. I shall take it from 1787 because I left Paris and its environs for the first time then.

Mme de Genlis had visited Spa in 1774 and enjoyed it immensely, and she had always wanted to make a second visit. In 1787 she managed to persuade my father and mother to pay the place a visit. The Low Countries and Holland were in turmoil at this time, and in the spring plans had been discussed for sending armed support for the Dutch Patriot party.† Although I was still only thirteen, I would have had to take part

* This seems a lot. However, in her memoirs, Mme de Genlis mentions that Louis-Philippe was strong.—ED.

† In the struggle between the Prince of Orange (Stadtholder) and his opponents, Prussia and England supported the Prince, to whom both their royal families were related, and France supported the Democrats (the name was used), since the foreign policy of the Ancien Régime had never been influenced by ideological considerations. In 1787 Prussia intervened militarily, and France prepared to do the same. But in September the Prime Minister, Loménie de Brienne, decided against intervention on financial grounds. Partly because of this the Minister of War, Ségur, and the Minister

in this campaign. I was colonel in chief* of the infantry regiment of Chartres that was then stationed at Givet, where it was planned to assemble the troops, and it was on the direct route to Spa. It would also give me the chance to see something of the troops and to gain a bit more experience of the world, which was considered essential before I embarked on a career in the army, where it would be virtually impossible to continue my education.

We left for Spa at the beginning of July 1878 with Mme de Genlis, who had limited our escort to M. Mirys and M. Conade the surgeon, an odd decision considering we had to traverse the great garrison towns and the whole of the Low Countries. When we reached Lille,† Mme de Genlis was given ample opportunity to appreciate the inadequacy of her arrangements for our journey. M. le Prince de Robecq, the commandant of Lille, was notified of our arrival when our courier was questioned at the gates, as is usual with frontier towns; and because a Prince of the Blood was not supposed to travel in France *incognito,* he prepared forthwith to give us the customary honors. He ordered the garrison to present arms and the regiment of Montmorency Dragoons to escort us to the glacis where he awaited us.

You can imagine how embarrassing it would have been at this juncture if our escort had been limited to M. Mirys, M. Conade, and Mme de Genlis, even though she was our governess; but by a lucky accident her brother M. Ducrest, who was my father's chancellor, happened to arrive at Lille at the same time we did. He was making for the coast of Flanders where my father had considerable landed property, and he broke his journey to accompany us. The presence of a soldier who was a Knight of the Order of Saint-Louis and in my father's service saved us from the ridicule to which we should otherwise have been exposed. I was in uniform, which was the way in which my father and, I think, all the Princes of the Blood traveled in France; I dismounted as soon as I saw M. de Robecq, and crossed the town on foot in the middle of a vast crowd. The troops were presenting arms and formed a line stretching from the gates to the house where we were staying. There I found a guard of honor with a flag of the Auvergne regiment, and I dismissed them in the usual way.

We spent the next day profitably at Lille, visiting the citadel, the

---

of the Marine, Castries, resigned. Castries had advocated a naval war to the knife with England as the solution to the régime's difficulties. He may have been right. During the period of his ministry, 1780–87, he had built up a superb navy for this purpose, regardless of cost and the complaints of the Finance Minister.—ED.

* At this time the Princes of the Blood owned the regiments that bore their names, and a lieutenant colonel commanded them for them.

† We did not have to pass through Lille and it was not on our route, but once Mme de Genlis realized that it was not much out of our way, she decided to satisfy her curiosity.

fortifications, the arsenals, and the military hospitals; we went to the parade where I gave the order of command, and after all that I had to attend a formal luncheon and the garrison's maneuvers. I do not know how I would have brought it off without M. Ducrest, because I was too young to have acquired the art of appearing in public and to have learned how to receive the honors. This visit cost Lille five hundred gold louis* that had to be given to the garrison. Instead of going straight from Lille to Brussels, we went by Valenciennes in order to pick up the road we had left to visit Lille. We arranged it so that we arrived at Valenciennes at night to avoid the honors. I warned the commandant, M. d'Esterhazy, that we would be leaving very early in the morning so that we could cross the Low Countries without having to stop—which the government was as keen for us to do as we were because of the disturbances there at this time.†

And we did get across quickly, even bypassing Brussels so as not to be seen. All the same, we could not but notice the Bourgeois Militia‡ everywhere mounting guard. The people were wearing cockades, and altogether it was a scene likely to ripen the seeds of Revolution in minds already greatly disposed toward it.

There is little to say about our stay in Spa. My mother kept open house on a grand scale. After lunch people played faro, which was necessary because at Spa nearly everyone is a gambler or an invalid. It was during this trip that the Chevalier de Chatellux fell for the charms and conversation of Miss Plunkett and decided to marry her. Mme de Genlis, I think, played her part in bringing about this marriage or at least helped to get the future Mme de Chatellux the promise of a place as lady in waiting to my mother.

There had been some trouble at Spa before we arrived. A new casino had been set up in competition with the existing one in which the Bishop of Liège had a share, and this new casino had built a hall which was much finer than that of its rival.

The Bishop, as sovereign ruler of Spa, had the new casino closed. But his authority was not recognized, and play continued despite the orders of the magistrates. Then he sent his guards in with no more success, and while we were at Spa he sent along a strong detachment of troops with

---

* A gold louis was worth twenty-four *livres* or francs, i.e., about the same as a pound sterling.—ED.

† The troubles in the Austrian Netherlands (Belgium) were caused by the Emperor Joseph II's attack on their "ancient liberties" in his drive toward uniformity and centralization in all the Hapsburg lands. In 1789 the Austrian garrison was driven out. Joseph's brother and successor, Leopold II (1790–92), was able to reassert Austrian authority by playing off the "Aristocrats" against the "Democrats," many of whom sought refuge in France, where they propagated democratic notions in general and the idea of a French invasion of Belgium in particular. The latter took place in 1792.—ED.

‡ The equivalent of the French National Guard, formed in 1789.—ED.

two cannons to stop the gaming in the new casino. This deployment of force to defend the profits of a faro bank was not very edifying, especially coming from a bishop, and was calculated to increase our horror of *despotism* and arbitrary power.

Meanwhile in France the resistance of the *parlements* to the government was increasing. The Parlement of Paris was exiled to Troyes. The plan to send troops to Holland was called off,* and at Spa the people expressed their discontent quite openly.

Returning from Spa, we went to Givet, where my infantry regiment was stationed. The lieutenant colonel in command at this time was M. de Vernon du Maget, and his second in command was M. de Valence, who, after a fashion, carried out the honors. I took command of the regiment for two days, which were spent in festivities and maneuvers. M. d'Esterhazy was in command at Givet with the rank of *maréchal de camp*.†

We left Givet with my mother and went to Sillery, where M. de Sillery‡ laid on magnificent festivities for us for eight or ten days, and we then returned to Paris at the end of September.

Discontent was increasing daily. The Parlement refused to register the government's financial legislation, declaring that these matters were outside its competence and that only the Estates-General had the necessary *competence*.§ The King came to Paris on November 19, 1787, to preside

* See note †, page 18.—ED.

† This rank was between that of brigadier and that of lieutenant general.—ED.

‡ At this time Mme de Genlis's husband, the Comte de Genlis, was styled Marquis de Sillery after the death of the Maréchale d'Estrées, who had made him her sole heir and left him the estate of Sillery. He was guillotined in 1793, and after his death Mme de Genlis chose to resume her first title and abandon that of Sillery. The Comte de Genlis's family name was Brulart, and he used this name as well for a time during the Revolution, after the National Assembly had suppressed the use of titles and names deriving from a landed estate. I am only going into such detail in order to explain how it was that Mme de Genlis changed her name so often although she was only married once.

§ The thirteen *parlements,* of which that of Paris was by far the most important, were primarily courts of law. Their involvement in the legislative process stemmed from their role, more or less acknowledged by the King, as custodians of the "fundamental laws," or unwritten constitution, of the kingdom. Their registration of an edict amounted to a declaration that it did not contravene the fundamental laws and, by extension, the best interests of the King. Their role was a capital one in the period 1614–1789, when the Estates-General, the equivalent of the English Parliament, was not summoned. The Parlement would inevitably be eclipsed by the presence of the Estates-General, and just why it demanded them in 1787 has never satisfactorily been explained. For what it is worth, the present writer considers that the Parlement was reacting to the King's decision to convene the Assembly of Notables, which had met in February 1787, in an attempt to outflank parliamentary resistance to his financial legislation. It must have appeared to the Parlement as a unilateral repudiation of the entente, the agreement on essentials, which had enabled the King and the Parlement to rule France during the past century and a half without reference to representative institutions at the national level. At all events, the

21

over what was called a *séance royale,* that is, *a lit de justice without ceremonial.** However, I remember that the *Gardes-françaises* and the Swiss Guards were armed and lined the quays from the Barrière de la Conférence to the Palais de Justice. The King allowed the councilors of the Parlement to give their opinions and to speak for quite a long time; then he stopped the discussion and ordered the Parlement to register the edict establishing a loan of a hundred and twenty-five million francs, as well as the other edicts. At this point my father sprang up and protested against a registration that he regarded as illegal.

The King merely replied to him dryly: "It is perfectly legal, sir." Then the registration took place. That night M. Fréteau and the Abbé Sabatier, the two councilors who had opposed the registration the most vigorously, were arrested by *lettre de cachet*† and escorted as prisoners of state to the châteaux of Dourlens and Mont-Saint-Michel respectively.

The following evening the Baron de Breteuil, minister for the *Maison du Roi,*‡ came to my father on the King's orders with instructions that he should leave Paris before midnight, spend the night at Raincy, and arrive at Villers-Cotterêts§ the next day. The King forbade him to receive anyone there except his family and Household. The Baron added that it was very painful for him to be the bearer of such tidings, since he was much beholden to the House of Orléans. He did not, however, in spite of that, in any way relax the King's orders about who could visit Villers-Cotterêts. My father carried out the King's orders to the letter, leaving the Palais Royal at eleven in the evening for Raincy and arriving the next day at Villers-Cotterêts. Before he set out he came to Belle-Chasse to tell Mme de Genlis what had happened, and he gave her the news in much the same

---

National Assembly abolished the *parlements,* and of all the institutions of the Ancien Régime they sank with the least trace and the least regret.—ED.

* If the King wanted to force the Parlement to register an edict, he held a *lit de justice,* which Fontenelle described as "a bed where justice sleeps." The theory of the *lit de justice* derived from the Roman law maxim: "In the presence of the delegator, the power of the delegate ceases." The difficulty was that the *parlements* were in-increasingly challenging the legality of the *lit de justice* (as Louis-Philippe's father does on this occasion) and also that the people would less readily obey a law when they knew that the Parlement's registration was not free. This was especially so when, as in this instance, the controversial edict was concerned with floating a loan, to which the response was necessarily voluntary. Accordingly, the idea of a *séance royale* was adopted to give a semblance of a free registration: The councilors gave their opinions but were not allowed to proceed to a vote.—ED.

† A *lettre de cachet* was simply a letter sealed with the King's sign manual, the small seal that he wore on his finger. It is usually regarded as being synonymous with all the abuses of the Ancien Régime; however, though its operation was, strictly speaking, arbitrary, the vast majority of the letters were issued at the request of the head of a family to restrain his errant offspring; a good example of this is to be found on page 25 of this volume.—ED.

‡ The minister for the *Maison du Roi* was, in effect, the Minister of the Interior.—ED.

§ The principal country seat of the House of Orléans.—ED.

way as he would have spoken to her about anything else. His first words were: *"My God, madam, I am an exile."*

My mother went to Villers-Cotterêts straightaway, and we left a few days afterward. As soon as he heard that my father had been exiled, M. de Biron, then Duc de Lauzun,* asked in vain for permission to go to Villers-Cotterêts, but at the same time permission was granted to the entire personnel of my grandfather's old Household. This gave rise to my father's remark that there seemed to be some fear that he would have too good a time at Villers-Cotterêts, since all these people had been sent along but his friends were not allowed to see him. However, the boredom that he experienced was one of the least of the ills resulting from his exile, for at Villers-Cotterêts a group sprang up that was against my father and sowed the seeds of the lamentable rupture between him and my mother that was to occur sometime later. Hitherto the peace and harmony of the Palais Royal had never been disturbed, since my mother had the wisdom to shut her eyes to my father's affairs, which she could have allowed to upset her. All the Princes of the Blood came to Villers-Cotterêts to express to my father the pain that his exile caused them. Would to God he had continued to act with the moderation and dignity he showed then. But he could not endure the boredom of life at Villers-Cotterêts and *begged* to be allowed to return. At the end of five or six weeks he managed, through the intermediary of my grandfather (the Duc de Penthièvre),† to get permission to remove to Raincy on the condition that he did not come to Paris. This made possible our return to Paris because we were able to go to Raincy every Sunday. My mother remained with my father at Raincy.

My father was exiled at Raincy for four or five months and acted with nothing like the same dignity he had displayed at Villers-Cotterêts. During this period of exile Mme de Chatellux profited from Mme de Genlis's absence and other circumstances to find a way of gaining my mother's entire confidence. Mme de Genlis soon noticed this and was able to turn the dislike that my father already felt for Mme de Chatellux into bitterness. Moreover, my father was painfully aware that the group that had come into being at Villers-Cotterêts continued to cut my mother off from him at the Palais Royal. He was easily convinced that Mme de Chatellux wanted to rule the roost there, cause a breach between my mother and Mme de Genlis and in consequence with himself, and thus gain control over his children's education. For her part, my mother was very annoyed with Mme de Genlis: She demanded her dismissal, and so developed those awful intrigues that caused us so much pain.

* Armand-Louis de Gontaut, Duc de Biron, 1747–93.—ED.
† Louis de Bourbon, Duc de Penthièvre, 1725–93, the last male descendant of Louis XIV's legitimated children and father of Louis-Philippe's mother, from whom he inherited vast estates and a striking resemblance to *le Grand Monarque.*—ED.

My father returned to Paris in April or May 1786, though I do not think he was allowed to appear at Court at first. Because of this exile, I received the Order of the Holy Spirit a year later than the other Princes of the Blood, though I was baptized in June of this year with the Duc de Montpensier, the King and Queen acting as godparents. Shortly afterward we set off with Mme de Genlis to spend the summer at Lamotte, an estate that my father had just bought, situated in Normandy by the sea.

My father and mother came to spend some time with us, and afterward Mme de Genlis conceived of the idea of returning to Paris slowly through Normandy, without bothering to obtain my father's authorization for this. We went from Rouen to Le Havre and thence to Cherbourg, where we were received by the Duc de Beuvron, the commandant of the province. General Dumouriez* was commandant of Cherbourg at this time, but he was away when we passed through. We were shown the work being done on the fortifications of the harbor in great detail. Having got as far as Cherbourg, Mme de Genlis was tempted to go farther afield, and she took us off on a tour of Brittany, still without my father's consent, on the grounds that we had to avoid Rennes, where the Estates of Brittany were in session and there was considerable disorder. In fact we could easily have returned directly from Cherbourg to Paris without having to go through Rennes, because Rennes was not even on the most direct route, but Mme de Genlis preferred to take us to Brest, whence we returned to Paris via Nantes, Tours, Châteaudun, Chartres, etc. I know that my father strongly disapproved of this trip and was very upset. Mme de Genlis's only motive was the desire to see some provinces she did not know very well and to give us a pleasant and educational tour, showing us the naval establishments at Brest, Cherbourg, Le Havre, Saint-Malo, etc. It must be said that the circumstances of our journey were extraordinary. We traveled in a carriage that was called a *voiture à douze* because it really could take twelve people. M. Lebrun did not come with us, and it was M. de la Woestine who looked after the expenditure and officiated as the senior member of our party. We were not very closely supervised, and we thoroughly enjoyed our trip and wished it could have been prolonged. One rather unusual visit we made was to Mont-Saint-Michel, where the Abbé Sabatier had recently been a prisoner. Mont-Saint-Michel was a Benedictine abbey just off the coast of Normandy and built on a sugar-loaf rock surrounded by sea at high tide. The prior of the convent was governor of the fortress and, as such, in charge of the prisoners of state who were sent there by *lettres de cachet*. We arrived in the evening and were waiting for supper with the monks when one of their number rushed in like a man inspired and gave a pompous rendition of an ode he had just composed in my honor that began with this baroque line:

"Bourbon, we see you on this rock!"

* Charles-François Dumouriez, 1739–1823, minister, general, Louis-Philippe's commanding officer in the campaign of 1792–93.—ED.

Then we had supper. While we were at table a few prisoners were allowed to come in, and each one told us his story. Among them was a Breton gentleman called M. de Bélissue, whose arrest had caused a great stir. He was an officer in the Bassigny regiment and had just been imprisoned at Mont-Saint-Michel by *lettre de cachet* for having disobeyed his superior officer in refusing to order his picket to fire on the crowd at Rennes. Instead of going before a court-martial, which would have been the natural way of trying him, he was cashiered without a trial simply on the say-so of the Minister of War. He spoke with great vehemence about all the issues of the day, and he gloried in the persecution he was enduring for having defended the liberties of his province, as he put it.* Another prisoner was M. Lion, son of M. Lion de la Houssaye, a merchant from Honfleur. He was not a political prisoner, but had been imprisoned for love. He was very young, and in despair at not being allowed to marry a woman with whom he was madly in love, he had tried to blow his brains out but had missed, the bullet merely grazing his forehead and leaving a bruise. Particles of gunpowder were embedded in his face, and he looked very sad and abstracted. As Honfleur belonged to my father, we gladly undertook to ask his family to let him go, which was agreed to on the condition that he went to Santo Domingo. There he went on to elope with the sister of Mlle de Sercey.

The things we saw and heard during our extraordinary visit were like something out of an adventure story. It made a great impression on me, which was made even deeper the next day when we walked through the subterranean vaults and dungeons. We asked to see the famous cage where the author of the *Gazette d'Hollande* had *been shut up for seventeen years for writing something against Louis XIV,* and we actually saw it! It was made out of thick pieces of timber placed in a fearful, damp dungeon. On one of the posts there was a flower that the wretched man had carved with a nail. The prior told us that the cage was scarcely ever used, except that occasionally a prisoner was put in for a day or two as a special punishment. He said that he had often toyed with the idea of demolishing it as a relic of barbaric times, and we promptly asked him to do this to mark our visit. The prior cheerfully consented, to the great joy of the prisoners who were following us. The only person who seemed to miss the cage was the Swiss guard, and his regret was natural because visitors gave him money to show it to them, but he was quickly consoled

---

* The disturbances in the summer of 1788 were occasioned by the Keeper of the Seals Lamoignon's edicts of May 8, which transferred the political role of the *parlements* to a Plenary Court. Registration by this body was to replace the separate registration by each of the thirteen *parlements* that had rendered general legislation impossible. In addition, the range of cases tried by the *parlements* was reduced, as was the vast territorial area of the Parlement of Paris. It is difficult to estimate the magnitude of the unrest throughout France, but at all events Lamoignon was dismissed in September 1788 and killed himself the following year.—ED.

by a hefty tip and by being reassured that he would get just as much for pointing out *the dungeon where the cage had been.* It was not destroyed in our presence, as was said at the time, because the work could not have been done in a single day. They just removed the door.

I have gone into such detail about our visit to Mont-Saint-Michel to show how everything combined to increase our ardor for the ideals of the Revolution. The rest of our journey had no special importance. On our return we learned that Cardinal de Loménie had been replaced by M. Necker as head of the ministry and that the Notables had just been convoked to give their opinion about the composition of the Estates-General.* What had to be decided was whether the three Orders should each have the same number of deputies and, if not, what the proportion between them should be. The Notables were divided into seven working committees, each presided over by one of the King's two brothers or by one of the five Princes of the Blood currently Knights of the Order of the Holy Spirit. The committee presided over by *Monsieur* (Comte de Provence) was the only one to recommend that the Third Estate be given as many deputies as the other two Orders put together, and yet its advice was followed. The Estates-General were convoked on December 24, 1788, and the letters of convocation for Poitou were sent to me as governor of the province.

I was nominated a Knight of the Order of the Holy Spirit on January 1, 1789, and installed a month after Candlemas. Nothing remarkable happened during the winter, which was very quiet. We were inundated with pamphlets of an increasingly democratic nature. At this time the Abbé Siéyès's famous pamphlet appeared, called "What is the Third Estate?" to which the obvious reply was, "It is everything, and the other two Orders are nothing."

These matters were the only topic of conversation, and the general ferment went on increasing. At this time we began a course of natural, civil, and constitutional law. Mme de Genlis chose as our tutor M. Gauthier de Biaurat, the nephew of a barrister of this name who was deputy for the Auvergne to the Estates-General. The law course was on the same lines as the rest of our education. The basis for our studies in natural law was *The Social Contract,* the *Discourse on Inequality,* and the

* Necker, the popular ex-Minister of Finance, was reappointed on August 25 and became *de facto* Prime Minister. On September 23 the exiled Parlement entered Paris in triumph, but on September 25 it had lost its popularity overnight by declaring that the Estates-General should be composed as they had been in 1614—i.e., that the clergy and the nobility together should have almost double the number of deputies possessed by the Third Estate. Necker referred the matter to the Assembly of Notables, a body of some 150 of the leading ecclesiastics, soldiers, and mayors, nominated by the King, which was surprising in view of their opposition to change when they had met in 1787.—ED.

other works of Rousseau. In civil law we went back to the origins of the different laws and customs of the kingdom of France. This study made us look at both Roman history and that of our monarchy in a new light, and brought us to the conclusion that all our laws were contradictory and oppressive and that our institutions and codes of law were in need of total renovation. The course in constitutional law consisted of an examination of all the forms of government, and we drew the conclusion that the constitutions of the American states came nearest to perfection.

The Chevalier de Chatellux died in the course of this winter. I do not know what passed between his widow and Mme de Genlis at this time, but the rupture became complete, and Mme de Chatellux even stopped coming to Belle-Chasse.

In the spring of 1789 M. le Comte d'Artois and my father arranged a marriage between M. le Duc d'Angoulême and my sister. The marriage was announced immediately, but its celebration was to be deferred till the feast of Saint-Louis (that is, August 25 of the same year) because my sister would not reach the legal age for marriage until August 23. This marriage was broken off without any explanation after the events of July 14, 1789, when M. le Comte d'Artois and his children emigrated. Everything that has been advanced on this subject is a tissue of absurdities.

The Estates-General were to meet on April 27, but this was deferred till May 4. For some time there was uncertainty about the venue: Orléans was considered because it was central and seemed far enough away from Paris to escape from the ferment that possessed this great city, and then there was talk of Soissons, with the Court established at Compiègne. It is probable that the choice of either of these places would have furnished more opportunities of preventing the Revolution. However, the expense of transporting the Court on the one hand and laziness on the other, and perhaps also the observation that these two towns belonged to my father, led to the decision to stay put and to choose Versailles. I can say with impartiality that if my father's influence was anywhere to be feared, it was at Paris rather than at Orléans or Soissons, whose populations were too small for there to be great popular risings. Thus, as is so often the case, the very danger is encountered that one has been trying to avoid, for later events have amply demonstrated that if the object was to remove the Estates-General from the influence of Paris, Versailles was a bad choice.

At the end of April 1789, there was a considerable riot at Paris. A crowd gathered in the Rue Saint-Antoine outside the wallpaper factory belonging to M. Réveillon. I cannot remember now exactly what had excited the populace; I think the workers wanted an increase in their wages, which Réveillon was refusing,[*] and the indignation against him became so great that all his workshops were destroyed. The *Gardes-françaises* were sent to the spot together with the Swiss Guards, but they

[*] Actually, Réveillon paid above-average wages and was referring to a reduction in wages in the abstract, not with reference to his own work force.—ED.

arrived too late to save the factory. They showed no reluctance about obeying the order to disperse the crowd and to fire on anyone who resisted. I remember that at this period the people were very discontented with the *Gardes-françaises,* and I think the authorities could have profited from this disposition, nourished it, and perhaps thereby have prevented the defection of this regiment, which played a vital part in the success of the Revolution. Be that as it may, the Réveillon riots had no consequences, and no one was punished except for a very small number of people who were killed or wounded on the spot.*

The Estates-General met a few days after this scandalous scene. On May 3 the deputies of the three Orders were presented to the King, each separately and following a different ceremonial. Both sides of the door were opened for the clergy and one for the nobility, while the King received the deputies for the Third Estate in a completely different room. The King ordered distinctive costumes for the members of the three Orders: The deputies for the clergy wore the costume appropriate to their rank within the Church, all the deputies for the nobility wore the costume of a peer of France, while the deputies for the Third Estate wore barristers' gowns, which was especially impolitic because there were, in fact, a large number of barristers among them. A peasant from Brittany (old Gérard, elected by his province) refused to wear a barrister's gown and stood out in this ceremony and all those that followed by wearing a peasant's smock, his hair short and unpowdered. The costume of old Gérard seemed an excellent criticism of those the Court had prescribed and of all the little squabbles over etiquette that were already being ridiculed on all sides.

On May 4 there was a great and solemn procession through the whole town of Versailles. It left from the church of Our Lady where all the deputies had assembled, and they marched in two files in front of the canopy containing the Holy Sacrament, which was carried by the King's two brothers and two nephews and immediately followed by the King, and then again two files to the right and left. The left-hand file was composed of all the Princesses, with the Queen at the head, while I found myself at the head of the file on the right, composed of the Princes and the peers, in the place of my father, who had wanted to take his place among the deputies. The procession made its way to the church of Saint-Louis, where we heard high mass and a sermon preached by the Bishop of Nancy, which concluded the ceremony.

The next day, May 5, I followed the King in his carriage with his two brothers and two nephews to the chamber of the Estates-General. The

* The King set up a commission of inquiry into these riots in the Parlement, but then transferred the hearings to a conciliar commission, presumably because he believed the Parlement had instigated the riot. This is the last indication we have that Louis XVI still regarded the judicial nobility rather than the Third Estate as his opponents.—ED.

Queen had gone there in advance and was sitting on a throne to the left of the King's and lower down. Monsieur and all the Princes of the Blood had stools to the right of the King's throne, and the Princesses were likewise seated to the left of the Queen. The peers were also seated on the platform where the throne stood, but in a second line behind the Princes. There was nothing remarkable about this session except the solemnity of the ceremony, which was enhanced by the beauty of the setting. It lasted for a very long time because a memorandum of M. Necker was read out. I returned with the King to the Palace of Versailles, then I went back to Paris, and finally in the evening we returned to Saint-Leu.

Some troops had already been brought up to the outskirts of Paris and Versailles, and more were summoned in the course of June. Three regiments of Swiss troops were encamped in the Champ-de-Mars and policed the markets of Paris, where bread was becoming very expensive; but there were still not many troops in Paris because of the fear that they would lose their discipline there. The authorities had even gone so far as to prevent the Swiss troops encamped in the Champ-de-Mars from communicating with the Parisians, and yet with inexplicable inconsistency the King left in the middle of Paris the regiment of the *Gardes-françaises,* composed of six battalions, which had been there ever since the Peace of Aix-la-Chapelle in 1748. At this point I should mention that this privileged regiment used to be the refuge of every scoundrel until the worthy Marshal Biron succeeded in improving its morale and intake by forming an excellent body of noncommissioned officers whose vigor and firmness made up for the laziness and indifference of most of the officers. These gentlemen had got into the habit of serving only when their companies were at Versailles, which meant that in fact they only served one week in seven or eight because there were only four companies in attendance on the King. This continued absence on the part of the officers was one of the main causes of the defection of this regiment, and it is worth noting that the four companies that were in attendance on the King on July 14, 1789, remained there loyally for five weeks and returned to Paris only after the King had disbanded the regiment. It is my belief that if the King had brought the whole regiment to Versailles on the pretext that the Estates-General should have a guard, this measure might have prevented its defection, because it seemed perfectly loyal at the time of the Réveillon riots. The organization of the Swiss Guards was very different and much tighter, and they were rarely in Paris. Nearly all their barracks were out of town and the officers were constantly with their companies, with the result that officers and soldiers had a mutual confidence, and discipline was very tight. These circumstances and, to be fair, the spirit of rivalry between the two accounted for the fact that unlike the *Gardes-françaises,* the Swiss Guards did not disband. However, it has been said with some justice that if Marshal Biron had lived, he would probably have preserved the *Gardes-françaises* because he was their idol and he had commanded them for forty-four years, ever since their command had been given to him by Louis XV on the field of battle at Fontenoy. Unfortunately he had died the winter before, and his successor, the Duc de Châtelet, had made innovations and altered the Marshal's organization of the regiment, causing discontent among the noncommissioned officers and the soldiers. An inconceivable act of weakness completed the ruin of the regiment. At the end of June or the beginning of July 1789, when signs of discontent had already been noticed in the regiment and there was reason to distrust its mood, some soldiers were put in the Abbaye* for a grave breach of discipline. A crowd broke into the prison, set itself up as the *liberator of oppressed soldiers,* and carried them in triumph to the Palais Royal and through all the streets of Paris. All this was accepted with docility, and a dangerous example went without punishment. The people and their ringleaders drew the conclusion from this lamentable act of weakness that a bit of boldness was enough to intimidate the authorities and paralyze the armed force that was being deployed in such an ostentatious and threatening way.

We remained in peace at Saint-Leu while the Estates-General debated whether voting should be by Order or by head, or in other words, whether the first two Orders or the last should have the majority of votes.

M. le Dauphin died at the beginning of June, and I was obliged to accompany his heart to the Val-de-Grace since my father's role as a deputy did not leave him the time to attend functions. The ceremony lasted seven hours. The tombs of my branch of the Dukes of Orléans were in the same vault where the hearts of the Kings were placed, and the abbess, pointing to the place that was waiting for me, said: "We shall have you there someday." This was charming and seemed a certainty at the time, but now I fear that she will never have the pleasure of having me in her vault.

On June 22 I was at Saint-Leu, dressed as usual in my coarse clothes, when I received an order from the King to be at Versailles the following morning at seven o'clock dressed as a peer. I arrived punctually. The King was alone in his closet with his two brothers and his two nephews, waiting for the deputies to take their seats. As this was taking some time, he asked for a large armchair to be brought in, as well as a list of the deputies, which he began to read out loud, making comments on those whose names were known to him. In general he was not very complimentary, and he kept repeating: "What the devil is he doing there?" as though he disapproved of anyone who was a member of this Assembly he had convoked himself, or wanted the Assembly to be composed of unknowns! There were all too many of these as it was, but it seemed that the Court disapproved of a man putting himself forward as a deputy, and I think that this was because the deputies were not nominated by the King and

* At that time, L'Abbaye was the military prison for the *Gardes-françaises.*

did not derive their powers from him. It is true that in proceeding to make elections the people were only carrying out the King's orders, but when passions are inflamed people rarely make rational judgments based on first principles.

The Court wanted neither a National Assembly nor Estates-General; and the King had only consented to convoke them as a result of his financial difficulties and in the hope of getting some money from the nation by making this concession, which the Court expected would only be temporary. After giving the necessary financial assistance, the Estates-General would be sent home without being allowed to meddle in affairs of State, and if they thought otherwise the King and his troops would put them to rights.

We waited for five hours in the King's closet, and I spent them all standing up because I was not given permission to sit. I did not dare ask permission, still less take it without asking, although I noticed that the other Princes had placed themselves on tables in odd corners so that they were not directly facing the King.

The cause of this long delay was the difficulties made by the Third Estate in complying with the King's instructions on how to enter the hall and on seating arrangements. It will be recalled that on June 17 the deputies of this Order, on a motion of the Abbé Siéyès, had constituted themselves as a *National Assembly,* simply inviting the deputies of the other two Orders to join them and check their credentials together. At the same time, they had abolished all the existing taxes and restored them provisionally and only as long as they remained in existence as the National Assembly. The King had closed their chamber, and on June 30 they had taken refuge in the tennis court where they swore their famous oath not to separate till they had righted abuses, etc. Now after all these declarations, they no longer considered themselves as deputies of the Third Estate for such and such a constituency,* but as representatives of the nation, and they did not want the order in which they entered the hall and took their seats to be determined by their constituency. Finally they won their point, and the only concession they made was that they would not occupy the benches reserved for the clergy and nobility. Because of these difficulties, the King was detained at the palace for five hours. Finally the King and his cortège set off. All the streets were lined with troops, and the approaches to the hall were guarded by strong detachments. Inside, the arrangements were the same as for the opening ceremony, except that in her absence, the Queen's throne had been removed and the Princes and peers sat on both sides of the King on the platform. The deputies of the clergy were to the right, those of the nobility to the left, and those of the Third Estate were at the back facing the throne. It is notable that even before they formed themselves into the National Assembly, the Third Estate never accepted the name of Third Estate, and

* The constituencies were known as *baillages,* or bailiwicks.—ED.

31

when they referred to themselves they always spoke of the *Common of France* to equate themselves with the House of Commons in England. There was a deep and mournful silence in the chamber, which contrasted with the cries of "Long live the King" that had echoed on all sides at the opening ceremony. This silence was made even more impressive by the absence of women and spectators, who had filled the room on the first occasion. The King made a speech that can be found anywhere, annulled the decrees of June 17 and the days following, forbade the use of the phrase *National Assembly,* and had read aloud what became known as the Declaration of June 23,* which granted provincial Assemblies organized on a new basis and Estates-General every three years, etc. Then he ordered the three Orders to withdraw and departed himself, followed by his suite. M. Necker was not present at this ceremony.

The first two Orders left immediately after the King, but as the third remained behind, M. de Brézé, the grand master of ceremonies, repeated the King's orders and received Mirabeau's famous reply: "Go and tell your master that we are here at the behest of the people and will only leave at the point of bayonets." I was still with the King when M. de Brézé, quite beside himself and very downcast, came to make his report. The King turned white with anger and said with an oath: "Get them out!" Then he straightaway retired to his private apartments, to which I did not follow him. M. de Brézé lost no time in returning to carry out his new orders, but he found no one there. The Third Estate, having upheld all its decrees and protested against what had just happened, had dispersed very peaceably.

There is nothing more dangerous than taking highhanded action merely to test out one's strength, and the height of folly is to repeat such action after experience has demonstrated that one neither can nor knows how to follow it up. A wise and enlightened government will never undertake something unless it has the ability and the will to carry it through. If one looked merely at results, it would be tempting to say that the purpose of all this pomp and glitter, this highhandedness and display of troops, was to discredit royal authority instead of consolidating it, and that these measures had been suggested by treacherous advisers who wished to ruin the King and his Court. But nothing would be further from the truth, for the Court always exaggerated its own strength and the weakness of its enemies, and thought it could cow them and reduce them to obedience by a mere display of force—though as soon as it came to a choice between actually using the troops or climbing down, the latter course was always adopted. The success of all the stages of the Revolution can be attributed to this inconsistency on the part of the Court, this faulty relationship between its plans and its actions. The people were conscious of royal authority only when it was menacing and unpredict-

* It was adopted by the Counterrevolution as the basis for its program, as being the King's last free expression of his will.—ED.

able. The best way of demonstrating the truth of my argument is to give a brief account of the events that followed the *séance royale* of June 23, though the later events of the Revolution furnish many other examples. On June 24 a few *curés* joined the Third Estate, which had already been reinforced by the nobility of Dauphiné. The next day forty-seven deputies of the nobility, including my father, also joined the Third Estate. These forty-seven deputies formed almost the whole of the minority of the nobility, who had always voted that the credentials of deputies of all the Orders should be examined together and that the Estates-General should deliberate as a whole and not by Orders. On the 26th members of the clergy continued to flock to the Assembly of the Third Estate, so that a large majority of the Estates-General was already to be found there. On the 27th the King ordered the members of the clergy and the nobility to do precisely that! And so resistance always ended in giving way, and the sole purpose of the struggle seemed to be to give the popular party a triumph, to increase its demands, and to give it to understand that it would obtain everything it dared to ask for.

This victory was acclaimed at Paris because it was rightly regarded as a decisive stroke. It did not, for all that, stop the unrest from increasing, because it was easy to see that it was not a voluntary concession and that instead of being made in good faith, it was designed only to gain time. The Palais Royal, which was rightly called the *Capital of Paris,* had always been the place where those who dabbled in politics assembled; news had always been exchanged in its gardens. In England people are less sociable; they talk only when they really have something to say, and they gladly leave the task of circulating news to the newspapers. In France, however, the newspapers have always had to limit what they print to what the censors allow the public to know, and so anyone wanting to keep abreast of what is going on goes to the public places, to the gardens and the cafés, since news is always spread by conversation rather than by the newspapers. Accordingly, it is easy to imagine that at such a critical juncture, with matters of the greatest importance arising every minute, the Palais Royal was turned into a vast political club and a terrible hotbed of enthusiasm and unrest. Nor is it more surprising that as the Palais Royal was increasingly taken over by the orators and the crowd that was always at their side, so it was deserted by peaceable men, and though it was perfectly natural that they should retire from the field of battle, the triumph of men of violent persuasions was facilitated thereby. It was very hot in 1789, and the marvelous summer proved a valuable ally of the Revolution: Frequent downpours would have made excellent agents of repression and would have been an excellent way of dispersing gatherings large and small. It was noticed during the Revolution that the riots and popular movements always took place during the fine season and never in winter.

Public unrest in Paris was increased by something which was especially dangerous in that it has always stirred the people at all times and in all places, namely the high price of bread and the shortage of wheat. I do not know whether this dearth was real or whether it was engineered, but what is certain is that it got progressively worse during the course of the summer, the autumn, and even the winter. I believe that the cause was bad administration, illegal associations, and even monopolies, which happened in 1774 and on other occasions, and I do not believe that its causes were political, that is to say, that one of the two parties contrived it to ruin the other. They have accused each other of this, and if either of them could have made the accusation stick it would have done so, from which I conclude that neither of them had anything to do with it.

I think I have already gone into so many reasons for unrest that you would be prepared for anything to happen. And yet I know that for a great number of people these reasons do not seem sufficient, and they believe that there were others. They will insist that money was a principal cause of the Revolution so that they can delude themselves about its real causes, and since my father was the only one among the revolutionary party who was rich enough to use this means, they claim that the Revolution was accomplished by means of the Duc d'Orléans's money.

I swear that this is a falsehood, and God knows that nothing would make me give my word unless I were absolutely sure! Nevertheless, I am aware that however much people might be disposed to believe me, on such a matter my testimony cannot be enough, and so I shall attempt to prove my assertion.

I shall repeat here the same argument that I used when talking about the shortage of grain: If my father had bought a revolution, his enemies would have discovered the proof and made it public. I will not accept the argument that they could not or did not dare to do it, and still less that they did not want to because of their *regard* for my father. For never has a man been hounded so relentlessly. Only a violent hatred could have inspired all the black calumnies that were employed to ruin him. The sole object of many newspapers, lampoons, and tracts seemed to be to libel him by concocting the most ridiculous stories about him, by collecting and distorting all the anecdotes that could possibly harm him, and by carefully digging out material that could give an unfavorable impression of anyone who had ever been his friend. His relatives and even his ancestors received no better treatment, and all Grange-Chancel's lampoons on M. le Régent were carefully reread to refresh the memory of the public and draw conclusions unfavorable to my father. Therefore it seems evident that if he really had distributed money to the people, at least some of his agents would have been discovered or some of those who had received money, either from him or from others; but no positive proof has ever been brought forward, and people fell back on the vague accusation of his *having distributed money to the people.* This seems to me an irrefutable proof that the accusation is without foundation, and I would leave it at that except that the strength of the hostility that my father's enemies displayed toward him furnishes me with even more conclusive evidence in his favor. Relentlessly and with minute attention to detail, they built up everything into a tissue of ridiculous lies that would be specious enough to justify the persecution they had in mind and to give a court of law, or rather one of perverted justice,* an excuse to condemn. They failed in both their objectives, and the best proof of this is to read the proceedings of the Châtelet's inquiry† into the risings of October 5 and 6, which they themselves instituted and which are in print.

So far as possible I shall not anticipate my account either of these baleful riots or of the inquiry, but I must say something here to establish the conclusions that I think can be drawn from these events in favor of my assertion that my father did not use money to bring about the Revolution.

This inquiry was set up in November 1789. From then until the following August, that is, for more than eight months, anyone who wanted to give evidence against my father could come to the registry of the Châtelet. Care was taken to make everyone come forward who was known to be prejudiced or have a grudge against him, without a single person being summoned who could be said to be on his side. I have read through these iniquitous proceedings in their entirety, and I can say that if they had not been published I would have had them printed immediately, because it is impossible to read them without being struck with the absurdity of the accusation and without recognizing that for anyone of good faith, there can be no greater vindication than that provided by reading them. The witnesses do not give a single positive fact, and their evidence is composed of hearsay and vague conjectures that have no semblance of truth and are often contradictory. There is not even a single person accused of being my father's agent in dealings with the people, and not one accused of having distributed or received the smallest sum. Now, since this investigation did not come up with a single piece of evidence that my father or anyone else distributed money to the people, this lack of evidence, after judicial proceedings of such length and exhaustive detail, is the equivalent of positive proof that my father was not concerned. Unfortunately, the transcript takes up two volumes, and it is difficult to get through them without a strong personal motive. I even suppose that the transcript was *unreadable* on purpose and that all that was wanted was for M. Boucher d'Argis‡ to be able to appear before the National Assembly with a voluminous procedure directed against the Duc d'Orléans and exclaim rhetorically: "See, now this terrible secret is exposed!"

Before I leave this subject, I must dispel one more myth that has

* Anyone who doubts that these courts dealt in perverted justice has only to read the transcripts of the Marquis de Favras's trial!
† Paris's main criminal court of first instance under the monarchy.—ED.
‡ One of the magistrates of the Châtelet.

played a big part in lending credibility to the belief that my father used great sums to bring about the Revolution. It was claimed that his later financial embarrassment could only be the result of his enormous expense for this object. I am convinced, and I hope I have proved it, that he spent nothing on this, but it will be even easier to prove that his financial embarrassment resulted from other causes, which I shall now try to elaborate.

It is well known that although the Duc d'Orléans had great riches, he also had great debts. The Revolution diminished his revenue, but not all the burdens on it, with the inevitable result that his financial embarrassment was considerable. The contraction of his revenue was enormous, as I shall demonstrate.

In the first place, the weakening of authority in the kingdom and the difficulty in using force meant that from the beginning of the Revolution, the collection of revenue was very slow and uncertain. Yet, however insufficient the sums collected, my father's treasury had to pay at fixed intervals the sums due on the land bonds and life annuities,* and this in itself would have been enough to bring about difficulties.

(2) There was much wasteful expenditure on some parts of his estates, which naturally diminished his revenues and gave those who owed him money an excuse not to pay.

(3) The legislation of the National Assembly on feudal rights would have been enough in itself to throw my father's finances into disorder. The decrees of the National Assembly divided feudal rights into two categories.† Those in the first class were abolished without compensation. My father had to bear this loss like all the landed proprietors, but it resulted in a considerable loss in revenue. Feudal rights in the second category were declared to be *redeemable,* that is to say that the new laws allowed those who payed them the chance to extricate themselves by repaying the capital to the proprietor, but under these laws payment had to continue until the redemption had been effected. But nothing of the sort happened: The redeemable dues were no more paid than those that had been abolished without indemnity. The pretext for refusing to pay was always that the size of the indemnity was under negotiation, but no one ever paid an indemnity. There was not sufficient capital in France to pay for such an operation, especially at this time, when all the spare capital in the countryside was going on buying the lands of the clergy which were up for sale.

(4) Finally, the greatest blow to my father's financial position was the

* It was possible for corporations and wealthy private individuals, as well as the Crown, to raise a loan by public subscription.—ED.
† The rights in the first category were those regarded as involving "personal servitude"—e.g., the obligation to send your corn to the lord's mill for grinding— while those in the second category corresponded to straight rent for the land.—ED.

National Assembly's legislation on the *apanages*,* and of all the frequent injustices committed by the various French Assemblies, it is impossible to deny that this was one of the most shocking. The main cause of this injustice was the ill will that a large part of the Constituent National Assembly bore toward my father. The existence of this ill will is a fact I think I can prove, and the conduct of the Assembly in the matter of the *apanages*, which I shall recount in detail, is in itself very strong proof. For present purposes it is enough to demonstrate that since the work of the National Assembly entirely ruined my father, this was not brought about by the expenditure that, according to his enemies, he is supposed to have incurred for the purpose of stirring up revolution.

At the end of 1790 the Constituent National Assembly, apparently not content with having to sell the whole of the Church lands† and the greater part of the Crown lands, and seemingly wanting to throw the public treasury deeper into debt than it already was by the payment of the pensions accorded to clergymen who had lost their livings and by paying all those whose jobs had not been suppressed, in its wisdom decided to revoke all the grants of Crown lands, or *apanages*, that the Kings of France had made to their brothers or younger sons. They, too, would receive an income from the public treasury instead, and in accordance with the current mania for mathematical equality in everything, all the cadet branches would receive the same. Accordingly, all the Princes who had an *apanage* were asked to disclose the amount of income they derived from it. There were only three Princes with *apanages* in France, the King's two brothers and my father. Monsieur,‡ Comte de Provence, put his at 1,500,000 francs,§ M. le Comte d'Artois's only came to 500,000, and my father's to 4,500,000, from which it can be seen that the object of the scheme was to rob my father and ruin him. But I am going to make this even clearer. The Assembly decided that each of the three Princes with *apanages* should receive instead an income of 1,000,000, which should be equally divided among all their male descendants in perpetuity. In addition, each of the King's two brothers was given a life annuity of 1,000,000 for the upkeep of his Household, and the nation undertook to pay off the 900,000 francs of life annuities that M. le Comte d'Artois had raised to satisfy his creditors. However, my father only got a million a year for twenty years to pay off his debts, and the Assembly did not grant him a million a year for life for the upkeep of his Household as it had

---

* The name given to the property with which the King's younger sons or younger brothers were endowed.—ED.

† In 1789 the Church lands were confiscated by the National Assembly, which undertook to pay the clergy's salaries. Since there was already a glut of land on the market, the measure was of dubious financial advantage.—ED.

‡ The King's next brother was referred to as Monsieur in Bourbon etiquette.—ED.

§ There were roughly twenty-four francs to the pound sterling.—ED.

done for each of the King's brothers, despite the fact that their *apanages* were worth much less.

I should weaken the impression that these proceedings must make on anyone who is impartial if I tried to hammer home their injustice. The concession of the Luxembourg Palace to Monsieur as part of his *apanage* was confirmed, as was that of the Palais Royal to my father, and M. le Comte d'Artois was promised a similar residence (the Temple belonging to the Order of Malta, of which his eldest son was Grand Prior). Yet here I must point out again that these confirmations were inspired by the same animosity and unfairness toward my father. The terms by which Louis XIV granted the Palais Royal to Monsieur (the first Duc d'Orléans of my branch) stipulated that if the property reverted to the Crown, any new buildings or improvements undertaken by Monsieur, brother of Louis XIV, or his male descendants would be accepted *ad valorem* and paid for by the treasury to their daughters or heirs in the female line. And since the various Dukes of Orléans had rebuilt the Palais Royal from scratch over the years, the Assembly would have had to buy it over again, which it had no desire to do just as much because it would not have known what to do with it as because the work was unfinished. As a result, it was regarded as more of a burden and left to my father. He protested in vain against this series of injustices and harassments; and in vain he pointed out that since Louis XIV's grant, our *apanage* had quadrupled in value because of the money we had constantly spent in improvements instead of buying more property, which we had a perfect right to do. His complaints were ignored, for his ruin had been resolved, and it was accomplished.

I assume that anyone who has taken the trouble to read these details will agree that the causes I have just given are sufficient to explain his well-known financial difficulties in 1792 when he concluded a concordat with his creditors.

To sum up this long section in a few words, *my father's income was reduced to a quarter while his debts remained the same.* And what will you think when I tell you that even of this revenue thus reduced to a quarter, the annual payment of a million francs for the *apanage* and the million payable for twenty years were never paid in whole or in part?

This digression has made me interrupt the thread of my narrative, but I daresay no one will be surprised that I have made it. Its conclusion is important because it seems to me to prove that despite what many people think, money was not used to bring about the Revolution. Now, if the Revolution was not paid for, the only other possible cause could be the state of public opinion, and one of the main objects of these memoirs is to prove this. Something else I hope I have achieved by this digression is to refute a baseless accusation against my father. Because, unhappily, I cannot justify all his actions, it is especially important for me to defend him when I can and to refute attacks that are unjust and without foundation. And now I pick up the narrative.

I have already said that the three Orders met in one Assembly in accordance with the King's orders of June 29, 1789, and I have discussed the effects of this in Paris. There is no doubt that the King's orders of the 29th contradicted those of the 23rd, for he recognized, at least tacitly, the step that the Third Estate had taken in setting itself up as the National Assembly since he ordered the first two Orders to join this Assembly. This order was directly opposed to those he had given only six days earlier at the *séance royale* of the 23rd that the Third Estate should not use the designation "National Assembly" and that each of the three Orders should deliberate separately in its own chamber.

I am not in a position to say whether, according to the laws then in force, the King had the right or not to give such orders to the Estates-General. I do not know these laws well enough to be able to give a definite opinion, though I am inclined to believe that he did not have the right; but whether he had the right or not, it is clear that his orders of the 29th prescribed what those of the 23rd had forbidden.

This contradictory manner of proceeding is at once a cause and an effect of the approach that I have said the King and his Court had always followed. They never formed the correct assessment of what line to follow in dealing with the nation and its representatives, whether these representatives were the *parlements* and the provincial Estates or the Estates-General and the National Assembly. On nearly every occasion the conduct of the Court divides into three contradictory phases. In the first there is a show of total and inflexible resistance, which is accompanied by terrible threats against those who try to disobey. In the second period, more threats but also partial concessions, which satisfy no one because they are clearly extracted by force and granted because they cannot be refused, and are always accompanied by secret reservations that leave some with the hope and others with the fear that the concessions will be withdrawn. In the third period some throw down their arms and others flee, while the enemies of the Court win a victory so unexpected and so complete that they no longer know what to do with it and often ruin it themselves, because success has gone to their heads. One can say that the Court regularly followed this progression throughout the whole course of the Revolution.

There is no doubt that in 1789 all France wanted a reform in the system of government and the creation of an elected Assembly. This demand was unanimous, and it was conveyed to the King in such a formal manner that it would have been wise not to oppose it.

As soon as the Estates-General had met, the King should have instructed his ministers to collaborate with the deputies of the three Orders in working out a draft Constitution that would have guaranteed the nation the rights it was demanding.

I believe the work would have been easy and its success complete if the King and his Court had so desired, but this was not what they wanted. They sought only to sow discord within the Estates-General, to turn the Orders against each other and paralyze their activity. They flattered themselves that this would demonstrate the futility of the Estates-General and make the nation weary of them, and it would then be easier to dissolve them, to rid themselves of any form of representative institutions at the national level and snatch from the nation its few remaining rights. What never occurred to them was that the same irresistible pressure of public opinion that had already forced them to grant the concession they wanted to withdraw would never let them do it with impunity. Thus, though they had in turn agreed and refused to summon the Estates-General, ordered and forbidden block voting by Order and individual voting, separate chambers for the Orders and then the one Assembly, they now managed to believe that the King had the power to dissolve by force an Assembly whose convocation he had not dared refuse and that after the terrible example that he was proposing to make of it, no one in France would think of asking for more Estates-General, and still less would want to be a deputy.

If one took the view that the first acts of the National Assembly were seditious, then the King should certainly have dissolved it, even, if necessary, by force. Then, however, it would have been absolutely necessary that the King, after such a display of authority, use the sovereign power that this act of authority had temporarily placed in his hands to give the nation the rights that were being demanded on all sides. I believe that this would have been the one way to consolidate the monarchy. In these circumstances his concessions would have been greeted with confidence and thanks, and the fear of royalist reprisals, an important cause of violence throughout the Revolution, would have gone forever. A wise constitutional government and above all good internal administration would soon have healed the wounds of the State and covered this miserable deficit of fifty-six million francs that caused such a stir.

Either way, whether the King had come to a sincere understanding with the Assembly or whether he had dissolved it, I think that such a grave crisis would have been very salutary, and looking back, it is very painful to compare what has happened with what might have been.

Be that as it may, the main thing for the King to do was that whatever policy he adopted, he should carry it out openly and with determination. Unfortunately he did precisely the opposite. He was constantly changing his plans and his actions, and this hapless inconsistency was one of the main causes of his misfortunes and ours. It destroyed what little confidence was left in the King's promises and undertakings, and there is no denying that the time that elapsed between two contradictory measures, such as those of the 23rd and the 29th of June, was sometimes so short that it was difficult not to see them as part of an overall plan based on deception and treachery. This impression of duplicity was reinforced when the King told the clergy and the nobility to join the Third Estate, constituted as the *National Assembly,* and then, maybe with the same breath, gave orders to surround Paris and Versailles with troops and prepared to use force to dissolve an Assembly whose combined meeting he had just ordered and whose legality he had just recognized. Not surprisingly the public, which was already nervous and suspicious, regarded the first of these orders as a cloak designed to cover the second.

After the union of the three Orders, the National Assembly was divided into thirty committees to speed up its work. After a few days the three Orders voted that the Archbishop of Vienne* should replace M. Bailly, who had topped the poll in the election of the deputies for the Third Estate of Paris and who had been elected president for a fortnight when the Third Estate had constituted itself the National Assembly. When the fortnight was up—that is, after the terrible events of July 14—my father was elected president, but declined.

The union of the Orders calmed the public for a bit as they waited for the Assembly to start its work, but the approach of the troops soon reawakened the unrest. By degrees, nearly all the foreign troops, German or Swiss, currently in the service of France arrived at the outskirts of Paris. The French regiments whose colonels seemed loyal to the Court party were also summoned, and these troop movements made it quite clear that the Court was planning a spectacular reassertion of authority. I think that the plans for carrying out this *coup* had not been settled, and that the Court was under the illusion that the mere presence of troops would be enough to frighten both Paris and the Assembly into submission and to destroy all authority that did not emanate from the King. I have good reason to believe that the Court was resolved to follow this up by making what were termed *examples* out of the most prominent members of the Assembly and to employ force to eliminate anything that could restrict the exercise of absolutism. Yet, though it was well known that M. Necker would not be a party to these projects, the King had not yet been prevailed upon to determine the composition of a new ministry. I have it from Monsieur, Comte d'Artois, that the nomination of the Baron de Breteuil was a matter of chance. The Queen said to him: "Whom do we have to replace M. Necker?" To which he replied: "The Baron de Breteuil can act with firmness and will do very well until we have the time to make a satisfactory final choice." According to Monsieur, these few words determined M. de Breteuil's choice, and it would have been the same if he had proposed anyone who had come to mind. He added that afterward he reproached himself heartily for making this suggestion.

I am persuaded that the King could have reduced Paris and the Assembly by the use of troops, but this can be judged by recounting the

* M. Lefranc de Pompignan.

41

facts. Clearly, the Assembly at Versailles was in the King's power, and all that was needed for success was boldness and speed—especially speed, first to stop the troops from disbanding and going over to the Parisians, and then so that the ringleaders in Paris and the Assembly would not have time to organize their defense, for men become very brave and enterprising when they believe they are lost and see their only hope of safety in reckless audacity. The Court did not bother to disguise its intentions, and everyone was made well aware of the fate that awaited him if he fell into their hands. The violence and anger displayed by the Court exasperated people and disposed them to push to the limit the advantage they derived from the weakness that, when it came to the test, always went with or followed the Court's threats.

The King dismissed M. Necker on July 11, and the people took this as a declaration of war which removed any consideration but that of saving themselves and attacking the enemy when possible. M. Necker went from Versailles in great secrecy and left France immediately, in accordance with the King's orders. In one of his works, he says that the King's motive in giving him this order had been to save him so that he would not be obliged to include him among the number of *examples* he was preparing to make.

The news of M. Necker's dismissal spread during the course of the 12th, and the turmoil it produced was indescribable. Crowds gathered all over Paris; the troops on the spot were ordered to take up arms, and more troops were called in. There were three Swiss regiments in the Champ-de-Mars, and M. de Lambesc was at the head of his cavalry regiment, the Royal German, on the Place Louis XV, accompanied by the Royal Dragoons; behind him, in the Champs-Elysées and in the Cours-la-Reine, came a considerable body of troops that could be reinforced at a moment's notice by numerous detachments placed all along the roads to Versailles and Rouen and in the area of Saint-Denis. To the left of the Prince de Lambesc was a line of infantry, though here, admittedly, the bulk of the *Gardes-françaises* was positioned. The line stretched from the Place Louis XV, all along the boulevards and almost as far as the Bastille. These troops were under the orders of the Baron de Besenwald [*sic*], lieutenant colonel of the Swiss Guards. Quite apart from these troop dispositions inside Paris, the city was surrounded by an army of about twenty-five thousand men under Marshal Broglie, whom the King had appointed Minister of War on M. Necker's dismissal. Consequently, on the evening of the 12th all Paris was in the grip of fear. M. de Lambesc, at the head of his regiment, had entered the Tuileries gardens by the swing-bridge at a gallop, and this sight had struck fear into everyone. That day Paris was in the King's power, as was Versailles, the Assembly, and the whole of France. Everything seemed tied up, and would have been if they had dared to believe it. But instead of getting down to a military occupation of Paris and to dispersing the mob, a portion of the troops was left under arms but without employment throughout the night. The *Gardes-françaises* were positioned on the boulevards, and for fourteen or fifteen hours the Parisians brought everything into play to win them over. The ensuing interchange was what finally led to the defection of the regiment. It is hard to imagine why this regiment was kept in Paris, when it could and should have been removed; and this was not all, for it was left there *alone, the only body of soldiers* to remain in the courtyard of the Dépôt* throughout the 13th.

The Place Louis XV was abandoned, and already the day seemed to be conceded. This hesitation gave the crowd the courage it lacked, the assemblies were larger than ever, the orators more audacious, and finally the terrible cry *To arms!* went out from the Palais Royal and spread like lightning through all the districts of Paris. The tocsin was sounded, drums beat out the call to arms, and in an instant Paris became an army. An orator, Camille Desmoulins, pistol in hand, got up on a table in the Palais Royal and told people to wear a cockade so that they could be recognized. Green was the color he proposed as being that of liberty, and it was adopted, but a moment later the green cockades were trampled underfoot when it was realized that green was the color of M. le Comte d'Artois's livery; and the people sported the colors of red, white, and blue, because they were the colors of the House of Orléans. Another orator proposed that they should seize the Invalides to get possession of the artillery and arms that were kept there and use them for the defense of Paris. They rushed there and, almost unbelievably, found that the ordinary guard of old pensioners had not been reinforced! This guard was soon overwhelmed, the arms carried off, and the artillery placed on the bridges, on the quays, and at the various points of access where it was feared the King would send in troops. Meanwhile, on the boulevards, the people were haranguing the *Gardes-françaises* and demanding that they take their stand *for* or *against*. They joined the people, and then the whole throng bore down on the Bastille, which was already surrounded by a considerable crowd demanding that the governor open the gates.

All these movements only appeared spontaneous: The events of July 11 and 12 had given the revolutionaries notice that the moment had come when they must either succeed or go under, and the electors of the Third Estate of Paris,† meeting in the Hôtel de Ville during the course of the 13th, had directed all these operations. It provided a striking example, and one too often forgotten, of the advantage to be gained by seizing

---

* The Dépôt was a large barracks on the boulevard at the corner of the Chaussée d'Antin.
† At the time of the election of the deputies for the Third Estate of Paris, the town was divided into sixty districts, to which all the bourgeois repaired and chose one elector for every hundred bourgeois voters, and these electors met in the Hôtel de Ville to elect the twenty deputies for the Third Estate of Paris to the Estates-General.

authority in moments of crisis; for then the man who takes it on himself to give orders will be obeyed, since men need to obey something and will recognize any authority. There was more than one example of this during the Revolution. This electoral assembly, then, having on its own authority made itself the government of Paris, convoked the electoral assemblies of the districts on July 13 as focal points to which it could address its orders, and it lost no time in organizing all the bourgeois of each district into companies and battalions. This became known as the National Guard, and one man in every eight was a soldier from the *Gardes-françaises* who taught seven bourgeois how to march, handle a rifle, and perform military service. On the orders of the electors, this National Guard immediately occupied all the military posts in Paris.

The Bastille was one of the most important of these military posts, and so on the 14th at seven o'clock in the morning one of the electors, M. Thuriot de la Rosière, later a deputy to the Legislative Assembly and the Convention, was at the gates of the Bastille negotiating with the governor. Meanwhile, the people were arming themselves at the Invalides, the defection of the regiment of the *Gardes-françaises* was being decided, and all the gates into Paris were seized without difficulty, even the Porte de Chaillot and the Porte de la Conférence: All the approaches were barricaded off and guards placed at the gates. Finally, all Paris except the Bastille was removed from royal authority and placed under that of the electoral assembly.

It would have been easy to throw a few troops into the Bastille, and it is hard to believe that its whole garrison consisted of thirty men from the Swiss regiment of Salis-Samade under Lieutenant de Flue plus the company from the Invalides that mounted the usual guard. Furthermore, it seems that there was so little expectation that this post could be threatened or besieged that no extra provisions had been laid in, and there was not even enough food to feed this small garrison for a *single day!* Therefore the governor could offer no resistance, but he prevaricated for some time, probably in the entirely reasonable expectation that the King's troops would come to his aid. This, however, was not even attempted, and toward four in the afternoon, seeing that no one was coming to his rescue, he decided to capitulate. I am writing from memory, and I would rather leave out details than report them inaccurately. I make no claim to be writing the history of the Revolution, but only tell what I know. I am not very well informed about what happened at the Bastille, though I do know that there were negotiations between the deputies of the electoral assembly and the governor of the Bastille, who agreed to let in men who were empowered to discuss terms, but I do not remember the details of this negotiation. What I am reasonably sure of is that it was just when the drawbridge was being lowered to let in the agents of the people and the electors that the multitude rushed in, and in this way resolved all points of difference. This was the only military exploit, and however prejudice or ignorance might have distorted this great event, I am sure that this is how the Bastille was taken. At the time, however, it seemed very important to present the popular victory as a brilliant and courageous action, for it was necessary that the people learn to think little of their opponents and to persuade themselves they were invincible. So the Parisians believed that they were a race of heroes, which gave them self-confidence and intimidated their opponents.

The unlucky governor of the Bastille, M. de Launay, was escorted to the Hôtel de Ville, but he did not arrive there alive, being slain *en route*—some say on the steps of the Hôtel de Ville and others at the Place Baudoyer not far distant! It is certain that he was already a fair distance from the Bastille when he was slain. The same fate befell several of his officers, and their heads and his were carried on pikes through the gardens of the Palais Royal and to every corner of Paris, providing an appalling prelude to the horror this city was about to witness. It is hard to imagine what the King was doing with his army at the time of the risings of the 13th and the 14th. It is generally admitted that Paris would not, could not, have offered any serious resistance. It is equally clear that at this time the troops would have obeyed *any* order coming from the King. Therefore, one can only explain his inactivity in terms of the incompetence or feebleness of those who were then at the head of the government. For a long time in France it had been accepted that the mere presence of troops was sufficient to overawe the people.* I even think they expected the mere arrival of troops would be enough to contain Paris and that it would not be necessary to fire a shot. Instead of that, the people of Paris played the role that in other times the troops have played: They made the King and his Court tremble without firing a shot. However, there is one detail that I must not omit, which, in reality or in appearance, had a great influence on the King's conduct at this juncture and on all the events that followed. The Archbishop of Paris† betook himself to the King at Versailles and played on his conscience by talking of the innocent blood that would be shed if his troops came to grips with the Parisians because, he said, in such confusion it would be impossible to distinguish the innocent from the guilty, both would perish together, and a King would be responsible to God for the innocent blood he had caused to be shed. The Archbishop urged the King to remove the troops and to use methods of conciliation instead. It is said that the King gave him this promise. Once this argument is admitted, it is impossible to justify war in any circum-

* This is an important point. However, a former Minister of Police, Lenoir, notes in his memoirs that in Louis XVI's reign, as opposed to that of Louis XV, excessive use of troops had been made, so that their effect had been diminished. The decision to use troops as instruments of internal police had been taken right at the beginning of the reign, in 1774.—ED.
† M. de Juigné.

45

stances, because all blood then shed is innocent. It was said at the time that this initiative of the Archbishop's was made with the King's prior knowledge, to give him a plausible pretext to withdraw the troops without appearing to give way to the Assembly or the city of Paris.

On July 15 the King went to the National Assembly to assure it that he did not want to cut himself off from it. The Assembly asked for the dismissal of his ministers, the withdrawal of the troops, and the recall of M. Necker. It obtained all these demands, and the King appointed to the ministry several of the deputies who had always advocated that the Orders should sit together. When the Assembly learned that the King was adopting all its measures, its enthusiasm knew no bounds, and in a spontaneous gesture all the deputies got up and escorted the King back to the palace.

The same day M. le Comte d'Artois and his children, M. le Prince de Condé, M. le Duc de Bourbon, M. le Duc d'Enghien, and M. le Prince de Conti, left France and, with the exception of the last, never returned during the Revolution. There is no denying that these Princes were very unpopular at the time and that the people of Paris had displayed great animosity toward them.

On July 17 the King made his way to Paris, preceded by a numerous deputation from the National Assembly. He was met at the Porte de la Conférence by M. Bailly, the new mayor, who had been elected without consulting the King.

To get to the Hôtel de Ville, the King had to pass through an immense, armed crowd that was completely silent, but when he appeared on the balcony of the Hôtel de Ville and fastened a tricolored cockade to his hat, the air resounded with cries of *"Long live the King!"* and cheers that were kept up till he left Paris. The same evening he returned to Versailles, and the deputation from the Assembly escorted him as far as the city walls and then attended a solemn *Te Deum* at Notre-Dame.

The electoral assembly nominated M. de La Fayette commander in chief of the Parisian National Guard, but he accepted only on the condition that the nomination be ratified by the King, who presented no difficulties. The electoral assembly continued to govern Paris for several months as easily as if it had had legal authority.

During this amazing series of events, my father spent his whole time at Versailles, occupied with his duties as a deputy. My mother was at Raincy, and we were at Saint-Leu with Mme de Genlis, who was very frightened because the spectacle of the Swiss Guards, the hussars, and so many troops left her in no doubt that the Court would win. Furthermore, communications had become so difficult and imperfect that she had only a very vague idea of what was going on in Paris and knew even less about Versailles, where my father and M. de Sillery, her husband, were at the top of the list of intended victims. She expected us all to be carried off at any moment by hussars, and every evening she took precautions so as to be warned of their arrival and have time to escape through the park in the forest of Montmorency. That would not have saved her even if she had got there, having avoided the suspicious and prying eyes of the large numbers of ordinary people and servants who occupied Saint-Leu at the time. No one was worse than Mme de Genlis at laying a good plan of escape and executing it, and her realization of this doubtless increased her fears. She became so frightened that on July 15, when everything was over (which, to be fair, she did not know), she dared not sleep in the château. On the pretext of taking us to Raincy, where my mother was, she led us along byroads, but in a coach-and-six, to the house of the Abbé Mastin at Boissy, where we knew we would be alone. This house was only three-quarters of a league from Saint-Leu, to which we returned next morning. Everyone knew the same evening that we were spending the night at Boissy, and our ridiculous expedition was a source of amusement to them.

My mother, too, had her worries about our safety at Saint-Leu, and she let Mme de Genlis known through a trusted intermediary that she wanted to have us at Raincy, but Mme de Genlis refused categorically, which greatly displeased my mother.

I remember going for a walk at this time with an Englishman who was helping with our education. I was very enthusiastic about the victory of the people, and he said to me: "Not so fast, you don't know what you are celebrating. You think this has saved your father, but it will lead to his ruin." "How so?" I replied. "Because," he said, "the leaders of a popular revolution have never derived any advantage from it and have always become its victims. You are very young, and I don't know what will become of you, but your father is too prominent to escape." I did not believe him, but his words made a strong impression on me, and I have never forgotten them.

Toward the end of July the wave of panic about the so-called brigands* reached Saint-Leu. It is one of the most extraordinary developments of the Revolution. The deputies of the popular party thought that the formation of National Guards in the provinces was going too slowly, and Mirabeau, who knew perfectly how to play on the credulity of the people, suggested that the process could be speeded up by simultaneously spreading a panic throughout France, which would force the nation to take up arms and form itself into contingents of National Guards. This strange plan was tried and was completely successful. It only took a very small number of letters to spread the rumor everywhere that not far from

* The cause of what has come to be known as the Great Fear is shrouded in mystery. Louis-Philippe's explanation, that it was engineered by Mirabeau, has no more substance than the more widely held contemporary view that it was part of an aristocratic plot.—ED.

each spot, there was a band of brigands cutting down the ripening corn to increase the famine, and that these brigands were burning villages and châteaux. All France was taken in, there was general panic, and the whole nation took up arms at once. In no time at all National Guards sprang up everywhere and rushed to the areas where they thought the brigands were to be found. They did not find anyone, but the nation was under arms, organized in units of National Guards with their commanders, officers, and noncommissioned officers. The aim was achieved because once set up, this institution would keep going of its own accord, for it gave security to the inhabitants of each area, who also would like the idea of wearing a uniform and could regard themselves as soldiers—something which flatters everyone's vanity and especially that of the French.

This panic frightened Mme de Genlis at first, but she soon recovered. However, the decrees of August 4 reawakened her anxiety. She did not want to stay at Saint-Leu any longer, and she went back to Paris almost immediately. There is no doubt that these decrees, which were called resolutions* at the time, had a great effect on the peasants, which was not surprising considering that their general purpose was to abolish feudal rights and the financial advantages of the clergy and the nobility. This sudden and somewhat unexpected abolition gave a tremendous jolt and was the signal for the burning and laying waste of châteaux in the provinces, and these fearful scenes lasted for several months. The peasants wanted to break into the châteaux to destroy the archives where the original titles of feudal and other dues were to be found so that they could never be reintroduced. In addition to these motives, there were personal and party animosities that brought disorder to its limit.

There is no point in my dwelling on the details of this famous night of August 4, when so much was done without discussion or reflection, in a sort of state of intoxication. The Vicomte de Noailles passes for the author of these decrees because he did in fact make the first proposal. I do not remember what he proposed, but I remember very well that he was followed by a large number of deputies of the clergy and the nobility from the opposite party, who capped his proposal with ones that were even more absurd, so that they brought about their own spoliation. It would be difficult to explain such madness except in terms of a *politique du pire*. This system consisted in driving one's opponents to adopt extreme measures in the hope that they would be impossible to execute and would lead to anarchy and a general confusion, for many people were foolish enough to believe that this state of affairs would lead to the restoration of an absolute monarchy and of those very privileges whose abolition they had themselves just brought about.

Mme de Genlis's return to Paris did nothing to calm her anxiety; and she wanted to find a house near town that would be near enough to avoid the risk of being cut off in the countryside, but at the same time far

* Or *arrêtés,* i.e., not a full legislative act.—ED.

enough away to be free from the fear of popular disturbances, which were in fact only too likely at this time. M. de Boulainvilliers's house at Passy combined these two advantages, and my father asked him if he would be willing to let it to her. He refused, but he offered to lend it, and his offer was accepted. We moved in there at the end of August. It was later spread about that Mme de Genlis had taken this house for purposes of intrigue and that she held cabals there. This is absolute nonsense. There is no doubt that her only motives were the ones I have given, and she never lived in such seclusion as then. Even my father saw very little of her; and M. de Sillery, who was very regular in attending the sittings of the National Assembly at Versailles, came only on Sundays when the Assembly was not in session. Mme de Genlis's brother, M. Ducrest, came only two or three times during the six weeks or so that we spent at Passy, and M. de la Touche-Fréville, my father's chancellor, came *once only*. The rumors that went around at this time about what went on at Passy were so absurd that these details are engraved in my memory, and I can vouch for their authenticity.

On the feast of Saint-Louis we went as usual with my father to Versailles to celebrate the King's saint's-day. We found that the National Guard of Versailles had taken over the positions formerly assigned to the *Gardes-françaises*. The Swiss Guards were at their usual posts and viewed with unconcern the National Guard in the place that the *Gardes-françaises* had occupied beside them. The Bodyguard and the Hundred Swiss Guards were on duty inside the palace, and the organization here had not been altered. M. Bailly, as mayor of Paris, and M. de La Fayette, as commander of the National Guard of Paris, came to Versailles on this day to pay their respects to the King on his saint's-day. They arrived in several carriages escorted by a mounted detachment of the National Guard. M. de La Fayette and all his aides-de-camp were wearing the uniform of the National Guard; in their buttonholes they wore the medal that the city of Paris had conferred upon the *Gardes-françaises* and that distinguished them from the other National Guards.

Mme de Genlis wanted to see the National Assembly, and I very much wanted to follow its proceedings. One day she took us into the gallery reserved for the substitute deputies. These gentlemen kindly let us enter their gallery every time we wanted to attend a sitting, and as long as the Assembly met at Versailles we went there often with M. Lebrun.

At this period the Assembly still retained a certain measure of dignity. Many of the deputies attended in court dress or in the costume of the Third Estate. The simple and noble style of the chamber and its fine proportions helped them, more than was realized, to act in a manner befitting the high functions with which they were entrusted. There is no doubt that the location of an Assembly has a great influence on its conduct and its debates. The chamber at Versailles was both elegant and convenient. When the orators spoke from the rostrum they could be heard in all parts of the chamber, which meant that few people spoke from their place. The rostrum was in an elevated and central position, so that it was a natural focal point for everyone. This exercised a restraining influence on the orators and prevented them from forgetting themselves as often as they were later to do. The commanding height of the president's chair was also very useful in maintaining good order, because he could see at a glance everything that was going on in the chamber. Finally, the size of the place and the ease with which one could walk from one spot to another prevented the various parties from claiming their own area as later happened, playing a greater part than is supposed in making them irritable and violent. A large chamber has yet another advantage even more real than appears at first sight—namely, that it never gets too hot. I am persuaded that many great misfortunes could have been avoided if the Versailles chamber could have been transported to Paris, because the Riding School* was just a long corridor and had all the disadvantages to match the advantages to which I have just referred. In addition, the public galleries, whose influence has been so baleful, were much more prominent in the Riding School, and so the cheers and the boos that the spectators frequently indulged in had much more influence at Paris than at Versailles. A craving for applause was always the weak spot of all the French Assemblies, and provided that they got it, they were not very particular about who gave it.

The debates of the Assembly can be considered as falling into two categories. The first consisted of debates on great constitutional issues and other issues which they wished to discuss from all angles. The second, on the other hand, consisted of the debates that took place after the discussions on the important matters and of debates on matters arising.

The debates in the first category were scarcely more than a series of prepared speeches. A list with two columns was drawn up on the table of the Assembly, and the members who wished to speak entered their names on it, giving notice whether they were speaking *for* or *against*. The president then invited the orators on each side to speak alternately and in their order on the list, so that one never heard two orators of the same opinion in succession. Each of these orators mounted the rostrum with a written speech in his pocket, and very often these debates bore more resemblance to a school exercise than a true discussion. Gradually a few orators got used to speaking *ex tempore,* but no one spoke without notes. This kind of discussion, then, prevented a proper debate because, as speeches had been written in advance, it was impossible to reply and refute one's opponent's arguments on the spot. These pompous speeches lasted till the Assembly's patience was exhausted, for there was never a shortage

* After the rising of October 5 and 6 the National Assembly was transferred to the Riding School of the Tuileries Palace.—ED.

of orators. It is true that the patience of the Assembly was not great; and I think that no discussion of this type took up more than four sittings, and less, I think, after the Assembly had been installed in the Riding School. Motions were *forced* through like a town taken by force—the word was actually used. When the Assembly thought it had heard enough orators to escape the reproach of having decided *lightly* (because this reproach, often richly deserved, was one of the ones they dreaded the most), it closed the discussion, and it was then that the other kind of debates began, which were much more meaningful than the first kind. Laughable were the long faces of those who had worked hard to compose a speech and were now forced to leave it in their pocket, but they normally got their revenge by having it printed.

The ending of the discussion always marked the beginning of a storm, for the Assembly was about to exercise its power, and passions were consequently inflamed. It was, in fact, the only time when people got worked up. Moreover, the fact that each orator was speaking in reply to the man who was termed, in the language of the National Assembly, the *préopinant** and that there were no more written speeches was in itself enough to make the orators more vehement and to lead the various parties to heap abuse on each other. That is why the most animated debates did not begin until after the period of discussion had ended, because then the set speeches were over and the debates took on the form of a sort of conversation. A few details will be enough to illustrate this.

As soon as the Assembly had brought the period of discussion to a close, it proceeded to give priority to one of the bills that had been proposed, that is to say, the Assembly decided which bill the president should put to the vote, article by article. When the bill had been chosen, each party tried to modify it to its own views by carrying amendments on the preamble and each successive article and subamendments and amendments of amendments. One can envisage the ill-assorted mixture of contradictions that resulted from this way of legislating. And very often one can get a better picture of this by reading the decrees than by anything that could be said on the subject.

There was yet another kind of debate which was spontaneous and therefore rowdy. These debates were on *motions incidentes,* that is to say, on matters arising. Their aim was nearly always to give the Assembly powers that it did not legally possess and that consequently it should not have exercised.

It must further be observed that the evening sittings were nearly always stormy: Men make more noise after dinner than on an empty stomach. It was in these sittings that the Assembly allowed itself to be led into committing its most absurd actions.

* I.e., the orator who had just spoken. Louis-Philippe has a keen ear for the pompous jargon that grew up with the Revolution and makes so many of its utterances difficult to interpret.—ED.

The dividing lines between the various parties in the Assembly were not as sharp as they later became. In September 1789 they were still blurred, or rather the lines between the parties were different from what they were after the Assembly had been transferred to Paris. Those of the deputies of the clergy and the nobility who had been opposed to the Orders sitting together formed the party that was called the *Aristocrats*. This label would have been more suitable for the advocates of a bicameral system of government. And in fact those who were called *Aristocrats* should have been called *Royal Absolutists,* but at this period each party still boasted of its royalism, and the revolutionary party feared lest the label *royalist* be given exclusively to its opponents. By using the word *aristocrats* they wanted to accustom the public to think of their opponents as men who were obstinately defending their own privileges, to the detriment of the true interests of the King and the people, and who were opposed to any reform whatsoever. This party was very strong in the Assembly and much more powerful than was generally believed, because the slightest division among their opponents gave them the majority.

The party that advocated a two-chamber system of government was always weak and small. Something that future generations will find it hard to believe is that the majority of the deputies of the clergy and nobility who had wanted separation of the Orders voted for a single-chamber legislature! I was there when this memorable and disastrous decision was made. There were more votes cast than for any other issue, 1,082 if my memory serves me right, of which 872 came out in favor of a single chamber, 88 for two, while 122 refused to vote, saying that they had *no opinion* on this great question. It is impossible to explain this strange result except in terms of that *politique du pire,* which I have already mentioned in connection with the decrees of August 4. The Court feared that two chambers acting as a moderating influence on each other would strike root and be more difficult to eradicate than a single one. The popular party feared that the division of the legislative body into two chambers would diminish its force and paralyze its operations.

The party that advocated two chambers did not survive the events of October 5. After this MM. de Lally, Mounier, and Bergasse left the Assembly, and MM. de Clermont-Tonnerre, Malouet, etc., who remained, found themselves for the most part lost among the Royal Absolutist party, while the others joined the party that voted with M. de La Fayette and sat on their side of the Assembly.

The divisions among the rest of the Assembly remained slight until after the rising of October 5. It is time to talk of the causes that led up to the popular demonstration on this day.

The King had brought the Berwick regiment to Versailles as a temporary replacement for the *Gardes-françaises,* which he disbanded, and to act as his personal guard. This motive seemed perfectly natural, and at the least it provided an excellent excuse to keep an infantry regiment of the line at Versailles, where there was not normally one stationed. But the Berwick regiment worried the Assembly and even the Parisians. People complained that the King had a foreign regiment with him and that he was surrounding himself with redcoats.* There was another ground for complaint, namely, that the Berwick regiment was attached to the Court party and would have done anything the King wanted. It was later to emigrate *en masse*. But the King did not dare keep it at Versailles, and he replaced it with the Flanders regiment whose colonel, M. de Lusignan, was one of the forty-seven deputies of the nobility who were the first to join the Assembly of the Third Estate, and he nearly always voted with the majority in the National Assembly. So this choice was very prudent as regards the colonel, whose political opinions could not give any grounds for anxiety either to the Assembly or to the people of Paris. But M. de Lusignan was a deputy and could not take command of his regiment; and his officers expressed opinions which were pleasing to the Court but disturbing for the people of Paris and the Assembly.

On the first of October the King's Bodyguard gave a banquet for the officers of the Flanders regiment. I do not know if everything that happened there was premeditated, but their conduct was very imprudent. They sang ecstatically the famous air from the opera *Richard the Lion-Hearted:*

> O Richard, O my king
> The world casts you aside
> In all the earth I alone
> Have your interests at heart.

The national cockade was trampled underfoot,† and handkerchiefs were torn up to make white cockades, which were sported enthusiastically; this brought from an old officer of the Swiss Guards I knew the very fair comment: "We always give pinpricks to receive back bodyblows." This banquet gave a lot of offense to the popular party and was regarded in Paris as a signal for the Counterrevolution. Unfortunately it was not the only one that people thought they could detect, and these fears greatly increased the unrest.

A great many factors came together at this time to foster this unrest. In the first place the scarcity of grain, which always produced popular agitation, continued to be felt to a very alarming degree.

(2) The liberty, or I should have said the license, of the press since July 14 had led to a flood of newspapers, pamphlets, and lampoons in Paris and the rest of the kingdom, which continued to be devoured as avidly as when they were still illegal. These various writings inflamed the

---

* The Berwick regiment was an Irish regiment formed by James II, and its members still wore a red uniform with black facings.
† This fact has been denied, and I do not guarantee it, though I think it at least probable.

passions and distorted judgment. Personalities were not spared, and the more the enemies of the Revolution strove to persuade the nation that the King was going to recover his absolute power, the easier it was for their opponents to excite the people against them, to make them see conspiracies everywhere, even in the most natural and least suspicious associations, and so drive them to commit the most reprehensible outrages. It was at this time, in the month of September 1789, that *Marat, The Friend of the People** began to put in print what he had repeated so many times, namely, that the Revolution would not be complete and indestructible until it had rid itself of two hundred thousand people who would always work to bring about the Counterrevolution.

(3) Another cause of alarm and therefore of agitation was the fear that the King would separate himself from the Assembly and retire to Metz or somewhere else and that from there, surrounded by his troops, he would be able to effect the Counterrevolution. These rumors certainly had a wide currency both in Paris and in the Assembly. It is certain, and as much is acknowledged, that projects of this kind were discussed in the King's Council, and that his departure had been settled the next day but that in the evening there had been a change of plan.

(4) Finally, the lack of understanding between the National Assembly and M. Necker had almost destroyed his popularity and that of his ministerial colleagues, especially as they were known to have favored the two-chamber system of government, for this had become almost as unpopular as the Counterrevolution, so unreasonable had men become by that time.

Such were certainly the main causes of the unfortunate event I am now going to discuss. But who directed the operations? The Duc d'Orléans? M. de La Fayette? To this I say boldly, categorically, neither. It was done by a group usually known by the name of the Cordelier party. It is as interesting to know the composition of this party as it is essential to study its workings if one wants to have a clear understanding of the causes of the Revolution and the way in which it was brought about. It was the same party that engineered the rising of August 10, 1792, and that succeeded in founding the anarchy and tyranny of the Republic on the ruins of those theories, each more absurd than the one before, which people had been foolish enough to regard as sublime political concepts.

The powerhouse of this party was in Paris in the Cordelier quarter, which was almost always the most violent of all. It was made up of men who were at the time unknown, drawn from the lowest of the classes who receive some education—that is to say, a large number of scribes, clerks, attorneys, students of medicine and surgery, junior schoolmasters, printers, etc. Danton, a King's counsel and president of the district, was one of the leaders. Those who know the topography of Paris will have a good idea of the class of person who made up the district assembly when they

* This was the title of Marat's paper.

realize that the Rue de la Harpe and the Rue Serpente were to be found within the boundaries of the district. From there went out all the pamphlets and popular eloquence of Paris. The inhabitants of this district associated with the lower classes with whom, in point of manners, they had much in common, and they acquired a considerable ascendancy over them by dint of their superior education. They were the orators at meetings and the leaders of the risings.

The fact that the district assemblies remained in session after July 14 meant that anyone who wanted could go and exercise his eloquence there, and the people in the neighborhood of the Cordelier district had skillfully profited from the opportunity to make themselves well known, to form acquaintances and, in short, to form a party and secretly prepare the execution of their plans. It was this party that planned and executed the popular rising of October 5 to force the King and the Assembly to establish themselves in Paris. As this party controlled the populace of this great city, it was certain to exercise a powerful influence on the government as soon as it could manage to get it transferred there. The history of this party is one of the most curious and the most important aspects of the Revolution, and I have not yet found it described anywhere.

At the time, no one understood the influence of this party. It was not even realized that it existed, because its members were lost in the crowd. People imagined that the crowd must be led by the famous popular heroes or by the members of the Assembly, and they were wrong, because the men in both categories were not and never had been more than the instruments. From the time Paris was removed from the King's authority, public opinion there was directed by the mob orators, and these orators were members of, or affiliated with, the Cordelier Club, which itself was a separate party, independent of the others, and had, I believe, no connection with any of the great names of the day.

By a singular and unfortunate coincidence I was present at Versailles at the very sitting of the National Assembly on October 5. But fairly early on, a man on horseback sent from Passy by Mme de Genlis gave me a note telling me to return to Passy as quickly as possible. She instructed me to take the Saint-Cloud road in order to avoid the bands of fishwives who were going to Versailles via the Sèvres road and who were telling everyone that they were going to search out the King and the Assembly and bring them back to Paris to stop the aristocrats from abducting them.

I immediately left the substitute deputies' gallery where I was sitting with my brother,* and we returned to Passy by the route indicated. We

* It has been claimed, and this deposition figures in the proceedings instituted by the Châtelet, that on this day I said in this gallery *that it was necessary to hang all the aristocrats*. Neither my brother nor I ever said this, there or anywhere else, and though I like to think that such a denial is superfluous, nevertheless I formally declare that it is a falsehood.

did not come across anyone until we reached the Bois de Boulogne, but between the Rond-de-Mortemart and the Château de la Muette we encountered one of these bands of fishwives. They recognized the livery of the House of Orléans and wanted to stop our carriage, probably to take us with them to Versailles. But the road was very wide, and we got past them easily. Expecting similar encounters, I had given the coachman express orders to be on his guard and to stop for nothing, and as we went by, I just heard the women shouting at us: "Dear God, my fine Duke, since you are in such a hurry, these are the women of Paris!" The National Guard of Passy was under arms in the main street. They saluted us when we passed. These good people seemed not to know what to do; some wanted to go to Versailles and the others did not, but they all felt obliged to remain under arms *in order to save the Fatherland and liberty,* because in general men console themselves for doing nothing by convincing themselves that they are doing a lot. When we arrived at Passy I found Mme de Genlis very frightened. M. Ducrest, her brother, was alone with her. My father had come to Passy in the morning; he had spent the night at the Palais Royal and planned to go to the Assembly, but when we heard that the fishwives were proceeding to Versailles, he thought it would be sensible to keep away so as not to give a handle to those who would defame him, and to have absolutely no involvement with anything that might happen. With this in mind, he withdrew to Mousseaux, where he spent the day—a wise precaution no doubt, but one which did not help him at the time. May it at least one day procure him the benefit that he expected from it!

Watching from the windows at Passy, we saw an amazing sight along the road to Sèvres. We saw a constant stream of women in groups and men of the people who were making for Versailles very calmly. Their number was increasing the whole time, and for the most part they said: "Let's go, we must find out what is happening at Versailles, there'll be a lot of people there already." Everyone, the lemonade sellers shouting "All freshly made," those who sold spiced bread, prostitutes, the women with their hurdy-gurdies, etc., all went off to Versailles as happily as if they had just been going to watch the fountains. But despite this carefree air, they were using the most fearful language about all the enemies of the Revolution, especially the Queen.

There was the greatest agitation in Paris. Since the assemblies of a few districts had ordered the tocsin to be rung, panic had spread to all the quarters, and the National Guard ran to take up arms. It was fairly late when it assembled on the quays to the number of more than thirty thousand men. They did not know what was going on at Versailles, though they were well aware that great numbers of people had proceeded there during the course of the day, and this lack of information allowed the most absurd rumors to gain credence. All the Parisian youth wanted to make an expedition, a soldiers' march; perhaps their real fear was that they had assembled for nothing. What is certain is that when the whole National Guard was under arms, they unanimously expressed the desire to march on Versailles in order to defend the National Assembly and prevent the King from leaving. There is no doubt that the idea of the King's departure was regarded as synonymous with the start of the Counterrevolution.

M. Bailly and M. de La Fayette were at the Hôtel de Ville, and they did not know how to extricate themselves from what was a very difficult situation. They knew that they possessed only the shadow of power, and that despite their offices, it was not for them to give orders but to receive them. It seems that M. de La Fayette would have liked to prevent this expedition, but when he saw that the National Guard was determined to leave without him if he did not put himself at their heads, he decided to do so and marched on Versailles with the Parisian army, its artillery and a considerable crowd in tow. We saw them pass before Passy about nine in the evening, in very good order, and silence was so well observed that our only warning of their approach was the sound of artillery in motion. The column took a long time to file past, and the darkness made the sight even more impressive.

The King was hunting when the first news of the activity at Paris reached Versailles. He was told immediately and returned to the palace. It is hard to know exactly what the King's intentions were because they were forever changing. He certainly adopted measures that were in contradiction with each other. I think there was considerable disagreement within the palace. The Queen disliked M. Necker and the ministers then in office, and she had a great deal of influence on the King. M. Necker has said in one of his works that during the course of this unfortunate day, the Queen had, within a few hours, two contradictory opinions about the advantages and disadvantages of leaving, and this explains only too well the King's fumbling indecisiveness. At times he wanted to go, and at times he no longer wanted to. During one of the periods when he had resolved to leave, he ordered the carriages, and the horses were harnessed to them; but the people of Versailles, together with a few of the Paris fishwives, crowded around the carriages and ended by cutting the traces.

The decision to leave was abandoned and that of defending the palace was adopted, and the first thing the King did after making this decision was to invite the National Assembly to come and join him. Immediately it left the chamber where it held its sittings and repaired to the palace, where it occupied the Salon d'Hercule. I think that it was in some perplexity as to what it was going to do there, and this perplexity could only increase that of the King and his Council. Still, they had to give the appearance of activity, and the Assembly decreed *that it was inseparable from the King's person*. The sense of this decree was that the *King's person* should always remain *beside the Assembly* and that he should not be allowed to remove himself from the place where it sat.

Nothing notable happened at Versailles in the afternoon except that the crowd from Paris tried to cut across a line formed by the Bodyguard, there were a few rifle shots, and M. de Savonnières, one of their officers, was wounded in the arm. However, this incident had no consequence other than that of adding to the animosity felt by the people toward the Bodyguard.

In the evening, the call to arms was sounded. M. d'Estaing, commander of the National Guard of Versailles, put it into battle array on the Place d'Armes in front of the palace, and the Flanders regiment was placed in the second line, taking up the Cour des Ministres, the gates of which were closed at eleven o'clock in the evening. When it was known that the Parisian army was approaching, there was a drum roll, and M. d'Estaing informed the troops *that the King's orders were to repel force with force*. But despite these preparations and such a positive declaration, there was not even an attempt at resistance; and as soon as M. de La Fayette arrived at the head of the Parisian column, the King put him in command of the palace, and the Parisian National Guards immediately occupied all the posts there.

By the time these arrangements had been carried out, it was very late. Versailles was filled with a hundred thousand men and women from Paris in a terrifying state of turbulence. It was greatly to be feared that this multitude would be carried to even more reprehensible extremes than it did in fact reach. But M. de La Fayette was tired out and fell asleep. He has been bitterly reproached for this sleep; and although I want to do him all the justice that is due him, there is no denying that since he had taken over command of the palace, he was responsible for its safety, and he should have taken care of it himself or at the least have taken steps to be warned of the first signs of movement from the populace. But I am far from suggesting, as his enemies have attempted to do, that M. de La Fayette wanted to leave the way open to the crimes that sullied this horrifying night. No part of his conduct can be construed in this sense, and it should not be forgotten that if he was on the side of the Revolution, he paid the price for trying to stop it running to extremes.

Be that as it may, in the middle of the night a group of ruffians entered the palace and got as far as the Queen's apartments, scarcely giving her time to seek refuge with the King. These same ruffians seized some of the Bodyguard and slew them* in the Cour de Marbre beneath the King's windows. Their heads were carried in triumph on pikes and sent to Paris to announce to the capital the arrival of its hapless monarch! M. de La Fayette was finally informed of the atrocities that were being committed and ran down to put a stop to them. He managed to save the rest of the poor devils who had already been marked out as victims of the people's rage.

* I think to the number of eight.

From my window at Passy I saw something going by that I could not properly make out. I raised my eyeglass to inspect it, and it dropped from my hands when I saw two bloody heads carried on pikes. And hard as it is to believe, I witnessed an even greater atrocity! These monsters, noticing the ribbon on the wig of one of these heads was out of place, made a wigmaker rearrange it and repowder it, and then they *peacefully* went on their way!!! I saw it with my own eyes!

Shortly afterward the crowd began to return from Versailles, and they displayed the same nonchalance that they had when going there the previous day. The whole route was buzzing with the news that the King and the National Assembly would be passing on their way to Paris *in accordance with the wishes of the people*. They certainly did go by, preceded by the National Guard of Paris and, in their midst, the Bodyguard, on foot and unarmed. The soldiers of the Flanders regiment were scattered but armed, with their haversacks on their backs. This grim procession was accompanied by an enormous crowd that kept shouting *Long live the nation!* and shooting loaded rifles in the air to right and left, though from what I have heard no one got hurt. The King, the Queen, M. le Dauphin, Madame the King's daughter, and Madame Elisabeth* were in the same carriage and seemed very calm. They got out at the Tuileries. The National Assembly was going to hold its meetings in one of the rooms of the Archbishop's palace till the one that was being prepared in the Riding School of the Tuileries was ready to receive it.

These events aroused much speculation and suspicion, which naturally fell on the most prominent members of the popular party, who at the time were undoubtedly my father and M. de La Fayette, so they were both of them suspected and accused. It is easy to understand why this accusation was directed principally toward my father.

The Court and consequently all its adherents feared and hated my father infinitely more than M. de La Fayette. My father was in himself much more important. The Court had always heaped insults on him and dealt with him very shabbily, while M. de La Fayette had received several important marks of favor. Therefore, the Court must have expected to be more hated by my father than by M. de La Fayette. Moreover, my father's rank was so exalted that the only possible object for his ambition was to exercise royal power either by becoming Lieutenant General of the Kingdom or by dethroning the elder branch and assuming the Crown. This was so obvious that he was openly accused of it. Yet he was far from wanting it, and whatever the stories about him that were circulated, I am convinced that he was devoid of ambition. Deep down, all he wanted, before the Revolution, was to be safe from the capricious ill will of the Court, and afterward a guarantee against persecution and vengeance from it. I cannot repeat too often that this policy of persecution and vengeance on the part of the Court was one of the main factors in fathering this

* Elisabeth de France, sister of Louis XVI.—ED.

dreadful storm against it, in which it was destroyed. At least may this unhappy example teach governments which find themselves in a similar situation that if there is a time to punish, there is never one to persecute.

M. de La Fayette's situation in relation to the Court was very different from my father's. Despite his family motto (*Cur non?*), he could scarcely be suspected of aspiring to the throne. The worst ambition of which he could be suspected was that of wanting to seize power and govern in the name of the King.

Consequently, faced with the choice, the Court preferred M. de La Fayette's influence to that of my father, and though it hoped one day to have the chance to break M. de La Fayette, it gladly seized the opportunity to use him in the process of ruining the principal object of its hatred. I do not make this accusation lightly or out of personal bias, and I think that the following details will show that my father's banishment was meant to be only a preliminary to his complete fall; that far from trying to make the banishment he voluntarily underwent more pleasant by giving him a suitable role to play, he was loaded with insults and humiliations, and an attempt was made to blacken his reputation and bring down legal retribution on his head.

However, the Court party was not the only one that wanted my father out of the way. Many others did as well, because they feared that they would be regarded as *members of the Orléaniste party*. M. de La Fayette desperately wanted my father to absent himself. It was said at the time that this was because he wanted to rid himself of a popular rival who overshadowed him, and there may be some truth in this. It was also said that he wanted to throw onto my father all the odium of the events of October 5 and 6 so that his own conduct at the time would escape examination, but this, I think, is unfounded. In the first place, I am perfectly sure that M. de La Fayette was no more their author or accomplice than was my father. Also, it seems hard to believe that placed as he was at the time, M. de La Fayette did not know what were in fact the secret springs of these events. He must have known that they were not inspired by my father, and he did know because he told him as much. Nevertheless, he thought that it was expedient that my father leave France just then, so he worked to persuade him to leave and, once he had gone, to prevent him from returning.

Be that as it may, a few days after October 5, 1789, M. de La Fayette sent to ask my father to suggest the house of a third party where they could meet. My father suggested the house of Mme de Coigny. M. de La Fayette told him that as he was responsible for the maintenance of public order, it was his duty to tell him that troublemakers were making use of his name to disturb the peace, that he was being accused of engineering the events of October 5, that he believed all these rumors were without foundation, but that the King required a big sacrifice of him and that his orders were to ask him to make his departure and leave France. (I am writing from memory, and I only vouch for the general drift of this). My father replied that he wished to act in accordance with the King's wishes, but that he could not abandon his work in the Assembly in this way and seem to fear a possible inquiry into his conduct; that on the contrary, he wanted as much light as possible to be shed on it, etc. This was followed by explanations, proposals, and counterproposals, and in the end it was agreed, on certain conditions, that the King should entrust my father with a secret mission to the King of England and that he should leave immediately for London; that although the object of the mission must remain a secret, M. de Montmorin, the Minister of Foreign Affairs, would inform the Assembly on the part of the King that my father had been entrusted with a secret mission to the King of England; and that then my father, as a deputy, should ask the Assembly to give him a passport, which did not raise any difficulties.

This mission was concerned with the troubles in Brabant. It seems that the idea was to tempt my father with the hope of becoming Duke of Brabant, but they were very careful only to drop him the hint without committing themselves. It is certain that nothing would have been more in accordance with my father's wishes and indications than to renounce his rights in France in this way. He knew that as long as he remained in France, he would be an object of suspicion to the King and even to all the parties. An arrangement of this kind, putting him beyond the reach of spiteful talk and persecution, would have been the summit of his desires and ambitions. It seems that if the only motive of the Court of France in removing my father had been to preserve the peace of the kingdom, then it should seriously have tried to give him a brilliant role abroad which befitted his rank. But they only wanted to remove him, to weaken and to ruin him, and far from trying to arrange a brilliant future for him, they spent all their time preventing him from achieving it.

Nevertheless, as it was necessary to give him a real mission to make him leave, my father went to the Tuileries to receive his instructions from the King, who gave them to him himself. His terms of reference were very precise, although they were accompanied by every conceivable restriction that could possibly weaken them. These same instructions were later found among my father's papers at the Palais Royal and published, along with all his correspondence with M. de Montmorin relative to this mission.*

* Extract from the "Memorandum to serve as instructions for His Serene Highness the Duc d'Orléans," dated from Paris, October 13, 1789; signed *Louis* and countersigned the "Comte de Montmorin":[a]

"M. le Duc d'Orléans's inquiries should definitely not be confined to ascertaining what may be the attitude of the Court of London toward us; they will also have reference to another matter in which France, as all the other European Powers, is interested—namely the Austrian Netherlands.

[a] N.B. This memorandum is printed in the collection entitled *Correspondance de Louis-Philippe Joseph d'Orléans, Paris.*

The Duc de Biron,* who had been a friend of my father's since his youth and who, with his nobility and loyalty of heart, remained faithful to him till his dying breath, tried in vain to prevent him from leaving. "If you go," he told him, "it will look as though you are running away. Ask to be judged and say that until you have been, you will leave neither the Assembly nor France, but that afterward you will undertake anything that the King sees fit to entrust you with."

"M. le Duc d'Orléans will not be unaware of the extreme unrest in the Belgian provinces; of the spirit of rebellion that has been displayed among the inhabitants and of their apparent desire to withdraw their allegiance to the Emperor.

"We are inclined to believe that the people of Brabant are strengthened in this resolve by the Courts of London and Berlin and the States-General, or rather the Stadtholder; but as to this we have only suspicions. It would be of great value to the King to know the truth, and H.M. trusts that M. le Duc d'Orléans will do all in his power to discover it.

"In the absence of definite knowledge, we are obliged to rely on suppositions. Thus it is on the supposition that the Court of London is fomenting troubles in the Low Countries that the King has decided to give M. le Duc d'Orléans instructions on this matter.

"The Court of London's aim must be either to join the Low Countries to the Confederation of the United Provinces or to form them into an independent Republic or, lastly, to put them under a Prince not from the House of Austria.

"In the first hypothesis the Court of London would give the United Provinces a strength that would not be without inconveniences for England herself.

"The second hypothesis would bring about a state of affairs that would not, of itself, influence the balance of power in Europe.

"As for the third hypothesis, it deserves the most serious consideration, and the following will inform the Duc d'Orléans of the way in which the King envisages it.

"If the Belgian Provinces are to come under another rule, the King would prefer that they have their own sovereign, but the difficulty will lie in the choice. M. le Duc d'Orléans will not need to be told that the King naturally wants to have a say in this choice and that it is a matter of importance to him that the Prince on whom it falls should be acceptable to him. M. le Duc d'Orléans will surely realize the delicacy of this matter and how much dexterity on his part it demands; and this all the more so because on the one hand, the objectives that the Court of London may evince will determine either the King's opposition or his assent, and on the other, it is possible that the result may turn to the personal advantage of the Duc d'Orléans. The King feels that for the moment, he should confine himself to these general observations: Before disclosing his intentions and objectives, His Majesty will wait until he has received precise clarification on those of the Court of London, and then he will put the Duc d'Orléans in a position to speak authoritatively on the matter at issue. From this the Prince will conclude that at first he must do no more than sound out the dispositions of the English ministers, win their confidence without angling for it, and prepare the way for serious negotiations, while it is advisable not to begin until there is a fair chance of success.

"If the Court of London is resolved to remove the Low Countries from Austrian rule and shows a readiness to act in concert with the King on the ways of effecting this revolution, the negotiations must proceed from two prerequisites: (1) the explicit consent of the Emperor; (2) fair compensation for the loss this monarch will incur. To act without the cooperation of Joseph II would be necessarily to expose Europe to a general war, and dispossessing this Prince without compensation would

* Armand-Louis de Gontaut, Duc de Biron, 1747–1793, deputy and general.—ED.

This advice was excellent, but a combination of my father's natural inclinations, the arguments put forward by his entourage, and the belief that by going he would put an end to calumny by demonstrating that he had no desire to seize power in France determined him to accept the mission. He left on the evening of October 14 under the illusion that through going he would obtain the justice he thought was his due. That was certainly his main objective, because the actual terms of reference of his instructions should have shown him that the Court of France had no desire to see him Duke of Brabant. He had hardly left when the outcry against him became almost general, and to add to it the Court spread the rumor that he did not have a real mission and insinuated everywhere that he had merely been given a pretext to leave. They tried to discredit him in England and to thwart him at every turn. His correspondence with M. de Montmorin, which was later published, makes this abundantly clear. The Minister's side of this correspondence is a veritable mockery, but it suffices to prove: (1) that my father preferred to keep clear of the internal affairs of France, where he did not want to be a source of rivalry to the King any longer; (2) that he had been promised and given a real mission, but that it had been made illusory as much by the actual terms of reference as by the vexations and impediments of every description with which it was accompanied. So I think I have reason to say that the main objective in removing him was to ruin his reputation by persuading one side that he was guilty of bringing about the events of October 5 and 6 and the other that like a coward he was abandoning them as well as the cause whose defense he had undertaken. But even this was not enough for his enemies. Having induced, I could say ordered, him to stay away, they needed either to get a judicial condemnation of him or, if that aim could not be achieved straightaway, to reinforce the public outcry with a body of legal proceedings that it was hoped could be used later and that at the same time would seem like proof of guilt to a fickle public which had managed to spin a web of lies around him it was no longer in his power to undo. After he had left, not a moment was lost in getting down to this.

As early as the month of November 1789 the court of the Châtelet of Paris, to which the National Assembly—out of jealousy for the *parlements*—had given cognizance of crimes of *lèse-nation*,* began secret

---

be an injustice which nothing could justify and in which it would be impossible for the King to participate: His Majesty would even be forced to oppose it by virtue of the undertakings which bind him to His Imperial Majesty. Assuming this Prince gives his consent, it is then a matter of ascertaining what compensation, or what *quid pro quo,* the Court of London sees fit to propose to him. When the state of the negotiations permits, the Duc d'Orléans will get the English ministers to give a frank and precise statement on this point, and he will gently but firmly deflect them from any ideas they may entertain of getting the King to make the first step."

* I.e., crimes against the nation—a self-conscious revolutionary adaptation of lese majesty.—ED.

criminal proceedings in connection with offenses committed on October 5 and 6.

The best way of proceeding in this matter would appear to have been to ascertain in the first place the identity of those who had murdered the members of the Bodyguard, which surely would not have been difficult. Then the murderers should have been arrested so that it could be discovered *from them* who the ringleaders were and who might have paid them, so that they could be arrested in their turn; and the guilty should have been prosecuted and punished with the full rigor of the law. Thus one could have got straight the facts, and the mystery would have been completely unraveled. But instead of adopting this simple and natural course of action, the authorities neglected to investigate the murders or to seek out the murderers. All they were concerned with was discovering the *grands coupables,* as they pompously put it; so the Commission of the Châtelet restricted itself to collecting all the individual conjectures of my father's numerous enemies as well as all the public gossip that could implicate him. They heard, I think, two thousand witnesses, and during this long hearing it was let out that the Châtelet was conducting criminal proceedings in connection with the events of October 5 and 6, and that the Duc d'Orléans was heavily implicated and had had to seek refuge in England, where he remained for the sake of his safety. At the same time, the Court used every means of discrediting him in England and of keeping him there.

Finally, after a seven-month stay in England, and wearied by all his trials and all the intrigues against him, my father lost patience and decided to return to France to brave the storm that had been stirred up against him, and by his presence either to quell it or make it burst. As soon as he had made known his intention to return, everything was put into play to prevent him, and M. de La Fayette even sent one of his aides-de-camp, M. de Boinville, to London to try to keep him there. But he had made his decision, and nothing would stop him. He returned to Paris for the great Federation of 1790.*

His arrival momentarily disconcerted his enemies and made them realize that the proceedings of the Châtelet did not frighten him. These proceedings had hitherto been shrouded in mystery, but his return precipitated a dramatic move. His enemies were only waiting for the excitement caused by the Federation to die down a little so that this matter could become an object of importance and occupy the attention of the public to the exclusion of everything else. According to the laws then in force, no member of the National Assembly could be put on trial unless the Assembly had passed a decree of accusation against him. Consequently, toward the middle of August, after eight months of secret proceedings, M.

* When the provinces sent delegates to Paris to celebrate the first anniversary of the fall of the Bastille.—ED.

Boucher d'Argis, *lieutenant particulier** of the Châtelet, presented himself at the bar of the National Assembly and asked for the necessary decree of accusation against my father and M. Mirabeau so that the court of the Châtelet could try them. This request was accompanied by a theatrical speech calculated to prejudice the public more and more against men whom they claimed they wanted to judge.

The Assembly ordered all the depositions to be printed and sent them to be examined by its Report Committee; shortly afterward M. Chabroust, its spokesman, proposed that the Assembly should declare that there *were no grounds for an accusation,* and this decree was passed by a very large majority. Then my father's enemies claimed that this decree did not vindicate him, because the Assembly was not a court of law. They even went so far as to assert that the Assembly was predisposed in his favor, whereas the exact opposite was the case. This is what I said I would try to demonstrate, and I shall make every effort to succeed. After that, I shall consider whether or not the Assembly was competent to pronounce on these proceedings.

At the time, the Assembly was divided into three main parties. The first was the one that sat to the right of the president. This was the party that had been called at first the *Aristocrats* and was later referred to in the Assembly as the *Blacks* on account of the large number of clergy in its ranks. I have already said that this party was for the most part made up of the bishops, the abbots, a fairly large number of curés, the majority of the deputies of the nobility, and a few from the Third Estate. This party comprised more than a third of the Assembly, about four hundred and thirty or forty deputies, which made it the biggest single party, but its strength was only fully recognized by its enemies.

The two other parties formed what was called the *left wing* because it sat to the left of the president. One was the party that held its gatherings at the 1789 Club. M. de La Fayette, M. Bailly, M. de Talleyrand, MM. de Crillon, de Latour-Maubourg, Roederer, Thouret, Le Chapelier, Démeunier, the Abbé Siéyès, Mathieu de Montmorency, and a few other deputies for the nobility on the side of the Revolution belonged to that party, which over and above included landowners, merchants, and rich people in general. Other deputies who passed as *independents* because they voted with no particular party, such as M. Dandré, de Montesquiou, Bouche, Le Camus, Lanjuinais, Fréteau, Tracy, etc., often joined with the party of the 1789 Club.

The second party of the left wing was the Jacobins, led at the time by MM. de Lameth, Barnave, Pétion, Adrien Duport, Alexandre Beauharnais, the Duc d'Aiguillon, the Prince de Broglie, etc. My father and the Duc de Biron nearly always voted with this party. It was the smallest party in the Assembly but had the most tactical skill.

* The *lieutenant particulier* was the deputy of the *lieutenant général de police* and presided over a court dealing with matters of public order.—ED.

The foregoing represents only a rough idea of the party divisions within the Assembly. There were many subdivisions, which I should have difficulty in remembering today and which would be of little interest. For example, Mirabeau, who virtually constituted a party by himself, went from the 1789 Club to the Jacobins without really being committed to either for long. He detested M. de La Fayette and MM. de Lameth alike: He detested everyone, and he acted in concert with no one; he believed he was strong enough to hold his own against everybody, and this belief brought him success more than once.

Having indicated the main parties in the Assembly, I shall examine their dispositions toward my father. It is well known that the right wing had an inveterate hatred for him, and so nearly all its members voted that he should be put on trial. I say *nearly* all because there were some deputies of the right wing who departed from the party line on this issue. But the whole of the left wing, with four or five exceptions, voted that he should not have to stand trial.

I have no need either to say that M. de La Fayette and all his partisans were hostile to my father: The fact and his reasons for it are well known. These two categories by themselves already formed a majority of the Assembly. The rest were always disposed to *vote against the Duc d'Or-léans* for the simple and all too human reason that they dared not seem to belong to the *Orléaniste party*.

I state this fact categorically and with all solemnity: *There never was an Orléaniste party.* One of the best proofs of this that I can give is that every party that existed in France during the Revolution, from that advocating two chambers to Danton and Robespierre, was in turn accused without distinction of being the Orléaniste party. But the less foundation there was in this accusation, the more it terrified those against whom it was leveled, and there is no doubt that from the very beginning of the Revolution the Court possessed in the trite accusation of being a member of the Orléaniste party a gorgon's head that turned its enemies to stone, sowed dissension among them, and impeded all their activities. It was precisely because no one wanted to elevate the Duc d'Orléans to the throne that everyone feared such an accusation, and this accusation upset everyone's plans and calculations. So everyone sought to defend himself from the charge, and this attitude led to a general feeling of ill will toward my father, for all the parties feared to have him in their ranks and each wished to disown him.

I know that when the forty-seven deputies of the nobility who first joined the Third Estate decided on this course of action, several of them wished that my father would not do so at the same time. "We shall seem to be following in your train," M. de Montesquiou said to him, "and we shall be regarded as being members *of your party,* which will be damaging for you and for us."

In fact these gentlemen were immediately accused by their opponents

66

of wanting to place him on the throne, and as they had no such intention and, on the contrary, sincerely desired to maintain the King there, from then on they looked for every opportunity to dissociate themselves from my father so as to dispel a suspicion that was too dangerous. I have to admit, though it wrings my heart to think of it, that my father's lack of concern for his reputation and the errors of his youth contributed all too much to the fear of appearing to be attached to him; for it is very true that this or that action of a man is never judged in isolation, but the general effect of his whole life always weighs in the balance and determines the judgment that is pronounced upon him.

This disposition to dissociate oneself from my father and to show him, if not ill will, at least great indifference, manifested itself from the month of September 1789, before the Assembly had left Versailles. When the Assembly regulated the order of succession to the Crown from male to male in order of primogeniture, it added (I might say without any pretext): *without intending to prejudge in any way the validity of the renunciations,* the aim of which was to give the Spanish branch of the Bourbons, to the detriment of our branch and in contempt of the treaties and the sacred charter of the renunciations, a means of claiming its hereditary right to the French throne, and thereby diminishing the importance of my father and making it easy to interpose a branch as numerous as that of Spain between us and the Crown.*

I have already dealt with the matter of the *apanages,* which seems to me another very striking proof of the Assembly's ill will, and I have nothing to add to what I have said on this subject. I merely recall it.

I think I have demonstrated that a very large majority of the National Assembly was very badly disposed toward my father. But before I conclude this discussion, I am going to take another look at the composition of the Jacobin party of the time so as to add new proofs to those I have already given.

The deputies of this party I have just named were at the time on very bad terms with M. de La Fayette, although not long afterward the majority were reconciled to him, but they feared that they would be regarded as being the Orléaniste party, and without any ill will for my father, they kept their distance from him. There were also in the Jacobin party of this time a few of the deputies who were later, in the National Convention, to split into Girondins and *Robespiéristes.* They were small in numbers in the Constituent Assembly, but even here the germ of division between the two parties was certainly noticeable. They knew very

---

* In return for international recognition of his title to the Spanish throne, Louis XIV's grandson, Philip V of Spain, renounced his claim to the French throne. This placed the Regent Orléans next in line of succession of Louis XV. However, many people in France did not consider that man-made treaties (especially ones imposed by foreign Powers) could alter the natural law of succession. The diarist Saint-Simon, though a friend of the Regent, told him that if Louis XV died he would have to recognize Philip because *"he would be king."*—ED.

well that since the Revolution, the influence of my father had been so reduced that his assistance was no longer of any value; they further knew that the Court, and consequently all the parties in alliance with it, had sworn my father's ruin, and that his only hope of salvation lay in the victory of the popular party and that he was *forced* to join it. This was enough to make them at least lukewarm toward him, and it is common knowledge that of the first two subdivisions of the party I have just mentioned, one (the Girondins) strove to ruin him in the National Convention, in which for eight months they were his open enemy, and the other (the *Robespiéristes*) made him one of their first victims.

As for Mirabeau, who, as I said just now, constituted a party by himself through the force of his eloquence and his talents, he had always had but few dealings with my father, and despite all that has been said on the subject, he was no more anxious than the others to pass for a member of the Orléaniste party: His enemies had linked his name with that of my father so that this association would damage them both; for as Mirabeau said himself, when the depositions made at the Châtelet were being examined, the only mention of him was that made in the speech that M. Boucher d'Argis pronounced at the bar of the National Assembly.

I could be wrong, but it seems to me that after what I have just said about this Assembly, it could no longer be suspected of bias in favor of my father and that its decision should have all the more weight in this case because it is the only time when it did not decide against him.

As for the objection that only a court of law could *clear* my father and that the Assembly was not a court of law, I will observe that one does not need to know the laws to pronounce on a matter of this kind, since the only point at issue was to determine whether or not my father had a part in the popular commotions of October 5 and 6 and whether he had instigated them. Consequently, the National Assembly, before whose eyes these events had taken place, seems to have been perfectly competent from every point of view to give the decision that it did.

May I further be permitted to add that if it is true that it is easy to convince others when one is absolutely convinced oneself, I must fully have succeeded with those who may read this work, because I have advanced nothing of which I am not absolutely convinced. However, I have not yet said everything that I could on a subject of such great importance for me, but the rest of my observations will find their place when I speak of later events.

I have demonstrated that my father had no influence on the National Assembly, and now I am going to reveal the secret mechanisms by which the National Assembly operated, and I hope to prove the assertion that I have already made that it was itself led by the political clubs which directed public opinion, that irresistible lever in modern times of all the convulsions which we have witnessed already and of those which are perhaps still in preparation. To give this exposition, I must take up the story a little earlier in order to give a proper explanation of how the political clubs were formed and in what ways they brought their influence to bear on the Assembly and the nation.

Brittany had been the first province to be stirred up before the convocation of the Estates-General. Since the reunion of this province to the French Crown,* despite the encroachments of royal authority, the Bretons had, by their energy, managed to keep their representative institutions. Like the English, with whom they share a common origin, they are tenacious and jealous of their rights; they defend them vigorously, and in the same way they defend a government with which they identify themselves. It is worth remarking that it should be in this province that the establishment of the Republic encountered the greatest obstacles and that it should be among the Bretons that the *Chouans* were formed.† The demand for the Estates-General was unanimous in Brittany; it was even made with violence; and this same nobility of Brittany, which later emigrated *en masse,* nevertheless at this time employed every device to attack royal authority. This is what happened more or less to all the enemies of the Revolution. There is not one among them who at one time or another did not help to bring it about.

In 1788 the demands of the nobility of Brittany seemed so dangerous to the King that he had the sixteen Breton noblemen who came to present them put in the Bastille. But once the King had ordained that in the forthcoming Estates-General the representation of the Third Estate would be equal to that of the other two Orders combined, the matter took on a different aspect, and the nobility of Brittany, which had insisted so forcefully on the convocation of the Estates-General, refused to recognize any constituted in this manner and steadfastly refused to send deputies to them. Their services were dispensed with. The higher clergy of Brittany (that is to say, the bishops and the abbots holding *in commendam*) made the same objection, and the lower clergy (that is to say, the curés) nominated by themselves the deputies who were allowed to vote in the Estates-General as deputies of all *the clergy of Brittany.* This short exposé should be enough to give a picture of the corporate mentality of the different Orders in Brittany and how passionately each one adopted its standpoint. This attitude resulted in the deputies for the Third Estate of Brittany forming a phalanx in the middle of the National Assembly; and the tactical skill with which they conducted themselves, even more than their talents and their impassioned state of mind, rallied to their phalanx those members of the Assembly who had opinions analogous to theirs.

After they had arrived at Versailles, the several deputies from Brittany assembled every day in a private house to draw up a concerted plan of

* This occurred in 1532.
† The Chouans were royalist rebels who maintained guerrilla warfare against the Republic for many years in the west of France.—ED.

campaign. There they determined in what sense they would write to their constituents* on the day's events and the activities of the Assembly. They discussed in advance the questions that were going to be discussed by the Assembly. They settled the way they would vote, and in this way they always arrived at the Assembly ready to maneuver it, like a densely massed column in the middle of a disunited multitude. This private gathering was called *The Breton Club*. The deputies from the province of Dauphiné, whose conduct bore a great resemblance to that of Brittany before the Estates-General, also formed a phalanx in the Assembly until the issue of the two chambers, of which they were the main advocates; but then they quarreled among themselves and split up. Moreover, they were less numerous than the deputies of Brittany, and unlike them, they were not composed of homogeneous elements, since there were no nobles among the deputies for Brittany and there were a lot of them among the deputies for Dauphiné.

In the Assembly it was not difficult to perceive the influence that this association in a club gave the deputies of Brittany, and in consequence other members wanted to be associated with it to share in this influence. The Bretons, sensing that these admissions to their club increased the strength of their party, made no difficulties, and their club became numerous. When the Assembly was transferred to Paris, they sought premises for their meetings near the place where it held its sittings, and they obtained from the Jacobin monks of the Rue Saint-Honoré a basement room in their monastery. Strangely enough, this room was precisely the one where in former times the famous League had been signed at the period of the Wars of Religion.† After their installation in this monastery, the title *Jacobin Club* was substituted for that of *Breton Club*. Since there were many people in this club, it realized the necessity of regulating its discussions. As a result, it nominated a president and two secretaries as in the National Assembly, and its sittings became regular. It became the custom to hold them in the evening, because at that time the Assembly scarcely met except in the morning,‡ and consequently the deputies could attend the sittings of the Jacobins without missing those of the Assembly.

* The deputies to the French Assemblies took their responsibility to their constituents much more seriously than their English counterparts. The idea that the deputy had to act within the scope of the mandate given to him by his constituents did not originate in the period of the National Convention, when radicals pressed this approach to direct democracy, but was present from the start of the Estates-General. In fact it was the right-wing deputies who were most insistent that they were only "mandatories" and as such did not have the authority to consent to changes in the organization of the Estates-General. The "letters to my constituents" that most deputies published did not therefore stem only from a desire for publicity or from the current obsession with self-justification.—ED.

† The League was a Catholic confederation to exclude from the throne Henry III's heir, the Protestant Henry of Navarre.—ED.

‡ Later the Assembly also held evening sittings; at first these were only three times a week, alternating with those of the Jacobins; later they had them every evening.

At first this club was frequented by nearly all the deputies of the left wing, so that it became a rehearsal room for the National Assembly, which in turn became a puppet whose strings were pulled by the Jacobins. This was bound to give, and in fact did give, this club a considerable importance. At first only members of the Assembly and substitute deputies were admitted to it; but soon, on the pretext of gathering the opinions of informed men, sometimes on one issue, sometimes on another, people who had absolutely nothing to do with the Assembly were also admitted, and soon they were to be found there in greater numbers than the deputies. The nature of the discussions changed. They were no longer restricted to the issues that were going to be the subject of the Assembly's deliberations; people digressed, and each day it became more difficult to contain the club within reasonable limits. The sensible men there took alarm at this tendency and successively began to withdraw. They did in the Jacobin Club what they did everywhere in France during the Revolution: They abandoned the field of battle to the extremists, who only kept it until some who were even more fanatical came along to whom they yielded it for the same reason.

However, it was realized that this club was becoming a real power, and with the intention of forming a counterweight, M. de La Fayette and all the deputies who wanted to leave the Jacobins broke away from it completely and founded a new club. Prominent among these were the Abbé Siéyès, Mirabeau, Talleyrand, Roederer, Volney, Barère, Démeunier, Le Chapelier, Condorcet (the last was not a deputy), etc.

This gathering took the name of the *1789 Club* in order to indicate that it included only friends of the Revolution and true patriots, and thereby to acquire popularity; but this did not produce the desired effect, and the public was not taken in. A charming suite of rooms facing the gardens of the Palais Royal was chosen as the venue for the sittings. In one of the rooms there was a rostrum and benches for the discussions; in others, people met to chat or often to dine, since they had provided themselves with an excellent chef. This establishment should have been alluring, and its members were under the illusion that it would bring about the fall of the Jacobins by taking all its deputies from it. They were deceived; the 89 Club was always very unpopular and only served to strengthen and popularize its rival and to push it more rapidly toward demagogy.

I have already indicated above those who directed the people of Paris and from what class of men the mob orators were drawn. Now I have to prove that the men who gave the impetus to the people of Paris thereby controlled the Assembly and *led its leaders instead of being led by them,* as people have persisted in believing. As long as the Assembly had to struggle against royal power and against the resistance of the first two Orders, it was possible to believe that it was the driving force, because in the presence of an agreed program it was impossible to discern the dominating influence. This was all the more so since the Assembly did not even dare attempt to have the murders of July 14 and of the 25th of the same month punished (when Bertier de Sauvigny and Foulon were slaughtered by the people of Paris) and therefore could not yet be attacked by the real leaders of the crowd. But a few days after the night of August 4, 1789, they attempted their first attack on it and warned it that they would give them support only for destructive measures. It was in connection with the tithes; the Abbé Siéyès spoke in favor of their retention and pronounced this famous phrase: "You want to be free, and you do not know how to be just." The Assembly hesitated. But the opinion of Paris declared itself so strongly that the Assembly yielded and decreed the abolition of tithes. The Abbé Siéyès was the subject of a personal attack of such a kind that afterward he scarcely ever appeared on the rostrum. He was accused of not being a true patriot and of abandoning the interests of the people to defend his own.

The affair of the *veto* was even more striking. The Assembly wanted to give the King this prerogative and in effect did give it to him; but the gatherings at the Palais Royal became so tumultuous, and opposed the veto with such force, that the Assembly declared by a second decree that the veto would only be suspensive and not absolute, and this retraction gave the people of Paris (and its leaders) the impression that it was they who dictated the laws and that the Assembly was only their organ. Despite this concession, those members of the Assembly who had voted for the veto had a tarnished reputation in the eyes of the people of Paris, and this alleged stain always disposed them to sacrifice their opinions to the desire to efface it and to that of recovering their reputation as true patriots. In Paris it was the custom to judge a man's patriotism by the extremism of his opinions, and the number of those in favor diminished with each day. I think that with a majority of issues the Assembly was influenced by similar motives and that it often yielded to popular opinion without ever having been able to direct or master it. The same thing took place, from their standpoint, with the *émigrés,* and the same thing will happen everywhere, whenever the leaders allow themselves to be carried along by the extreme opinions of the mass of their party. I regard it as a positive and certain fact that the opinion of Paris regulated that of the Assembly. What is at question now is to examine by whom and how this opinion of Paris was formed. That will bring us back to the political clubs of which I was speaking.

After July 14, 1789, when royal authority in Paris was annihilated, the new authorities realized that they depended for their existence on their obedience to the people, and that when the people became tired of them they were left without any means of forcing them to obey. On their side the mob, or at least its orators, realized that these authorities were only figureheads who could not restrain them. From then on they began to *rule by terror* over those whose offices gave them the right to give orders. This led to real anarchy. The leaders of the Assembly had apparent power whenever their speeches and acts tended to augment the extremism of opinions; but once they wanted to act or even speak in an opposite sense to that of the leaders of Paris, they had none. It even seems that their efforts to arrest the alarming progress of this extremism only increased it; for in general these efforts inspired the people with distrust of those who made them, and the reduction of their influence on public opinion added to the power of the leaders of Paris. The interplay of all these political wheels always eluded the observation of the enemies of the Revolution, who only heeded the opinion of their *salons* without troubling themselves with the way in which the opinion of their adversaries was formed and directed. Always preoccupied with discovering wrongs or crimes to justify the persecution that they wanted to make them suffer, they persistently failed to recognize the real ringleaders and considered as such those who, whatever their rank, their importance, and their talents, were only instruments. I return to the internal organization of the city of Paris after July 14, 1789.

Paris was divided, as I have already said, into sixty districts, and each of these furnished a battalion of National Guards. The district assemblies came to be in permanent session in the sixty churches where they were held; but gradually the men of peace who had a profession to follow or other occupations tired of these assemblies, which were often riotous and always useless; and by retiring they caused the lower classes and the unemployed who frequented them to fall even more into the hands of those orators who were bent on playing a role and whose voice never gave out. When these people were not declaiming in front of a crowd, they were at the rostrum in the districts, engaged in stirring up their fellow citizens, in giving them high notions about their strength and importance, and in propagating the foolish seeds of democracy that had been well sown in everyone's mind. These district assemblies were all the more formidable because each district furnished a battalion of National Guards, and the National Guard was the only armed force in Paris. Another factor further increased the difficulty, already considerable, of governing Paris. The men of peace, as was to be expected, tired of performing their service in the National Guard and of supervising the policing of Paris themselves; they took to paying vagrants thirty *sous** to perform their watch, and this became their trade. These details should give an even deeper impression of the truth of what I said when speaking of the causes of the rising of October 5 and enable one to appreciate how it was that the mayor and commander in chief of the National Guard were forced to obey those whom they were supposed to be commanding. As a result, shortly after the rising of October 5, fairly sensible measures were adopted to remove the National Guard from the influence of the

* 1.50 francs.—ED.

district assemblies, and they met with a certain amount of success. The success would have been complete if the general policies of the government of the time had not prevented the detailed application of these measures from being carried out successfully.

The first of these measures was a rearrangement of the topography of the city of Paris. The sixty districts were amalgamated into forty-eight divisions that were called *sections* so as to efface the very memory of the districts. But care was taken to leave the division of the National Guard into sixty battalions intact, so that as a result of this operation, the armed force found itself separated from the deliberative assemblies, and consequently easier to discipline and render subordinate to its commanding officers. In addition, the assemblies were forbidden to remain in permanent session, and each section could not assemble until it had fulfilled certain formalities. Henceforth, the influence of these assemblies was reduced to insignificant proportions.

The other measures consisted of internal regulations for the National Guard: in the first place, the obligation to wear a uniform when on duty, which flattered the vanity of the bourgeoisie and made them take on, to a certain degree, a military *esprit de corps;* secondly, the formation of companies of grenadiers and riflemen where those who enrolled undertook to perform their service in person and to proceed to wherever they might be directed. There were many young men to be found who were delighted to be grenadiers, to have a busby and red epaulets, and since one had to pay for the cost and upkeep of this equipment and at the same time be able to perform duties that were pretty tiring and expensive in the loss of time incurred, these companies were composed of men of substance who consequently had an interest in maintaining public order, and their morale became excellent. Some advantage was derived from this, and I believe even more use could have been made of them.

Care had been taken in the new division of Paris to split up completely those districts which had shown themselves to be the most hotheaded and to scatter them as much as possible. Particular care was taken with the Cordelier district, as it had been the most prominent. However, it circumvented this wise precaution and became even more dangerous; for as soon as it saw itself suppressed, *it constituted itself as a club* and calmly continued to hold its sessions in the same place and with the same forms as previously under the name of *The Cordelier Club*. At the head of this club were the men who later figured in the National Convention and the Commune of Paris as *Robespiéristes,* such as Danton, Fabre d'Eglantine, Camille Desmoulins, Robert, Keraglio, Panis, Sergeant [*sic*], Billaut [*sic*] de Varennes, Chaumette, Hébert, Fréron, etc.

The Cordelier Club became for the Jacobins what the latter was for the Assembly and what the Assembly in turn was for the King, that is to say, the *tribune of the people*. This gradation was very noticeable and became more pronounced with each day, until the different parties of which it was composed brought about their own downfall in the order that I have just indicated. The Cordeliers infiltrated the Jacobin Club furtively and one by one, and it was not until they were already there in considerable strength that the members of the National Assembly perceived that their oratorical talents were no longer producing the same effect as when they were deliberating among themselves. They thought to remedy this and to restore their club to the footing on which it had been before these ill-considered admissions by forming the 89 Club, that impolitic schism which succeeded in weakening them and in rendering the Jacobin Club even more dangerous by assisting the development of demagogy there. Mirabeau soon realized this, because having left the Jacobins for the 89 Club, he was not long in going back; and on his return, although the prejudice against him there was considerable, the force of his talents and of his eloquence always swayed this Assembly, even when he was hazarding opinions contrary to those which it professed at the time. Despite the great advantages which the Cordeliers derived from the schism of the 89 Club with that of the Jacobins, they still needed to win two further victories over their opponents and to cause many members of the Jacobin Club to leave in order that their opinions should enjoy complete success there.

The 89 Club was never more than a social gathering, and despite the great oratorical talents of some of its members, its debates had no political importance, nor any influence on public opinion.

The Jacobin Club soon became too numerous to fit into the room where the League was signed. It moved to the library of the same monastery in the summer of 1790, and in the spring of 1791 it established itself in the chapel, which was arranged along the same lines as the chamber of the National Assembly. Then for the first time, there were public galleries that filled up with people during the sessions, and that greatly added to the influence of this club. There were more than three thousand members at this period, each paying nine francs a quarter to cover expenses. At the beginning of 1790 the club adopted the title *Society for the Friends of the Constitution*. People tried to pour ridicule on this title by saying that the Constitution was not finished, but its foundations had been laid, and there is no denying that they were well known.

All the provincial towns followed the example of Paris, and more or less numerous assemblies were formed everywhere, which likewise adopted the title *Society for the Friends of the Constitution*. Their assemblies were organized in the same manner, with presidents, secretaries, etc. They affiliated themselves with the Parisian society, which was called the *Mother Society*. They corresponded with it, informed it of everything that was going on in their towns or departments and received its advice on what they should do. At first their correspondence was conducted by the secretaries of the Parisian society, who read it out at the meetings; but later on it became so voluminous that a committee was formed to conduct it, nominated by ballot and called the *Corresponding Committee,* and then only extracts of the correspondence were read out at the rostrum. The affiliations and the correspondence gave the Jacobins of Paris great influence and even real power. The members of the affiliated societies had right of entry to the Mother Society when they came to Paris, and likewise the members of the Parisian society had right of entry to all those in the provinces. The form of address among them was always *Brothers and friends!*

When the Jacobins left the room where the League was signed, a society was formed there that was called the Fraternal Society. It was composed of the lowest class, and men and women were admitted without distinction. Sometimes the papers were read aloud; sometimes mob orators, very demagogic, followed each other at the rostrum to declaim before their audience, to send them to sleep, and yet to send them home a little more inflamed than when they had left. By and large these orators were of too crude a caliber to dare mount the rostrum of the Jacobins, although later nothing was too crude for them. But at this period a semblance of decorum was still preserved, at least in comparison with what later obtained. This period was that of the mania for clubs, because all the parties regarded them as a means of influence. And yet there was only the Jacobin Club that had real influence. It even exercised a surveillance over the other clubs that was so active that no club could remain in existence without its permission. Often in provincial towns two clubs would be formed in competition with each other, with both soliciting the honor of being affiliated with the Mother Society; and as this affiliation would determine which one would have the victory, no means were neglected to procure it. Then the Mother Society became a tribunal that heard witnesses and instituted proceedings; and when it had ascertained which of the two clubs was the more extreme, that one was granted the affiliation and the other went into liquidation. Nothing was more vexatious or destructive of order than these little provincial clubs. Idleness gives men a disposition to interfere and to gossip, a disposition that flourishes in small towns; and as the majority of these clubs had nothing to do and did not know how to make themselves important, they merely spent their time in discovering things that were in reality trifling, but which they could represent to the Mother Society as *great conspiracies.* This tendency to be suspicious of everything, to make the most ridiculous denunciations, and to be frightened of the most insignificant things also derived from the people's credulity and from the distrust with which it was inspired by the dispositions of the Court and of the nobility and clergy. The provincial clubs tormented and terrorized their whole neighborhood with these absurdities. In garrison towns they were reinforced by the smooth-talkers in the army who, in general, have been troublemakers at all times. The slightest disciplinary punishment was depicted as harassment and an abuse of power, the slightest indulgence on the part of the commanding officers as a means of corruption to win the confidence and affection of the troops and thus engage them to support the Counterrevolution. But at the same time I ought to say that those colonels and officers who passed as patriots could do pretty well what they liked without being denounced.

Later, under the Reign of Terror, when these provincial clubs became Revolutionary Committees* and the accusations they formulated were death sentences, they continued to see conspiracies everywhere; and it was in this way that so many innocent victims were sacrificed to the credulity of some and the wickedness of others. I shall terminate this digression and resume my account.

Having left Passy shortly after the rising of October 5, 1789, Mme de Genlis returned to Belle-Chasse and we went to the Palais Royal. Our style of life was the same as in the preceding years. My mother displayed increasing dissatisfaction with Mme de Genlis's conduct. To the best of my belief there were even quarrels that resulted in my mother's ceasing to see her. But there was not yet any open rupture during this winter. These harrowing scenes only took place the following winter, that of 1790–1791. During the course of the winter of 1789–1790, Mme de Genlis did not receive any member of the Assembly at Belle-Chasse, and I do not recall that there was any change in her circle of friends.

With the return of the fine season, we went to Saint-Leu as in the previous years, and it was there that we found ourselves on my father's return from England, a few days before the great Federation that took place on July 14, 1790, to celebrate the anniversary of the fall of the Bastille. We returned to Paris the day before to take part in this ceremony. Mme de Genlis went with my sister to spend the night at the Convent of the Visitation at Chaillot so as to be within reach of the Champ-de-Mars, where the Federation was to be held. My brothers and I spent the night at the Palais Royal; and the following morning, as carriages were forbidden throughout Paris, we went on foot to Chaillot with M. Lebrun.

A temporary bridge had been constructed over the Seine opposite the École Militaire. At the entrance to the Champ-de-Mars a triumphal arch had been erected, and we wanted to see it at close quarters. Rather inadvisedly we proceeded there. I was recognized, and immediately men from the crowd surrounding us got hold of me, placed me on their shoulders, and made ready to carry me like this to the Altar of the Fatherland, which was the last thing I wanted. In the end, partly by force and partly by persuasion, I got down from their shoulders and thus avoided the slightly embarrassing triumph with which I was threatened.

* These committees, instituted by a law of March 21, 1793, performed such functions as rounding up "suspects."—ED.

We recrossed the bridge as quickly as possible and positioned ourselves on a terrace from which we saw the ceremony in perfect comfort. It was magnificent. A hundred and fifty thousand representatives of the army of the line and of all the National Guards of France had been summoned to Paris to take an oath of loyalty to the nation, the law, and the King, and to maintain the Constitution decreed by the National Assembly and accepted by the King. The federal army assembled at daybreak on the Boulevard de la Bastille. The National Guards took up position according to their department, and the departments took their rank in alphabetical order, so that the march was led by the Department of the Ain, with that of the Yonne bringing up the rear. The representatives of the army of the line were placed in the center, as was the National Assembly, which marched as a body in the midst of this immense column. All of the federal army had saber in hand. It entered the Champ-de-Mars to the sound of numerous salvos of artillery. The level of the Champ-de-Mars had been lowered by a few feet so as to form an earthen amphitheater around the perimeter on which an immense crowd had gathered.

The King had made his way to the apartments at the front of the École Militaire, and from there he proceeded to a throne placed above the tier occupied by the National Assembly. He took the oath first, and it was then repeated enthusiastically by the whole federal army and by all of the spectators. Nothing could have been more solemn or more fine. Then M. de Talleyrand, Bishop of Autun, celebrated High Mass on the Altar of the Fatherland. There was a heavy downpour of rain during the ceremony, and many people said by way of a joke, as the Ancients might have done, that this was a bad omen.

The consequences of this great assembly were, to my way of thinking, very different from those that had been expected. People imagined that all these provincials and all these old soldiers would be *democratized* a little during their stay in Paris; but rather they were *royalized*. As the representatives of the army were the most senior from each detachment, they were for the most part imbued with royalist notions. As for the representatives of the National Guards, the sight of the King, which was so rare a treat in the provinces, the benevolence with which he greeted them, and the gravity with which he took his oath—which persuaded them that *it was impossible that the King's acceptance of the Revolution was not in good faith*—all aroused the enthusiasm of these representatives, and it was even feared that they might make some demonstration in favor of the King. How many similar opportunities presented themselves without the hapless Louis XVI ever taking advantage of them! But the Court had no desire for the King to employ such methods to reestablish the independence of action of royal authority because they would always have led to a more or less constitutional outcome, which the Court was above all anxious to avoid. The Court considered as enemies of the King all those who wished for the slightest modifications in the Ancien Régime, that is to say, the whole nation, because one can say that there was no one in France who did not desire a change in one direction or the other.

Mme de Genlis had been very alarmed at my father's departure for England, and she was equally alarmed by his return. She felt cut off at Saint-Leu; she feared the Parisian risings (although at this period she had nothing to fear from that quarter), and she did not feel at ease anywhere. At the beginning of August she was seized with panic for reasons unknown to me. It is unlikely that there was a connection with the Châtelet's investigation into the rising of October 5, because if this had been the case she would not have installed herself at Paris just when this storm broke. She suddenly announced, I think it was on August 8 or 9, 1790, that the spring water we drank, which was excellent, had become tainted and that for the sake of her health and ours we must not spend another second at Saint-Leu. It was only a pretext, but we left the same day without my ever being able to ascertain the real reason for our precipitate departure. We returned to the Palais Royal and she to Belle-Chasse. The Châtelet affair broke out a few days later.

I was seventeen in the month of October of this year, and as had been determined a long time before the Revolution in accordance with an old family custom, the day I reached that age I became *my own master,* that is to say that I was no longer subject to any tutor, that I was no longer bound to do anything except of my own free will, and that I could even do anything I liked. The same day my father gave me the apartments he had occupied during my grandfather's lifetime when he was Duc de Chartres. These apartments were refurnished and greatly enlarged by the destruction of the Opera House, which had restricted their development. In addition, my father allowed me to put there any of the paintings in his collection that suited me, which greatly improved its appearance.

My independence did not make any difference to my habits, or at least very little. When the new laws abolished ownership of regiments, those owner-colonels who were not staff officers were given the option of taking command of one of their regiments or of leaving the service. I decided to give up my infantry regiment and become the ordinary colonel of my regiment of dragoons in the place of M. de Valence, who was its lieutenant colonel and who passed to a regiment of riflemen. This decision obliged me to rejoin my regiment the following summer, and as I foresaw that I would have few opportunities of continuing my studies in the future, I resolved to employ this winter much as the preceding ones. I continued with the periods of study at Belle-Chasse, and at the same time I regularly followed the sittings of the National Assembly, where I had obtained access to the substitute deputies' gallery.

At the time it seemed essential to gain a knowledge of parliamentary tactics and to practice public speaking. I was forcefully impressed with this necessity, and my father and Mme de Genlis were no less so. Virtually the only way I could achieve this aim was by frequenting the 89

Club or the Jacobins* so as to take part in their debates. My father did not care for me to go to the 89 Club, and I did not want this any more than he did. There was little debate in this club, while in the Jacobins there was a regular series of debates. My father did not see any harm in my going to their meetings, and I shared his opinion: He just recommended me to exercise great circumspection and not to become involved with anyone in this club. I scrupulously followed this advice.

It was M. de Sillery who presented me to the Jacobin Club, as my father was not yet a member. The composition of this club was very different from what it later was. At the time there were only six or seven hundred members, about three hundred of whom were deputies. The outlook of the Jacobins at the beginning was not what it later became. Events subsequent to the time when I frequented this club have attached a sanguinary connotation to the label *Jacobins* that makes me regret having been a member of this society. But at this period it was not yet a power in the State, and people only spent their time there in preparing for the debates in the National Assembly.

My mother was very upset that I should be going to the Jacobins. Vainly she strove with my father to make him put a stop to it, and she also expressed to me her desire that I cease to go there. Long before this period she had already expressed views hostile to the Revolution, which I attributed to the influence of her circle, because at the time I believed that opposition to the Revolution stemmed either from one's being led astray or from motives of self-interest, which I regarded as being without effect on my mother. It is undeniable that by an unfortunate coincidence, nobles and the majority of individuals who opposed the Revolution had advocated its principles until the moment when they experienced personal losses, whether through the abolition of privileges or of abuses or otherwise. This led to the belief that they had attacked the authority of the Court at first only to augment their own and that they were defending it subsequently only to prolong the existence of the privileges and abuses from which they profited. This opinion was general among all the partisans of the Revolution, and it was natural that it should produce a great effect on me. The greater my losses, the more I prided myself in making them nobly. I thought I was sacrificing myself for the general good, and this confidence carried me away. Youth is presumptuous; I regarded all the fine results with which my imagination presented me as assured, and in the strength of this conviction, I had no doubt that my conduct would receive the justice that was its due.

A few days after my introduction to the Jacobins I was nominated to the Entrance Committee for a limited period. This committee, which was entrusted with vetting those who wished to be admitted to the society, had a membership of thirty, a third of whom were renewed at a time. It met

* This club was called the Society for the Friends of the Constitution.

every Thursday evening in a room that housed a natural history collection near the library, where its sittings were held at the time. No one could be admitted to the society unless he was proposed by six members who had signed the proposal. Then the committee made its examination and drew up a list that was read to the society at three separate sessions and posted up on the rostrum for a week. The committee took a great deal of care that the society not be infiltrated by false comrades, but despite all its care it would have been easy to elude its vigilance and deceive it. But this method was never employed, although it would have been the surest way of destroying the Jacobins. It seems that people should have attached greater importance to being admitted to this society, but this was far from being the case. I was very assiduous in this committee while I was a member of it because I pride myself on punctiliously carrying out the duties with which I am charged. I can vouch for the fact that of the thirty members, there were rarely more than eight or nine who attended the sessions of the committee. I was always reproaching the members, above all those who were deputies, for this negligence which allowed so many dangerous and unsuitable men to slip into a society whose importance was not sufficiently foreseen, but the reply to anything that I could say was: "My God, this is just too boring for words!" They were right in this, and it was more boring for me than for anyone, because not knowing any of the men proposed, I was always obliged to rely on other people. For the rest, while I was in the Jacobins I restricted myself, as I have already said, to attending its sessions fairly regularly, and I had no special dealings there with anyone whatsoever.

Since the winter of 1789–1790 my mother had expressed her dissatisfaction at virtually never being allowed by Mme de Genlis to be alone with her children, especially with my sister, and at not being allowed to see us as often as she wanted. In the winter of 1790–1791 I dined with my mother three times a week, and my brothers and sisters dined there every Sunday. In addition, it was agreed that my mother should come to Belle-Chasse a certain number of times a week to take charge of my sister and that she should keep her as long as she liked. But there were other difficulties. Mme de Genlis had been for a long time openly at loggerheads with Mme de Chatellux. My mother was no longer on speaking terms with Mme de Genlis, nor was my father with Mme de Chatellux. He was dissatisfied with the company my mother kept, and the difference in political opinions succeeded in arousing discord in the midst of the Palais Royal, to the great satisfaction of many people whose animosity against us was carried to such extremes that they derived enjoyment from our misfortunes. Their justifiable expectation was that the removal of my mother's influence would be very detrimental to my father. These fatal divisions, then, reached their peak and produced the unfortunate scandal that I would feign not have to mention.

Early one morning in the month of April 1791, my mother arrived at

Belle-Chasse. She went into Mme de Genlis's apartments and read her a memorandum, the contents of which I have never known except that in it she asked her to resign her position with my sister and to leave her immediately. Mme de Genlis gave this promise, provided that she could remain for three more weeks to complete my sister's preparation for her first communion. I arrived at Belle-Chasse that day as usual. My father came there a little afterward, and after talking a fair while to Mme de Genlis, he summoned me to come and speak with him. In her presence he told me of the morning's happenings, that he knew in advance that anything he might try to say on the subject to my mother would be without effect, that he saw me as the only person who could shake her resolution, and that consequently he wished me to go to see her and try and persuade her to desist from her demand, because otherwise Mme de Genlis would certainly leave. I went around my mother's apartments in the Palais Royal straightaway; she received me with her usual kindness, but asked me as soon as she saw me not to speak to her about the object for which I had come. I did, however, but I had the satisfaction of doing it in a manner that did not cause offense. I tried to make her imagine the effect that this separation would have on my sister and that the scandal would have on the public, the difficulty of replacing Mme de Genlis in times such as those, and I added that my father had just intimated to me his determination not to give my sister back to anyone in my mother's current entourage. She was very touched, but she remained inflexible and confined herself to telling me that she had considered in advance all the arguments that I was putting forward to her, that she had very strong reasons for what she was doing, that she could not yet tell me them but that I would know them one day, and that she was sure that then I would approve the course of action she was adopting.

For his part, my father decided to demand of my mother the banishment of Mme de Chatellux; the result of this step was that my mother suddenly left the Palais Royal and retired to the town of Eu, where the Duc de Penthièvre, her father, was. It is not for me to trace these unhappy scenes and those that followed in detail, but I owe it equally to my father and to my mother to give the lie here directly to the odious calumnies that were carefully circulated among the public about the way in which my father behaved toward my mother in the talks he had with her at this unfortunate time. It is the last word I shall say about events of such painful memory to me.

During this period my father was seriously engaged in finding a replacement for Mme de Genlis, who was due to leave in a fortnight. He did not known which way to turn, and as he did not see a suitable replacement for Mme de Genlis with my sister, he hit on the idea of attaching only a menial to her and of having her education finished in a provincial convent. He even made proposals to the nuns of two abbeys near Rouen that we had chosen together from the map. It was one of my men who was charged with making the proposals, and my father had forbidden him to let it get out that he had been sent by him. The reply was unfavorable; these nuns were uncertain of their future because of the Assembly's decrees on ecclesiastical property, and did not want to admit anyone into their convents. This refusal increased my father's difficulties, although he always believed that he would find some other convent where he could place my sister because the Assembly had decreed that a certain number of these establishments should be kept in existence.

My sister made her first communion at Easter, and Mme de Genlis profited from a moment when my sister had gone out to the baths to leave Belle-Chasse without her noticing. She proceeded directly to Auvergne and was to return via Lyon and Franche-Comté at the end of about three weeks. After that I do not think that she had any definite plans; sometimes she seemed to have it in mind to withdraw to Puysieux in Champagne, to a little *château* of M. de Sillery's; sometimes she spoke of leaving France and going to set herself up in Germany because she was afraid of what she foresaw as bound to happen in France, where she regarded the success of the Counterrevolution as very probable. The only people she took with her to the Auvergne were Pamela, M. Myris, and her chambermaid. My father had consented to allow Mlle de Sercey to remain with my sister so that she would not be left entirely alone and, insofar as was possible, to make up for the deficiencies of the person to whom provisionally he entrusted my sister. This person was a woman of sixty called Mme Topin.

My sister did not learn of the resignation of Mme de Genlis until after her departure. She had a violent attack of nerves, which was followed by several others, and her state became alarming. She had long convinced herself that she could not bear to be separated from Mme de Genlis, and she had a great fear of the kind of life in store for her if this separation became permanent. Her mind had been adjusted to this in more ways than one. In the first place, excessive sensibility had been represented to her as the best proof of a good heart. From early on Mme de Genlis had instilled in her, as in all her pupils, the notion that to enjoy a good reputation it was necessary to profess for her affection and even devotion without limit. Nothing was better calculated than all this to encourage my sister to allow herself to give way to the admittedly very real and very natural grief that Mme de Genlis's removal caused her.

If my mother had still been at the Palais Royal at this period, she would constantly have been at Belle-Chasse; I do not know what would have happened, because her presence would have calmed my sister to a certain degree, and it is hard to say whether my father would not have lent himself to the arrangements that she thought appropriate. I know that afterward he often expressed to me the desire to give my sister back to my mother; but that after the scandal that my mother's departure had caused, he had an intense repugnance against sending her to the town of Eu. As for Mme de Genlis's return, it is more exact to say that my father *lent himself to it* than that he *asked for it*. I confess that I earnestly desired it, and the state in which I saw my sister convinced me that this desire was a duty. We all wrote to Mme de Genlis to engage her to hasten her return and to take up her place again at Belle-Chasse. It was at Lyon that she decided to return directly to Paris, and she arrived a few days afterward at Belle-Chasse, where she was immediately restored to the same footing as before her departure.

I spent the rest of the month of May in Paris, and at the beginning of June I made ready to rejoin my regiment of dragoons at Vendôme. I went to the Tuileries to take my leave of the King and Queen, who received me very coldly. I had constantly gone to the Tuileries to discharge my duties toward Their Majesties since they had been installed there, and this was the last time that I had the honor of paying them my court. I also went, with my father and my brother the Duc de Montpensier,* to see M. le Dauphin, Madame the King's daughter, Madame Elisabeth, as well as Monsieur, Comte de Provence, and Madame, who occupied the Petit Luxembourg. After a rapid journey to the town of Eu to see my mother and the Duc de Penthièvre, my grandfather, I left Paris on June 14, 1791, taking with me only M. Pieyre, who had been attached to me for some time in the capacity of Keeper of the Seals.† I arrived at Vendôme on the 15th; and on the 16th I was received as colonel at the head of the regiment by its lieutenant colonel, M. de Lagondie.

In accordance with the new army regulations suppressing the old names of regiments and substituting for them a number determined by the order of their foundation in their respective arm, my regiment had ceased to bear the name *Chartres* and was called the 14th Regiment of Dragoons. At Vendôme I found only the staff officers of the regiment and three companies, the rest having been dispersed some time ago. Before going into garrison at Vendôme, the regiment had been stationed at Le Mans for over two years. A quarrel that some of the officers had at the theater with the inhabitants of this town about remarks with a political bearing had led to a popular demonstration against the regiment, which had at all times remained perfectly loyal to its commanders. The Council of the Department of the Sarthe, of which Le Mans is the administrative center, had required the commander of the regiment to leave the town immediately and go into quarters in the surrounding district, and the Minister of War, M. Duportail, had subsequently dispersed it: The staff officers and three companies had been sent to Vendôme, one company to Le Montoir, four leagues away, a squadron to Caen in Normandy, and several detach-

---

* The Comte de Beaujolais was too young to accompany us; he had not yet been presented at Court.

† *Secrétaire des Commandements.* All the Princes had then to counter-sign and seal their documents.—ED.

ments in various directions to protect the circulation of grain, which was still causing anxiety.* This dispersal was very annoying. It necessarily involved an unfortunate relaxation of discipline and dress. It was harmful to training, it tired the horses by making them carry out the duties of mounted police, it spoiled equipment and led to a general deterioration of the regiment. As a result I was very keen, and I made strong representations to this effect, that my regiment should be reassembled and sent to some frontier town where it could be installed in good quarters and be among the first to take the field should war break out, which became more probable each day. I was afraid that under the pretext of needing troops at home, those which happened to be there would be left where they were, and that in this way I would be successfully excluded from active service.

The King, the Queen, and all the members of the Royal Family departed mysteriously from the Tuileries during the night of June 20–21, 1791, and immediately left Paris. The gates of Paris had been closed for a few hours as soon as it was realized that the King had left, so I did not receive the news at Vendôme until the morning of Thursday the 23rd, and I was only informed of his arrest at Varennes in the course of the evening. This Thursday just happened to be that of the feast of the Holy Sacrament, and the solemn procession with which it was accompanied was bound to attract a vast concourse of people from the surrounding countryside to Vendôme. Fearing the ferment that this news must produce, I went to see the mayor (M. de Frémant) in good time to coordinate with him such police measures as might become necessary. We agreed that as it would be perfectly natural for the regiment to be on horseback for the procession, nothing more needed to be done except to keep the horses saddled until nightfall and to confine the dragoons to their barracks. There were no incidents during the procession, and everything went off very quietly. At two o'clock, just when I was going to sit down to table, one of my servants, quite out of breath, came to warn me that a crowd of people had collected in the main street and wanted to lynch two men. I sped there straightaway with M. Pieyre and two officers, MM. Dubois and d'Albis, whom I had invited for lunch. And I did find a fairly considerable crowd who were shouting: "They are lawbreakers; they must be hanged; string them up from the lamppost." The mayor was with some National Guards, few in number, in front of the door of the house containing the two objects of the popular fury. These were an old nonjuring† priest and his father, whom the people accused of having made a

* The inhabitants of a province were always very reluctant to let grain leave that province, even if it had a surplus and the grain was being sent to an area of dearth. Internal free trade in corn had not been introduced until 1763, and then only temporarily, and it was still a controversial matter.—ED.

† I.e., one who had refused to take the oath to uphold the Civil Constitution of the Clergy voted by the National Assembly in 1790. Those who did take the oath (about half the clergy) were known as the "constitutional" priests.—ED.

face at the "constitutional" *curé* when he had gone by carrying the Holy Sacrament to the procession. The mayor told me that he had sent someone to look for a carriage, which would come in a minute, and that he hoped that with the assistance of the National Guards he would succeed in getting them out of the town. However, the people's wrath was increasing, and it was mooted in the crowd that the door of the house should be forced. At this point I got up on a small stone bench in front of the door, and having obtained silence, I harangued the crowd to the best of my ability to bring home to them the horror of the crime that they wanted to commit. Perceiving that the silence I had obtained calmed the people, who are always animated by noise, I prolonged my harangue as much as I could in the hope that the carriage would arrive. In the end a voice shouted from the midst of the crowd: *"You are a good patriot and we shall spare them out of consideration for you."*—*"Do you promise me?"* I shouted out immediately;—*"Yes, yes, yes, yes."*—*"All right then,"* I said to them, *"I shall take your word and go and look for them."* I entered the house immediately, and I shall never forget the spectacle that I saw. These two old men were sitting facing each other in front of a table, their heads sunk on their chests, in complete silence. I said to them: "There is not a moment to lose, trust me, we must *leave here.*"—*"My God!"* one of them cried, *"leave here! The people will tear us to shreds!"*—*"If you stay here you are lost without hope, because the people will force the door. Believe me, let us leave as fast as possible."* They made up their minds to it. As soon as they appeared in the street they were greeted by a general hiss. I wanted to have the carriage brought forward, which, in accordance with the mayor's explicit request, was only escorted by two dragoons, but there was general opposition from the people to this proposal: "Let them walk, let them walk so that we can hiss at them at our leisure!" was shouted on all sides. I got onto the bench again to harangue the crowd once more. I recalled the promise that had been made to me, and I consented to have the two old men leave on foot only on the condition that they would be peacefully escorted out of the town. The people seemed satisfied, and we began to walk. One of the two old men walked between the mayor and myself, and we gave him our arm. The other followed immediately behind us and gave his arm to the two officers. This passed off all right as long as we were in the town, but as we were leaving we were assailed by an angry band of armed peasants who were shouting: *"Hanged, hanged, all the rotten b———s must be hanged,"* and without hearing anything or listening to anything, they threw themselves on me to snatch away my old priest. I grabbed one around the waist and the other by the arm, the mayor was carried off some distance by the crowd, and I had great difficulty, with the help of the two officers, in defending these two unfortunate men against this new fury. Finally, seeing that there was no other way to save them, I shouted at the top of my voice *"They must be tried, to the prison, take them to the prison,"* and immediately the whole of this crowd proceeded to echo: *"To prison, to prison!"* and we returned toward the town. A few minutes afterward M. de Lagondie arrived with the regiment. The sight of the troops reawakened the people's fury and directed it against me, whom they immediately accused of deceiving them. But I obtained room for maneuver by announcing that I was going to dismiss the dragoons, who had come without my knowledge. In fact, I stepped forward and shouted to M. de Lagondie to withdraw the regiment. This brought an end to the matter. I conducted the two unfortunate men to prison without difficulty. I committed them in front of the gate, and in front of all the people I recommended the jailer to keep an eye on them. Then I had the prison locked up; the crowd broke up and to the best of my knowledge thought no more of the matter. In the evening I was at the prison with the mayor. The jailer, faithful to my advice, had kept them separate. We caused them to be reunited, and the good old men embraced in the most touching manner. They spent two more days in prison; after which, in concert with the municipal authorities, we drew up a document attesting that during these two days no one had come forward to give evidence against them, and consequently at eleven o'clock at night they got into a post chaise and departed. On the morrow of the riot I had a visit from two or three of those who had shown the most animosity, the town crier among others. They came in tears to present me with some fruit and to thank me for having prevented them from committing a great crime.*

Although the King's flight and his arrest at Varennes had absolutely nothing to do with me, they are relevant to the aim I have in view in this work, and it is necessary to know the facts about them to be in a position to understand the consequences arising from them. So I shall recount the salient features.†

* I have recounted this anecdote in detail because it seemed to me to give an impression of the times, and also because in the course of the Châtelet's proceedings, some people were pleased to give evidence that they *had heard me express the wish that all the Aristocrats should be strung up,* and I thought that the incident that I have just recounted was a good reply to their calumny.
† Before going into details of the King's departure and his arrest at Varennes, I am going to produce some letters of Mme de Genlis, which may serve to give further amplification of her advice and of the direction she tried to give to my conduct and opinions.

Fragments from letters that Mme de Genlis wrote to me from Paris during my stay at Vendôme.

June 13, 1791

"It is true that I have private troubles, but I have enough courage to support them patiently: My way with you is not to dwell on that, but on a series of things I have disapproved of in you: I see you becoming lax in matters of religion; (2) that you are letting yourself become indolent; that you make promises and do not keep them; that you do not possess that keen desire to be considerate and to do good in which

Monsieur, Comte de Provence, left from the Luxembourg with M. d'Avaray and reached the Flemish frontier without difficulty, crossing by the Pont-sur-Sambre. Madame likewise left at the same time. The King and Queen, M. Le Dauphin, Madame the King's daughter, and Madame Elisabeth with Mme de Tourzel, governess of the Children of France, had promised each other not to separate. They left the Tuileries on foot during the night of the 20th–21st, and a short distance from the palace they continued in a carriage that had been prepared for their journey, which the Comte de Fersen, acting as coachman, conducted as far as Bondy. The Queen had a passport under the name of a Russian lady (the

---

true goodness consists. You had promised me that you would keep your diary,[a] and yet for six weeks you have left it where it was despite the fact that all your time is your own. If you *were* industrious, if you really were patriotic, you would, in addition, have written an abstract and commentary of *The Social Contract* and *The Institutions of Poland*.[b] What I should regard as real tokens of affection, and what would make me happy, would be for you to bring and show me tangible proof of time usefully, and therefore virtuously, employed." . . . Etc., etc.

Second letter, midnight, the same day

"Dear child, farewell! Keep in mind your promises and the holy love that binds us. Think of my happiness; it rests with your success and above all with your virtues. Be such as my heart desires; you can be if you are determined to overcome completely your lack of concern and laziness. Conduct yourself as your tenderhearted second mother would wish, and I shall see you again with inexpressible transports of joy. Life is short, my son, but the soul does not perish, and fame is immortal: All is vanity, all is illusion on earth, except virtue and friendship. Farewell, my son, come back worthy of a friend who would give up her life this instant to ensure the success of yours. Trust that in your absence I shall attend to all your affairs without forgetting any. Tell our friend whom you are taking with you (M. Pieyre) that I hope he will write to me and inform me of the details concerning you. I give him my word that I shall reply. Always appreciate this worthy friend who will never conceal the truth from you. Mention me sometimes, I will be thinking of you every day. Farewell, my beloved son, and bless you; does not my maternal tenderness give me this right?—Write to Mme d'Orléans and M. d'Orléans from the first night's stop; once you are at Vendôme, never fail to write every four or five days to your mother, do not write to me when M. Pieyre can do so. Farewell, dear Théodore."[c]

June 15

My child,

"There's one day gone. I am very impatient to hear your news, especially from Vendôme. I recommend that you try to win the hearts of the National Guard and to get your soldiers to line in harmony with them; it is the only way to neutralize the traps that are being laid for you. Charge your attendants and *valets de chambre* to make friends among them: Do not forget that. I have one anxiety: You know how to

---

[a] A diary that I then kept at the instigation of Mme de Genlis was found in my apartment at the Palais Royal. I was done the disservice of having fragments of this diary published. It is only too obviously the work of a young man who has only just emerged from childhood, but, such as it is, it seems to me to demonstrate the sincerity of my opinions and that I unfeignedly did what seemed to me good and honorable.

[b] Both by Jean-Jacques Rousseau.—ED.

[c] A reference to Mme de Genlis's novel *Adèle et Théodore,* published shortly before.—ED.

Baroness Korff), and the King was supposed to be her *valet de chambre*. The first part of the enterprise was remarkably successful. The King took the road for Châlons. He only had three of his Bodyguards with him in disguise. After Châlons M. de Bouillé, the military commandant of this region and of Lorraine, had posted detachments of dragoons along the route by which the King was to pass with orders to escort a *treasure;* however as no one knew, or was supposed to know, what this treasure was, it was unlikely that these detachments would be of any service to the King, and their presence along the route by which the King was to pass could not but arouse suspicion. It is probable that M. de Bouillé was

---

ride a horse only in the English manner; I entreat you to take some lessons in this, either from an officer who rides well or from a riding school if there is one. I beseech you also to practice pistol-shooting two or three times a week. Do not forget to write immediately to M. and Mme d'Orléans. While not disguising your high principles, display also some lightheartedness. I advise you to arrange a good game of prisoner's base with the soldiers of the National Guard, to play hard, and to be very gay and pleasant to everyone. Mention this to M. Pieyre; if there are no difficulties, this would be a success, would amuse you and make you popular. Often such methods are more successful than greater ones. In the town, try to associate with those with a reputation for good judgment. When making your first round of visits, follow the general custom of colonels. This is absolutely essential: Nothing would be more Aristocratic than not to pay the customary visits that all colonels pay on arriving in a garrison town. They visit the most prominent ladies, the commandant, etc. Find out about all this. If there is a theater in the town, go to it, and however bad it is, be careful not to denigrate it. Behave there in an open and unaffected manner, and do not ostentatiously applaud the allusions.[d] In the streets and parades be very careful to greet people courteously. Please do not lapse into your habit of walking with a stoop: Try to assume a noble air of poise. Do not eat milk foods, salt meat, and pastry, dear child, I beg you; and take lots of exercise, on foot and on horseback, to make sure you grow to your full size and strengthen your frame. Also swim, I beg you earnestly: You display an assurance which is a pleasure to watch. In your walks and in all your games, always take people with you and vary the company. Never be alone or unsociable except during the time set aside for study; in all other activities, make sure you are observed—it will be to your advantage. If any chaste, pleasant ladies receive you, be polite to them, attentive, and amiable. In short, overlook nothing that may make you popular: That constitutes my own happiness, and I entrust it to your care. I should like you to show this letter to M. Pieyre so that he can add his observations. I beseech you to reread the last letter but one I wrote you here because, with this one, it constitutes all the advice which your dear friend can give you. Farewell, my son, write to me in detail about everything that concerns you—what kind of reception you get from the officers, the soldiers, and the inhabitants and whom you have visited, etc. . . . How did you find the club,[e] is it a large one, etc. . . . Do not forget to go and see the churches and the antique collections, if there are any; do find out about everything of interest to be seen, to display the greatest appreciation of the arts and everything relating to education. Do this when you receive people, make everyone speak, and question them on what they know most about, and make sure you listen with an air of interest, etc. . . . Farewell, then, dear child, I embrace you from the depths of my heart.

---

[d] I.e., to events in the Revolution. As the Revolution progressed, the theater became increasingly, even exclusively, topical.—ED.

[e] I.e., the local Jacobin Club.—ED.

under the illusion that if the King were recognized, the commanding officers of these detachments would be able to persuade them to protect the King's passage and stop people from arresting him: The event was to prove that he was deceived. While the King was changing horses at Sainte-Menehould, he was recognized. The postmaster of the place, Drouet, had a horse saddled on the spot; and profiting from the fact that the King, following the main road, would pass through Clermont on the way to Varennes, he went there directly through the forest of Argonne and arrived a long time before the King. He informed Sausse, the town clerk of Varennes, of his discovery, and the two of them together made ready

---

"P.S. (to the preceding letter).

"When you are writing letters that you want to be well written, such as to M. de Beauharnais, write them yourself, but make rough copies and show them to M. Pieyre so as to receive some words of advice on matters of style, the elegant turning of phrases, etc. . . . and then rewrite them in accordance with his advice. —It is essential that you write a friendly little letter to M. de Valence, and soon. In it you will tell him that the friendship he has always shown you emboldens you to give him some news about your reception: a few vague details and above all, no criticism, no complaint about any person or thing whatsoever; a few compliments, to tell him that you have *boasted* in his friendship for you, that you have had the pleasure of hearing him eulogized, etc. Finish, in a postscript, by begging him to offer *the homage of your respect* to Mme de Valence and to Mme de Montesson."

June 21

My friend,

"The King and all the Royal Family have escaped in the night. All Paris is in turmoil, as you can well imagine. The people and all good patriots are behaving perfectly. So far there have been no excesses and the greatest patriotism in many gatherings; the people have spoken of you with tender concern. —It is claimed that the King, who escaped in disguise, has been stopped at Meaux: He escaped along the subterranean passages of the Tuileries kitchens. —My son, summon up all your prudence, all your courage: I have no anxieties as to your conduct; faithful to the Fatherland, to honor, to your oath, you will shed, if need be, the last drop of your blood for the cause of liberty. Farewell, dear child, I entrust your destiny to God: He will watch over you, whose soul is so pure and noble."

The same day, two o'clock

"Dear child, that is what I wrote at ten o'clock, but it is impossible to dispatch the courier I wished to send you. The prohibition is categorical and without exceptions. M. the Keeper of the Seals came to inform the Assembly that the King had left behind a letter for him in which he forbade him to use the seal and enjoined him to consider as null and void the orders of the National Assembly and any other kind of orders. M. de Cazalès and M. de Clermont-Tonnerre have been ill-treated by the people, but the National Guard has restored them safe and sound to the Assembly. The whole Assembly displays the greatest vigor, and there is only one opinion now voiced. I shall not post this letter until tomorrow; as reliable information comes in, I shall write it down. —I received your letter, dear friend, and it gave me very great pleasure. Ah! Would that I were with you!"

Wednesday morning, June 22

"An admirable state of order and the greatest patriotism continue to reign in Paris. Wednesday evening—I have just learned that the King has been stopped at Varennes,

to stop the King. I have been to Varennes since, and I took good note of its landmarks, so I can speak of them with certainty. Arriving at Varennes from Clermont, one passes under a long, dark arch that is, or was, the town gate. Next, one enters a street that goes down fairly steeply, then one turns to the right to cross a very narrow bridge over the Aire River, which is fordable at several points in summer. It was under the arch I have just described that Sausse went to take up position with three or four National Guards to await the King. A detachment of hussars from Lauzun's regiment, under the command of an officer named Délon, was stationed in the street near the turning that leads to the bridge, and on the

five leagues from the frontier, this is positive. M. de Bouillé's conduct is suspected: The Assembly has provisionally cashiered him. —M. d'Orléans has been at the Jacobins this evening and was universally applauded.[f] M. de La Fayette and all the members of the 89 Club were there: All the friends of liberty are closely reunited. Good night, dear friend. I await news of you with extreme impatience, and I embrace you from the depths of my heart."

Midnight, June 24

Oh my son!

"This evening I received the letter containing the details of your charming deed:[g] I shall not describe to you what it made me experience! I leave that task to your heart. Your glory is mine, it is my joy, it is my happiness, it is for me as it is for you; would that I could likewise share your perils! Would that I could have been with you in those moments when I should have contemplated you with such emotion and such pride! . . . Having wept, exclaimed, and above all thanked Heaven, which guides and inspires you, in short, having read this letter five or six times, I wondered at that margin that, as in the others, was there to receive my criticisms. This time, my friend, my criticism is lacking: Such a style as that will find no censors.

"But while my child is performing heroic deeds and his noble soul is troubled with anxiety for us, we enjoy perfect calm: Never did the people display such grandeur. I would already have sent you three couriers if it had been possible, but the prohibition is categorical. Yesterday at the National Assembly, I saw all the National Guards and all the people of Paris take an oath. What a spectacle! Oh, my child, it would have transported you! All this was done with enthusiasm and without confusion; I melted into tears. —The King is speaking tomorrow night, Saturday, at Meaux, and will be here on Sunday at two or three o'clock. There is a lot of talk of a regency: In that case it is absolutely certain to be offered to M. d'Orléans, who has irrevocably decided to refuse it, as well as any kind of position which would show ambition. At the same time, he will accept all those in which he could serve the Fatherland, whether on land or sea. I strongly approve this conduct, especially after the unworthy calumnies with which people have sought to blacken his reputation. You would be of this opinion, dear friend, who, I am perfectly sure, would refuse the throne if it were offered to you and if you could not ascend it without doing an injustice. For you have the morals and the soul of a Spartan. Pursue, my child, pursue your noble career. Thanks to the Revolution, we live in a century when the man himself and not his rank makes his reputation. Oh! what a lesson for the friends of morality and virtue is that which we are now witnessing! A village mayor arrests the King of France in his domains and scornfully rejects his offers and his promises. . . . *What can you offer me that is worth the glory of saving my country?*

---

[f] My father had never been at the Jacobins before this period.
[g] Rescuing the two priests, see pages 85–87.—ED.

other side of the bridge there was a change of horses for the King and a considerable escort of cavalry. I think there was also some infantry (the Nassau regiment and another German regiment). But it would seem that the officers in command of these troops were not informed in time that the King had arrived and been stopped. It also seems that the King was reckoning to change horses near the arch at the entrance to the town and that he did not know that his change of horses was awaiting him on the other side of the bridge. When the King's carriage arrived, Sausse stopped it and asked for the passport: When he had been given it, he pretended that he needed to take it home to examine it, where he pronounced that it

---

Two commoners (Barnave and Pétion) protect the King and his children and undertake to preserve him from all insults! Virtue, talents, are no longer useless gifts. More or less high-sounding names, decorations, ribbons, the kind of seat one sits on, or the particular design of a small *bâton* are now only chimeras or objects before which one no longer bends the knee, and there is a very strong likelihood that these knickknacks will pass out of fashion. —My portrait for you, dear friend, is finished and framed. I am waiting for a safe opportunity to send it to you, together with the box with the hard-stone top. Farewell, child of my heart: I am publishing with a mother's pride—other than which there is none higher—M. Pieyre's letter. Extracts of it will be in the papers, and your brother is planning to read it to the Jacobins tomorrow. He performed a very fine deed the day of the flight. He rushed, completely alone, to his district, and there he said: 'The Fatherland is in danger, I rush [to its aid]; I am only fifteen, but make use of me, I am ready to shed all my blood for liberty.' This had the greatest success; he did his guard duty, and he looks charming in his National Guard uniform. —Good night, dear friend. This letter is for you and M. Pieyre: What a friend you have there! What a consolation it is for me to know that you are together! Farewell, my dear and virtuous friends. Give me news of you as often as you can."

Midnight, June 25

Dear child,

"I saw several deputies today and read my dear letter from M. Pieyre eight or nine times. An extract of it will appear the day after next in the *Chronicle* and in three other papers. M. d'Orléans does not want M. de Montpensier to read it to the Jacobins; we will have it read by someone else. Ah! how I relish your glory! Mark well that if the people had not seen you set an example of piety, you would not have had the same influence on them: They would have seen in your eagerness to save those wretches only contempt for the religion they had insulted. What weight morals and piety give to actions! what a prize to courage and an ascendancy to a man in authority! and how much pleased and sparkling youth embellishes and sets all that off!

"The King, the Queen, their children, and Mme Elisabeth arrived intact today. The people showed themselves to be truly worthy of the liberty they have conquered. Here is what the Faubourg Saint-Antoine proclaimed: *The first man to shout Long live the King will be beaten; the first to insult him will be hanged.* All the people abided by this convention. There was the greatest order and, in general, profound silence. As you may well imagine, there were no cannons fired and no Honors whatsoever. The Guards who were in attendance at the Tuileries were standing easy, everyone with his hat on his head. Two men who did not have a hat were forced to put their handkerchiefs on their heads so they would not be uncovered. The King and the queen had two separate Guards, all the private doors of their apartments are bricked up. The Assembly has decided to dispense with the royal assent until

was false; I do not know how, but one way or another he persuaded the King and Queen to get down from their carriage and to step into his house, which was nearby. It seems that a lash of the whip administered to the horses at this point would have saved the King; but for whatever reason, it was not given, and the King and his family entered Sausse's house. It was nearly eleven o'clock when the King was stopped, which made it very difficult to assemble the National Guard. The proximity of the troops on the other side of the river added considerably to the difficulty and danger of assembling them. However, Sausse brought it off;

---

the Constitution has been completed and that it will appoint a governor for M. le Dauphin. There was a slight commotion for five minutes on the subject of three of the Bodyguards who followed the King; they were made fast and tied behind their carriages.[h] The people wanted only to lead them to prison; but the sacred word of *law* promptly contained them. Good night, my son, good night, my dear friends. I await news of you with extreme impatience. Our deputies are dining here tomorrow; I will write to you about all the reliable details I learn. Tomorrow's letter will be to M. Pieyre, to whom I owe so many thanks. I embrace you from the depths of my heart, dear child. Write, then, to your papa and to Mme d'Orléans about your feat. She is in the town of Eu."

June 28

Dear friend,

"I have received your letter of the 25th. Your fine deed is the talk of the town here and wins the universal acclaim it deserves. How much I rejoice in it! How happy it makes me! How much I love you, my dear and good child! . . . Everything here is in perfect tranquillity: the Aristocrats are totally defeated. The Assembly decided today that it would appoint a governor for M. le Dauphin and that he would not be chosen from among their number. The deputies are drawing up lists, and the decision will be made by ballots based on three lists. I am having M. Pieyre put on the list: He is more deserving, in all respects, than those I hear being put forward. I do not flatter myself that he will be elected, but he will certainly win some votes, and if he has friends here apart from ourselves who can serve him in this matter, let him not remain in the background! As for myself, I shall do what I can. . . . I beg you to write immediately to M. de Beauharnais, who covered himself with glory during his memorable presidency. It was he who proposed to move on to the order of the day, which was really sublime, which settled public opinion and maintained the peace. Congratulate him on that: Tell him that we have taken the most lively interest in his successes and in his reputation, and thank him for kindly undertaking to have your regiment reassembled and its destination changed—he has spoken about this to M. Duportail. Testify to a great desire to go to places where war can be fought, and write to him without delay. Then write a charming and tender little letter to Mme de Bourbon. She has become an absolute *democrat* and displays a lively interest in you, your brother, and your sister. Mme de Montesson has written me a charming letter on the subject of your action. She would be enchanted if you wrote her a little letter telling her that I have told you she has written me a letter full of affection about you; that you never forget the kindness she has shown you ever since you were a child; that through your affection, you will always deserve the interest she takes in you and upon which you place so high a price; that you would be very happy to learn her news directly from her. *End by begging her to accept the homage of your respect* and of the lifelong attachment to her you have vowed. You

---

[h] This is an error; the three Bodyguards were not bound.

93

he had a wagon of manure upturned on the bridge, and this prevented communication between the two banks as effectively as if the river had been unfordable. As a crowning piece of bad luck, or rather incompetence, the officer from the Lauzun regiment (M. Délon) did not speak German or spoke it so badly that he could not make himself understood by his hussars, who were all Germans; and an officer of the National Guard from Alsace or Lorraine came and harangued the men of this detachment in their own language. As soon as M. Délon was informed of what was happening at the top of the town, he proceeded to Sausse's house to take the King's orders, but it seems he was unable to see the King alone and that the King ordered him in Sausse's presence to remain

---

would give me pleasure by writing that when you have written first to M. de Beauharnais and then to Mme de Bourbon; do not forget to show your sympathy for the latter's fears about war and to assure her that you are deeply affected by her troubles. —I will say, as regards your style, dear friend, that you write too negligently. You repeat the same word thousands of times, and you often make grammatical mistakes such as this: "It is now twenty-four hours since we received *no* news from you." You will be well aware that in this phrase there is a negative too many: It should be *since we received any*. This mistake is very gross. You also write the choir of a church *coeur,* which is a spelling mistake. One writes *le coeur humain* and *le choeur d'une eglise* or *les choeurs d'Athalie,* etc. Watch out for all this, and take more care with your style. Farewell, dear child, tell me, then, how I may send you my portrait? I beseech you to find a way of swimming, you may be sure that people will be delighted by your proficiency at this sport and at seeing you diving in headfirst. Your dragoons will be enchanted with this. Believe me, things of this kind are not unimportant. If you are marching with your dragoons, I very much hope that you will march and line as they do and that thereby they will clearly see how much you despise luxury—that will succeed in making you adored. As far as possible, dear friend, do not neglect your studies and reading. Farewell, my son, a thousand remembrances from me to our agreeable and worthy friend."

July 30

"A decree passed today has abolished the Orders [of Chivalry] except that of Malta; but its Knights will be regarded as foreigners and will not be active citizens. M. d'Orléans has already given up his ribbon and star. Give yours up immediately. In this connection I advise you to make some patriotic little speech,[i] either to the Society for the Friends of the Constitution or to the troops. Say that as you have not yet personally merited any decoration, you were loath to wear it; that you will do your utmost to merit a patriotic decoration, which should be the prize for valor and services rendered to the Fatherland, etc. . . . Do this with good grace. The Order of Saint-Louis is being kept until further orders. I do not know what you should do with the medal, which is consecrated, and with the collar of the Order.[j] I shall find out and tell you. —The [question of] the governor [for the Dauphin] has been adjourned once again today. —Good night, dear friend. I ask you, as a favor, to make me a little pocketbook written in your own hand and containing a detailed and scrupulously accurate account of everything of interest that you have seen in Vendôme and its surroundings, including the noteworthy views, the châteaux, the gardens, the collections of curios, if there are any at Vendôme, and also the customs,

---

[i] I thought it better to dispense with this.
[j] I left them in my apartments in the Palais Royal, where they were found after my departure from France in 1793 and brought to the National Convention.

calm; however, we are assured that the Queen said to him in German: *Retten Sie den König* ("Save the King"), and probably he did not understand her, because he made no move to carry this out. He returned to his detachment, which had been taken over by the National Guard in his absence, and stuck to the order that he had received from the King. Meanwhile at Varennes and the surrounding district, the National Guards on the left bank of the Aire River were assembled, and armed peasants arrived from all sides, some with forks, others with shovels and pickaxes, a decrepit cannon *without ammunition* was trained on the principal ford above the bridge; and in the morning, as soon as it was quite light, the King set off again in his carriage for Paris, surrounded by an already considerable crowd.

M. de Bouillé was only informed belatedly that the King had been stopped. He rushed up with the Royal German regiment, but it was too late, and the slightest movement on his part could have caused the King and Queen to be murdered. It would certainly have been easy to save them during the night, and I have no doubt that they would have been rescued if M. de Bouillé had been warned in time. The three Bodyguards who accompanied the King were unquestionably loyal, and it is probable, since they did nothing to rescue him from this predicament and to warn M. de Bouillé, either by trying to cross the river or by some other means, that they did not know where he and the troops were or that they were prevented for reasons unknown to us. It is certain that the King had made

---

if there are any peculiar to the area, etc. . . . . I beg you to work on this straightaway, because otherwise what you have seen will become confused in your mind, and if you leave Vendôme it will be too late to do it accurately. Do this little piece of work, which will please me a lot. If there happens to be a sketcher at Vendôme, I should very much like this little book to be embellished with one or two small sketches taken from life. —You had promised me to let blood[k] from time to time; if you do not practice this at all, you will forget how to do it, and that would greatly grieve me. All in all I count on your promises because mine are inviolable and because I esteem you as much as I love you. If you were to neglect to fulfill them, you would cause me infinite pain. I understand that your intention is to remain linked with the Jacobins, and I strongly approve; but while assuring them of your loyalty, be careful not to seem critical of those who have caused the schism and of the members of the Feuillant Club.[1] M. d'Orléans does not wish your brother to return to the Jacobins, at least for the present; but in this matter he leaves you a free hand to do as you like. As you are absent, I do not think that you have, yourself, to do anything for the moment; however, as those who are remaining in this club are registering their names, I will know for certain tomorrow what an absentee who wants to remain a member should do, and I will tell you. Meanwhile, for your part, will you inform me immediately of your decision on this matter and that of the club in the town where you are. I would add that the Jacobins have put themselves in the right and are behaving very wisely. Farewell, my dear child, I embrace you with all my heart."

---

[k] I had learned how to let blood at the Hôtel-Dieu of Paris, where I often underwent the prescribed bleeding.

[1] See page 100.—ED.

95

his escape much more difficult by refusing to be separated from his family.

The crowd escorting the King swelled so rapidly that it became difficult to provide food for such a multitude (the papers put it at a hundred and fifty thousand souls). The three commissioners whom the Assembly had nominated to go before the King met him near Châlons. They had great difficulty in dismissing part of this vast crowd, because everyone wanted to escort the King's carriage all the way to Paris. These commissioners were MM. de Latour-Maubourg, Barnave, and Pétion; that is to say, a friend of M. de La Fayette, a friend of MM. de Lameth, and one of the out-and-out Jacobins.

Paris and the Assembly were thrown into consternation by the news of the King's departure. The alarm was sounded, the tocsin rang out, everyone ran to take up arms without knowing either what would or what should be done. In the Assembly M. Regnaud de Saint-Jean d'Angély proposed, and it was adopted unanimously by the Assembly, that the Minister of the Interior (M. Delessart) should immediately dispatch couriers to all the departments ordering the arrest of all persons leaving the kingdom and also preventing the exit of provisions of war, arms, etc.

Next, at the proposal of M. le Chapelier, it voted a short address to the citizens of Paris and to all Frenchmen.

The King's ministers proceeded to the Assembly, and M. Duport du Tertre, Minister of Justice, informed it that in a note he had only just received, the King had forbidden his ministers to sign or seal anything in his name until further orders from him and had enjoined him, the Minister of Justice, to send him the Great Seal when he required it. Then, at the proposal of M. Dandré, seconded by MM. de Cazalès,* Custine, and Démeunier, the Assembly unanimously passed a provisional decree providing that its decrees be executed by the ministers, and that the Great Seal of the State be affixed to them without the need for the royal consent, and that they would provisionally have the force of law throughout the kingdom. M. de la Porte (in charge of administering the Civil List, and executed in the month of August 1792) came to present to the Assembly a memorandum from the King in which he gave an exposé of the reasons that had led him to withdraw from Paris, but which was remarkable for the care with which he avoided disclosing his future intentions. The Assembly immediately ordered one of the secretaries to read it out. As soon as this was finished M. de Beauharnais,† who was presiding, declared: *"Let us move on to the agenda for the day!"* and the Assembly enthusiastically adopted this excellent means of getting out of an embarrassing situation and avoiding any discussion of this important document.

---

* M. de Cazalès was one of the most notably talented members of the right wing.
† M. le Vicomte de Beauharnais, father of Prince Eugène.

The item on the agenda was the Penal Code, which generally aroused very little interest. M. Lepeletier de Saint-Fargeau mounted the rostrum with his draft decrees to make his report, and the Assembly concentrated on turning them into laws, article by article, with that nonchalance that had caused it to be christened the Decree Factory.

However, fear was general, and in the French Revolution fear was always the precursor and one of the main causes of violence. The fear of being massacred by the people imposed silence on the right wing in the Assembly; the fear of royal reprisals rallied the whole of the left wing around the Jacobins: I am speaking of the immediate reaction. M. de La Fayette and his friends in the 89 Club realized that the loss of the King's person destroyed their power. Hitherto, their power had been based on their position as intermediaries between the King and the people. They reigned over the King through his fear of the people, and over the people through their fear of the King. Such power is necessarily precarious and ends up by placing its possessors at the mercy of one or the other party, sometimes of both: The political reversals in Denmark in 1660 and in Sweden in 1772 are examples of this,* and I am disposed to believe that if Louis XVI had known how to and wanted to adopt the method of frankly making common cause with the people, as Dumouriez was later to advise him, he would have provided a third example. M. de La Fayette and his friends, then, ran at one and the same time the very dangers the two other parties each ran separately. Their previous conduct exposed them to a royalist reaction; and the mistrust of the people, in whose power they found themselves and who had frequently suspected them of playing a double game, exposed them to being butchered if they did not come out against the King. Consequently, they adopted this course of action unanimously and returned to the Jacobins, where they were greeted with applause, but addressed in such a way as to make them realize that it was perfectly well understood they were seeking a protection against the double danger to which they were manifestly exposed. Danton, who happened to be at the Jacobins when M. de La Fayette arrived, made a point of saying this to him in an unmistakable manner. There were some deputies of the left wing who, as they had never belonged to any club, did not present themselves before the Jacobins; but they were few in number.

The silence of the right wing on the one hand and on the other M. de La Fayette's union with the Jacobins made the latter masters of the field of battle, and it was they who, in the name of the Assembly, were to repel the King's attacks and direct the nation's resistance. The King's flight confirmed the suspicions that had always been entertained about his real intentions: In a single blow it destroyed the effect of so many initiatives by means of which he had vainly tried to make people believe in the

* In both these "revolutions," the King turned the tables on the ruling aristocracy by allying himself with the Third Estate.—ED.

sincerity of his professions. Thus the Jacobins easily managed to persuade the public *that the King and his Court were absolutely incorrigible and that they would never be brought to govern in a constitutional manner and to respect the nation's liberty in good faith.* The King's flight seemed a positive proof of the existence of those plots and conspiracies to bring about the Counterrevolution that filled the papers at the time. But although the Jacobins desired that the King cease to be the head of state, it did not follow that they wished to place my father on the throne. Certainly not; those who have adopted this belief are considerably in error. From then on the leading Jacobins were absolutely bent on a republic, and they made this fairly clear shortly afterward. But it was then that this terrible republicanism grew up, and it must be admitted that it resulted as much from the democratic ideas that, as I have already said, had penetrated into everyone's thinking as from the impossibility of determining the Kings and their Courts, as well as their ministers and agents, to make in good faith the concessions necessary if the nations and individuals were to enjoy the advantages they had a right to demand. I cannot be positive about what I am going to say, and I only put it forward as a personal conjecture. As soon as the King had departed, *M. de La Fayette wanted the Republic;* but after the King had been brought back to Paris, *he ceased to want it,* and his only consideration then was consolidating the monarchy and the King's throne by causing him [the King] to surround himself with ministers who accepted the Constitution and to govern in a constitutional manner. I am persuaded that at the time this was the only plan capable of preserving monarchical government in France and of preventing the King from being dethroned; but the event was to prove that this plan was impracticable and that the King was bound to be dragged to his ruin by the irresistible influence of his entourage. If, as I believe, M. de La Fayette momentarily wanted a republic, it was probably out of fear that a regency or some other form of administration would cause power to fall into the hands of my father. If the monarchy were retained, my father would be the natural depository of royal power in the absence of the King and the Princes of the elder branch; whereas this would be very difficult in a republic, where it would always be easy either to ruin my father or at least to keep him from power by causing him to be suspected of aiming for the throne. It was in this way that Brissot, Roland, and the Gironde successfully attacked my father in the National Convention in 1792, and it is probable that if a republican government had been set up in France at the time of the King's departure in 1791, the post of commander in chief of the Parisian National Guard that M. de La Fayette occupied at the time and the influence that he exercised on the ministers and on the part of the Assembly would have given him great opportunities to become the center of power by adopting this procedure. For the rest, I can only formulate conjectures about this, but I am going to try to demonstrate that those I make are not without foundation.

When news of the King's departure spread through Paris, the first person to speak of a republic was *Achille Duchâtelet,* otherwise known as the Marquis du Châtelet. He had served in the American War, and he had continued to be associated with M. de La Fayette and had been his aide-de-camp in Paris. It is the same M. Duchâtelet who wrote to M. de Bouillé in October 1789 about M. de La Fayette: "You certainly have correspondents sufficiently exact to be informed of the events which have taken place; you know they have raised Lafayette to the summit of power, and that by his firmness he has just got rid of the duke of Orléans."* On the day of the King's departure or the day after, M. Duchâtelet had a poster stuck up, in which he invited the French people to constitute themselves as a republic, seeing that a King was a *political superficiality. He* will certainly not be suspected of having wanted to work for my father.† The second person was Condorcet, who published a pamphlet to demonstrate *that a King has no useful function in a constitution.* I think that at this period Condorcet was still working with M. de La Fayette, while he certainly was not with my father. Finally, the third person to propose a republic was Brissot, who was as much my father's enemy as M. de La Fayette's friend and who only broke with the latter after the King's return from Varennes. Brissot has publicly affirmed what I am advancing as a conjecture. He has said that M. de La Fayette had planned to create a republic and that he would have proposed it if the King had not been stopped at Varennes, that the King's return had altered his plan, and that it was then that he, Brissot, had detached himself from M. de La Fayette and had concentrated on bringing about the creation of a republic by other methods. For the rest, this had no importance except in ascertaining how the Republic was introduced in France, because either way, M. de La Fayette did not long desire one; and whether it was despite him or with his consent that people associated him with the proposition to establish a republican government, it is certain that he opposed it from the moment the King was stopped and brought to Paris; but the momentum given to opinion favorable to a republic by the King's flight, and the resultant proposals, did not stop and was one of the main causes of the establishment of a republican government in 1792, that is, fifteen months afterward.

I often saw, in the debates of the National Assembly, that after rash motions had been put forward, their authors wanted to withdraw them to prevent the Assembly from discussing them; but then those whose purposes they suited declared: "Your motion no longer belongs to you, it

---

* As I only have in front of me an English edition of the *Mémoires de Bouillé,* printed in London in 1797, I should say at this point that the above passage is translated from the English, and in this note I give the English text verbatim, which is taken from page 102. (The English version appears above.—ED.)

† Those who suspect M. Duchâtelet of this have not read the *Mémoires de Bouillé,* where two letters from him are to be found.

belongs to the Assembly because it is no longer in your power to take away its cognizance of the matter." That is what happened to those who proposed the Republic; a proposition like that is not withdrawn, and this one was strenuously supported. The Jacobins went into an uproar and resolved to present a petition to the National Assembly. I do not recall exactly what the object of this petition was, still less in what terms it was couched. I think it was to request that the King not be restored to his constitutional authority without the explicit consent of the nation, and that it should be considered whether he ought to be declared to have forfeited his throne. At least it was something like that. In order to give greater weight to this petition, the Jacobins resolved to proceed to the Champ-de-Mars, to place it on the Altar of the Fatherland and to invite all the friends of liberty to come and sign it. Immediately M. de La Fayette marched there with a large detachment of the National Guard, and M. de Bailly, as mayor of Paris, carried the red flag that announced the proclamation of martial law. Three times he called on the crowd surrounding the Altar of the Fatherland to disperse, and seeing that his orders had not been obeyed, he required M. de La Fayette to disperse them by force, which was easily done by means of a few volleys. I do not know how many men were killed. I think that it has never been known. Later, in the same Champ-de-Mars, the unfortunate Bailly was put to death with a studied ferocity that makes one shudder and that he endured with the greatest courage.

The "massacre" of the Champ-de-Mars arrested the progress of republicanism temporarily. Those who had supported this step [i.e., holding a meeting—Ed.] were cowed. Robespierre, although he was a deputy, Brissot, and several others who were not, even went into hiding for a period. The Jacobin Club was almost abandoned. M. de La Fayette and MM. de Lameth left it altogether, and they worked together to found a new club along the same lines as the Jacobin Club. It was a second edition of the 89 Club, and this second attempt was even more disastrous than the first. The new club met in the church of the Feuillants* right by the National Assembly. For this reason it was called the Feuillant Club, and the label *Feuillants* was given to its members, as that of *Jacobins* had been given to the members of the original club. The Feuillant Club had only an ephemeral existence, although that of the party which was formed there was much longer.

A small number of individuals who, braving the storm, continued to meet at the Jacobins was the nucleus around which this society reconstituted itself, more powerful and more dangerous than before, since it had resisted the shock and rid itself of the majority of those who wished to confine it within the bounds of moderation. A great number of those who at first had joined the Feuillants returned to the Jacobins, of which Pétion

* A monastic order named after the village of Feuillant in Burgundy, where its principal abbey was situated.—ED.

100

was elected president. The crush became so great that the Jacobins feared that all the Feuillants would come back to their society, and they carried out what was called a *purge,* that is to say, a new examination of their members ending with the expulsion of all those who had stood out against them in the schism with the Feuillants. The provincial clubs were invited by the two clubs of the Feuillants and the Jacobins to correspond with them. A small number came out straightaway for one side or the other; but the majority waited for one of the two clubs to crush the other before declaring themselves, and then the correspondence was returned to the Jacobins.

It has been said, and I believe it to be the case, that if Mirabeau had lived, this coalition between MM. de Lameth and M. de La Fayette would not have taken place. Mirabeau and the Lameths were a counterpoise to the Jacobins, and this counterpoise restrained the Cordelier faction, which worked on the Jacobin Club for a long time before gaining control of it. Mirabeau and the Lameths detested each other, but they detested M. de La Fayette even more, and it is difficult to envisage what Mirabeau would have done if he had been alive at the time of the departure and arrest of the King; but as it is likely he was sold to the Court,* I think

---

* It is believed that Mirabeau sold himself to the Court in February 1791, or rather it was at this time that it was thought it had been discovered. MM. de Lameth and Adrien Duport, with whom they were closely associated, profited from a rather remarkable incident to denounce Mirabeau's intrigues to the Jacobins. On the 28th of this month (February 1791) there was some trouble at Vincennes; the folk from the Faubourg Saint-Antoine wanted to demolish the dungeon, and they had begun when M. de La Fayette arrived on the spot and with the help of the National Guard restored order. Meanwhile, a fairly large number of men whose opinions were opposed to the Revolution became anxious about the King's safety and that of the Royal Family and went, inopportunely, to assemble at the Tuileries to defend them in case of need. It is probable that they would not have succeeded in this if there really had been an attack, but there was none; however, the National Guard, which was on duty at the palace, became anxious in their turn about this extraordinary assemblage, and they wanted to make these gentlemen leave. They resisted, and force was employed to compel them. It was claimed that daggers were found which some of them had hidden under their cloaks, so that they were called the Knights of the Dagger—an unfortunate name that caused a lot of harm; and so that no element of ridicule should be lacking in this affair, it was pleasantly christened the Battle of Canes because it was said that canes were the only weapons that had been employed to drive them out. These labels have more effect in France than is generally thought, because with us a good joke is often worth more than a good argument, and the people there are often so credulous that a bad label is enough to turn them against those to whom it is applied. I was at the Jacobins that evening. Duport and Alexandre Lameth profited from the unrest occasioned by these disturbances to attack Mirabeau and make public his secret dealings with the Court. This denunciation had the greatest effect, and it seemed that Mirabeau was going to be expelled from the Jacobins and consequently to lose his popularity. He was not present at the beginning of the attack, but he arrived in time to hear the end, and he positioned himself behind the rostrum with a solemn air. As soon as Alexandre de Lameth had left it, he appeared there. He was greeted with boos all round and with

---

that if they had formed a coalition in his lifetime, he would have squashed them between the King and the people. He held them in check by the force of his eloquence and his talents and left them no way of playing a role other than that of turning themselves into *tribunes of the people;* this they were as long as he lived; but he died on April 2, 1791, that is to say, about a month after that memorable scene in the Jacobins of February 28, 1791, details of which are given in the note, and his death gave MM. de Lameth and their friends a way of coming to terms with M. de La Fayette. They agreed on a compromise, and the *Coalition* was formed. They undertook together to recast all the isolated decrees that the National Assembly had passed with reference to the *future* constitution of the *State* into a single constitutional document. At the same time they agreed to modify and complete them. This great work was what was called the *revision.* The result was that it is known under the name of the Constitution of 1791. What it was has been very well expressed by saying that it was a *royal democracy.* It was difficult to prevent the royal power and the democratic power from destroying each other. It was even more to be feared that this struggle would become a struggle to the death, as unfortunately happened, since in France people rarely force themselves to make the mutual sacrifices that alone can moderate men's passions. The French have a great tendency to press their advantages to the limit; in general they lack restraint and nearly always permit themselves to do everything it is in their power to do. It is remarkable that the French language cannot express in a single word that admirable English word *forbearance,* which is the noun for *"to abstain voluntarily from doing what one could do if one wanted"*—a sublime quality without which there can be neither a constitution nor liberty and which I regard as the cornerstone of the English political system! In France, popular power conquered royal power as soon as it could. Royal power had done as much in the opposite direction long before and was ready to begin again.

---

cries of *Down with him, down with him,* which proceeded from all corners of the room. He was not disconcerted, and gave them warning that he was determined to make himself heard and that they would do better to hear him in silence; that a veteran like himself in the army of liberty had some right to the indulgence of his supporters, especially when it was clear that no one had dared attack him to his face, when it was clear that the moment when he was absent had been chosen to blacken him with unworthy calumnies and to whip up such an outcry against him and such prejudice that the voice of his innocence could no longer make itself heard; that they had wanted to ruin his reputation with those whose esteem was most precious to him and whose opinion was rightly regarded as the regulator of public opinion; that he saw very well why they wanted to ruin him; that he knew about the factious projects of his enemies and that they were blackening his reputation with this society in order that he would not be believed when he unmasked them, etc. He stopped from time to time to allow applause and only got a deep silence; but finally someone broke the spell and began to applaud; immediately the whole room joined in with redoubled effort, and he ended by carrying off a complete victory over his adversaries, although it was believed that they had spoken the truth.

The revision greatly diminished the power that the previous decrees had attributed to the people and to the Assembly. It made important additions to that of the King. I think the Feuillants would have liked to further add to it, but their position and the state of affairs were such that they must have counted themselves lucky to have obtained so much. As from the day after the King's departure, the right wing of the Assembly had resolved to take no further part in its proceedings. This step certainly has an admirable side to it, considering their opinions, but I find it impossible not to consider it impolitic. I realize that perhaps a super-human degree of courage and firmness was necessary for them to con-tinue in functions so opposed to their opinions; this should even have made them consider such devotion as the highest degree of honor and duty, but men's passions dealt otherwise with all this, and according to them, *honor* required that they leave the Assembly; so they did. It was in vain that M. Malouet at their private meeting made strong remonstrances against this impolitic step; he persuaded only a few members. I even know that M. de Wimpfen,* one of the members of the left wing, was sent to the right wing to ask merely for their votes *to increase the King's power and that this was refused him.* The number of those who ceased to vote was about three hundred. M. de Espréménil announced it on their behalf from the rostrum. I have no doubt that if the members of the right wing had stayed in the Assembly they would have obtained much more than was gained in the revision, because everything leads me to believe that the *revisionists* wanted to go much further than they did, and the combination of the *Blacks*† and the revisionists would have formed a big majority. It is incontestable that whatever the conduct of the Assembly in other circum-stances, in this one they *voluntarily reestablished* the King and the mon-archy, because they *could* have destroyed them. It even needed some skill and courage not to end up at this extremity; and sufficient credit for this has not been given to the Constituent Assembly or to those who led it at the time. What am I saying—they have not been given enough credit! Alas, it is only too probable that they would have carried their heads to the scaffold if they had had power sufficient to match their desire. The long, unjust, and impolitic captivity that M. de La Fayette and those alone of his companions in misfortune who had been members of the Constituent Assembly were later made to endure proves only too well the truth of my assertion.

Let no one suppose that I am trying indirectly to praise the Constitu-tion of 1791, still less the Assembly whose work it was. I have only said what I believe to be fact, and I am convinced that it was already very difficult to stop the progress of republicanism. This political system would have been immediately triumphant if the Assembly had been disposed to

* I have this fact from M. Guilhermy, one of the members of the right wing.
† Sobriquet given to the members of the right wing because of the large number of ecclesiastics who sat there, as I have already said.

take advantage of it, as so many men led astray by their passions and blinded by their partisan approach have claimed, and it is even probable that the Assembly would have been carried away by the torrent if it had not opposed it with such force and perseverance. At the time, the King fell far short of having as many resources with which to oppose it as he later had in 1792: These resources had been given him by that very Constitution of 1791, which has nevertheless been represented since as having paralyzed his authority and delivered him defenseless to his enemies.

I come to one of the most difficult points to deal with in the work that I have undertaken. It is to the Emigration, its causes and effects, that I am going to turn my thoughts. The difficulty of this discussion, very great in itself, is further increased by my personal position. I may be considered prejudiced, influenced by memories, embittered by resentment at personal injuries, motivated by the desire to defend the course of action I embraced at the time. It is for my readers to judge whether I have been influenced by these considerations and whether my arguments are good or bad. The notoriety of the facts upon which I have based them makes it superfluous for me to attest the scrupulous exactitude with which I have reported them. This discussion is too important and demands too much elaboration for me to confine myself, as I embark on it, to a strict examination of the events of the period of the great Emigration, and I shall often have to go back to what I have already spoken of and to anticipate events whose details I have still to give. This will involve me in a brief examination of the King's conduct and of the feebleness and inconsistency of the means that were employed to stop the progress of the Revolution.

I regard the Emigration as having been a false step. I respect the honorable motives that may have dictated it, but I repeat that one of my main objects is to demonstrate that rectitude of intentions is unrelated to good judgment, that the violence of passions and of party spirit misleads and blinds people even to their own best interests and to the best way of achieving their desired aim; and that when they allow themselves to be carried away by the torrent, they can become very prejudicial to the cause they are striving to defend. One of the principal sources of the misfortunes of the Revolution was the complete and general ignorance of the course of action that everyone should maintain in such a crisis; and this ignorance was common to men of all parties and all shades of opinion. There were no longer any clearly defined duties; all was confused and overturned; morality itself, which it would seem should be immutable, was no longer a sufficient guide, and the steps that people believed best calculated to achieve their aim led to a result often opposite and nearly always different from the one expected. Consequently, men with the same intentions and the same object in mind often adopted opposite courses of action. And so nothing is more difficult than to judge men by their opinions and their political conduct; nor is it less so to judge that conduct and those opinions with impartiality. The more this difficulty was felt, the more it seems people should have been disposed to be indulgent. But such indulgence was very little practiced. Alas, they went further still and represented those who preached and practiced it as secret enemies,* while violence and intolerance seemed proofs of a man's loyalty and the firmness of his principles. However, people made mistakes on all sides and in all parties, and it would be desirable if everyone were persuaded of this. People would have fewer pretensions about themselves and more indulgence for others.

The Emigration began in July 1789 with the departure of M. le Comte d'Artois and his two sons, M. le Duc d'Angoulême and M. le Duc de Berri, of M. le Prince de Condé and of his son and grandson, M. le Duc de Bourbon and M. le Duc d'Enghien, of M. le Prince de Conti, and their attendants. It is probable that at first the Princes had no other object than their safety; but soon they concentrated on becoming the nucleus of a gathering outside France. The Constituent Assembly desired their return.† They viewed with concern the absence of the majority of the French Princes and the hostile stance they had adopted toward the Constitution. They thought it necessary for the consolidation of their work that they come to range themselves around the constitutional throne. But perhaps this same point of view operated on the Princes in the opposite sense, and I am not a long way from thinking that one of the main reasons preventing their return was the fear that the constitutional régime would be consolidated by their presence.

From 1789 people began to withdraw from the King and the kingdom to go and join the French Princes on foreign soil. This is what was called *emigrating*. There was not much emigration in 1789. There was much more in 1790, and the Great Emigration took place in 1791 and continued into 1792, until the campaign of the Champagne. The desire to put themselves out of reach of the dangers to which they were exposed in France at the time was one of the early motives for the Emigration.

I understand very well that a slackening in law enforcement, riots going unpunished, and the pillaging of the châteaux (which nevertheless had taken place long before the Great Emigration) determined a great many people to seek a peaceful refuge in foreign lands; but the majority were determined by other motives. It is common knowledge that promises and

---

* Louis-Philippe is referring in particular to a group of men associated with Danton and christened the Indulgents, who in the winter of 1793–94 unsuccessfully attempted to scale down the Terror.—ED.

† It strove as hard as it could for that of M. le Comte d'Artois by giving him great advantages in the matter of the *apanages*. In accordance with one of its decrees, M. Duveyrier was sent by the King to M. le Prince de Condé for the same object and with no more success.

threats were lavished in turn to engage those who had not yet emigrated to leave France, and it is only too well known that several people were fairly badly received at Coblenz and elsewhere for having arrived too late.* So people made it a point of honor to emigrate, and so they emigrated *to fulfill a duty* and not *to fly from a danger*. The Emigration was thus a voluntary act, and should be considered as such, since it was decided on by choice and not by necessity.

From 1789 to 1790, the enemies of the Revolution began to maintain that one would be dishonored by accepting a post under the new régime or even by continuing in the one with which one had been invested under the old régime. This false notion of honor, this ill-founded fear of dishonoring oneself, reduced to insignificance the majority of those who wanted to dedicate themselves to the defense of the King and the support of the monarchy, while their opponents daily increased their strength by accepting all the employment they could obtain. It is certain that this sophism about honor made a substantial contribution to the fall of the monarchy. And yet it seems easy to recognize that one was more powerful in than out of office, and that one had more power exercising any function whatsoever within the kingdom than in voluntarily reducing one's influence to that of an ordinary Prussian or Austrian soldier. But one must have reference to the times and not lose sight of the profound ignorance of people in France of the nature of the political convulsions and of what the appropriate course of action was in those difficult circumstances.

People interested themselves in the Revolution as they would in a new novel. It was spoken of like a piece of news, and it was reserved to a very small number of individuals to examine it attentively, to try to discover its nature and progress.† With such a frivolous attitude, it was impossible that the enemies of the Revolution should have a clear idea of the strength of their opponents, and that they should not be in complete ignorance both as to what was happening and to what course of action they should adopt to achieve their aims. They should have sought to hinder the progress of the Revolution by profiting from the faults and blunders of their opponents. They should have striven to win the people

---

* It is claimed that this reproach of having arrived *too late* was addressed to M. d'Arçon, one of the most distinguished engineers in the French army, when he presented himself at Coblenz in the month of March 1792 and that he replied coldly: "I will still be in time for the other side." In fact, M. d'Arçon returned to France immediately, asked to be put on active service, was attached to the Committee of War, and later directed the sieges of Breda and Gertruydenburg under General Dumouriez.

† People prided themselves on adopting the attitude of a woman toward this; and they believed, or they claimed to believe, that to concern oneself with politics was *pedantry;* that to read the papers and keep abreast of the day's events *was to be bored to death;* and, as for reading the debates of the National Assembly, oh fie! They prided themselves on holding it in *horror* and on not pronouncing that word without *an air of distaste.*

back by concessions, but their blind confidence in the support they expected from abroad made them disdain all the methods of acting within the country and of procuring for themselves the support of a part of the nation.

The almost general opinion at the time among the enemies of the Revolution was, to use the favorite expression of the day, that *all that* could not last. This opinion stemmed in large part from the ignorance of which I have just spoken. It produced a very unfortunate effect on the enemies of *all that* because it led them to lay their plans for gaining advantages for themselves when *all that* had been overthrown rather than to ensure this overthrow. I believe that this excessive confidence in the overthrow of *all that* is one of the main reasons why *all that* is still in existence, and I am persuaded that a very large number of those who emigrated would not have left their regiments and employments if they had not been persuaded that when *all that* had been overthrown *the King would strip of their rank all his nobles who had not emigrated.** Thus did the enemies of the Revolution cooperate with their adversaries in expelling their partisans from all the posts they occupied in France!

As soon as the National Assembly began to organize the new system, that is to say, the courts of law, local administration, and the army, the popular party evinced a strong disposition to remove the King's right of nomination to employments. Nomination to the councils of the departments, with which they wanted to replace the intendants and the provincial Assemblies,† was assigned to the people.

The manner of nominating judges for the law courts was hotly debated in the Assembly because the right wing and a part of the left wing wanted their nomination to be assigned to the monarch, and the judges to be appointed for life and irremovable except by being put on trial. But they lost the issue, and the nomination of judges was assigned to the people. It

---

* The French reads: ". . . *le Roi casserait et dégraderait ses Nobles; tous ceux qui n'auraient pas émigré.*" Nobles lost their status (*déroger*) if they did anything regarded as *dishonorable,* such as engaging in retail trade. As the core of a nobleman's honor was devotion to the King, it was argued, wrongly, that since the King *really* wanted his nobility to enlist abroad to restore his Crown to its former splendor, those who remained behind were not acting honorably. However, loyalty was to the person of the King, the actual man Louis XVI, and it was common knowledge that Louis was on very bad terms with the *émigrés,* who still held to the beliefs that had sought to limit the power of the King in the period 1787–88.—ED.

† The intendant was the principal agent of the Crown in the provinces in the seventeenth and eighteenth centuries. He was universally criticized (as being too powerful and arbitrary) in the Assembly of Notables. Louis XVI, however, thought that he was the best part of the system. Provincial Assemblies, nominated by the King rather than elected, were set up in the provinces that had lost their elective Estates, by Loménie de Brienne in 1787–88 in an attempt to widen the government's basis of support. They acted in an advisory capacity to the intendant but had little independent power; what little they had was concerned with matters such as distribution of taxation and upkeep of roads.—ED.

was decided that they should serve *for a term* and not *for life,* and a commissioner of the King, holding his employment for life, was attached to each court. These commissioners were charged with seeing that the laws were not infringed. They did not have a say in the verdict, but the extent of their functions gave them great power. The choice of bishops and of those ecclesiastics destined to lower ranks was likewise taken from the King. It was thus clear that the partisans of the Revolution wanted all public functionaries to be replaced.

This desire was even more pronounced in matters concerning the army, because the consolidation or overthrow of the Constitution depended on the party that it adopted, and consequently the dispositions and political opinions of the officers became matters of the greatest importance. The opinion of the old officers was well known, and as long as they were at the head of the army it was always to be feared that they would manage to use it against the new order. To consolidate it, therefore, it was vital that the officers should cease to be opposed to it or that a way of discharging and replacing them should be found, which would have presented the greatest of difficulties had they not taken themselves off of their own accord. The orators of the Cordelier Club were strongly of the opinion that all the army officers should be dismissed and immediately replaced by a general measure. But the Assembly rejected this proposal almost unanimously, and it preferred to strive to make the officers as favorable to the Constitution as were the noncommissioned officers and the troops. It made only very slight changes in the organization of the army. The main one was a new mode of military promotion, which was calculated on the one hand to preserve the King's right of nomination and on the other to reconcile those below the rank of staff officers to its operations. Seniority was given enormous advantages, which was very favorable to that numerous class of nobility that was called the *provincial nobility,* for whom formerly appointment as a lieutenant colonel was like being given the *bâton* of a Marshal of France: It must be remembered that under the Ancien Régime the nonstaff officers were condemned to the humiliation of *being directly under someone's orders,* which is the most painful of all conditions when one had no hope of escaping it. Under the new régime they not only had the hope but the certainty of so doing; nevertheless, the places reserved for the King's nomination opened a path of very rapid advancement to favor and merit. There was also another innovation whose object was to satisfy the noncommissioned officers and consequently the ordinary soldiers. It was to give one sublieutenancy out of four falling vacant to the noncommissioned officers of the unit, alternately by seniority and by the choice of the officers. The three other posts of sublieutenant were entirely in the gift of the King. The ratio between promotion by seniority and by choice was perhaps badly worked out, but the principle was just, and experience could easily have rectified possible defects in its application. I confess that the method of promotion prescribed by the Constituent Assembly seemed to me sensible and well thought out, and I think that it put right the complaints that had been formulated on this subject before the Revolution.

Although emigration had been fairly heavy in 1790 among colonels and general officers, the leaders of the Cordelier Club found that this was going too slowly and that they were not getting rid of the *Aristocrats* or counterrevolutionaries quickly enough. In the spring of 1791 Dubois de Crancé, a Knight of the Order of Saint-Louis who had nevertheless seen little service and who was one of the members of the Constituent Assembly whose opinions were most in conformity with those of the Cordeliers, proposed to disband the army and to reorganize its elements under a new format, by means of which the counterrevolutionaries were to be eliminated. His plan was to form a national army by means of military conscription instead of the voluntary recruitment that had always been employed in France. This proposal aroused some debates in the assembly, but as neither the Lameths, nor Mirabeau, nor La Fayette, nor the right wing favored it (each for different reasons), the proposal was very quickly dropped. It was not the same in the Jacobins, where the Cordelier party strongly supported total disbanding and military conscription.*

* Robespierre supported this proposal by saying that "public liberty could never become established as long as the bulk of the officers in the army were counterrevolutionaries; that no matter how well disposed most of the troops were, they would be paralyzed by the officers; that as long as they were at the head of the army they would have only too many ways of hatching plots and conspiring against the Fatherland; that the army was being disorganized by their plots and by their daily desertions; that they were emigrating in batches; that one day a regiment had its full quota of officers and the next there was not a single one to be found; that there was less danger in replacing all the army officers in one go than in being continually exposed to their desertions and treason, and that unless the Assembly promptly adopted some sweeping measure, France was going to find herself in no position to resist the insults and attacks of the foreign Powers; that the more hostile the neighboring Powers appeared, the more important it was to put the army on a sound footing and to purge it without delay." Etc.

It is extraordinary that considering that such speeches were given in public and printed in all the papers, those who were qualified as counterrevolutionaries could be mistaken as to the intentions of their opponents, but I repeat, they were so little *au fait* with what was going on that they had no idea of the nuances and subdivisions among the partisans of the Revolution and particularly with the National Assembly. So as a result of this ignorance, their animosities were often in inverse ratio to what they should have been; and I am persuaded that the majority of them detested the Duc de La Rochefoucauld more than Robespierre, and M. de La Fayette more than Marat. It is therefore possible, and even probable, that if they had been informed that the debates of which I have just spoken had taken place in the Assembly, they would have formed a false impression of them that would have succeeded in making their mistake about what course of action they should adopt total—that is to say that if they had ever known that the disbanding of the army officers had been proposed in the Assembly and that the Assembly had rejected it, and that M. de La Fayette, M. de La Rochefoucauld, and so many others had voted for this rejection, they would properly have understood that the Assembly did not want them to be

109

However, they were forced to abandon it for the time being; but, in their usual fashion, they returned to the charge on several occasions and succeeded in getting successive parts adopted, until gradually the system was found to be established in its entirety—which did not take place, however, until the summer of 1793.* One of the first parts of this system, adopted as early as the month of July 1791, was the levy of ninety-one thousand *National Volunteers* ordered by the Constituent Assembly during the period of alarm occasioned by the flight of the King. There can be no mistaking the intention behind this measure. It was to form a counterpoise to the army of the line; but by playing it right, this measure could have been turned against the Assembly and used to turn the army of the line against it and make it favor the King. This seemed all the more to be feared by the partisans of the Revolution in that the Assembly, wishing to make of these national volunteers a *popular army,* gave them a wage of fifteen sous a day, that is to say, double that of the troops of the line; and it ordered that the *officers of these units should be elected by the soldiers!* This in itself would have sufficed to set up jealousy between these two kinds of troops. The difference in their uniform was another source of bitterness between them; the troops of the line at the time were dressed in white, and the National Volunteers in blue, like the National Guards. From this arose all the play on words about the *blue pottery that was fine but would not stand the fire* and the *blue plates for fifteen sous,* etc.

In general the various oaths that were demanded of the old officers are regarded as one of the main motives that determined them to emigrate. I do not think this is so. I can see that there are different ways of looking at them, although to my way of thinking they did not contain any clause that was contrary to their honor and their obligations. I am speaking here only of the oaths that were required between 1789 and the moment when people stopped emigrating (September 1792). At the time of the Federation of 1790, it was prescribed that the army take an oath of loyalty to the nation, to the law, and to the King, and to maintain with all its power the decrees of the National Assembly that had received the royal assent.†

---

disbanded; but they would have concluded from that that the officers should take themselves off for the good of their cause, because that was what the Assembly did not want; and as for discerning that this measure had been proposed by those of the most extreme opinions, as for comprehending that the Assembly had rejected it in order to arrest the progress of anarchy and demagogy—in a word, as for getting it into their heads that there was a party in France more demagogic and more anarchical than the Constituent Assembly itself, I believe it was absolutely beyond them, and it seemed to me that they were not even convinced when the National Convention proceeded to such violent measures.

* With the famous *levée en masse.*—ED.

† I am not speaking about the oath that was taken in 1789, since it differed little from this one, and the King was even mentioned second because this formula provided that one should be loyal *to the nation, to the King, and to the law,* whereas that of 1790 provided that one should be loyal *to the nation, to the law, and to the King.*

Nearly all the regimental officers below the rank of staff officers had taken this oath. Many colonels and staff officers had gotten out of it or had refused. But neither the King nor the Assembly had taken any measures in this respect. My opinion is that what was new in this oath was illusory and that all the officers should have rushed to take it, because it did not bring any change to their previous engagements.

This oath of allegiance was divided into three parts: *the nation, the law, and the King.* It could only inspire scruples in those who, regarding Kings as God's representatives on earth, believed that nations have no rights and that men should totally and blindly obey everything that the Kings ordain. Consequently it is only for them, however small their number today, that I am examining the question; because for those who consider that Kings are only the first magistrates of the nation, this oath could not have caused any hesitation or presented any difficulty. Therefore there is no point in spending time here on their opinions in this respect.

A nation is a collective body whose composition is constantly changing, which is always scattered and therefore can never be assembled in one place, and of which one could say in a word, as has been said of the divinity, *it is everywhere and it is nowhere.* Nevertheless nations are capable of having two mouthpieces; one is that of public opinion and the other that of national representation. These two organs are often imperfect, and the latter is, of necessity, always so. There can sometimes be difficulty in knowing the true state of public opinion; but when the inquiry is made in good faith, these difficulties, which are nearly always artificial, are overcome, and an exact knowledge of it is acquired. Now it is of capital importance for a government to have a good knowledge of it, because it is public opinion that makes for its strength or weakness. My object here is not to examine how a nation ought to be represented. It seems incontestable to me that the King and the Estates-General or the National Assembly were perfectly competent to make laws in France;* and whether or not the National Assemblies represented the French nation fairly and accurately, they never claimed to do anything (until the month of August 1792) without the participation of the King, who—whether *in reality* or at least *nominally*—had the power to refuse it (with the exception of the two and a half months following the departure of the King in June 1791). I shall examine this difference later on, as well as the objections that could be based on the steps that the Constituent Assembly

* Louis-Philippe seems to be referring to the argument advanced in 1788–89 that certain things, such as the "capitulations" worked out when a province joined France, or the rights of the nobility, or even the wishes of the electors as expressed in the *cahiers de doléances,* could not be altered without the consent of the parties concerned. Such arguments amounted to a denial of parliamentary sovereignty, since in the past they had been a great theoretical and practical limitation of royal sovereignty, and were doubly inappropriate when people were claiming for the Assembly what Siéyès called "the dictatorship of constituent power."—ED.

took after the flight of the King. The fact is that in the case of which I am speaking, their decrees did not become law until they had received the royal assent and that it was the King who promulgated them in his own name. This oath of allegiance *to the nation,* therefore, signified nothing but an oath of allegiance to the State, which is the absolute duty of every man of honor whether or not it is explicitly stated in the oath that he takes; and I do not see in what way this obligation could be regarded as a new duty or a new engagement. I think, therefore, that I am justified in saying that after having taken the first part of the oath, one found oneself in the same situation in which one had been previously with respect to one's engagements and duties.

The second part of the oath is relative *to the law.* This word, taken in its literal sense, expresses something to which I think no one can deny his allegiance. If a difference of opinion were possible here, it would be concerned with what should be recognized as law. But here this difference of opinion could not exist, because it was always the King who gave the order, and there was no question in any way of obeying what he had not ordered. This applies equally to the last phrase relative *to the decrees that have been given the royal assent.* Consequently, one could avoid obeying only by disobeying the King. I know that the objection was made that the King was not free. I shall examine this question thoroughly, but for the moment I shall confine myself to the observation that one of two things is true: Either one believes that promises made in captivity are valid, or one believes that they are not. In the first case there can be no hesitation about the line of conduct one should follow, and in the second there should be no more hesitation, because if the royal assent is found to be null, the oath is *ipso facto* annulled. I believe, therefore, that this second part of the oath in no way diminished the duties and the existing oaths of the officers, the soldiers, and, generally, all the King's subjects; and I repeat, it left them in exactly the same situation as they were in before.

Since the first two parts of the oath contained nothing which contradicted the third—that of loyalty to the King—it seems that the more one was attached to the King, the less one should have refused to take an oath that, without making any changes in the duties of those who were loyal to him, to some extent renewed and revivified the engagements toward him of those whose loyalty seemed suspect. Consequently, I think I have demonstrated that one could take this oath without scruple. But I shall go still further, because I think that it would have been good politics to take it with alacrity.

If, instead of evading this oath, of seeming to fear it, and of taking it only with regret, those who passed for being attached to the King in preference to everything else had shown eagerness in taking it and had seemed to consider it merely as a new tie between the King and the army, the mass of the army and the people would not have been able to regard it as a victory won against royal authority; and that in itself would have been a very real victory for royal authority. By taking the oath with good grace, they would have lessened popular mistrust and calmed the unrest of the army. With the popular party reassured, the Assembly would have granted greater provision for discipline, because it was restrained more by the fear of displeasing this party than by its own views. It is probable that by adopting this approach, the officers would have remained in their posts until the moment for action or until the storm had abated for other reasons.

The late King Louis XVI sensed that it was to his advantage that this oath should be taken by those on whose loyalty he counted because he ordered M. de Bouillé to take it; and if M. de Bouillé had not done so, he would not have found himself in a position to be of use to him in the month of June 1791.

It is easy to understand that if the dispositions of the officers caused anxiety before the King's flight on June 21, 1791, they caused very much more after this event. There were already large numbers of *émigrés* at this time, and their assemblies outside France swelled with each day. On June 11, 1791, the Assembly, after hearing M. Bureaux de Pusy's report, had ordered that a new oath be taken, aimed at making the officers declare their hand unequivocally.* But the events of the 21st annulled this measure, and the oath decreed on the 11th was neither required nor taken; consequently, it would be useless to discuss it. On the 21st the

* Extract from *le Moniteur* for Sunday, June 12 and Thursday, June 23, 1791.

That of the 11th contains M. Bureaux de Pusy's report in the name of six committees together, as well as the wording of the oath which in accordance with the decree of June 11, 1791, had to be taken by all the officers on active service but which was never required of them because of the events of June 21, 1791. Here is the wording:

"I promise on my honor to be loyal to the nation, the law, and the King; not to take part in, either directly or indirectly, but on the contrary to resist with all my strength, any conspiracies, machinations, or plots that should come to my attention—whether directed against the nation and the King or the Constitution passed by the National Assembly and accepted by the King, who is its head—and to employ all the means entrusted to me by the National Assembly that have received the royal assent or been accepted by the King, to see that they are observed by those who are put under me by those same decrees; and if I do not carry out this undertaking, I consent to be considered as dishonored, unworthy to bear arms and be included in the number of French citizens."

Article 4 (of the same decree): "In case of refusal, those refusing will be regarded as having been retired, and they will be given a retirement pension, a quarter of the salary of their (present) rank or the one to which they would have been entitled in virtue of their seniority."

A section of the report dealing with officers:

"Once they have contracted in writing—I do not say to *like,* but to *obey* and to *respect the Constitution*—they will never go back on this." (*Murmurs from the left wing.*) "I would guarantee with my life that an officer would not go back on his word."

Article 8 of the same decree: "The King will dispatch a letter of confirmation to the officers who have satisfied [the terms] of the present decree."

Assembly in practice suspended the exercise of royal authority, or at least removed it for the moment from the King, by ordering that its decrees should be carried out without the royal assent and by enjoining the ministers to continue in their functions and to countersign in the name of the King. It ordered that the army take a new oath, whose wording again I give below,* and it pronounced that those officers who refused to take it be deemed to have handed in their resignation. The decree ordered the Minister of War to replace them immediately in accordance with the regulations for military promotion, but observed that for this time only the sublieutenants should be equally divided between the noncommissioned officers and the sons of active citizens. Every man who paid in taxes the equivalent of three days' work, each day being reckoned at a *livre tournois,* was an active citizen.†

There is no point in examining whether the Assembly had the right or not to take such measures, and whether the extraordinary circumstances in which it found itself placed justified it in taking them or not. It is certain that it had the necessary power, for it took them and had them executed; these measures then presented the officers with the alternative of taking the new oath or of losing their employments; and consequently,

---

* Formula of the oath as prescribed by the decree of June 22, 1791:

"I swear to employ the arms placed once more in my hands in the defense of the Fatherland and to uphold the Constitution decreed by the National Assembly against all the enemies from within and from abroad, to die rather than suffer the invasion of French territory by foreign troops, and to obey orders only given in virtue of the decrees of the National Assembly."

The Assembly decreed that commissioners taken from its number should be charged with seeing that this *oath* was taken in the armies. Two members of the Assembly took the oath conditionally. A third swore an oath of loyalty to the King. M. de Folleville (a Knight of Saint-Louis and member of the right wing) said: "I demand that the decree apply only to public officials." (Violent murmurs.) "I did not ask to speak in order to propose restrictions—one does not propose such a measure when the salvation of one's country is at stake—but I think that in the present circumstances the oath decreed should be taken by all Frenchmen, because all Frenchmen must take up arms in the defense of the Fatherland."

M. de Folleville took the oath, MM. d'Ambly, d'Avaray, de la Gaussonnière, d'Aigalliers, de Mercy, de Crussol, de Mortemart, de Lamberty, etc., all from the right wing, took the oath without any reservations.

M. Fermont said: "I demand that all the members absent from the Assembly be recalled immediately; (2) that there should be a roll call on July 12 to determine the number of members present; (3) that until further notice, no one should be granted leave."

M. de Murinais and several other members of the right wing who had not been present at the opening took the oath and went to sign at the desk.

† Only "active" citizens had the vote. The distinction between active and passive citizens was designed to get around the embarrassing fact that despite the Declaration of the Rights of Man, the Constitution of 1791 did not confer anything like manhood suffrage.

The *livre tournois,* i.e., of Tours, was the standard monetary unit synonymous with the franc.—ED.

it is sufficient to examine whether the oath that was demanded of them contained any new obligations that conflicted with the old, and whether it was more advantageous to the monarchy that the existing officers keep their positions by taking the oath or give them up by refusing it.

I readily agree that this new oath could cause doubts among upright men of conscience that, to my way of thinking, the previous oath could never have occasioned. It materially differed from it in that the name of the King was removed, and certainly this omission made the proceedings very delicate. It can even be maintained that if the King had made good his escape, it would have been even more consistent with the previous oaths to refuse it than to take it, at least until it was known whether the King was in France at the head of a party or of any sort of force. It would then have been necessary to decide for or against the King, for or against the Assembly, which is a very different question from the one with which I am concerned and one I see no point in discussing, since the necessity for this choice did not arise. The fact is that when the troops took this oath, the King had been recaptured and confined to the Tuileries; that there was no force whatsoever supporting his cause against that of the Assembly, whose decrees were recognized without difficulty or opposition throughout France; and that the King was too well guarded for people to speculate on the possibility of a second escape. For the rest, even admitting this possibility, I do not think that this destroyed the argument.

It seems to me that those who took this oath argued along similar lines to those I am going to expound.

Does the oath contain promises that could prevent us from serving the King in conformity with our previous oaths or oblige us to break them?

To this the reply was No.

It seems that in effect the renewal of the oath of allegiance to the Constitution decreed by the National Assembly was a new promise of allegiance to the monarchy, because although this Constitution had not yet been finally crystallized, there was no doubt that it would be monarchical.

Moreover, the engagements resulting from this oath were only temporary and in no way permanent; it was evident that they had to cease as soon as the Constitution was put into operation; and since royal power was only suspended, this single word necessarily implied that it would be *restored;* it must also be observed that during this suspension the government kept the monarchical forms; that all the proceedings continued to be made in the name of the King; that the partisans of the Republic were forced into silence by this same Assembly upon which everything depended at the time. Finally (and this last reason will perhaps seem stronger than all the others), *in no case* did this oath impose the obligation to act against the King; it did not mention previous oaths, which consequently were not *withdrawn;* the position of the King made it highly unlikely that he could give orders that contradicted those of the National

115

Assembly before it had itself restored him to the exercise of the royal authority, more or less limited by the establishment of the Constitution; and if the position of the King had changed, it is probable that many people would have believed they could obey him without breaking the new oath *only to obey orders given as a result of the decrees of the National Assembly* since, long before the period of which I am speaking, these decrees had already *placed the supreme executive power* in the hands of the King and he had been declared by them Supreme Head of the Army, etc. I could easily present a thousand loopholes if need be, but all I want to demonstrate is that one could take this new oath without breaking the old ones or violating any duty.

If I have succeeded in proving that this was possible, it will not be difficult for me to demonstrate that it would have been better to take this oath than to refuse it. I think it was very desirable and very advantageous for the King that the officers should take the oath, and that it was very harmful to his interests and to theirs that they should refuse it.

Assuming that there was nothing that could be done in France and that there would be no movement of any kind in favor of the King until the moment when the Constitution would be put into operation, it was clear that by taking the oath required of them the officers were not losing any opportunity they might regret; and given their viewpoint, they ought to have considered it a very great advantage to find themselves still at the head of troops and in possession of military authority at the moment when the King resumed the exercise of his constitutional authority. Even supposing that there were royalist insurrections in France before the King had been reinstated (which did not happen and was highly unlikely), they would have had to take place very quickly for the officers still to have been at the head of the troops at the moment when they took place, since refusal of an oath involved immediate dismissal and replacement. Consequently, after this refusal the officers were no more than private citizens without influence or any kind of authority whatsoever, and by this ill-considered action they handed over the posts, the arms, the plans, and the military power to those whom they generally regarded as the enemies of the King and of the monarchy. They were surely not under the illusion that the troops would refuse to take the required oath. They knew perfectly well that they were very ready to conform to it. The very terms of the decrees left them no option because they did not grant those soldiers who might have wished to refuse it the right to ask for their discharge and to leave the army; and to get out of the new oath there was no other resource left to them but that of trying to desert. Thus, except in the case of a general insurrection in the army (which in the circumstances of the time no one could have regarded as possible), it was clear that the officers could indeed abandon their posts, but that the soldiers could not and that consequently they would remain in them. It was equally clear that it was impossible then to draw the mass of the army (or, if you like,

116

its real force) away from its obedience to the Assembly.* There could have been no more doubt that this obedience of the army to the Assembly, and this authority of the Assembly over the army, would become infinitely more complete and indestructible after the old officers had been replaced by others whose attachment to the Revolution was all the greater because the retention of their employment and of their new ranks depended on its success. Contemporaries were convinced that these new officers would never learn how to command troops and that the departure of the old officers would necessarily disorganize the army and would make it unfit to stand up to the foreign armies whose attack was already confidently predicted. Later, there were enough opportunities to recognize how greatly people were mistaken in this respect to allow me to dispense with the need to stop to demonstrate it.

It remains for me to make only one more observation on this oath, and I think I have a special duty to make it, because those who took the oaths required at this time have been bitterly reproached with perjury. It is fair to say everything that can correct people's thinking on this matter. Therefore I shall recall that every man admitted to the French army, whether as an officer or as a private, swears solemnly under his regimental colors *never to abandon them, and to shed the last drop of his blood to defend them and to prevent them from falling into the hands of an enemy of the King.* Now, it is a fact that refusing the oath forced those who refused it to abandon their colors and to let them fall into the hands of those whom they accused of being the enemies of the King. It seems to me that this consideration ought to have militated strongly in favor of taking the oath. I know that to deal with this objection, one would find one's regimental colors in the assemblies of *émigrés* that were building up outside France, but (without insisting on this subterfuge) one did not find there either the soldiers or the power; one became oneself a *soldier* instead of an *officer,* and although this exchange could have been considered *honorable,* it is certain that it was a loss of power. However, nearly all those who refused the oath rushed to leave the kingdom to go (still as individuals) to swell the assemblies formed under the auspices of the *émigré* Princes in order, they said, to prevent the fall of the throne and the overthrow of the monarchy.

I have given in detail the reasons that lead me to think these oaths could have been taken without violating those taken previously and without any breach of duty. I must assume that a great number of individuals refused the oaths because of an opinion opposite to the one I have advanced. But—I say it with regret—the oaths had no more than a slight influence on the majority of people! The proof that it was not these oaths which occasioned or prevented the officers from emigrating is that people emigrated equally *before* and *after* taking them, according to each

* It is common knowledge that there were only three or four regiments, all foreign, who left *en masse* to join the *émigrés* outside France.

117

one's convenience, his turn of mind, and the mood of his acquaintances. The oaths were not regarded as binding because they were considered as having been taken under duress and therefore of little consequence. It was accepted that when one took them it was for one's personal safety, and that by refusing them one was exposing oneself to being murdered. However, it is a fact that when the commissioners of the Constituent Assembly went from garrison to garrison for the taking or refusing of this oath, there were regiments where nearly all the officers refused it without a single one of them being *murdered;* it is equally a fact that the day after this refusal some went home, others to Paris or left the kingdom without experiencing any difficulty. But they needed to justify what they had made up their minds to consider as a necessary step; and it was in adopting this miserable subterfuge that men full of honor and accustomed to respect themselves allowed themselves to be involved in juggling with oaths and to give such a disastrous example to their inferiors. How many times did we see whole batches of officers take the oath, and the day after leave France and go and join the Princes. However, until the time of the rising of August 10, 1792, when the King was deprived of the exercise of his constitutional authority, there was no argument that could explain or justify the departure of the officers who had taken the oaths required since 1789. But nevertheless it is certain that nothing stopped the Emigration except the retreat of the combined armies that had penetrated Champagne in September 1792, because then the Counterrevolution was regarded as having failed; and it began to sink through that *all that* could well last longer than had at first been thought. The consequences of such a false way of thinking must leap to the eye of anyone who has the least knowledge of human nature. The result was a general distrust that caused people to see plots and treason everywhere, and this distrust added to the slackening of every aspect of discipline. The soldiers said openly: "When we face the enemy we shall begin by firing on our officers if we see that they are not acting in good faith." And assuredly one cannot be surprised after what I have just related.

In leaving the army and France, the officers, in common with all those who emigrated, made no effort to hide, and on the contrary strove to publicize the fact that they counted on the support of the foreign Powers and that it was with the help of their armies that they expected to overthrow the new Constitution, to recover their places, to reestablish feudal dues, tithes, and everything that had been abolished by decrees of the Assembly which had received the royal assent, and finally to inflict exemplary punishment on all those who seemed to them to have merited it. It was believed at the time that once the old officers were no longer there, there would no longer be an army in France; and the conclusion was that France would be in no position to resist the invasion with which it was threatened.

It was impossible that the nation should not be exceedingly alarmed by this state of affairs. It saw itself about to be delivered defenseless to a servitude all the more odious for coming from abroad. Even a great number of the declared enemies of the Revolution were frightened at the prospect, and the Duc de Penthièvre, my grandfather, said: "I have not so far forgotten my old notions as to put up with the Emperor and King of Prussia sending their armies to Versailles to dictate terms to the King under the guise of putting him back on the throne."

But such were not the sentiments of the French Princes outside France. They were constantly calling to their side *all Frenchmen loyal to their King,* and they claimed that *as the King was a prisoner* it was for them to proclaim his true intentions. This necessarily leads to an examination of the position of the King, upon which were based the appeals and other actions of the French Princes outside the kingdom and their general behavior, as well as that of the *émigrés.*

The position of the King varied according to the circumstances. To get a decent grasp of what it was, it must be examined at three different periods. The first was from October 5, 1789, to June 21, 1791, that is to say, from the day when the King moved from Versailles to the Tuileries up to that of his flight. The second was from his arrest at Varennes on June 21, 1791, to September 14, of the same year, when he accepted the Constitution. Finally, the third period ran from this last date to August 10, 1792, which was the space of time during which the Constitution of 1791 was in operation.

On October 5, 1789, the King was forced to take up residence in Paris. He was *forced* to send away his Bodyguard. Of all his former Household, only his Swiss Guard remained to him (a remarkable circumstance and one too little commented upon),* and the Parisian National Guard took over the Household duties that had previously been performed by the Bodyguard and the *Gardes-françaises.* The Parisian National Guard was not dependent on the King: They were under the orders of M. de La Fayette, their commander in chief, who in turn received, or was supposed to receive, those of the mayor and council of Paris. No one will deny that such was the King's situation from October 5, 1789, to June 21, 1791, when he attempted to leave Paris. It is literally how he depicted it himself in the declaration that he caused to be handed to the Assembly after he had effected his departure from the Tuileries and Paris on June 21, 1791. No one will suspect the King of having disguised his feelings in this document. It was not drafted by a popular or "constitutional" minister or by an agent of the Assembly. The author was not a partisan of the

* No one ever succeeded in making the Swiss Guard understand the theory of Emigration or in persuading them that it was necessary to leave the King to defend him properly. They insisted on remaining at their post, obeying his orders and those of their commanders until the moment when they honorably succumbed on August 10, 1792.

Revolution, and I am quite sure that its author was the King himself. In it the King said that he had been a prisoner in the Tuileries since October 5, 1789, that he had been stripped of several of his royal prerogatives, and that he had been hindered several times in the exercise of his authority; he specifically complained that the Assembly had not taken any notice of the remonstrances that he had made to it on February 4, 1790, on the state of the finances, and the way in which he spoke of that day proves that he had acted on his own initiative.* He said again that he had been perfectly happy to reside in Paris as long as he believed this could be useful, and that he was only taking himself away from the Assembly because the hopes he had entertained were found to be misplaced. He said, speaking

* On February 4, 1790, the King proceeded unexpectedly to the National Assembly. No one knew what he was going to do there; and the Assembly, always inclined to be mistrustful, feared for a moment that the King had come to upbraid it. But it appeared that the purpose the King had in mind was, as he put it in his speech, "to associate himself even more expressly and openly in the successful execution of all that the Assembly was undertaking for the good of France." Having congratulated the Assembly in particular on the great enterprise it had just brought to such a successful conclusion (that of the division of the kingdom into eighty-three departments enjoying the same laws and the same rights), the King said to the Assembly: "I will encourage, I will promote, with all the means at my disposal, the success of this vast reorganization on which, I believe, the salvation of France depends. And I believe it necessary to say that I am too concerned with the internal situation of the kingdom, too aware of the dangers of all kinds surrounding us, not to realize fully that given the present state of mind and the state of public affairs, either a new order must take root calmly and peacefully or the kingdom must be exposed to all the calamities of anarchy.

"Let true citizens reflect on that, as I have done, fastening their attention solely on the good of the State, and they will see that even with differing opinions, an overriding interest should bring them together today. Time will correct possible defects remaining in the collection of laws that constitute the work of this Assembly. But any enterprise tending to shake the foundations of the Constitution, any project aiming to destroy or weaken its sublime influence, would serve only to introduce the fearful scourge of discord among us. And if such an attempt against my people and myself were successful, it would permanently deprive us of the various blessings that a new order shows us in prospect." And the King concluded this speech, which I invite [the reader] to read in its entirety, with this remarkable exhortation addressed to the enemies of the Constitution: "Let those still wanting in a spirit of concord, which has become so necessary, make me the sacrifice of all the memories that torment them, and I will repay them with my gratitude and my appreciation. From this day forward I set you the example—let us all declare but one interest, one mind: attachment to the new Constitution and ardent desire for the peace, happiness, and prosperity of France!"

The Assembly was drunk with joy. It sent the King's speech to the forty-four thousand municipalities; it ordered that it be read from the pulpit in all the parishes in the kingdom, and it transported itself bodily in a procession to Notre-Dame, where it caused a solemn *Te Deum* to be sung in gratitude for this happy event. This fine ceremony made so strong an impression on me that I can still remember it as if I had just come from it. The enthusiasm was general, and from the Tuileries to Notre-Dame was heard just one, prolonged cry of *Long live the King and the National Assembly!* People persuaded themselves that all the *émigrés* were going to

of the Federation of 1790, in which he swore loyalty to the nation and to the law and to maintain with all his power the Constitution voted by the National Assembly and accepted by himself, that despite several disagreeable incidents, *it was the most agreeable moment* he had experienced since October 5, 1789. He made no reference to the *émigrés*; he merely invited Frenchmen of all parties to rally around him, and he promised them a reasonable degree of liberty, solidly based, etc. I suggest a reading of this document; through a marked hostility toward the Assembly and above all toward the Jacobins of the time will be seen the argument I am putting forward.

Does the King's position during the first period permit one to say that the King was not free? Yes, without doubt: The King was not free to go where he liked, and the journey he was allowed to make to Saint-Cloud in 1790 proves nothing except that people did not want to give the impression of keeping him in captivity; and it is worthy of note that this same journey, which was made without difficulty in 1790, was attempted in vain in the month of April 1791, because popular distrust had made alarming progress since the year before. M. de La Fayette strove in vain to enable the King to make his journey; in vain he threatened to hand in his resignation, to break his sword etc. They shouted at him that he could do as he pleased, but that the King only wanted to go to Saint-Cloud in order to *go still further and that people did not want him to be taken from them to operate the Counterrevolution.* But it does not follow from the fact that the King was not free to go where he liked that he was in captivity—that is to say, in a position analogous to that of his ancestor Saint-Louis* when he was taken by the Saracens. That, however, was the impression the enemies of the Revolution wanted to convey when they said: *The King is a prisoner.* They thought to prove by this assertion that the King was left with no power and that his authority was now merely nominal, while I believe I can prove that he exercised a considerable portion of his authority; I am convinced that when the King did not exercise it, it was because he believed it expedient not to do so, and that it was out of calculation and not necessity.†

During the second period, from the moment the King was stopped at Varennes in June 1791 till the moment the Constitution was offered to and accepted by him on September 14 following, that is to say, for less

---

return, and already they expected to see the Princes back in Paris. But no! M. le Prince de Conti alone returned. On arrival, he went to his district to take the civic oath, that is to say the one *to be loyal to the nation, to the law, and to the King, and to uphold, with all one's strength, the decrees of the National Assembly, having received the royal assent.*

* Louis IX, 1226–70, who most perfectly fulfilled the medieval ideal of kingship, was canonized.—ED.

† I remember that a large number of deputies from the left wing of the Assembly often complained of the inertia of the executive power, and Mirabeau said with his usual originality: "The executive power is playing dead."

than three months, the King's captivity in the full sense of the word was complete, and it was not only real but evident to everyone's eyes and frankly admitted. Nevertheless the King still retained a portion of his authority, which was very real although based only on sentiment and which affected people only in this way. An important part of this consisted in the certainty that he would be restored to his position as a constitutional ruler; another part lay in the belief of a large number of people at the time that the Counterrevolution would probably be successful; and finally, a third part consisted in the belief, though badly shaken, that was still present in many people's thinking—that obedience to the King was the primary duty. It is true that the *émigré* assertion that the King's position did not permit him to show his *real intentions* seriously diminished the advantages he could have derived from this kind of authority. But be that as it may, he was never deprived of its exercise, and he made use of it until he was shut up in the Temple and unable to communicate with anyone.

During the third period, which is that when the Constitution of 1791 was in operation, the King enjoyed a considerable measure of personal freedom, though one could not deny that there were still some restrictions. It is only in times of perfect tranquillity that Kings and sovereigns can enjoy unlimited personal freedom, especially when there is reason to fear that they wish to absent themselves from the kingdom. It is incontestable that the Constitution attributed to the King the exercise of considerable power, and that it gave him great legal resources to defend himself against the attacks with which the legislature and the popular element in the Constitution might threaten him. Thus the King could be attacked only by a direct and manifest violation of the Constitution.

As to the resources of physical force that the Constitution put at the King's disposal, not to speak of the considerable authority it gave him over the army of the line, it assured him, apart from the two thousand Swiss Guards, a military Household of eighteen hundred men that was organized immediately and formed from the pick of the soldiers taken from the army of the line. He nominated the officers himself, and these, as well as the soldiers, consisted of men who were devoted to him. It is true that the King had to pay them out of the Civil List; but it seems to me that this was an advantage for the King and that this could not have been a very heavy charge, because the Civil List amounted to twenty-five million a year drawn on the public treasury, plus about seven million of landed revenue. Thus the King had in Paris entirely at his disposal a force of four thousand men; and however small this force seems at first glance, it was perfectly adequate then to repel the attacks that were to be feared; and the events of August 10, 1792, would never have taken place if the King had not himself previously consented to dispense with the greater part of this force, as I shall explain when I come to speak of these events.

I think that one can neither deny that the establishment of the Constitution restored to the King the freedom to exercise in full the power that it attributed to him, nor that this power was bound to strengthen that authority, based on sentiment (as I have already mentioned), of which nothing could deprive the King—a power far greater than is generally believed, which Shakespeare has depicted for us so accurately and strikingly by placing the following lines in the mouth of Richard III:

> Besides the King's name is a tower of strength
> Which they upon the adverse faction want.

I must not forget to mention another very important advantage that the establishment of the Constitution procured for the King: It was that the limits of royal authority and of the legislative power were fixed in a clear and precise way. During the first phase of the King's residence at the Tuileries, which was when the Assembly was working on the Constitution, article by article, everything was vague and uncertain, and neither the King nor the Assembly could know the extent and limits of the power that was going to be assigned to them; while the establishment of the Constitution had put an end to this uncertainty, and the King could deploy the full extent of his constitutional authority without anyone having occasion to complain or to legally oppose him. The King used his powers often, and on several occasions it was in opposition to strongly pronounced popular opinion; and yet he was not hindered. My object is not to examine whether he acted well or badly; it is enough for me to prove that he was acting of his own free will and that he made use of his constitutional authority when he judged it appropriate to do so. I am going to cite some striking examples of this. While the Constitution was in operation, the King made use of his right of veto three times. The first time was over the decree on *émigrés* passed at the end of 1791. The second occasion was in connection with a decree on the nonjuring priests (that is to say, those who had not sworn to maintain the Civil Constitution of the Clergy). The King did not think his conscience permitted him to give it the royal assent. The third occasion was in connection with a decree passed in June 1792 at the proposal of his Minister of War, M. Servan. This decree ordered the formation of a camp of twenty thousand volunteer National Guards inside France, intended to proceed to any part of the frontier that might be attacked. The King thought that this army could be used to dethrone him, and appended his royal veto to the decree. These vetoes had their effect as long as the Constitution remained in force, and the rising of June 20* did not in any way impair them. It seems to me that these facts prove that the King *could* exercise his constitutional authority, all the more so because the prerogative of the veto is the one

* On June 20, 1792, a crowd entered the Tuileries and the royal apartments in protest against the King's use of the veto. On this occasion they were persuaded to leave.—ED.

123

that causes the most offense to the people. The King of England has not used it for more than a century, and yet he is not a *prisoner* and no one tries to say he is, although neither he nor the heir apparent can leave the kingdom without an Act of Parliament; but in England they no longer wish to overthrow the Constitution, and that is what was desired in France by those who sought to persuade people that the King was a prisoner.

Having made known what the position was, I shall examine the conduct that this position, just as much as the state of affairs, imposed on those who wished to serve the kingdom, by comparing my conception of what that conduct should have been with what it in fact was.

I think, as I have already said, that those who held offices should have tried to maintain themselves in them for as long as they could. As for those who did not have any, or who had lost those they held as a result of abolition or reorganization, they should have sought to obtain new ones in order to increase the number and strength of the King's party and to be ready to seize opportunities of serving the cause for which they believed *their honor* demanded the sacrifice of everything—in a word, to keep ourselves in a position to profit from the opportunities that the course of events was bound to present. But they did the opposite. I have already spoken of what happened in the army. A similar course of action was followed by the judiciary, although in general the magistrates were much more tenacious of power than the officers.* They had more experience and learning, and they knew that it is less difficult to defend the power one has than to reconquer that which one has abandoned. Moreover, no oath was required of the judiciary: They lost their places without having, like the officers, the alternative of keeping them. The Assembly had been much bolder in dealing with the judges than with the officers—in the first place because the barristers were very numerous in the Constituent Assembly, and they detested the former judges whose places they wanted; then again because they saw no way of immediately replacing all the officers, whereas the barristers were quite ready to supply as many judges as were wanted.

An attempt was also made to make the great landed proprietors emigrate, and its success was fairly general: the royalists outside France continuing, unconsciously, to help the Jacobins at home in their favorite project of depriving the King of all those around him who wanted to serve

---

* There were several bodies of magistrates who took the decision not to emigrate and to brave the storm, among which was the Parlement of Toulouse, nearly all of whose members were executed in 1794. Those magistrates who were called the *grand-banc*[a] of the Parlement of Paris took the same decision and suffered the same fate at about the same time: unfortunate victims of a real and not imagined devotion to duty, because if everyone had remained faithful to it, it is probable that this slaughter would not have taken place.

[a] The *grand-banc* comprised those senior judges called, after the mortarboards they were entitled to wear, *présidents à mortier*.—ED.

him and who could defend him. It was only long after, when the Emigration began to lack funds, that it was discovered too late that the property had not followed the proprietor into emigration, and that by this act of wisdom one had abandoned to the adverse faction in France both the influence that goes with office and the power that results from territorial possessions, while one had plunged one's friends and partisans into misery, and, in addition, got them expatriated.

Distaste for democracy made the enemies of the Revolution wish to return to the Age of Chivalry, and it was to these dim and often mythical times that they looked for models of conduct. It is easier to read old novels or even old chronicles than to study one's own century and the progress of human affairs. The Crusades were the model that was chosen, and the Emigration was to be *a modern crusade.* In its results it resembled them only too much! But to conclude, absurd as it was, the great landed proprietors, the army officers, the magistrates, a host of retired officers or those who had lost their jobs through reorganization, small landowners, and also, I think, a goodly number of adventurers of all kinds set off on this new crusade, and acting on this false idea of duty that *honor* imposed on them, they abandoned the monarch and the monarchy, their families, and their fortunes in the vain hope of defending them the better later on!!! . . .

As I have already said, the Emigration was openly and publicly instigated by those of the French Princes who had left France in July 1789. As early as the end of that year, they had begun to summon the nobility to them, and later individuals of all conditions who were discontented with the new régime. They had formed them into small gatherings on the French frontiers that threatened various points and gave rise to some anxiety about the security of the fortresses and garrisons. They kept up correspondence, which increased suspicion and unrest within the kingdom, to little avail, because they were not worth so much as a single fortress to the Princes and barely procured them a few deserters.

Although the aim of these assemblies was the destruction of democracy, the democratic spirit had nevertheless penetrated their internal organization, and the lack of financial means had resulted in all ranks being mixed up. Officers, soldiers, and domestics lived together in positive equality. Distinctions of rank were promptly effaced by such an intermingling, especially at a time when the lower classes had such a tendency to consider as their equals those who thought they were above them.

When Monsieur (Comte de Provence), the King's brother, left the kingdom at the time of the King's flight on June 21, 1791, he proceeded to Brussels, where a gathering of a large number of magistrates was formed whose aim was to examine what conduct Monsieur and the other French Princes should follow in view of the position in which the King and M. le Dauphin found themselves in the Tuileries. I have heard it said that there were two opinions: One was that Monsieur should declare himself Regent of the Kingdom and M. le Comte d'Artois Lieutenant General; the other was that Monsieur should simply declare himself Lieutenant General, and this was the advice that Monsieur adopted.

Monsieur, having declared himself Lieutenant General of the Kingdom, joined forces with the other Princes who had emigrated before him to persuade all those who were inclined to emigrate to do so. They ordered this in circular letters that were dispatched in all directions, and they did not neglect any means of bringing it about. Agents of the Princes, distributed in all the Courts of Europe, made all the governments understand the necessity of making war on France to restore the monarchy, which was regarded as destroyed because it had been limited; and M. le Comte d'Artois proceeded to Pillnitz, where he joined in the conferences which culminated in the treaty between Austria and Prussia that was concluded there for this object on August 18, 1791. Three weeks afterward King Louis XVI accepted the Constitution, and his constitutional authority was restored; this event momentarily delayed the execution of the Treaty of Pillnitz, though this delay does not seem to have brought about any change in the conduct and the projects of the *émigrés,* nor in those of the foreign Powers.

It is worth remarking that at the time of his flight on June 21, 1791, the King was not reckoning on leaving France; and I am convinced that his intention was to arrest the buildup of *émigrés* around M. le Comte d'Artois and the other French Princes and to rally them around his person at Montmédy. I believe that the King disapproved of the Emigration as a political measure, and it is a fact that he restrained several people who wanted to leave. Several *émigrés* have told me the King had secretly informed them that he did not want them to emigrate. The Emigration deprived the King of the only supporters to whom he was disposed to give his confidence; he sensed that it weakened him, and he feared to fall into a state of tutelage if the new order were reversed by anyone but himself. I know for a fact that the Queen expressed herself on the subject and that she said: "We do not want the Constitution, but no more do we want to be in tutelage under the King's brothers or anyone else; and if these gentlemen came here as liberators, they would want to act the master." It does not seem that the King delegated any power to his brothers, still less to the other *émigré* Princes. I do not doubt that if there had been documents of this kind, they would have been made public when their publication could no longer be harmful. There are a large number of printed documents in existence that prove the opposite, but as they are *official,* their validity is contested by the *émigrés,* who refuse to accept as the expression of the King's wishes any of the instruments countersigned by his constitutional ministers; consequently, I shall set them aside from the discussion on which I am engaged at the moment. Later I shall examine both the validity of these documents in themselves and the influence they were to have on the conduct of the royalists. At the moment I am concerned with unraveling the secret and real intentions of the King in order to prove that, even admitting that the King's thoughts should be the political guide for his subjects (which is not my own view), the royalists should have eschewed the Emigration because the King regarded it as a dangerous measure for his cause and for himself. Nevertheless, it would be difficult to affirm that the King always acted in accordance with this opinion. It is well known that the King's conduct was continually changing, sometimes through the influence of the various depositaries of his confidence, sometimes through that of circumstances, often even through the conversation of those who came up to him; it is incontestable that this fluctuation of opinions and conduct was one of the main causes of his misfortunes and those of the French monarchy.

It is known that the King gave several missions to various individuals, who made no secret of it after his death. The Baron de Vioménil was employed by the King in this way, and Mallet-du-Pan was also the bearer of similar instructions. His task was to engage the *émigrés* to break up their assemblies and return to France to defend the King there. He even had a secret political mission to the Emperor of Germany to discharge at Frankfurt at the time of the Coronation in 1792, and although I cannot remember the precise terms of this mission, I know that its object was to prevent the Emperor from allowing himself to follow the promptings of the *émigrés*. The most remarkable mission was the one that the King entrusted to the Baron de Breteuil, to whom he gave plenipotential powers under the Privy Seal to negotiate in his name. In the note below, I give a copy of these powers as well as extracts from letters of the King and Queen that prove my assertion about their true attitude toward the *émigrés* and the opinion they had of the results that their conduct was bound to produce. I shall append the whole of this correspondence, copies of which were given to me by one of the agents employed by the Baron de Breteuil in 1810.*

* Powers given to M. le Baron de Breteuil by King Louis XVI.

"Monsieur le Baron de Breteuil, knowing all your zeal and loyalty and wanting to give you a new mark of my confidence, I have chosen to entrust the interests of my Crown to you. As circumstances do not permit me to give you my instructions on such and such a matter and to maintain a continuous correspondence with you, I send you these presents to serve as plenipotential powers and authority vis-à-vis the various Powers with whom you may have occasion to deal on my behalf. You know my intentions, and I leave it to your discretion to make what use of this authorization you judge necessary to achieve my goal, which is the restoration of my legitimate authority and the prosperity of my peoples. Upon which, Monsieur le Baron, I pray that God may help you under his holy protection. Paris, Nov. 20, 1790." (Signed) "Louis."

Letter of Queen Marie-Antoinette to Emperor Leopold, May 22, 1791.
"My dear brother,

I am delighted that you are putting your trust in M. de Bombelles; he is also the one whom we are charging to speak to you on our behalf, and the Baron de Breteuil will inform him of all our plans. I am astounded that you should know so little of

I have already said that I have refrained from making use of all the arguments the King's public conduct and orders would have furnished me in abundance because I only wished to employ arguments whose validity would be recognized by the *émigrés* themselves. However, I think I have proved that although the King wished to overturn the Constitution and the new order, it was not through the Emigration that he proposed to attain this end; and that the conduct of the *émigrés* was neither the result of his orders nor even in conformity with his intentions. It is possible that many of the *émigrés* were in error in this respect, but considering only the

---

our real intentions. Here they are, in a few words, because the code is very difficult.

We have always intended to extricate ourselves from the appalling situation we are in, and for this we have addressed ourselves to M. de Bouillé on the one hand, and the Baron de Breteuil on the other: There are only these two in the secret and a third person[a] here who has undertaken the preparation for our departure and our connections. In accordance with these measures, we are to proceed to Montmédy: M. de Bouillé has undertaken to bring provisions and troops to this place, but he ardently desires that you place a detachment of eight to ten thousand troops in Luxembourg, which should be available at our request (naturally this will not be until we are in safety) to enter Montmédy, both to serve as an example to our troops and to hold them in check. I have already written about this several times to M. de Mercy, who can certainly have troops march to the border, but cannot allow them to enter the town without your authorization. As time is extremely pressing, it is to be desired that you give your orders promptly.

"The Princes, the Comte d'Artois, and their whole entourage want to act no matter what; they have no real resources and will ruin us. Because of their indiscretion and the men who lead them, we will not let them into our secret till the last moment.

"I have no inkling of what you tell me about a man and dispatches you are supposed to have received from us: I repeat what I have already told you this winter: Do not believe that anything is from us unless it comes via M. de Mercy or the Baron de Breteuil. Fontbrune and the others are wretched intriguers.

"We are annoyed that the Comte d'Artois should have left Italy; anywhere else he can only compromise us, and there he could have served us usefully and thus enhanced his reputation.

"Our gratitude for all the concern you show for us can only be equaled by the tender love with which I embrace you."

Letter of Louis XVI to M. le Baron de Breteuil, December 3, 1791.

"Monsieur le Baron de Breteuil, I enclose herewith letters that the Queen and I are writing to the Kings of Spain, Sweden, Prussia, and to the Empress of Russia, together with the duplicates of all these letters, which will acquaint you with their contents. I have charged the Bishop of Pamiers (M. de Agoult) to write to the Marquis de Bombelles telling him to go to you, and I believe that you will consider him a suitable person to pursue my interests at Petersburg: You will send someone in your confidence to Spain, and you will charge the Duc de La Vauguyon with the negotiations. You will entrust the Comte de Fersen with the letter to the King of Sweden, who will, I think, be very happy to resume the direction of my affairs; and if the Marquis de Bressac, who served me with such zeal and intelligence last year at Berlin, is free and within reach of you, I desire you to entrust him with the Prussian mission.

"I do not know whether you will approve the measures I propose—doubtless they will seem to you too leisurely—but you are not in a position, as I am, to judge the

---

[a] The Comte de Fersen.—ED.

128

facts, one must agree that their conduct was in contradiction with their own principles and with what they themselves pompously called the *fundamental principles of the monarchy.*

It is generally recognized that hereditary monarchies are exposed to buffetings and crises whenever it becomes necessary to invest a cadet member of the dynasty with the royal authority *pro tempore* during the lifetime of the King and the heir presumptive to the throne. The history of every regency is a positive proof of this;* they have always been times of trouble and factions. But with what in history can one compare the

degree of exaltation here and how necessary it is to mind public opinion. I think I can be certain that as soon as a respectable force appears on the frontier, a rising will take place inside the kingdom that will provide a better ordering of things without the loss of blood. Moreover, abandoned as I am by the Emperor, who does not even deign to reply to my letters, and vexed by my brothers, who are given over to treacherous advisers and whose every step tends to increase the damage, I thought that there was no other course of action open to me than the one I have adopted.

"You will keep me informed of everything via the same channel you employed to write to me when you were at Soleure, and I will likewise use it when I have something to let you know.

"Though I certainly do not suspect the sincerity of their intentions, my brothers are nonetheless a continued source of anxiety. They are surrounded by people who seem to have sworn my ruin and that of my family. Every measure that is taken at Coblenz increases my difficulties. Any time now I am going to be forced to threaten the German Princes with war if they do not dispatch the *émigrés* from their territories, and none of this would have happened if my brothers had observed a wiser conduct than the one that had been put into their heads. The height of misfortune would be if they attempted to enter the kingdom: They do not know its temper nor the state of the troops, and if they were led to this fully with the meager resources at their command, they would reckon on perishing there with all their followers and on causing us, here, to be slaughtered. It is a question, therefore, of trying to hold them back, and the means I would consider most appropriate to this end would be that they correspond with me through you and through the Marshal Castries. The Baron de Vioménil, whom I am charging to explain to them my wishes on this point, will be passing through Brussels and will confer with you; but if this correspondence is established, you must be very careful not to tell them my secret, because they are unable to keep any. You must confine yourself to attempting to get them to do nothing except in concert with you, to submit their plans to me and let me know their resources, and above all, it would be desirable if they chose as their agents men wiser and more capable than those they have employed hitherto. Finally, I authorize you, for this object and for all the others, to do everything that you believe to be in the interests of my service, relying absolutely on your intelligence, your zeal, and your loyalty. I pray God, Monsieur le Baron de Breteuil, that He may keep you under His holy protection." (Signed) "Louis."

Extract from King Louis XVI's letter to Charles IV of Spain, December 3, 1791.

". . . A reason that makes me desire even more eagerly the convening of a Congress and that Your Majesty should assume its direction is the position in which my brothers and other French *émigrés* find themselves. I should regard it as a great

* I.e., that of Catherine de Medici in the sixteenth century; of Marie de Medici for Louis XIII, and Anne of Austria for Louis XIV in the seventeenth century; and of the Duc d'Orléans for Louis XV in the eighteenth century.—ED.

proceedings by which the French Princes, having retired to Coblenz, declared themselves to be invested with the royal authority and signified to the French nation that it was no longer to recognize any orders other than theirs on pain of severe penalties, which they never failed to enumerate in full on every occasion. The Prince who declared himself Lieutenant General of the Kingdom and who, in this capacity, undertook to exercise royal authority did not reside in France, nor could he reside there. He had no way of gaining public recognition, in any part of the kingdom, of the right he claimed to exercise the royal authority during the lifetime of the King and of M. le Dauphin, and still less of enforcing his orders and those

---

misfortune for France and for all Frenchmen if they carried out an armed invasion. Without reckoning the degree of confidence and love among the people that I personally should forfeit, what would affect me much more would be the certain ruin of the nobility, the clergy, and all decent people. I have written to my brothers several times in this vein, but their position is very difficult: Surrounded as they are by men who are embittered by their misfortunes and who believe they can overcome everything by their courage, my brothers are not free to do what they want or even to keep their plans secret. The Congress, by holding out to the *émigrés* reasonable expectations, would abate their passion and (something that I regard as being of the utmost advantage) enable us to arrive at a better arrangement without their intervention. The reasons I have just given, about the position of my brothers and the lack of secrecy of their entourage, have prevented me from informing them of my proceedings, and I beg Your Majesty, in his dealings with them, if he likes my ideas, only to communicate them as coming from himself. He will readily conceive of all the precautions that my position demands. I believe that this National Assembly's conduct toward the foreign Powers constitutes a very strong reason for convening a Congress; I have also written about this to the Empress of Russia and to the King of Sweden, whom I know to be well disposed toward me, and I beg Your Majesty to use his credit with them to support me. I have informed the Baron de Breteuil of all my projects and have charged him to take up all their details with Your Majesty. What pleasure will I not have to be indebted to Your Majesty for the restoration of order in my kingdom and the strengthening of my authority on stable foundations. It is with great confidence that I place my interests in Your Majesty's hands, in the sure knowledge that I could not find a better relative and friend."

Extract from the letter of December 3, 1791, from Queen Marie-Antoinette to the King of Sweden, Gustavus III.

". . . The copy of the letter that I am writing with the King's consent to the Empress of Russia will be placed before your eyes. Y.M. will see there what our thinking is about the present situation and what we think can be done to reach our goal. The King is likewise writing to Spain to beg the King, his cousin, to take upon himself, in concert with you and the Empress, everything relating to this plan. There is another paragraph in my letter that I greatly desire you properly understand in order to assess our [position]. It [concerns] our own conduct and the reasons that have obliged the King to give his assent. Our position *vis-à-vis* the King's brothers is also enlarged upon there: If we could isolate them from their whole entourage, we would not hesitate to speak to them with all the confidence of the most loving friendship, but at the moment they are unable to maintain silence before all those who have sacrificed themselves to follow their fate, and for us the slightest indiscretion would forever ruin all our plans. Would Y.M., therefore, be so good as to guide and restrain them. If they chose to act foolishly, they would infallibly ruin us and, what would

of the other Princes. The tacit recognition of this right and of those orders must have seemed a very delicate matter of conscience even to the most uncompromising royalists because instead of having, as in an ordinary regency, a silent King who never spoke except through the organ of the regent, there was in Paris a King who, for whatever reason, *spoke, acted,* and *gave orders* that contradicted those of the Prince who was Lieutenant General and those of the other *émigré* Princes, and the orders of this King were recognized and obeyed in the whole of France. Next, given that it was a fact that the Prince who declared himself to be invested with the royal authority as Lieutenant General of the Kingdom was at the time unable to exercise it anywhere within France, I find it impossible to accept that this step was *necessary* to bring about the restoration of all that it was desired to restore. The King's situation, in the midst of those who were accused of wanting to destroy him, should have led to even more caution over proceedings that are always inherently delicate and were particularly so in the case I am speaking of, because one could

---

cause us more grief, all decent people with us. It is absolutely essential that when you speak to them, they never suspect that we are in correspondence with you, and to this end there must only be the Baron de Breteuil and the Comte de Fersen in our secret. We must thank you once again for the generous offers you have made us to speak to the King of Prussia, but as he has personally expressed his interest, the King has thought he should write to him himself to thank him and thereby secure him further in our cause without, however, entering into details with him."

Extract from a letter from Queen Marie-Antoinette to the Empress of Russia, Catherine II, December 3, 1791.

". . . The extreme caution we must employ in all our projects and all our actions means that it has been impossible for us to inform the King's brothers of our ideas. God forbid that there should be the slightest mistrust between us (as people have wished to spread abroad). We judge their hearts by our own, and we know that they are concerned only with us. But not all of their entourage is the same. The loyalty of some, the indiscretion of others, indeed the ambition of a few, all impose on our hearts the heavy duty of not speaking to them with the unbounded confidence that their personal sentiments deserve. It is, therefore, to Y.M., Madam, with the influence over them that you must be presumed to have in virtue of your generosity, that we confide our dearest interests. Be so good as to guide them in the direction which, without disclosing our plans to them, may be useful to us by demonstrating to them fully that they could only ruin their unfortunate country by acting in isolation, and that even if with stronger forces something could be undertaken, it would still be necessary for the Princes and every Frenchman to stay behind. The rot begins to be felt here. A little steadfastness and patience will bring us to our goal within France, but for this there must be, outside, a formidable force that can only be justified with impunity by an armed Congress which, restraining the Princes on the one hand, quells the men of faction on the other and gives the moderates on all sides force and a rallying point. It is with this in mind that we are writing to the Kings of Spain and Sweden, on whose concern we must entirely rely because of the frank and noble way in which they are acting. The King is also to write to the King of Prussia thanking him, but without entering into details of our plan. Vouchsafe to employ your good offices at this Court and that of Denmark; also engage the Emperor to show himself to be my brother at last."

131

derive advantage from it only by giving currency to the idea that one was acting in accordance with the intentions and orders of the King. Now, the establishment of this opinion was bound to have the most disastrous consequences by preventing the party that was then dominant in France from putting any trust in the King's sincerity and by destroying the effect of all the measures by means of which he was constantly striving to inspire it.

It seems that a *politique du pire* had been adopted at Coblenz, that is to say that the more troubles there were in France and the more crimes committed, the less likely the Constitution was to last, and the more the success of the Counterrevolution in its totality would be assured. Everything that tended to contain the Revolution within sensible limits was regarded as a misfortune because that could make the constitutional government last a little longer and because they believed that once it was so clogged "that it could no longer work" (that was the favorite expression), *"all that* would of absolute necessity crumble"; and then, according to the same people, "the King, rid of his jailers, would naturally resume all of his former authority and would put things back on the same footing as they had been for so many centuries." The result of this illusion was that it was not even suspected that the fall of the constitutional government could lead to the establishment of the Republic, and those who were politically sound* were forbidden even to conceive of the possibility of this. And yet this is what happened, and it was thus that this illusion materially contributed to bring about the crash we witnessed, whose first shudderings involved the destruction of the King and his family and the ruin of the *émigrés*. It is certain that the Emigration did incalculable damage to the King and his cause. Each day he felt a greater need to surround himself with faithful servants, and each day he saw them abandon him to go to defend the monarchy at Coblenz, at Worms, or at Brussels; and each day the number of those to whom he would have liked to entrust the important places and functions at his disposal grew smaller. Appointments were turned down, the places that he offered as a constitutional King were disdained, and it became the rule that to show proof of one's royalism, it was necessary to disobey the King. *"The King is a prisoner!"* it was said, and by uttering this phrase with the accents of grief, people thought they had acquired the right to disregard orders and to treat them with no more respect than those of a lunatic shut up in an asylum. People seemed to think that by those magic words—*The King is a prisoner!*—they had brought about the forfeiture of his throne and released from their oaths all those who had sworn allegiance to him. And yet that was how the *émigrés* behaved toward the King! And great God! at what a time, at a time when the throne was shaken up by an unparal-

* Among the *émigrés,* you were called *sound* if you professed all their opinions, and the more extreme you were, the *sounder.*

132

leled concatenation of circumstances each more terrible than the one before; at a time when the progress of democratic and republican principles had unloosed all the ties that bound the peoples to their sovereigns; at a time, finally, when, as the *émigrés* never tired of repeating, *the King's life, his throne, and his Crown ran the greatest of dangers!* . . . It was at such a time that the *émigrés* taxed with *dishonor* the man who consented to be the minister of their King, and it was in the middle of a crisis whose magnitude they were striving to convey that they themselves frustrated all the initiatives and hampered all the measures this unfortunate King thought necessary for his personal safety and that of his throne! Let me not be accused of overstating the case! No: I have not said a word too much. I ask you, those of you who emigrated, have I said a single thing which does not conform with the truth? Is it not literally true that whenever the King thought he ought to make some initiative to win popularity, you hastened to say that he was doing it *despite himself* and *that he was forced to do it?* When he was assuring France and Europe of his good faith and of his desire to maintain the Constitution, was it not you who were assuring that on the contrary, it was nothing of the sort and that he wanted to overthrow it? When he invited all Frenchmen to remain in their employments and in the kingdom, was it not you who said, "Don't be in the least taken in by it, and emigrate as fast as you can under pain of losing your employments and being dishonored"? And finally, when this hapless King, groaning at the ills caused by the financial disorders and realizing the necessity of making great sacrifices to arrest its progress, had given the royal assent to the decree providing for the creation of *assignats,** merely expressing his regret that it was only *a partial remedy and a temporary alleviation,*† where did the presses to counterfeit them begin to be set up? Who were the counterfeiters of this currency bearing the effigy of your sovereign? . . . I shall not push this painful discussion any further. I think I have said enough to prove that your reckless conduct and your petulance launched you along a road leading in exactly the opposite direction from the one you intended, and that you were assisting the enemies of the throne to undermine and overthrow it. You paralyzed the efforts of the Constituent Assembly to sustain and consolidate the throne; and to complete your deplorable work, hardly anyone remained in France who did not have to fear for his

* Paper money secured initially against the confiscated Church lands.—ED.
† See the King's declaration of June 21, 1791. (One can appreciate the King's interest in financial matters when one recalls that it was on account of the deficit that Louis XVI had consented to convoke the Estates-General in the first place. Imagine his ironic bitterness when the result of the powers he had shed after 1789 was a deterioration of the financial situation! Another point is that Louis XVI had a very clear grasp of financial matters—witness the devastating criticism he made of the financial program that Loménie de Brienne proposed to lay before the Assembly of Notables in 1787.—ED.)

personal safety in the event of your success and to whom your foolish threats did not constantly present the scaffold lying behind the King's victory and your own! . . .

I now take up the thread of my narrative, which has been interrupted by this discussion, doubtless very long but essential to the goal I have set myself in these memoirs.

I received at Vendôme at the beginning of July 1791 the decree of the Assembly on the new oath for officers,* which had been dispatched to me by the Minister of War. I immediately communicated it to the officers, informing them that I should carry out the decree within the required time limit. They kept silent. In the morning I learned that one of the captains (M. de Mastin) had left during the night, and I was given a very polite letter from him in which he expressed to me his regret at leaving his guidons; he added that it was impossible for him to take the required oath unless I allowed him to introduce the word *King* into the formula after the *nation* and the *law,* and that if I agreed to this he would return to his post with as much eagerness as he experienced pain in leaving it. The other officers made the same request, informing me verbally of their resolution to refuse the oath if I did not yield to their desires. I replied that it was not in my power to change anything in the wording of the required oath, that I was simply required to ask them to take it or to refuse it so that I could inform the Minister; that they saw that by the terms of the decree they ceased to be officers from the moment they refused the oath, that I was sorry to see them go and that I trusted that although we had been together only a short time, this regret would be mutual. They assured me it was and said some very nice things. Some of them were moved and appeared to be very affected at leaving the regiment. The lieutenant colonel, M. de Lagondie, asked me in the name of them all to relieve them from the spectacle of publicly refusing the oath and even begged me not to speak of their decision for the moment so that they could leave quietly during the night. I gladly granted all that they asked of me, and we parted very amicably. A moment later M. de Lagondie returned to my quarters to tell me that the town council was refusing them passports and that my good offices were necessary to procure them for them. I went to the town hall straightaway and found the council in session, and indeed the councilors were alarmed that such a large number of officers were asking them for passports. I told them that as all these officers had decided to refuse the new oath, I had agreed to spare them the unpleasantness of refusing in public, and I explained that since, after refusing, they would no longer be officers, they could not then be denied passports and that consequently it would be better to issue them with them straightaway; and the councilors agreed to do this.

A regiment of dragoons of the time was composed of three squadrons and twenty-eight officers. Only eight took the oath. They were all—with

* See page 114.

134

the exception of myself, whom I include in the eight—what was called at the time *officers of fortune,** that is to say, officers who had risen from the ranks. For the four companies that I had at Vendôme, consisting of about two hundred and forty dragoons, I was left with four officers only; the three others were detached. I confess that as I was only seventeen at the time and had never seen any service (I had only been three weeks at Vendôme), I was very disturbed at commanding a regiment denuded of its officers. I knew that the regiment was very attached to its officers, and I feared the effect that their departure might have on the dragoons. But they expressed resentment rather than regret at being *abandoned* by their officers—that was the expression they used: "Why," they said, "have they *abandoned* us, as well as the guidons, when they know perfectly well that we cannot leave them? We have always conducted ourselves like true dragoons, perfectly obedient to our commanders; they have nothing with which to reproach the regiment, and we do not deserve this from them." During the night one of the companies (Mastin's) in which there was not a single officer left panicked and sent to inquire at my quarters whether it was true that I had left, taking the guidons with me; but with the assurance of the sentinel who was at my door that I was peacefully in my room, as were the guidons, they returned to their quarters, where their comrades had already saddled the horses to set off in pursuit of their guidons.

Next day the regiment mounted on horseback, and the oath was taken in the presence of the town council and of a sizable crowd that shouted: *Long live the nation and the Chartres Dragoons!* Everything went on in the regiment almost exactly as before the departure of the officers, and discipline was well maintained by the small number who had remained.

It was not till the end of July 1791 that the National Assembly pronounced the abolition of all the orders of chivalry (with the exception of the Order of Saint-Louis, which was retained as an ordinary *military decoration*); my father then stopped wearing the Order of the Holy Ghost, and I did the same. I had hitherto worn it all the time. I took no other steps in this connection, and I only recount this circumstance, which is fairly trivial in itself, in order to find the opportunity of giving the lie to all the absurdities that have been uttered on the subject. It was said that I had gone to the bar of the Assembly to strip off my blue ribbon and make an offering of my collar of the Order. This is entirely false. I can even add that after my departure from France in 1793, my collar of the Order was found in my apartments in the Palais Royal and was carried in triumph to the National Convention, as if an important discovery or capture had been made.

Nothing further happened during my stay at Vendôme worth the

* These seven officers were MM. Ducastaing, Tousch, Vilmet, Logan, Roussel, Perrin, and the quartermaster Jacquemin.

135

trouble of telling until the time I finally got permission for my regiment to be sent to the frontier and reassembled there.

The Minister of War sent me orders to conduct it to Valenciennes. A few days before I left Vendôme I had the good fortune to rescue from the water a drowning man* who had already lost consciousness; and this, added to the adventure of the two priests I recounted above, was worth an address of thanks from the town council, which was as unexpected as it was little deserved.

I left Vendôme in the month of August 1791 and set off with the regiment. We were marching in one-day stages, and we passed through Chartres, where we were received with great magnificence. A considerable crowd went before us to a point quite far beyond the town. At the gates I found the heads of the administrative bodies of the town and of the National Guard, who escorted me to an abbey where the departmental authorities had prepared a great banquet. The dragoons were put up free and entertained in the houses where they were lodged, which naturally delighted them. I need not recall that in my father's lifetime I had borne the title "Duc de Chartres" and that the 14th Dragoons, which I commanded, were still habitually referred to as the Chartres Dragoons, which surely contributed to the reception we were given at Chartres. I am even more inclined to believe this because the National Assembly had already taken from my father the dues he collected at Chartres and the surrounding area in virtue of his *apanage*. It is true that since the majority of these dues were at this time collected by the government, I believe that the inhabitants experienced less indulgence and more vexation on the part of the fisc than they had previously from our private administration.

I made the journey from Vendôme to Valenciennes at the head of the regiment. I absented myself only for two days to make a trip to Paris, which we passed by very nearby. I found Belle-Chasse in a state not at all to my liking. Mme de Genlis's anxieties had made alarming progress since my departure from Paris. She feared the King, M. de La Fayette, the Assembly, the people of Paris—in short, everything she could fear—and in her constant search for protectors she had increased the number of deputies she had been accustomed to receive during the previous winter, and this increase made a pretty bizarre circle. I sought in vain to reassure her; it was impossible, and probably the only result of my efforts was to lead her to hide from me with even greater care the plan that she had certainly already formed of going off to England and taking my sister with her. Assuredly, if I had known about it then, I could perhaps have succeeded in preventing my father from consenting to it because he strongly disapproved of this expedition, and Mme de Genlis only extracted his consent by promising to return at the end of a month.

When I returned to my regiment, I took with me the Duc de Montpensier, my brother, to whom I had given one of the vacant sublieutenancies

* M. Siret, an engineer from the Department of Roads and Bridges.

so that we would be together, which we both wanted all the more for never having been separated. It was, moreover, according to the new laws, the only way of beginning one's service, and a great garrison like Valenciennes was bound to strike us as a good training ground. This arrangement had the additional advantage of getting him out of Paris and especially Belle-Chasse, of which he was tired and where my father, with good reason, did not care for him to remain any longer. I admitted him as an officer at Montdidier, and we arrived at Valenciennes at the end of August 1791.

Valenciennes was then the headquarters of the command of the frontier departments from Dunkirk to Bitche. The troops stationed in these departments were to form the *Army of the North,* and the lieutenant general, the Comte de Rochambeau (who was made a Marshal of France in the following winter of 1791–1792), was entrusted with this command. This appellation *Army of the North* gave me hopes of active service, but on my arrival at Valenciennes I saw, to my great regret, that there was no assembly of troops nor any desire to assemble them. I tried to persuade M. de Rochambeau to mobilize a part of his army: I pointed out to him that as our troops had not fought for nearly thirty years (except those he had commanded with distinction in America),* it would be of great importance to have them under canvas and to assemble a sufficient number to carry out warlike maneuvers. I added that this would create a good impression in France and abroad—in France because of the confidence this would inspire both as to the intentions of the government and the army chiefs and as to our means of resisting the aggression with which we were threatened; and abroad by giving the foreign rulers to understand that the invasion of France and the Counterrevolution would not be as easy to accomplish as the *émigrés* were saying. But I was not successful in persuading M. de Rochambeau. He replied that I was not to concern myself with any of this; that it was none of my business; that I was too young to be involved in such matters; that I struck him as being a little impetuous and that I must cool off; that I had a regiment to command, and it was with that I should be concerning myself and not with anything else. Then I asked him if he would be so kind as to assist me by granting me such facilities as would enable me to put my regiment in a position to fight with distinction. I explained to him that the first need of this regiment was for officers (and I earnestly begged him to speed up their nomination); that the dispersal of this regiment between Vendôme and Caen and the constant duties it had been obliged to perform to protect the circulation of corn had been very detrimental to its training,

* The Seven Years' War ended in 1763 and was the last European war in which France was engaged before the Revolution. She entered the War of American Independence in 1778 and sent a small force to help the insurgents. This absence of wars contributed to the discontent of the nobility, whose only training was for the career of arms.—ED.

armament, and equipment; that I hoped he would permit me to have recourse to him over these matters and that he would give me his advice and assistance.

He replied dryly that as for his advice, since he had always served in the infantry, he had none to give me regarding a regiment of mounted troops; that as for assistance, he did not interfere in the running of individual regiments; that for all these matters I should address myself to M. de Fléchin, the *maréchal de camp* in command at Valenciennes; and he begged me never to speak of the matter again. This unexpected beginning was only the prelude to the coldness that ever since has always subsisted between him and me, from that moment until the time he left the command in May 1792. But such was then the unfortunate effect of differences in political opinions. Marshal Rochambeau in a sense belonged to the Palais Royal, where I believe he was born, the Marquise de Rochambeau, his mother, having been lady in waiting to the widow of the Regent Orléans, then my father's governess in his childhood when he was still in the hands of women,* and finally my own governess and that of my second brother during our infancy. M. de Rochambeau had been aide-de-camp to the Duc d'Orléans, my grandfather, at the beginning of the Seven Years' War,† and it seemed that the combination of so many circumstances would have inspired him with more interest in two young Princes, one aged eighteen and the other sixteen, who had come to carry out their apprenticeship in war under his orders. I was all the more hopeful of inspiring him with this interest because, as he had taken the oath required by the Assembly and undertaken the command of the principal frontier, he must have known that the *émigrés* and the counter-revolutionaries would not forgive him for having taken this line. But it was precisely because he had taken this line that he thought he had to keep his distance from me and behave coldly to me. He loathed the Revolution and the whole constitutional setup. I do not know what had determined him to take the oath at the bar of the Assembly, but I know that he constantly regretted having taken it. The contrast between his former relationship with my family and his present views made it very disagreeable for him that I should come under his orders. Frequently he scarcely concealed this from me, and he was only concerned with maintaining an attitude toward my brother and myself that preserved him from the suspicion of favoring, and above all being a member of, what was called at the time the Orléaniste faction. Although his attitude toward me piqued me all the more because I believed I had the right to different treatment from him, nevertheless this never prevented me from doing justice to his personal qualities as a man of honor and a good soldier.

I went to find M. de Fléchin to tell him that M. de Rochambeau had referred me to him and to beg him to take into consideration the state of

* French Princes were given male tutors at about the age of six.—ED.
† This began in 1756.—ED.

the regiment I commanded. I found him very civil, but I obtained no more assistance from him than from M. de Rochambeau. Like him, he had only ever served in the infantry, and he had only taken over the command of Valenciennes two days before my arrival, replacing M. de Sarre-la-Brousse, who I believe had refused the oath. M. de Fléchin had taken it; however, he emigrated a few days afterward, which was a blow to Marshal Rochambeau, under whom M. de Fléchin had served in America with great distinction. The Marshal temporarily replaced M. de Fléchin with Colonel Théobald Dillon, whose seniority in his present rank made it certain that he would become a *maréchal de camp* at any moment. But Colonel Dillon only carried out the duties of *maréchal de camp* at Valenciennes for a very short time and until he had been replaced by M. de Chalus, who had been a *maréchal de camp* and inspector of cavalry before the Revolution. M. de Rochambeau liked M. de Chalus very much. He, too, had served under him in America, and during the few weeks that he was in command at Valenciennes I had nothing but praise for him in every respect; but he, too, emigrated, and in a manner sufficiently curious for me to recount it here.

A few days after M. de Chalus had been made a lieutenant general, he came to me on parade and asked me if I would be so kind as to present him to the Society for the Friends of the Constitution, that is to say, to the Jacobin Club of Valenciennes. "Certainly, General," I said, "if you are making a serious request I should be delighted to introduce you." —"Oh! I am perfectly serious," he replied. —"Very well," I said, "whenever you like; but tell me then, my dear General, how has your conversion come about; because hitherto I thought I had detected that your opinions were none too pronounced in that direction." —"It is no longer a matter of opinions," he replied, "I think it could be useful for me to be a member of this society, and that is what has decided me."* Then we agreed that I should present him the same day. I proposed that the society admit him by acclamation, together with M. de la Roche, his aide-de-camp, and they were received immediately amid great applause. The following morning M. de Chalus emigrated. As soon as it had been reported to me, I betook myself to the Marshal's quarters to inform him. I found him in front of a great map that was hanging in his room, pointing out to M. de la Roche with his cane which was the most direct route from Valenciennes to Béthune. He begged me to allow him to finish his explanation before listening to what I had to say to him: "Perhaps you will find there is no need," I said, "when you have heard me; because if M. de la Roche's intention is to go and rejoin M. de Chalus, he should not go and look for

---

* It was certainly very useful then for the generals and officers to go to the clubs because their presence there could not do any harm, and it inspired confidence in their patriotism and the soundness of their opinions at the same time as it muzzled those who sought to inflame the people by making them see treason and conspiracies everywhere. It is true that nothing was more calculated to increase popular distrust than to see a staff officer *emigrate* the day after he had himself been admitted by the Jacobins.

139

him at Béthune, but at Ath."*—"How so?" the Marshal said to me with surprise. —"Because M. de Chalus has emigrated, and the sentry on the gates at Quévrain has just come and reported it to me." —"And you are surely going to do the same?" the Marshal resumed, turning toward M. de la Roche. —"No," he replied, "but I do not wish to serve any longer, and I am going to withdraw to my home."†

After M. de Chalus, we had successively as commander at Valenciennes the Duc d'Aumont, a lieutenant general, and Théobald Dillon, *maréchal de camp* (the same who had provisionally commanded there after M. de Fléchin). Finally the Duc de Biron, a lieutenant general, was definitively appointed to this command. He came to Valenciennes in the month of December 1791. From the moment of his arrival he displayed to me, as well as to the Duc de Montpensier, my brother, some of the long-standing, constant, and loyal friendship that he always had for my father until his dying breath.

The garrison of Valenciennes at the time when I carried out the functions of commandant of the castle consisted of two infantry regiments (Navarre and Royal Swedish, or the 5th and the 8th of the line) and two of dragoons (Chartres and Schomberg, or the 14th and 17th Dragoons) —that is to say, of two German and two French regiments. I was the most senior colonel of the garrison (my colonel's *brevet* being dated November 20, 1785), and as such I performed the functions of the King's lieutenant, or of *commandant of the castle,* because general staffs for fortresses had been suppressed.

These duties as commandant of the castle obliged me to make continuous tours of inspection, day and night, visiting the watches, hospitals, prisons, stores, arsenals, ovens, etc., and in addition M. de Rochambeau sometimes amused himself by making me carry out rather singular duties. For example, when quarrels broke out in the garrison between the soldiers in the French regiments and those in the German ones that were sufficiently serious to cause the Marshal some anxiety, he ordered me to put the whole garrison on patrols so that the soldiers would no longer be able to fight among themselves. He required me to put myself at the head of these patrols with the senior officer for the day, and I was perfectly ready to carry out this order. But he was not content with that, and he ordered me to go in person to visit the brothels to arrest all the soldiers who were found there on the spot. I protested that I would do nothing of the sort, that what he was ordering me to perform were police duties and in no way those for soldiers, and that all that the troops of the line had to

* At the time there was an assembly at Ath of *émigré* officers incorporated into a regiment.

† After Louis-Philippe supplanted his cousin Charles X in 1830, the latter ordered his loyal supporters not to emigrate, but to resign from all public office. It was called *l'émigration à l'intérieur.* During the Great Revolution, attention is normally focused on the kind of protest that took the form of external emigration, but one imagines that our M. de la Roche was not alone.—ED.

do was to give armed assistance to the civil arm if it should meet with resistance. The Marshal realized that I was right and summoned the municipal officers who undertook to make the visit, and I confined myself to carrying out patrols in the adjacent streets.

I obtained fairly promptly from the Minister of War (M. Duportail) the replacement of those officers who had left the regiment. He sent me two very good officers for lieutenant colonels, M. de Sahuguet d'Espagnac, who came from the 7th Horse (Royal and Foreign), and M. de Valabris, who came from the 1st Mounted Rifles. As for the captains, as they were nearly all taken according to seniority from among all the lieutenants in the cavalry arm, there were some among those who were sent me who were too old for active service. Captain Clarke, later Duc de Feltre, who was at the time an acting captain, was nominated to a company in my regiment; he joined it at Valenciennes, but he only stayed there for a few days.

During the autumn of 1791 M. de Rochambeau had the garrisons of Valenciennes and Quesnoy brought out several times and made them carry out maneuvers against each other in the plains which lie between these two places; but he never wanted to carry out large-scale maneuvers or troop mobilizations.

At Valenciennes I had taken a house near the citadel, where I stayed with my brother. M. Pieyre, who was attached to my service and whom we both very much appreciated, and M. Mirys, who was attached to that of my brother and who helped him to cultivate successfully his talent for painting, lived there with us. Our establishment was comfortable but in no way magnificent, and yet I had some difficulty in meeting the cost. My father's income at this period was so greatly reduced, both for the reasons I have already dwelt on and because of the Constituent Assembly's nonpayment of the income it had voted him to replace the *apanage,* of which he never received a sou, that the allowance he made me to defray my expenses only amounted to fifty thousand francs. I had in addition four thousand francs salary as a colonel of dragoons, and so my total revenue only came to fifty-four thousand francs. It needed all the methodical and economical instincts of M. Pieyre, who regulated my household, for us to be able to live in a manner befitting our rank on such a slender income, yet neither my brother nor myself ever contracted any debt. M. Pieyre gave me some very good lessons of this sort and I regard this as a great service he did me. My brother's allowance only came to two thousand francs a month, so, as was right, I supported the expense of the household alone.

We led a very uniform life at Valenciennes, the regularity of which was indeed very monotonous. I went punctiliously to the barracks every morning before lunch and to the parade at noon. Three times a week we had four or five officers to dinner, and the other days we dined alone. Often in the evening M. Pieyre made music with M. de Sahuguet and some musicians. At other times we went to the quarters of Marshal Rochambeau, who played whist every evening. We also went to the theater when it was open, but it was often closed. It was usually mediocre; however, given the isolation of our life at Valenciennes, we still found it very agreeable.

The garrison at Lille would have offered us much greater advantages and comforts. I greatly desired the Marshal to send my regiment there. This was up to him, because he had the power to distribute the troops in his command as he saw fit, but I could never get his consent. At Valenciennes I did not find the military advantages I could have desired, and this garrison had great drawbacks. The barracks that my regiment occupied there were execrable and greatly inferior to the ones occupied by the 17th Dragoons. They were so bad, and so dilapidated, that for some time they had ceased to be used for troops; part of the stables was in a fearful state, and it was necessary for the regiment to leave these barracks for the good of the service; but M. de Rochambeau was inexorable. In vain I begged him to come and inspect the barracks himself; he found this proposition beneath the dignity of a commander in chief and would never consent to carry out this inspection. Furthermore, I did not dare press him too hard on this point because he threatened to send us away from the frontier if the barracks were recognized to be uninhabitable, and this was precisely what I wanted above all to avoid so as to be sure that my regiment would form part of the army when it was finally decided to mobilize it.

In this way I spent nearly seven months at Valenciennes, from the end of August 1791 till the beginning of March 1792, occupying myself principally with the command of my regiment and of the citadel of Valenciennes that had devolved on me, as I have already said.

In the course of October 1791, I received a letter at Valenciennes from Mme de Genlis informing me that she was on the point of leaving for England with my sister and that my father would explain to me the reasons for this trip, which would not be a long one. My father wrote to me at the same time in such a way as to let me see that he was agreeing to this journey more through indulgence than the belief that it would be useful or suitable. Mme de Genlis promised to return in a month or six weeks at the latest, and this promise persuaded my father to let her go; but she did not keep it, and my father was not long in repenting this mistaken indulgence.

Although, according to all the calculations I could make about Mme de Genlis's timetable, it was probable that I would not succeed in reaching her before she left France, nevertheless my brother and I determined to make for Calais immediately, where it was possible that we would still find her if she had been detained by the wind and especially if she had not embarked at Boulogne, which we had reason to fear. I went immediately to Marshal Rochambeau's quarters to ask his permission to make this journey, and he gave it to me, but only for three days; and he asked for my word that I would appear on parade the fourth day and not leave the limits of his command, which included Calais; however, as he was a great stickler for the military hierarchy, before finally granting my request he further required that I go to get M. Dillon's permission and that it should be M. Dillon who presented the request to him in accordance with the rules and regulation of the service.

As soon as we had obtained all these permissions, I left with my brother, and our departure was so precipitate that we did not take any money to pay for the post horses, and we left a bundle of one hundred sous *assignats* (which were called *corsets* at the time after the name of the man who signed them and which we had earmarked for the expenses of our journey). We did not realize we had forgotten it until we had covered more than three leagues,* so we decided to send back a courier to look for the money and to attempt to travel post on the strength of our honest looks. This plan succeeded excellently. At each relay post we announced that the courier behind us would be paying, and this passed for ready money. In this way we traveled without difficulty from Valenciennes to Béthune, where we were joined by our courier, who restored to us our *assignats* and who had paid for our horses along the whole route.

Since we had to pass through several garrison towns, we encountered difficulties in continuing our journey at night. However, at Aire the commandant (M. de Henisdale) kindly let us pass; but the commandant at Saint-Omer was inflexible, and he did not even want to allow the departure of our advance courier, who had arrived before the gates were closed. The postilion who had conducted us to Saint-Omer was prepared to leave us in a wretched inn and was even beginning to unharness his horses when, by getting the local people to talk, I learned that there was a very rough road by which one could skirt the town and reach the road to Ardres; then, by giving the postilion money, I persuaded him to conduct us along this road, which was indeed very bad but which we covered without accident. We arrived at Calais the following morning at eight o'clock.

We learned to our great satisfaction that Mme de Genlis and my sister were still there, but that they were due to embark at ten o'clock in the morning. Consequently, I had time to talk to Mme de Genlis about her journey, of which I greatly disapproved. Her constant anxiety in France for her safety was the main reason that had determined her to undertake it. She had the greatest fears for her safety, and as she had decided to make this journey at the time when the Constituent Assembly finished its term,† she persuaded two fairly prominent deputies to accompany her as

---

* A league was somewhat less than three miles.—ED.

† Having drafted the Constitution and completed its self-appointed task, the Constituent Assembly gave way to the Legislative Assembly, which met on October 1, 1791. Members of the Constituent Assembly were debarred from being members of the Legislative.—ED.

far as London in order that the popularity of their names (they were MM. Pétion and Voidel) might serve to protect her on the way. She was frightened of being stopped by popular disorders, which were highly unlikely at this period, and she did not fear—though this was nevertheless much more dangerous—the talk to which this journey was bound to, and did indeed, give rise. These gentlemen were supposed to be going only as far as London, and in fact that was as far as they went. Mme de Genlis was going to Bath because the pretext for the journey was that the waters of this place were necessary for my sister's health, though in reality she had no need of them. The result of this bad arrangement was that once she had arrived in London, Mme de Genlis was going to find herself alone in England with my sister and her two companions, Mlle de Sercey and Pamela, without any men apart from domestics, and this circumstance added greatly to all the anxieties this journey caused me. I strongly insisted on this point when I saw Mme de Genlis at Calais, and she strove in vain to reassure me by saying she had so many friends in England that she did not need anyone and that if, for one reason or another, she prolonged her stay, she promised me to summon someone suitable who could save her from difficulties if such an occasion arose.

In fact, soon after, she summoned MM. Alyon and Lepeintre, who may have been agreeable to her personally but who could not fulfill the objective or seem fit traveling companions in the eyes of the public. Moreover, she did not keep them with her for long, and she even hastened to send them back to France together with the chambermaids and domestics she had brought to England, with the exception of a single footman called Drancy. She stayed only a few weeks at Bath, but instead of returning in the month of November or at the latest in December 1791, as had been agreed with my father, she took my sister to Bury Saint-Edmunds in Suffolk, where she took a house; and she did not bring her back to France till the month of November 1792, and even then my father had to employ very strong means of persuading her.

I saw clearly from my conversation at Calais with Mme de Genlis that she was going away with the intention of not returning for a long time, and I was in no way duped by the hope she held out to me that she would return at the end of six weeks. But my father, who had been taken in, was justly irritated by the prolongation of Mme de Genlis's and my sister's stay in England, and when I tried to excuse her to him by saying that it was her constant anxiety for her safety that prevented her from returning and bringing my sister back to France, he replied very fairly: "If she is frightened, let her go and stay abroad, nothing is more reasonable; but it is not reasonable that she should make use of my daughter for the purpose and keep her in a foreign country against my wishes and at the risk of having her classed among those who have emigrated" (which is what in effect happened). However, it is fair to say that in the month of October 1791, at the time of Mme de Genlis's departure with my sister for England, there was not yet any law on emigration. On the contrary, it was hoped that the acceptance of the Constitution, which had just taken place, would have a soothing effect and cause many *émigrés* to return to France. Nothing of the sort happened, but people expected it, and in this hope the laws relating to passports had been abolished; there was complete liberty to enter and leave France, and consequently there was no indication that a journey to England for pleasure or instruction could be equated with those to Coblenz.

My brother and I accompanied Mme de Genlis and my sister to the packet on which they embarked in fine weather and with a good wind. We then returned to the inn at Dessain, and we set off immediately back to Valenciennes. On our way to Calais we had passed through Bouchain, Douai, Lens, Béthune, Aire, and Saint-Omer, and we returned via Saint-Omer, Cassel, Bailleul, Armentières, Lille, Orchies, and Saint-Amand. We were very struck by the beauty of the countryside surrounding Cassel, with the view that can be seen from it, and with the richness of the country we passed through between Cassel and Lille.

We had read such fulsome descriptions of the *floating islands* of Saint-Omer that we felt obliged to go to see them, but I think there have never been more deceptive descriptions. We took a boat, and having sailed for a very long time in the fens of Saint-Omer, our boatman announced a *floating island*. We looked in all directions and could see nothing, but the boatman, taking his boat hook, proceeded to push in front of him a piece of turf, straw, and reeds, in the midst of which was a small willow, the whole being no more than seven or eight feet in diameter. "There," he pronounced, "is a floating island." Technically, the island did float, but we were very disappointed and very annoyed at having spent several hours on this expedition when we had so little time left to arrive at Valenciennes within the time prescribed.

We arrived at Lille the same evening, but the gates had already been closed. Luckily, the commandant of that garrison town, more obliging than the one at Saint-Omer, had them opened for us. This commandant was the Comte de Grave, then colonel of the 90th Foot (Chartres) who was the senior colonel of the garrison at Lille and who was made a *maréchal de camp* shortly afterward. The Comte de Grave was my first groom before the Revolution, and through all the course of my life he maintained the friendship for me that he had pledged from my earliest youth.

We had the satisfaction of arriving at Valenciennes before the time for the parade. There was none that day because it was raining; but I went off immediately to the Marshal's quarters to prove to him my punctuality.

Toward the end of February 1792, Marshal Rochambeau left Valenciennes to go to Paris, to which he had been summoned by the minister of War (M. de Narbonne). As he was about to leave, I went with my brother to ask his permission to make a visit to Paris, since I could be sure that nothing important would occur on the frontier while he was absent, but he refused me categorically, adding that I could have nothing to do at Paris and that it was better that I stay with my regiment. In the absence of M. de Biron, who at that time was in England,* the Marquis de Crillon, a lieutenant general (the elder of the two brothers of this name who were members of the Constituent Assembly) was left as second in command at Valenciennes. I had always found him ready to oblige me, so that after waiting for a fortnight for the permission that the Marshal had refused me, I addressed myself to him. He replied that the Marshal, on his departure, had forbidden him to grant it; but that as this prohibition struck him as eccentric and out of place, he would grant me what it was in his power to grant, that is to say, *permission to be absent for three days without leaving the area of his command;* he added that with this permission I had only to go to Paris, which he would *not know,* and that he was sure that on my arrival the Minister of War would tell me to stay there as long as suited me.

I eagerly followed M. de Crillon's considerate advice. I scarcely took time to thank him, and I left immediately for Paris with my brother. On arrival I went to see M. de Narbonne, and I told him that as M. de Crillon was not authorized to give leave of absence for more than three days, I had come to ask his permission to remain in Paris until further orders, and I assured him that should any army be mobilized I would rejoin my regiment without delay. M. de Narbonne seemed not to doubt my zeal, and he very kindly granted my request.

After leaving him, I went to see Marshal Rochambeau, who was a little startled to see me. "I hope," he said as soon as he saw me and without waiting for what I had to say to him, "that you are going to set off immediately back to Valenciennes and that you do not intend to remain in Paris." —"I am sorry," I said to him, "but that is precisely what I have in mind." —"But how *could* M. de Crillon?" —"M. de Crillon could do nothing at all," I resumed, "you made sure of that; but he gave me permission to be absent for three days, and the Minister of War has kindly prolonged it for me indefinitely." —"I am not surprised," the Marshal said, "he wants to oblige you and," he continued in an ironic tone, "except for me, his consideration for you would have gone a little too far, because he wanted to get the King to use his choice to make you a *maréchal de camp,* but I advised him to do nothing of the sort. At your age it is better to command a regiment; and then with your patriotism and ideas I thought you would not care to be promoted by the choice of the King, and I think that the King would not be any more anxious to grant you this favor." —"You have read my thoughts very well," I said;

* The Duc de Biron had just been sent to England on a diplomatic mission with M. de Talleyrand and M. de Chauvelin; ostensibly M. de Chauvelin was the only one charged with this mission so as to get around the decree that forbade those who had been members of the Constituent Assembly from accepting any employment in the gift of the Crown during a specified period.

"Marshal, I much prefer the King not to grant me any favors whatsoever, and I shall be very happy to fight as an ordinary colonel, provided we make war *in earnest*. Moreover, at the rate the Emigration is going, a few months from now I shall become a *maréchal de camp* by seniority, and so I in no way regret the favor that you have made me miss, and I merely see it as a gratuitous mark of your consideration for me."

This took place a very few days before M. de Narbonne was dismissed from the ministry. When M. de Grave was installed there in his place, he wished, out of his long-standing friendship for me, to have me made a *maréchal de camp* through the King's choice. He mentioned it to me, and he did not disguise the fact that he expected to meet with some difficulties from the King; but he thought he could overcome them, and he attached some importance to attempting it. I dissuaded him; and after relating what had happened with M. de Rochambeau, I assured him, which was perfectly sincere on my part, that I should prefer to remain a colonel until I was appointed a *maréchal de camp* through seniority. In fact I only waited two months, and my *maréchal de camp's* commission was still signed by the Comte de Grave a few days before he left the ministry.

As soon as he saw me in Paris, Marshal Rochambeau lost no time in withdrawing my regiment from the frontier. He sent it to Laon without taking the trouble of telling me. It grieved me because the way things were going I foresaw what indeed happened—that hostilities would soon break out on the Flemish border—and I feared that with my regiment being at Laon it would be too far away to be present at the opening of the campaign. Moreover, I had reason to fear that this withdrawal was arranged on purpose to have a pretext for leaving me on the home front during the war. I complained bitterly to the Marshal about this change of garrison. He replied that I was wrong, since I was dissatisfied with the barracks at Valenciennes and the ones he had just assigned to me were some of the finest in France; but the Marshal knew perfectly well that this change would be disagreeable to me, since he had ordered it without informing me. All my efforts to get him to send my regiment to Valenciennes, or Lille, or Maubeuge, were in vain, and he kept repeating that he could not have the troops sent hither and thither in this way like valets, that my regiment would be perfectly all right at Laon, and that it must remain there. I then addressed myself to the Comte de Grave; but although he was Minister of War, he could not order troop movements within the area covered by each commander in chief, and the most he could do was to promise me that if hostilities began he would make sure I would not be overlooked.

I proceeded to Laon as soon as I knew that my regiment had been installed there, taking with me the new tricolored guidons, whose issue had been delayed until then on various pretexts by the officials in the War Ministry. I presented them to the regiment in the presence of the Council of the Department of the Aisne and of all the authorities, and then I sent the old guidons bearing my arms to the War Ministry in conformity with the military regulation decreed by the National Assembly and accepted by the King, of which one of the articles prevented colonels from keeping colors, standards, and guidons that had been abolished so that they would not reappear if there were a Counterrevolution or be taken off to Coblenz, as some colonels had vainly attempted. I stayed only a few days at Laon, and at the end of March I returned to Paris, where I remained from then until the declaration of war, which occurred on April 20, 1792.

At this point I shall suspend the account of what concerns me personally to present a picture of the King's conduct relative to his acceptance of the Constitution in 1791 and of his relations with the Assembly. To this I shall add a survey of what was going on at the time both in France and in Europe, and I shall indicate the main causes of the war, the early events of which I shall have to describe.

When the Constitution was presented for the King's acceptance, it is clear that he had to choose between two courses of action, namely, *to accept it or to refuse it*. He accepted, but he did it in such a way as to nullify the effect of this, because his object was not to consolidate the Constitution that he had sworn to maintain but to destroy it, which he thought he could achieve by gaining time.

I think that in accepting the Constitution the King should have resigned himself in good faith to becoming purely and simply the head of the nation, as laid down by the Constitution presented for his acceptance.

But if the King did not think he could carry out his resolution, then he should have refused to accept the Constitution, basing his refusal on the fact that it was impracticable and that consequently by accepting it he would be putting himself in a position where it would be impossible for him to fulfill his duties toward the nation and the State.

By adopting one or other of these two courses of action and following it vigorously, the King would have traced for himself a simple and honorable line of conduct. He did nothing of the sort, and the impracticable policy he preferred added to the misfortunes of which he was one of the principal causes—that of exposing himself to the just reproach of having played a double game and of having successively deceived and abandoned all the parties. I am going to try to give a clear idea of his policy.

The King wanted to give his political conduct a different appearance in the eyes of the French nation from that which he wanted it to have in the eyes of all the Courts of Europe. I do not know how he expected to succeed in a project whose execution was impossible; but it is certain that in attempting it, he exposed himself to the danger of losing the confidence of the nation forever when his conduct was found out, which could not fail to happen.

The King wanted people in France to believe that he had sincerely

148

accepted the Constitution, that the love of his people had triumphed over the repugnance he had felt, that he was sacrificing all to the wishes of the nation, that time would show whether the Constitution would work in its existing form, that he feared this was impossible but that experience must reveal its shortcomings; and that as for himself, having no object other than the happiness of France and national prosperity, he would in good faith give all his attention to making the Constitution work, so that if in practice it did not come up to the nation's expectations, the blame for it could not be imputed to him. Again, he wanted to persuade the nation that the conduct of his brothers caused him great pain, that he disapproved of it as well as that of the *émigrés,* that he realized the damage it did him, that he had done and would continue to do all he could to determine them to change it and to enjoin them to return to France; and that if he did not succeed with them by means of persuasion and by negotiation with the foreign Powers, he would be the first to bring about the armament of the nation and to have recourse to war if provocations abroad made it necessary.

But the King would have been very much put out if the European Powers had believed that such were his real intentions. On the contrary, he missed no opportunity to justify himself to them for what he was *constrained* to do by his position, by his lack of any kind of power, and above all *by the captivity in which he and his family were held by the revolutionaries;* because with the shameful pretext that this *captivity* nullified all the engagements he contracted, even all the letters that he wrote and all the words that passed his lips, he salved his conscience and rid himself of the scruples that could have given him pause in this subterfuge; and disregarding the example of so many martyrs of the Christian religion (whose prayers and intercessions in his favor he nevertheless solicited every day), he forgot that they had died under torture rather than declare *that they believed what they did not believe,* and although sham and dissimulation might have saved their lives; they had preferred to be tortured and to die rather than to betray their beliefs and fail in their duty.

The secret letters that the King and Queen wrote to various sovereigns of Europe and that I give as an appendix are concrete proof that the policy of the King was in truth such as I present it.* I do not doubt the

* The King says in his secret letter to the King of Spain, Charles IV, dated December 3, 1791:

"I accepted the Constitution and, in performing this act, I had to appear to be doing so freely. I thought I ought to adopt this course, however painful it was for me, because, given the situation of my kingdom, I thought it was necessary to do so to calm the spirits of the errant multitude who, without really knowing why and urged on by the novelty-mongers, passionately desired a new Constitution, although many still retained a residual attachment to the monarchy. I thought it necessary to profit from this residual attachment to win the people's confidence, to my mind the only way left of operating inside France. If I had pursued a contrary line of conduct and

authenticity of these letters, but I realize that one can have a different opinion and dispute the matter with me; this, however, would not invalidate at all the *exposé* I have just given of the King's policy, since I have based my argument on facts that are common knowledge throughout Europe. This policy was always perfectly understood by all those contemporaries who were in a position to observe the course of events. This knowledge, unfortunately, was not confined to the King's servants, to his friends, or even to the royalists; it was general among all the parties that were opposed to him, and especially the republicans. The debates in the Convention at the time of the lamentable catastrophe that terminated his life bear this out conclusively.

---

had refused, all the ties that still bind the people to the monarchy would have been broken. The republicans, who seek only anarchy, would have had the upper hand, the kingdom would have been set alight and turned upside down from one end to the other, and the life and property of decent men and those who still remain truly attached to me would everywhere have been exposed to the greatest dangers.[a] These are the considerations that determined me, and perforce I did not take any action to show that I was not free, thinking that the facts would speak sufficiently for themselves and that when people were enlightened they would of themselves desire a return, at least partial, to the *status quo ante,* and that for this I should have only to acquiesce in the general desire. A further deciding factor was the disjointed and formless nature of the new system. It is impossible to establish a rational arrangement and one that could operate the machinery of any form of government by the means laid down in the Constitution. It must collapse of itself and perhaps, even, in a short period of time. For the good of my subjects and for my own, I must, by then, have sufficiently won the people's confidence to make it impossible for them to attribute to me any of the woes they will experience and to make them turn back to me. It is to arrive at this salutary goal that I accepted the Constitution as I did and afterward followed the path I have laid down for myself. It is impossible to hide from oneself the fact that at present, real power resides in the people: To arrive at a more desirable arrangement without a violent jolt, we must gain the confidence and win back the love of the French for the King and the monarchy. To achieve this I must give the appearance of complete sincerity in the policy I have adopted by following the letter of the Constitution and by not taking any step that could give grounds for distrust. To proceed in accordance with the letter of the Constitution is the surest way to make everyone realize its defects and illogicality."

The Queen in her secret letter of the same day to the Empress of Russia, Catherine II:

"The King has accepted the Constitution; not that he thinks it is good, or even that it can be executed, but he has accepted it so as not to be the pretext for greater disturbances and misfortunes in the kingdom that the men of faction would not have failed to attribute to his refusal. He has accepted it in the hope of demonstrating all its defects the better by appearing sincerely to desire to execute it and to demonstrate by the very act that it cannot *work;* finally, he accepted it because of his total ignorance of the disposition of the other Powers toward him."

a Who would have believed that the man who so judiciously described here what would have happened if he had not accepted the Constitution was the selfsame as the one who was under the illusion that once experience had shown the people that the Constitution was incapable of *working,* the people would beg him to resume the exercise of his absolute authority? The people saw, indeed, that the Constitution was not *working* because the King wanted to overthrow it, and they shattered them both.

But at the period when the King accepted the Constitution, a considerable portion of the nation was still under the illusion that he would sincerely undertake to consolidate it and that once the King had sworn to observe it, only factious people and agitators would continue to have doubts as to his good faith in carrying out his promises. Consequently, it is impossible to describe the nation's transports of joy at the moment when the King accepted the Constitution, and it was not only in Paris that this joy was manifested but throughout France. It was believed then, as it was believed so many times afterward, that the *Revolution was terminated,* and perhaps it really would have been if the King and Court had wanted it so. But then it would have been necessary to bend, in good faith, to the nation's will and to public opinion, and that is what they never wanted to do; they would have had to desist from begging for the assistance of the foreign Powers and give up the hope of making them intervene in our internal affairs; they would have had to content themselves with ruling France *constitutionally* in good faith, and above all, they would have had to make the *émigrés* return and completely bring an end to all hostile postures on their part on foreign soil.

The nation's joy was of short duration, and in the event it could not have been otherwise, since it was founded on an illusion and since the King had only accepted the Constitution in the hope that his acceptance would give him more resources to destroy it subsequently and to restore royal authority to its former limits.

Now, once the King began to act with this intention, it was impossible that the Assembly, that the whole of France, should not perceive it sooner or later, and it was perceived very quickly. The consequence of this discovery was easily foreseeable; that the nation's outburst of feeling in favor of the King was extinguished and gave way to suspicion, to the desire to see precautions taken against the Court's plots, against the intrigues and threats of the *émigrés*—in short, to see the measures adopted that were demanded by the language and attitude of the foreign Powers, who, even at this stage, disguised neither their desire to destroy the Constitution nor their intention to do so by armed force, and to invade France as soon as they had completed their preparations for this enterprise. This change in the nation's attitude toward the King was doubly unfortunate for him because he was denuded of all armed resources within the kingdom, because the Emigration, by taking all the royalists out of France, succeeded in enervating this party and, as I have already said, in making it absolutely impossible for him to undertake anything by himself.*

* Perhaps the rising in the Vendée in 1793 will be cited as a proof that this was not impossible. I do not think that any of these royalist movements could have been carried out earlier; but it would take too long to embark here on an explanation of the forces that always paralyzed these risings. I shall confine myself to referring the reader to the various memoirs that have been published on these events, and in particular those of Mme de La Rochejacquelein [*sic*].

151

The King concurred with the *émigrés'* aim of overthrowing the Constitution and obtaining the support of the foreign Powers; but I think it is a great mistake to think that the *émigrés'* conduct was directed by his orders or was entirely in conformity with his views. The King and Queen were disturbed by and jealous of the ascendancy and authority that the Emigration gave the *émigré* Princes, and particularly the King's brothers, over the mass of the nobility and clergy. They were equally jealous of the credit and advantages that the position of these Princes gave them in relation to the foreign Powers; and without wanting themselves to act in accordance with the Constitution, they did not want to allow themselves to be represented by the *émigré* Princes, and they often tried to obstruct their operations; there resulted from this a clash in the activities of those who claimed to serve the King that was very damaging to him.

There were at the time outside France three kinds of French diplomatic agents, all claiming that they were the true representatives of the King of France and that their rivals should not be considered as possessing any character which could be recognized by the Powers to which they were accredited. These three kinds of agent were

(1) The ambassadors and ministers formally accredited by Louis XVI in his capacity of constitutional King, or to use the expression employed in the Constitution, in his capacity as King of the French.

(2) The secret agents of the King, such as the Baron de Breteuil, Mallet Dupan, and many others, whose mission was to keep an eye on the *émigrés,* to put a stop to their more foolish exploits, and to preserve for the King the principal influence and direction of affairs in dealing both with the mass of French *émigrés* and with the foreign rulers. Above all, they were to see to it that if the Counterrevolution succeeded, the foreign Powers would prevent the King and Queen from falling into dependence on the *émigré* Princes.

(3) The agents of the *émigré* Princes who claimed to discount the other two categories of agents, the former as *rebels,* the latter as *intriguers,* neither of whom had powers that the European Powers could recognize, since the King, being a prisoner, could not have supplied them, and these agents maintained that the King's brothers were, by right of birth, the only people who could legitimately speak and act in his name. It seems that these agents of the Princes were those whom the foreign Powers at the time received most favorably.

It is easy to see the confusion that must have resulted from the use of such contradictory agencies and how much this confusion was bound to weaken the King. The King sensed this weakening, probably without fathoming its real cause. He shared the misconception that is only too common among Princes and Courts that a monarchy can be stable only when the monarch is invested with absolute power; and of the nation, he considered that only the nobles and priests were attached to the conservation of the monarchy because they were the only ones seeking the restoration of the Ancien Régime. He believed, as a result of the same mistake, that they were the only ones who were well affected toward him and in whom he could place his trust. But every day he saw them withdrawing from him and going to join his brothers outside France. The result, as I have already said, was that the Emigration deprived the King of the assistance of the only part of the nation on which he relied, while his brothers had already seized control even of that and therefore found themselves in control of the only force of Frenchmen that the King considered as royalist and wanted to lead. Therefore, as soon as the King saw that the current toward emigration was becoming too strong to be dammed or even channeled by him, his only thought was to take up position in a place where he would be able to draw it toward him and prevent it from flowing toward the *émigré* Princes, and surely that is one of the main reasons that determined him to undertake the withdrawal to Montmédy in 1791.

Nevertheless, the King realized the weakness of this party, and he saw no other way of bringing about its victory than by reinforcing it with foreign armies. This error was one of the main causes of his own misfortunes and of those of his family, of the overthrow of the monarchy in France, and of all the calamities that the excesses of the Revolution have brought down on France and Europe.

Because of the King's opinion about the necessity for the cooperation of the foreign Powers to restore absolute power and its former institutions, the relations of the *émigré* Princes with these Powers became another subject of jealousy and anxiety for him; and yet the King found as few means in this case as in the other of conducting these relations himself in accordance with his own views and of preventing his brothers and their agents of exercising the principal influence on the European Courts in matters relating to France. These Courts rapidly became populated with *émigrés* of both sexes propagating their opinions, their prejudices, and their illusions in all the drawing rooms, in every circle, and above all among the Princes and sovereigns, because the latter, being themselves very anxious about the results the French Revolution could produce in their own states, eagerly welcomed everything that presented it to their people in an unfavorable light, and similarly rejected everything that would have led to a different interpretation. The result of this bizarre conjunction of circumstances, which are as extraordinary as they are generally misunderstood, was that in reality this unfortunate King exercised far less influence and authority over those who boasted that they were defending his cause than over the kingdom which was represented throughout Europe as being in rebellion against him and which he himself was probably weak enough to consider as really being so.

We have seen how the King's authority over the *émigrés* and his influence with the foreign Powers had been paralyzed or even destroyed. We shall see how these same factors operated inside the kingdom on public opinion, on the working of the government, and on the King's position in general.

At Court there was a complete lack of appreciation of the vigor and resourcefulness with which, despite the greatest difficulties, M. de La Fayette, together with MM. de Lameth and the majority of the "constitutional" wing of the Constituent Assembly, had halted the republican movement and maintained monarchical government in the person of the King; nor were the *émigrés* any fairer toward them in this respect. No matter what services they might have been able to perform for the King, they would still have been *constitutionalists,* and as such, the Court would never have ceased to regard them as *enemies of the King and of the monarchy.* However, as the royalist party was not carrying out any rising in France or showing itself anywhere, and because all its leaders were hastening to leave the kingdom, the result was that despite the King's repugnance for the constitutionalists, he had no other support in France than these *enemies;* and so had to resign himself to employing them and had, to a certain point, to appear to adopt their ideas until the arrival of the foreign armies allowed him to dispense with them and probably to take some measure against them even more severe than that.

I believe that the King, by uniting with the constitutionalists sincerely and by deciding unequivocally to defend France with them and with the nation against any form of foreign invasion, would have acquired an incalculable strength, and that this strength would not only have stifled the seed of republicanism but would have established his authority on a more solid foundation than any other. But because this union was only apparent and had nothing real or sincere about it, it was impossible that the result should have been other than the overthrow of the Constitution; and it is well known that when this happened, it entailed the fall of the King and that of the constitutionalists, whose position was especially critical because they had no way of holding their ground and because their ruin was assured whether the Constitution was overthrown by the Republic, as in fact happened, or by the victory of the foreign armies and the *émigrés.*

Having presented this general picture of the King's policy and action, I shall pass to the details that I think provided even more numerous proofs of what I have just put forward.

It was on September 3 that the Constituent National Assembly finished the work of revision and that the Constitutional Act was presented for the King's acceptance by a deputation of sixty members.

On September 13 the King notified the Assembly, in a message that was conveyed by the Minister of Justice, that he accepted the Constitutional Act and that he would come down to the Assembly at noon on the following day to pronounce his formal acceptance. In this message the King gave fairly long details about the considerations that had always guided his conduct, and he declared that these same considerations inclined him to accept the Constitution. The message was concluded with the request that prosecutions arising out of the events of the Revolution should be dropped as part of a general reconciliation.

On the proposal of M. de La Fayette, the Assembly decreed by acclamation that all those detained for reasons connected with the Revolution should immediately be freed, and that all proceedings instituted in connection with these matters should be dropped. Then it added to this a general amnesty in favor of both soldiers and *émigrés,* permitting all Frenchmen to travel freely within the kingdom and to leave it without a passport. This decree received the royal assent on the 15th.

On September 14, 1791, the King proceeded to the Assembly, and having solemnly declared that he accepted the Constitutional Act, he swore "to be faithful to the nation and the law, to employ all the power that had been delegated to him to maintain the Constitution decreed by the Constituent National Assembly, and to see to the execution of the laws." As the King was leaving, the whole Assembly rose in a spontaneous movement, left the chamber where it held its sittings,* and, crossing the Tuileries gardens to the noise of the people's acclamations, escorted the King back to his apartments.

The obligations imposed on the King by his oath would seem to have been expressed with clarity and precision; however, I am persuaded that quite apart from the grounds of nullity that the King thought he could extract from his self-styled state of captivity, he had managed to interpret to himself the obligations imposed by this oath in such a way as to convince himself that even after taking it, he was not obliged to maintain the Constitution. It is easy to demonstrate that such really was the impression the King formed of his engagements relative to the Constitution.

The Assembly, in drafting the wording of this oath,† certainly had in mind to make the King recognize that he had no other power than that *delegated* to him by the Constitution, but I think the King envisaged this oath in the opposite sense. He saw in it the obligation to employ the authority that the Constitution conferred on him to maintain the Constitution and see that it was executed, but nothing more; and since, to his mind, this authority was distinct and different from that which he believed he held from God and his ancestors alone, for the exercise of this divine authority he did not regard himself as being bound by the engagements he was contracting in relation to his constitutional authority. I agree that this must appear paradoxical and even *Jesuitical,* but I believe that such was the King's manner of thinking. He regarded the Constitution as illegal because it was not he who had granted it, and he had not partici-

* The apartments of the Riding School, now destroyed, which adjoined the terrace of the Feuillants.
† This formula was prescribed by Article 4 of the first section of the second chapter of the Constitutional Act.

pated in its formulation; he believed that it was impossible to execute, and his only concern was to expose this *impossibility* by restricting the resources of government as much as he could and by adhering strictly to the letter of the Constitution. Thus, when a constitutional minister or any other agent of the executive power came to ask the King what were his orders, [he replied] "Apply the Constitution, those are my orders," [and] the minister retired, a little nonplused by the latitude of the royal instructions he had just received; and then some courtier coming up to the King's ear, said to him, smiling: "Your Majesty has given him a commission that I absolutely defy him to execute properly," to which the King replied, shrugging his shoulders: *"Now I have given him it, it is his affair and not mine."*

The King's intentions will be made even clearer by quoting his own words in his personal communications with the Assembly.

The King said in his message of September 13, 1791:*

"Gentlemen, I have examined with attention the constitutional instrument you have presented for my acceptance. I accept it and shall see that it is executed."

These are the first words, and they seem to me important: *The King accepts and will have it executed.* In the whole of the King's message, one searches in vain for signs of eagerness that the Constitution should take root; there are none at all. *The King will have it executed;* he says nothing more. In consequence, if—as the King did not doubt—his constitutional powers, applied literally but with ill grace, were insufficient to make the Constitution work and to prevent its fall, then consequently the King was no longer to blame if it were overthrown, and thus he was under the illusion that he could get rid of it without anyone being able to put the blame for it on him.

"I accept then the Constitution," he said further on, "I undertake to maintain it at home, to defend it against attacks from abroad, to use *all the means that it places in my power* to have it executed.† I declare that, being informed of the adherence that the vast majority of the people gives to the Constitution, I renounce my claim to have participated in this work, and that as I am responsible only to the nation, no one else has the right to complain when I make this renunciation."‡ (*The left wing of the Assembly and all the galleries rang with applause.*) "Nevertheless, I should be telling rather less than the truth if I said that I saw in the means of execution and administration all the energy necessary to impart direc-

---

* See *le Moniteur* for Wednesday, September 14, 1791.
† This specification of the means that the Constitution put in the power of the King seems to imply the exclusion of those that he could have personally.
‡ This bears some resemblance to what is called in English law a caveat, that is to say, an insurance against possible events. It was at once a protest against the violation of what King regarded as his right and a way of preparing to reassert it in the case of the Constitution's being overthrown.

tion to such a vast empire* and to preserve unity in all its parts; but since opinions are divided on these topics today, I consent to let *experience alone decide.* When I have honestly brought into play *all the resources that have been delivered to me, no reproach can be addressed to me;* and the nation, whose interests alone should serve as a guide, will deliver its verdict in the way reserved for it by the Constitution." (*Renewed applause.*) If the King had been able to express his whole mind, I think he would have added: "And I, too, will deliver my verdict then by the means I have received from God and my ancestors."

The same intentions are expressed anew in the speech the King pronounced on September 30, 1791, to the Constituent Assembly when he went to perform the closing [ceremony].† The following passage is to be found there:

Having *accepted* the Constitution *you have given* to the kingdom, I shall employ all that I have received from it in the way of force and resources to assure that the laws receive the respect and obedience which is their due."

It seems to me that nothing is more striking than the affectation with which the King repeats that he will only employ in the execution of the Constitution *the resources he has received from it;* and because he announces at the same time that these resources seemed insufficient to him, there can remain no doubt as to the result that he foresaw.

Immediately after this *séance royale,* the National Assembly, called the *Constituent,* was dissolved by its president (M. Thouret) in these terms: "The Constituent National Assembly declares that it has accomplished its mission and that all its sittings are over." This Assembly was replaced as from the following day, October 1, 1791, by what was called the *National Legislative Assembly* because it was the first legislature elected and assembled in accordance with the forms prescribed by the Constitution.

The Legislative Assembly was composed entirely of newly chosen members because the Constituent Assembly had decreed that none of its members could be reelected. It had also decreed that none of its members could accept a place in the ministry or any employment whatsoever in the King's gift until a period of four years had elapsed from the day it was dissolved. These exclusions could have been dictated by honorable motives of disinterestedness. Many people thought they were dictated by the mutual animosity of the various parties. Whatever the motives behind them, the result was disastrous because it excluded from the ministry

---

* The energy concerned here is the extent of royal power. The use of the word "empire" here is an example of the grandiloquence of the revolutionary jargon. It also takes up an older theme that France should be self-sufficient both economically and diplomatically. (The word was first used in the Middle Ages to stress that the King's sovereignty was not limited by the Pope.) All these senses are appropriate at this time of crisis.—ED.

† See *le Moniteur* for Sunday, October 2, 1791.

those whom it would have been desirable for the King to have been able to appoint. Given the state of affairs in France at the time, and people's state of mind, the King could scarcely expect to have any support other than that which he received from the members of the Constituent Assembly who had carried out the revision. For many reasons they had the most interest in defending their work and in supporting the Constitution; thus it would have been better if they had openly been the King's ministers, with all the advantages of the ministry and all the weight of ministerial responsibility, instead of being what in fact they were—secret ministers hiding behind the *ostensible ministers* for whose appointment they were nearly always responsible, but whom they were never able either to defend or support. No more than the members of the old Assembly were members of the new able to become ministers, with the result that the King's choice was infinitely restricted, and he could not strengthen his ministry with any prominent member either of the former or the current Assembly.

This new Assembly immediately divided into a *left and a right wing,* like the one that it replaced. The constitutionalists, who were then the supporters of the King and his ministers, positioned themselves on the right on the same benches where, in the first Assembly, those people had sat who gloried in the fact that they wanted no Constitution, and this was very bad tactics on their part. There was no one in the Legislative Assembly who professed opinions contrary to the Constitution; but the public, which too often judges only by appearances, confounded a man's place with his opinions. It must be admitted that it was all the easier to fall into this error because whatever the constitutional principles of those who sat on the right in the Legislative Assembly, their opinions were constantly being distorted by the necessity in which they had placed themselves of defending a Court whose conduct and intentions were in opposition with their own; and this same Court, always thankless, rejoiced in the power of representing them to the nation as apostates to the cause of liberty—a cause which the nation had won over that of despotism and absolute power. Thus, with its own hands the Court broke the sole instruments remaining in France to support and defend it.

To the *left* of the president sat other constitutionalists who, mistrusting the intentions of the Court, thought it necessary to take more precautions against it and to observe all its activities with great vigilance. These last sat in the lower portion of the left wing that was called *the Plain.* Further along, in the part of the chamber where the tiers of seats rose up very steeply and which in consequence was called *the Mountain,* sat men who became justly famous on account of their great talents and their misfortunes; they declared themselves to be *republicans,* and I think they would have preferred that form of government; but at the same time I think they would have made do with liberty under the Constitution, if the existence of the Court as it then was had not seemed to them incompatible with any form of liberty, and if it had not been impressed upon them that this Court was trying to deliver France into the hands of the foreign armies by paralyzing its means of defense. These men were those whom their opponents designated as *Brissotins,* from the name of Brissot de Warville (deputy for Paris to the Legislative Assembly and then deputy for the Department of Eure-et-Loire [Chartres] to the National Convention); but they are better known as the *Girondins,* because the Department of the Gironde [Bordeaux] had produced the majority of the talents who shone in their ranks, such as Guadet, Vergniaud, Gensonné, Ducos, Fonfrède, Grangeneuve, etc.

I think, then, that the majority of this Assembly accepted the Constitution and that if the King, for his part, had carried out a policy which frankly accepted the Constitution, it would have sustained him very effectively. In revolutions, more than at other times, there are circumstances that do not permit men to act in perfect conformity with their beliefs, and often one is lucky if one can prevent a little harm rather than effecting the good that one would have liked to do. It would be unfair to judge the opinions of the Legislative Assembly by its acts subsequent to the rising of August 10, 1792, because at that period it was deserted by half its members, and the current was too strong for those who remained to attempt to resist it, had they so desired. It is not that I am claiming to set myself up as the defender of the Legislative Assembly from the moment it was opened on October 4, 1791, till the rising of August 10; for on the contrary, I believe that several of its acts were unconstitutional, unjust, and impolitic and that, as with the Constituent Assembly, it constantly lacked foresight, a sense of proportion, and dignity. But I think it is very difficult to judge its conduct fairly and with impartiality because of the difficult and alarming circumstances in which it found itself placed. And with how many reefs was it not in fact surrounded? In Paris it was placed between the Court and the Jacobins; it served as a kind of battleground for the two parties, and yet I think that the majority did not want either party to win a total victory. It wished to contain them by putting them in balance. It would have liked the Constitution to have been a success, which is precisely what the Court did not want, as I have more than once observed and I think I have demonstrated. The result of this was that all the Court's proceedings bore the stamp of duplicity that the Jacobins of the day easily unmasked before the public.

The Jacobin Assembly, which continued to call itself the Society for the Friends of the Constitution, was then fulfilling the functions of a *Tribune of the people* in a most active and formidable manner. It was already far removed from what it had been when I was introduced there in October 1790.

The Feuillants's schism, which had momentarily shaken it, had given it new strength instead of weakening it, and it was composed of about three to four thousand individuals, not counting the numerous spectators who filled the vast galleries open to the public, where people grabbed seats for themselves. There were scarcely any other members of the Legislative Assembly who frequented the Jacobins at the time but the deputies from the Gironde. They exercised their eloquence in this society where they disputed the supremacy with Robespierre, Danton, and the other leaders of the *Cordelier Party,* the same who later became the leaders of the *Mountain* in the National Convention and who sent the *Girondins* to the scaffold.

The functions of *tribune of the people* which the Jacobin Assembly had arrogated to itself were at the time only too easy to fulfill, and it was impossible for the nation and the Legislative Assembly to ignore the mass of evidence that was every day presented to them of the duplicity in the Court's conduct, of the hatred it bore for the very Constitution that it claimed it wished to defend, and of its constant efforts to render France powerless to resist the invasion that the foreign Powers, in concert with this same Court and the *émigrés,* were preparing against her. In vain the Assembly sought in the Constitutional Act for means to remedy this ill and to force the executive power* to act in good faith in accordance with the Constitution, and above all to take efficacious measures to prevent the invasion of France or, if it became impossible to prevent it, to resist and repel it. The executive power likewise dug itself in behind the Constitution and claimed that there was nothing it could do. This inactivity caused the Jacobins and the papers to fulminate—in a word, it inflamed public opinion; the Assembly took fright, the King dismissed his ministers and took others who neither did nor could do any better than their predecessors, and the only reactions that these repeated jolts produced at Court were simply a smile of satisfaction followed by the usual comment that the *Constitution would never be able to work.* But in the Assembly, in the nation, and in the army, whose strength was already at two hundred and forty thousand effectives (including the new levies of National Volunteers), hopes based on deceptive appearances gave way to indignation, and indignation to fury as they saw France delivered up defenseless to the invasion of the foreign and *émigré* armies, who scarcely dissimulated their plans for vengeance and executions. It is incontestable that nothing was more difficult than the conduct of a National Assembly in such circumstances, since it was clear that it could not save the Constitution by itself; and consequently it fell into the dreadful uncertainty of seeing that it would necessarily be violated and of not knowing what measures to adopt to stamp out anarchy, to repress violence at home, and finally to save France and defend her national independence against foreign invasion. I believe that to resolve this problem exceeded human wisdom.

The hope that had been conceived that the acceptance of the Constitu-

* We should simply say the executive, but in the eighteenth century people wanted to stress the importance of the separation of powers arising, largely, from a misunderstanding of the English system of government.—ED.

tion would determine the *émigrés* to return to France had evaporated. Instead of breaking up, their assemblies constantly continued to swell on all the frontiers; they were already armed and put in regiments; they performed military service and wore the white cockade. The King made a proclamation on October 14, 1791, in which *he invited all the émigrés to return to France.* As this measure also had no effect, the Legislative Assembly passed a decree on October 28, 1791, requiring, in the terms of the Constitution, *Louis Stanislas Xavier, French Prince* (that was the constitutional title of Monsieur, Comte de Provence) to return to the kingdom within two months or forfeit his contingent rights to the Regency if he had not returned within the time stated. The King gave his assent to the decree, and in dispatching it he wrote to both of his brothers to engage them to return, which they refused in letters that were printed at the time and are to be found in back numbers of *le Moniteur.**

As this decree and the King's letters made no change in the *émigrés'* attitude, the Assembly thought that it should take a tougher line with them. On November 9, 1791, it passed a decree† against them declaring that Frenchmen assembled outside the frontiers of the kingdom would hitherto be suspected of conspiring against France,‡ and if they were still in a state of assembly on January 1, 1792, proceedings would be taken against them as being guilty of conspiracy against France, and they would be punished by death. The same decree declared that their goods would be sequestered if they did not return, as would the income, for life, of those condemned in their absence, except for the rights of wives, children, and creditors. The King found this decree unconstitutional, and I think he was right. He visited it with the royal veto in the sitting of December 12, 1791; but as the public was already too irritated not to suspect that the King's main object in this action was to paralyze a measure that could put the enemies of the Constitution off their stride, the King felt the necessity of accompanying this veto with some initiative that would serve him as an excuse and calm the public for the moment. On the same day he published a proclamation in which he exhorted the *émigrés* once more to break up their concentrations and return to France;§ in terms remarkable enough to be worth quoting, he informed them of the veto he had just appended to the decree against them. He told them "that those who

* See *le Moniteur* for Tuesday, December 13, 1791, no. 347.
† See *le Moniteur* for November 16, 1791, no. 320.
‡ An early example of what was to be commonplace in the period of the Terror. The argument was that in a time of national crisis measures could be taken against people merely suspected of crimes, though nothing had been proved. Admittedly these measures were usually of a preventive nature, e.g., house arrest. As here, whole categories of people were suspect; later on it sufficed merely to *be* a nobleman to be prevented from living in Paris. This is possibly what Louis-Philippe means when he says that he agreed with the King in considering these measures unconstitutional or, as we would say, not in accordance with the rule of law.—ED.
§ See *le Moniteur* for Monday, November 14, 1791, no. 318.

supposed that he had another will from the one he had expressed publicly and who based their conduct and their hopes on such an error would be strangely deceived; whatever pretext they might have had with which to cloak their conduct, there no longer existed any; that in exercising his prerogative in connection with punitive measures against them, he was giving them a proof of his liberty that they could neither disregard nor contradict; and that to doubt the sincerity of his resolutions when they should be convinced of his freedom would be to do him an injury." And further on the King said "that people had no right to indict the disturbances in their country when by collusive absence and suspect assemblies they were working to foment anxiety and agitation in its midst; that they had no right to lament that the laws were not executed and that the government was feeble when they were giving an example of disobedience themselves and were refusing to recognize as binding the combined will of the nation and its King."

None of these initiatives had any more effect than the preceding ones: The *émigrés* did not return, their assemblies continued, and their hostile attitude and their menaces, far from weakening, merely increased with every new day. French merchants and travelers could no longer appear outside France—above all in the Rhineland, which was the center of the Emigration—without being exposed to snubs and insults. A Frenchman who had not emigrated, in the eyes of those who had, passed for a revolutionary and an enemy of the King and monarchy. The *émigrés* were too carried away by their feelings to realize the drawbacks there were for themselves in assuming this right of surveillance in foreign countries and to perceive that by this conduct they were making a tacit avowal that all those who had not emigrated—that is to say, nearly the whole nation— did not share their opinions.

It was impossible that such a state of affairs should not daily increase the exasperation that was already general in France, and on November 29, 1791, the Legislative Assembly decreed that a message be presented to the King* requiring him to take efficacious measures against the *émigré* concentrations and the invasions with which France was threatened on all sides: "Sire," the Assembly said in this address which was drawn up and presented to the King by M. de Vaublanc, "it is for you to cause these hostile preparations, these threats of invasion, to cease . . . what ambassador has adopted the necessary tone in your name? None. . . . Sire, your interest, your dignity, the greatness of an outraged nation require of you a language different from that of diplomacy. The nation expects of you strong representations in the circles† of the Upper and Lower Rhineland, to the Electors of Trier and Mainz, and to the Bishop of Speyer. Let

* See *le Moniteur* for Thursday and Friday, December 1 and 2, 1791, nos. 335 and 336.
† The divisions of the Holy Roman Empire were called circles.—ED.

them be such that the *émigré* hordes will at once be dissipated. Lay down a short period of time after which no dilatory reply will be received; let your declaration be backed up by movements of troops that are entrusted to you, and let the nation know who are its friends and who its enemies. We will recognize the defender of the Constitution in this striking initiative. Thus you will ensure the tranquillity of the Empire that is inseparable from your own, etc."

At the time the King made only a trivial reply, and it was not until December 14, that is to say, more than a fortnight after the Assembly's message, that the King decided to proceed there and in their midst to pronounce a speech* that made a tremendous impression, which would have been even greater had the measures he announced been taken up with the wholeheartedness and vigor this speech might have led one to expect. I shall quote the main passages from it.

The King said to the Assembly: "You desire that I make it known to the neighboring Princes, who protect these assemblies in contravention of the rules of good neighborliness and of the principles of the law of nations, that the French nation cannot any longer tolerate this lack of respect and this covert hostility.

"Finally, you have given me to understand that the nation is swept along by a general movement and that the cry of all Frenchmen is *Better war than a ruinous and humiliating patience* . . .

. . . .

"The Emperor (Leopold) has performed what was to be expected of a faithful ally by forbidding and dispersing all assemblies in his dominions. The measures I have taken in relation to some of the other Princes have not met with the same success: The replies to my requests were scarcely measured in their language. These unjust refusals prompt resolutions of another kind. The nation has declared its will; you have brought it together; you have weighed its consequences and expressed it to me by your message. Gentlemen, you have not forestalled me: Representing, as I do, the people, its injury has touched me, and I shall communicate to you the resolution I have adopted to such reparation.

"I am having the Elector of Trier† told that if before January 15 he has not brought to an end all concentrations and all hostile posturings on the part of Frenchmen who have taken refuge there, I shall no longer regard him as anything but an enemy of France." (*Repeated applause broke out, accompanied by shouts of "Long live the King!"*) "I shall make a similar declaration to all those who likewise countenance assemblies that disturb the tranquillity of the kingdom, and while guaranteeing

---

* See *le Moniteur* for Friday, December 16, 1791, no. 350, where the King's speech is reported.

† The Elector of Trier was a Prince of Saxony, brother of Madame la Dauphine, the mother of Louis XVI and his brothers.

foreigners all the protection they have a right to expect from our laws, I will have a perfect right to require that such outrages as Frenchmen may have received be promptly and fully made good. (*Applause.*)

. . . .

"At the same time I am adopting the military measures best calculated to ensure that these declarations are respected. (*Applause.*)

"And if they are not heeded, then, gentlemen, I shall be left with no alternative than to declare war—war, which a people who have solemnly renounced conquests makes only when forced to it, but which a valiant and free nation does not flinch from when its own security, when honor, requires it. (*Renewed applause.*)

"I will faithfully preserve the trust of the Constitution inviolate, and no consideration will have power to persuade me to allow it to suffer harm. Those who observe the proceedings of the government attentively, though without ill will, must recognize that I never deviate from constitutional rectitude and that I am profoundly aware how fine it is to be King of a free people." (*Applause was kept up for several minutes. Several . . . voices could be heard in the Assembly and in the galleries shouting "Long live the King of the French!"*)

It would have been easy for the King to take advantage of this enthusiasm by adopting a stance that would have been equally advantageous for France and for himself if he had wanted to act in this sense; but such was not his desire. The Assembly's message of Nobember 29, the sensation that had been produced on December 12 by his appending the veto to the decree on the *émigrés,* and the fear that the general exasperation instilled in him had decided him to take this initiative of December 14, which, to be of use to him, would have had to have been dictated by other motives and made with other objectives. It would have been necessary for the King to recognize that when so many circumstances combined to warn France of the danger that threatened her, that when the Treaty of Pillnitz* was in all the papers and its objective consequently known by everyone, it was impossible that there should not develop in the French nation a strong desire to defend its independence, to oppose any violation of its territory, and, in a word, to repel the aggression of the foreign Powers and the *émigrés.* The King's duty, as well as his true interest, was to carry out wholeheartedly what he announced in his speech. Head of state, no matter what his title, his duty was to defend it and to oppose invasion by foreigners; he had therefore to put himself at the head of the national movement and put off to another time the paltry question of determining whether he exercised a greater or lesser part of the power in France, whether he reigned there in his capacity of *King of the French by the Grace of God and the Constitution*

* See *le Moniteur* for September 23, 1792, no. 267.

*of the State** or whether it should be as *King of France and Navarre*† and purely and simply by the *Grace of God* without there being any *constitutional law* in the State,‡ which at that time was the *utopia* of the *émigrés* and many other Courts.

On December 7, in the interval between the Assembly's message to the King (on November 27) and the King's speech to the Assembly (on December 14), the Minister of War had been changed, and Comte Louis de Narbonne, friend of M. de La Fayette and designated by him for this ministry, had been appointed, as possessing more energy and dispatch than M. Duportail. Indeed, M. de Narbonne lost no time in taking more decided measures than those of his predecessor. On December 14, 1791, after the King had left the Assembly and while it was still thoroughly electrified§ by the speech it had just heard, M. de Narbonne announced‖ "that the King had just ordered him to assemble a hundred and fifty thousand men on the borders within a month; that he was going to leave to inspect the state of the army and of the fortress towns; that he would say to the officers that if former preconceptions and a too uncritical love for their King had possibly excused their conduct for a time, nevertheless the word *treason* was not in any language, etc." M. de Narbonne added "that three armies had seemed necessary and that as the nation marked out MM. de Rochambeau, Luckner, and La Fayette to command them, the King had given them the commands."

These three armies were to be known as the *armies of the North, of the Center, and of the Rhine.* That of *the North* was to remain under M. de Rochambeau, whose command was restricted to that portion of the frontier stretching from Dunkirk to Maubeuge inclusively. The command of *the Army of the Center* from Philippeville and Givet to Bitche was given to M. de La Fayette, and that of *the Army of the Rhine* from Landau to Huningue, to M. de Luckner. At the same time *the Army of the South* was formed to defend the frontier from Geneva to Nice. Command of it was given to M. de Wittgenstein.

Informing the Assembly of this nomination of three commanders in

---

* This was the formula in the Constitution of 1791.

† This had been the title borne by the French Kings since Henri IV, King of Navarre, won his way to the French throne.—ED.

‡ Louis-Philippe must be taken to be referring to the specific Constitution of 1791 and not public law in general. The *émigrés,* of course, recognized the existence of a constitution comprised of the "fundamental" laws of the kingdom and the "capitularies" or contracts that the various provinces had made or could be supposed to have made when being incorporated into France. These "laws" all tended to limit royal absolutism, which was, in fact, defended by scarcely anyone but a few aging Crown lawyers like Calonne.—ED.

§ A word very much in vogue during the Revolution, following Benjamin Franklin's experiments.—ED.

‖ See *le Moniteur* for December 16, 1791, no. 350.

165

chief, M. de Narbonne asked for and obtained the restoration of the rank or dignity of Marshal of France, which had been abolished as part of the reorganization of the army, and the King immediately nominated MM. de Rochambeau and Luckner as Marshals of France.*

M. de Narbonne spoke in the Assembly with much grace and even eloquence. He promised lofty and fine-sounding measures, but he was not as fortunate in the realization of his promises. Perhaps it did not depend upon him to fulfill them; what is certain is that the hundred and fifty thousand men who were meant to be mobilized immediately were not, and that at the end of the month prescribed by the King we were scarcely further advanced than before.

The greater the enthusiasm at the time of the King's speech, the greater the discontent when it was seen that none of his promises had been carried out. It is incontestable that the agents of the executive power at this time acted with a dilatoriness and a bad faith that paralyzed everything. In general they made no secret of their opinion that any defense would be in vain, since France could not, according to them, resist the storm that was about to break on her; and they were scarcely better at hiding their desire that she should succumb. On all sides, commanders and officers were to be seen leaving one after the other, to swell the *émigré* concentrations; and even when they did not leave, their opinions and conversation caused even more irritation through the fear in France that they would keep up a secret correspondence with the *émigrés* and the foreigners and that they would hand over our strongholds and our arsenals. The declarations of the *émigrés,* their proclamations and manifestos, arrived in France from all sides. All these writings were penned with unbelievable ferocity, both in substance and in form. The only talk was of vengeance, punishment, and executions, and people whose only hope of accomplishing projects as unworthy as they were absurd lay in the measure of support that the foreign Powers thought it was in their own interest to grant them, claimed that they were dealing mercifully with the French nation by confining themselves to decimating it. In their writings, the *émigrés* always spoke *in the name of the King,* and they lost no opportunity of assuring the French nation and Europe that the sentiments expressed in these writings were those that the King would have professed openly if he had been free to express himself without constraint. Consequently, it was at this time that in the clubs and the papers, people began to draw the nation's attention to Article 6 of the first section of the second chapter of the Constitutional Act, which declared that the *King would forfeit the throne* in the eventuality of his not categorically opposing

---

* They proceeded to Metz, where M. de La Fayette had his headquarters, to receive the [Marshal's] *bâton* from the hands of M. de Narbonne. I was then at Valenciennes, and when M. de Rochambeau returned from Metz I went to congratulate him and asked him how he felt after his journey. "Ah, my dear Prince," he replied, "you see an old marshal worn out with fatigue."

attempts that might be made in his name to destroy the Constitution.*

The nation's increasing mistrust of the King and his ministers made their position more difficult each day and encouraged the Legislative Assembly's encroachments on the executive power. Like the Constituent Assembly, it contained a large number of committees, named after the matters with which they had been entrusted, and each exercised a surveillance over the government department whose name they bore. It was perfectly natural that the Assembly should seek to be informed in its labors by the preliminary discussions of its committees; but it would have been necessary for the Assembly to limit their number to the number of objects of which, constitutionally and legally, it could and should have taken cognizance and, at the same time, for it to reject any proposal tending to involve it in the exercise of functions that the Constitution had not attributed to it and that belonged to the executive power. This moderation, this wise restraint, would have been the true practice of what, as I explained earlier, the English call in their language "forbearance," that is to say, *the voluntary abstention from doing what one knows to be in one's power but which, nevertheless, one knows one should not do;* but perhaps it is asking too much of men in general to hope that they should be so able to appreciate their true interests as to confine themselves voluntarily to these terms of reference and only do what can truly be useful. The Legislative Assembly did not possess this merit. It listened with pleasure to all the reports these committees saw fit to make to it on matters that were none of its business and that exceeded the limits of its competence; it made no scruple about interfering by means of its decrees in all the measures of the executive power. The ministers of the King saw themselves continuously reduced to being merely the secretaries of the Assembly's committees. The King and his Court, who detested them, took a secret pleasure in their humiliation and merely regarded this as an additional proof that the *Constitution could never work.* They did not realize that it was the merited distrust they inspired in the nation that gave the Assembly reasons or pretexts for these continual encroachments, and that this progressive degradation and whittling away of the King's constitutional authority concentrated the government in the Assembly and established, at least *de facto,* a republican system of government. Moreover, it was perhaps difficult for it to be otherwise, since the King did not wish to govern and thought it advantageous to reduce himself voluntarily to being simply (as one of the popular orators of the day had it) *a political superfluity who presented the greatest of dangers for liberty without possessing any utility, still less appeal.*

Among the committees formed by the Assembly, there was one called

* This article is couched in the following terms:

"If the King puts himself at the head of an army and directs its forces against the nation, or if he does not explicitly countermand such an enterprise carried out in his name, he shall be deemed to have abdicated."

the Diplomatic Committee; one would have thought that nothing would have been more disapproved of by the public than the direct influence of a committee of the Legislative Assembly on that branch of the executive power that was the most alien to the Assembly's functions; however, as it was generally believed at the time that the King was in collusion with the foreign Powers to let their armies reach Paris and to overthrow the Constitution with their assistance, it is certain that the Assembly was in a manner supported in this encroachment by the public, who merely saw in it a salutary precaution. As soon as the Minister of Foreign Affairs made any communication to the Assembly, it passed it on to its Diplomatic Committee for examination before taking any decision. The Minister would be summoned straightaway and questions put to him to which he was obliged to reply, because in the committee, unlike in the Assembly, he could not base his silence on the fear and danger of publicity.

M. Delessart was then Minister of Foreign Affairs. He was the subject of lively attacks in the Assembly, as well as in the Jacobins and among the public, on account of the manner in which he was conducting France's negotiations with the foreign Powers. These were very complicated in themselves, and new circumstances increased their difficulty at every moment. I shall not undertake to give a detailed consideration of them here, but I must give a glimpse.

The original object, real or pretended, of the Powers' complaints was the rights of the Princes of the Empire* in Alsace and Lorraine. These rights were abolished by the Constitution or by the decrees of the Assembly on feudal dues, which had received the royal assent. France wanted to indemnify the Princes who had possessions in these provinces and redeem the rights that had been suppressed. A few of these Princes were perfectly willing to enter into negotiations and allow themselves to be bought out. Others, on the contrary, took the matter to the Diet of the Empire and to the Emperor of Germany (Leopold), as head of the Germanic Federation, so as to force France to respect the treaties guaranteeing their possessions in Alsace and Lorraine.

The second point of grievance was the incorporation† of Avignon and the County Venaissin into France; but since here again France consented to enter into arrangements with the Pope for financial indemnity, it is probable that it would have been easy to conclude these negotiations if the European Powers had not wanted to retain pretexts for a rupture.

To these negotiations were joined the complaints of France relative to the protection accorded to the French *émigrés* and to the encouragement given to their armament and their hostile preparations.

---

* When these German territories were annexed by France—Alsace in 1648, and Lorraine, finally, in 1738—the rights, feudal and otherwise, of German Princes with property in these provinces had been guaranteed by treaty.—ED.

† Avignon had, since the fourteenth century, been a papal enclave in France. It was annexed in September 1791.—ED.

The declaration that the King had made to some of the German Princes, and in particular to the Elector of Trier, in accordance with his announcement to the Legislative Assembly of December 14, 1791, determined the Emperor Leopold to order Marshal Bender, who had the command in the Low Countries—which were Austrian at the time—to look to the defense of the Electorate of Trier and to protect it with his troops in case of a French attack, provided that the Elector adopted the same police regulations in relation to the French *émigrés* obtained in the Austrian territories. This condition was all the easier to fulfill because it amounted to nothing; and it was impossible that France should be satisfied with it, since the police regulations in the Austrian territories merely obliged the *émigrés* to submit to a few restraints that were more apparent than real and that did not prevent them from forming troop concentrations there and from doing just about what they pleased. The Elector of Trier promised to conform to the Emperor's request, and at the same time he himself declared that the ice and the rigors of winter prevented the *émigré* Princes from dispersing their troops and artillery* before the better weather.

M. Delessart communicated these imaginary impossibilities to the Assembly, and no one was fooled by them. It was but too well known throughout France that the notes of M. Delessart and the King's declaration of December 14 were objects of jest and sarcasm in the German Courts and among the *émigrés*. Their concentrations, far from dispersing, were becoming more and more menacing and hostile. The Princes concluded agreements with various people, among others with a Prince of Hohenlohe, to raise regiments that were to remain in the pay of France after the Counterrevolution had been effected. It was asked how the Princes found the means to pay for such enormous expenses, and there is no doubt that a part they procured by the considerable debts they contracted. I have already spoken of the third resource resulting from the fabrication of *forged assignats*. It was said that the King also had contributed to these expenses, but I do not believe that the King effected any payment to the *émigrés* after July 1, 1791, that is to say, after the period when he accepted the Constitution and in public declarations invited the *émigrés* to return. I base my opinion on the accounts of the Civil List, which were printed at the end of 1792 and establish that until July 1791 the King had paid the [members of his] Bodyguard at Coblenz and that at this period he had ceased to do so.

The replies of the Princes of the Empire to the King's declaration, as well as the notes from the Court of Vienna supporting them, could leave no doubt that the Powers would not defer to any remonstrances and that the attack on France was resolved. However, the current ministers of the day seemed to believe that it would still be possible for them to prevent it, and of this they tried to persuade the Assembly. But it was unlikely that

* It is admitted in the following notes that they had no artillery.

the Assembly would retain such a hope when it was given cognizance of the documents they had to communicate to it. It was in the sitting of December 31, 1791,* that M. Delessart went to make these dangerous confidences and presented the official note dated December 21, 1791, from Prince Kaunitz, Chancellor of the Empire,† to the Marquis de Noailles (later Duc de Noailles), who had continued to be France's ambassador to Vienna during the Revolution. The Emperor informed the King in this note of the orders he had given Marshal Bender for the protection of the Electorate of Trier. He added‡ that "he was too strongly attached to the King not to desire to avoid the shocks that would inevitably result from the execution of the measures which would have to be taken, whether by the states and head of the Empire *or the other sovereigns acting in concert for the maintenance of public tranquillity and for the honor of their Crowns.*"

This last phrase amounted to an admission of the existence of a Coalition of all the sovereigns of Europe to repress the French Revolution and to send their armies to Paris to overthrow the Constitution and restore the *Ancien Régime.* This notification on the part of the Emperor (Leopold) had an effect all the more harmful because the King had told the Assembly a fortnight previously: "The Emperor (Leopold) has carried out what ought to be expected of a loyal ally"; and it was this *loyal ally* who, in reply to the King's request to employ his good offices to determine the Elector of Trier to disperse the *émigrés,* ordered his generals to give him the most efficacious aid and to protect the Electorate with Austrian troops in case of attack. Again it was this *loyal ally* who announced a *Concert of Sovereigns for the maintenance of* public tranquillity and for the honor of their Crowns. It would be rather interesting to know whether the King, when he made his declaration to the Elector of Trier, had been informed that this Prince would be supported by Austria. I know almost for a certainty that the King, and above all the Queen, wanted France herself to be the one that provoked war, to make sure that nothing would prevent its outbreak and their profiting from the result they regarded as certain, without any likelihood of being held responsible. M. de La Fayette, MM. de Lameth, the ministers of the day, and their friends shared the Court's opinion about the impossibility that France would not be crushed in the struggle, but this opinion led them to a standpoint in opposition to the secret standpoint of the King and Queen. They were opposed to a declaration of war by France and wished to confine themselves to a defensive policy that probably would have opened the way to

* See *le Moniteur* for January 1, 1792, no. 1.
† Strictly, Kaunitz was Chancellor of Austria and Bohemia, and not of the Holy Roman Empire.—ED.
‡ See the report of the Diplomatic Committee in the sitting of January 14, 1792, in *le Moniteur* for the following day, no. 15.

the capital to the foreign armies and that seems to me to have been one of the main reasons for their fall.*

The Jacobins, on the other hand, and the vast majority of those who had favored the Revolution were burning for war and demanded its declaration with a sort of fury. It is rather remarkable, however, that Robespierre, almost alone, opposed it; and it was over this issue that he came out against Brissot, who, like the Girondins,† was decidedly in favor of war.

The King, foreseeing the effect of the communication that M. Delessart was to make to the Assembly, had written at the same time to the president to show his astonishment at the note from Austria and give an assurance that he would continue with his measures against the Elector of Trier unless the *émigré* concentrations were *effectively and really dispersed*.‡

The very next day, January 1, 1792, a decree was passed unanimously by the Legislative Assembly arraigning the two Princes who were the King's brothers, and M. le Prince de Condé.§

On January 14, 1792, the same Assembly, again unanimously, "declared|| that any agent of the executive power, and any Frenchman who took any part directly or indirectly in a Congress whose object was to obtain the modification of the French Constitution, would be pronounced infamous, traitors to the Fatherland, etc." At the same time it invited the King to make known to all the European Powers, in the name of the French nation, that, "resolved to maintain its Constitution in its entirety or perish with it, it would regard as an enemy any Prince who wished to damage it."

This decree was taken to the King by a deputation and received the royal assent the same evening.

Meanwhile, the Assembly had received the report of its Diplomatic Committee on the dispatch of the Emperor, and the public had learned from this report about a quantity of documents that, although official, had never officially been communicated to the French government because they were all directed against it. These documents consisted of treaties, private conventions, circulars, rescripts, conclusions, etc., and other acts that under the various categories of the old diplomacy uniformly proved that the foreign Powers were resolved to wage war with France and to

---

* The Feuillant ministry was replaced by one of Girondin complexion in March 1792.—ED.

† It is not clear whether Louis-Philippe is trying to differentiate Brissot from those we normally refer to as the Girondins. The latter were usually referred to as Brissotins at the time, though there are examples of the later usage.—ED.

‡ See *le Moniteur* for January 1, 1792.

§ See *le Moniteur* for January 2, 1792.

|| See *le Moniteur* for January 15, 1792.

invade her so as to overthrow the Constitution, etc. The report that M. Koch made on this subject, in the name of the Diplomatic Committee, gave rise to very long and very heated debates, in the course of which nearly all the orators of the Assembly spoke in succession.

M. Delessart tried hard to calm spirits. He took the news he received to the Assembly to prove that the steps the Emperor had taken in respect of the Elector of Trier had been positive; and despite the snow, the ice, and the various obstacles that the Elector had at first regarded as insurmountable, all the *émigré* troop concentrations had finally left the Electorate. In fact they had not gone far. For form's sake, a few companies of *émigrés* had been sent outside the Electorate, and all they had done was to cross the Rhine and go into quarters in the territories of the Princes of Nassau; but the Bodyguard had remained at Coblenz as the Princes' guard, and all the *émigrés* who were not armed (but who soon could be) remained, fully organized, in the Electorate. Recourse had been had to the same subterfuges in the Upper Rhine. M. Delessart drew the conclusion that there was no further risk of danger here and that one could continue to negotiate on the other subjects. But the majority of the Assembly, and of the public, did not share this opinion and saw nothing substantive in these measures. M. Delessart wanted to give the Assembly the impression that he could secure the neutrality of the Court of Vienna. I do not know if this was possible, though I think not; but the manner in which M. Delessart conducted these negotiations led many people to think that he was betraying the cause he was supposed to be serving, and that he wanted to gain time to prevent France from attacking her neighbors before the Powers were ready to begin the execution of their projects.

Consequently, his efforts were useless, and on January 25, 1792, the Assembly decreed* "that the King should be invited to ask the Emperor whether he intended to live in peace and good understanding with the French nation, and whether he renounced all treaties or conventions directed against the sovereignty, the independence, and the safety of the nation, declaring to him at the same time that unless he gave the nation, before March 1 next, full and entire satisfaction on the above-mentioned points, his silence or any evasive or dilatory reply would be regarded as a declaration of war."

The King replied to the Assembly in a message dated January 28, 1792,† and reproached it with having interfered with matters that concerned him alone. He also complained of the form, which was in fact offensive to the Emperor, and he assured the Assembly that a fortnight before he had asked the Emperor for a categorical statement about the main points contained in the Assembly's demand.

The whole month of February went by without notification of the Emperor's reply. Finally, on March 1 M. Delessart communicated to the

* See *le Moniteur* for January 26, 1792.
† See *le Moniteur* for January 29, 1792.

Assembly* his dispatch of January 21, the official notes in which Prince Kaunitz had replied to him in the name of the Emperor Leopold, and a note from Count von Goltz, the Prussian minister at Paris, "which recalled that he had already made it known that an invasion by French troops of Imperial territory would be regarded as a declaration of war by the Germanic Body and that consequently His Prussian Majesty could not but oppose it with all his forces, in conjunction with his Imperial Majesty"; and M. de Goltz added that "Prince Kaunitz's notes contained a statement of the principles on which the Courts of Vienna and Berlin were in perfect agreement."†

These notes of Prince Kaunitz are very long. They are to be found in *le Moniteur*.‡

It seems that the principal object was to throw the blame for the provocation of war back onto France, and to represent the other Powers as being forced to defend themselves and to curb the attacks to which the King was exposed in France, as well as the revolutionary and republican principles that appeared to be dominant there.

Prince Kaunitz admitted the formation of the *Concert* of Powers and declared that the execution of the measures for which it provided was only suspended. This concert, Prince Kaunitz said, had been proposed by the Emperor to the other sovereigns after the arrest of the King at Varennes in the month of July 1791, in the form of a declaration defining its objectives, which I shall give.§

"All the sovereigns regard the cause of the Most Christian King‖ as their own.

"They demand that this Prince and his family be immediately placed in complete freedom by granting them the power to proceed wherever they think best, and they claim for all these royal personages the inviolability and the respect that natural and human law requires of subjects toward their Princes.

"They would unite to avenge in the most striking manner all subsequent attempts whatsoever that might be committed or allowed against the liberty, honor, and safety of the King, the Queen, and the Royal Family.

"Finally, the only constitutional laws that they will recognize as legitimately established in France will be those invested with the voluntary consent of the King in the enjoyment of complete freedom; but in the opposite case they will employ, in concert, all the means in their power to

* See *le Moniteur* for March 2, 1792.
† See *le Moniteur* for March 3, 1792.
‡ See *le Moniteur* for March 3, 1792, no. 63.
§ See *le Moniteur* for March 3, 1792, no. 63, in the second article, explanations about the Concert of Powers.
‖ The title which the Pope had conferred on the French King in the sixteenth century and by which he was known in diplomatic language.—ED.

put an end to the scandal of a usurpation of power bearing the character of an open revolt whose baleful example it behooves all the governments of Europe to suppress."

The [King's] acceptance of the Constitution had determined [the Powers] to suspend the execution of the measures for which this concert provided, but the state of affairs in France presented them too many grounds for anxiety for them not to keep the concert in existence and hold themselves *in readiness to act when they considered that circumstances imposed on them their duty.*

Such was the sense of Prince Kaunitz's explanation on the subject of the *Concert of Powers to maintain the honor and dignity of the Crowned heads.*

There was another, very long explanation that did not seem any more satisfactory on the subject of the orders given to Marshal Bender and of those relative to the *émigrés* and their armaments, matters with which Prince Kaunitz considered France ought not to have concerned herself. According to him, "all Europe was convinced, like the Emperor, that these people, known by the name of the Jacobin party, had wished to incite the nation first to take up arms and then to make a rupture with the Emperor; and that having made the assemblies in the territories of Trier the pretext for the former, they were now seeking to bring about these pretexts for war by demanding explanations from His Imperial Majesty in such a manner, and with such attendant circumstances, as were openly calculated to make it difficult for this Prince to reconcile, in his replies, the pacific and amicable intentions with which he was animated with the feeling that his dignity had been wounded and his repose disturbed by the fruits of their maneuvers."

Later on Prince Kaunitz says again: "The Emperor believes he owes it to the well-being of France and of the whole of Europe, as well as being authorized thereto by the provocations and the dangerous intrigues of the Jacobin party, to unmask and denounce publicly this pernicious sect as the enemies of the Most Christian King and of the fundamental laws of the present Constitution and as disturbers of the peace. Will the illegal ascendancy of this sect win the day against justice, truth, and the welfare of the nation? This is the question to which all the others are reduced. Whatever the result, the cause of the Emperor is that of all the Powers."

After all these documents had been read to the Assembly, M. Delessart informed it that as the Emperor had moved a detachment of thirty thousand men from Bohemia to reinforce his armies in Brisgau, Luxembourg, and especially in the Low Countries, where he already had about fifty thousand men, at any moment there would be ninety thousand Austrians on the frontiers of France. At this period people were not yet used to the large armies that were seen later, so that this concentration of ninety thousand men seemed very considerable.

At the same time M. Delessart communicated his reply to the nobles of

Austria. In this reply the King requested the Emperor* "to bring to an end the Concert of Powers; he offered him, or rather renewed, the assurance of concord and peace; he asked him for a similar declaration of his sentiments and intentions; he asked that it should be prompt, frank, and explicit."

So far so good, and M. Delessart's reply could not have been either different or better, but the conclusion did not seem to correspond to the beginning. Here it is:

"As a token of loyalty to one another, the King promised that as soon as the Emperor undertook to cause all preparations for war in his territories to cease and to restore his military forces in the Low Countries and Brisgau to the same footing as on April 1, 1791, His Majesty would likewise cease all preparations and reduce the French troops in the frontier departments to the usual state of garrisons.

. . . .

"Finally, the ambassador was instructed to observe that after so loyal and explicit an invitation, the King could only interpret a reply that was not in the same spirit as a desire to prolong a situation in which France neither would nor could any longer remain."

The Assembly sent all these documents for examination by its Diplomatic Committee before allowing a discussion of them, but an immediate impression was formed of the minister's reply, and it was not favorable. Indeed, this reply no more conformed to what the Austrian notes and the situation seemed imperiously to dictate than to the King's declarations on several previous occasions. Was it politic, was it fitting, that after reading these hostile notes, the minister of the King should announce at the same time that, on the one hand, *the Austrian armies were on the march,* and, on the other, that he was instructing the French ambassador to Vienna *to propose even a conditional disarmament?* It was certainly not what France expected or had a right to expect, above all from the King and from those same ministers who had surrounded him on the night of December 14, 1791, when he had declared† "that he was taking the military measures most appropriate to make his declarations respected, and that if they were not heeded it would only remain to him to declare *war;* war, which a people who have solemnly renounced conquests never makes except through necessity, but which a generous and free nation knows how to undertake when its own security, when honor, commands it." Assuredly it was *war* that the honor and security of the nation required, after receiving the communications from the Court of Vienna whose drift I have just indicated. They show conclusively the hostile intentions of this Court and the existence of a Coalition of Powers that only awaited the end of their preparations to attack France. It is note-

* See *le Moniteur* for March 3, 1792, no. 63.
† See above, page 163.

worthy that the same day that the Court of Vienna dispatched these official notes, it signed a convention with the Court of Berlin, which I give here in its entirety because I think that having read it, one can no longer remain in doubt as to the intentions of the Powers toward France and above all toward the French Constitution,* and it was agreed by this convention that Austria and Prussia would undertake to put more than two hundred and forty thousand men in the field to restore the French

* Extract from *le Moniteur* for April 13, 1792, no. 104. Convention signed at Vienna on February 18, 1792, between His Excellency the Count von Colloredo, empowered by the Emperor for this purpose, and the Baron von Bischoffswerder, minister plenipotentiary of H.M. the King of Prussia.

(1) It is agreed that there shall subsist between His Majesty the Emperor and His Majesty the King of Prussia a solid and durable concert, both between themselves and their respective allies, aimed at taking the most appropriate measures, whenever the occasion demands, to uphold the honor and dignity of Crowned heads against any injury that may be done them by men of faction, whether they be their own subjects or those of their allies or those of any Prince or potentate whatsoever whose sovereign dignity may be exposed to insult.

(2) The two high contracting parties reciprocally undertake to preserve themselves and likewise their respective allies from any change or innovation whatsoever in the rights, prerogatives, and powers that they enjoy in their states or that, by ancient laws or customs, are found to belong to them.

(3) Their aforementioned Majesties undertake, on their own behalf and that of their allies, to take no part in any revolt or rebellion that may arise in a neighboring state, but on the contrary, to employ all their power to suppress it. To this end they will not allow any subject of another state to enter their territories without the knowledge and approval of the sovereign of that state: They will be seized and handed back at the first request. All export of arms and ammunition from their states will be forbidden, and likewise all sales of these same commodities abroad.

(4) The two high contrasting parties agree to employ all their power to restore to the Crown of France the former rights and prerogatives belonging to it. To this end, as soon as the season permits, they will employ the following forces: His Imperial Majesty and his allies undertake to put a hundred and eighty thousand men in the field, and His Prussian Majesty and his allies undertake to supply sixty thousand over and above their contingent in the Imperial armies. These troops will act as shall be subsequently agreed between the parties and will be paid by their respective sovereigns, His Imperial Majesty reserving to himself the right to make arrangements with his allies in respect of the number that each shall supply, as does His Prussian Majesty. If, contrary to all expectation, these forces prove inadequate, Their Imperial and Prussian Majesties will take all further measures to increase the size of their armies that are deemed necessary.

(5) A Congress shall be set up to which Their Imperial and Prussian Majesties and their allies shall send envoys with the task of ascertaining the nature and extent of those prerogatives belonging to the Crown of France which require to be reinstituted to restore that Crown to its dignity. If the Congress were to be informed that the high contracting parties or any of their allies had suffered any injury to or usurpation of their authority in their dominions, the decision of the Congress will be considered as final and binding on all parties, and if gentler measures fail, they will employ the above-mentioned forces or a part thereof, but always in the same proportion, as the occasion requires to restore the injured party to the exercise of his legitimate authority and also to defend, in every possible eventuality, the dignity of sovereigns from all violation, insults, and usurpations.

Crown and the ancient rights and prerogatives that belonged to it, and it was established by the communications that M. Delessart had just made to the Assembly that the Austrian troops were already on the march and making for the frontiers of France. Consequently, there should no longer have been any hesitation; the King should have immediately notified the Emperor that France was not going to wait until her enemies were ready to attack her before declaring war, that he therefore required of him the immediate dissolution of the Concert of Powers, that he warned him that upon receipt of his latest communications he had ordered the mobilization of French forces on the frontier with the Low Countries, and that his reply would determine the orders he would give them. That if the Emperor gave him a satisfactory reply and countermanded the march of his troops, etc., the French troops would return to their garrisons; but that if he received any more hostile replies, or even merely evasive ones, the French armies would cross the frontier immediately and attack the Low Countries. That is what I thought at the time, and what I feel I should still think in a similar situation, and it was also what was demanded with reason as much as justice, not only by the Assembly but by the whole of France.

To this point of view it was objected that France was in no position to make war, that it was impossible for her to resist the combined attack of Austria and Prussia; but the mass of the people did not accept this impossibility; already they were aware of a potentiality later realized under leaders who, whatever their opinions, had at least a frank and sincere desire to maintain their national independence and to sustain the glory and honor of their arms. The Minister of War, M. de Narbonne, had promised in the sitting of December 14, 1791 (when the King had announced that he was granting only a month's delay to the Elector of Trier and other Princes of the Empire) that when this limit had expired —that is to say, on January 15, 1792—France would have a hundred and fifty thousand men on her frontiers divided into three armies ready to take the field. January 15 had gone by; so, too, had the month of February; now we were even at the beginning of March and still no army had been mobilized, and the nation saw no preparations corresponding to the desire it had so openly and loudly proclaimed of taking up arms for its defense and to the solemn promises that the King had made on this point.

The position of this ministry was thus very critical, above all that of M. de Narbonne, who had promised the promptest and most efficacious measures, and who could see the foreign armies marching toward our frontiers without any of his promises having been realized and without anything in France being ready to resist the invasion. In this dilemma M. de Narbonne, who had summoned the three commanders in chief, MM. de Rochambeau, de Luckner, and de La Fayette, to Paris to coordinate with them the military measures demanded by the circumstances together with the particular arrangements of their own armies, had the idea of bringing them to the King's Council so that they might discuss the matter in person with the King and his ministers. This step, which was not agreed upon with his colleagues, could have had no other purpose but that of diminishing the risk of his being held responsible and of assuring himself the cooperation of these generals in the measures he wanted to have adopted. However, the other ministers saw it differently. Access to the Council was considered then as a great source of influence and power, and the ministers, who were perhaps jealous of M. de Narbonne's successes in the Assembly and who, it was said, had often suspected him of wanting to dominate them, saw in the introduction of the generals to the Council an attempt by M. de Narbonne to obtain supremacy there: They profited from this circumstance to have him dismissed.*

On March 10, at the opening of the morning sitting, the Assembly received a letter from the King† announcing that he had just nominated M. de Grave to the Ministry of War in place of M. de Narbonne.

The dismissal of M. de Narbonne was already public knowledge, and as he was believed to hold views more in accordance with those of the Assembly than the other ministers, it occasioned some agitation and an extra degree of irritation. M. Brissot was already announcing from the rostrum that the Diplomatic Committee (of which he was a member) was divided in its examination of the official dispatch of the Emperor and the dispatches of M. Delessart—one portion of the committee seemed disposed to let the accusation against this minister drop, but the other believed that France and the Assembly were surrounded by malevolence and treason—and that he demanded that his criticisms of M. Delessart be heard. They were, and he delivered a very long speech, which he concluded by proposing that the accusation of M. Delessart be decreed on several grounds, *for having neglected his duties and betrayed the nation.*

M. Vergniaud succeeded him at the rostrum. He had one of those flights of eloquence whose effects on the French Assemblies were often very strong. I feel it is remarkable enough for me to quote it here, because such quotations often give a better understanding of the times, the state of affairs, and men's opinions than all the descriptions of them one could give. Having discussed the question, M. Vergniaud concluded his speech as follows:‡ "Allow me to make an observation. When the decree giving the Christian religion§ despotic powers was proposed to the Constituent Assembly, Mirabeau pronounced these words: *'From this very rostrum from which I am addressing you can be seen the window from which the*

---

* It was common practice during the Ancien Régime to summon experts to the Council to give advice on a particular topic, and this in itself could not have caused offense.—ED.

† See *le Moniteur* for March 11, 1792, no. 71.

‡ See *le Moniteur* for March 12, 1792, no. 72.

§ I have copied *le Moniteur*'s exact words. I think there is an error and that instead of *Christian,* one should read *Catholic.*

hand of a French monarch,* armed against his subjects by execrable factions that mingled private interests with the sacred interests of religion, fired the harquebus that was the signal for the massacre of Saint-Bartholomew's Day.' And I, too, proclaim: From this rostrum from which I address you, one can see the palace where false councilors mislead and deceive the King whom the Constitution has given us, forge the irons with which they wish to enchain us, and prepare the maneuvers that must deliver us to the House of Austria. I see the windows of the palace where the Counterrevolution is being plotted, where the means are being contrived of plunging us once more into the horrors of slavery after making us pass through all the disorders of anarchy and all the fury of civil war. *(The chamber echoed with applause.)*

"The day has come when you can put an end to such effrontery, such insolence, and finally confound the conspirators. In ancient times, and in the name of despotism, fright and terror have often issued from this famous palace. Thither let them return today in the name of the law! *(Redoubled and prolonged applause.)* There let them penetrate every heart! Let all those who inhabit it know that our Constitution grants immunity to the King alone.† Let them know that the law will reach everyone there who is guilty without distinction, and that not a single one convicted of crimes can escape its punishment! I demand that the decree of accusation be put to the vote."

The decree of accusation was put to the vote and passed immediately with a very large majority, without its victim being heard: A sad example—and one too often repeated during the course of the Revolution—of the injustice to which enthusiasm can lead when it is not tempered by reflection and the fear of going too far.

After the Assembly has passed the decree of accusation, M. Gensonné added a further proposal that is sufficiently noteworthy for me to relate it: "I beg leave," he said, "to put forward a fourteenth article to the preamble of M. Brissot's proposed decree. The Minister's conduct must be envisaged in relation to the nation and in relation to the King because the same facts proclaim that he has, at the least, exposed the King to the suspicion of favoring the Concert of foreign Powers. I demand, therefore, that mention should be made of it in the indictment."

M. Delessart could have escaped if he had wished, but he gave himself up, declaring that as his conscience had nothing with which to reproach him, he wanted to be judged. He was transferred to Orléans, where the National High Court charged with trying those accused of high treason was due to meet.‡

* Henri III.

† A cowardly threat to the Queen. According to the Constitution, the King "could do no wrong."—ED.

‡ M. Delessart was later slaughtered in the month of September 1792, as were all those sent to be judged before the High Court by decree of the Legislative Assembly.

The decree accusing the Minister of Foreign Affairs was a thunderbolt for the other ministers and for the Court. All the ministers (except the Comte de Grave, who had been nominated the same day) resigned immediately, so that on his entry to the ministry M. de Grave found himself momentarily charged with the portfolios of all the departments. The downfall of the whole ministry was the Assembly's main purpose in the decree with which it had just visited M. Delessart. I think that it could have achieved the same end and by less violent means; and that it would have been wiser, and above all more just, to have acted less precipitately.

It is said that the King was hard pressed to form a new ministry at this juncture, and this was necessarily so because he could not compose it of people of the same political color as those who had just resigned. It is, moreover, doubtful whether he would have found any of them willing to accept so slippery and dangerous a post. Still less could he seek ministers among those who were called *the denizens of the Court* because, as their opinions were in direct opposition to those then prevalent in France, he might as well have chosen them from the ranks of the *émigrés* at Coblenz. The King therefore realized that he had no other course open to him than to turn to those whose opinions could be taken to be roughly in line with those of the Girondins; this is why General Dumouriez was summoned to the Ministry of Foreign Affairs. The Ministry of the Interior was given to M. Roland de la Platière, husband of the famous Mme Roland; that of Public Contributions—that is to say, of Finances—went to M. Clavière, and the Marine to M. Lacoste. The Ministry of Justice was offered to M. Garnier, and when he refused it, it was given to M. Duranton. M. de Grave remained at the Ministry of War.

The events of March 10 should have convinced the King that the defeat of those constitutionalists who had undertaken to support him was also a defeat for him and his Court; and that their departure from office, far from bringing in those whom the Court preferred by virtue of their sentiments of opposition to the Constitution, would necessarily bring in men of decidedly more "popular" hue, of whom the majority were members of the Jacobin Society. The King should have seen that as the cause of this upset was the suspicion inspired by the duplicity of the executive power's conduct toward France and the foreign Powers, a change of policy was indispensable; but this warning was spurned; the Court persisted in its policies, and the popular thunderbolt, which on March 10 had struck only the ministers, on August 10 struck the King* and shattered his throne at the very moment when the foreign armies were crossing the frontiers and making for Paris. Thus it was that that which he regarded as the sole means of strengthening his throne was the cause of his downfall!

The fall of the old administration and the choice of the new ministers made war a certainty, and the remaining negotiations offer nothing more

* It was on August 10, 1792, that Louis XVI was deprived of the exercise of his royal authority based on the Constitution.

worth the effort of reporting. It is, however, remarkable that it was only then that France had knowledge of the important document I mentioned above: the convention that had been signed at Vienna on February 18, 1792, between Austria and Prussia, by which these two Powers undertook to put two hundred and forty thousand men in the field against France. Another event, more noteworthy than decisive, was the death of the Emperor Leopold, which occurred on March 2, 1792. This event produced no change* in the progress of the negotiations and the relations of Austria with the other Powers, since the new monarch, Francis II, left his father's ministry unchanged.†

As the Court of Vienna declared in its note of April 7, in reply to the one addressed to it by the new Minister of Foreign Affairs (General Dumouriez), that it adhered to the intentions expressed in the name of the late Emperor Leopold and that it did not wish to make any reply other than the one it had made in the note of February 18, of which I spoke earlier, General Dumouriez made his report to the King in the Council on April 18. The conclusion of this report was that *"His Majesty, surrounded by his ministers, should proceed to the National Assembly to propose war against Austria."*‡ The King adopted this conclusion on the unanimous advice of his Council and proceeded to the National Assembly on April 20 at noon, and having ordered General Dumouriez to read to the Assembly the report he had made to the Council, *"he proposed war on the King of Hungary and Bohemia."*§ I was placed in a private gallery, exactly above the King, when he made this memorable proposal. It was received in complete silence, and when the King had left the chamber, the Assembly adjourned and decided that it would deal with the King's proposal in the evening sitting. I returned to be present at the debates, which were not long. There were only eight or ten members who opposed the Assembly adopting the King's proposal, and the declaration of war was passed almost unanimously. As the president announced it, the spectators gathered in the public galleries showed their enthusiasm by rising spontaneously and keeping up their applause for several minutes. A

---

* Only the protocol will be changed by substituting the title *King of Bohemia and Hungary* for that of *Emperor of Germany*.

† Here modern scholars would take serious issue with Louis-Philippe. The change in rulers was decisive. Leopold was more cautious, wiser, and more liberal (he had granted a constitution to Tuscany when he was Grand Duke) than his son. His consistent advice to Louis XVI was to make a success of being a constitutional monarch. The concert of *all* the Powers with which Louis-Philippe makes such play was purposely ineffective for that very reason: Unless all the Powers intervened in France, *none* was obliged to.—ED.

‡ See *le Moniteur* for Saturday, April 21, 1792, no. 112.

§ The second article of the first section of the third chapter of the Constitution was couched in the following terms:

"War cannot be decided upon except by a decree of the legislative body, passed upon the King's formal and necessary proposition and receiving his assent."

deputation of twenty-four members was sent immediately to present the decree to the King, who gave his assent on the spot.

In the second part of these memoirs I shall unfold the events that followed the declaration of war, and I shall continue the account of what concerns me, but before finishing the first part, I must make known my father's position and his relations with the Court at various periods. This knowledge is necessary for an impartial appraisal of what I shall subsequently have to relate concerning him, and to cause all the lies and calumnies that were related about him through the frenzy of party spirit to be appreciated at their true value.

When I returned from Valenciennes to Paris in the month of February 1792, I found my father in a highly distressing condition. His financial difficulties resulting, as I have already said,* from the suppression of his *apanage,* from the losses he had sustained in the Revolution, and from the nonpayment of a considerable portion of what he retained, while the burden of his expenditure was maintained in its entirety, exposed him to continuous harassments by his creditors and had forced him to reduce his establishment to a very modest level of expenditure. However, nothing ever altered the gentleness and charm of his character; he enumerated his worries and his difficulties as though he were speaking of those of someone else. He had adopted a very withdrawn and even monotonous style of life. The theater was a sort of compulsion for him; he went nearly every night, which did not prevent him from being very bored: Since he had never had a taste for work or become accustomed to it, he did not know how to fill his day, and often it seemed to him overlong. He felt himself more isolated with every new day, and my arrival with my brother caused him great pleasure. It was a real change for him. How little understood was the manner of life that he led at this time! How much his enemies distorted everything concerning him! Assuredly, he was very far from concerning himself with all that has been imputed to him. He dreamed only of living quietly and safeguarding himself from the relentless persecutions of his enemies; they were such that they did not leave him a moment's peace. The future also was the source of considerable anxiety to him because he was fully aware that he could expect no real support from the partisans of the Revolution, and that he even had a fairly substantial number of political enemies among them; and he knew that on the part of the Court and the *émigrés,* his ruin was irrevocably resolved. He was certain that their main objective was to ruin him at all costs. However, it was not he who had provoked this state of hostility. Indeed, he had often vainly sought a reconciliation with the King, and he would have been delighted to have been on good terms with the Court, provided that this reconciliation had not been purchased by the sacrifice of his constitutionalist principles, which no consideration could have made him

* See pages 36–37.

renounce. Rightly, he considered the establishment of the constitutional régime as absolutely necessary for the prosperity and the tranquillity of France, as the sole means of obtaining the freedom of the individual—the only guarantee that he personally could have against the persecutions to which he was exposed.

My father had not taken part in public affairs from his return from England in July 1790 until the dissolution of the Constituent Assembly on September 30, 1791, except in giving his personal vote in the deliberations of this Assembly, of which he was a member. In the course of October he was nominated *admiral,* a promotion to which the established procedure for promotion entitled him, since he was one of the most senior lieutenant generals in the navy. This new rank did not give him any functions to fulfill; but he wanted to profit from this opportunity to be reconciled with the King, and with this in mind, he addressed himself to M. Bertrand de Molleville, then Minister of the Marine. M. Bertrand de Molleville, whose testimony concerning my father cannot be suspected of partiality toward him since he had collected in his works all the calumnious tittle-tattle that his enemies ceaselessly worked to spread against him, relates the following anecdote in his works on the Revolution. I shall give his own words, as I have copied them from his *History of the French Revolution during the Last Years of the Reign of Louis XVI,* part two, volume six, chapter seven, page 289.

Having said that the batch of promotions made by M. Thévenard (his predecessor) had not gone down very well in the navy as a whole, M. de Bertrand adds that among the small number of officers who had acknowledged receipt of the letter in which he had informed them of their promotion to a new rank, there had been very few, with the exception of the Duc d'Orléans and the Comte d'Estaing, who had not sent him their resignations, and he continues as follows:

"The Duc d'Orléans did not merely notify me in writing of his acceptance of the rank of admiral: He came to see me and told me, among other things, that he attached great importance to the grace the King had just accorded him because it would place him in a position to make known to His Majesty his true sentiments, which he claimed had been so unjustly misrepresented. This declaration, which was mainly notable for the frank and loyal air with which it was accompanied, was followed by several equally singular outpourings of his heart. 'I am very wretched,' he told me, 'and certainly I have not deserved it; my name has been used for a thousand atrocities that have been placed at my door, though I had not the slightest knowledge of them, and I have been blamed for them because I wanted to avoid the shame of justifying myself; you are the first minister to whom I have said as much because you are the only one to inspire me with confidence; you will soon be in a position to judge whether my conduct fails to bear out my words.'

"The tone and looks with which the Duc d'Orléans addressed this phrase to me did not give me leave to doubt that it was suggested to him by the air of astonishment and distrust with which he perceived I was listening to him. I replied that the fear of not transmitting the full strength of the sentiments he had just expressed to me, in the account of them that he begged me to give to the King, made me wish that he would communicate them directly to His Majesty. He told me that he asked for nothing better if he might hope the King would receive and hear him, and that he had it in mind to present himself the next day at the palace to pay his court.

"The same day I made a report to the Council of the Duc d'Orléans's visit to me and of our conversation. The King decided to receive him, and the next day he had a conversation with him lasting more than half an hour, with which His Majesty appeared to us to have been highly satisfied. 'Like you,' the King told me, 'I think that he has had a genuine change of heart and that he will do all he can to repair the damage he has done, in which it is possible he has not had so large a part as we thought.'

"The following Sunday he went to the King's *levée,* where he was greeted in the most humiliating manner by the courtiers, who were in ignorance of what had happened, and by the royalists, who were accustomed to proceed *en masse* to the palace on that day to make their court to the Royal Family. They pressed around him, they affected to tread on his feet and to push him toward the door so as to prevent him from entering. He went down to the Queen's apartments, where the table was already set; as soon as he appeared, people exclaimed on all sides: *Gentlemen, keep an eye on the plates!* as though they had been persuaded that his pockets were full of poison.

"The insulting murmurs that his presence everywhere excited forced him to withdraw without seeing the Royal Family; he was pursued as far as the Queen's staircase; as he was descending, a lump of spit landed on his head, and several others on his shoulders. Rage and spite were seen painted in his face; he left the palace convinced that the instigators of the indignities he had undergone were the King and Queen, who had no inkling of them and were indeed much distressed that they had taken place. From that moment he swore an implacable hatred for them, and he was all too true to this horrible vow. I was at the palace that day and witnessed all the facts that I have just related."

The basis of this anecdote is true, though I do not think that all the details are accurately reported. It is not true that people trod on my father's feet or that they proceeded to the other extremes related by M. de Bertrand, which my father would certainly have instantly checked; but with that exception, it is true that his reception at Court was such as M. de Bertrand describes it, and I seem to recall the history of the *plates*.

M. de Bertrand relates that the King appeared to have been very satisfied with the discussion he had had with my father. However, I recall that my father, telling me with some pride about the attempt he had made to be reconciled with the King through the mediation of M. de Bertrand, said that he had told the King that he placed the highest price on convincing His Majesty of the absurdity of the calumnies which had blackened him in his eyes, above all those tending to accuse him of having worked to dethrone the King in order to supplant him; that he was ready to reply to all the questions His Majesty thought fit to ask, and that he was certain he could demonstrate the falsity of everything of which he was accused; but that nevertheless, the King had replied that he was not the judge, that his future conduct would determine the opinion he would form about his past conduct. And I remember my father telling me that the manner with which the King had treated him left him little hope the King would revise his opinion of him.

Elsewhere, M. de Bertrand says *that the King and Queen were unaware of and were even very put out* by the conduct of their courtiers toward my father when he had been at the Tuileries to pay his respects publicly to Their Majesties. It seems to me that if the King and Queen had been as put out as M. de Bertrand claims, it would have been very easy for them to show some regret at what had happened, or at least to let him know that they hoped this would not prevent him from returning to Court or that his appearance there would give Their Majesties pleasure. But my father received no message whatever, directly or indirectly, of a sort to recall him to Court, still less disclaiming responsibility for the treatment he had suffered. It is, therefore, impossible not to conclude from this silence that if Their Majesties had not themselves encouraged this conduct, at least they had not disapproved of it, and that those who had taken it upon themselves to act like this had not misunderstood their intentions. For the rest, I have never seen a Court where the courtiers mistook the real intentions of the King, and it is often easier to discover what these are from what the courtiers say than from what he says himself.

M. de Bertrand is no nearer the truth when he supposes that *from that moment my father swore an implacable hatred for the King and Queen.* Nothing was less characteristic of my father than to have *an implacable hatred* for anyone, and those who believe it was hatred that dictated the vote I wish he had not given* are sadly mistaken. His reception at the Tuileries, far from inspiring such sentiments in him, did not prevent him sometime afterward from making a new attempt at a reconciliation with the King.

When the Comte de Grave was nominated Minister of War, my father sought him out and told him of his sincere desire to remove the King's prejudices against him, as well as his desire to be able to uphold, constitutionally, his rights and his authority. M. de Grave had great pleasure in undertaking this commission. A few days afterward he came to confide

* In Louis XVI's trial before the National Convention.—ED.

his embarrassment to me and told me that the terms of the King's reply to him were such that he did not feel able to repeat them to my father. "Never mention his name to me again," the King had said, "no reconciliation between him and me will ever be possible, etc." The rest of this reply is too dreadful for me to relate, but it will never be effaced from my memory. It is sufficient that I give the gist of his reply, *that no reconciliation between the King and the Duc d'Orléans was ever possible.*

I promised the Comte de Grave absolute secrecy about this reply, although the King had in no way imposed it on him,* and all my father ever knew of it was what M. de Grave told him, that is to say, "that the King had given a cool reception to what he had reported to him on his behalf, and that he thought my father would do better to await different circumstances to attempt a reconciliation with the King." My father was not at all surprised by this reply: He hardly could have been. He was endowed with too great a power of observation and judgment not to understand the Court, and he understood it perfectly. He had had an aversion to it all his life, and undoubtedly this sentiment was fully returned.

The first impulse in this direction had been given him by the Prince de Conti, his uncle.† The Prince de Conti was a man of great intelligence and merit. His talents made him the true leader of the party of the Princes of the Blood, who were very numerous in his time. He brought them together under his roof every time there was a question of resisting the Court, whether when those great issues arose in which the *parlements* tried to oppose a barrier to ministerial despotism that ceaselessly and ubiquitously worked to extinguish the nation's few remaining privileges, or whether it was merely a question of repulsing the continuous and systematic encroachments of Court etiquette on the prerogatives of the Princes of the Blood. I have often heard my father relating how the Prince de Conti spoke to them in their private gatherings: "Forward, gentlemen," he told them, "no equivocation; if we falter we shall be treated like valets, as already we are only too much. We must make the Court realize that we are Princes and peers of the kingdom and that, as such, it is up to us to set the example of resistance to arbitrary authority and to prevent the Court from invading our privileges and those of the nation." My father, then very young and just as anxious not to allow himself to be humiliated as to defend his privileges and those of the nation, would have liked there and then to cap his uncle's suggestion, but the Prince de Conti restrained him, and addressing the Duc d'Orléans, my

* This has the ring of truth, for such lack of delicacy was completely characteristic of Louis XVI.—ED.

† The Prince de Conti, who lived in the Temple in his capacity of Grand Prior of the Order of Malta. He was at once son-in-law of the Duc d'Orléans, Regent of the kingdom during the minority of Louis XV, and brother-in-law of the Duc d'Orléans my grandfather, who had married his sister.

grandfather, as the head of the Princes of the Blood, he said to him, tapping him on the belly: "Go on then, Chief, you are the eldest, it is for you to speak to these gentlemen: What do you have to say to them?" And then my grandfather eagerly recognized the necessity of resisting what was demanded of them, and all the Princes agreed that it was impossible to submit to the Court's caprices, that the moment had come to draw up joint remonstrances to the King, or in other words, to do what the Prince de Conti wanted them to do. It was in this way that all the Princes of the Blood—except the Comte de la Marche, the only son of the Prince de Conti—united in 1771 to oppose the suppression of the existing *parlements* and the establishment of those of M. de Maupeou, for which resistance they were barred from the Court.*

This union of the Princes ended with the Prince de Conti, who died in 1776, but his advice, his policies, and the conversation of the people who formed his circle had made an indelible impression on my father, and it is in large measure to these same contacts that must be attributed those youthful errors with which he was later reproached with such bitterness and spitefulness. In his youth, my father had always been greatly struck by the insignificance of the majority of the Princes, and he attributed it to etiquette, to the laxity of their education and life style, and to the flattery with which they were surrounded and which left them no means of knowing the world and their fellow men. This opinion, or rather this attitude, led him to take every means of avoiding what he regarded as the cause of the limited faculties of the Princes; and from this derived his lifelong propensity to do nothing as they did and to detach himself from them, as well as his constant desire that the public should not pass the same judgment on him as he knew they passed on the majority of the Princes. It was the same reason that determined him to serve in the navy.

My father's successes in this career (successes that were so grotesquely distorted afterward) stirred the Court's jealousy and pique, and it was the applause he received in Paris for his conduct in the Battle of Ouessant in 1778 that determined the King to require him to leave the navy. The inconceivable calumnies that were put out about his conduct on this occasion were not dreamed up until long afterward, and for two reasons; one was to give a plausible pretext for having forced him to leave active service in the navy in the middle of a war with England, which had been censured at the time; the other reason was to harm him in public opinion by substituting damaging suspicions for the favorable impression that his

* In 1771 Louis XV and his chancellor, Maupeou, forced a conclusion in their struggle with the *parlements* by restaffing the Parlement of Paris and effecting lesser purges in the provincial *parlements*. The effect of these measures, and the degree of their acceptance in the country, will never be known because in 1774, a few months after his accession, Louis XVI recalled the old Parlement. What can be said, however, is that the refusal of the Princes of the Blood to recognize the new Parlement was a major source of uncertainty as to the duration of Maupeou's "revolution," as it was called at the time.—ED.

187

conduct had created. I think there was the further aim of acquiring pretexts to avoid giving him the dignity of Grand Admiral when it became vacant by the death of his father-in-law, the Duc de Penthièvre, who was invested with it, so that it could be disposed in favor of one of the Princes of the Royal Family. These calumnies consisted of insinuating that he had lacked courage in the Battle of Ouessant and that he had not supported the commander in chief (M. d'Orvilliers) as he should have done. However, it is a fact—as the official dispatches, which they dared not suppress at the time, establish—that when the vanguard of the French fleet, composed of five vessels, discovered the English fleet off Ouessant, my father, who commanded this vanguard, contented himself with signaling to the commander in chief that the enemy was in sight and that he was going to engage in combat without awaiting either his orders or the rest of the fleet. This in fact he did, and the *Holy Spirit,* a vessel of eighty guns that he commanded, sustained by itself the fire of three English ships for a very long time; indeed, of all the French ships, it was the one that lost the most men, and it was only this unequal struggle (which at the time did my father the greatest honor both in France and England, where details of it resounded in the press) that gave M. d'Orvilliers time to come up with the fleet. Then the English fleet set sail for the coast of England without being pursued by the French fleet, which returned to Brest; but this return was M. d'Orvilliers's doing, and not only did my father have nothing to do with it, but I seem to recall that he expressed his disapproval of it to M. d'Orvilliers. I am writing from memory, but no one will be able to contradict these facts, and I am sure that if I had collections of newspapers or other documents beside me, it would be easy for me to present numerous proofs of what I advance.

My father returned immediately to Paris, where he found it more agreeable to stay than at Brest, and this was a mistake; if he had remained at Brest, one would perhaps not have dared recall him thence, but he was prevented from returning thither. Then people began to say at Court that he had attacked *recklessly,* that he had jeopardized the fleet and that therein lay the disadvantage of employing Princes in the navy; that the navy was always given to insubordination, that a Prince in its midst encouraged this tendency, and that, for the maintenance of discipline and the authority of the commanders in chief, there should be no more Princes under their orders. The aim of these insinuations was to prepare the public for the decision that the King wanted to adopt of no longer employing my father in the navy. But it was not till much later that they thought of secretly casting aspersions on an action that at the time had been universally admired. They had to wait until these details had been forgotten, as everything is in the long run; they had above all to wait till a party had been formed, ruthlessly dedicated to blackening my father's name and ruining him no matter how, before they dared to publicly authorize this calumny. It would have been easy to demonstrate its falsity, and it was not the difficulty of doing it that prevented my father from refuting it chapter and verse, but solely because he scorned this calumny; and when people tried to get him to refute it, he declared: "Oh goodness, this is a little too steep, they won't seriously accuse me of that!" and he added: *"Qui s'excuse s'accuse!"* which it was his custom to say whenever he was pressed to rebut one of the calumnies against him that were constantly being put about.*

Among the complaints about him that my father's detractors sought to exploit, one which they got the most out of, was his *Anglomania,* as it was usually called. Before speaking of its causes and its so-called effects, let me point out that Anglomania was prevalent among the wealthy clan of the French nation during the reign of Louis XVI. It was even so by the end of the reign of Louis XV, who was disturbed by its progress. It is well known that when the Comte de Lauraguais returned to Versailles from a trip to England, Louis XV asked him what he had gone there to learn. —"To think, Sire," replied M. de Lauraguais.—"Of horses, no doubt," the King said, turning his back on him. And Louis XV died on May 10, 1774, so this anecdote is earlier than this date, and therefore this *Anglomania* was already prevalent in France at least ten or twelve years before my father had ever been to England.† Thus, if they had reflected, if they had been prepared to consider an accusation before launching it, they would have seen that the spirit of the age had already propagated English ideas, and that the taste for things English had spread before my father could have given them their first impetus.

The taste for magnificence, for great palaces and sumptuous châteaux, had almost died out with Louis XIV. Very little such building went on under Louis XV, and at the end of his reign people no longer cared even to inhabit those they possessed; all the owners of these buildings had their *little houses,* which they preferred; it was there that they broke free from the restrictive grandeur of etiquette, and for magnificence and display they substituted comfort and freedom. Thus the Duc d'Orléans my grandfather (whom no one ever thought of taxing with *Anglomania*) left the Palais Royal to live in a little house in the Rue de Provence, and Saint-Cloud for Saint-Assise, where he also laid out an *English garden,* and he was neither the first nor the last to follow this fashion. What were called *English gardens* won preference everywhere over those that Le Nôtre‡ had planted: Everything has its time, and every time its fashion, and without the sad experience that revealed to me the true origins of all the calumnies that have hounded my father, I would never have conceived how tastes of this kind could have occasioned them; I would still less have

* M. de Bertrand relates that my father spoke to him in the same sense; see above, pages 183–85.
† I believe it was in 1783 that he went there for the first time.
‡ Le Nôtre laid out great gardens in the reign of Louis XIV, including those of Versailles and Vaux-le-Vicomte.—ED.

conceived why people spoke so much about his *Anglomania* and so little about other people's; why people laid such emphasis on the fact that he had built *Mouceaux,* that he had installed English stables there, and that he had English hunters and racehorses, while no one seemed to recall the *Anglomania* of M. le Comte d'Artois, whom Mr. Baldwin had also taught English, who had built *Bagatelle* and laid out an English garden, who started an English stable of racehorses at Vincennes, and who bet on them in just as English a way as my father. "Nothing is more true," someone to whom I was making this reproach said one day. "Your father is no more blameworthy in this respect than M. le Comte d'Artois and so many others; but later on there was a great difference: M. le Comte d'Artois was at Coblenz, and your father sat in the National Convention." It is only too true that such differences, distorted by party spirit, are in general the cause of the conflicting way in which the same actions and the same conduct are often judged by contemporaries.

There is no doubt that as regards *Anglomania,* the *effect* was taken for the *cause,* which happens only too often, giving rise to many errors. Instead of considering my father's *Anglomania* as the result of the inclinations of the age and his personal habits, as had been done at first during his youth, people later wanted to see in it a deep laid plan to propagate *Anglomania* in Paris in order to bring about a revolution there. However absurd was this pretended discovery, people wanted to believe in it, and they did believe in it despite all the recollections and proofs that should have given it the lie. Afterward, when the disasters of the Revolution had become irreparable and had facilitated the propagation of calumnies against my father, the perspicacity of certain people increased in proportion, and they thought to see in this *Anglomania* the proof of a secret understanding between the English government and the Duc d'Orléans to put him on the throne by overthrowing Louis XVI; and they were astonished that they had not realized this sooner because, according to them, it was clear that the Duc d'Orléans had plotted the French Revolution with the English government during his visits to England, and they did not even doubt that they had *shared the cost.* When one thinks about this objectively, it is hard to believe that anyone could have credited such absurdities; but this way of looking at the causes of the Revolution seemed to a great many people to fit very well; it offered them a double advantage: in the first place, calumniating the Duc d'Orléans by representing his efforts to make France enjoy the judicious liberty enjoyed by England under her institutions as the culpable maneuvers of a French Prince conspiring with an enemy Power to rend and overturn his country in the detestable hope of dethroning his King and reigning in his place; secondly, distorting the true causes of the Revolution and reducing them to the hired intrigues and the venality of a few wretches. Really, by such willful self-deception, they lost sight of the true, I daresay almost the only, cause of the Revolution, *public opinion.* Now it is clear that once one has mistaken the nature of a disease, it becomes impossible to find the remedy and cure it; and this is precisely what happened. But to make myself even clearer, I should say that the first concern of the people or the party of whom I am speaking was not to forestall or stop the excesses of the Revolution; it was first of all to ruin all those whom it suited them to consider as its instigators, then to destroy all the institutions created by the Revolution, and above all to wipe out the barriers that had been set up against arbitrary authority;* because only then could they reestablish all that had been abolished during the Revolution and restore the Court and the privileged classes to the enjoyment of all the rights and all the abuses of power the exercise of which very rightly became hateful to the nation.

In vain did each day's experience demonstrate that this Revolution, entirely accomplished by the propagation of opinions that had become almost unanimous, neither had, nor could have, leaders, and that those who were thought to be such were, as I have said earlier, swept along by the masses rather than in control of them. At first they were convinced that there must have been subordinate leaders, that these subordinate leaders must have been directed by a principal leader, and they concluded that this principal leader was necessarily my father. From that it resulted that destroying him was regarded as the most efficacious way of disorganizing the Revolution, and it was believed that the success of the Counterrevolution would be assured if they managed to destroy him. Therefore, the highest priority was given to his destruction, and he was destroyed. But his death had no effect on the course of the Revolution. It procured no advantage to his enemies, not even that of showing them the uselessness of all the persecutions and calumnies to which he had been a prey. If my father's enemies had managed to destroy him earlier, if this event had taken place at some other period of the Revolution, it is possible that it might have had harmful consequences for them, but it seems to me impossible that they would have derived from it any advantages whatsoever. I think I can prove it.

It is well known that at Court and at Coblenz it was believed that the supporters of the Revolution would be placed in the greatest difficulty if those regarded as their leaders disappeared from the public scene for any reason. However, it is equally well known that during the whole course of the Revolution it was always easy to find substitutes with whom to replace them. This was consistently borne out with reference to the army, the ministry, the Assemblies, and finally to the King himself, whose rule was replaced without any difficulty by so many successive substitutes. But

* This may be taken to have been the King's objective, but it was certainly not that of the bulk of the nobility who had resisted the King in 1787–88 and then emigrated. They had fought the King in defense of aristocratic privilege, certainly, but against "arbitrary authority" as well, or they would never have succeeded in enlisting popular support. They would have resisted this authority with the Estates-General and provincial Estates rather than with a National Assembly; that is the difference.—ED.

at Court and among the *émigrés,* only one danger was perceived, and it was thought that that danger was always to be seen in the person of the Duc d'Orléans: *"Because,"* they said, *"when all is said and done, he is of the stuff Kings are made of, and as long as these gentlemen hold him in reserve, they will not be in difficulties; but if once they should lose him they must necessarily submit because they would be left with no way of dispensing with the King, and they could no longer expect to replace him should they manage to destroy him."* Thus did they see the whole Revolution in the Duc d'Orléans, and they convinced themselves that without him the Revolution would no longer be but a body without a soul and would disappear like a phantom. In vain they realized, after the fall of the King, after his death and that of my father, that the Revolution was marching on with giant steps, and the revolutionary governments that had replaced the King were deploying an energy and were obtaining successes unparalleled in the annals of the monarchy. They concerned themselves only with the internal faults of these governments, in which they saw obstacles to their long continuance; but instead of drawing the conclusion that when these internal faults had destroyed these governments, others of the same complexion would be formed, they went on thinking that the success of the Counterrevolution and the restoration of the King would be the immediate and necessary consequences of the fall of the National Convention or of that of the Executive Directory.* It is amazing that when the successive fall of all these ephemeral governments had carried Buonaparte to supreme power, when neither the King nor the Duc d'Orléans nor any Prince of the Blood had profited from the weariness and distaste occasioned in France by the governments of the Convention and the Directory, but a *Corsican* who at the beginning of the Revolution had been *merely an ordinary lieutenant in the artillery* unknown to the whole nation—when, in short, they saw all the powers of the State concentrated in the person of Buonaparte, they still persisted in their error and continued to believe that the *Revolution had leaders,* that the late Duc d'Orléans had been the *leader of the leaders,* and that there was nothing to fear except from the Duc d'Orléans's son; because *he alone could be a danger to them.*

This error is fundamental. It stems from the fact that the enemies of the Revolution never formed a sound judgment as to its causes and the means by which it was brought about. I have said it before, and I repeat: Nothing was caused, nothing was effected, by hired intrigues; of this I have a deep-seated conviction. I think one can hire a riot, but not a revolution. If the French Revolution had been paid for by England, traces of it would have been found in the reports made to the English Parliament on the use made of its money. These accounts demonstrate that for

* The National Convention was replaced in 1795 by a five-man executive with two legislative chambers, which in turn was replaced by Bonaparte's Consulate in 1799.—ED.

a long time before the Revolution and during the first four years of its course—that is to say, until the period when war broke out between France and England in February 1793—England spent no large sums in fomenting disorder in France. Besides, if it were true that English money brought about the Revolution in France, it is probable that the same means would have destroyed it or stopped it in its tracks, for these same accounts that I have just cited show that since the outbreak of war, England has devoted vast sums to supporting the royalists of the Vendée, the Chouans, and, in general, the cause they were upholding. However, it is well known that these enormous sums have not produced any results and that they have not overthrown any French government. This seems to me very clear proof that revolutions are not produced by means of money. Revolutions are only brought about by *public opinion,* that is to say, when the majority of individual opinions in a nation coincide in preferring this or that system of government and there results from this a general will to bring about changes in its political organization.* It is this convergence of opinions, brought about by enlightenment, education, reading, conversation, sometimes even by the prevailing fashion, that forms what I call *public opinion,* and public opinion, so defined, seems to me an irresistible force. It infiltrates everywhere, directs everything, governs everything, nothing is safe from its influence, and it breaks everything that does not bend before it: It alone makes and breaks revolutions. The French Revolution was effected by *public opinion,* and consequently there was only public opinion that could have stopped its progress. One had, therefore, to apply oneself to obtaining a good knowledge of the nation's opinion; then strive to make it favorable by concessions, agreements, or, much better still, by speaking in earnest and faithfully performing one's promises. In short, one way or another, what was needed was to attune oneself with the times and above all with the nation.

It would have been well to remember that at no time have violent means triumphed over political or religious opinions. The suffering of the first Christians had no effect other than that of propagating and strengthening the *doctrine* (that is to say, the *opinions*) it was desired to stamp out by these persecutions. Then, too, it was at the *leaders,* it was at the propagators of the proscribed doctrine, that they wanted to strike; and the faster the leaders and the propagators were struck down, the faster new ones emerged and the further their successes extended and increased. Now, the Revolution was based on a code of opinions that in many respects had the characteristics of a new religion and that already had its variants and its different sects like an old religion, which proves that these opinions were not as recent as people would have liked to have us believe and that they had been discussed for a long time before having become general enough to produce an explosion.

* In this section, heavily indebted to Rousseau's *Social Contract,* Louis-Philippe shows the effects of the educational diet provided by Mme de Genlis.—ED.

193

The most marked opponents of the Revolution, as well as its supporters, admit that it was prepared and brought to a head by the writings of Voltaire, Rousseau, Raynal, Mably, and almost all the writers of the reign of Louis XV. They likewise admit, as concomitant causes, the more general study of the English language, the speeches of the orators of that nation in their Parliament, the freedom to print and of their press, and finally, the war of the United States of America against England, which had caused a reverberation throughout Europe and above all in France, of the American declarations of the rights of man, their republican constitutions, and the feelings of independence, patriotism, and love of liberty that had brought the American people to undertake that memorable struggle in which French help had facilitated their victory.

I could still give a great many other causes of this kind, from Fénelon's *Télémaque** and the sermons of Massillon† to the *Comtes rendus* of M. Necker,‡ but the more I recognize the existence and the force of these causes, the less I understand the logic of those who accept them and yet do not reject as an insult to reason the absurd assertion that the Revolution was paid for by England and by the Duc d'Orléans.

I think I have demonstrated that the Revolution neither had, nor could have had, leaders, and that in consequence my father was not such. This granted, it is easy for me to show how difficult my father's position was. Not only did he not have any party strength, but the fear felt by the supporters of the Revolution that he should be thought their leader constantly deprived him of their support and was the reason he was but feebly defended when he was not entirely abandoned or sacrificed. He remained, therefore, exposed to vengeance, to persecution, and above all to the calumnies of his enemies without having any support other than that which he could expect from the protection of the law—a feeble support in those times when anarchy and despotism reigned by turns! Thus the party that wished to overthrow and destroy the Revolution was seen during its course to lack audacity in almost all its enterprises except that it never slackened for a moment the violence of its attacks against the Duc d'Orléans. It was seen pursuing him with as much assurance as if the Counterrevolution had been effected and the trail of the Duc d'Orléans had already been instituted in the Parlement of Paris. This assurance had no cause other than complete understanding of their opponents' half-heartedness for my father's interests and the certitude that he would never be defended zealously or efficaciously by them. In fact, he never seemed anything but an embarrassment or a burden to all the parties with which

* *Les Aventures de Télémaque* by Fénelon, Archbishop of Cambrai and tutor to Louis XIV's grandchildren, put forward aristocratic, antiabsolutist ideas.—ED.
† Jean-Baptiste Massillon, Bishop of Clermont.—ED.
‡ Necker's *Comte rendu au Roi* of 1781 disclosed to the public, for the first time, the state of royal finances, hitherto regarded as arcane. Its tone was one of cozy confidentiality, and its content deliberately misleading, giving as it did the impression that revenue exceeded expenditure, when the reverse was the case.—ED.

he acted in turn. His alliance with them was always represented by their opponents as being based on the intention to place him on the throne, which frightened those of whom the reproach had been made all the more because they themselves always had other projects whose execution was hindered by this reproach. During the first three years of the Revolution there were effectively only two schemes: One was to bring the King around to a policy of constitutionalism and to keep him there; the other was to demonstrate the impossibility of making a sincere constitutional monarch out of the King and, by demonstrating this impossibility, to prepare the way for establishing the Republic. Now it is clear that the Duc d'Orléans's cooperation was of no use in the execution of these two schemes, and that it exposed those who were working for them to the danger of their aims being distorted by the suspicion of preparing to place him on the throne; and this was why several of the parties favorable to the Revolution helped the Court in its hostility toward him, while those who would not participate in this hostility because they were convinced of its injustice confined themselves to never mentioning his name.

The catastrophe that ended my father's life ought at least to have dulled animosity and calumny against an unfortunate victim from whom nothing further was to be feared. But my father's vote in the trial of Louis XVI had seemed to a large section of the public as the confirmation of all the rumors that had been spread about him and of all the calumnies that people had sought to prove against him; and people persisted in believing that he had perished only because he had failed in his ambitious projects. I had foreseen that opinion would take this direction, and I had even made this prediction to my father in striving to dissuade him from giving the vote that causes me so much regret. In this I very nearly succeeded; and they are greatly mistaken who believe that my father bore the King an implacable hatred and that it was this hatred which pursued that unfortunate monarch before the National Convention and which there determined my father to cast the fatal vote. They have no better understanding of my father than of the appalling circumstances in which he found himself. However painful this subject is for me, I shall treat it in detail when my account has reached this grievous period. I shall not attempt, however, to justify what I find unjustifiable; my opinion has never changed on this point; on the contrary, I displayed it at a time when this exposed me to great difficulties, and this is so well known that even my enemies have been forced to do me justice. I hope, therefore, that I have even more right than I would otherwise have had to be heeded with confidence, not in order to justify my father's vote, but in order to rebut the calamitous accusations that people have wished to base on this vote. My father never desired the King's death, and he only voted for it because he was *swept along* and forced to give a pledge, as this vote was qualified, by the party with which he had aligned himself politically. This party, I regret to say, was the group in the National Convention *that wanted the*

King's death, and my father was then a prey to the attacks of all the rest of the Assembly, as well as all the other parties; and he was driven by the fear of losing this last, solitary support—the only one remaining to him, the only one perhaps that he could hope to obtain—into giving this deplorable vote. They required *this guarantee,** as they called it, of the future sentiments and intentions of my father before undertaking to defend him against his enemies; but having obtained it, they soon changed their tune; they sent him to the scaffold by the same decree that sent their common enemies (the Girondins) to the guillotine—the very faction against whose hostility they had promised him their assistance. One can hardly marvel over this, but was one to expect that the catastrophe that ended my father's life would have redoubled the relentlessness of his enemies! All he left behind him was a widow deserving concern and, I dare to say, universal respect, and children whose tender age and misfortunes seemed to give them some rights at least to forbearance. But no! His family became the objects of unparalleled persecution, both in France and in the foreign countries to which, even during my father's lifetime, I had thought it best to withdraw as much for my safety as to avoid the misfortune—to my mind worse than any other—of passing, even unjustly, as the accomplice of the atrocities that he could not prevent. It was at that time that they took pleasure in aggravating their misfortunes by publishing a multitude of writings that defamed the memory of the Duke, which could have no other object than that of hurting his family and which were especially cowardly because it was well known that no voice would be raised to refute and confound them, however easy that might have been. It was then that Montjoie's *History of the Orléans' Conspiracy* appeared, and all those absurd fables that in other circumstances would have inspired general contempt. But in those times of political sensitivity and dissension, all these works were avidly received, and the absurdities that they contained were repeated without scruple both by those who, wanting to write the history of their times, had no other source of information and by those who, well knowing the falsity and injustice of these charges, thought by repeating them to escape suspicion of belonging to an Orléaniste faction that never existed. It is this junction of those who could not be suspected of personal animosity toward my father with those whose relentless pursuit of him was carried to the highest degree that resulted in that torrent of unfavorable opinions, which it was certainly difficult to resist. I am not seeking to recriminate against those whom it bore along: I know human weakness and the nature of the times in which we live too well. I am only trying to explain the reasons the general

* One can see why the vote in the King's trial was regarded as the acid test of political orthodoxy. Regicides could expect no mercy if the Counterrevolution were successful, and as such could be taken as being loyal to the Republic. As if to emphasize the point, the renegade aristocrat Lepeletier de Saint-Fargeau was assassinated shortly after voting for the King's death.—ED.

opinion about my father took a turn that was as unjust and mistaken as it was painful for his family and for those who were attached to him and who knew, like me, the falsity of all these assertions.

I shall add only one more observation to end this long digression. I loved my father; I have never had anything but praise for him; I honor his memory, I know the accusations that cloud it (with the exception of his vote in the trial of Louis XVI) are unworthy calumnies, and I believe I can prove it. I know more: I know that it is no longer against him that these calumnies are directed but against me, and that, not daring to attack my conduct and reputation openly, they attack my father ceaselessly in the hope of throwing on me the blame for the harm imputed to him. For more than twenty years I have endured these attacks in silence; powerful considerations have made me hold my peace, and I still do not know when it will be possible to let my voice be heard. Now I ask, what judgment should be made about such accusations when it is probable that those who have made them know their falseness themselves, and when it is certain that they were not unaware of the fact that we were prevented by our position from refuting them? And what is one to think of those who, not content with the misfortunes of every kind with which we have been overwhelmed, have had the unworthiness to aggravate them by all sorts of insults and persecutions?

I have already given a general idea of the attitude displayed toward France by the principal Courts of Europe at the time when France declared war on Austria by the decree that the National Assembly passed on April 20, 1792, after King Louis XVI had come down in person to propose it. The aim of his ministry in bringing about this declaration was to upset the plans of the Coalition already formed against France by making a rapid invasion of Belgium. The calculation was that a military occupation of Belgium would be easy because at this time there were still very few Austrian troops in the region between the Meuse and the sea, and it was believed that as soon as they had been expelled, the native population would come out against Austria and raise armies that would act in concert with ours to defend their independence. I believe that this plan really could have succeeded if both the Court and the generals and officers then at the head of the French armies had sincerely wanted it to, but whatever their differing motives, they were agreed in not wanting this. The first undertakings of the war were unsuccessful because of this general absence of the will to win rather than because the plan was unworkable as was claimed.

It was highly important that France should have a successful beginning to this war, and yet the measures adopted were not calculated to pave the way for victories. However, this is not to say that the ministry did not sincerely wish the war to be successful: it was even very much in its interests that it should be because only thus could it maintain itself in office. I have already said that the ministry of the time consisted of (1) M. de Grave, the Minister of War, who had been appointed under the previous ministry when it was about to collapse but who had remained in the new one; (2) General Dumouriez, Minister of Foreign Affairs, and MM. Roland, Clavière, Duranton and Lacoste, Ministers of the Interior, Finance, Justice, and the Marine respectively. This ministry was supported by that part of the Legislative Assembly that was already coming to be known as the *Gironde* because among its members, the deputies from Bordeaux* had drawn attention to themselves by their superior talents. At this time the Girondins were the popular party, and they owed this popularity principally to the opinions they had expressed about the Court, the *émigrés,* and the foreign Powers. They had argued that the Court was not acting in good faith, that it was sacrificing the interests of France to its desire to overthrow the Constitution and restore the Ancien Régime, that its disavowal of the *émigrés* was in appearance only, that it was not taking effective steps to thwart their plots, that it was counting on the assistance of the foreign Powers to achieve its aims, and that it had an understanding with them to paralyze France's means of defense so that the kingdom would be opened up to the foreign armies. These opinions were not only true but were already shared by a large part of the nation, and they became more general with each day because as events unfolded, their truth was increasingly recognized. This belief led to a general desire to see all the forces at the nation's disposal being wholeheartedly directed to resisting the Coalition of foreign Powers and to anticipating their threatened attack on France by carrying the war abroad. So when the ministry, in obedience to the promptings of the Girondins, strove to conduct the war with vigor and speed, it was acting in accordance with public opinion and the interests of France. It is therefore probable that it would have become unassailable if it had obtained the success that the sincerity of its opinions and conduct led the nation to hope for. The truth of this was only too well realized by the enemies of the ministry. They formed two very distinct parties whose principles and opinions were so opposed that this was practically the only occasion when they were seen to come together.† These two parties were that of the Court and the *émigrés,* and that of which M. de La Fayette was considered at the time to be the leader. This latter party was made up of MM. de Lameth and of a fairly large number of former members of the Constituent Assembly. It was they who had in turn founded the 1789 Club and the Feuillant Club and who had revised the Constitution before presenting it for the King's

* Bordeaux is the main town of the Department of the Gironde.—ED.
† I use the phrase "come together" because I do not know of a weaker one; because in fact there was no true coming together of these two parties, as later events abundantly demonstrated. All they had in common was their opposition to certain measures and to the policy that was being carried out by the Girondins and the Jacobins at the same time.

acceptance in 1791. I am sure that they sincerely believed in the Constitution; they wanted the Constitution to be maintained and King Louis XVI to remain the head of state; but they had always been opposed to the war, and right up to the last moment they were under the illusion that the foreign Powers would not attack France provided that she did not attack them and that the King remained at the head of the government: I even think they were still under this illusion after the declaration of war. Be that as it may, they always strove to keep military operations within the strict limits of a defensive war and said on every occasion that this kind of war suited them better than an offensive one, given the state of France and of the French armies at the time. The other party, on the contrary, that of the Court and the *émigrés,* wanted the foreign Powers to attack France; they loudly proclaimed the desire that their armies would enter the country and above all reach Paris to overthrow the Constitution and back them up in their plans for reaction and vengeance that would be directed especially against this same constitutional party which they hated and to which—despite their momentary agreement to block the plans of the ministry and bring about the failure of the military operations—they held out no more hope of mercy than before. It was this mistake of the principal leaders of the constitutional party that led to their downfall by causing them to become confused in the public mind with those who wanted to deliver France to the foreigners for the restoration of the Ancien Régime. It was a mistake from which they never recovered, and their conduct in this respect was one of the main reasons the nation acquired this suspicion of everything, which had such fatal consequences and caused the death of so many victims on the scaffold.

The combined opposition of these two parties was strong enough to block the activity of the ministry on all sides. Everywhere they found a lack of cooperation. None of the measures of the ministers was adopted in its entirety; they always had to choose between abandoning their plans or agreeing to mutilate them by concessions that their enemies demanded as the *sine qua non* of their cooperation, but that were nearly always designed to bring about the failure of everything the ministers undertook and yet to enable them to cast the same responsibility for defeats on the ministers as if their projects had been adopted in their entirety.

I have already said that at the moment when war was declared, the frontier of France from Huningue as far as Dunkirk was divided into three commands, each made up of an army under three independent commanders in chief. These three commanders were the Marshals Rochambeau and Luckner and Lieutenant General La Fayette. Marshal Luckner's command, the Army of the Rhine, stretched from Huningue to Landau. This army was supposed to remain on the defensive until the movements of the armies to its left enabled it to proceed down the left bank of the Rhine toward Mainz.

M. de La Fayette's command, or the Army of the Center, stretched from Bitche to Givet and Philippeville inclusive, and that of M. de Rochambeau from there to Dunkirk. It was called the Army of the North.

The ministry wanted to put the armies of the North and the Center into action immediately. M. de La Fayette received the order to assemble his troops at Givet, where a train of siege artillery had already arrived from Metz. He was then to proceed to Namur, lay siege to its fortifications, whose garrison was very small, and having taken them, march down the Meuse on Liège, or perform such other operations as the circumstances would seem to suggest—that is to say, he would have turned his army toward Brussels if the Army of the North had needed his help, or on the other hand, if it had already overcome the obstacles between it and Brussels and the Meuse, then the two armies would have joined forces at Liège so as to march together to the Rhine in readiness to combat the armies that the Coalition was going to send against France. They imagined that the French armies would be aided in these operations by the discontent of the people of Belgium, on which the ministry believed it could count.

The Army of the North was to proceed in three main bodies: The first, leaving from Valenciennes and Maubeuge, was to make for Mons; the second to go from Lille to Tournay, and the third from Dunkirk to Furnes, Ypres, and Courtray; and all three were to reassemble at Brussels. But when the ministry wanted to execute this project, it encountered an obstacle that determined it to make one of those fatal concessions I have already discussed, which was necessarily going to decrease the chances of success. Marshal Rochambeau, who was in command of the Army of the North, refused to undertake the execution of the plan of campaign, and he even went as far as declaring that he would not cooperate in carrying out any operations relative to an offensive war. It seemed a necessary consequence that the Marshal should be replaced as commander in chief, but the ministry dared not, or rather could not, do this, and it thought to extricate itself from its difficulties by leaving him as nominal commander in chief while giving the real command to another officer on the general staff. As a result the command of the detachment at Valenciennes and Maubeuge was given to Lieutenant General le Duc de Biron, but he had to remain subordinate to the Marshal because he retained overall command. The detachment at Lille was to be commanded by the *maréchal de camp** Théobald Dillon and that at Dunkirk by Lieutenant General de Carle. The result of these arrangements was that, as these two generals were less senior than M. de Biron, they would find themselves under him if their operations were carried beyond France, especially if the three detachments came together at Brussels according to plan. On the other hand, if they were obliged to fall back on French

* The rank between brigadier and lieutenant general.—ED.

territory, which is precisely what happened, they would necessarily come under Marshal Rochambeau again.

As for the means of execution of this plan, I shall confine myself to the observation that at this period the arsenals of France were abundantly supplied in all things and that there was a vast artillery in excellent shape. In the following June, the Army of the North, encamped at La Madeleine near Lille, had a total of twenty-eight thousand men, and the Army of the Center consisted of thirty-three thousand, not counting the admittedly tiny garrisons that had been left in all the fortified towns. Now, one cannot deny that what was possible in the month of June would have been possible from April on if it had been desired, and consequently it can be said without exaggeration that France was able to put sixty thousand men into Belgium at the moment she declared war on Austria, to which Belgium belonged at the time.

It is more difficult to evaluate the number of troops that Austria had on the spot to resist this attack. But I think she did not have thirty thousand men all told between Luxembourg and the sea, and I have never heard anyone, at the time or later, say that she had more, which makes it a strong presumption at the least that she did not. I can say further that what we saw of her forces led us to believe that they were indeed well below this number. Now, with such insufficient means at her disposal, Austria would not have been able to resist a French army of sixty thousand or even fifty thousand men in completely open country, where the fortifications had been dismantled and where the attachment of the inhabitants to Austrian rule was more than suspect, since two years previously they had thrown off its yoke and had only been subdued by force of arms.

Having given this glimpse of the plans and the state of affairs, I move on to a detailed consideration of what concerns me personally; at the same time I shall consider the general operations of the war and the political shifts that accompanied or followed them. I shall often have to go into excessive detail to give an accurate picture of this and to convey a sense of the incompetence and above all the intrigue and bad faith that produced the misfortunes which I witnessed and which at first paralyzed the nation's noble drive to defend its liberty and independence.

Although I was only eighteen and a half at the time when war was declared, because of the incidence of emigration among those of the rank of staff and senior officers and above, I was the most senior colonel in the army on active service: I had been made a colonel because I was a Prince of the Blood, and my commission was dated November 20, 1785. I have already said that a few weeks previously the regiment that I was commanding, the 14th Dragoons, had been sent from Valenciennes to Laon, and so it was no longer right on the frontier. The Minister of War, the Comte de Grave, had promised me that if war were declared, he would arrange for my regiment to be part of the army that took part in the campaign. So I went to see him the day after war was declared, that is to say on April 21, and asked him to carry out his promise, which he did with the same kindness he had always displayed in everything that concerned me personally, on account of his long-standing and unwavering affection for me. However, since he could not order troop movements in the areas under the jurisdiction of the commanders in chief of the armies, who had retained this power, he could do no more than ask Marshal Rochambeau to bring my regiment back to the frontier and include it among those that were going to make up M. de Biron's detachment. M. de Grave knew as well as I did that M. de Rochambeau would be in no hurry to bow to this order from the Minister; and to get around this difficulty, he gave me special instructions to join M. de Biron immediately at Valenciennes together with the Duc de Montpensier, my brother, who was a sublieutenant in the regiment I commanded. He told M. de Biron to use us as volunteer officers on his staff until our regiment had joined his detachment of the army.

Armed with this order from the Minister of War, I left Paris for Valenciennes with my brother on April 23 and arrived there on the 24th. I found M. de Biron closeted with the Marshal in his study: I was announced and they came out together. The Marshal said dryly to me: "I don't know what you are doing here, but your regiment is at Laon, so just return there immediately." I gave him to understand that I had come to Valenciennes on the orders of the Minister of War to receive those of M. de Biron. The Marshal replied with pique that when he was giving the orders, M. de Biron had no need to, and asked if they had nothing better to do than make colonels without regiments. But M. de Biron took him on one side, and he calmed down and came over to tell me that he would not insist that I leave and that since M. de Biron wanted to keep me with him, he would not object further. Having cleared this first hurdle, it was then easier to get the Marshal to order my regiment to leave Laon and proceed to Valenciennes. However, it took so long for this letter to be dispatched that my regiment did not reach Valenciennes till April 30, that is to say, the very day that the ridiculous expedition made by M. de Biron's detachment came to an end, so that my regiment was not able to take part in it.

Instead of immediately putting into the field every possible man from the Army of the North and the Army of the Center, they assembled only a part of the troops, on the grounds that they could not employ more without stripping the fortified towns of their garrisons and risking their safety. Despite the absurdity of this contention, since the Austrians had no means of attacking them, the ministry felt obliged to make this further concession and thus agreed that the execution of its plans, which was easy to accomplish with large forces, should be undertaken with very small ones. The detachment of M. de Biron was composed of only eight thousand four hundred men; that of M. Dillon, at Lille, of three thousand six hundred; and that of M. de Carle, at Dunkirk, of fourteen thousand men. The detachment that M. de La Fayette encamped at Rancennes near Givet was said to consist of ten thousand men. Thus, they entered the campaign with at the very most twenty-four thousand men when they could have tripled the number if they had wanted to; and yet, even with this force as it stood, they could have mopped up the country as far as the Meuse if they had not used their authority to paralyze its operations when they should have directed them.

It was during the night of April 27–28 that the troops from the different garrisons that were to form M. de Biron's detachment met at Valenciennes, with the exception of those from Maubeuge, which had orders to make straight for the frontier at Quiévrain. They were under the orders of M. de Rochambeau, the son of the Marshal, who was still only a *maréchal de camp*. As my horses and those of my brother had not yet arrived at Valenciennes, M. de Biron was kind enough to lend us one each, and we accompanied the expedition in the capacity of volunteer officers serving on the general staff.*

Our little detachment set off on April 28 at daybreak and set up camp right on the frontier. The camp straddled the main road from Valenciennes to Mons, with its right flank at Quiévrechain and its left at the Abbey of Crespin. Before our front line lay the village of Quiévrain, situated on an eminence, with the Ronelle River between us, separating French and Austrian territory here. The boundary of the frontier was between two bridges. A few Uhlans and an Austrian officer were stationed on the bridge on their side. General Biron sent Colonel Dampierre with a trumpeter to notify them of France's declaration of war. This was prob-

---

* General Biron's general staff consisted of General Rochambeau, Colonels Alexandre Beauharnais[a] and La Tour-Foissac, adjutants general; MM. Lafitte, a colonel in the sappers, and Dupuch, a colonel in the artillery, and MM. de Pressac and Le Vasseur, aides-de-camp to the General; MM. d'Hédouville[b] and de Pontavice, adjutants to the adjutants general. Colonel Alexandre Berthier, at the time adjutant general and later Marshal of France and Prince de Wagram, was sent on a mission to M. de Biron during this expedition. I am writing from memory, and I am not in a position to give a precise enumeration of the troops that composed this little army. I do remember, however, that there were four regiments of Horse that provided only eleven squadrons, or about fifteen to sixteen hundred horses, namely the 3rd Hussars (Esterhazy), commanded by Colonel Froissy, who emigrated the following August; the 3rd Cavalry (general commission), under the command of Colonel de Flers, who was later commander in chief of the Army of the North and who died on the scaffold; the 5th Dragoons (colonel in chief), commanded by Colonel Dampierre, who was later commander in chief of the Army of the North and was killed in the Battle of Famars in 1793; and the 6th Dragoons (the Queen's), commanded by Colonel Duval, who died later with the rank of commander in chief.

a Alexandre Beauharnais, who had been a member of the Constituent Assembly. He was then commander in chief of the Army of the Rhine and died on the scaffold in 1794. He was the first husband of the Empress Josephine, by whom he had Prince Eugène and the Duchesse de Saint-Leu.

b Later a commander in chief and today a peer of France.

ably the last time that this formality was observed. Shortly afterward General Biron, seeing that the Austrians were not going to withdraw, sent a few skirmishers forward, followed by a squadron from the 5th Regiment of Dragoons; the Uhlans emptied their rifles on them and then made off at a gallop. The village of Quiévrain was occupied immediately, and as some of the troops had come from distant garrisons and had marched all through the night, we carried out no further measures that day.

On April 29 the troops continued their march toward Mons along the main road, the hussars clearing the way. We met with some resistance in the village of Boussu, which our hussars entered rashly. Some Tyrolean riflemen from the Leloup detachment who were hidden behind the hedges fired a few shots at them and forced them to withdraw sharply. However, we lost only Lieutenant General Cazenove, whose horse was killed and who was taken prisoner. General Biron ordered the company of grenadiers from the 74th Regiment (Beaujolais), commanded by Colonel Freytag, to advance and followed it up with all his infantry so that the Austrian riflemen were soon driven back; on our side there was not even a single grenadier lightly wounded. But a little further on, still on the main road to Mons, we encountered more resistance. The Austrians had taken up position at the gates of Quaregnon, which dominates a fair stretch of the road in a straight line, and they had three-pounder cannons. As General Biron was marching in the midst of his skirmishers, we were subjected to several discharges before we managed to dislodge the Austrians, which was done promptly. There were some wounded on our side, including Colonel Dupuch of the artillery, who was hit in the arm.

After this skirmish we noticed a small body of Austrian troops on the heights of Quaregnon and Jemappes, which lay before us. Then General Biron thought the best thing to do was to stop and to deploy his little army on the plain to the right of the gates of Quaregnon. Our front line was covered by a stream, and we had to our right and our left the villages of Wasmes, Pâturages and Wasnielles, where we merely placed lookouts. We learned from peasants and travelers that the Austrian troops we saw before us had just been reinforced by a few companies of grenadiers who had arrived the day before from Brussels to oppose our progress.* General Biron ordered soup to be made and decided not to advance any further that evening, but he told us that he proposed to attack the Austrians the following morning. The troops bivouacked in two lines. The first was composed of infantry, and the second, which was a fair distance behind the first, was composed of the heavy cavalry and the dragoons. General Biron set up his headquarters in an isolated house in the village of Hornu; this house was on the main road, exactly to the left of the place where the dragoons had bivouacked. He gave orders that no matter what,

* General Beaulieu, who was in command of the Austrian troops, said in his official report that he had only eighteen hundred infantrymen and about fourteen to fifteen hundred cavalry (see le Moniteur for May 8, 1792).

the horses should be kept saddled throughout the night; that night he slept fully dressed in a low-ceilinged room in the house, and we went to sleep on the hay in the attic with M. de Beauharnais and a few other officers. We remained there quietly until about ten at night, when we were awakened by a few pistol shots very near to the house where we were. Immediately afterward we heard a great tumult and many cries of "To horse, to horse!" We thought that the enemy was attacking us or that some patrol had penetrated our lines. We leaped down from the attic to look for our horses, and we encountered M. de Biron and the whole staff of the headquarters mounting their horses and each asking what was happening. Scarcely had we left the courtyard of the house when we discovered that the main road was entirely blocked* and that we were surrounded by a large column of our dragoons going at a fast trot and shouting: "Every man for himself! We are betrayed, given over to the enemy, let us go back to our own territory and get to our strongholds!" The night was very dark, and we could not even see who the troops surrounding us were. It was equally impossible to avoid being swept along by the movement of this column, in whose midst we found ourselves trapped, carried off by a completely irresistible force. I stayed by the General's side the whole time during this *débâcle,* and I had great difficulty in avoiding being separated from him. In this way we covered a league and a half going back toward France without being able to fathom the cause of such a strange movement. M. de Biron was in a state of despair and rage. Ten times we tried to face about but always in vain, for the road was so narrow and so congested that it was impossible to wheel our horses around. Finally, after we had passed through the village of Boussu in this way, M. de Biron thought that he would try giving regular commands to the throng that surrounded us; he shouted in a firm voice: *"Attention! Column, slow march!"* and to our great amazement, all the horses fell into a walk. Then he whispered to the officers near him to be ready to assist him as soon as he gave a second command, and when he shouted *"To the right, in battle order, march!"* we all lunged suddenly to our right into a field with an open gate. In this way we managed to extricate ourselves from the column, a large part of which responded to the impetus we had given and came to form up on our right, while the others continued to follow the main road; but when they realized how few they were in number, they turned in their tracks one after the other, and nearly all of them had rejoined their regiments by daybreak. As soon as we were in the field we regrouped the companies as best we could, and then we learned that the troop that had carried us off consisted of only three or four hundred dragoons and a few officers.† The General did not waste

* The roads in Flanders are narrow and have deep ditches at the sides, and the fields are closed by gates.
† I like to recall that these dragoons were not from my regiment, which did not take part in the expedition.

precious time finding out the cause of this unbelievable movement; he hastened to go to see what was happening in his camp, and breaking away to the right, he set off at as fast a gallop as before, in the direction from which we had started out. When we arrived there, we were pleasantly surprised to find that the other troops had noticed nothing. We went to the place where the infantry was bivouacked, and all were sleeping peacefully. The dragoons resumed their place beside the heavy cavalry, which had not moved; and General Biron, having summoned the senior officers of the dragoons and questioned them about what they had seen and heard, received from them all the assurance that they had seen and heard nothing apart from the four or five pistol shots we had all heard. We never discovered who had fired them, but General Biron remained convinced, as did I and many others, that this movement had been prearranged and that the pistol shots had been a signal. This seems all the more likely in that our outposts were so positioned that it was virtually impossible for any enemy patrol to penetrate as far as the house where the headquarters was established without being seen by them, and they were all at one in declaring that they had seen nothing. What happened in the course of the following day served to confirm us in our opinion that it was a *coup* got up by a few officers because the rout on that day was in large measure brought about by these same dragoons, and it is rather striking that a large numbers of officers from these regiments emigrated a few days later.

The rest of the night passed quietly, but we did not enter the house again, and we awaited the dawn in the courtyard, wrapped up in our cloaks.

Early in the morning of April 30 M. Duvigneau, aide-de-camp to Marshal Rochambeau, arrived with dispatches for M. de Biron in which the Marshal informed him of the unfortunate outcome of the expedition from Lille and urged him to retire to the frontier. He told him that General Dillon had left Lille on April 28 with his detachment and found enemy outposts on the main road to Tournay between the villages of Hertain and Marquain. He had attacked them with his advance guard, which had then been seized with panic and fled in disarray,* his cavalry tumbling over his infantry and killing many; the flight had then become general, and after making vain attempts to reestablish order, General Dillon had himself been accused of treason by the disbanded troops and had taken refuge in a barn to escape their fury, but had been slain there together with Lieutenant Colonel Bertois of the engineer corps. All the troops had reentered Lille, where the greatest panic and unrest reigned.

After receiving this sad news, General Biron decided to defer to Marshal Rochambeau's request and to fall back on the frontier behind the

* It is worth noting that this movement was exactly the same as the one that had taken place in M. de Biron's detachment and is another piece of evidence that they were prearranged.

Ronelle. He entrusted General Rochambeau with the command of his rear guard, which he formed out of the 18th Infantry Regiment (Royal Auvergne), commanded by Colonel Tourville, and the 3rd Hussars (Esterhazy) under Colonel Froissy. The retreat was carried out at first in perfect order. General Beaulieu, the Austrian commander, seeing that we were withdrawing, advanced his troops and attacked our rear guard; but General Rochambeau repulsed this attack vigorously and covered the retreat for three leagues without sustaining any losses. When he reached Quiévrain General Biron placed two infantry battalions, the 68th of the line (Beauce), commanded by M. de Montchoisy, and the 2nd of National Volunteers from the Department of the Nord with their four fieldpieces, in the brickfields on both sides of the road to Mons covering the center of the village. The walls of unfired brick were at right angles to the main road. They were placed in several parallel lines in pits and formed trenches that should have been regarded as impregnable, especially against a cavalry attack. The whole of our little army filed through the village of Quiévrain in very good order and again took up the position behind the Ronelle that it had occupied on the 28th. Marshal Rochambeau preceded M. de Biron as far as Quiévrain and told him that he had positioned the 1st Regiment of Mounted Riflemen, commanded by Vicomte Louis de Noailles, *maréchal de camp,* near Honain and that the 5th and 89th Foot (Navarre and Royal Swedish) were on the heights of Saint-Sauve with my regiment of dragoons (the 14th), which had just arrived, as had the 17th of the same arm (Schomberg). The Marshal only remained a few moments with M. de Biron and then returned to the heights of Saint-Sauve, from where he could observe all that was going on in the plain. It was believed then, and with reason, that everything was finished for the day, but suddenly we saw the two battalions to whom the defense of the brickfields had been entrusted arriving in confusion and on the run. They had been seized by blind panic at the sight of two or three hundred Uhlans, commanded, I have been told, by the Count von Zinzendorf, advancing boldly along the main road to sound out the village of Quiévrain. The battalion from the Nord abandoned the brickfield immediately, crying: "We are betrayed! Every man for himself!" The 68th followed this fatal example despite the efforts of Colonel Montchoisy (later a lieutenant general, who was to die as governor of Genoa in 1814). Some—the majority—fled by way of the village of Quiévrain, and the rest spread out to the right and left in the villages, but they all made off fast. Then the Uhlans entered Quiévrain at a gallop, sabering those of the fugitives they could catch, and in this way they advanced along the main road to within thirty paces of the infantry line that had just been formed on the ground where it was going to camp. Because of the way the trees were spaced and the nature of the terrain, the Uhlans could only be seen by the battalion that was on the main road. This battalion was the 74th, commanded by Colonel Freytag, who ordered a few volleys to be fired at them and drove them off immediately. But just at the time when this fusillade took place and when the arrival of the soldiers from the two disbanded battalions was beginning to spread the alarm, the 3rd Horse, which had crossed the Ronelle at Quiévrain, was advancing in a column to take its place on the right of the infantry. Colonel de Flers, seeing rifle fire on the road, put his column into a trot in order to arrive more quickly, and because they were obscured by the cloud of dust around them, the troops who were already in the camp believed they were a column of Austrian cavalry taking them on the flank at the same time as their front was being attacked, and disorder broke out immediately. The dragoons of the 6th Regiment, who were behind the infantry, themselves set the example for disorder instead of trying to check it, and they disbanded shouting: "Every man for himself! We have been delivered to the enemy!" General Biron ran to them with all his officers to try to hold them back; but it was impossible to make them understand anything, and in an instant the flight became general. The artillery and the ammunition wagons left at a gallop in all directions. The wagoners crossed the plain knocking over everything in their way; the hedges and the ditches did not stop them; they left behind their cannons and their ammunition wagons and cut their traces with saber blows to get out more quickly. No description can give an idea of the sight that this plain presented then. Fortunately the Austrians did not make even the slightest attempt to profit from this confusion. General Biron was everywhere, but to no avail. General Rochambeau did as much with no more success: He could not even hold back his own regiment, the 18th, which had conducted itself so well in the morning by repelling the attack of the Austrian infantry. He had such an outburst of anger that he broke his sword and threw the bits into their midst, saying they would never see him at their head again.*

When General Biron saw that all was in vain and that his efforts could no longer arrest the disorder, he sent me to give General Noailles the order to advance immediately with his three regiments of riflemen; at the same time he told me to go and find my regiment on the heights of Saint-Sauve and to beg the Marshal to send him all the troops that were there in reserve. Exhausted as my horse now was,† I lost no time, and I went with my brother to give the Vicomte de Noailles General Biron's order. He did not know what to do with it because I think he was acting in good faith and genuinely wanted to prevent the Austrians from profiting from our confusion; but he replied to me that the Marshal had forbidden him to advance without an express order from him and that in consequence he could not obey General Biron's order immediately; however, he told me

* In fact he left in the evening for Paris and never returned to the army; but a few months afterward he was appointed governor of Martinique and saw some service again in America.
† This was still the one that M. de Biron had lent me. I had had no other for three days, and it died the next day from exhaustion.

to point out to the Marshal in his name that there was not a moment to lose and to tell him that he would answer for the restoration of order if he would authorize him to act and merely send him the two regiments of dragoons that were at Saint-Sauve. So I went to find the Marshal, who was standing with the elder M. de Crillon and his general staff by the windmill of Saint-Sauve, coldly observing everything that was happening with his eyeglass. I discharged M. de Biron's commission and that of M. de Noailles, and all the reply that the Marshal gave me was: "I do not want M. de Noailles to go forward, nor you. Your regiment is here, put yourself at its head and await my orders without moving." "But Marshal," I said to him, "I hope at least that you will not condemn me to watch this fearful *débâcle* without trying to stop it or do something about it, and that when M. de Biron asks you to order an advance and M. de Noailles joins him in this request, you will not take it upon yourself to refuse them?" Then for an answer the Marshal merely told me that I had no knowledge of men and that he knew what he was doing; and he added, turning to M. de Crillon: "These gentlemen wanted to go to war, they must get themselves out of it." So I went to my regiment, which was a hundred paces behind the Marshal, and I spent the rest of the day there, during which he did not decide to make or allow any movement.

However, there was one infantry battalion which had not broken up. It was the 49th of the line (Vintimille), commanded by Colonel Casabianca.* It was at the extremity of the left flank in front of the Abbey of Crespin, and this position enabled its commander to preserve it from contagion. M. de Biron put himself at its head to dislodge the Austrians from the village of Quiévrain, which he assumed they had occupied after our troops had abandoned it; however, he found no one there, and when he was quite satisfied that the Austrians had not moved and did not intend to give chase, he sent to the Marshal to inform him of the fact and beg him to accelerate his advance; but the Marshal persisted in not doing so, and M. de Biron was informed that the best thing he could do was withdraw. And so they abandoned seven or eight pieces of cannon that had remained in the ditches and camping equipment for eight thousand men, not to mention the rifles, bags, pans, etc., that littered the plain. It was not until night that the Austrians dared come to see what was going on in our camp; and it was then, but only then,† that finding it abandoned, they lit fires and burned all our effects that they could not transport and that they feared, with reason, we might finally decide to go to recover.

Toward evening the Marshal summoned me to tell me that the troops that were on the heights of Saint-Sauve would bivouac there for the night and that he would be sleeping in a nearby house. I then replied that since he seemed determined to give us nothing to do, I wanted permission to go

* Later a lieutenant general, senator, and one of the peers of France who were removed by the ordinance of July 24, 1815.
† I believe it was not till two in the morning.

to Valenciennes (which is only half a league from the place where we were) to ascertain what had happened to General Biron, about whom I was very concerned, especially considering what had happened the day before at Lille and the tragedy of M. de Dillon. The Marshal replied that he would allow me to go to Valenciennes if I wanted, but that it was very rash and that I could be done a mischief there in the midst of the unrest caused by the reverses in the war. I replied that that was my affair, but that I had nothing to fear from this unrest because I was certain that no one suspected the sincerity of my opinions or the good faith of my conduct, and immediately I made for Valenciennes alone with my brother.

As we approached the place, we were exposed to a score of rifle shots that the soldiers, spread along the ramparts, were shooting off into the fields. We entered without any other difficulty and made straight for the Hôtel de Ville. The squares and streets were full of soldiers sitting on the ground and seemingly disposed to spend the night there. All the regiments were mixed up and there was complete confusion, but in the midst of this disorder there were no excesses committed, although the soldiers showed their discontent by the violent language they used when discussing the officers and the Marshal; but they did not display any animosity toward M. de Biron, and they were all agreed in saying that he was a gallant man. He was at the Hôtel de Ville when I arrived there, and the first thing he did was to express his fear that the Marshal had come to Valenciennes, which was worthy of his loyal character and well founded because if the Marshal had gone there that day, it would have been difficult to keep him from the soldiers' fury. General Biron told me that it was impossible that evening to sort out the chaos that was obstructing all the streets of the town, but that he hoped the different battalions would be reorganized the next day and ready to proceed to the quarters around Valenciennes he had assigned to them while they awaited new orders.

Such was the shameful beginning to a war from which the French nation was later to reap such glory. I have dwelt at such length on these events because I have not seen an accurate and detailed account of them anywhere. Those that were produced at the time were designed to suppress the truth rather than make it known. There is no doubt that if the war went badly then, it was because they feared the consequences of success. These were the sentiments of the Court and its supporters. However chimerical their hopes may have been, there was a crowd of people who considered that their realization was a certainty. The result, as should have been expected at the time, was that the nation, far from acknowledging its so-called weakness and inability to resist, laid the blame on the incompetence of its leaders and its government; it believed that they were sacrificing the honor and interests of the nation to the vain hope of restoring the Ancien Régime, and was led to place the direction of its destiny in other hands.

Scarcely were the disasters I have just recounted known in France when everyone put their minds to discovering their true causes, and they were not long in unraveling them. It was in vain that no inquiry was made into the proceedings of the dragoons on the night of the 29th, or into the *débâcle* at Lille, that they tried to conceal the fact that several officers from these regiments had emigrated on the morrow of their return to Valenciennes, that no inquiry was made into the *débâcle* of the 30th, that Marshal Rochambeau's inactivity during that unfortunate day was likewise hushed up, and that they tried to place the blame for the setbacks France had just experienced on the ministry that had planned the enterprise and on the troops who had failed to carry it out. Neither the nation nor the army was deceived, and on all sides the outcry against the Marshal and those who did not want to fight the war wholeheartedly became so great that they were forced to relieve the Marshal of his command, despite the renewed efforts that were made to preserve him in it. But finally he went, and the clamor calmed down. However, they persisted in a policy of inaction and of total obstruction, and the clamor broke out again with more vehemence than before. Experience did not make them wiser, and the approach of the foreign armies made them bolder; they thought they could resist the voice of the nation, they tried it, and they fell. At least such was my way of looking at things at the time, and such it still is today. I hope that the rest of my story will go some way toward justifying this view.

The day after the *débâcle* the Marshal sent my regiment into quarters at Frith-Saint-Léger, a village on the Scheldt behind Valenciennes. The 1st Regiment of Mounted Rifles withdrew to Marly, which is a suburb of this garrison town, so that all the frontier villages were left without any protection against the incursions of the enemy's light troops, and they did not fail to send in their patrols, though without causing great damage. Representations were made to the Marshal about the distribution of these quarters, and after a few days his permission was obtained to bring them nearer to the frontier. My regiment was then placed in the villages of Saultain and Curgies, on the road to Maubeuge, with four companies of grenadiers who were placed under me. The 3rd Hussars were placed at Jalain; we formed a chain of posts before these villages, and the frontier was a little better protected. I remained only a few days at Saultain before being relieved by the 5th Regiment of Mounted Rifles, commanded by Lieutenant Colonel Richardot.* It was then decided that the dragoons would cease to serve as light troops and that they would be employed in the line like the heavy cavalry. My regiment was made up into a brigade with the 17th, commanded by Colonel Prilly, and this brigade received orders to join the camp at Famars.

I was made a *maréchal de camp* in order of seniority on May 7, at the

* A very keen and active officer who killed himself in the Conciergerie in 1794 when he was due to appear before the Revolutionary Tribunal.

same time as Colonel Alexandre Berthier, the next ranking colonel. He was made chief of general staff of the Army of the North, and I kept my command, as *maréchal de camp,* of the brigade of dragoons with which I was encamped at Famars. Lieutenant Colonel Sahuguet d'Espagnac, who was my second in command in the 14th Dragoons, became its colonel in my place, and I took the Duc de Montpensier, my brother, as my aide-de-camp.

Troops were successively brought to the camp at Famars, and about twelve thousand men were assembled there; however, they continued not to undertake offensive operations despite the enthusiasm of the nation and the general discontent aroused by this inactivity. Instead of profiting from the precious time before the enemy had gathered its forces, they merely spent their time in intrigues to change the ministry or to keep or change the generals. Marshal Rochambeau, after addressing very strong representations to the King, the ministers, and the Assembly about the enterprises that had been undertaken against his advice and about the necessity of confining themselves to a policy of defensive warfare, resigned on May 8, and the ministers recalled Marshal Luckner from Alsace to replace him. This marshal had often declared himself in favor of an offensive, and his nomination looked as if it would satisfy the nation and the army. However, the party that wanted to retain M. de Rochambeau managed once again to prevent Marshal Luckner from being definitively nominated to the command of the Army of the North. They tried to get the staff officers and the body of regimental officers to declare that they would leave the service if Marshal Rochambeau left the army, and some lent themselves to the idea, though the majority refused. They even presented the Assembly with a proposed resolution inviting the Marshal to keep his command, but it was rejected on the grounds that to interfere in the choice of generals would be impinging on the functions of the executive, and at the same time the Assembly directed its president to write to Marshal Luckner thanking him for the proclamations he had addressed to the troops under his command on the occasion of the declaration of war. Immediately afterward it passed a decree fulminating against the *débâcle* of the 30th, ordering that the 5th and 6th Dragoons should be summoned to reveal the names of those who had sown disorder among them and that unless they complied with this demand within the time prescribed by the General, the two regiments would be disbanded, their colors burned at the head of the army, and their numbers left vacant for all time as a perpetual reminder of the chastisement that had been inflicted on them by an outraged nation. But like so many others, this decree was never executed,* and as I have already said, there was not even an inquiry into the events of April 29 and 30. However, they thought it advisable to send Marshal Luckner to the Army of the North, but before he left, the King summoned him and ordered him publicly to express to

* See the issues of *le Moniteur* for May 12 and 13, 1792.

212

Marshal Rochambeau his personal wish that he keep the command, and he even forbade him to accept it as long as he was able to obtain the Marshal's consent not to relinquish it and to stay in the army.

It was, I think, on May 14 or 15 that Marshal Luckner arrived at Valenciennes. I was present at some of the meetings that took place between the two marshals, and the compliments they paid each other were truly ludicrous. Marshal Luckner claimed that he had only come to the army to obtain Marshal Rochambeau's consent not to relinquish its command, while Marshal Rochambeau pretended that he was only staying on to obtain Marshal Luckner's consent to be good enough to undertake it. All the time that this battle of good manners was going on, Marshal Rochambeau kept the command; he often made the troops leave camp to amuse his colleague with maneuvers; but they continued to remain inactive, as though they were in the middle of peace and war had not been declared.

There was, however, a little encounter on May 17. The Austrians, to the number of about twenty-five hundred men, overran a garrison of eighty men of the 49th Foot at Bavay. A few hussars from the 3rd Regiment who happened to be with them and who escaped capture reported the Austrian maneuver. Marshal Rochambeau came immediately to the camp at Famars to put himself at the head of the troops, and Marshal Luckner took command of the vanguard under his orders. We set out to march to Bavay, but we had scarcely covered half the distance when we discovered that the Austrians had retired immediately, taking their prisoners with them, so that no longer having anyone to fight, we returned to the camp at Famars without firing a shot.

A few days afterward, Marshal Rochambeau formally relinquished command of the Army of the North and handed it over to Marshal Luckner.

It was at this period that my father came to the Army of the North and spent about six weeks there. He was an admiral and would have liked employment in the navy appropriate to his rank, but this he was refused. He asked to be employed as a lieutenant general in one of the armies but was no more successful. Then he asked for permission to accompany the headquarters of the Army of the North as an ordinary volunteer, and after the Minister of the Marine, M. de Lacoste, had written to him saying that the King left him free to take what action he thought appropriate in this respect, at the end of May he proceeded to Valenciennes, where he rented a house that would serve him as a base while he accompanied the army. Then, as he wanted to be nearer to the camp where my brother and I were and to the village of Famars where his old friend M. de Biron was lodging, he took a house, where we went as often as our duties permitted. People have tried to find hidden motives behind this visit that my father made to the Army of the North. I can affirm that there were none. My father made no secret of the motives that determined him to undertake it.

213

He considered that in his position and with the political opinions he had professed, it was not right that he should remain inactive at Paris when war was raging on the frontiers, and he was very glad to play his part in the same army in which his two sons were serving. He had the further motive of wishing to take his third son, the Comte de Beaujolais, there himself; he was only twelve at the time and was with him during this trip. Moreover, my father's position in Paris had become painful in many respects, as much by the contraction of his income as by the total isolation in which he now found himself, that it was perfectly natural that he should try to withdraw and make another kind of life for himself by following the activities of one of the armies. Circumstances did not permit him to continue to do this, which I much regretted. I resume my account.

The Comte de Grave, wearied of a ministry where he was harassed by all the parties without being able to satisfy any of them, gave in his resignation on May 8, that is to say, the day after he had made me a *maréchal de camp*. He was replaced by M. Servan. As the Comte de Grave had been brought into the ministry by the party that opposed his colleagues, it seemed that his leaving would bring about a greater unity of action within the government. However, it had the opposite effect; it was the signal for the disunity which crept into the ministry and led to its fall at the end of a month. M. de Grave's wise and conciliatory nature, as much as his detachment from the two parties, maintained an equilibrium in the Council that moderated the claims of both much more than they themselves realized. As soon as he had been replaced by M. Servan, the Girondins, realizing that this appointment increased their strength, became more exacting toward General Dumouriez, and he, for the same reason, sought ways of making himself more independent of them; the result was the disputes and the disunity that caused the schism in the ministry, the details of which I shall give after I have carried the account of the army operations up to the point where it erupted.

When Marshal Luckner had finally taken over command of the Army of the North, responsibility for Maubeuge was transferred to the Army of the Center, which was commanded by M. de La Fayette, who set up his headquarters there. The troops in the entrenched camp of Maubeuge were reinforced by the infantry brigade of M. Alexandre Lameth, *maréchal de camp* at the time, and all the other troops of the Army of the North encamped at Famars set off on the march to Lille. There was only one garrison left at Valenciennes, command of which was entrusted to Lieutenant General d'Harville.

Here are the details of the new plan of campaign that was adopted then and was not carried any further than the previous one. All the available troops of the Army of the North were to be assembled near Lille at the Madeleine camp, while those of the Army of the Center were to be assembled at the camp at Maubeuge. And assembled they were, to the number of sixty thousand men: Those of the Army of the North

214

amounted to twenty-eight thousand men and those of the Army of the Center to thirty-three thousand. The Army of the North was then to enter Belgium via Menin and Courtray and to proceed from behind the Lys and the Scheldt toward Gand, to draw off the Austrians in this directon. Then after this movement had been brought about, the Army of the Center would have attacked Mons, which is only four leagues from Maubeuge, and would then have proceeded toward Brussels if it had succeeded in taking Mons.

This plan was perhaps less methodical than the first, since it did not envisage sending a detachment to besiege Namur and follow the Meuse to make the Austrians anxious about their communications with Germany, but it was easy to execute; and I consider that given the superiority of the troops then at our disposal, all these plans would have been equally good, for to win Belgium all that was needed was to desire it and to march.

Marshal Luckner left Valenciennes on June 10 with the detachment of the army that was encamped at Famars, to which the brigade of dragoons that I commanded belonged. We camped on the 10th and the 11th at Saint-Amand, on the 12th at Orchies, and on the 13th at La Madeleine near Lille, where we were reinforced by different troops taken from the garrisons and by two regiments of carabineers that had been brought from Strasbourg at Marshal Luckner's request.

This army was composed for the most part of troops of the line. There were, however, a few battalions of National Volunteers, but they had been chosen from among those whose military bearing and discipline was the most advanced, and this army both looked good and was good, There were only two lieutenant generals, M. de Biron and M. de Carle. The *maréchaux de camp* were Alexandre Berthier, chief of general staff; Jarry, commanding the vanguard; Valence, commanding the reserve made up of six squadrons of carabineers and a few battalions of grenadiers formed from companies of different regiments; d'Aboville, in command of the artillery; Charles Lameth, commanding a brigade of cuirassiers; Duhoux and myself, each commanding a brigade of dragoons; Lynch and Beurnonville,* commanding infantry brigades; the other brigades were commanded by colonels, pending the arrival of the *maréchaux de camp* who had not yet rejoined their regiments and who never did. The colonels were Courcy, of the 1st Regiment of Foot, Casabianca of the 49th, Desforêts of the 78th, Dupuch of the 81st, etc. Marshal Luckner's aides-de-camp were Colonel Ihler, who was killed serving with the Army of the Rhine in 1793, Lieutenant Colonel d'Aoust, who died on the scaffold after being commander in chief of the Army of the Eastern Pyrenees, and Captains Mathieu de Montmorency and La Grange.† The adjutants general were

* Captain MacDonald, later Marshal of France and Duke of Tarento, was at that time General Beurnonville's aide-de-camp.

† M. de La Grange is today a lieutenant general. He lost an arm and in 1814 was commanding one of the companies of musketeers.

Alexandre Beauharnais, César Berthier, Chancel,* Hédouville, etc.

Our army remained encamped at La Madeleine near Lille on June 14 and 15, and on the 16th it marched on Werwicke, where it crossed the Lys and the frontier and entered Belgium. The same day Marshal Luckner had pressed straight on with the vanguard to Menin, where the Austrians put up some resistance and were dislodged by main force. My father was present at this action with my younger brother the Comte de Beaujolais, who acquitted himself very well.

On the 17th the Marshal brought the whole army up to Menin, encamped it near this town, and pushed the vanguard and the infantry from the reserve as far as Vevelghem, between Menin and Courtray.

It was then that we received the news that there had been a partial renewal of the ministry. We learned that the King had dismissed MM. Servan, Roland, and Clavière, that General Dumouriez had passed to the Ministry of War, that MM. Duranton and Lacoste were kept on in the same ministries, and that MM. Naillac and Hourgues had been appointed Ministers of Foreign Affairs and the Interior respectively. The Ministry of Finance remained vacant. It was easy to foresee that this change in the ministry would bring about a change in the conduct of affairs; but as General Dumouriez had been the main advocate of an offensive war, it was probable that if the new ministry managed to become established, the war, instead of being conducted more feebly, would be conducted with more vigor than hitherto. We had as yet no details, and everyone abandoned himself to his own conjectures. Those who wanted the war to be prosecuted wholeheartedly told the Marshal that the new ministry would surely speed up operations and that he would be wise to continue them himself, while those who wanted to reduce the war or were entirely opposed to it (and unfortunately these were in a majority among the Marshal's entourage) advised him to halt the march and await orders. The Marshal inclined toward the first group, but he had not yet entirely made up his mind to adopt its policy.

I was having lunch with him on June 18, as was customary at the period for the *maréchal de camp* on duty for the day, when he received a letter from Generals Valence and Jarry informing him that the enemy was in force before them at Nederbecke, that he appeared to be maneuvering to attack them, that their position at Vevelghem was bad, and that as they must consequently decide on the spot whether to attack the enemy or withdraw the vanguard, they were asking for his orders. It was then two o'clock in the afternoon. Having read the letter, the Marshal asked M. de La Grange to rise from the table—he was one of those who advocated that the war should become offensive—and charged him to reply to the two generals that he was proceeding to the vanguard to decide for himself what would have to be done and that meanwhile he relied on them to ensure that nothing went wrong. Such was the substance of the order

* M. de Chancel perished on the scaffold.

given by the Marshal, seated at the head of the table; he then calmly finished his luncheon without more ado. M. de La Grange, profiting from the latitude that the Marshal had allowed him, drafted his note in such a way that the two generals would interpret it as an authorization to attack the enemy if they thought this opportune, which he knew they wanted to do, and he sent it off to them without submitting it to the Marshal. In fact, they mobilized their troops as soon as they received it. These details may seem excessive, but I thought it right to relate them because they portray the times and the way in which the different parties exploited everything to arrive at their objective. The lively debates to which this note gave rise have etched these details so deeply in my memory that I can vouch for the accuracy of my account.

When the Marshal had finished his luncheon, he mounted horse with his general staff. As I was on duty for the day, I accompanied him with my brother Montpensier. I saw to it that my father was notified, and he joined us, too. We went to Vevelghem, which all the troops had already vacated as they advanced. The Marshal was very surprised to find they were no longer there: It made him very angry, and he began to swear, which was his wont on every occasion. We continued to follow the main road from Menin to Courtray, and we encountered General Valence, who was making his dispositions to attack the entrenchments the Austrians had made at Nederbecke, while General Jarry had proceeded to our left to turn them from this direction, as the course of the Lys prevented us from turning them to our right. M. de Valence was on the road with Colonel Delage of the 90th Foot (Chartres) and Lieutenant Colonel Brice de Montigny, who commanded the battalions of grenadiers. There was then a fairly lively exchange between the Marshal and M. de Valence, the one claiming that they were attacking without his orders and the other that M. de La Grange's note had authorized the attack. The discussion was interrupted by the shooting that we heard on our left, and the Marshal immediately galloped away toward it without giving precise orders to M. de Valence.

When we arrived they were already fairly heavily engaged in battle. The Belgian Riflemen,* commanded by Colonels Rosière and Dumonceau,† were dislodging the Austrian light infantry hedge by hedge. At first the Marshal wanted to begin with General Jarry the same discussion as he had had with General Valence, but his attitude was changed by the sight of the combat. He was a good hussar and he liked war, so that his natural inclinations won the day over political considerations. He saw the possibility of defeating the enemy, and he could not resist the temptation.

---

* The Belgian Riflemen were new levies and made up of what were called at the time the *Patriots of Brabant,* that is to say, the Belgians who had sought refuge in France after the Austrian troops had reconquered Belgium and dispersed their army in 1790.

† Later commander in chief of the Dutch army.

General Jarry profited very adroitly from the Marshal's state of mind by pointing out to him that the Austrians were much weaker than had been thought. "If you stop me," he told the Marshal, "you will be taking on yourself a responsibility all the greater, because the Austrians who are weak today may be strong tomorrow; you will be blamed throughout France, and there will be a terrible outcry against you. If, on the other hand, you leave me free to act, success is assured, and you will reap the benefit." The Marshal was entirely won over by this argument, and he was fired to such a point that he hardly allowed General Jarry to finish: "Come on then," he told him, "let us march and order all your troops to advance so that this will go quickly," and at the same time he sent orders to General Valence to continue his operations. Then he went to mingle with the skirmishers and did the best he could to animate the troops by his example and his enthusiasm. However, having driven the Austrians back for some time without much difficulty, our riflemen were held up at a stream behind which was a hedge lined with Austrian infantrymen, who turned a very sharp fire on them. The Marshal ordered a battalion of grenadier Volunteers to advance to force the passage of the stream, but this battalion was repulsed and dispersed. The Marshal rallied it promptly and led it to the attack a second time himself. The passage of the stream was forced, and the Austrians withdrew in haste, leaving a few prisoners in our hands. While this was going on on the left, General Valence was attacking the Austrian entrenchments on the road, and we could hear a fairly sharp cannonade from his direction. It is worth pointing out that the paving of this road had been partially removed, and a fraise had been constructed with palisades and a ditch, so that there could have been no doubt that the Austrians had realized for some time that we intended to attack them from this direction. It must also be observed that at the point where they obviously seemed to be expecting us, they only opposed us with, at the very most, two to three thousand men, from which one must conclude that they were much weaker than was generally thought.

General Valence took the entrenchment with the grenadiers and captured a cannon. Colonel Delage had a horse shot from under him. The Austrians then made their retreat in very good order. While M. de Valence was advancing on Courtray by road, our vanguard was continuing its operation on the left with the Marshal, and we entered the town by one gate while M. de Valence was entering by another. We were very surprised that the Austrians had abandoned Courtray without even attempting to make a stand there because a good defense of this town is possible on account of its position astride the Lys and in the middle of flat and, in some places, even marshy country. Moreover, the walls were good, and there were dykes, the majority of which, I seem to remember, were full of water.

The inhabitants of Courtray welcomed us with transports of joy. The women cheered us and in all the streets we heard shouts of: *"Long live the French nation, long live the French, down with the Austrians, down with the Germans!"* The Marshal was enchanted, and he announced publicly that he would order the army to march the next day to continue the operations. The same evening he had artillery placed on the ramparts of Courtray, and he did not resume his march toward Menin until he had made the necessary arrangements to put the town in a state of defense. I returned to Menin with him. On our way there, General Berthier, his chief of staff, who had openly opposed the operations we had carried out, approached him and reproached him with having lightly undertaken to have the army march the next day. "Oh, and who will prevent it from marching when I have so ordered?" replied the Marshal. —"The fact is that no preparations have been made," replied General Berthier, "we have not even decided our order of battle." —"That can be done to-night," M. de Beauharnais said for the party opposed to that of General Berthier. —"No," replied the Marshal, "Berthier is right, we must settle the battle order tomorrow, and we shall march the day after, it's the same thing." We all knew that it was very different, but it was impossible to bring him back to his first opinion.

On the 19th we learned that the new ministry had fallen immediately after being formed. We read in the newspapers that when General Dumouriez had presented himself to the National Assembly, he had been booed so much that he had had great difficulty finishing reading a memorandum on the organization of the army and that the ministers had handed in their resignations to the King on leaving the room. We were informed at the same time that the new ministry would be chosen from those whose opinions were opposed to those of the previous one. It needed no more to prevent the Marshal from carrying out the operation he had announced. In fact, he decided to remain in the position he occupied at the time, there to await the orders of the new ministers.

Now I shall give details about these changes in the ministry, their principal causes and the results that they produced.

In the first days of June, since the King's Bodyguard, consisting of only eighteen hundred men, had been disbanded by virtue of a decree of the National Assembly sanctioned by the King,* the only troops in Paris,

---

* The Constitution of 1791 gave the King the right to have about him at his disposal a Military Household; its strength, however, was limited to eighteen hundred men. The Constituent Assembly had not introduced any changes in the organization of the Swiss troops serving in France because it had been fearful of contravening the treaties between France and the various Swiss cantons. Thus, in addition to the eighteen hundred men of his Bodyguard, the King had another two thousand Swiss Guards about him, which made about four thousand men at his disposal. In a period of calm, this force would have been regarded as insignificant, but in a time of revolution and in the midst of the unrest which then reigned constantly in Paris, it caused the popular party anxiety, and this anxiety was nurtured by the very hope that the Court had the folly to base on this support. I believe the King should have realized that if this force could defend his person against a rising, it could not serve

apart from the National Guard, were the Swiss Guards, which were two thousand strong, and what were called at the time the National Gendarmes, which was a police force.* The popular party and even the whole nation were alarmed that such an important place should be so stripped of its means of defense. It was feared that Paris and the King, who resided there as did the Assembly, would be exposed if the French armies suffered defeats and were unable to prevent the foreign armies that were approaching the frontier from marching straight on the capital. There was the further fear that the Court, supported by the Swiss Guards† and its partisans, would attempt some move against the Assembly. The new Minister of War, M. Servan, in concert with the Girondin leaders, profited from this state of mind to get the Assembly to adopt a measure that was

him as a support against the feelings of the nation—still less in a struggle with the power of the Assembly or in resisting its decrees. If this truth had been recognized, the Court would have avoided everything that could have provoked a conflict in which it would be bound to fight at such a great disadvantage. But it never knew how to assess its strength at its true level, and it always deluded itself in this respect. Instead of recognizing its weakness and seeking, in good faith, to reach agreement with its opponents, it thought only of threatening them, without realizing that the attempts it made to intimidate them seemed only to reveal to them the bankruptcy of its resources and to demonstrate the incompatibility of its existence together with their safety, the maintenance of the constitutional régime, and the defense of national independence against enemies at home and abroad. The Court thought it had brought off a victory by getting the Constituent Assembly to agree that the King should have a Military Household, that is to say, a Bodyguard depending on him alone and separate from the rest of the army—a circumstance which in itself was sufficient to make this guard an object of suspicion and hostility. The Court saw in this Bodyguard nothing more than an addition of force and power to arrive at its goal and lost no time in forming it from all those whose views were most consonant with its own and most opposed to the constitutional régime. This method of selection, which the Court in its blindness thought essential to its safety, was, however, the surest way of compromising it further, for it was bound to provoke an attack on the Bodyguard, and in fact it did. On May 29 M. Basire delivered a long speech on the composition of this guard and declared that it was unconstitutional, and the same evening the Assembly passed a decree ordering that it should be disbanded immediately and steps taken without delay to reorganize it. This decree was blatantly unconstitutional, and yet the King made no difficulties over giving the royal assent. The Bodyguard was disbanded, but it was not reorganized. At the same time a decree was passed accusing the Duc de Brissac, its commanding officer, and he was sent to Orléans to be tried by the National High Court. But this tribunal did not carry out any trials, and in the month of September following, after the Duc de Brissac had been transferred to Versailles together with all the wretches accused by the Assembly, they were all put to death there by the *septembriseurs* from Paris.

* There were still in Paris the three regiments of the line, the 102nd, the 103rd, and the 104th, which had been formed in Paris out of what were called the hard-core companies of the National Guard, or the *paid force;* but they inspired little confidence, and the inclination was to send them to the front.

† In addition to the Swiss Guards at Paris, there were also ten Swiss regiments in the border fortresses that had refused to take any part in the war and whose well-known attitude also caused a great deal of anxiety.

Louis-Philippe
in his cradle,
his father
bent over him

Louise-Marie-Adélaïde
de Bourbon-Penthièvre,
Duchesse d'Orléans,
mother of
Louis-Philippe

Philippe Égalité,
his children,
and Mme de Genlis

View of the house at the convent of Belle-Chasse,
built by the Duc d'Orléans for the education of his daughters

Portrait of Louis XVI
by Duplessis
(detail)

Portrait of
Marie-Antoinette
by Roslin

Louis XVI inaugurating the first session of the Estates-General,
Versailles, May 5, 1789

Louis XVI driving to the Hôtel de Ville, July 17, 1789

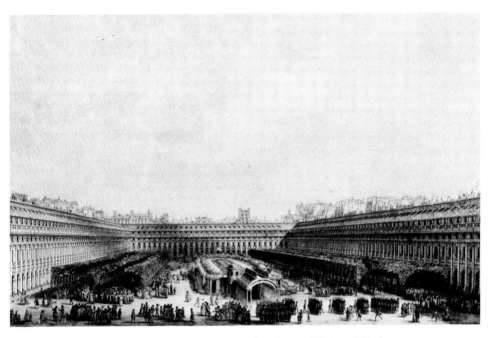

The inner courtyard and galleries of the Palais Royal, Paris

Storming of the Bastille and arrest of its governor, July 14, 1789

"To Versailles, to Versailles," October 5, 1789

Place de Grève, October 6, 1789.
The heads of two Bodyguards triumphantly carried on pikes

Louis XVI returning to Paris with his family, October 6, 1789

Champs de Mars, preparations for the Feast of the Federation,
July 14, 1790

Louis-Philippe, Duc de Chartres, in 1790

Drawing of Louis-Philippe's father,
Philippe Égalité,
by Angelika Kauffmann

Arrest of Louis XVI and his family at Varennes, June 22, 1791

Louis XVI accepting
the Constitution at
the National Assembly,
September 14, 1791

Session at the Jacobin Club, January 11, 1792

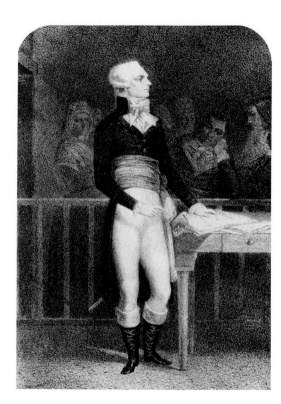

Robespierre

Marat

Council of War at Courtray, June 26, 1792.
Left to right: Berthier, Lameth, Beurnonville, Biron, Luckner,
Louis-Philippe (standing), Valence, Duhoux, d'Aboville, and Lynch

Proclamation of "La Patrie est en danger," July 22, 1792

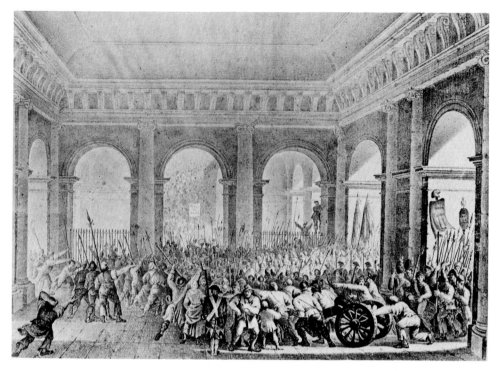

The people of Paris entering the Tuileries, June 20, 1792

Siege and storming of the Tuileries, August 10, 1792

Louis-Philippe,
Duc de Chartres,
in officer's uniform,
1792

General Dumouriez

Danton

Louis the Last and his family on their way to prison in the Temple,
August 13, 1792

The first meal of the royal family in the Temple prison

The Battle of Valmy, September 20, 1792

The Battle of Jemappes, November 6, 1792

Louis XVI as defendant before the Convention, December 1792

Execution of Louis XVI

the immediate cause of the schism within the ministry and that shortly afterward led to its complete dissolution. On June 4 M. Servan proceeded to the Assembly, and without having obtained the King's assent or that of the Council, without even having notified General Dumouriez and the majority of his colleagues, proposed that it should decree that each canton, of which there were four thousand at the time in France, should be obliged to send five National Guards to Paris, completely armed and equipped, to renew the oath of Federation of July 14; that after their arrival in Paris, these National Guards should be organized into companies and battalions and that they should form there a camp of twenty thousand men specially assigned to the defense of the capital. The Assembly gave an enthusiastic reception to this proposal and translated it into law on the spot. These proceedings of M. Servan's gave rise to the most lively exchanges between the ministers. It was approved by MM. Roland and Clavière and censured by General Dumouriez and MM. Lacoste and Duranton. The King was at once irritated and frightened by it: It is even claimed that he went as far as to say that the aim of this decree was to gather in Paris an army of ruffians to dethrone and butcher him; what *is* fact is that he refused to submit the decree to his Council for examination and that he announced his intention to visit it with his *veto.* Apart from the decree on the twenty thousand *fédérés,* the Assembly had passed another on what were called the *refractory* priests* containing strong sanctions against them; and the King, out of a scruple of conscience, was determined to visit it likewise with his veto, against the unanimous advice of his Council, who wished him to sanction it. It was on this occasion that Roland wrote his letter of June 10 to the King that caused so much stir at the time.†

The King, who wanted to rid himself of the whole ministry, profited from this letter and M. Servan's conduct in proposing the camp of twenty thousand men without his consent, to tell General Dumouriez that it was impossible for him to tolerate the three ministers—Roland, Servan, and Clavière—any longer and that it was necessary to dismiss them immediately. At the same time the King told General Dumouriez that it was his intention to retain him and to entrust him with the formation of the new ministry. Dumouriez gave his consent; it was a mistake that caused a rift with the Girondins and created an attitude of mistrust toward him that he could never entirely efface, despite the energy he was later to display in the defense of France and the brilliant victories he obtained for her. He hoped that the dismissal of the Girondin ministers would win him the confidence and good will of the King; that this measure would reassure at once the Court and the constitutional party, both equally alarmed by the strength and the projects of the Jacobins, and that he would reconcile the

* They were called *refractory* because they had refused to take the oath required of them as the *sine qua non* of keeping their ecclesiastical employments.
† Here Louis-Philippe gives extracts from Roland's letter.—ED.

221

King and the nation by his open support of the Constitution at home and conduct of the war against the foreign Powers.* He was mistaken. Instead of his becoming a *via media* between all the parties, as he expected, they all came together to rebuff him and to deny him any kind of support. The Court, the Assembly, the Jacobins who were then a power in the State, united to attack the new ministry, and it had scarcely been formed before it was overthrown. It was on June 13, as I have already said, that the King informed the Assembly that he had thought fit to dismiss MM. Servan, Roland, and Clavière and to replace them by General Dumouriez, M. Naillac, and M. Hourgues and that he had not yet filled the Ministry of Finance. The Assembly replied at once to this communication with a decree pronouncing that in leaving the ministry, the three ministers dismissed by the King took with them the regrets of the nation. Nevertheless, General Dumouriez presented himself before the Assembly as soon as it had passed this decree, and without discussing or making any reference to it, he communicated to them a dispatch from General La Fayette giving details of an action at the front that had taken place on June 9 between Maubeuge and Mons, in which General Gouvion had been killed, together with the two lieutenant colonels of a battalion of Volunteers from the Côte-d'Or. After making this communication, General Dumouriez read the Assembly a long memorandum that he had composed the night before on the organization of the army and the administration of the War Ministry. This piece of work was very well done, and some of the proposals it contained were very wise and necessary by any standards; but such was the General's unpopularity with the Assembly just then that he was frequently interrupted by boos, and he needed all his perseverance to manage to finish reading his memorandum.

In agreeing to undertake the formation of a new ministry and to be a member of it himself, General Dumouriez had extracted from the King his sanction of the two decrees on the camp of twenty thousand men and on the refractory priests because he believed that no ministry, not even the King himself, could maintain itself without granting this point; and he relates in his memoirs that the King first promised him this and then refused it. General Dumouriez proposed modifying the decree on the camp of twenty thousand men in the way in which he reckoned to carry it out. In the first place he wanted to resist the formation of new contingents envisaged by the decree because he found it absurd to create new ones before the old ones, which were still lacking forty thousand men, had been brought up to strength. In effect, his memorandum to the Assembly proposed that all the men procured by the new levy should be distributed among the old formations. In addition, he wanted the reserve force of

* The hope M. Dumouriez had cherished of winning the Court's confidence was based on the influence over the mind of the King and Queen that he believed should be exercised to this end by M. Delaporte, comptroller of the Civil List, with whom he had been well-acquainted for a long time.

twenty thousand men designated to cover Paris to be composed of existing formations that had had a period of training, and to be placed at Soissons (which he planned to fortify) because if the reserve force were placed at Soissons, it would cover Paris better than if it had been at Paris itself, as Soissons was midway between Paris and the border, and the reserve could easily proceed from there to anywhere where reinforcements might be needed; and from another point of view, since it would be twenty leagues from the capital, it could not take part as easily in the political movements whose eruption was feared by the Court. It seemed then that this modification in the execution of the decree would guarantee the nation all the military advantages of this measure for the defense of Paris and support for the armies on the frontiers, and that it would reassure the King and his Court by removing the dangers to which they believed they would be exposed by the presence of these twenty thousand men in Paris.

Immediately after General Dumouriez had resigned, the King formed a new ministry that was chosen from those who professed the same opinions as M. Delessart's ministry and the previous ones. M. de Lajard, who was nominated Minister of War, had been one of M. de La Fayette's adjutants general while he was commander of the Parisian National Guard. M. de La Fayette thought that the moment when the supporters of the Girondins were leaving the ministry was a propitious one to get the Assembly to clamp down on the political clubs that were organized throughout France under the direction of the Jacobin Club of Paris, which was called the *Mother Society,* and on June 16 he addressed a letter to the Assembly to persuade it to adopt severe measures toward them. This letter was read to the Assembly almost at the same time as the new ministers were announcing that the King had just put the formula *le Roi examinera* on the two decrees relative to the priests and the camp of twenty thousand men, which was the mode described by the Constitution of 1791 to veto those decrees of the legislative body to which the King wished to refuse his consent. The Assembly did not adopt any of the measures requested by M. de La Fayette, and the only effect that his letter had was to increase the Jacobins' exasperation with him; but the Assembly adopted a more hostile attitude toward the King's rejection of the two decrees. It summoned the ministers and directed its president to question them in its name on the measures that the King had taken to ensure the defense of the capital and to check the intrigues of the priests. They did appear and asked for a short delay, which was granted, to enable them to prepare a detailed reply.

However, public unrest was so increased by all these circumstances that a very alarming popular disturbance broke out in Paris.

In the course of June 20 the people assembled riotously in the Faubourgs Saint-Antoine and Saint-Marceau, took up arms, and proceeded *en masse* to the Tuileries to present, as they said, petitions to the King demanding his assent to the two decrees and the recall of the dismissed ministers. At first, the King had the gates of the palace closed; but as the people were breaking them down with axes, he ordered that there should be no resistance and that the gates should be opened. At the time he advanced as far as the room preceding the one later known as the Marshals',* accompanied by the Queen, who was holding M. le Dauphin in her arms, Madame the King's daughter, Madame Elisabeth, and a deputation from the departmental administration of Paris at whose head was the Duc de La Rochefoucauld, its president; and M. Roederer, the deputy public prosecutor of the Commune, also came, but later, with a deputation from the Hôtel de Ville. The deputation that the National Assembly sent to watch over the safety of the King and the Royal Family did not arrive at the palace till sometime later. The crowd made way for it and greeted it with a big display of its loyalty and respect. The Assembly declared itself to be in permanent session and ordered that it be given an hourly report of what was happening. The mass of the people entered the palace and climbed up to the King's apartments by the great staircase, crying furiously: *"Down with the veto, down with traitors, the assent or death,"* and they mingled with these cries the most violent abuse, though protesting all the while that their only aim was to exercise the right of petition. The King heard all the harangues and consequently all the threats that were addressed to him with perfect calm, replying the whole time that he merely wanted the Constitution to be upheld;† but it is claimed that he carefully avoided making any promise to give his assent to the two decrees or to recall the ministers. As the people complained that they were unable to see the King, he stood on a chair in the embrasure of a window so as to be more visible. They then demanded that he put a red bonnet on his head, which was claimed at the time as the symbol of liberty but which soon became that of terror and popular excesses; the King submitted to this. As the speeches drew to a close, the people filed out through the Gallery of Diana, and as the crowd went by, the King kept on shouting "Long live the nation." On leaving the palace, the people proceeded toward the chamber of the National Assembly, and having read a few addresses,‡ they asked, as before, to walk in procession

* Napoleon's marshals.—ED.
† See the editions of *le Moniteur* for June 21 and 22, 1792, nos. 173 and 174.
‡ Extract from one of these addresses inserted in *le Moniteur* for June 22, 1792, no. 174:

"We are complaining, gentlemen, about the inactivity of our armies. We demand that you discover the cause of this: If it stems from the executive power, let it be abolished!

"A single man should not affect the wishes of twenty-five million men. If, out of consideration, we maintain him in his office, it is on the condition that he fulfills it constitutionally: If he departs from this line, the French people will no longer have anything to do with him."

through the middle of the Assembly, which was granted. The crowds then broke up, and everyone returned home.

Though no blood had been shed during this rising, it was clear that blood soon would flow, and the sentiments that the people had displayed were a clear indication that they would soon proceed to the greatest excesses unless the public unrest could be calmed one way or another by removing the causes that had produced it. Always obsessed with the same idea, a large number of those who were called at the time the constitutional party seemed to think that this growing unrest was merely the artificial product of Jacobin intrigues, and of the means given them by their daily debates and their affiliated clubs throughout France to poison public opinion and sour its attitude toward the King, the ministers, and generally toward anyone entrusted with authority. They seemed to think that everything would quiet down if they managed to get the Assembly to pass laws of repression against the clubs and severe measures against all those who took part in popular disturbances. The Assembly was solicited to adopt these measures alike by a part of its members and by a large number of petitions. For their part the Girondins, the popular party, and the Jacobins were not less active and got up a large number of addresses and petitions in the opposite sense. Since, according to the Constitution, armies were forbidden to make collective petitions, individual ones were made. On June 28 Marshal Luckner wrote the King a long letter that was printed in its entirety in *le Moniteur* of July 1, 1792. It was in the same sense as that of M. de La Fayette. The staff officers and most of the unit commanders wrote to the King in a similar vein, each expressing his feelings and opinions as he thought fit. My father, who was still with Luckner's army, wanted me to write to the King as well, so I addressed a respectful letter to him in which I merely said that "I had sworn to be loyal to the nation, to the law, and to the King, to defend with all my strength the Constitution voted by the National Assembly and accepted by His Majesty, and that I would be faithful to my oath."* M. de La Fayette expressed his feelings in an order of the day, and leaving Maubeuge, where his army was, he proceeded to Paris and presented himself before the bar of the National Assembly on June 29. He delivered a very strong speech on the rising of June 20 and on the dangers to which the Jacobins were exposing France. He concluded by demanding the Assembly to order (1) that the leaders and instigators of the disturbances of June 20 should be prosecuted and punished for the crime of *lèse-nation;* (2) that it should destroy *the sect*† of the Jacobins; (3) that it should

---

* The King did not give me any reply; but he kept my letter, and he even locked it in the famous iron chest that was discovered in the Tuileries after he had been moved to the Temple. My letter was found there. If this collection were still in my possession, I would transcribe it literally, but I think that I am reporting it accurately.
† Many people, at the time and later, were to point out the affinities between the Revolution and a religious movement.—ED.

take effective measures to give the army the assurance that the Constitution would in no way be attacked within France while brave Frenchmen were lavishing their blood for its defense on the frontiers.*

This initiative of M. de La Fayette produced no results and only increased the irritation that his letter of June 16 had caused the popular party. The Assembly referred the examination of his petition to the Committee of Twelve, the usual grave of all the proposals it did not care to pronounce upon, and it was never heard of again. The Girondins wanted to obtain a vote of censure against the conduct of M. de La Fayette and demanded that the Minister of War should be questioned to find out whether M. de La Fayette had his permission to leave his army to go to Paris; but the Assembly rejected this proposal by a majority of 339 votes to 234, and he returned to Maubeuge without achieving the results that he expected from his visit.

I think M. de La Fayette was mistaken in taking the clubs to be the cause of the public unrest and disturbances. To my way of thinking he was taking the effect for the cause. I think that these assemblies would have ended spontaneously or certainly would have ceased to be dangerous if one could have removed their underlying cause. Now, the cause of the unrest was the mistrust that the intentions, the opinions, the language, and the conduct of the King and the Court inspired. It was impossible that the nation should forget that the King, who was entrusted with the defense of its liberties and the Constitution, was surrounded by that same Court and those same advisers who had placed so many obstacles in the way of their establishment. This was made all the more impossible in that the Court did not even take the trouble to conceal how much it regretted the Ancien Régime, and that it no more concealed its desire to restore it nor its hopes of accomplishing this with the help of the foreign armies. Often, indeed, the Court boasted about having summoned such armies in concert with the *émigrés*. It was impossible for the nation to be calm in the middle of such a crisis. Impossible for them to watch without indignation the very men entrusted with the defense of their territory paralyzing their efforts themselves. The Jacobin orators increasingly brought national opinion around to them, while the efforts of the constitutional party to justify the conduct of the Court and its agents were disowned by the very Court they wished to defend, which only accepted their services in order to hold them up to ridicule. Thus the constitutional party, discredited by their alliance with a Court that wanted to overthrow the Constitution, grew weaker every day, and in proportion as they lost their strength through losing the nation's confidence, the Jacobins took hold of it, so that the only result of the attacks directed against them was to render them more dear to the nation and to make them its veritable leaders. But none of this was understood at the time. Admittedly it was no longer believed, as in 1789, that the popular disturbances were paid

* See *le Moniteur* for July 1, 1792, no. 183.

for, because my father was ruined and it was well known that the Jacobins did not have a penny. However, it was believed that the unrest resulted from the proclamations of the clubs instead of recognizing that these proclamations were only the consequence and the echo of this unrest. Once the true state of affairs is misunderstood and one starts from a false premise, one always goes from error to error; and so they persuaded themselves that if they closed the clubs and treated their orators as men guilty of crimes of *lèse-nation,* they would frighten some and destroy the others' taste for meddling in public affairs. Nothing could have been, and nothing was, more fatal than this illusion.

I do not think that M. de La Fayette ever had this project in mind. He forgot or misunderstood the intentions and conduct of the Court; he thought he could bring the King to accept that constitutional throne in defense of which M. de La Fayette succumbed without any notice being taken of his loyalty. I think he was beguiled by the prospect of saving France from popular anarchy and of defending the constitutional monarchy against the attacks of the people, just as he had defended the rights of the nation against the attacks of the Court; but I do not understand why he did not realize sooner that he was duped and that the only service the Court wanted from him was to assist it in deceiving the nation with the personal confidence to which he had a right and which the Court could no longer inspire. It seems to me that the events of June 20, instead of being regarded as a crime requiring exemplary punishment, should have been taken as a terrible warning that there was not a moment to lose in changing policy completely and in changing it sincerely. It was evident that if the policy that had been followed hitherto continued to be followed, the people of Paris would not wait much longer before making a second visit to the Tuileries Palace and that this time, instead of confining themselves to half-measures, they would strike a decisive blow. In fact this second visit took place on August 10, 1792, that is to say, seven weeks later; but this time it was no longer to exercise the right of petition, it was to dethrone Louis XVI and overthrow the monarchy.

It would be superfluous to go into details about the discussions arising from the report given by the ministers in reply to the questions the Assembly asked them about the measures the King was to have taken in place of executing the two decrees. The result was that the King maintained a strict veto on the decree relating to the refractory priests but that he agreed to a compromise on the camp of twenty thousand men. He wrote a letter to the president of the Assembly, countersigned by the Minister of War, M. de Lajard, which was read in the evening sitting of June 22 and in which he proposed to order the formation of forty-two battalions of National Volunteers designed to form a camp of reserves at Soissons, where he would have provisions sent. The Assembly decreed this measure, but it was executed so feebly that I seem to remember there were still only seven or eight battalions formed at Soissons at the time of the rising of August 10, when the great political change that then took place gave to the defense of France the resilience and energy the King would have been wise to have given himself.

While these events were going on in Paris, Luckner's army remained immobile in its camp at Menin, with its vanguard still at Courtray. The Austrian troops were too inferior in numbers to ours for them to be able to attack us, but they formed a cordon of light troops before Courtray. Duke Albert of Saxe-Teschen was their commander in chief. At Mons, General Beaulieu commanded the detachment opposed to M. de La Fayette's army, which was at Maubeuge. At Tournay, General Happen-court commanded a detachment that was estimated at fourteen thousand men. However, I do not vouch for the accuracy of these details, which I am writing down from memory; what is certain is that Marshal Luckner and General La Fayette had sixty thousand effectives in the field at the time. The Austrians were content to push along the left bank of the Lys with a body of four or five thousand men under General Clairfayt so as to cover Gand and Bruges. This small detachment went to take up its position at Deynse, and while it was carrying out its operations, the Austrians covered it by making a reconnaissance of Courtray, which was soon repulsed. M. Achille Duchâtelet, *maréchal de camp,* who normally replaced M. de Valence as commander of the reserve force of grenadiers, was wounded in this little action; he had the calf of a leg blown off by a cannonball. This wound deprived the army of the services of this staff officer, who had only rejoined the regiment two or three days previously. He did not perform any further service.*

I have already explained how the operations of the army had been suspended after the capture of Courtray. Marshal Luckner was still waiting for the new ministry to send him orders about what he had to do, and these orders did not arrive. He said publicly that he had submitted a plan of campaign to the King's Council, and yet nothing was decided. This indecision and this inactivity of the armies, at a time when there was every indication that they were superior to those opposed to them, caused general discontent: It was manifested several times in the Assembly, and several members called upon the Minister of War to inform them if it was true that Marshal Luckner had suspended operations on his orders. M. de Lajard stated that he had never given such an order, and to free himself entirely from blame—perhaps also to rid himself of all responsibility for the actions of Marshal Luckner, who was secretly being urged to with-draw—he sent him *carte blanche* to take whatever action he judged appropriate, with the single proviso that he act in concert with M. de La

* Achille Duchâtelet was a man of great merit who had served in the American War with distinction. He had acquired a sort of celebrity by the petition he had presented to the Constituent Assembly on June 21, 1791, at the time of the King's departure for Varennes, in which he demanded that it proclaim a republic. Nevertheless, he was incarcerated in 1793 in the prison of La Force and poisoned himself there when informed that he was due to appear before the Revolutionary Tribunal.

Fayette. At the same time he informed the Assembly of this measure in an official letter, which was read in the evening sitting of the 25th.* This intimation was greeted in the Assembly by repeated applause, which was taken up in the galleries, because no one in Paris doubted that the Marshal would be eager to act vigorously; however, the news of the extension of his powers produced a very different effect on him, and I was in a position to notice that it gave him no pleasure. He had just received this news when I called on him, as staff officer on duty for the day, to report that I had inspected the pickets and that there was nothing new to report about the army. He was in his shirtsleeves and was pacing up and down his bedroom and seemed very agitated: "What ails you, then, Marshal?" I said to him. —"Ah, what ails me?" he replied. "I have *carte blanche!*" —"How so, *carte blanche?* What do you mean?" —"That's it," he replied, "instead of sending me orders, they send me *carte blanche.* What does it signify to give *carte blanche* to an old soldier like me? Tell him 'do this,' and he does it. But *carte blanche!* . . . I have never had *carte blanche* in my life, nor do I understand the least thing about it. One tells me 'advance' and the other 'retreat,' I do not know which one to listen to, I am in despair and in the cruelest dilemma!" And putting both hands to his face, he dissolved into tears. "Calm yourself, Marshal," I replied, "doubtless the Minister of War has sent you *carte blanche?*" —"Yes, it's him," he replied with an oath, "and devil take him, him and his *carte blanche* and his whole show!" —"Well then," I said laughing, "maybe the devil will take him and his whole show if you take advantage of his *carte blanche* to attack the enemy, to give it a good thrashing; have a go!" —"Ah, Prince," he replied, "I am well aware of your opinion, I know that you are one of those who want us to forge ahead, but it is not for that that the ministers are sending me *carte blanche.*" —"What do their reasons matter to you? Since they are giving you *carte blanche* they can't complain if you profit from it to act." —Then he said, "My dear Prince, you may be right. You have always treated me *very honorably,†* and since I have been with the army I have had nothing but praise for you; but you are too young for me to decide on your advice. I have got to ponder all this and consult my colleagues." After this conversation, which I thought was piquant enough to be reported, I returned to the camp, and after an hour or two I received an order from the Marshal, which was transmitted to me by General Berthier, enjoining me to proceed immediately to headquarters, where the Marshal intended to hold a Council of War composed of all the staff officers present in the army.

I left the camp to go to the Marshal at the same time as General Duhoux, whose cavalry brigade was camped beside mine. This general was a good soldier who understood nothing about politics and prided

---

* See *le Moniteur* for June 27, 1792, no. 179.

† I am reporting his expressions and even his Germanic usages as literally as I can, though I delete the numerous expletives with which he seasoned his utterances.

himself on the fact. I thought it important to gain his vote for the opinion that I wanted to win that day in the council, and I had the pleasure of succeeding in this, which was all the more fortunate because he would probably have voted the other way if I had not encountered him. General Duhoux was a crude but good man, and we got on very well together. "Do you know," I said to him as we went along, "why we have been summoned?" —"No," he replied, "I haven't a clue, and I can't think what they want with us, because they don't have to make us come to give us orders, they only have to send them. Actually all this general staff doesn't know much about its job." —"That may well be so," I replied, "but for my part I have made myself a set of rules for this which saves me from any difficulties; when I am given orders, I obey and execute them to the best of my ability; but when my advice is asked . . ." —"Ah, no advice," Duhoux went on, brusquely interrupting me, "I don't know what advice is, and if they ask me for any, I will send them about their business." —"Yes," I said, "so would I, if I were at the head of my brigade; but according to my set of rules, when the commander in chief summons me to his headquarters to ask my advice, the case is altered, and in this eventuality I shall always have one piece of advice to put at his disposal, which is brief and worthy of a good soldier; I shall tell him, without details or explanations: *General, no retreat, go forward!*" —"Ah! that is well said," General Duhoux said to me, *"gnia qu'ça, faut ça."** ("That's the only thing to do, we must do that," an expression he was accustomed to use the whole time.) *"Always advance, by jingo, gnia qu'ça, faut ça;* I will say as much, and I am very grateful to you for having made me think of it. Ah! I tell you that if they ask for my advice I will give that, and firmly. I shall say that if they want Duhoux's advice, here it is, *Go forward, no retreat, always forward, gnia qu'ça, faut ça!"†*

The Council of War was composed of nine staff officers not including the Marshal, namely: M. de Biron, lieutenant general, and the *maréchaux de camp* d'Aboville, Valence, Charles Lameth, Duhoux, Lynch, Alexandre Berthier, Beurnonville, and myself. MM. de Carle and de Jarry were at Courtray and consequently could not attend. The Marshal began by ordering General Berthier, his chief of staff, to read to the council the letter by which the Minister of War had just given him *carte blanche* to take whatever action he thought appropriate, though recommending him to act in concert with M. de La Fayette. The Marshal then told us that as

---

* Corruption of *il n'y a que cela, il faut cela.*—ED.
† General Duhoux defended Lille vigorously during the Austrian bombardment in the month of September 1792, though his only means of defense was a handful of troops and the help of the inhabitants who, it is true, worked with tremendous enthusiasm. In 1793 he was arrested and summoned before the bar of the National Convention, where, against precedent, his frankness and soldier's language got him out of difficulties. He was set free and continued to serve until his death. Before the Revolution he had served in the Gendarmerie, which was a privileged body.

this extension of his powers greatly increased his responsibility, he had wanted, before coming to a decision, to consult a Council of War comprised of staff officers in order that their advice might enlighten him as to the best course of action. He added that it seemed useless to him to advance any further in the Low Countries because the inhabitants were not making any efforts to aid our operations, and it was clear that the hopes General Dumouriez had raised about this were without foundation. He thought, moreover, that he had insufficient means at his disposal to attack the Austrians with advantage, and consequently he recommended that the council examine whether it was preferable to wait any longer at Menin and Courtray for the inhabitants of Belgium to come out in favor of France or whether it was not better to retire to the border straightaway and admit that the invasion of Belgium was impracticable and should be abandoned. "That is to say," replied M. de Biron, who spoke with facility and was a very good debater, "that before devoting ourselves to any other matter, we must decide whether or not it is necessary for the army to abandon Menin and Courtray and withdraw to France. I must admit that I did not expect the result of the *carte blanche* the Minister has just sent the Marshal would be that we should be called upon to examine whether he should not profit from this extension of his powers to abandon offensive operations once and for all and to make the army withdraw. I had rather expected that if the Minister, misled by false reports, had ordered the army to retreat, the Marshal would have summoned all the staff officers to a Council of War in order that they could add their remonstrances to those it would have been his duty to make against such an order. But, in short, since the Marshal wants us to begin by deciding whether it appears necessary to us or not that the army leave Menin and Courtray and withdraw to France, let us begin by saying that not only does this retreat seem to us unnecessary but that nothing is forcing it and that we would find it unjustified. Next, when we have agreed on this premise, we shall examine, if the Marshal thinks it in order, the various operations that the army can undertake, and we will recommend to him those that seem to us preferable."

M. de Valence strongly supported this opinion, but I shall not undertake the task of reporting the rest of the very long and very lively debates that then began in the council. It had been summoned in the expectation that the staff officers in the army would recommend to Marshal Luckner that he abandon offensive operations and withdraw to France, and the views of some of them were uncertain enough for this expectation to seem founded; but General Duhoux's vote upset this plan. He kept repeating, despite all the efforts to make him change his mind: *"No retreat, go forward, always forward, gnia gnia qu'ça, faut ça";* so that instead of being in a minority, as expected, we found ourselves with a majority of one against our opponents, that is to say, five against four. The five who declared that retreat would be unjustified and that it would be equally so to discontinue offensive operations were MM. de Biron, de Valence, Duhoux, Beurnonville, and myself, and the four who recommended to the Marshal to withdraw to France and to discontinue offensive operations were MM. Charles Lameth, d'Aboville, Lynch, and Berthier.

This unexpected result of the Council of War determined the Marshal to suspend his retreat temporarily, but for all that the project was not abandoned, because it took place three days afterward. Nevertheless, the Marshal wrote a letter the same evening to the Minister of War, which was read to the National Assembly and inserted in *le Moniteur,* in which he said: "Our position is still the same, and there is nothing in it sufficiently disquieting to make me fall back on Lille. I have reinforced my vanguard at Courtray, and with the defenses I am going to construct,* this position is very good."† M. de Valence, who was obliged to go to Paris for private reasons, was in addition charged to give the Minister any details he might require about the state of affairs and morale; but though there is no doubt that M. de Valence presented things as they really were, and although it is equally certain that he stressed to the ministers the importance of continuing offensive operations, the replies that the Marshal received obliged him to withdraw precipitately toward Lille on the night of June 29–30, that is to say, three days after he had affirmed that he would do nothing of the sort and without this retreat being necessitated by any attack or even by any movement of the Austrians.‡

A very unfortunate incident occurred during the retreat. General Jarry, who was in command at Courtray under Lieutenant General Carle, thought it was necessary to set fire to the suburbs of the town in order to prevent the enemy from seeing his movements and harassing his retreat, and he started the fire without giving the inhabitants time to recover the linen that was in the bleaching-houses and that constituted the wealth of the district. The loss was all the greater because the fire spread rapidly, and all the premises from Courtray to Harlebeck became a prey to the flames. The Assembly thought it detected in this fire a counterrevolutionary plot to make the French odious to the Belgians: The very moment it received the news, it decreed that the owners of the establishments destroyed by fire should be indemnified at the expense of France, and it nearly decreed that General Jarry should be accused and brought before the High Court-Martial. I think that these suspicions were without foun-

* Menin and Courtray still had very good walls, the remains of the ancient fortifications demolished under Joseph II, and it was easy to restore them to a state of defense. But work was carried out only at Courtray, and even here it was done very halfheartedly.

† See *le Moniteur* for June 30, 1792, no. 182, which carries Marshal Luckner's letter dated from the headquarters at Menin, June 26, 1792, the year IV of Liberty.

‡ Recourse was had to all kinds of means to persuade the Marshal to retreat: Among other things he had been persuaded that a Prussian column commanded, it was said, by General Knobelsdorff, had arrived at Gand, although this did not have the slightest foundation and was impossible.

dation. General Jarry had served in Prussia for most of his life, and he detested the Austrians* and took a pleasure in doing them all the harm possible. As he was, furthermore, of a violent and irascible disposition, he had been driven to the height of exasperation by Austrian snipers slipping every day into the houses and gardens of the suburbs of Courtray to kill some of our men, and as he had himself nearly been killed several times in this way, he had seized on a plausible pretext to take revenge.†

The retreat of Marshal Luckner's army produced the sensation that was to be expected. News of it spread through Paris as early as July 1 without the Minister of War informing the Assembly, which therefore decreed on the 2nd that he should be summoned forthwith to give an account of the retreat and also of the burning of the suburbs of Courtray, news of which was likewise being spread unofficially. M. de Lajard declared that he had received no news from Marshal Luckner since the letter that he had communicated to the Assembly.‡ It was not until the sitting of July 3 that the retreat of the army was officially announced to the Assembly by the communication of a long letter from Marshal Luckner, who gave as his reasons for the retreat the fact that the Belgians had not risen up against the Austrians as he had been led to hope, and that since Prussian and Austrian columns were marching on Coblenz§ it was necessary to concentrate on defending Lorraine and to stop dreaming of an invasion of the Low Countries. He added that he was going to fall back on Valenciennes so that General La Fayette could proceed to Lorraine, and he announced that General Lanoue, who had remained encamped with five thousand men at Maulde while we were at Menin and Courtray, had already left with his troops to relieve those of M. de La Fayette at Maubeuge. The Marshal concluded his letter by asking for the *carte blanche* that had been given him to be revoked, declaring that he

* Austro-Prussian enmity formed the basis of European diplomacy between Frederick the Great's invasion of Silesia in 1740 and the French Revolution.—ED.

† Although General Jarry was not cashiered for this action and legal proceedings were not taken against him, he was exposed to so many attacks in the newspapers that he thought he could no longer continue to serve in France, nor even remain in safety there after the rising of August 10, and he went abroad at the same time as M. de La Fayette. Like him, he was arrested by the Austrians and locked up in a dungeon where the *émigrés* came every day to look at him through the grill and insult him in his misfortune and shower him with abuse. He told me that one day an entire *émigré* contingent had come for this amusement and that literally each one in turn had spat in his face. He recounted these details to me in England, where he had retired and where he died as director of the military academy at Wycombe. Time had not calmed his resentment at these insults, and judging by the anger with which he told me of them ten years later, one could have thought that what he was talking about had just happened that very minute.

‡ That of June 26, in which the Marshal said that there was nothing sufficiently disquieting to make him decide to retreat.

§ Consequently, these armies were still on the other side of the Rhine and too far removed to oppose the operations of the French army in Belgium.

would continue to keep the command of the army only if the King's Council undertook the direction of its operations.

This communication produced considerable unrest in the Assembly, and consequently in Paris and the whole of France. The Minister of War declared that he had not given the order to retreat, but the Assembly was skeptical about this assertion. It ordered him to show one of its committees all his official correspondence with Marshal Luckner; he did so, and the formal order to retreat was not found there. People did not fail to say that if his private correspondence had likewise been examined, the search would not have been as fruitless. However, since there was nothing official and since, at least ostensibly, Marshal Luckner had *carte blanche* for his operations, it seemed that he must be held solely responsible. But it was quite otherwise. The Assembly and the public detected that the Marshal had been ensnared by a Court intrigue, and it was the Court and the ministry who carried the blame for the retreat. There was more: The fear of compromising the Marshal gave the Assembly pause and stopped it taking severe measures when it realized that it could not indict the ministers without including him in the indictment. At the time there was so little experience of war in France* that people thought they could not manage without some experienced general like Luckner to command the French armies; and as he was almost the only one they thought they could count on, it would have been regarded as a national calamity to be deprived of the services of this old man who, eighteen months later, was dragged out of retirement to be sent to the scaffold. The Assembly then considered it essential to keep Luckner as commander of the army, and consequently it sought itself to guard him from the suspicions that the retreat from Menin must naturally have inspired about him. It was for this reason that on the proposition of M. de Kersaint, it decreed unanimously that *Marshal Luckner had retained the full confidence of the nation.* Nevertheless, the attacks against the Court only became stronger and more acrimonious for this, and the most violent speeches were delivered at the rostrum. I shall report a few lines from Vergniaud's speech, which was one of the most striking:

". . . *It is in the King's name* that the French Princes have attempted to rouse all the Courts of Europe against the nation; it was *to avenge the King's dignity* that the Treaty of Pillnitz and the unnatural alliance between the Courts of Vienna and Berlin were concluded. . . . In short, it is the *King's name alone* that is the pretext or the cause of all the ills our enemies strive to gather around our heads and of all those we have to fear.

"Now I read in the Constitution, Chapter II, Section I, Article 6: If the King puts himself at the head of an army and turns its forces against the

---

* Because before the Revolution, nearly all the officers were nobles, and many of these had emigrated. Also France had not been engaged in a full-scale war on land for a generation.—ED.

234

nation or if he does not explicitly oppose such an enterprise carried out in his name, he shall be deemed to have abdicated the throne.

. . . .

"I propose that the following be decreed:
"(1) *That the Fatherland is in danger.*
"(2) That the ministers are responsible for all internal disturbances, having religion as their pretext.
"(3) That they are equally so for any invasion of French territory arising out of their failure to take the necessary precautions to replace, in time, the camp whose formation was decreed by the Assembly."

M. Vergniaud then proposed a Message to the King and an Address to the French People, urging them to take the measures that were indispensable in the circumstances, etc.*

The Assembly voted for the Message to the King and the Address to the French People, but it did not declare immediately that the Fatherland was in danger.† For the moment it merely drafted a long decree specifying all the measures that would be taken when it judged it right to make this declaration. Vergniaud's speech had a prodigious effect on the Assembly and on the public. It produced no real change in the policy of the Court and in the conduct of the ministry; however, it gave rise in the Assembly to a movement which, if it had been followed with the consistency necessary to consolidate its impact, could have had favorable consequences for France and for the King.

In the sitting of July 7 M. Lamourette,‡ constitutional§ Bishop of Lyon, interrupted the discussion that was in progress, on the measures for national security necessitated by the danger to the country, to propose an incidental motion. He said "that the best measure for national security the Assembly could adopt was the coming together of the parties which divided it; that all that was needed to succeed in this was mutual understanding; that the cause of the division was that one part of the Assembly credited the other with the seditious ambition of wanting to destroy the monarchy, while the other credited the first with the desire to destroy constitutional equality and with favoring the establishment of the aristocratic form of government known by the name of *two chambers.* "Very well, gentlemen," Bishop Lamourette exclaimed, "let us anathematize, in a single condemnation and by an irrevocable oath, both a republican form of government and that by two chambers!" (*The chamber resounded with universal applause from the Assembly and the galleries and with shouts, several times repeated, of "Yes, yes we want the Constitution and the Constitution alone."*) "Let us swear to have but one mind, one heart, to

---

* See the editions of *le Moniteur* for July 4 and 5, 1792, nos. 186 and 187.
† The formula prescribed for declaring a state of emergency.—ED.
‡ M. Lamourette and M. Vergniaud perished on the scaffold the following year.
§ See *le Moniteur* for July 8, 1792, no. 190.

blend into a single body of free men, terrible alike to the spirit of anarchy and that of feudalism. And the moment when foreigners see that we only want stability and that we all want the same thing will be the moment when liberty is triumphant and France is saved." (*The same applause broke out again and continued*). "I demand that the president [of the Assembly] put this simple proposal to the vote: that those who abjure and execrate both a republican form of government and one based on two chambers stand up." (*The applause from the galleries continued.*)

The Assembly was electrified by this speech: The whole Assembly rose in a spontaneous movement, and all its members, standing as to take the oath, declared that they would never allow any alteration to be made to the Constitution, whether by introducing a republican form of government or one based on the two chambers. This first wave of emotion was followed by a general desire for reconciliation. The members sitting on the extreme left immediately rushed to mingle with those from the opposite side, who welcomed them with embraces and in turn went to take up position in the ranks of the left.

At the same time the Assembly sent a deputation of twenty-four members to present the King with the extract of the minutes of the sitting containing the details of this remarkable reconciliation. The King left immediately to proceed in person to the chamber of the Assembly. He entered it, preceded by the deputation and accompanied by all his ministers, which led one to suppose he had advance warning of the proposal that had just been adopted with such abandon. The King was greeted with repeated shouts of *Long live the nation* and *Long live the King*. He positioned himself next to the president and said "that he was deeply moved at the sight of everyone coming together in their desire to save the Fatherland; that for a long time he had desired this salutary moment; that the nation and its King were indivisible; that their coming together would save France; that they should all defend the Constitution and that in this the King would always set them an example." The president (M. Stanislas de Girardin) replied to him "that the memorable day when all the constituted authorities came together would be a symbol of joy for all the friends of liberty and of terror for all its enemies, that from this union would stem the strength necessary to overcome the tyrants in league against France, and that it was a sure guarantee of victory." The King, according to *le Moniteur,* appeared moved and added: "I tell you, Monsieur le Président, I could not wait for the deputation to arrive so that I could rush to the Assembly." Then the King left the Assembly in the midst of applause and the same slogans that had been heard on his arrival.

It would have been as wise as it would have been easy for the King to turn this movement to account. All that was needed was for him to make up his mind to perform sincerely what he had just said again it was his intention to do. He had only to give up his reliance on the foreign Powers and all hope, as all desire, to overthrow the Constitution and reestablish his absolute power. But the King did not change his policy at all, and so the enthusiasm of this sitting led nowhere and was of short duration, while M. Vergniaud's quotation of the article of the Constitution defining the case where the King should be deemed to have abdicated the Crown germinated in everyone's mind and became the theme of numerous petitions that were presented to the Assembly asking it to declare, in the terms of the Constitution, *that Louis XVI had forfeited the throne.*

Luckner's army, having withdrawn from Menin toward Lille on the night of June 29–30, camped at Orchies on July 1, at Saint-Amand on the 2nd, and on the 3rd returned to the protection of its camp at Famars below Valenciennes. Lieutenant General Carle returned to Dunkirk with the troops that he had brought from that town.

La Fayette's army left Maubeuge at the same time and began its movement toward Sedan. It stopped for a few days at La Chapelle, which was the nearest point to Paris on its route. This stop, for which there was no apparent military reason, gave rise to a lot of conjecture. It was believed that it had a political object, and it is certain that this conjecture was well founded. It is claimed that this object was to engage the King to take advantage of the moment when M. de La Fayette's army found itself close to him, to try to make his way there. It is even claimed that M. de La Fayette charged M. Adrien Duport, a former member of the Constituent Assembly, to make the proposal to the King and that when Mr. Duport discharged this commission the Queen, who was present, told him *that he must be mad to think that the King would happily go and place himself in the hands of his jailer again.** It is added that M. Duport replied as he withdrew *that he desired that their Majesties should never have more grounds of complaint against any jailer than they had had against M. de La Fayette.* I think that this anecdote is authentic, but I am not sure enough to vouch for it. Be that as it may, the King made no attempt to leave Paris, and after stopping for a few days at La Chapelle, the army of M. de La Fayette continued its march and made for Sedan, where it remained till the time of the rising of August 10.

I have said nothing further of General Dumouriez since he left the ministry. He had had the foresight to profit from the twenty-four hours when he had been Minister of War to give himself letters accrediting him to serve with the Army of the North with his rank of lieutenant general; but since a general measure, taken in virtue of a decree of the Assembly, forbade all those who had been ministers to leave Paris before they had given a statement of their accounts, he had been forced to remain there until they had been examined. However, he managed to get this operation

* This makes reference to the fact that M. de La Fayette had been entrusted with guarding the person of the King and that of the Royal Family at the Tuileries after the return from Varennes.

completed at the beginning of July, and as soon as it was finished he proceeded to the army in which he was employed, at Valenciennes.

General Dumouriez was very badly received by Marshal Luckner and his entourage. They affected not to speak to him and even not to look at him. For several days General Berthier refused to put it in orders that he was employed in this army. However, the evening of his arrival, he followed the Marshal to the camp where I happened to be with M. de Biron. I had never seen him, but M. de Biron, who had served with him in Corsica and who liked him very much, brought me over to him, and we became acquainted. Having toured the camp, we were all returning together by the main road when General Dumouriez, without bothering about the ugly looks that were being given him, came up to the Marshal and said to him: "When you took command of this army I was a minister, and you blamed Marshal Rochambeau so much for having taken up position in this camp that I cannot imagine who could have persuaded you to return to it." —"It's all the same to me if you can't imagine it," the Marshal replied testily. —"My God," Dumouriez continued, as though he had not noticed the interruption, "your criticism of it was well founded, and I find it even worse than I expected. If you are attacked here you will be thrown into the Scheldt, which you have your back against. Instead of staying here and doing nothing, you would do well," he continued, pointing to the plain that stretched as far as the border, "to cover this fine land instead of letting it be pillaged by the Austrians. I don't see why you don't take up a position that is less timid and at the same time more defensible than this by going to camp at Quiévrain on enemy territory?" —"You are not here to give advice," the Marshal said to him dryly, "but to receive orders, when I give you them." —"It seems to me," Dumouriez replied, "that a lieutenant general has a perfect right to give you his advice, especially when it appears so necessary." The discussion did not proceed any further, but Dumouriez had it out with the Marshal several times like this and in a very lively fashion, and to get rid of him, the Marshal sent him to take command of eight battalions and two squadrons that were to camp at Maulde before Saint-Amand, to cover this part of the border. General Beurnonville, who was still only a *maréchal de camp,* was sent there as General Dumouriez's second in command. At the same time an order from the Minister of War removed General Biron from us. He was sent to Strasbourg to take command of the troops that had hitherto been under General Lamorlière, who had to be replaced, it was said, because of his age and infirmities. We saw in this change a way of separating and isolating those who had expressed opinions favoring an offensive war and who wanted it to be fought wholeheartedly. It was a wrench to part from General Biron; I had great confidence in him, and I was keenly aware of my need for his advice and of its utility. I did not see him again after that, and I regretted it very deeply, as much for the friendship that he retained for my father till his dying breath as for that which he had for my brother and myself.

After all plans for offensive operations had been totally abandoned, a defensive plan was drawn up that was very defective. They conceived of sending Marshal Luckner's army, whose depots were in Flanders, to Lorraine, while that of M. de La Fayette, whose depots were in Lorraine, had to furnish the troops assigned to the defense of Flanders. The result was that in future it became impossible for the troops on campaign to draw from their depots the different replacements they needed in men, horses, equipment, clothing, etc. Another drawback was the long march that the armies had to make to reach their respective destinations, and moreover, there was no denying that this exercise was bound to appear absolutely pointless. Therefore, it became the butt of public satire and ridicule, and it was gaily christened the Army Square Dance. As a result of this arrangement, Marshal Luckner was entrusted with the command on the border from Bitche to Longwy inclusive, and M. de La Fayette with that from Montmédy to Dunkirk.

For the purpose of proceeding from Flanders to Lorraine, Luckner's army was divided into two divisions, the first of which, under Lieutenant General d'Harville, was to leave immediately, and the second, under Lieutenant General Dumouriez, was to await the arrival of the troops from La Fayette's army, which was supposed to replace it. Consequently, General Dumouriez remained under General La Fayette until his division set off. I was placed with my brigade of dragoons in General d'Harville's division. This was around twelve thousand men strong. We left the camp of Famars on July 12, and we went to camp at Landrecies, where the division remained until the 13th.

My father accompanied us on this first stage of the march, but it seemed to him useless to remain any longer with an army that was simply going to move across France to change its location; he returned to Paris and took my youngest brother, the Comte de Beaujolais, with him. The Duc de Montpensier remained with me. My father intended to rejoin the army when it had reached Metz, but the King forbade Marshal Luckner to receive him there and charged him to communicate this prohibition to my father, who was then obliged to abandon this project.

The Marshal came to Landrecies, where he had an interview with M. de La Fayette, as a result of which he left for Paris. Nearly all the staff officers did as much, and M. d'Harville handed over command of his division to General d'Aboville, who was the most senior of those remaining there. These were Generals Berthier, Lynch, and myself.

On the 14th we went to camp at Guise, where we celebrated the anniversary of the Federation, as was the custom at the time.

The division, continuing its march toward Lorraine, camped at Marle on the 15th, at Montcornet on the 16th and 17th, at Seraincourt and

Rémaucourt on the 18th, at Rethel-Mazarin on the 19th, at Vouziers on the 20th, at Grandpré on the 21st and 22nd (where it crossed the passes of the Argonne), at Varennes on the 23rd, at Verdun on the 24th, at Mars-la-Tour on the 25th, and on the 26th at Metz, that is to say, near to this town on the banks of the Moselle between Longeville and Moulins. I was quartered in a pretty little château that had belonged to Marshal Fabert. We remained in this position till the return of Marshal Luckner, who came to Metz after he had visited the Army of the Rhine, which the King had placed under his orders.

While the French armies lost precious time strolling through France, the foreign armies were rapidly approaching our frontiers. They built up their stores in the neighboring countries that were still regarded as neutral: As war had only been declared on Austria, the German Empire continued to enjoy a neutrality under cover of which the troops of the small states comprising it assembled to join the Prussian and Austrian armies and prepared to make common cause with them against France. These circumstances determined the National Assembly to pass a decree providing "that the King was charged to repel by force of arms every declared enemy that has begun or is about to begin hostilities against the French nation and to see that it is attacked and harried wherever the military dispositions are suitable."* This decree was passed in the sitting of July 16 on the proposal of M. Pozzo di Borgo,† the spokesman for the Commission of Twelve and the combined military and diplomatic committees.

The Assembly accompanied this decree with the formal declaration that *the Fatherland was in danger.* This was announced with great ceremony on July 22 and 23 in all the districts of Paris by municipal officers on horseback. Here is the proclamation that was read on this occasion in conformity with the decree of the Assembly.‡

"Large forces are advancing on our frontiers. All those who hold liberty in dread are taking up arms against our Constitution. *Citizens, the Fatherland is in danger!*

"Let those who are to have the honor of being the first to march to the defense of all they hold most dear remember always that they are Frenchmen and free; let their fellow citizens maintain security of person and of property at home; let the magistrates of the people be vigilant; let everyone with calm courage—the attribute of true strength—await a legal signal to act, *and the Fatherland will be saved!*"

The decree authorizing the King to see that assemblies of enemy troops were attacked regardless of the country in which they had been formed

* See *le Moniteur* for July 18, 1792, no. 200.
† Then deputy for Corsica to the National Legislative Assembly, later a general in the service of the Emperor of Russia and his minister plenipotentiary in Paris.
‡ Here Louis-Philippe gives Pozzo's speech.—ED.

was not executed, and the French generals did not attempt any attack on the Electorate of Trier, nor on the Duchy of Zweibrücken, the Bishopric of Speyer, etc.

For their part, the Girondins made a futile attempt to obtain a decree of accusation against M. de La Fayette. The Assembly declared an August 8 by a majority of 406 votes to 224 that there were no grounds for accusation against him.* The grounds of accusation that this minority put forward against M. de La Fayette boiled down to three main ones, namely (1) having wished to make his army march on Paris and having proposed to Marshal Luckner to act in concert with him to execute this project; (2) having allowed his army to deliberate on the events of June 20, having encouraged petitions on the subject although the Constitution forbade all armed bodies to make collective petitions, and having come himself to present one at the bar of the National Assembly without first obtaining permission to leave his army; (3) having kept his army inactive and having failed to support the operations undertaken by Marshal Luckner.

The first part of the accusation related to a project of which there was no proof, although there were indications that this project had existed. As to the second, the provisions of the law allowed individual petitions, so M. de La Fayette could not legally be prosecuted for those he had presented; and as to the third, the orders and instructions of the ministers had screened him from responsibility. It was, therefore, just that the result of the deliberations should have been as it was; but party animosity was carried to such a pitch in Paris that those deputies who had voted to absolve M. de La Fayette were insulted everywhere, and it is probable that the fury felt by the people at this declaration of the Assembly accelerated the agitation that erupted on August 10, that is to say, two days after this sitting.

When Marshal Luckner arrived at Metz, he informed all the staff officers who were gathered around him that as General Dumouriez had not carried out the orders he had left him on leaving Valenciennes, he was going to be arrested and transferred to the citadel of Metz, where he would be put on trial for disobedience. This disobedience consisted of the following: The Marshal had ordered General Dumouriez to leave the camp at Maulde on July 20 with his division and to proceed to Metz; but instead of leaving, General Dumouriez had assembled a Council of War at Valenciennes on the 18th and, at the request of the administrative and municipal bodies, had pointed out to it that the departure of his division was going to leave the Department of the Nord without defense against the incursions of the enemy, and that it seemed to him necessary to suspend the march of his division until it had been relieved by the troops which General La Fayette was to detach from his army to replace it. The council had unanimously endorsed this opinion, and General Dumouriez,

* See *le Moniteur* for August 9, 1792, no. 222.

241

who had only assembled it to fortify himself with its advice, had taken the further precaution of immediately informing the National Assembly of the resolution of the council, which certainly contravened the regulations of the military hierarchy but which had so awed the King's ministers that they did not dare insist that the orders of the commander in chief be executed immediately. However, General Arthur Dillon,* who was senior to General Dumouriez, had been sent to Valenciennes to be M. de La Fayette's second in command in the Department of the Nord; and as a result General Dumouriez was subordinate to him, although he continued to be in command of the camp at Maulde, the striking of which was suspended. General Lanoue continued likewise to command the camp at Maubeuge, and General Chazot took command of the troops that General Dillon had assembled at Pont-sur-Sambre, where he established his headquarters.

On August 4, 1792, Marshal Luckner left Metz with the division that included the brigade of dragoons I commanded, and he brought it to camp at Richemont, between Metz and Thionville. The Marshal established his headquarters in the château of Pépinville. I was quartered in the village of Boussange, and Generals d'Harville and Valence, who were back with the army, took up quarters in the village of Hukange. General Desprez de Crassier was sent to Fontoy on the road to Longwy with a feeble advance guard, though one that had been reinforced with the few troops the Marshal had thought he could withdraw from the garrisons of Lorraine. M. de Belmont, a lieutenant general, was in command at Metz, and M. Félix de Wimpfen,† *maréchal de camp,* was in command at Thionville, which was almost the only fortress town on this frontier where real preparations for defense had been made. General Wimpfen had repaired the fortifications, and all the outworks were lined with palisades. He had stocked up with provisions and blocked up the windows of the churches in the town so that they could be used as shelters in case of bombardment. In short, he was ready to withstand a siege, and he announced his intention to put up a vigorous defense if he were attacked. He was, and he kept his promise.

The Marshal sent General Berruyer‡ to take command of Longwy, where there was no staff officer, but after two days General Berruyer returned to headquarters and told the Marshal that the stronghold was in too bad a state for him to undertake its defense. The Marshal went into a frenzy and threatened to have him arrested and put on trial like Dumou-

---

* General Arthur Dillon perished the following year on the scaffold. He had been a member of the Constituent Assembly.

† A former member of the Constituent Assembly. A decree of accusation was passed against him the following year, and as they could not manage to arrest him, he was made an outlaw.

‡ General Berruyer was an old officer who had served with distinction. He had just been made a *maréchal de camp* and was later a commander in chief.

riez for having disobeyed him. However, he did nothing of the sort; but unfortunately he did not take any measures as regards Longwy, where the command remained with Colonel Lavergne of the 34th Foot, who was the man who surrendered the town a fortnight later when the Duke of Brunswick summoned him to capitulate.

Verdun, which was much weaker than Longwy, had been even more neglected, and nothing had been done to put this fortress in a state of defense. Montmédy, which was in a very strong situation, had been much better cared for, and General Ligneville, who was in command there, was ready to withstand a siege. When the fortress was invested, he declined the summonses to capitulate and defended himself vigorously with well-planned sorties. Montmédy was not taken, and yet the following year General Ligneville was accused of wanting to hand over this fortress to the enemy; he was summoned before the Revolutionary Tribunal on this absurd accusation and was about to be executed when he was saved by the death of Robespierre.

At this time General La Fayette occupied the camp of Vau near Sedan with about twenty-three thousand men. Marshal Luckner had from thirteen to fourteen thousand men between Metz and Thionville. General Kellermann* was encamped near Weissembourg with a body of seven to eight thousand men. General Custine† was in command of Landau, and General Lamorlière of Strasbourg. General Biron was entrusted with the command of the troops assembled near this last stronghold.

Such, in outline, was the state of the frontier when the combined armies of Prussia, Austria, and the Princes of the Empire entered France at the beginning of August 1792. The Prussian army under King Frederick William and the Duke of Brunswick was fifty-two thousand men strong. The Austrian army under General Clairfayt consisted of only thirteen thousand. The Hessians, Brunswickers, Württembergers, etc., came to about eighteen to twenty thousand men. In addition to these armies, that of the French *émigrés* must be included. It was said to be about fourteen thousand strong, including the foreign contingents that had been raised and taken into their pay with the promise that the King of France would take them into his service; but it was divided into three sections under the orders of *émigré* Princes. The most considerable, reported to be between five and six thousand men, was attached to the Prussian army under the immediate command of Monsieur, Comte de Provence, who had taken the title Lieutenant General of the Kingdom for his brother, King Louis XVI, and of M. le Comte d'Artois.‡ So the

---

* Later Marshal of France and Duc de Valmy.

† Later commander in chief of the Army of the Rhine and of that of the North; died on the scaffold in the month of August 1793.

‡ The two other *émigré* contingents were commanded by M. le Prince de Condé and M. le Duc de Bourbon. That of the Prince de Condé was to operate on the Rhine and was then employed at the siege of Thionville. That of the Duc de Bourbon was sent to Flanders.

combined strength of the army that entered France at this time was about one hundred and ten thousand men.* It was under the Duke of Brunswick, whom the Powers in the Coalition had chosen as their generalissimo.

The Duke of Brunswick prefaced the entry into France of the armies he commanded with two declarations dated from the headquarters at Coblenz, July 25 and 27; they are too long for me to give in full.† These declarations, as well as the counterdeclarations of the Courts of Berlin and Vienna of June 26 and July 7, correspond exactly. The Duke of Brunswick announced to the inhabitants of France that the object of the allied Courts was to restore the German Princes with possessions in Alsace and Lorraine to their rights and property,‡ "to bring the anarchy in France to an end, to stop the attacks carried out on the Throne and the Altar, to restore legal authority, to give the King back the safety and liberty of which he has been deprived, and to put him in a position to exercise the legitimate authority that is his due." It was further declared that "Their Imperial and Royal Majesties had no intention of interfering in the internal government of France, that they wanted only to deliver the King, the Queen, and the Royal Family from their captivity; but that they could only recognize as laws in France those that emanated from the King in perfect enjoyment of his liberty; that they protested in advance against the authenticity of all the declarations that may be made in the name of His Most Christian Majesty as long as his sacred person, that of the Queen, and of all the Royal Family were not really in safety; for which purpose, their Imperial and Royal Majesties invited and urged His Most

* I am not including in this number the Austrian troops stationed in Flanders who were to operate on this frontier.

† These two pieces were put in the editions of le Moniteur of August 3 and 8, 1792, nos. 216 and 221. I am transcribing here Article 8 of that of July 25, which concerns particularly the city of Paris and from which one can get an idea of the rest.

(8) "The city of Paris and all its inhabitants without exception will be bound to submit to the King on the spot and without delay, to place this Prince in full and entire liberty, and to assure him, and likewise all the royal personages, that inviolability and respect which the law of nature and of nations demands of subjects toward sovereigns. Their Imperial and Royal Majesties render all the members of the National Assembly, of the District, Municipality, and National Guard of Paris, the judges of the peace, and all others concerned personally accountable with their lives, on pain of military punishment with no hope of reprieve for whatever happens. Their said Majesties furthermore declare, on the word of honor of an Emperor and a King, that if the Tuileries Palace is broken into or stormed, if the slightest violence, the slightest affront, is offered to Their Majesties the King, the Queen, and the Royal Family, and if immediate provision is not made for their safety, their preservation, and their liberty, they will exact an exemplary and unforgettable vengeance by turning the city of Paris over to military execution and total ruin, and the rebels guilty of these outrages to the punishment they deserve. If, on the contrary, the inhabitants of the city of Paris obey the above injunction promptly and to the letter, Their Imperial and Royal Majesties promise to employ their good offices with His Most Christian Majesty to obtain pardon for their wrongs and errors and to take the most active measures to safeguard their person and their property."

‡ The quotation marks indicate the passages that are transcribed word for word.

Christian Majesty to designate the town in his kingdom nearest to his frontiers to which he judged it most expedient to retire with the Queen and his family, under a good and safe escort that would be sent to him for this purpose, in order that His Most Christian Majesty should be able, in full security, to summon to him the ministers and councilors it pleased him to designate and to make such convocations as seemed to him appropriate to provide for the restoration of good order and regulate the administration of his kingdom."*

It was further stated in the Duke of Brunswick's supplementary declaration of July 27 that "Their Imperial and Royal Majesties would not accept that His Most Christian Majesty had been free to choose the place to which he would withdraw, assuming he saw fit to accept the invitation that they had made him, unless this withdrawal were effected under the escort that they had offered him.† That any manifestos whatsoever in the name of His Most Christian Majesty *running counter to the objective insisted upon by Their Imperial and Royal Majesties* should in consequence be regarded as null and void."

That "if contrary to all expectations, through the perfidy and cowardice of any of the inhabitants of Paris, the King, the Queen, or any other member of the Royal Family were to be abducted from the town, all the places and towns whatsoever that had not opposed their passage and prevented their progress would undergo the same fate as would be inflicted on the city of Paris, and that the route that had been followed by the abductors of the King and the Royal Family would be marked by a continuous sequence of examples of the punishment due to all the accomplices as well as to all the authors of unpardonable crimes."

That "all the inhabitants of France in general must consider themselves duly warned of the danger that threatened them and from which they could not escape if they did not oppose the passage of the King and the Royal Family with all their force and with all their means, wherever the criminals might attempt to take them."‡

It was also announced that "those of the National Guards who fought the troops of the Allied Courts and were taken arms in hand would be treated as enemies and rebels to their King and disturbers of the peace. The generals, officers, noncommissioned officers, and soldiers of the French armies of the line were likewise summoned to submit immediately to the King, etc."§

This Manifesto of the Duke of Brunswick produced in France more

---

* See the manifesto of the Duke of Brunswick of July 25, in *le Moniteur* for August 3, 1792, no. 216.

† Which means, provided that the King of France were surrounded by foreign armies and able to rule as he wished to rule.

‡ See the supplementary Manifesto of the Duke of Brunswick of July 27 in *le Moniteur* for August 8, 1792, no. 221.

§ See *le Moniteur* for August 3, 1792, no. 216.

enthusiasm for the defense of the Fatherland and national independence than all the addresses of the Assembly and all the popular societies put together could have done.* It was printed in all the papers, and the Assembly nearly decreed that it be sent to all the forty-four thousand municipalities so that all Frenchmen should know in their fullest extent the intentions of the Allied Powers toward them and the fate that awaited them if they triumphed. This proposal was made to the Assembly, but it was rejected, as the King had informed it, in a formal communication of August 3,† "that the declarations of the Duke of Brunswick had not been transmitted to him by any of his residents at the German Courts *closest to the borders* and that consequently the copies of them that had been circulating for some days had no official character."

Nothing could have been more dangerous for the King personally than the publication of this Manifesto, which was bound to lend weight to the opinion, already very widespread, that he was in league with the foreign Powers and that what he wanted was the success of their armies. This Manifesto had the result of convincing the popular party and a large part of the nation that the replacement of the executive power was the only means of preventing France from falling under the yoke of the foreigner and the restoration of the Ancien Régime; this conviction led to the call to arms of August 10 and resulted in the establishment of the republican government.

It is probable that the King wanted to temporize with the Assembly and with Paris until the foreign armies had arrived in the capital, for no one at Court doubted that they would easily get there. But the King feared lest the people of Paris proceed to violence against him or lest the Assembly carry him off in its train when the approach of the foreign armies obliged it to withdraw from Paris. The Manifesto of the Duke of Brunswick gave a clear indication that these were the only dangers they thought they had to fear. To preserve itself from them, the Court sought to assemble around the King a body capable of defending the Tuileries against a popular attack and of resisting the Assembly if it tried to involve the King in its flight. I have already said that since the Assembly's decree of May 29 providing for the disbanding of the King's Bodyguard, he was left with no more than four battalions of Swiss Guards that would each have been two thousand strong if they had been at full strength, which it is claimed they were not. What is certain is that these forces had remained

* It is fairly remarkable that it should be precisely at the moment when the Manifesto of the Duke of Brunswick became known in France that the *Hymne des Marseillais* should become a national anthem. It had been composed shortly before for a gathering of National Guards by M. Rouget de Lisle, a captain in the engineer corps. It was found that it replied to the Manifesto, and it was this coincidence that gave it the vogue it has had. It is unquestionable that the majority of the couplets adapt themselves perfectly to this object and that they express with great vigor the feelings the Manifesto had aroused in the nation.

† See *le Moniteur* for August 4 and 5, 1792, nos. 217 and 218.

in Paris despite three decrees of the Assembly requiring them to withdraw in accordance with an article of the Constitution* and that their presence gave rise to considerable suspicion from the Assembly, the popular party, and the people of Paris. In general, this regiment aroused the suspicions of the public. They were still further increased when they saw a concentration of all those whose political opinions were against the new order of things building up around the King inside his palace. The King regarded them as faithful servants coming to make him a rampart from their very bodies and to sacrifice themselves for his defense; but the people simply regarded them as the enemies of liberty and the supporters of the *émigrés* and foreigners assembling to assist in the execution of their projects. The courtyards of the Tuileries were not then, as they are today, enclosed by railings that make it possible to see everything that is going on; they were flanked by a line of low houses separating them from the Carrousel, and

---

* The Constitution of 1791 provided (Part III, Chapter III, Section I, Article 6): "The executive power may not cause any body of troops of the line to pass or remain within the distance of thirty-five miles from the legislative body unless at its request or with its authorization." As early as July 15 the Assembly, on the grounds of the Article, had declared that it did not authorize the Swiss Guards to remain in Paris. In consequence it had enjoined the Minister of War to order them to leave and withdraw from the place of its sittings, in accordance with the Constitution. On the 17th the Minister (M. d'Abancourt) informed the Assembly that M. d'Affry, colonel of the Swiss Guards, was claiming that the treaties permitted only two battalions of the Swiss Guards to be employed in capacity other than as the King's Bodyguard on the condition that the other two battalions would remain about his person, and that consequently he declared he could not consent to the departure of the whole regiment without special authorization from the cantons. So the Assembly, taking the view that the Swiss Guards' contracts had expired in 1789 and that they had not been renewed, referred examination of M. d'Affry's claim to its Diplomatic Committee and for the moment told the Minister of War to have two battalions leave Paris immediately, which M. d'Affry recognized that he could not oppose. But this second decree was no more carried out than the first. The Minister of War first sought to gain time and to drag the matter out. But finally, pressed for an explanation he informed the Assembly on August 4 that he had ordered M. d'Affry to have two battalions leave for Cambrai, minus three hundred men whom the King wished to send to the Department of the Eure, where he thought they were needed to protect the movement of grain.ᵃ He added that these three hundred men would leave Paris on August 7 but that M. d'Affry was maintaining that he could not provide the two battalions required of him to reinforce the garrison of Cambrai. The Assembly passed a third decree to force the two battalions to leave, and it instructed its Diplomatic Committee to investigate the conduct of the Minister of War and report back. Nevertheless, the three hundred Swiss Guards assigned to the Eure Department were the only ones to leave, and the rest of the regiment was kept at Paris. After the rising of August 10 a decree of accusation against M. d'Abancourt was passed on account of this, and he perished on the scaffold.

(See the issues of *le Moniteur* for July 17 and 19, 1792, nos. 199, 201, and 219.)

ᵃ It is claimed that at this period, the King was making preparations at Rouen through M. de Liancourt, its commandant, and that he was considering withdrawing there. It is probable that this detachment of three hundred Swiss Guards near Rouen had some connection with this plan.

the public was denied access to them. The people of Paris regarded this walled-off area as the hotbed of the Counterrevolution, and this opinion acquired more credibility when it was discovered that arms and ammunition were being carried into the Tuileries. It is possible, even probable, that the King merely wanted to put himself in a state of defense against attacks from the people of the *faubourgs* and above all against those coming from the men, then in Paris in large numbers, called the *fédérés* because they had come from Marseille and a good many other places to celebrate the Federation of July 14 in Paris.* But these preparations caused increasing hostility. On both sides, preparations were being made for a conflict, and an explosion was inevitable. Expectancy of such an event kept spirits in the greatest state of agitation: No one any longer regarded himself as safe in his own house; some saw themselves threatened by a royalist Saint-Bartholomew's Day Massacre and the others by one from the populace; fear was general, and when matters had reached such a pass, no more than a spark was needed to set everything alight. That is what happened on the night of August 9–10.

There are different versions of what led to the taking up of arms. The most likely one is that a false patrol composed of unofficial servitors of the King,† which had left the Tuileries about eleven in the evening to observe what was going on in Paris, was stopped at the Place Vendôme by the National Guard, and when it was recognized as a false patrol, a violent scuffle ensued, in the course of which some were killed and the rest made their escape; but this incident raised the alarm in the district, and they began to ring the tocsin and beat the drum. These terrible signals were immediately relayed, and in a moment they were resounding throughout Paris. All the inhabitants ran to arms, and the public functionaries to their posts; and the members of the Assembly, no less afraid for their personal safety than the others, hastened to seek refuge in their chamber. Soon they were assembled there in sufficient numbers to form a quorum, and at two o'clock in the morning, the sitting was opened.

In its ignorance of what was happening, the Assembly began by summoning the mayor of Paris to the bar to inform them. M. Pétion was at the Tuileries, and already the word had gone out that he was being kept there as a hostage. But this rumor was without foundation because he appeared at the bar shortly afterward and informed the Assembly of the measures he assured them he had taken to prevent the tocsin being rung and to disperse the crowds that were gathering in the *faubourgs*. I do not know what these measures were, but they were ineffectual, and I think that nothing could have stemmed the tide once the floodgates had been

---

* However, I think that the number of these *fédérés,* and the part they played in the rising of August 10, has been greatly exaggerated.

† A man of letters named Suleau, who was very well known at the time for various works and pamphlets he had published against the Revolution, was one of the leaders of this false patrol and was killed in this incident.

opened. As M. Pétion was leaving the Assembly, the people got hold of him and conducted him to the mayor's residence in the Rue des Capucines, near the Place Vendôme, where he was detained without being allowed to return to the palace or the Hôtel de Ville. It was claimed that this was for his safety, but the real reason was to prevent him from exercising his functions.*

After hearing M. Pétion, the Assembly found itself in the same dilemma as before. In a vain attempt to conceal this, the reporter of the Committees for the Navy and Colonies was summoned to the rostrum and proposed the sequel of a projected decree on the progressive abolition of the slave trade. Doubtless the hope was that the insignificance of this discussion at such a critical juncture would give the Assembly's stance an appearance of grandeur, but they were mistaken, and no one was deceived as to why they embarked upon it. The reason was that the Assembly knew that the people accounted it for nothing and that it could exercise no influence over their actions. So the discussion on the slave trade was not of long duration.

At the sound of the tocsin and the drums, the forty-eight sections of Paris had assembled spontaneously. They notified the Assembly successively that they had placed themselves in a state of insurrection against the perfidious authorities who were betraying France and that they would so remain until the fall of the monarchy had been pronounced and efficacious measures had been taken to preserve the Fatherland and liberty from the dangers threatening them. At the same time the sections sent extraordinary deputies to the Hôtel de Ville, who constituted themselves as the Assembly of the Representatives of the Commune of Paris and thus supplanted the legal municipality, at whose head were Pétion and Manuel. The people's confidence in these two officers was still too complete for anyone to dare attack them openly, and the new Assembly of the Commune speedily recognized their maintenance in office; but this sudden reorganization of the Paris Commune was a deadly blow to the Girondin party, with which Pétion and Manuel were closely associated. It destroyed their ascendancy over a considerable portion of the popular party and over the people of Paris, which they never managed to recover. Henceforth, the Paris Commune was composed of those men who, in the National Convention, were to form what was called the *Montagnard party*. They skillfully profited from the absence of Pétion and Manuel to organize themselves without them and to set the insurrection on a course in line with the sanguinary projects of their party. Robespierre was proclaimed president and Tallien secretary of this Assembly.

After the suppression of the office of commander in chief of the Parisian National Guard, its functions were carried out in rotation by the six divisional commanders of the Guard. M. Mandat (a former officer in

* This detail may seem unimportant, but I think that the rest of my account will demonstrate that it was not without significance.

the *Gardes-françaises*) was slain on the steps of the Hôtel de Ville* for refusing to obey the orders of the new Commune. M. Carle and some others who also refused suffered the same fate. Santerre† was proclaimed commander in chief, and a numerous general staff was immediately organized. The Arsenal was forced, and the arms and munitions found there were distributed to the people and the *fédérés*. At the same time, the battery by the statue of Henry IV on the Pont-Neuf was disarmed by order of the Commune, and the detachments of the National Guard occupying this important post were sent elsewhere. As on June 20, all the people in arms proceeded toward the Tuileries; but it was no longer to demand the royal assent for such and such a decree or the recall of such and such a minister: The unanimous cries of these furious masses were for *the dethronement of the King and the punishment of the traitors.*

During this general activity, the preparations for resistance inside the palace had continued. The battalion of the National Guard for the Filles-Saint-Thomas district, on whom it was believed the King could rely, had been brought in, so that with the Swiss Guards and all those who had been led there by their opinions and their attachment to the King, there was a fairly considerable force at hand. It was divided between the gardens and the three courtyards of the palace. The Swiss occupied the middle one. At daybreak the King, the Queen, M. le Dauphin, and all the Royal Family had gone down to the courtyards to ask these troops to defend them, and it is said that they had been well received, though with the exception of the gunners of the National Guard who were in the courtyard of the Marsan wing. Deputations from the departmental administration and of the municipality had accompanied the King, and M. Roederer, deputy attorney general of the department, had read out at the head of the troops the various articles of the laws authorizing and even obliging them to repel force by force; but, as M. Roederer said himself in the report he gave to the Assembly of what had happened at the palace, the reply of the gunners from the National Guard made it clear that they would do nothing to defend it, because they unloaded their cannons there and then.

Having made his tour of inspection of the courtyards, the King went back to his apartments, and M. Roederer and his colleagues proceeded to the Place du Carrousel to engage the people, already assembled there in considerable strength, to withdraw peaceably; but his exhortations were in vain, and cries of anger gave him notice that the people would not withdraw until they had obtained the assurances that the dethronement of the

* It is said that M. Mandat was at the Tuileries organizing the maneuvers of the National Guard when an orderly brought him an order to proceed immediately to the Hôtel de Ville to confer with the municipality. This order was just a trap set for M. Mandat so as to disorganize the command. He would probably not have been taken in by it had he been informed of the changes in the municipality, but in his ignorance he rushed to the Hôtel de Ville, where he was slain.

† A brewer from the Faubourg Saint-Antoine in command of a battalion.

King would be pronounced. M. Roederer returned to the palace to inform the King of the state of affairs and of the futility of his efforts. At the same time he advised him, as did his colleagues, to withdraw to the National Assembly, because the attack on the palace seemed inevitable. Before adopting this advice the King charged the Minister of Justice (M. Joly) to go and ask the Assembly, on his behalf, to send him a deputation to look to the safety of his person and that of his family and to engage the people to withdraw. But it seems that before the Assembly had come to a decision on this request, the King decided to leave the palace: He left accompanied by his family, his ministers, and deputations from the department and the municipality; he had crossed the Tuileries Gardens and had proceeded to the chamber of the Assembly via the Feuillant Terrace. "Gentlemen," he told them on entering, "I have come here to prevent a great crime, and I can think of no greater security than to be in your midst." The president replied to the King: "Sire, you can count on the steadfastness of the National Assembly; its members have sworn to die in support of the rights of the people and of the constituted authorities." The King then placed himself beside the president. By then it was eight-thirty in the morning.

The Assembly, which was maintaining itself without powers or force in the midst of this terrible crisis, fell into consternation at the King's arrival. Uncertain of events, still more uncertain of what it wanted itself and of what it wanted to do, it eagerly seized upon the expedient suggested to it by one of its members, who reminded it that according to the terms of the Constitution, it could not deliberate in the presence of the King. Then the King and his family withdrew behind the president's chair to the recorder's gallery, which was outside the chamber but from which one could see and hear everything that was going on. Having in this way managed to rid itself of the immediate presence of the King, the Assembly turned its attention to hearing the report given it by M. Roederer of what had happened at the palace, of the steps that he had taken, in conjunction with the deputations from the department and the municipality, of their fruitless efforts to engage the people to withdraw, and finally, of the disappearance of the commander in chief of the National Guard, which made it legally impossible for them to take measures for the defense of the palace. In this dilemma, M. Roederer requested the Assembly to prescribe for him the line he should follow.

The noise of cannon and of the discharge of muskets that made itself heard at the end of M. Roederer's speech threw the Assembly into such confusion that it became impossible for it to reply to his request. The King, according to le Moniteur, hurriedly informed the president that he had just dispatched orders to the Swiss Guard that they were not to fire; but it was too late. This is what had happened at the palace after the King's departure.

The people had drawn up in front of the Hôtel d'Elbeuf some pieces of

251

cannon that fired on the King's apartments while the crowd gathered on the Carrousel strove to force the gates of the palace. Then the middle gate opened to reveal two or three cannons charged with grapeshot, which were fired on the multitude and put it to flight. The Swiss, swiftly following up this advantage, debouched in a column onto the square, beating the charge and firing on all sides at the people, who began to flee along the adjoining streets where they rushed headlong, one on top of the other.* In an instant, not a single one of the people remained in a square where, a few seconds before, there had been an immense crowd.

But when the Swiss Guard had entirely cleared the Carrousel and had seized the cannons at the Hôtel d'Elbeuf, General Bachmann,† their commander, received simultaneously the news that the King was no longer at the palace and his order forbidding them to continue resisting the people and to fire on them. His men were so incensed by this order that as soon as he had communicated it to them (which he did at the corner of the Rue Saint-Nicaise, in front of the gates of the Hôtel de Longueville)‡ they threw their arms to the ground and shouted to the people that they could come back and do anything they liked because they would no longer fight against them. The people did come back, but they came back still further enraged, and throwing themselves at the troops, they began to massacre them. Then the Swiss tried to resume their arms and regroup, but there was no longer time; the people returned pell-mell with them into the courtyards and the palace, indiscriminately butchering all those they could lay their hands on. A single company of the Swiss Guard (the Salis company), having managed to regroup, crossed the palace and the gardens unharmed; but it encountered such a mass of people on the Place Louis XV that it could not clear a way and leave Paris as it had planned. It was obliged to fall back on the Rue Royale, with its back to the building that was then the place where the crown jewels were guarded.§ It was in this spot that the unfortunate members of this company, having spent their cartridges, were butchered like their comrades.

Such are the most accurate details I could obtain on this event. I know that there are different versions, but I have been in a position to hear and to compare the accounts of the two sides, and it is in accordance with this that I have given the preceding account. . . .‖

* My brother Beaujolais, who was at the Palais Royal at the time, witnessed this flight, which lasted for nearly a quarter of an hour.
† General Bachmann was a major in the regiment of Swiss Guards; he perished on the scaffold a fortnight later.
‡ Later the King's Stables.
§ Today the Ministry of the Marine.
‖ Here, quotations given by Louis-Philippe on the debates of August 10 in the Assembly have been deleted.—ED.

The actions of the National Assembly, both during the course of August 10 and of the days that followed, give a clear indication, to my way of thinking, of how prepared it would have been to uphold the King's constitutional authority if it had been in its power to do so.

At the same time, it is worth pointing out that these actions were the work of the minority whose hostility was feared by the King, for of the 747 members who made up the Legislative Assembly, only 630 had voted on August 8 on the motion relative to M. de La Fayette, while the roll call of August 10 produced no more than 384 votes;* thus the Assembly had lost nearly half its members and the Girondins had become the majority party in the Assembly, instead of being the minority as hitherto. However, this Assembly, so reduced, refused to pronounce that the King had forfeited his Crown, and confined itself to adopting the same measure the Constituent Assembly had taken the previous year at the time of the King's flight to Varennes—that is to say, that it merely suspended his exercise of the executive power until the nation had declared its will through the organ of a *National Convention,*† which it was asked to nominate immediately, given the Assembly's acknowledged incompetence to pronounce on the weighty questions whose solution was demanded by the present state.

At the same time as the National Assembly suspended the King's

* This roll call was the largest there was between August 10 and September 20, when this Assembly ceased to sit. Thus, since the 224 members of the Gironde remained till the end and those absent were all members of the majority, it is true to say that after they withdrew, all the deeds of the Assembly were those of the Gironde, since out of the 384 members then comprising the Assembly, 224 were Girondins or voted with that party.

† The idea of a *National Convention,* as well as the name, which was new to the French language, was taken from the Constitutions of the United States of America with which everyone was much exercised at the time and to which people sought to approximate the Constitution of France insofar as this was permitted by the different circumstances of the political and moral situation of the two nations. In America, National Conventions are assemblies to which people of each state delegate the specific power of revising or amending the Constitution or even of drafting a new one, depending upon the requirements of the case; but this assembly called a *National Convention* can concern itself only with these objects and can take no part in the exercise of government. Unfortunately the National Convention in France followed a contrary course of action and instead of *setting up* a government, it took it over and was concerned only with governing itself.

(Louis-Philippe is rather unfair here, as the Convention drafted no fewer than three constitutions and was very conscious that this was its prime responsibility. Moreover, even in its heyday, the Committee of Public Safety was never technically the government—it merely supervised the Council of Ministers—and attempts to make it this were viewed with great suspicion. A further point is that an assembly invested with the power to draft a new constitution was, almost necessarily, going to be the most powerful body in the country, possessing—as Siéyès put it—the "dictatorship of constituent power." This is one reason the Legislative Assembly was never as strong as the Constituent Assembly and was in August 1792 obliged to bow to popular pressure and summon a National Convention.—ED.)

exercise of the executive power, it instructed its Extraordinary Commission to present it, within the day, with a draft decree concerning the nomination of a governor for the Prince Royal,* which indicates that the intention and wishes of the Assembly were that this child be called to the throne after the dethronement of the King, his father, had been pronounced. This measure obviously gave so much offense to those who wanted a republic pure and simple that the Assembly abandoned it and dared not take it up again.

Custody of the King's person while he was suspended from office was another question the Assembly had originally decided upon, a decision contrary to the one that the Commune prevailed on it to carry out. As early as August 10 the Assembly had chosen the Luxembourg Palace as the King's residence and that of his family. It had charged the Department [of Paris] to prepare for them within the day quarters where, as it put it, they would be placed under the safeguard of the citizens and the law.† The Assembly was still ignorant of the fact, or pretended to be, that there no longer was a department and that a power existed in Paris superior to its own. The Commune of Paris lost no time in enlightening it on this point. As early as August 11‡ it informed the Assembly that it had relieved the officeholders and Council of the Department of Paris of their jurisdiction over the city of Paris; that it had likewise suspended the Committees of the sections and the justices of the peace, and that it had charged the General Assemblies of the sections to exercise their functions. The Commune (no doubt to soften the effect that this arrogation of all the powers must have produced on the National Assembly and on the public) announced that M. Pétion, the mayor of Paris, whom it continued to confine to the town hall on the pretext that assassins wanted to do away with him, would shortly be given his freedom in full. But the Commune protested against the Assembly's choice of the Luxembourg as the King's residence and demanded that he be placed in the Temple.§ However, the Assembly refused to adopt this proposal. It gave up the idea of housing the King in the Luxembourg, but it decreed|| that he should occupy the residence of the Minister of Justice, in the Place Vendôme; that, as during his suspension in 1791, his guard should be under the orders of the commanding officer of the National Guard and under the surveillance of the mayor of Paris; and that a sum of five hundred thousand francs should be granted the King for the upkeep of his House-

* The name given to the Dauphin under the Constitution of 1791, Dauphiné having ceased to exist.—ED.
† See *le Moniteur* for August 12, 1792, no. 225.
‡ See *le Moniteur* for August 13, 1792, no. 226.
§ A fortified monastery in Paris, in the tower of which Louis XVI was imprisoned.
—ED.
|| This second decree was passed on the 12th (see *le Moniteur* for August 14, 1792, no. 227).

hold until the National Convention met. This second decree found no more favor with the Commune than the first; it demanded its repeal, and not only did the Assembly have the weakness to do this, but in addition it decreed that it would leave the task of determining the King's residence to the Commune, to which it was entrusting custody over him. Then the King was transferred to the Temple with his family and abandoned to all the vexations and bad treatment that the Commune saw fit to make him suffer.

Likewise, the Assembly submitted to the wishes of the Commune over the matter of the Department of Paris. As soon as it had been informed that the Commune had suspended the officers and Council of the Department, it ordered that steps should be taken without delay for the formation of a new departmental authority, and it thought it could reconcile the Commune to this measure by decreeing that the Commune would not be subordinated to it as would an ordinary municipality, and that the department could only concern itself with general administration. However, the Commune opposed the formation of the new department, and it was not formed.

It was over the creation of an extraordinary criminal tribunal that the Assembly tried to put up a special resistance to the Commune's wishes and that, for its part, the latter deployed the most audacity to force the Assembly's compliance. The Assembly had not known what to do with the Swiss officers and men who had not perished on August 10 and who were provisionally confined in the Palais Bourbon, and had, therefore, ordered that they should be brought before a court-martial, which should judge their conduct and pronounce on their fate. But this was not what the Commune wanted, and on August 13* it asked the Assembly to decree that a special tribunal be formed whose members should be nominated by the Paris sections and which should be invested with the power to judge not only the Swiss but all those in general who had wanted to spark off civil war in France. As the Assembly did not immediately give legislative effect to this demand, a second deputation from the Commune presented itself at the bar on the 14th, at six o'clock in the morning,† to repeat the request, and later the same day a third one came, which simply said to the Assembly: "The Commune has deputed us to ask for the decree on the court-martial. If it is not passed, our mission is to wait until it is." This imperative manner gave rise to lively complaints from several deputies. Nevertheless, the Assembly repealed its original decree and attributed judgment of the crimes of which the court-martial was to have taken cognizance to the ordinary tribunals, at the same time authorizing each of the Paris sections to nominate two of the jurors who were to decide whether there were ground for an accusation, and two for

* See *le Moniteur* for August 15, 1792, no. 228.
† See *le Moniteur* for August 17, 1792, no. 230.

giving judgment,* because, it said, some of the jurors who had previously been nominated did not enjoy the confidence of the citizens. But the Commune of Paris was not satisfied with being met halfway, and on August 15 at seven in the evening† Robespierre presented himself at the bar at the head of a deputation from the Commune and pronounced the following speech, which is sufficiently striking for me to quote it in its entirety:

"If the maintenance of the peace and, above all, of liberty depends on the punishment of guilty men, you must secure the machinery for this. Since the 10th the people's just desire for vengeance has not yet been satisfied. I cannot conceive of what insurmountable obstacles apparently stand in the way. The decree you have passed seems to us inadequate and, to dwell on the preamble, I find that it contains no explanation at all of the nature and extent of the crimes that the people must punish. Reference is still made only to crimes committed during the rising of August 10, and this is to restrict the people's vengeance too much, because these crimes go back well before then. The most guilty of the conspirators made no appearance during the rising of the tenth, and according to the law it would be impossible to punish them. Those men who have covered themselves with the mask of patriotism in order to kill it, those men who affected the language of legality in order to overthrow all the laws, that La Fayette who perhaps was not in Paris but who could have been would then escape the nation's vengeance! (Applause.) No longer mistake the times we are living in. Look at principles, look at public necessity, look at the efforts the people have made to be free. The people need a government worthy of them, they need new judges specially created for the circumstances, because if you gave them back the old judges you would restore prevaricating judges and we would return to that chaos which very nearly ruined the nation. The people enfold you in their confidence: Return that confidence, and do not spurn the glory of saving liberty in order to prolong a state of pride and injustice, without profit for yourselves, at the expense of equality, and in contempt of justice. The people are resting, but they are not sleeping. They want the guilty punished, and they are right. You should not give them laws that contradict their unanimous desire. We beg you to rid us of constituted authorities in which we have no confidence; to abolish that two-tier system of justice‡ that by building in delays guarantees impunity. We demand that the guilty be tried by commissioners taken from each section, sitting as a court of final appeal." (Applause.)

"The Deputation obtained the honors of the sitting."

On the proposal of M. Chabot, the Assembly decreed in principle that

* Members of the *jury* were called *jurors*.
† See *le Moniteur* for August 17, 1792, no. 230.
‡ There were at the time two levels of jury that had to pronounce in turn on criminal matters: the jury of accusation and the jury of judgment.

256

a popular court should try the culprits, and referred the manner of its execution to the Extraordinary Commission, instructing it to make its report during the current sitting. This report was delivered shortly afterward by M. Brissot, and as he proposed, the Assembly persisted in its refusal to create the extraordinary criminal tribunal demanded by the Commune of Paris; it upheld its decree sending the accused before the ordinary tribunals and confined itself to ordering that to make justice more expeditious, the condemned should not have the right of appeal.*

It was to be expected that this refusal would redouble the rage of the Commune, so the Assembly was careful to accompany it with an Address to the People of Paris to try to bring them around to more equitable sentiments; but it did not succeed in this, and on the 17th a provisional representative of the Commune came to the bar and addressed the following speech to the Assembly: †

"I come to tell you, as a citizen, as a magistrate of the people, that at midnight tonight the tocsin will be rung and the alarm drum beaten. The people are weary of waiting to be avenged. Beware lest they carry out justice themselves. I demand that you decree on the spot that one citizen per section be nominated to form a criminal tribunal. I demand that this tribunal be established at the Tuileries and that Louis XVI and Marie-Antoinette should slake their great thirst for the blood of the people by seeing that of their villainous satellites flow."

After hearing these threats, the Assembly put up no further resistance: On the spot it decreed unanimously that an electoral body should be formed of forty-eight members chosen by the Paris sections and charged with nominating the members of a criminal tribunal designed to judge *the crimes committed during the rising of August 10 of the present month, and other crimes thereto appertaining; the circumstances and contributory factors, etc.*

This tribunal was immediately set up, but the party that dominated Paris considered it was too slow in its proceedings (although in the course of a few days it had condemned four or five wretches to death, who were executed in the Place du Carrousel), so recourse was had to a more expeditious method, that of carrying out a general massacre of the prisoners, which took place on September 2 and the days following.

It is only with extreme repugnance that I embark on giving an account of an event I would rather be able to efface from our annals; but however painful the task, I must carry it out in order to show how it was possible to give the course of events an impetus that became impossible to stop and that submitted France to that régime of terror and blood whose remembrance is so bitter and whose consequences have been so appalling.

* See *le Moniteur* for August 17, 1792, no. 230.
† See *le Moniteur* for August 19, 1792, no. 232.

Especially must I give this account because it was the horror with which it inspired me (which, with more frankness than prudence, I habitually displayed) that more than anything brought down on my head the persecution from which I nearly perished and which, to all the misfortunes overwhelming me, added that of being forced to expatriate myself and of no longer being able to defend the cause I had espoused.

From the beginning of the Revolution, Marat's paper called *l'Ami du Peuple,* that of *Père Duchesne,* edited by Hébert, and some other sheets of this kind had never ceased repeating that liberty would never be solidly established in France until all its enemies, without exception, had been exterminated; and from this they drew the conclusion that to consolidate it, two or three thousand people must necessarily be sacrificed—that being, according to them, the number of the enemies of the new order. Such was the absurd origin of the execrable policy that has stained the Revolution with blood, altered its course, and produced the deplorable crimes that have rightly revolted and horrified all civilized nations.

It was among the advocates of this policy, which had made considerable inroads into the popular mentality, that the Paris sections chose the members of the Assembly of provisional representatives of the Commune, which was formed spontaneously during the night of August 9–10 and which directed the operations of the populace. As soon as this party had seized power, its sole concern became that of consolidating its hold on it and of making it formidable by establishing a reign of terror that humored the passion and rage of the people. Up until August 10, everyone's desires had seemed to aim toward the same goal—that of making the government proceed in the direction the nation wanted—but when the impossibility of achieving this had brought about the overthrow of the government, matters assumed a different form, and disunion broke out in the popular party. Only on one point did they remain in agreement, that of preventing the Counterrevolution from being effected and of repulsing the foreign invasion; but there were divergences on all the rest, and people became indifferent on all matters that seemed of only secondary importance provided that this great aim was achieved. The National Assembly found itself without the force to strip the Commune of Paris of its power, and it perceived too late that there was no longer any other authority in the State than that which had just overthrown the government. Thenceforth, the decrees of the Assembly were nothing more than the repetition of the orders of the Commune of Paris, whose power was now untrammeled.

From August 10, the gates of Paris were closed to prevent the escape of those who were already designated as victims of the popular fury: No one could now leave Paris without obtaining a passport from the Commune, which granted them only after making a great deal of difficulty. It instituted a Committee of Surveillance, which carried out domiciliary visits everywhere* and made numerous arrests. Several thousand individuals were thrown into the various prisons: The fuller the prisons became, the more the public clamored for the judgment of this mass of prisoners. The people already regarded them as guilty, and the new tribunal's lack of speed appeared to them as nothing but a device dreamed up by the supporters of the Counterrevolutionaries to snatch them from death. Therefore, the leaders of the Commune experienced no difficulty in ridding themselves of their prisoners by having them butchered *en masse*.

At daybreak on September 2, the Commune of Paris passed a resolution, which was immediately posted up all over the town and which began with these words, printed in large lettering: †

TO ARMS, CITIZENS, TO ARMS, THE ENEMY IS AT OUR GATES!

The Commune then announced that Verdun was besieged and could not hold out because it had been left without supplies, and that the enemy was going to make for Paris. Consequently, it invited all the citizens to assemble to march against them. It ordered all those whose age or infirmities did not permit of this to deposit their arms with their sections so that they could be distributed to those who could make use of them, and that all horses fit for service should be immediately seized and employed in the army. In addition, the Commune ordered that the alarm cannon be fired and the call to arms sounded, and that each of its members should proceed immediately to his section to announce these measures and to give his fellow citizens a vivid picture of the imminent danger of the Fatherland, and the treason with which they were surrounded or threatened, to make them realize that the aim of their enemies was to deliver France to the most ignominious slavery and that rather than endure it, they must bury themselves under the ruins of their country and not surrender their towns till they were no more than a pile of cinders.

While the population of Paris, electrified by this appeal, was going into action in the various quarters of the city, the rumor was carefully circulated that the prisoners had attempted an uprising in the prisons and had tried to force the gates: Some sections sent large patrols there to keep them under surveillance, the reports of attempted escapes attributed to the prisoners gained credence, and the popular orators hastened to take advantage of the fact to persuade the people to massacre them. *Le*

---

* One such visit was made to Brissot's house, and the Commune issued a warrant for the arrest of Girey-Dupré, his collaborator in editing the paper *le Patriote-Français*. The Assembly summoned the president of the Commune to the bar—at the time it was M. Huguenin—to give an account of his conduct in this matter. He justified himself on the grounds that *le Patriote-Français* had libeled the Commune. The Assembly made do with this explanation and in addition accorded him the honors of the sitting. (See *le Moniteur* for September 1 and 2, 1792, nos. 245 and 246.)

† See *le Moniteur* for September 3, 1792, no. 247, for the resolution of the General Council of the Commune of Paris, from which I quote fragments here.

Moniteur recounts how one of them who had just enlisted for the front declaimed: "Very well, let all the prisoners die! The danger to the Fatherland calls us, let us depart! But as we leave our families, let us not take with us the fear that our fellow citizens, who are depriving themselves of their arms for us, will be unable to defend our women and children against new plots; let all the scoundrels die!" This resolve spread with an incredible rapidity; from all sides the people proceeded to the prisons, and the massacre began.

Inside the gateway of each prison, a popular commission of twelve members was set up that obliged jailers to hand over the registers of committals. One by one, the prisoners were successively brought before this so-called tribunal whose president, it is said, asked them several questions. Then the twelve individuals who comprised the tribunal put their hands on the head of the prisoner and with a *yes* or a *no* answered the question the president put to them in these terms: "Do you think we can in conscience set free this gentleman?" The term *set free* was used by them with the understanding that it meant to *condemn,* so that if the reply was in the affirmative, the wretched prisoner went out and was immediately pierced with pike thrusts and put to death, but if it was in the negative, a shout of *Long live the nation* went up forthwith, the butchers made way for the prisoner, the crowd applauded, and he was restored to liberty. Unfortunately, there were only a very few prisoners saved in this way, and the number of those who perished was very considerable. It is said in the report to the Assembly by the three commissioners of the Commune—Truchot, Tallien, and Guiraud—that out of more than four hundred prisoners in L'Abbaye, only eleven were spared.*

The butchers proceeded successively to the prisons of L'Abbaye, La Force, Le Châtelet, the Conciergerie, Sainte-Pélagie, and the Carmelite Monastery where the priests were imprisoned, and the carnage lasted for three consecutive days: They sent a detachment to Bicêtre preceded by seven cannons, and this vast prison, where the prisoners were crowded together, was emptied in a few hours like those in Paris; another detachment was sent to Versailles, where the prisoners whom the National Assembly had sent before the High Court of the Nation were expected from Orléans; they did not arrive till September 9, that is to say, several days after the massacres in Paris had ceased; nevertheless, on their arrival they were put to death.†

It is remarkable that despite the people's indignation against the King

* I take these details from *le Moniteur* of Monday, September 4, 1792, no. 248.
† "After the National Assembly's refusal to pass the decree demanded of them to have the prisoners of Orléans transferred to Versailles, the Commune of Paris itself sent commissioners to Orléans who seized these wretches and forcibly effected their transfer. When it had been informed of this, the Assembly merely charged the Executive Council to send a commissioner to Versailles to look to the safety of the prisoners, which did not save them." (See the issues of *le Moniteur* for September 4, 6, 7, and 14, 1792, nos. 248, 250, 251, and 258.)

and especially against the Queen, no attempt was made during these days of disorder and confusion to break into the Temple, where they were detained with their family; but I believe that the leaders of the Commune did not want the people to end their days just then. A circumstance that it is painful for me to recall makes me assume that they had arranged in advance for the prisoners in the Temple to be spared. Three days before September 2, Mme la Princesse de Lamballe, my aunt, who had been led by devotion to the Queen to be imprisoned voluntarily with her in the Temple, was removed by order of the Commune and transferred to the prison of La Force along with Mme de Tourzel, Mlle de Tourzel her daughter, and Mme de Saint-Brice, who had likewise wanted to share the captivity of the King and the Royal Family. It is probable that the object of this transfer was to place them in a prison whose inmates were to perish: However, the three ladies who were escorted there at the same time as Mme de Lamballe were saved by the commissaries of the Commune, who arranged their escape, while they abandoned my aunt to her fate, and she was slain in front of the gates of La Force on September 3 at eight o'clock in the morning.*

The National Assembly made vain efforts to arrest the course of these atrocities; everywhere its authority was flouted. It sent commissioners to the prisons, and they were not even given a hearing. It issued a condemnation of the Executive Council requiring it to take effective measures, and the Executive Council, having no more authority than the Assembly, in turn ordered the commander in chief of the National Guard to employ armed force to guard the prisons and maintain public order; but he replied that the few troops he had at his disposal were guarding the gates and could not leave them. The orders sent to the Commune—and the Assembly did not even dare make these categorical—bore as little fruit: Everyone made speeches and addresses, the Assembly passed decree on decree requiring that it be kept informed of the situation and trying to moderate the fury of the people; but all was in vain, and the massacre continued without interruption until the prisons had been completely emptied and there were no more prisoners left to massacre.

It was in the midst of this execrable scene that the people of Paris gave the impetus for the nation's wonderful drive to defend its independence at this period and to repel the foreign invasion to which France had been delivered. In these three days, the city of Paris put thirty-two thousand men, fully armed and equipped, into service, who left for Châlons-sur-Marne where the mobilization was taking place. This was a fine response to the threat of *total destruction* that the Duke of Brunswick had made in

* My brother Beaujolais was having a lesson at the Palais Royal when, hearing noises in the courtyard, he looked out of the window to ascertain the cause and was struck with horror when he recognized my aunt's head being carried on the end of a pike by some of these wild creatures. Her body was dragged through the streets as far as the gardens of the Palais Royal, having been exposed to the greatest indignities.

the name of the Allied Powers. But what a difference there would have been for France, and even for all the civilized nations, if, while deploying such glorious *élan,* the French people had not been thrown by their abuse of liberty into that state of anarchy and disorder to which the horrors I have just related were merely the prelude.

Following the rising of August 10 and as soon as the Assembly had pronounced the suspension of Louis XVI, it had sent commissioners to the armies to assure itself of their obedience to its decrees. M. de La Fayette tried open resistance, and when three commissioners sent by the Assembly to his army—MM. Kersaint, Antonelle, and Péraldi— arrived at his headquarters, he required the General Council of the Commune of Sedan to have them arrested and escorted to prison, and this was carried out. M. de La Fayette then announced that as the decrees of the Assembly were unconstitutional, they would not be promulgated in the army under his command: He caused the oath of allegiance to the nation, the law, and the King to be renewed, and he addressed circulars to the neighboring departments engaging them not to recognize the decree ordering the suspension of the King and to take concerted action with him to oppose its execution. He was not, however, supported, and he soon realized that the resistance upon which he had embarked could not be sustained. Having issued some orders for the day in which he frankly expressed his political sentiments and principles, he resigned himself to taking the only course of action remaining to him if he were to escape certain death: He left the army during the night of August 19–20 and emigrated with those officers of his general staff who had decided to leave because of their opinions or out of fear of the dangers to which they were exposed in France through their adherence to his measures.

M. de La Fayette and all the officers who accompanied him were arrested at Rochefort, in Luxembourg, by the Austrians and taken to Namur. Those of them who had not been members of any [National] Assembly were shortly afterward released, being merely ordered to leave the Low Countries and Germany; but M. de La Fayette and MM. Alexandre Lameth, Latour-Maubourg, and Bureaux de Pusy, who had been members of the Constituent Assembly, were kept in prison, and it was then that their long captivity commenced. They were made to languish in the dungeons for seven years. It is hard to imagine what could have been the object of such an unjust and impolitic persecution. It seems that by reciprocal agreements, the Allied Powers had contracted with each other to keep them under lock and key until they could hand them over to the royal government to deal with, when they had restored it to France, and no secret was made of the hope that all four would be executed on the Place de Grève in Paris to serve as an example to all those who might be tempted to reform their political systems. M. de La Fayette's conduct and the political principles that seem to have guided him were misunderstood in France at that time and even more so abroad, where the extreme opinions of the *émigrés* had caused the most false ideas to be adopted about the origins and course of the Revolution and about the character of those who had taken part in it. The result was that M. de La Fayette was persecuted in France for wanting to defend the King and abroad for wanting to defend liberty in France.

M. de La Fayette's command also covered the Army of the North, which, as I have already said, General Arthur Dillon commanded under him. It was divided into two main camps, the one at Pont-sur-Sambre, which General Dillon commanded in person, and the one at Maulde, commanded by General Dumouriez. At first, General Dillon fell in with the orders of his commander in chief, M. de La Fayette: He refused to recognize the King's suspension; made the troops comprising the camp at Pont-sur-Sambre renew the oath to be faithful to the nation, the law, and the King; and ordered General Dumouriez to do the same in the camp at Maulde, though he refused. As soon as the Executive Council* had been informed of these circumstances, it removed the overall command from General Dillon and gave it to General Dumouriez; but before this decision had reached the army, General Dillon had been reconciled with the commissioners of the Assembly, MM. Delmas, Dubois-Dubay, and Bellegarde, and he had been confirmed in his command by them, so they were in some perplexity when they received the orders of the Executive Council. However, General Dillon agreed to serve under General Dumouriez and, as a result, just continued to be employed in the army with his rank of lieutenant general instead of being relieved of all his duties, as had at first been ordered by the Executive Council. General Dumouriez ordered him to leave immediately for Sedan, there to take provisional command of the army that M. de La Fayette had just left, and he sent General Chazot with him because there were scarcely any staff officers left in this army, command of which had even, momentarily, devolved by seniority on an old artillery officer (General d'Hangest), who himself confessed that he was incapable of exercising it. General Dumouriez remained a few days more in the Department of the Nord to set its defense in order and prepare for such troop movements as circumstances might require. He placed the camp at Maulde under General Beurnonville and that of Pont-sur-Sambre under General Duval and then departed for Sedan, where he arrived on August 28 to begin the important operations demanded by the Allies' invasion.

But before reporting these, it would be apt to recount what was going on in the army in which I was serving and which was then under the command of Marshal Luckner. As I have already said, it was about thirteen to fourteen thousand men strong and was encamped near Riche-

* The Provisional Executive Council was at this time composed of MM. Roland, Clavière, Servan, Danton, Monge, and Lebrun, ministers of the Interior, Finance, War, Justice, Marine, and Foreign Affairs, and M. Grouvelle, who was secretary to the Council. The first three were those who had quarreled with General Dumouriez during their first ministry.

mont, between Metz and Thionville, with an advance guard at Fontoy on the road to Longwy, when we heard the first news of the happenings of August 10. The Marshal was thrown into consternation and announced to the staff officers and even to the troops that he would recognize no orders other than those emanating from the King. However, he issued no general orders or proclamation, and a considerable fluctuation in his opinions was noted: They crystallized, however, as soon as M. de La Fayette's departure had brought all opposition to the decrees of the National Assembly and the orders of the Executive Council to an end. Then Marshal Luckner had no other consideration than that of maintaining himself in his command; in this, however, he was not able to succeed.

The National Assembly, which, for reasons unknown to me, had omitted to send commissioners to the army commanded by Marshal Luckner at the same time as it sent them to all the others, decided to do this on August 20,* and MM. Laporte, Lamarque, and Hua were charged with this mission. They arrived at Metz on the evening of the 21st, and having conferred with the Marshal, who was already informed of M. de La Fayette's departure, and finding him disposed to do everything they wanted of him, they decided to confirm him in his command. On the 22nd the army presented arms for the commissioners, the infantry forming a square around which the cavalry was drawn up. Marshal Luckner escorted them to the center, where M. Lamarque read aloud the decrees of the Assembly suspending the King's exercise of the executive power and ordering the formation of the Executive Council to exercise it provisionally. The troops responded to this communication with shouts of *Long live the nation,* and as no new oath was required, the case of anyone's expressing his personal opinion did not arise; but M. Hua, without notifying his colleagues, wanted to harangue the army, and when M. Lamarque had finished, he exclaimed: "Soldiers, a great lawsuit has been instituted between the nation and one man. . . ." The murmurs that immediately broke out in all ranks obliged him to be silent and prevented us from hearing the rest of what he intended to say to us. "What does he mean by his lawsuit?" they said. "We are soldiers and not judges. It is enough for us to know that Louis XVI has been suspended from his functions, and we have no need to hear any more." A drum roll brought these private conversations to an end, and they were not resumed. This incident is not the only one where I have had occasion to notice that civilian commissioners rarely know how to tackle troops and often manage to produce a result quite contrary to the one desired.

While the Assembly's commissioners were confirming Marshal Luckner in his command on August 22 at Metz, the Executive Council in Paris was removing him on the 23rd† and replacing him with General Keller-

* See *le Moniteur* for August 22, 1792, no. 235.

† This detail may seem insignificant, but I think the rest of my account will prove that it is not unimportant.

mann, who had hitherto commanded the troops assembled near Landau. As soon as the commissioners were informed of this, they hastened to send a courier to General Kellermann to dissuade him from coming, and at the same time they informed the Assembly and the Executive Council that they had confirmed the Marshal in his command and asked that his dismissal be revoked. But General Kellermann did not defer to their request; he came to Metz and insisted on taking up the command that the Executive Council had given him. As the Marshal did not want to give way, the commissioners found themselves in the greatest embarrassment. However, General Kellermann won the day. The Council maintained him in his command and rid themselves of Marshal Luckner by giving him, on August 29,* the empty title of Generalissimo of the French armies, with orders to proceed to Châlons-sur-Marne, there to command the great assembly of all the new recruits who were being directed to this point. The Marshal stayed only a short time at Châlons. He found himself in a very disagreeable position there, and as the generals in the army had not been made subordinate to him and he could not give them any orders, he was not slow in recognizing that his title of Generalissimo was a mockery. So he asked to withdraw to his estates at Strasbourg, a request which was granted him with pleasure. He lived there in retirement till the end of 1793 when Saint-Just, commissioner of the Convention,† came to uproot him and send him to the scaffold.

The light troops of the Duke of Brunswick's army entered France on August 8 or 9; on the 11th there were skirmishes at Sierck and Rodemack, as a result of which the outposts of the garrison of Thionville that occupied these little towns were driven back into the town itself. The enemy army made for Longwy, which was besieged on August 18. On the same day Prince Hohenlohe, a Prussian general, presented himself with his detachment before the camp of Fontoy, which was occupied by General Desprez de Crassier with the advance guard of our army. He sent to ask for a conference with the commandant of the French camp, and Desprez de Crassier proceeded there immediately with a few officers. Prince Hohenlohe was accompanied by the Prince of Nassau-Siegen, who had served in France; he made Desprez de Crassier propositions the object of which was to persuade him to emigrate, or at least to establish a correspondence with Marshal Luckner through him; but Desprez de Crassier refused point-blank any arrangement of this kind; he assured the Prince that he had been misled as to the nation's dispositions, and he told him that he must expect a vigorous resistance. "So," replied the Prince, "you want us to treat you as enemies, then?" —"Certainly," replied Desprez de Crassier, "as long as you seek to dictate the law to us." —"But I know," the Prince replied, "that you have very small numbers at Fontoy, that in addition your troops will not even try to fight against ours,

---

* See *le Moniteur* for August 30, 1792, no. 243.
† The term more usually employed was "representative-on-mission."—ED.

and that I have it in my power simply to take you by storm." —"That we shall see," said Desprez de Crassier in parting, and as soon as he had returned to his camp, he drew up an account of his conference with Prince Hohenlohe, which he has since shown to me and which I even think he included in the orders of the day.

The Prince attacked the camp at Fontoy on the 19th. Desprez de Crassier held out there throughout the day. There was a moment of panic among his troops, but a timely charge by the 4th Dragoons swung success in his favor, and the attack was finally repulsed. Nevertheless, as there was no doubt that it would soon be renewed with stronger forces, during the night Desprez de Crassier fell back on Uckange and Richemont, where we lay with our little army. Marshal Luckner judged it wiser not to remain in this position now that the passes of Fontoy were no longer guarded; he decided immediately to withdraw behind Metz with all his troops, and the maneuver was accomplished during the night of August 20–21. We pitched camp on the right bank of the Moselle near Frescaty, where he established his headquarters in the palace of the Bishop of Metz, and a pontoon bridge was thrown across the Moselle to allow communications with the left bank.

Such was the position in which we found ourselves when the commissioners of the National Assembly visited the army on August 21. We learned on the 25th that Longwy had put up no resistance and that Colonel Lavergne of the 34th, who was in command there, had capitulated on the 23rd. Our communications with Thionville had been cut off, and although the surrounding countryside was being ravaged by the enemy's light troops, the Marshal carried out no operations to protect it from their incursions. Finally, after ten days of complete inactivity, the fear of losing the command decided him to carry out a small maneuver, but it was so paltry that it would almost have been preferable if he had continued to do nothing.

I was summoned to headquarters on August 30 at ten in the evening. There was no sign there of the Marshal, who had already gone to bed, and I found only General Berthier, the chief of general staff, who handed me an order enjoining me to be ready to march at midnight with my brigade of dragoons as part of a detachment to be commanded by General Desprez de Crassier. I asked General Berthier the destination of this detachment, but he refused to divulge this to me, saying that the purpose of the operations we were going to carry out would only be confided to the commanding officer. I brought my brigade at midnight exactly to the main Longeville road as instructed; there I found General Desprez de Crassier, and we began our march, taking the Verdun road. Our detachment was composed of an infantry brigade of the line of four battalions, of my brigade of dragoons of four squadrons, and of a squadron from the 3rd Hussars. Each infantry battalion had two four-pounders, and the total strength did not amount to four thousand men. I was effectively second in command because I was the only staff officer attached to this army apart from Desprez de Crassier, and therefore he informed me immediately of the orders he had received. He told me that first of all he had to make for Étain to defend the crossing of the Ornes River, that if he could not succeed in this he must then fall back on the defiles of Vaux and Eix, where it was thought he could hold up the Prussian army long enough to receive reinforcements, and that finally, if that proved impossible, he was to throw his whole army corps into Verdun. I put to him that he had undertaken a task that could not be executed; that it was absurd to try to arrest the progress of an army of a hundred thousand combatants with an army corps of four thousand men and that, as for the order to take refuge in Verdun, it meant sacrificing the cavalry of our corps to no purpose and depriving France of troops at a time when she had such great need of them, for only infantry could be used in defending a fortress and it was certain that the dragoons and hussars would be of no service there. I added that it seemed the intention had been to ruin me by charging me with an intrinsically impossible mission whose probable outcome would be to throw me—and also my brother, who was my aide-de-camp—into the hands of the enemy Powers or of the *émigrés,* whose animosity toward our family and toward us was well known. "I know all that as well as you," said Desprez de Crassier, "but what do you want to do about it? Everyone must follow his destiny, and we soldiers must carry out the orders we are given. I confess I was astounded that you should have been sent on this expedition, but here you are, and all I can say to you is that I'll do my best to get you out of it all right." We marched together all night, and on the morning of the 31st we pitched camp near the village of Mars-la-Tour. We learned from peasant reports that Étain was already occupied by the Prussians. However, on September 1 we set off again, still following the main road to Verdun. The hussars, who were our scouts, were driven back on us by the Prussian hussars before Maizery, and we were obliged to come to a halt at the village of Harville, near which we pitched camp behind the Langeau River. Shortly afterward, we saw a Prussian camp being set up on the heights opposite us, and we learned from the peasants that the whole countryside was occupied by enemy troops and that Verdun was already under siege.

I camped with my brigade, and Desprez de Crassier put up in a neighboring house. A few hours later, he sent me his aide-de-camp, Captain Schérer,* to inform me that he was ill and that as he recognized that it was impossible for our corps to advance any further—all the roads being barred to us by superior forces—he proposed to return to Metz, and he was going to hand over command of the corps to me, leaving me free to decide on the best course of action. I went to him straightaway, and

* Later commander in chief of the Army of Italy and Minister of War under the Directory.

267

found him on a bed suffering from colic and in no mood to listen to my observations or discuss anything. He told me that in his condition it would be impossible for him to mount a horse and consequently to remain in command of the troops that had been entrusted to him; he added, however, that he realized we could neither advance nor stay where we were but that henceforth it was for me to decide, as he was no longer in command. I got nothing more out of him, and as his carriage had arrived, he got in and returned to Metz.

This position was in fact untenable, and it can be seen from a glance at the map how easy it would have been for the Prussians to cut off our retreat to Metz and to force us into the fairly difficult terrain to the south of the main road. I decided, therefore, to withdraw to the point where it was impossible to cut us off from Metz and where we could act as advance guard or observation corps for the little army then at Frescaty. I began my march on September 2 before daybreak. I withdrew beyond the village of Gravelotte, where I placed my squadron of hussars, and I took up position behind the gulley at the place where the different roads leading to Metz converge, so that I was in a position to observe all of them. I learned on arrival that Marshal Luckner had left the army the previous day, after handing over command to General Kellermann, to whom, in consequence, I hastened to write, informing him of the measures I had just taken and asking him for his orders. I signed my letter *Louis-Philippe, Prince Français* (as I was accustomed to do since the establishment of the Constitution of 1791, which had prescribed this signature for us), but I abbreviated the last two words to *Pce Fcais,* in accordance with the practice I had adopted to avoid the affectation of always putting *Prince Français* in full; and Kellermann, unable to decipher them, took them for part of my paraph; consequently, not even knowing that I was employed in the army, he believed that the man who was writing to him was a *maréchal de camp* called *Philippe,* and he replied to me, through one of his aides-de-camp, with a note addressed to General Philippe, commandant of the camp at Gravelotte, in which I was enjoined to hand over command of the corps temporarily to the most senior officer and to proceed immediately to Metz to receive the orders of the commander in chief concerning its future destination. When I received this note, I realized that Kellermann had clearly not understood who I was. I handed over the command in my absence to Colonel Sahuguet of the 14th Dragoons and left for Metz. When I entered Kellermann's quarters he looked me up and down with astonishment and said: "My God, I have never seen a staff officer as young as you before! What the devil have you done to be a general already?"—"Been the son of the man who made you a colonel," I replied coldly. —"Ah, can it be?" he then exclaimed. "And yet I should have realized. But, my Prince, I did not expect the honor of seeing you under my orders." —"And I very much look forward," I said, "to receiving them and executing them to the best of my ability." After this he expatiated a lot on my signature and on the fact that it was impossible to comprehend from it who it was who had written it; and when this subject was exhausted, we began to discuss the difficulties of our situation.

He told me that he had not yet unraveled what the Duke of Brunswick's real plan of campaign was; that the siege of Verdun could equally indicate the intention of marching on Paris or that of launching an attack on Lorraine; that he thought that Thionville was going to be besieged; that he feared to abandon Metz to its own forces, given the state in which he found its fortifications; that the garrison was small in relation to the extent of fortifications to be defended, and that the army whose command he had just assumed was so small that he could not embark on any operation until he had received the reinforcements which had been promised him; that, furthermore, he did not know what the army recently commanded by M. de La Fayette was doing, and he concluded by telling me to return to Gravelotte and to remain there in observation until he had decided what he would do.

I returned, therefore, to my corps immediately and resumed command of it the same evening. On the 4th a column of French soldiers, disarmed and marching in a disorderly manner, presented itself to my advance posts outside the village of Gravelotte. It was a portion of the garrison of Verdun, which had capitulated on the 2nd. I learned from them that before the surrender of Verdun, a Council of War had been assembled to deliberate on the Duke of Brunswick's summons to capitulate, and that after it had been resolved that resistance was impossible and that they must surrender, Lieutenant Colonel Beaurepaire of the first battalion of National Volunteers from Maine-et-Loire, who was in the chair as commandant of the fortress, had blown his brains out in the midst of the council rather than be a party to the capitulation.* I had these soldiers escorted to headquarters to be put at the disposal of the commander in chief, who immediately distributed them among the garrison of Metz; but their passage through my camp spread despondency there, and three captains of the 5th infantry regiment of the line (Navarre) went over to the enemy during the following night. These were the last officers to emigrate, at least to my knowledge.

Almost at the same time, we received news of the operations of General Dumouriez, who had taken command of M. de La Fayette's army and had arrived at Sedan on August 28, in the interval between the surrender of Longwy and that of Verdun. This army was at the time divided into two corps.† One, of about seventeen thousand men, was encamped on the heights dominating Sedan; the other, of about six thousand picked men, formed the advance guard and was encamped three

---

* For details of these events, see le Moniteur for September 8, 1792, no. 252.
† See the Mémoires of General Dumouriez, volume III, book V, chapter 5, pages 65 and following.

leagues away on the heights of Vaux on the right bank of the Meuse. "Consternation there was general," says General Dumouriez in his *Mémoires*, "the soldiers regarded all the officers as traitors and took this pretext to observe neither discipline nor obedience. The officers feared the soldiers and no longer dared to order anything. Nobody gave any orders, and certainly between the 22nd and the 28th, if the Duke of Brunswick had thrust a corps of only ten thousand men on Sedan, this army would have scattered to the fortresses or would have fled as far as Paris. The departmental and district authorities were expecting the Counterrevolution to succeed and did not mind. The three commissioners of the Assembly who had been arrested and released, as well as the three others who had been sent afterward, had returned precipitately to Paris, and their departure was augmented by confusion and alarm."

General Dumouriez was rather badly received by the troops, who were prejudiced against him, but he was not discouraged by this. He found only four staff officers in the army, Dillon and Chazot, whom he had sent there from Flanders, and Dietmann and d'Hangest, the only ones left of M. de La Fayette's general staff. As soon as he arrived on the 28th, he applied himself to reinforcing the garrison of Verdun, which was composed of only two battalions of National Volunteers. The same evening he ordered two battalions of infantry to leave, one of which was the 17th of the line (Auvergne), and he chose as their commander Lieutenant Colonel Galbaud, an old artillery officer who had formerly commanded at Verdun. He ordered him to throw his troops into this fortress, which was not a good one, but one whose situation and the provisions of all kinds that were there made it of great importance. He did not expect that it could resist a regular siege, but he wanted to oblige the Prussian army to conduct one, to halt its march and gain the time necessary to carry out the maneuver he intended and to receive the reinforcements he was awaiting. On charging Galbaud with this task, he took it upon himself to make him a *maréchal de camp;* then he appointed his adjutants general, completed the organization of his general staff in three days, and fixed the order of battle for his army so that he could act immediately.

In Paris it was desired that General Dumouriez bring his army closer to the capital, from which it was feared, with good cause, that the enemy would cut him off by a rapid march on Sainte-Menehould and Châlons. The Executive Council had expressed the wish that he withdraw behind the Marne without, however, ordering him to do so explicitly; but the General had another plan, and he believed, rightly, that the best way of defending Paris was to keep the enemy as far from it as he could. He sounded out the opinion of his staff officers; all advised him to withdraw behind the Marne, and even seemed to doubt whether he could get there before the enemy. Seeing then that he could not get them to recommend the plan he wanted to adopt, he did not disclose it to them, and he only confided it to Colonel Thouvenot (from the corps of geographical engineers), whom he had just made adjutant general, and M. Petier, his quartermaster. This plan was to occupy the defiles of the Argonne, a small chain of fairly difficult mountains separating the basin of the Meuse from the plain of Champagne and stretching from northwest to southeast. General Dumouriez says in his *Mémoires* that the Prussian army could only cross it at five points, le Chêne-Populeux (or Pouilleux), la Croix-aux-Bois, Grandpré, la Chalade, and les Islettes, which was the most important point because it was the one over which the main road passes from Verdun and Clermont to Sainte-Menehould and Châlons. It is only five leagues from Verdun to Clermont, two from Clermont to les Islettes, and two from les Islettes to Sainte-Menehould, making nine leagues from Verdun to Sainte-Menehould by a fine main road, while it is twelve from Sedan to Grandpré and six from Grandpré to Sainte-Menehould following the direct route by very bad country roads, along which it was to be expected that the enemy would be able to halt the march of the French army at every step. General Dumouriez had all the more cause to fear this because his army consisted of only twenty-three thousand men and was still at Sedan and Vaux, while General Clairfayt was already established at Stenay with twenty thousand Austrians. It was, therefore, probable that General Dumouriez would be outstripped by the Duke of Brunswick in the Argonne, but he calculated that the enemy would not embark on anything until Verdun had been taken, and his calculation proved right. He dared to execute the bold operation he had conceived, he followed his plan with tenacity despite the clamors with which he was besieged and the obstacles of all kinds which stood in the way of its execution, and his success was complete. In this way he managed to preserve France from the invasion of an army four or five times more numerous than the one he commanded at the time he conceived of an enterprise all the more glorious for its seeming, and necessarily so, to be impossible.

On August 30 General Dumouriez learned at Sedan that General Galbaud had been unable to penetrate as far as Verdun; that the enemy was already in force at Dun; and that he had only just escaped being taken there with his two battalions but that he had managed to take refuge in the forest of Argonne and to fall back on Sainte-Menehould, where he had found two of the disarmed battalions from the garrison of Longwy. General Dumouriez immediately ordered General Galbaud to occupy les Islettes, to construct abatis there, to raise entrenchments and batteries, to have arms and munitions brought posthaste from Châlons, to summon all the mounted police in the neighborhood, and to reinforce his corps with all the volunteers that the locality could provide. Galbaud executed all these orders punctually and occupied les Islettes; but the arrival at Varennes of a detachment of Prussians and *émigrés,* who wanted, as they said, to punish this small town where the King had been stopped in June 1791, caused a panic in his camp at les Islettes, which was abandoned without its even being attacked. Galbaud was carried along by his own troops as far as Sainte-Menehould; but luckily, the enemy did not notice this flight and did not take advantage of it: Galbaud managed to rally his small contingent and bring it back without difficulty to les Islettes, which the Prussians and the Hessians then attacked several times, always without success.

General Dumouriez divided his army into three corps.* He entrusted the command of the one of six thousand men that was at Vaux to General Dillon, and charged General Miaczincki to act as its advance guard. He reserved for himself the main body of twelve thousand men that was at Sedan and put his advance guard under Colonel Stengel, for whom he requested the rank of *maréchal de camp*. The third corps, composed of five thousand men also at Sedan, was put under Lieutenant General Chazot and charged with covering the movement of the artillery park and the wagon trains. He ordered General Dillon to proceed via Mouzon to Stenay on the 31st and to attack the Austrians there, but General Dillon did not think he was strong enough to execute this order and stopped at Mouzon, contenting himself with having General Miaczincki attack the forest of Neuville. It is claimed that this engagement was not to our advantage: However, it determined General Clairfayt to withdraw his advance guard from the left bank of the Meuse, to evacuate Stenay, and to take up position behind this town on the heights of Brouennes, where General Dumouriez did not take the trouble to pursue him. He left Sedan on September 1 with his twelve thousand men, making for Mouzon, where he was very vexed to find General Dillon still there, and proceeded with the two army corps to the forest of Neuville while General Chazot filed along behind him with the bulk of the artillery via Tannay and les Armoises. He camped by the side of the main road to Stenay and set up his headquarters in the village of Yonck. On the 2nd he camped at Berlière, and General Dillon at Saint-Pierremont. On the 3rd he remained at Berlière to allow General Chazot's column to pass, and General Dillon proceeded to Varennes, where he pitched camp. On the 4th General Dillon went through la Chalade and occupied Côte de Biesme and les Islettes, where he effected his junction with General Galbaud. The same day, General Dumouriez and General Chazot established themselves at the camp of Grandpré;† and the operation was accomplished without the enemy doing anything to interrupt it. General Dumouriez had a large number of empty tents erected in his camp, to make his army appear larger than it really was. The front of the camp, naturally in a very strong position, was bristling with batteries. Les Islettes and Côte de Biesme, as well as the defile of la Chalade, were likewise entrenched and furnished with a formidable artillery by the attentions of General Dillon and General Galbaud. The nature of the terrain made it unlikely that the enemy

---

* See General Dumouriez, *Mémoires,* volume III, book V, chapter 6, pages 86 and following.

† Here Louis-Philippe gives Dumouriez's description of the camp at Grandpré.—ED.

would attempt to penetrate between General Dumouriez's corps and General Dillon's, but on the other hand, the distance there was between them made it impossible for them to stand together or come to the other's aid in case of attack. The defect of this position was its great expanse, and it is certain that if the Duke of Brunswick had concentrated all his forces against a single point he would have stormed it, and this in itself would have caused all the others to fall. General Dumouriez was well aware of this, but he calculated that the Duke of Brunswick would be unwilling to sacrifice the number of men necessary to take such well-entrenched positions by storm, and his calculation proved as correct as the one he had made at the time of his operation in the Argonne, because the Duke of Brunswick contented himself with seeking to turn his position. To make this maneuver more difficult, General Dumouriez caused the defile of la Croix-aux-Bois on his left to be occupied by two infantry battalions and two squadrons of dragoons, and he ordered abatis to be constructed throughout all this part of the forest of Argonne in order to force the enemy to go back up as far as le Chêne-Populeux to find an opening into the plains of Champagne. He forewent guarding this opening which, being so far to his left, would have obliged the enemy to make a considerable detour to seek him out, would have cut them off from their supplies and led them by paths that were daily worsening as the season advanced, in an area devoid of resources and one where it was impossible for them to subsist. It was much more difficult to turn General Dillon from the right, but to make this maneuver absolutely impossible, General Dumouriez asked General Kellermann to proceed with his army immediately via Bar-le-Duc to Révigny-aux-Vaches, whence he could equally cover General Dillon's right and proceed to the left of General Dumouriez if the enemy army got through to Champagne.

Such was the state of affairs and the position of the armies on September 4 when, on arrival at Grandpré, General Dumouriez received news of the fall of Verdun. It was then that to forestall the discouraging effect this news was bound to have, he announced it himself to the Minister of War in a laconic letter that would make a fine inscription for the pedestal of his statue if ever the nation has the gratitude to raise one to him for not despairing of France's salvation when all had given up hope and for succeeding in repulsing an invasion it seemed impossible to resist. Here is this remarkable letter:*

"Verdun is taken, and I await the Prussians. The camp of Grandpré and that of les Islettes are the Thermopylaes of France, but I shall be more fortunate than Leonidas."

General Dumouriez's army was swollen every day by voluntary reinforcements furnished by the neighborhood and arriving from all parts,†

* See Dumouriez, *Mémoires,* volume III, book V, chapter 7, page 91.
† The city of Rheims alone sent fifteen hundred men, Saint-Mihiel five hundred, and the little town of Mouzon furnished a company of one hundred men and ten rifle-

273

but often these reinforcements were an embarrassment to him, as much by the difficulty of feeding as by the poor organization of these spontaneously recruited troops and the spirit of insubordination that reigned among them. He requested that only troops completely equipped and organized should be sent to the army and that the others should be directed to Rheims and Châlons until they were in a state to join his army. He also requested that they accelerate the movement of the troops from the camp at Pont-sur-Sambre under General Duval and those from the camp at Maulde under General Beurnonville, to whom he had given orders to come and join him by forced marches. But the point on which General Dumouriez most insisted was that Kellermann's army should be reinforced by troops from the Army of the Rhine and that it should be ordered to proceed immediately via Bar-le-Duc to Révigny-aux-Vaches, so that in future the two armies could act in concert. The Executive Council did not do exactly what General Dumouriez wanted in this respect; but it agreed in part, and the force of circumstances led to the rest. It ordered that a detachment of troops from the Army of the Rhine join Kellermann's army and that this army, thus reinforced, should immediately approach the Marne, behind which thinking Paris persisted in seeing the best line of defense for the capital.

General Kellermann began his movement on the night of September 5–6. I struck camp at Gravelotte at nine in the evening, and I made for Pont-à-Mousson along the left bank of the Moselle, arriving there on the 6th at seven in the morning. General Kellermann arrived there at the same hour by the right bank, leading the main corps coming from Frescaty, and at the same time we saw the column of the Army of the Rhine, commanded by General Muratel, emerge from the road to Alsace. The troops showed great pleasure at the moment when the three columns descended together into the basin of Pont-à-Mousson, and the junction was effected in the midst of cries of *Long live the nation* and *Long live France*. However, our army was still only twenty-seven thousand strong after the junction of these three corps; but we had not seen so many French troops together for a long time, and those that made up this army were almost the best there were then in France, both as regards training and discipline and their excellent morale.

We stopped only for a few hours at Pont-à-Mousson in order to give the soldiers time to rest and to make soup; and when this had been done, the army set off on its march in a single column. We followed the road to Nancy as far as Dieulouard, where we took the one to Toul. We bivouacked near this town at one in the morning, and it was not until the 7th, at daybreak, that we were able to have our camping equipment. The men and the horses were extremely tired by this long march, and the

men who followed the army. See *le Moniteur* for September 8, 1792, no. 251. I regret not having taken notes of what the different towns furnished in soldiers at this period. The city of Paris gave thirty-two thousand men.

route was covered with stragglers, overcome by weariness and sleep, but they all rejoined in the course of the 9th, because then not a single man deserted from our ranks.

We remained at Toul on the 7th. On the 8th the army camped at Void, and on the 9th at Ligny. On the 10th we went to camp on the other side of the Marne, at Saint-Dizier; we stayed there on the 11th, and on the 12th a false report that the Prussians were in strength at Saint-Mihiel determined General Kellermann to lead his army to Bar-le-Duc, where we learned that there were only light troops at Saint-Mihiel and that the bulk of the army was making for General Dumouriez's army at Grandpré. On the 13th we stayed at Bar-le-Duc, and on the 14th we withdrew via Heiltz-le-Maurupt to Vitry-le-François, where we remained on the 15th and 16th.

It was at Vitry-le-François that I learned that the Executive Council had made me a lieutenant general on September 11 and that it intended to entrust me with the command of the fortress of Strasbourg. I managed to avoid this new assignment and to remain with the army in which I was serving with my new rank. General Kellermann very kindly consented to this. This was precisely the moment when he was occupied with regulating the order of battle for his army and consequently the commands of each of the staff officers. Command of the vanguard was given to General Desprez de Crassier. General Valence was entrusted with the first line, in which were placed the sharpshooters and the battalions of grenadiers he had hitherto commanded as a reserve corps, and I was entrusted with the second line, made up of twelve infantry battalions (of which eleven were of the line) and six squadrons of cavalry. General Schauenbourg, who had just been made a *maréchal de camp,* was made chief of staff of our army in place of General Berthier, who had been recalled to Paris.

It is a good place now to give an account of what had been happening to General Dumouriez's army since it had occupied the camp at Grandpré on September 4. It had to suffer many privations and often went short of food, especially in the first days. "In addition," General Dumouriez says in his *Mémoires,** "the soldiers and the generals themselves were attacked by diarrhea, which was attributed to the poor quality of the water and the many cold showers of rain as well as to the necessity of frequent watches. Fortunately, this illness was not severe and had no consequences; but it left dysentery germs behind at Grandpré, which later were to be very bad for the Prussians." There was discontent; all means were put into play to have Grandpré abandoned and to persuade the General to retire behind the Marne. A few generals tried to present him with formal remonstrances: He imposed silence on them. The backbiting reached Paris; the Executive Council wrote to the General every day begging him to give up a project that they qualified as *unworkable* and trying to get him to retire behind the Marne. These representations became even more lively after

* See Dumouriez, *Mémoires,* volume III, book V, chapter 7, page 101.

he had been forced to fall back on Sainte-Menehould; but he resisted them, and it was his firmness that assured his success and saved France. To everything that was sent him, he replied: "Get Kellermann here, and once the junction of the armies has been effected I shall look after the rest, but stop opposing my plan of campaign."

The Prussian army lost a lot of time after taking Verdun, and it was not until the 8th that it reached the great plain stretching from Clermont to Buzancy. On the 9th, the French advance posts were attacked along the whole front, and everywhere the Prussians were repelled. On the 10th, General Clairfayt with the Austrians took up position before la Croix-aux-Bois, the King of Prussia and the Duke of Brunswick threatened Grand-pré, and Prince Hohenlohe made for les Islettes. General Duval arrived the same day at le Chêne-Populeux with the French troops from Pont-sur-Sambre, and General Dumouriez ordered him to leave only General Dubouquet there with four battalions of infantry to bar this pass to all the small enemy detachments and to proceed immediately to Grandpré with the rest of his troops, so that he soon had more than twenty thousand men to defend this position, apart from the camp at les Islettes and the other detachments.

On the 12th, after General Dumouriez had, with a carelessness for which he reproaches himself in his *Mémoires*,* allowed the colonel who commanded two battalions and two squadrons at la Croix-aux-Bois to return to the camp (at Grandpré) and, as this colonel proposed, to entrust the defense of this important position to a single battalion of National Volunteers from the Department of the Ardennes; it was attacked and carried on the 13th, at daybreak, by an Austrian corps under Prince Charles of Ligne.† General Dumouriez immediately sent General Chazot there with two brigades of infantry, six squadrons, and some emplacement artillery, and after a very fierce battle, in which Prince Charles of Ligne was killed, the Austrians were forced to withdraw, and the entrenchments of la Croix-aux-Bois were retaken the same day. But on the 14th General Clairfayt attacked them anew with considerable forces‡ before the abatis had been remade and took them a second time, and General Chazot made his retreat to Vouziers, with the loss of part of his artillery.

The same day the Prussian army made a general attack along the whole front of the camp at Grandpré, without obtaining any advantage: Everywhere it was repulsed. At the same time a corps of *émigrés* attacked General Dubouquet at le Chêne-Populeux and was likewise repulsed without breaking his line. But as the loss of la Croix-aux-Bois opened up

---

* See Dumouriez, *Mémoires*, volume III, book V, chapter 8, pages 111 and following.
† The eldest son of the Prince of Ligne, celebrated for his campaigns, his adventures, his verse, and his writings.
‡ General Chazot only had about five thousand men, and it is said that he was attacked by twelve thousand Austrians.

an entry into Champagne to the enemy army, it became necessary to change the line of defense, and General Dubouquet evacuated le Chêne-Populeux immediately and withdrew via Rethel to Rheims and Châlons. Then the *émigrés* went through le Chêne-Populeux without difficulty and made for Vouziers to back up the operations of General Clairfayt's Austrian corps.

It was only on the 14th, at seven in the evening, that General Dumouriez learned from a note from General Chazot* that the Austrians had retaken la Croix-aux-Bois and that he was falling back on Vouziers. It was impossible for General Dumouriez to remain at Grandpré, where his position was now turned and dominated, and where, moreover, he no longer had more than about fifteen thousand men since the separation of Chazot's detachment; but his retreat presented great dangers and great difficulties. If the Prussian army had followed up the operations of the Austrian corps, if it had thrown itself rapidly into the gap at la Croix-aux-Bois, and if some had pursued General Chazot while the others had made for the flank and rear of General Dumouriez via Olizy and Termes, they would have captured all his artillery at Senuc, and as he puts it himself in his *Mémoires,* "this village would have become his Caudine Forks."† But nothing of the sort happened. The Austrians, satisfied with having retaken la Croix-aux-Bois on the morning of the 14th, did not even pursue General Chazot in his retreat toward Vouziers, and undertook no operation whatsoever after obtaining this advantage. The Prussians remained equally inactive after failing in their attack on the front of the camp at Grandpré, and consequently nothing interrupted General Dumouriez's retreat along the heights of Autry, behind the Aisne River.

General Dumouriez immediately sent orders to General Chazot to leave Vouziers at midnight and to proceed via Vaux to Autry, where he told him his detachment would find the army. In the evening, he began filing his artillery park, which was at Senuc, across the bridges of Senuc and Grandchamp from the other side of the Aisne. At midnight, he ordered the camp at Grandpré to be struck, put his army on the march, and at eight o'clock in the morning he had already crossed the Aisne and put his army in battle array on the heights of Autry. He regarded it then as saved, and he had proceeded in person to the other side of the heights to put his artillery park in motion and direct it to Dommartin-sous-Hans, when he perceived a large number of men in flight arrive, shouting:

* General Dumouriez says in his *Mémoires,* volume III, book V, chapter 8, page 115, that it was on the 15th that General Chazot was beaten at la Croix-aux-Bois and wrote him this note, but it seems—according to *le Moniteur,* from which I have checked the dates—that he is mistaken and that it was the 14th (see *le Moniteur* for December 17, 1792, no. 261). It follows from this error that all the dates for his retreat from Grandpré to Sainte-Menehould are one day too early [*sic*] in his *Mémoires,* which he wrote later from memory in Germany without any documents to consult.

† See Dumouriez, *Mémoires,* volume III, book V, chapter 8, page 118.

"Every man for himself, all is lost, the army is in flight and the enemy is on our heels." He immediately turned in his tracks to try to check this disorder, the cause of which he did not understand. This is what had occasioned it:

The Prussians, perceiving that the camp at Grandpré had been abandoned, had detached about fifteen hundred hussars with a few pieces of horse-drawn artillery to harry the French rear guard commanded by Generals Duval and Stengel. The latter stopped them on the banks of the Aisne and were fighting them in very good order when General Chazot's detachment emerged from Vaux. The troops of which it was comprised, seeing a battle to their right and believing that Dumouriez's army was still at Grandpré, imagined that the Prussians were attacking it from the rear and that they were cut off from it. One must have served in the French army at this period, which had as yet no experience, to understand the effect that the fear of being *cut off* then produced. No sooner did people think themselves *cut off* than they had no further doubts but that they had been *betrayed,* and their only thought was to flee, which seemed the only way to avoid being *delivered* to the enemy. Chazot's troops, accordingly, disbanded in a moment; on their side, those from Dumouriez's army corps, seeing them in flight, thought that they had been pursued by the enemy and likewise began to flee, so that in a moment the flight became general. However, General Miranda, who had been serving in the French army for a few days with the rank of *maréchal de camp,* restrained the brigade that he was commanding and halted a part of the army corps' infantry. The rear guard continued to contain the Prussians and finally even drove them back, although they had managed to cross the Aisne and capture two cannons and some baggage from General Chazot's column; but they did not derive any further advantage from this flight of the army and quickly withdrew, once they were sure that they could not harm the rear guard.

General Dumouriez rallied the army on the heights of Berzieux, behind the Tourbe, and ordered General Duval to keep behind the marshes of Cernay until nightfall and then to take up position on the right bank of the Tourbe between this river and his camp. He hoped to spend the night quietly in this position, but at ten at night a new panic broke out among the troops, without his ever being able to unravel its cause. People began shouting *Let's go, let's go* in a few newly recruited battalions, and with these cries being repeated throughout the line, it broke spontaneously in disorder. The artillerymen hastened to couple up, everyone began to flee, and two cavalry regiments even rode down the infantry at a gallop. Men were crushed, wagons overturned, the troops got mixed up, and the whole army, except the rear guard, fell into a confusion which darkness soon made it impossible to sort out. General Dumouriez strove in vain to restore order, and it was only after some time that he managed, with the assistance of the generals and officers of all ranks who rallied around him, to stop the commotion and to prevent the prolongation of this flight, but he could not even begin during the night to clear up the chaos which had been created in his army. It was such that if an enemy corps, however small, had showed itself then, the army could not have put up the least resistance to it and would have disbanded in a moment; but the enemy did not appear. General Dumouriez made everyone bivouac wherever he happened to be when the commotion was stopped. He had large fires lit in all parts of the plain and resigned himself to awaiting the day in this state. More than two thousand men of all arms quitted the army during this night, and fleeing in all directions to the interior with inconceivable rapidity, they spread dismay and fear everywhere with the false rumors they put about. They insisted, among other things, that General Dumouriez had gone over to the enemy with his general staff and all his generals and that his army was entirely destroyed.

On the 16th, at daybreak, General Dumouriez began to restore order to his army. Each regiment was soon reconstituted and resumed its place in the line according to the order of battle. The enemy allowed him to accomplish, without hindrance, an operation that would have become impossible if they had attacked before it was finished. Then he crossed the Biesme in three columns and in the evening occupied the camp at Sainte-Menehould.

The support for this position was the area between the Biesme and Aisne rivers. Les Islettes and la Chalade, to which access was in any case very difficult, had, in addition, been carefully entrenched and were occupied by good troops under Generals Dillon and Galbaud, as I have already said. Vienne le-Château and Saint-Thomas, near the confluence of the Biesme and the Aisne, were likewise entrenched, and the defense of these posts was entrusted to General Duval. General Dumouriez fixed his headquarters at Sainte-Menehould and placed small intermediary detachments on the right bank of the Aisne, at Moiremont and Neuville-au-Pont. The latter village was to the right of the main position that he had his army occupy on the left bank of the Aisne, before Sainte-Menehould, and that stretched from this river to the village of Braux Sainte-Cohière. To give good coverage to his right, General Dumouriez caused a small detachment of three to four thousand men, left by General Kellermann at Bar-le-Duc under General Labarolière, to fall back on his army, and he placed it at Passavant, in the midst of pools and marshes to prevent any enemy corps from getting through to his rear and trying to spread alarm in his camp.

Although the French forces were still too extended in this new position, they were more concentrated than before. The area they occupied was sufficiently confined for an attack to present great difficulties to the enemy. This position had the advantage of covering a fertile area from which the French army could draw its provisions, while that which it offered to the Prussian army was arid and could not furnish it with any. Besides, as the occupation of this position by the French army barred the main road from Verdun to Châlons, in order to penetrate Champagne and push their advance guard on to Paris, the allies would have had to make a wide detour and travel with their artillery and baggage along very bad roads, which the advancing season was daily making worse and which could become impassable in the event of a retreat. If the allies' march on Paris was halted for any reason and they tried to establish themselves in Champagne, as in fact happened, they would then not only have to draw their provisions from Lorraine and bring them along these same bad roads but also to devote a sizable proportion of their troops to masking the French camps at les Islettes and la Chalade, covering their communications with Verdun and Longwy, and protecting the passage of their convoys along the whole length of the semicircle of the French position. These difficulties were so great that the Allies failed to surmount them; and when they tried to establish themselves in Champagne, it was equally impossible for them to procure provisions there or to protect the passage of their convoys—which, exposing them to a shortage of food, was one of the main reasons for their retreat. Such was the result of General Dumouriez's happy inspiration in occupying les Islettes and Côte de Biesme before the enemy. The Duke of Brunswick could then snatch these advantages from him only by attacking these positions and incurring the heavy casualties necessary to capture them; but he preferred to enter the plains of Champagne via Grandpré and Vouziers so as to turn the position and enable himself to attack the French army on its left flank, if it persisted in holding this position when the Prussian army was between it and Paris. It is true that this left flank was very weak and that it would have needed far more troops than General Dumouriez had to be able to resist an attack from the Prussian army. Thus it was to cover the left and reinforce it that he urged General Kellermann to come to join him with his army, but he could not order him to do this; and Kellermann had considerable difficulty in deciding to do this because he shared the views of those who wanted the French army to withdraw behind the Marne. However, he yielded to the promptings of his colleague, and on September 17, he left Vitry-le-François and directed his army to the left of General Dumouriez's. As he feared being attacked while crossing the open plains separating us from Sainte-Menehould, he had the army march in several columns very close to each other and in short, daily stages. On the 17th we camped at le Fresne, on the 18th at Dampierre-le-Château, and on the 19th on the heights to the north of the village of Dommartin-la-Planchette, where he set up his headquarters. In this way the junction of the two armies was effected without our having encountered the enemy or met with the slightest obstacle. The previous day General Beurnonville had rejoined Dumouriez's army with the nine to ten thousand men he had brought from Flanders. Their arrival had been delayed by the various countermarches he had been obliged to perform to avoid encountering the Prussian army, so that on the 19th the total number of French troops

280

assembled in the vicinity of Sainte-Menehould amounted to about seventy thousand men, not counting the great concentrations at Châlons and Rheims, which were, admittedly, only paper forces incapable of sustaining any assault.* The advance guard of the camp at Châlons was under the orders of Lieutenant General de Sparre on the road from Châlons to Sainte-Menehould.

On arrival at Dommartin-la-Planchette, General Kellermann ordered his army to camp in two lines in accordance with the order of battle he had established at Vitry-le-François. He sent General Desprez de Crassier to Hans with his advance guard; General Stengel occupied the village of Valmy with a detachment of light troops from Dumouriez's army, and the 1st Dragoons, commanded by Colonel Tolozan, was quartered in the village of Gizaucourt, which was on the left but a long way to the rear of our camp.

On the evening of the 19th, I accompanied General Kellermann to Sainte-Menehould, where we went to see General Dumouriez. There we learned that the Prussian army was advancing into Champagne from Grandpré; however, we did not as yet know how close to us it really was.

The following day, September 20, before daybreak, Köhler's Prussian hussars surprised the 1st Dragoons at Gizaucourt, which, as I have already said, was behind our camp. Colonel Tolozan only had time to get his regiment on horseback and leave the village, where he lost all his equipment. Luckily, the Prussians had no infantry with them, and consequently dared not remain at Gizaucourt, and this important post was shortly afterward retaken by our troops and never again captured. About half past six in the morning we heard a heavy cannonade from the direction of our advance guard, and the call to arms was sounded at the camp. Desprez de Crassier sent word to Kellermann that as he was being attacked by sizable forces, he was going to withdraw. He added that the thick mists that morning prevented him from clearly making out what body was attacking him, but that he believed it was the whole Prussian army that was marching on us. Desprez de Crassier followed up this intimation soon afterward and returned to the camp with our entire advance guard. Kellermann proceeded to Gizaucourt and placed his front line, under General Valence, before Orbeval, between the Auve River and the hill of Valmy, at right angles to the Châlons road. The second line,

---

* The disorder of the camp at Châlons made one tremble. There was a complete lack of discipline there, and all sorts of crimes were committed. Several officers, commissioners, and other individuals were murdered: Their heads were carried on pikes. On several occasions Marshal Luckner nearly became the victim of the suspicions and fury of these masses and soon abandoned this theater of horrors. After his departure, but still before the retreat of the Prussians, General Dumouriez requested and obtained the dispersal of this dangerous and useless assemblage. Nevertheless, he took forty battalions from it, in which strict discipline soon established good order and even made pretty good troops of them.

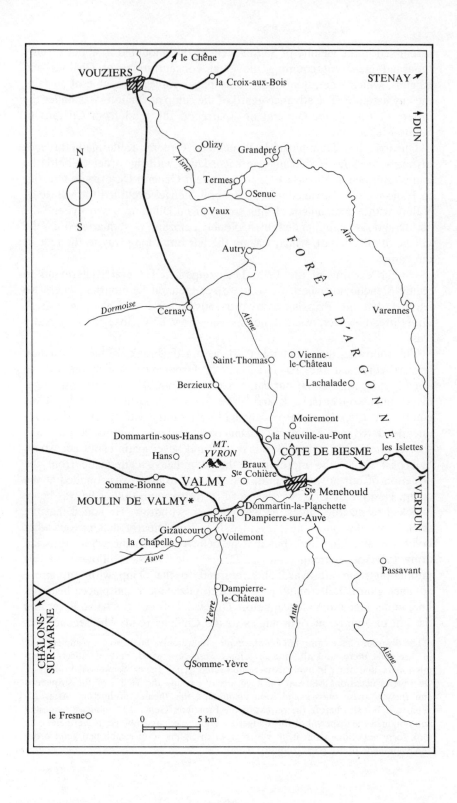

which I commanded, was placed parallel to the road and at right angles to the first line on the summit of the hill of Valmy, so that the two lines formed a square. A strong battery of heavy artillery was stationed at the windmill of Valmy, which was the highest point on these slopes. Despite my eagerness to be off, I lost so much time through the need to strike camp and load the pack horses* that it was nearly eight o'clock when I arrived at the windmill of Valmy at the head of my infantry. "Come on, then, take up your position," said General Stengel, "because I can't leave my post until I am relieved, but if I don't get there before the Prussians," he added, pointing to the side of the Yvron, "we shall be crushed here presently." At the same time, having ordered his infantry to follow him as best it could, he left at a gallop with a few squadrons of light troops he had under his orders and the two companies of horse-drawn artillery under Captains Barrois and Anique, rapidly traversed the village of Valmy and the valley that separated us from the slopes of the Yvron, and arrived there at the moment when a Prussian column was advancing to occupy it. But he repulsed this column and defended the Yvron throughout the day with the greatest vigor.

General Dumouriez, seeing that the attack was directed against us, sought out his colleague Kellermann and personally informed him of the dispositions he had made to support us. He had divided his army into three corps, which he had put on the march immediately, not counting the reserve that he had left in his camp. The leftmost corps, nine battalions and eight squadrons strong under General Chazot, proceeded along the Châlons road to the heights of Dampierre-sur-Auve and Gizaucourt to support General Desprez de Crassier and General Valence's left.† The central corps of sixteen battalions under General Beurnonville was directed to the side of the Yvron to support General Stengel; and the right-hand corps, consisting of twelve battalions and eight squadrons under General Leveneur, was ordered to extend the line to the right of Beurnonville, to try to engage the Prussian rear guard, and to seize their equipment.

The cannonade, which had already begun at the windmill at Valmy before I relieved General Stengel there, became very lively about ten

* I have already said that of the twelve battalions that made up the infantry division I commanded that day, only one was made up of National Volunteers, the first battalion of Saône-et-Loire. The morale of this battalion was so good and its rivalry with the troops of the line such that the soldiers assigned to guard the equipment refused to carry out this task, and the commandant could not find any willing to replace them. When he reported this to me in front of the battalion, a soldier stepped out of the ranks and told me in the name of his comrades: "General, we are here to defend the Fatherland, and we ask you not to require any of us to leave the colors of our battalion to go and guard the equipment." —"Very well, comrade," I said, "I do not require it. Your equipment will look after itself today, and your battalion will march intact with our comrades of the line to whom you will show that, just as much as they, you are French soldiers."

† See Dumouriez, *Mémoires,* volume III, book V, chapter 9, page 140.

o'clock.* The Prussians established two principal batteries against the windmill, which they later successively reinforced. One of them was on the continuation of the hill on which the windmill stood, and the other on the hill facing it in one direction of the road, in front of the small farm called La Lune, which this day made famous and where the King of Prussia set up his headquarters the next day. These batteries cost many men but did not shake the resolution of our troops, and there was only a moment's disorder in two battalions of my division† when a shell landed in their midst and caused two boxes full of cartridges to explode. This explosion momentarily scattered them, but they promptly rallied, despite the fire to which they were exposed, and immediately took their place in the line. The ardor of the troops that day was indeed so great that all the cavalrymen, carabineers, or dragoons whose horses had been killed or wounded, immediately ran, rifle on shoulders, to take their place in the infantry.

At about eleven o'clock, the mist entirely cleared to reveal the whole enemy army advancing in perfect order in several columns and deploying itself before us on the vast plain stretching from Somme-Bionne to La Chapelle-sur-Auve. The eye could then encompass more than a hundred thousand men ready to give battle, and this spectacle was all the more imposing in that we were not yet used to seeing armies as large as those which were later seen‡ and that at this period it was more than thirty years since Europe had fielded such a large concentration of combatants.

The deployment of the Prussian army was very slow, and it was not till about two o'clock, sometime after it had been completely effected, that we saw it break up into columns for attack. Then we thought that it was going to march on us and join battle, and immediately shouts of *Long live the nation* and *Long live France* were to be heard in all the ranks of our army; but whether the fine bearing of our troops had given the Duke of Brunswick an inkling that he would experience more resistance than he had at first reckoned on§ or whether (which is fairly likely) he wanted to

* It was then that the horse being ridden by General Kellermann was wounded, and General Senarmont of the artillery had his thigh grazed by a bullet, which obliged us to have him carried off. Colonel Lormier was killed shortly afterward.

† These two battalions were the former German regiments of Salm-Salm and Massan (the 94th and 96th). They were commanded by Colonels Rothenbourg and Rewbell (brother of the deputy in the Constituent Assembly, who was later a member of the Directory).

‡ The Revolutionary and Napoleonic wars brought the *levée en masse* in some degree to most of the combatants, which led to larger armies and a revolution in tactics. However, it should be remembered that Louis XIV at one time had 400,000 Frenchmen under arms, which was more purely French (as opposed to men from allies and satellites) than Napoleon ever commanded or than, indeed, was reached until the First World War.—ED.

§ The *émigrés* had persuaded nearly all the chancelleries of Europe that their departure from France had completely disorganized the French army, that there were no longer any officers or generals capable of commanding, that France was not in a

await General Clairfayt's Austrian contingent, which did not arrive till night, the Prussian columns formed and deployed themselves three times in succession, as they might have done on a parade ground, without ever deciding to attack us, and the battle was reduced merely to a cannonade that lasted throughout the day and only ceased when the darkness of night made it impossible to continue it further. The artillery officers estimated the number of cannon shots fired by the two armies at more than forty thousand, and the ammunition in our artillery park was nearly exhausted. I was unable to ascertain exactly how many men were killed on our side, but I think it was about fifteen to sixteen hundred,* and the Prussian officers of whom I later had occasion to ask the size of their losses told me that they had lost about two thousand men.

Toward evening, General Kellermann asked General Dumouriez to come and find him to discuss what measures should be taken; he came, accompanied by M. Thouvenot, his adjutant general. These two generals invited me to take part in their deliberations, with General Valence, General Stengel, and General Schauenbourg, chief of general staff of Kellermann's army.† There it was decided that we should change position during the night, that all of Dumouriez's army should return to the camp at Sainte-Menehould and occupy the village of Braux-Saint-Cohière, that Stengel's corps should occupy that of Dommartin-la-Planchette in order to protect communications between the two armies, that Kellermann's army should retire behind the Auve River, taking care to raise its level by means of dams, thus causing it to burst its banks and flood the surrounding country; that it should camp on the heights of Dampierre-sur-Auve, where its headquarters should be established, and that it should occupy the villages of Voilemont and Gizaucourt and fortify them.

Then I had the windmill at Valmy pulled down (it was made of wood and so riddled with bullet holes that there was danger of its falling down), and I had great fires lit at intervals along the hill we occupied. Then we began our maneuver. The distance we had to cover was very short, but unfortunately, there was only one bridge over the Auve River, across

---

position to put up any resistance, that at their approach the French army would disperse, and that the Duke of Brunswick's army would arrive in Paris without firing a shot.

* General Dumouriez in his *Mémoires* puts it at only three or four hundred, but I have already made the observation that he was writing from memory and without documents, and I believe he is mistaken. Our losses were certainly much more considerable, but I take no responsibility for the figure I give, and indeed I think that an exact count was not taken.

† These deliberations took place in the miller of Valmy's hut, where it was very dark. However, when we entered, we noticed a grenadier sitting in a chair, with his back to the door. We thought at first he was asleep, and General Dumouriez said to him, tapping him lightly on the shoulder: "Come on, friend, would you mind going and leaving us alone," but the man was dead and fell to the ground when Dumouriez touched him. A cannonball had ripped open his stomach, and he had just expired in this chair.

which the whole army had to file, and it was so bad that it gave way under the weight of the artillery. We lost a lot of time in mending it; it gave way again, and we even had to rebuild it several times, with the result that the troops, worn out with fatigue and lack of sleep, became impatient with the interruption of the march, broke ranks, and finished by being mixed up. If a few Prussian hussars had appeared then, it would have been the end of the army, and we would have had a fearful flight, which nothing could have prevented or brought to a halt; but the enemy did not show himself. We managed to cross the river, and at three o'clock in the morning the army and all its artillery (admittedly in complete disarray) were established on the heights of Dampierre-sur-Auve. During the night it was impossible to sort out the chaos that had been caused by the crossing of the river, and we awaited the dawn in this state; when it appeared, we all returned to our respective places, despite a thick fog; the camp was soon set up and order entirely restored before the enemy had noticed our change of position.

In the course of the 21st, a Prussian detachment set up camp on the side of the Yvron and positioned its outposts on the hill of Valmy; but the Prussian army carried out no further operations and made no attempt to interrupt the work we were carrying out—both to cause the Auve River to overflow [and protect] our front with inundations and to entrench our positions on the heights of Dampierre and Voilemont. As direct communications between Sainte-Menehould and Châlons were cut off, the Prussian army occupying the main road, Generals Dumouriez and Kellermann immediately took the necessary measures to safeguard communication by an indirect route and at the same time to cover the rear of our position. General Desprez de Crassier was posted at Dampierre-le-Château with the advance guard of Kellermann's army. Colonel Frégeville the Elder,* of the 11th Light Cavalry, was placed at Somme-Yèvre with a detachment of light troops from Dumouriez's army, and General Dubouquet at le Fresne, where he was in contact on one side with Colonel Frégeville and on the other with General Sparre, who occupied Notre-Dame-de-l'Épine before Châlons. This semicircle was admittedly very extended, but as the detachments manning it were meant to observe and hinder the enemy's movements rather than to defend the posts they occupied if they were attacked by superior forces, the Generals' objective was accomplished; our communications were assured and our convoys of food and munitions arrived without difficulty, while those of the enemy were often intercepted by our troops.

It was certainly more difficult to attack and defeat the French army in this new position than in the one it occupied the day of the cannonade at Valmy. This was all the more so in that the opinion of the Prussian army and its commanders of the French army had been altered by the firmness

* Colonel Henri de Frégeville was the elder brother of Charles de Frégeville, at the time colonel of the 2nd Hussars (Chamborant) and later a lieutenant general.

displayed by our troops on the day of September 20; that they no longer believed victory so easy and began to treat as myths all that the *émigrés* had made them believe, before their arrival in France, about the disorganization of the French army and the disposition of the nation to put up no resistance and to throw themselves into their arms as soon as they appeared. However, I believe that if the Duke of Brunswick had attacked our position on September 20, he would have taken it; but even if he had succeeded in this, I have no doubt that this victory would have cost him dearly. It is even probable that it would not have been complete and that after the losses he would have had to sustain to obtain it, he would not have been in a position to press home his advantage and break through Dumouriez's army, which was behind ours; and again, if we had turned out the victors, holding our position and repelling his attack, it is likely that the Prussian army would have been annihilated; because if it had been defeated at Valmy, it would have had great difficulty in regaining and crossing the defiles of Grandpré, la Croix-aux-Bois, and le Chêne-Populeux in order to withdraw to Lorraine. His artillery and baggage would have fallen into our hands, and the masses [of troops] that would have fallen on him from every side with the confidence of success and the enthusiasm with which they were then inspired would probably have wiped out his army in the midst of the arid plains of Champagne, where it had imprudently joined battle. This danger, already very great on the 20th, became more so on the 21st after the French army had improved its position and succeeded in getting onto a terrain that presented the attackers with far less chance of success than did Valmy. So this attack did not take place, and I consider that the Duke of Brunswick has been wrongly blamed for not risking it. Be that as it may, once the commanders of the Prussian army ceased to believe that they were in a position to attack us with advantage, they had to find some other way of extricating themselves from the awkward position in which they had placed themselves. It seems that for a moment, they hoped to succeed in this by negotiation with the commanders of the French army; but this hope, if it ever existed, soon vanished, and it is indeed fairly likely that the main motive of the Prussians in seeking communications with the French generals was to sound out their dispositions, as well as those of the troops and the nation. It must not be forgotten that at this time, the King had only been suspended from his functions and that the monarchy had not yet been formally abolished in France or, more precisely, that we did not know that it had been, since the decree of the Convention pronouncing its abolition was not passed until September 21 and we did not know of it until the 23rd or 24th. Thus the Prussian leaders, in opening these negotiations, may have been entertaining hopes of which the Convention's decree quickly deprived them.

On September 22, a Prussian officer of the Anspach Dragoons presented himself with a trumpeter to our advance guards, whence he was conducted to General Kellermann at Dampierre-sur-Auve. He handed him a letter from Colonel Manstein, first aide-de-camp to the King of Prussia, asking him for a parley and requesting his kind permission to visit his headquarters with the Baron de Heyman, a major general in the service of Prussia. General Kellermann replied to Colonel Manstein that he was willing to receive him and that as he regarded General Heyman as a Prussian officer, he would receive him as well.* Consequently, he invited them to dine the same day, and he sent to General Dumouriez requesting him to be so good as to come to his headquarters to take part in the conference. I, too, was at this dinner, together with Generals Valence and Schauenbourg, Colonel Thouvenot, whom General Dumouriez brought with him, and several officers from the two general staffs of our army. Colonel Manstein proposed to establish an agreement for the exchange of prisoners and to suspend hostilities between the two armies for the time being, each one to remain in its position, with their commanders retaining the option of breaking the armistice as soon as he saw fit. The French generals acceded to these proposals, though restricting the suspension of arms to the limit of the front lines of the camps of the two armies so that isolated detachments were not included, and [stipulating] that the generals of each army should remain free to carry out all the troop movements they saw fit to order. The armistice was concluded the same evening on this basis, and another meeting was agreed upon to make the final arrangements for the exchange of prisoners. As to the other points discussed in this conference, I can do no better than transcribe General Dumouriez's own account of them in his *Mémoires* because I believe that his account of them there is perfectly accurate.† But I want to add to this an anecdote that is personal to myself.

* General Heyman was an Alsatian who had reached the rank of *maréchal de camp* in the service of France. He had emigrated the previous year with M. de Bouillé, under whom he commanded at Metz, but he had not joined the *émigré* corps and had immediately entered the service of Prussia. As he had served in the hussars with General Kellermann throughout and both had, at least in large part, owed their advancement to the protection of my father, who worked directly with the King on appointments in this arm of which he was colonel in chief, he had been considered better qualified than any to carry out negotiations with Kellermann; but his quality of a French *émigré* constituted a barrier, and the two generals, Kellermann and Dumouriez, thought it necessary to ask him not to come to their headquarters any more, as his visits would not have failed to arouse suspicion.

† Extract from General Dumouriez's *Mémoires,* volume III, book V, chapter 11, pages 164 and following.

"On the 22nd Kellermann sent word to General Dumouriez that General Heyman had asked him for a conference on behalf of Colonel Manstein, adjutant general to the King of Prussia. He proceeded immediately to Kellermann's headquarters at Dampierre, where he found this colonel with Heyman, whom the King of Prussia had made a major general in his service after his flight with Bouillé. The pretext for this conference was the need to come to an agreement for the exchange of prisoners between the French and the Prussians.

After dinner, General Heyman took me to one side; first of all, he made me many protestations of gratitude and loyalty to my father; then he told me that he feared he had incurred his displeasure in emigrating, that he wanted to convey a letter to him in which he would ask him to maintain his good will toward him, and he asked me to be so good as to dispatch it to my father. I replied that if his letter contained no more than that I would gladly take charge of it. "Ah," he said, "if it contained only that, it would not be enough, because I should like the Prince, your father, to know that it perhaps rests with him to stop the scourge of the war. I know the intentions of the allied sovereigns; I know that what they

---

"After the first compliments had been exchanged, Colonel Manstein told Dumouriez that full justice was done to him in the Prussian army; that his great influence over his army was recognized; that it was in his power to bring this war to an end, and that very far from being impeded in his activities, he would have all the assistance he could desire if he wanted to bring to an end the anarchy in France; that he would be able to dictate the terms of peace and that he would render a service to his country and to the whole of Europe.

"He replied that France had not declared war on the King of Prussia, that nothing was easier than to have peace, that the Prussian army had only to withdraw to the frontiers and remain neutral, as the other sovereigns of the Empire; that soon the Imperial armies, left to themselves, and the King of Sardinia, unaided, would seek an accommodation, so that peace depended entirely on the King of Prussia; that as regards what was going on in France, although he disapproved of some of it, it was not for him to remedy it; that while he was obliged to devote all his attention to repelling such a formidable army, he could not even work on this. He concluded by saying that for the moment they must confine themselves to setting up the machinery for the exchange of prisoners.

"They sat down to table; after dinner the conversation became very friendly. Then, after Colonel Manstein had explained himself even more clearly, the General said to him: 'Colonel, you have told me that I am esteemed in the Prussian army; I should believe I am nothing of the sort if you continue to make me proposals that dishonor me. I desire to see you again and to cultivate your friendship, so let us speak no more of such proposals.'

"During this meeting it was agreed that Colonel Manstein would come to dine with General Dumouriez at Sainte-Menehould the day after next. MM. de Manstein and Heyman proposed that sniping along the front of the camps should cease, while themselves explicitly specifying that it should only be along the front. Dumouriez agreed that this sniping was pointless, and that very evening a cease-fire was arranged along the front of both armies.

. . . .

"Colonel Manstein came to dine with General Dumouriez on the 24th. They dealt with the arrangement for the exchange of prisoners. He wanted to discuss the émigrés, but it was pointed out to him that they were Frenchmen in arms against their country, making war on their own account with entirely French troop names such as Musketeers, Gendarmes, King's Regiment, etc., and that matters touching them did not concern the Prussians. Colonel Manstein abandoned this cause, and an agreement was made for the exchange of Prussian, Hessian, and Austrian troops.

"Dumouriez then embarked on a discussion about foreign policy to demonstrate that the King of Prussia was engaged in a war against his own interests; that the French were fighting this monarch very reluctantly; that an alliance between the two

desire above all is to preserve France from anarchy, and as it was thought likely that you would come here, I have been authorized to tell you and to give the Prince, your father, to understand that they would be reassured if they saw him at the head of the French government." —"Bah," I replied, laughing, "how can you think that my father or I would listen to such nonsense? No, General," I continued, "there is no more desire on your side than on ours that my father should be at the head of the government, and I know that my father is no more disposed than I am to entertain such propositions. I shall not, therefore, be able to pass anything on to him on that subject, and I would think that you would do better not to try

peoples would be mutually advantageous and that it was very easily accomplished. For his part, Colonel Manstein told him that the King of Prussia did not wish to continue the war against France, that he did not desire to meddle in its Constitution or government, and that his requirements were very moderate. At the same time he handed him some very wise proposals in six articles, the first of which provided that the King should be released from prison and restored to the authority he had exercised before August 10.

"In reply, Dumouriez handed him the bulletin which he had just officially received and which contained the decree transforming the National Assembly into a National Convention and the monarchy into a Republic. Colonel Manstein appeared very affected by this, and the General himself did not conceal from him the fact that he was very put out that matters should have reached this extremity, and all the more so because he did not see any chance of going back on it. Colonel Manstein left for his camp, and it was agreed that the following day Colonel Thouvenot should go to the headquarters at Hans[a] to sign the agreement for the exchange of prisoners.

"The General, learning that the King of Prussia lacked coffee and sugar, took the liberty of sending him twelve pounds, not having managed to find any more, and some fruit and white bread. The present was accepted, but he was told not to send any more. The greatest cordiality grew up between the advance posts of the two armies, and the French shared their bread with the Prussians, who were dying of hunger. Dysentery was causing the greatest ravages among them, and the foul water and fodder was killing off their horses, which they skinned and ate.

. . . .

"While Thouvenot was at the Prussian camp, Dumouriez drew up a memorandum in which he threw all the blame for the war on the House of Austria and sought to persuade the King of Prussia that it was in his interests to break off an alliance that was neither natural nor advantageous. He sent this memorandum to Colonel Manstein with the request that, in the interests of the two nations, he have it read to the King. Manstein promised to do so, but at the same time he advised him that this memorandum would not have any effect and that he disapproved of it.

"Dumouriez was then, in all good faith, not the personal, but the political, enemy of the House of Austria. We were at war, and he was doing his duty by trying to deprive it of an ally. Perhaps if he had succeeded, France's bloody catastrophe would not have occurred; perhaps peace would have been concluded the same year; perhaps the calamities that all Europe is suffering, and the still greater ones with which it is threatened,[b] would have been effaced from the Book of Destiny.

"On the 28th, in the morning, a Prussian aide-de-camp from the Duke of Brunswick announced himself, and on his orders handed a memorandum to the General.

a The headquarters of the King of Prussia and the Duke of Brunswick was then at Hans.
b Dumouriez's *Mémoires* were published in 1795.

to communicate with him about it." He insisted, but when he saw that my resolution was unshakable, he confined himself to asking for me to take charge of an ordinary letter for my father, which he would write in my presence and which would merely contain protestations of attachment and respect, but in which he would inform him of his desire to send further communications to him and asking him to indicate the means for this. I agreed to this, though not before consulting Generals Dumouriez and Kellermann, who advised me to take charge of his letter. I sent it, therefore, to my father by the courier who took their dispatches to Paris; but, as I fully expected, he would not even open it, and he hastened to deposit it on the table of the National Convention, declaring that he did not want to receive any communication from General Heyman. The

---

This document was so imperious, so harsh, and so misplaced that the General, after reading it twice, said to the aide-de-camp: 'Sir, I took the liberty of sending a memorandum to the King of Prussia; I certainly did not address myself to Monsieur the Duke of Brunswick. Doubtless he takes me for a burgomaster of Amsterdam. Tell him that as of now the truce is over and that I am giving the order in front of you.'

"He did indeed give the order there and then, and this order gave great pleasure to the whole army. Likewise, he wrote to Colonel Manstein, and all negotiations were broken off. The manifesto, which had been written by some *émigré* minister, had been written and in print for two months,[c] and it was all the more inappropriate for the Duke of Brunswick to deliver it then, because two days afterward he struck camp to carry out his retreat.

"All this parleying, all this coming and going of Prussian officers to the French camp and of French officers to the Prussian camp, did not for a moment affect the army's trust.

. . . .

"Such, precisely, were all the negotiations that took place between General Dumouriez and the Prussians. Their retreat, which followed closely, gave rise to a thousand absurd stories. He was believed to have so little hope of resisting so formidable an army that people sought to discover the reasons for his salvation in the shifts of a deep-seated stratagem. Then they passed from one extreme to another. After imagining that he had gotten out of his difficulties by deceiving the Prussians, when they learned of the debilitated state of that army and saw that it had been saved, they attributed the good fortune of this retreat to connivance between him and the King of Prussia; and a number of know-it-alls are still of a mind that first the salvation of the French army and then that of the Prussian were the results of an extremely subtle and abstruse stratagem."

---

c I must again point out that General Dumouriez was writing from memory and that he lacked the documents he would have needed to consult in order to rectify some slight errors into which he fell. Here he is clearly confusing two manifestos of the Duke of Brunswick: The first had indeed been published two months earlier, that is to say, on July 25 and 27, 1792, but the one that was handed to General Dumouriez at Sainte-Menehould was a second Manifesto, dated from Hans, September 28. It is true that it was drawn up in the same vein as the first, but it related to the events of August 10 and also to all that had occurred since the publication of the first Manifesto and, in particular, to the abolition of the monarchy and the introduction of the republican system of government in France. This second Manifesto of the Duke of Brunswick was inserted in its entirety in *le Moniteur* on October 20, 1792, no. 276, and the first is to be found in the issues of August 3 and 8, 1792, nos. 216 and 221.

Convention took note of his declaration and had the letter burned without hearing it read and without even unsealing it. It was Brissot, currently one of the secretaries, who burned it on the table, which is rather remarkable.

While these events were taking place at the front, Paris, the Assembly, the government, I could say the whole of France, were a prey to the keenest anxieties. No one had a clear idea of the situation and the position of the armies. After the retreat from Grandpré had opened up Champagne, and especially after the Prussian army had established itself between Sainte-Menehould and Châlons, that is to say, between the French army and Paris, all were at one in thinking that the capital lay open and that if the Prussian army marched on it, it would arrive there before the French army could stop its progress or even try to oppose it. This opinion was general, because a look at the map showed that the Prussian army was at least one march ahead of the French and that it could gain even more by maneuvering its rear guard in such a way as to prevent the French army from following it by the direct route. They did not consider the great difficulties and the great risks of such an operation: They forgot that if the Duke of Brunswick had thought he could march on Paris leaving the French army to his rear, he would have proceeded from Grandpré directly to Châlons or Meaux and would not have been deflected from this line, as he had been in coming to attack us at Valmy, and they did not recognize the truth of what General Dumouriez never ceased repeating and which was fully justified by the event, that as long as he occupied the strongholds of the Argonne, Sainte-Menehould, and Dampierre-sur-Auve, the Prussians would not dare to penetrate any further inside France nor, consequently, march on Paris.

Considering the state of affairs at the time, I find General Dumouriez's reasoning sound. I think the defensive plan he had conceived—and which he persisted in following, despite so many obstacles, with a tenacity that does as much credit to his talents as to his character—was the only way possible to paralyze the Prussian army and upset its plans. However, I also think that if the Duke of Brunswick had dared to march on Paris, leaving our armies in their strongholds and without troubling himself about the camp at Châlons and the other concentrations (which were in no position to impede his progress), the whole defensive plan of General Dumouriez would have automatically crumbled; for it is a fact that at this time Paris was without any means of defense despite the great work of construction that had been begun after August 10 to fortify it but had not been completed, and it is certain that the Duke of Brunswick would have taken it without difficulty had he attempted it. Once Paris had been taken, it would have become much more difficult for the nation and the French armies to continue the resistance they were then putting up to the foreign invasion because in a country organized like France, where all the threads of government are linked to the capital, this capital becomes in a sense its citadel because the existence of the government depends on its defense and preservation. The fall of Paris would necessarily have involved the dissolution of the National Convention and the Executive Council, and it is probable that the orders and proclamations of the new government that the King or the *émigrés* would not have failed to organize immediately under the protection of the foreign armies would have led to the submission of the French armies and of the whole of France. However, it is possible that the Convention and the Executive Council might have reassembled elsewhere, and judging by the nation's ardor for the defense of its liberty and independence, I cannot assert that it would not have managed to continue the defense successfully. Be that as it may, the danger to which the city of Paris was evidently exposed caused general anxiety and stirred up a very loud clamor against General Dumouriez's persistence in remaining in his strongholds when the Prussian army had placed itself between them and the capital. They did not see that this persistence was the best way of preventing the enemy from making himself master of the capital. On the contrary, it was characterized as *culpable obstinacy;** the most urgent and the strongest remonstrances were addressed to him every day to persuade him to withdraw behind the Marne, and the Executive Council itself went as far as categorically ordering him to do this. Nevertheless, Dumouriez refused to comply or, rather, he delayed executing this operation on the grounds that it would still be premature. He strove to demonstrate that there was nowhere behind the Marne where he could make a stand and that there was no surer way of attracting the Prussians to Paris than retiring behind this river as he had been ordered; he recalled what had happened at the time of the retreat from Grandpré to Sainte-Menehould in order to bring home the danger of undertaking a backward movement with armies such as ours then were, and he drew the conclusion that this should not be done unless strictly necessary. General Dumouriez had good reasons to give to prove that this necessity did not yet exist. He knew that the difficulties of the Prussian army were increasing daily, that it lacked everything, that people were literally dying of hunger, that dysentery was rampant, that there was an epidemic among the horses that was carrying them off by the hundreds, and finally, that it was equally unlikely that the Prussian army would dare remain any longer in the position it occupied or that it would dare risk a battle to force him to leave his position. He was justified, therefore, in asserting that not only did nothing oblige him to withdraw but that if he continued to stay put, the Prussian army would pretty soon decide to withdraw of its own accord because the force of circumstances would inevitably make it do this, and the only way of sparing it this disaster was the immediate execution of the order he had been given to voluntarily abandon positions whose occupation was the principal cause of all the Prussians' woes. He foresaw indeed that the longer they

* See Dumouriez, *Mémoires,* volume III, book V, chapter 10, page 158.

deferred their withdrawal, the more difficult their retreat would become when they did decide to embark upon it, because the rains were increasing and the roads were deteriorating everywhere and had soon to become impracticable. Moreover, while the Prussian army was experiencing such great suffering and was incurring fairly considerable losses through illness, the French army's state of health was very satisfactory; we had no sick, and although our convoys of provisions got stuck in the mud often enough to delay our distribution of food more than once, these delays were never so prolonged that the army suffered materially from them, and the privations that it experienced could not be compared with those that the Prussians were reduced to supporting. Nevertheless, our soldiers grumbled when the bread wagons were too long delayed, and one evening,* when these complaints had taken on a character especially disturbing because General Dumouriez had just learned that the wagons were bogged down two leagues to the rear and could not arrive till the morrow, he betook himself to his camp, where he was immediately surrounded by a crowd of soldiers demanding bread who let him hear some pretty bad language; but this did not disconcert him, and he said to them severely: "So, who are the bad citizens who are so cowardly that they do not know how to support hunger? Let their arms and uniforms be taken, and have them drummed out of the army. They are unworthy to share with us the honor of saving our country. You will not have any more bread today: Show yourselves to be soldiers capable of surmounting anything. No more complaints. Long live liberty!" And the crowd surrounding him began to shout: "Long live liberty! Long live our General!" Then he began to soften, and adopting a bantering tone, he told them: "The famous Marshal de Saxe† wrote a book on warfare in which he argues that at least once a week one must cause the distribution of bread to the troops to fail, so that in an emergency they will be less affected by this privation. That emergency has arrived, my friends, but you have not as much to complain of as the Prussians you see before you, who sometimes go four days without bread and eat their dead horses. You have bacon, rice, and flour; make biscuits, and liberty will season them." General Dumouriez knew the French character well. This little speech sufficed to restore the troops to their good humor, and they did without bread with very light hearts. But the main difficulties against which General Dumouriez had to struggle to maintain himself in his position and continue to deprive the Prussians of all the resources they would have found in the fertile country they covered did not come from the troops. These difficulties came from some of his generals and from the commissioners who were sent to him from Paris to force him to withdraw behind the Marne.

* I transcribe this anecdote from General Dumouriez's *Mémoires*, volume III, book V, chapter 10, pages 156–57.
† Marshal de Saxe, natural son of Augustus the Strong of Saxony-Poland, Marshal of France, victor of the Battle of Fontenoy in 1745.—ED.

General Kellermann had never approved of General Dumouriez's plan of defense. He had always advised withdrawal behind the Marne in order to take his stand between the Prussian army and Paris, and he was all the more insistent on constraining General Dumouriez to adopt this course because he was supported by the opinion of the Executive Council. Immediately after the engagement at Valmy, he announced his intention of leaving with his army without waiting for that of his colleague if the latter did not decide to carry out the same operation. However, General Dumouriez managed to restrain him by various means during the negotiation, but after the Executive Council had given categorical orders to withdraw behind the Marne, General Kellermann notified him that if he did not obey the orders of the Council, he would definitively separate his army from Dumouriez's and leave him alone with it at Sainte-Menehould and les Islettes. General Dumouriez, who was convinced that the Prussians were about to abandon the field, requested a further delay of three days and obtained it with the promise that if the Prussians had not withdrawn before this expired, he would do what was wanted of him. This took place, I believe, on September 28 precisely—that is to say, at the very moment when, after a Prussian aide-de-camp had officially communicated the new Manifesto of the Duke of Brunswick, dated that day, General Dumouriez declared that all negotiations were broken off, that he was abandoning the truce, and that he was giving orders that it be no longer observed. It is probable that it was this decision of General Dumouriez's that determined the Duke of Brunswick to defer his retreat no longer, because the Prussians struck their camp during the night of the 29th to the 30th; however, they only withdrew a league, to cover the movement of their artillery and extensive baggage, which filed toward Grandpré; but as this movement did not permit further doubt that their intention was to leave Champagne and to give up, at least for the present campaign, the idea of marching on Paris, there was no longer any question of the French army's carrying out the Executive Council's order to withdraw behind the Marne.

I did not have the satisfaction of being with the army at the moment the Prussians began their retreat. I left on September 27 with my brother the Duc de Montpensier to go to Paris for reasons I must make known in some detail. On September 26 I had received official notification that my place in Kellermann's army had been filled and an explicit order from the Executive Council to proceed to Douai, there to take up the position of second in command of the troops that were being assembled under the orders of General Labourdonnaye and that were designated for the relief of Lille, which had been bombarded for some days by the Austrians under Duke Albert of Saxe-Teschen. Despite the initial success of General Dumouriez's plan of defense and the admirable verve of the nation in putting such large masses of the population into action for the defense of the Fatherland, one was only too aware of what was lacking in the organization and discipline of these new troops, and it was a source of the keenest anxiety. The more the number of them surrounding us increased, the more determined were my brother and I not to let ourselves be deprived of the position in the front-line army, with all its opportunities for combat, that we held ourselves lucky to occupy, in order to be relegated to fortified towns and to what were termed *places of safety* for us. But our personal friends and all those who took an interest in us were at one in saying that my brother and I should certainly continue to serve our country, but that it should not be where we were too exposed to the risk of being taken prisoner or of being suddenly abducted, with all the hazards that were to be feared for us through the presence of the *émigrés* in the Duke of Brunswick's army. The Duc de Biron, my father's old and faithful friend, who at the time commanded the Army of the Rhine, and Alexandre Beauharnais, his chief of staff and my personal friend (though he always looked on the black side), were an inexhaustible source of remonstrances on this point with my father and with us. Finally, seeing that there was nothing to be gained from this, at least as far as we were concerned, they had me nominated *commandant of Strasbourg* without my knowledge and urged me in the strongest terms to proceed there immediately. I did nothing of the sort; I replied that I considered myself far too young and very little fitted to command such an important fortress, and I declared that my brother and I would remain at our post in Kellermann's army. It was, I believe, on September 10 that I was informed of this unfortunate nomination whose implementation I managed to prevent; and on the 12th, having received my commission as lieutenant general at Vitry-le-François, I presented it to General Kellermann at the very moment he was arranging his order of battle. He included me in it immediately according to my new rank, as I have already said, entrusting me with the command of the second line comprising twelve infantry battalions, six squadrons of cavalry, and artillery in proportion. It is to this circumstance that I owe the signal good fortune of commanding this second line a week later at the Battle of Valmy.

Although for France the consequences of winning this battle were enormous, they did not appear as such at first: Indeed, I think they only acquired this importance because General Dumouriez succeeded, as I have related above, in keeping us in our positions at Sainte-Menehould and in preventing our retreat behind the Marne despite all the attempts that were made to force this operation upon him. Be that as it may, and without reopening the discussion I devoted to that grave and important decision, it is sufficient here to explain why the Battle of Valmy had not calmed the anxiety of my father and our friends about our personal situation nor, consequently, lessened their desire to change it. So they wrote to persuade me and added that after the great success I had had the good fortune to obtain at Valmy, I should no longer have any regrets about changing my appointment. Alerted by my refusal of Strasbourg, they acted in such a way as to make a second refusal on my part impossible by having an official letter from the Ministry of War sent to me with orders to proceed to my new destination without delay and by having me simultaneously replaced in Kellermann's army by General Lynch, a *maréchal de camp* newly appointed lieutenant general.

This new appointment did not suit me in any respect, although the order was accompanied by very flattering expressions, and I was assured that it was dictated by their confidence in me and that which I was believed to be capable of inspiring in the troops. I felt real bitterness at being forced to part from those with whom I had fought the whole campaign. I was all the more distressed because Kellermann's army was just about the best, and the best composed, that there was in France at this period. Also, I had great confidence in the troops I commanded, and the knowledge that I had been in a position to acquire of the difference between these old troops and the newly recruited units that were being assembled at Douai gave me considerable concern about the new command to which I was summoned. However, realizing that I must obey, I adopted the course of proceeding to Paris in the hope that I might manage to persuade the Executive Council to exempt me from going to Douai to take up the command assigned to me and to restore me to the one I was relinquishing.

I set out on horseback with my brother to skirt by the south of the positions occupied by the Prussian army on the main road to Paris between Sainte-Menehould and Châlons-sur-Marne. We were obliged to go as far as le Fresne, where we had a few light troops and the 11th Light Cavalry (Normandy), commanded by Colonel Henri de Frégeville. Thence we proceeded to the camp of Notre-Dame-de-Lépine before Châlons, which was under the orders of General Dubouquet. We arrived there at the moment when the newly recruited battalions of National Volunteers, which constituted all this camp, were being passed in review by the three commissioners of the National Convention, Prieur (of the Marne), Brûlart-Sillery (Mme de Genlis's husband), and Carra (a journalist), and after accompanying them on this review, we boarded a carriage and took the road to Paris.

It was at the camp of Notre-Dame-de-Lépine that in the ranks of a battalion of volunteers from the section of Butte-des-Moulins, which covered Saint-Roch and the Palais Royal, I found young César Ducrest, Mme de Genlis's nephew. He had been brought up with us, and I had wanted to have him appointed a sublieutenant in my regiment of dragoons (the 14th) as the *son of an active citizen* at the time when the officers emigrated; but the Marquis Ducrest, his father and the brother of Mme de Genlis, who was an extreme *émigré*, had absolutely forbidden it. However, César Ducrest, who was then sixteen, had in turn absolutely refused to emigrate and follow his father to Coblenz. He had remained in

Paris, and in the moment of enthusiasm when the National Guard rushed forward en masse to march to the armies, he left as an ordinary rifleman in the Butte-des-Moulins battalion commanded by Auguste Lebrun, our former subgovernor, who died as director of the École Polytechnique in the reign of Napoleon.

I drew César Ducrest from the ranks of this battalion and took him as my second aide-de-camp. César Ducrest was afterward my faithful companion in the war and in exile. He accompanied me to Switzerland, but after *the Terror* he returned to France and died unfortunately in Paris in 1802 on the river when a firework fell on his head during the celebrations to mark the Peace of Amiens.

In 1791 and 1792 a club was formed, at first in secret then openly, which met at the former Hôtel de Soubise and where the principal members of the party that was later known as *the Mountain* met. One of the leading members of this club was Robert Keraglio, whose name has figured since in the events of his time. He was then an obscure writer. I had known him at the Jacobins, and after the rising of August 10 he proposed to my father, in the name of his club, to have me elected a member of the National Convention for Paris. I was not yet twenty-one, the age required by law; I was not even fully nineteen; but Robert Keraglio was little troubled by this difficulty; he said that the nation was sovereign, that it could elect anyone it liked without troubling with the laws, and that my nomination would produce a great effect. My father found the project rather ironical because he was very embarrassed by his position and himself wanted to avoid being elected to the Convention. In communicating this proposal to me he appeared fairly eager that I accept it. But I categorically refused, and I said in fitting terms: "I shall not exchange the saddle of my horse for a bench. My post is with the army, especially at a time when foreign armies are invading our territory, and I will not leave it to go to sit in an assembly." Furthermore, I did not conceal from my father that the role of deputy to the Convention, especially that of a deputy sent there by the Montagnard party, did not at all appeal to me; and the possibility, already too likely, of being called upon as such to decide the fate of the King was repugnant to me in the highest degree. I did all that I could to persuade my father not to allow himself to be elected either. But they told him that since they could not have me, they would elect him; and in fact he was elected as a deputy to the National Convention for the Department of the Seine (Paris), which nominated twenty-four deputies. Robespierre was the first on the list, and care had been taken to put my father last to demonstrate disdain for his title of Prince and to satisfy the ruling passion for social leveling. My father was very embarrassed by it; but he dared not get out of this assignment, however little it suited him, and he resigned himself to taking his seat in the Convention.

This took place at the end of August and in the first days of September

1792. My father was in Paris, at the Palais Royal, and I, with my brother, the Duc de Montpensier, was following the operations of the army in Lorraine and in Champagne. It was there that we learned by accident that my father had allowed himself to be saddled with the name *Égalité;* and would to God it were the only example I have been in a position to observe, in the course of my long career, of the difficulty of resisting the revolutionary torrent when once one has been carried along by its current.

I shall relate this unhappy episode; but before I do this, I must make clear exactly what my father's position was, and ours, and likewise that of all the Princes and all the branches of our family, relative to the names we bore, and explain the difficulties of reconciling this position with the requirements of the new laws that prescribed the suppression of titles and feudal denominations, or in other words, of the names of estates and fiefs. For these explanations to be intelligible, we must go back in time a little, because in the first place, one must remember that before the period of the Crusades, there were no *family names* but only *Christian names,* which, by their nature, could not become hereditary. Those who had similar Christian names were distinguished from one another by the addition of a *surname,* which sometimes expressed their physical and sometimes their moral qualities. Thus in the second dynasty* we had Pepin *the Short,* because he was little; Charle*magne* because, apart from his great conquests, he was of large stature; Charles *the Bald,* etc.; then, for other reasons, Louis *the Debonair,* Charles *the Simple;* and in the third dynasty, Hugues *Capet,* because he had a big head. His father was Hugues *the White,* his grandfather Robert *the Strong;* his son Robert *the Pious;* finally Louis *the Fat,* Louis *the Young,* Philippe-*Auguste,* etc.; and in England, William *the Conqueror* (at first *the Bastard*), then William *Rufus,* Richard *Coeur-de-Lion,* etc. At the time, it was a general usage. However, toward the end of the tenth century, sometime before the Crusades, people started adding the names of fiefs to the Christian names and surnames and having them preceded by titles. Before ascending the throne in 987, Hugues Capet was *Duke of France†* and *Burgundy, Count of Paris and Orléans.* There were then the Dukes of Normandy, the Dukes of Lorraine, the Counts of Vexin, of Dreux, of Champagne and Vermandois, etc. At his death Hugues Capet, whose son Robert succeeded to the throne of France, assigned the Duchy of Burgundy to his second son, Henri *the Old,* who was head of the branch called *old Burgundy.*

At the epoch of the Crusades, the knights who had taken the Cross bore the names of their fiefs when they led their vassals to the Holy Land, with their banners charged with armorials that were repeated on their

* The first dynasty was the Merovingians, the second the Carolingians, and the third the Capetians, who ruled till the Revolution.—ED.
† Duke of France because he held as a fief the province called the Isle de France, of which Paris was the capital.

armor. Then armorials, names, titles, all became hereditary like fiefs, domains or movables, and suzerainty. The names of fiefs and estates thus became *family names* for the nobles and feudal lords, while among the lower classes, families also added some name to their baptismal names; and this name likewise became their family name. One can see from the foregoing that our ancestors, the Kings of France, who occupied the throne of France in heredity before the Crusades, could not take any other family name but that of France; and that—especially since their first fief, before Hugues Capet's accession to the throne—was the Duchy of France, later called the *Isle de France,* like one of the provinces of the kingdom, as I have already said above. Such, however, was the importance and grandeur of this name *France,* even at such a remote period, that the Kings did not wish it to be borne as a family name by their collateral or cadet branches, and they reserved it exclusively for their sons and daughters, their immediate descendants. Thus it was only the sons and daughters of the King who were called *Sons and Daughters of France;* and then, as each *Son of France* became the *head of a cadet branch,* he transmitted the principal title among his fiefs as a family name to all his line so long as the order of succession did not summon him to ascend the throne; in this case the Prince who became King took the name of *France* for his senior line of descendants, as well as for his sons and daughters, and then gave the names of distinct branches to each line descended from his younger sons.*

From this derive the names of Valois, Anjou, Burgundy, Orléans, Brittany, Bourbon, Artois, Alençon, Évreux-Navarre, etc., borne successively by the various cadet branches of the House of France.

These names of the branches were always inserted as family names, between the Christian names and the particular title borne by each Prince. I shall take an example from the fourteenth century:

King Jean had four sons who bore the following names and titles.

(1) Charles de France, Dauphin, who became King Charles V.

(2) Louis de France, Duc d'Anjou, who became King of Sicily.

(3) Jean de France, Duc de Berri, who had no posterity.

* The title Grandson of France, invented under Louis XIV to soothe internal family intrigues or satisfy pretensions concerning rank, was never more than a mere courtesy title. The Duc d'Orléans, the Regent, the first Prince to enjoy it, was never Philippe of France, but only Philippe *d'Orléans,* Duc d'Orléans; and even when he became Regent of the kingdom after the death of Louis XIV, he always continued to sign *Philippe d'Orléans.*
After Louis XVIII had accorded to his two nephews the Duc d'Angoulême and the Duc de Berri the rank and honors of *Sons of France* wishing, as he said, to let them anticipate the enjoyment of what could belong to them after his death, nevertheless he did not permit them to assume this name in official documents. I myself saw him, at the time of the birth of Mademoiselle, daughter of the Duc de Berri, have excised from the document that was read to him the name of *France,* attributed to these Princes, to be replaced with that of *Artois.*

(4) Philippe de France (called the Bold), Duc de Bourgogne, who also had four sons:

(1) Jean de Bourgogne (called the Fearless), Duc de Bourgogne.

(2) Louis de Bourgogne, died young.

(3) Antoine de Bourgogne, Duc de Brabant.

(4) Philippe de Bourgogne, Comte de Nevers; and likewise with all the branches.

This usage was regularly observed and followed up to the Revolution of 1789, that is to say, till the eighteenth century; and at this period, in my branch of Orléans, we bore the following names and titles:

My father Louis-Philippe-Joseph d'Orléans, Duc d'Orléans.

Myself, Louis-Philippe d'Orléans, Duc de Chartres.

My two brothers,

Antoine-Philippe d'Orléans, Duc de Montpensier.

Louis-Charles d'Orléans, Comte de Beaujolais.

It was the same for the cadets of the elder branch, descended from Louis de France, Dauphin, the son of Louis XV, namely:

Louis-Stanislas-Xavier de France, Comte de Provence (later Louis XVIII), who had no posterity.

Charles-Philippe de France, Comte d'Artois (later Charles X), who then had two sons, namely:

Louis-Antoine d'Artois, Duc d'Angoulême.

Charles-Ferdinand d'Artois, Duc de Berri.

Thus, for seven or eight centuries, this internal regulation of the Royal House had been maintained with the wise respect that our fathers brought to our ancient usages, a respect so well expressed by this formula for proclamations that was venerated as a guarantee against arbitrariness and illegality, "according to the ancient law of the kingdom always herein preserved."

But while preserving this precious formula, its spirit had so often been violated by deplorable actions that in 1789 the prestige of this respect had disappeared, to give way to the opinions that hitherto everything had been abuse and privilege for some, and abasement, oppression, and slavery for the others. So that, instead of seeking to improve without destroying, on the contrary, people wanted to change everything, innovate everywhere, and above all indiscriminately proscribe everything that was old. In this they succeeded only too well.

The Constituent Assembly's decree of June 19, 1790, which became a law of the kingdom after receiving Louis XVI's assent, abolished all titles of nobility, feudal or otherwise, and consequently people began to call us simply Monsieur d'Orléans, Monsieur de Chartres, etc. But as these names still had a feudal origin, people were not long in wanting to forbid them, too, and to replace them by our family name, preceded by the baptismal names of each of us. That would have been all very well if there had been a *family name,* but all the researches that were conducted

301

to discover it had no result other than that of proving that the family had never had one. Then opinions differed about the names or—as they put it then—the denominations that should be assigned to us; but unfortunately agreement was reached only on the point of denying us the names that our family had borne for so many centuries; and it is sadly noticeable that this question, considered or decided three times in the space of a year and a half by three different Assemblies, received a different solution from each of them. These three Assemblies were

(1) The Constituent Assembly, drafting and voting the Constitutional Act of 1791.

(2) The Council of the Commune of Paris, where my father resided.

(3) The National Convention, on the occasion of the dolorous trial of the unfortunate Louis XVI.

The Constituent Assembly adopted a consistent policy in dealing with the names that should be borne by the Princes in line of succession to the Crown.

Article 6, Section III, Chapter II of the Constitutional Act of 1791 was couched in the following terms:

"The members of the Royal Family in line of succession to the throne will add *the denomination 'French Prince'* to the name that has been given them on their birth certificate; and this name may not be either patronymic or formed from any of the *categories abolished* by the present Constitution.

"The denomination 'Prince' may not be given to any other individual and carries with it no privilege nor any exemption from the common law of all Frenchmen."

In conformity with this constitutional article of 1791, my father was called Monsieur Louise-Philippe-Joseph, Prince français; I was called Monsieur Louis-Philippe, Prince français; and my brothers and the rest were to be the same, with the difference of their Christian names.

The Council of the Commune of Paris, ruling by virtue of the law attributing to it the exclusive right of giving a legal name to French citizens who did not possess one, assigned to my father the name of *Égalité,* as I shall explain.

The National Convention, casting aside all the traditions of history and forgetting the consideration that at the least it should have paid to the august but luckless man it dragged before its bar, decided that as *Hugues Capet* had been the first King of a dynasty of which, according to its decree, the man whom it was putting on trial was to be the last, the accused should be designated and called by the name of *Louis Capet.*

This unfortunate Prince had the courage to reply, on hearing this name for the first time: "I am not called *Capet,* and this name has never been more than a sobriquet."

But surmounting the pain that I have just experienced in tracing these last lines, I take up the threads of my narrative.

It was, I think, on September 10 or 11 that my father presented himself before the authorities of the Saint-Roch district, within whose boundaries the Palais Royal was situated, to exercise his rights as what was called then an *active citizen,* that is to say, an elector, of voting for the deputies who were to compose the National Convention. When asked his name, he replied "Louis-Philippe-Joseph d'Orléans." "That cannot be," he was told immediately; "it is a feudal name forbidden by the law, and it is not a family name. What is yours?" —"You know," my father said, "that the Constitution of 1791 laid down that we should add, after our baptismal names, the designation *Prince français,* which in a manner replaced the family name that we lack, but today I can no more adopt that designation than you could give me it." "Your argument is sound," the president said, "but the law has foreseen that difficulties of this kind could arise and has provided ways of resolving them by prescribing that in this case the difficulty should be submitted to the Council of the Commune where you reside. Besides, these Councils alone have the right to give a family name to citizens who do not possess one, such as bastards and foundlings. So, *nameless citizen,* proceed to the Hôtel de Ville, and when the Commune has come to a decision about you, come back and see us, and you will be allowed to vote."

My father resigned himself to this and proceeded to the Hôtel de Ville, where the Grand Council of the Commune of Paris, made up of a hundred and forty-four members, sat. Ushered into this assembly, as was anyone whatsoever who asked to be, my father explained the difficulty in which he had found himself with the district authorities of Saint-Roch respecting the exercise of his electoral rights and declared that, in accordance with the provisions of the law, he had been referred to the Council of the Commune to have the difficulty resolved. Then it was proposed, I do not know by whom, to commemorate his submission to the law abolishing privileges with a symbolical name, by assigning the name *Égalité* to him as his family name. My father told me himself that the ridiculousness of this name struck him straightaway and that he had been unable to prevent himself from grimacing. "Very well," the president had then replied, noticing it, "would you prefer the name *Publicola?*"* —"Certainly not," my father replied, and the name *Égalité* was assigned to him!

If my father had been in less of a hurry to have the matter decided so that he could vote in the course of the day and had not proceeded immediately to the Hôtel de Ville, I think he could have avoided this name, since, before the president of the Saint-Roch district's outburst, people had so little worried about this difficulty over family names that at that very moment, on September 11, the Executive Council dispatched

* Publius Valerius, called Publicola ("friend of the Commonwealth"). As Second Consul of the Republic, he had played a great part in the abolition of the monarchy and in liberating his country from the yoke of Tarquin, surnamed the Proud.

my commission as lieutenant general under the name of *le Sieur Louis-Philippe de Chartres*.

When I arrived from the army with my brother, we found my father in the great chamber that was later to be the Queen's bedchamber and where two of my sons, the Duc d'Aumale and the Duc de Penthièvre, were born. As soon as he saw me enter, he came up to me and said straight off: "I beg of you not to spoil the happiness I feel at seeing you after this battle and in rejoicing with you over the part you played in it, with Montpensier at your side, by speaking to me again about the new name that has been *clapped* on us." —"But," I said, "it is something I must discuss with you because—forgive me for saying so—it is a piece of nonsense that we must try to rid ourselves of; don't be annoyed." —"Alas," he said, sighing, "I cannot, I will not be angry with you over it. Moreover, you know how much I share your repugnance for everything that can look like affectation. But what do you expect me to do? There is nothing more to be done. It is an insult to which we must be resigned, and you will understand when I tell you all about it. But now I must dispatch you to the Ministry of War to see your Minister; but first, tell me briefly what you have in mind in coming here." —"Two things," I said; "one to avoid going to Douai to join M. de Labourdonnaye who, I think, has no more desire than I to undertake the impossible task of disciplining and organizing the provincial recruits." —"But I assure you," replied my father, "that the opinion they have of you, of the purity of your patriotism and of the confidence you inspire in the soldiers, leads them to believe that there is no one who can manage the provincial recruits as well as you." —"Bah!" I said, "I am very flattered by that opinion, but I know what the provincial recruits are, and I will not be lured to the camp at Douai." —"Very well, you must be sent somewhere else, but where do you want to go?" —"I am going to ask that I be sent back to Kellermann's army, where I know the troops and where I am known by them. I am very annoyed that you should have played a part in having me taken away." —"I only did it," he said, "because they have depressed me with anxieties about you and Montpensier; but after all, I don't ask more than that you return, and if you can obtain this, I shall not put any obstacles in your way."

I proceeded from there to the War Ministry, at that time the former Hôtel de Choiseul in the Rue Grange-Batelière on the spot where the Opéra is today. I was told that General Servan, then Minister, was ill and in bed; further, that all the ministers were assembled as the Executive Council* in his bedchamber and that no one could enter. However I insisted that he be informed that I had that moment arrived from the army and that I desired to know when he could see me. Someone went to tell him, and he bade me enter. I had never seen him before. He was

* When the ministers assembled, they were more than just the sum total of their members and formed the Executive Power in place of the King.—ED.

sitting up in bed with a bed table in front of him covered with papers and on his head a cotton nightcap with a tassel, attached by a satin ribbon. The Executive Council had no president, and all the ministers were merely seated round a table beside the recess for his bed. They were six in number, namely, Joseph Servan, Minister of War, Roland, Minister of the Interior, Clavière, Minister of Finance, Danton, Minister of Justice, Lebrun, Minister of Foreign Affairs and Lacoste, Minister of the Marine.*

"Please be seated, General," M. Servan said, "the Council would like to ask you a few questions and gather all the information that you can give it on the state and position of our armies." Then we entered into a long conversation whose details it would be pointless to relate even if my memory were in a position to do so. When it was over, I got up and, approaching M. Servan's bed, began my litany of complaints about being withdrawn from Kellermann's army and the appointment I had been given at Douai. M. Servan replied that the intention had not been to do anything that was disagreeable to me, but that my father and his friends had seemed to want this change. I continued to plead my cause when Danton came up behind me, tapped me on the shoulder, and said: "A word in your ear," and leading me to the embrasure of a window, he added: "Don't waste your time talking to that imbecile: Come and see me tomorrow morning at eight o'clock at the Chancellery in the Place Vendôme, and I will try to arrange your affairs to your satisfaction." I accepted this proposition with alacrity and withdrew.

I was on time for the appointment, and Danton received me in the chamber of the Seal of State—in that same room where, twenty-two years later in the month of May 1814, I found myself sitting with Chancellor Dambray at the same table near which I had been sitting beside Danton in 1792. And so this striking juxtaposition of the vicissitudes of my life had thrown me into a kind of reverie which Chancellor Dambray did not fail to notice, and he said to me: "You seem preoccupied?" —"That I am," I replied, "and I will tell you why. Twenty-two years ago I found myself sitting in the same place, beside one of your predecessors, beside Danton." —"Good God," exclaimed Chancellor Dambray, nearly falling backward on his chair, "Monseigneur, there is food for thought in that comparison."

My interview with Danton began, on my part, with the enumeration of my complaints at being withdrawn from Kellermann's army, of my desire to be reinstated in it, and of my repugnance for the appointment at Douai. "It is not our intention to force you to accept it," Danton said. "I have talked the matter over with my colleagues, and we will not insist on this point. But as for putting you back in Kellermann's army, this seemed to us just about impossible because that would oblige us to reverse the

* The Minister of the Marine was minister both for the Navy and for the Colonies. —ED.

305

translation of staff officers involved in replacing you in that army, and the Council cannot go back on this, at least for the moment. However, to reply to the desire with which I am delighted to see you animated to continue to serve in the most active manner, I thought that the army in which you could find the best opportunities was that of General Dumouriez. I have not yet said anything about it to my colleagues because above all I wanted to know if that would be satisfactory to you and to tell you that if you had another plan, I would be equally ready to help it succeed." —"I have none," I said. "I have no other desire than to return to Kellermann's army because its troops inspire me with great confidence, and I trust that this confidence is reciprocated by them. I have served in Kellermann's army for five months, while I know no more of Dumouriez's army than I am known by it; moreover, it must indeed be said, the large proportion of the troops of the line in Kellermann's army has maintained discipline on a better footing than I believe is present in Dumouriez's army. There are a great number of newly recruited battalions, and above all *fédérés,* who may in time become excellent but who, in their present state, cannot inspire us with the same confidence as the troops of the line, nor even as the battalions recruited in 1791. But to conclude, since my return to Kellermann's army is impossible, I prefer to transfer to that of Dumouriez." —"Very well," he replied, "that will be arranged; and I shall speak of the matter to the Council, where everyone is well disposed toward you. We want to give you another proof of this by making your brother, who moreover has fully deserved it by his fine conduct at Valmy, adjutant general lieutenant colonel." —"Ah, I thank you on behalf of my brother, although this promotion must separate us, we who have never left each other; but I know that this must be, and I am resigned to it. Only let me ask you to see that my brother's commission and my new credentials are promptly dispatched." —"You can count on it," he said, "and I will look after it myself."

This matter being concluded, I was about to leave when he restrained me and said: "For the moment you have finished with me, but I have not finished with you." —"How is that?" —"I want to profit from this opportunity of chatting with you, and perhaps my conversation will not be without its use to you because, for all that you are a lieutenant general, you are very young." —"I am approaching my nineteenth birthday." —"I know that your patriotism is ardent." —"That is true, and this sentiment rules my heart." —"I know also that you are a sincere friend of liberty, that although born a Prince, you have had the rare wisdom to relinquish without regrets the empty advantages of the rank in which you were placed by the accident of your birth, and I can tell you that already you are recompensed for this with the esteem, confidence, and affection of your fellow citizens. That is a good scenario for the long career that you may have to run; furthermore, we are not unmindful of the fact that you have loyally helped to oppose the invasion of the foreign armies with an efficacious resistance and to preserve France from the odious yoke of the *émigrés* and the horrors of the Counterrevolution. So, I can tell you that people are well disposed toward you, that you inspire complete confidence, and that you are believed to be sincerely devoted to the cause of the Fatherland and of liberty." —"Rightly. But the more I am, the more I suffer from seeing the cause I serve with so much ardor perverted—this cause which is so noble in my eyes, so dear to my heart—the more, in short, I am outraged by seeing it covered in blood by massacres and by all the horrors of which Paris has recently been the theater." —"Ah, there we have it," replied Danton with an ironic smile, "I was waiting for you to get around to it, my brave young man, and I thank you for not keeping me waiting any longer for this outburst, because it was precisely about that I wanted to take issue with you. I knew full well that the fine declamation you have just caused me to hear was your usual language and that you regaled with it everyone whom you could persuade to listen." —"Yes, that is true, and I should blush not to do so on every occasion." —"That is admirable, but let us leave those fine sentiments at that, and listen to me with the serious attention that everything I shall say to you deserves. I respect your candor and, as I wish you well, so I advise you not to allow yourself to be carried away like that. Know that it could easily bring down on your head—and perhaps also on those who are dearest to you—a storm of incalculable violence that would inevitably ruin you." —"But how do you expect me to contain my indignation when I see the cause whose defense I have undertaken drenched in blood by the murder of thousands of victims without trial?" —"And who are these victims whose fate you bemoan with such warmth and noble generosity? Do you not know that they were the implacable enemies of your father, yourself, your family, and all of us? Do you not know that they were, within France, the accomplices of the *émigrés*, the auxiliaries of those who wanted to deliver France to the Foreigner and men whose sanguinary projects could not be doubted by anyone? Like me, you have seen that abominable list drawn up and published at Coblenz on which I appear as a deputy, alongside your father and all those who have taken part in the Revolution, in the Assemblies or otherwise, and you cannot have forgotten that alongside each name on this list one of the three initials Q.B.H. has been marked to indicate those who, according to the degree of culpability attributed to them, are to be *quartered, broken on the wheel,* or *hanged?"* —"Yes, I have seen the list; but although I know only too well the blustering anger the *émigrés* often take a pride in exhibiting, I think that one can at least doubt the list's authenticity." —"But you cannot doubt the fate that awaited you and yours, together with all the patriots and friends of liberty, if they had been victorious and had been able to execute all the detestable projects with which they have never ceased to threaten us?: —"Even so, I cannot accept the principle of these odious reprisals, and even had the *émigrés* committed atrocities, that would not justify the September Massacres." —"Listen," said Danton in a severe tone, "you must give up this kind of talk, whose full consequences you do not understand because of your inexperience. In your youth you must learn as soon as possible not to give an opinion when you are not asked for one and above all not to censure, rightly or wrongly, everything that you do not like or do not think you can approve; because it often happens, especially during a revolution, that one has to be thankful for finding acts carried out that one might not, perhaps, have wished or dared to do oneself. So, in a word, do you know who gave the orders for those September Massacres you inveighed against so violently and irresponsibly? . . . It was I." —"You!" I exclaimed, with an uncontrollable expression of horror. —"Yes, that's right. But pray collect yourself and continue to hear me calmly. To judge such actions, you must envisage the situation in which we found ourselves as a whole. You must remember that when the entire male population of military age was speeding to the armies and leaving us without forces in Paris, the prisons were bulging with a mass of conspirators and wretches who were only waiting for the approach of the Foreigner to rise up and massacre us ourselves. I only acted to anticipate them and throw their plans for vengeance back at them by making them undergo the fate they planned for us. But I had further reasons. Don't think that I am deceived by these spurts of patriotic enthusiasm that carry away your youthful virtue. No, I know what reliance to place on this inconstancy, on these rapid transitions that so often expose us to panics, flight, shouts of *everyone for himself,* and even treason. So I did not want all these Parisian youths to arrive in Champagne until they were covered with blood, which for us would be a guarantee of their loyalty; I wanted to place a river of blood between them and the *émigrés* . . ."* "Monsieur Danton, you make me shudder." —"Very well, shudder as much as you like, but learn to control your shuddering instead of continually vaunting it; and believe me, this is the best advice you can be given." —"This advice is difficult to follow." —"Why? We are not asking for your approval; all we are asking from you is silence, instead of making yourself the echo of our enemies and yours. Listen, young man, I must tell you this, your father's patriotism is well known, his political opinions are properly appreciated, but his position is different from yours. As an ordinary deputy, he is not as prominent in the ranks of the Convention as you are in the army. So watch out. I warn you, more notice is taken of your activities than you think and perhaps than you could yourself appreciate, and mark well what I say to you: You will always be more closely observed than your father. All eyes will always be focused on you rather than on him, so simply try to contain your bursts of indignation." —"Ah, but I cannot undertake to do that," I exclaimed, interrupting him, "the cry of my conscience . . ." —"It is not

* I.e., a pledge on behalf of the soldiers, parallel to the one shortly to be given by the regicides in the Convention.—ED.

a question of your conscience," he replied, interrupting me in turn, "we are not asking you to task your conscience with anything, but merely to refrain from judging that of others. I shall say only a few more words to you, and I am sure that your father will confirm them for you himself. Restrict yourself to your military career, without concerning yourself with our actions and playing at politics. It is essential for you and yours, indeed it is for us and especially for your father," he said, giving me a meaningful look; then he added, "carry this advice to the army; it is motivated by genuine concern. Engrave it on your memory and keep your future open."

I left Danton's under the shadow of an impression that has never been effaced, and those who have read the account of this terrible conversation that I have just penned will doubtless not be surprised that the space of fifty-six years that has elapsed, in which I have experienced so many vicissitudes, has not weakened the remembrance of it.

During my stay in Paris, I was present at two sittings of the Convention, the only ones at which I was ever present. I say this explicitly in order to rebut the totally baseless assertion that I was present when the unfortunate Louis XVI was brought before the bar of the Convention. At the mournful time of the King's trial, I was in Belgium and therefore absent from Paris, to which I did not afterward return until 1814.

It was on Thursday, September 20, 1792 (the very same day was the Battle of Valmy), that the National Convention began its unhappy career. The deputies ot whom it was to be comprised met individually to have their credentials checked in the room in the Tuileries Palace then called the Chamber of the Hundred Swiss Guards and later the Marshals' Hall. After this procedure had been completed, they declared that they were constituted as a National Convention, and having assembled in the same chamber the following morning, September 21, they had this declaration intimated to the National Legislative Assembly, which was still represented by some hundred of its members meeting in the Riding School, where it had always held its sitting.*

As soon as that Assembly had received this notification, it started to process through the gardens, with its president (François de Neufchâteau) at its head, to seek out the National Convention and install it in its place in the Riding School, just as the Guard going off duty gives place to the one coming on.

* The Riding School of the Tuileries was built along the Terrace des Feuillants on the site of the Rue de Rivoli. It was converted into a chamber for an Assembly at the time of the transferring of the National Constituent Assembly from Versailles to Paris in October 1789, and it was in this chamber that successively the two National Assemblies (the Constituent and the Legislative) and the National Convention, until its sittings were transferred to the place where the theater of the Tuileries Palace now is, were to hold their sittings.

There Grégoire (the constitutional Bishop of Blois), began by saying:*

"Kings are, in the social order, what monsters are in the natural order. Courts are the factories of crimes and the dens of tyrants. The history of Kings is the martyrology of nations. Certainly none of us will ever propose to retain in France the fatal race of Kings.

"We know only too well that all the dynasties have never been anything but a devouring breed living off human flesh. But we must fully measure the friends of liberty! We must destroy this magic talisman whose power may still bewitch many men. I demand, therefore, that you consecrate the abolition of the monarchy by a solemn law." He then proposed the following wording:

"The National Convention decrees that the monarchy is abolished in France."

This proposal was acclaimed with the greatest enthusiasm and decreed on the spot without any discussion.

I was still with the army, and I did not arrive in Paris until several days later. The two sittings at which I was present were those of Wednesday and Thursday, October 3 and 4 (consequently well before the date when the King's trial began).

I was placed in the Recorder's gallery.† This gallery was something like the ground-floor boxes in the theater today, that is to say that it was below and behind a gallery projecting above it and also behind, to the right and very close to, the president's chair. The gallery and the bar below were facing the president's chair and the secretaries' table and therefore also the Recorder's gallery, from which one had a very good view of everything that went on in the Assembly. On entering this gallery, a crowd of diverse memories passed before me. In the first place, I knew that it was in this area of about twenty feet by ten or twelve that the unfortunate Louis XVI had spent three or four days and nights when he had been confined there on August 10 with Queen Marie-Antoinette, their children, and Madame Elisabeth, before their removal to the Temple. I knew also that it was from this same spot that my unhappy aunt, the Princesse de Lamballe, had been violently abducted to be shut up in the prison of La Force and murdered on September 2 before the gates of that prison!

Finally, I saw again the same chamber where I had assiduously followed the debates of the Constituent Assembly and so often heard the great orators whose eloquence had given it such distinction and a marked superiority over the Assemblies that followed it. Attending some of the sittings of the Legislative Assembly, I had already been struck by this

* See *le Moniteur* for Saturday, September 22, 1792, from which these passages have been transcribed word for word.
† The Record was a diary of great size in which it was said that the debates were taken down verbatim.

decline, but merely looking at the bearing of the National Convention, the comparison became even more painful; and I said to myself inwardly: "My God, is this, then, the Assembly that is going to determine the destiny of France in absolute sovereignty, with no other law than its good pleasure and no other brake to restrain its passions!"

As I let my eyes wander over this Assembly whose bearing had so little dignity, it was natural that I should look for my father and that he should be the first person I wanted to see. This search was not difficult, and it was, indeed, impossible not to distinguish him immediately, so great was the contrast between his simple and noble countenance and his dress—always careful, never affected—and that of the majority of the members of the Convention; their clothes, worse than neglected, smacked only too much of the spirit of an age that regarded vulgarity as a republican virtue, and politeness and gentlemanly conduct as aristocratic habits that should be banned from the revolutionary education they were striving to give the nation.

The first sitting I attended held no further interest for me than that of being able to put names to the faces of the members who answered successively to a roll call for the election of a Minister of War to replace General Servan, who had just resigned. Each member rose as his name was called out and pronounced his vote aloud. The majority of votes was collected for M. Pache,* and he was proclaimed Minister of War and a member of the Provisional Executive Council. The house rose immediately afterward, and I returned the next day to be present at a debate. It was a lucky chance, for this was a remarkable sitting.

The debate turned on an argument between the Convention's Surveillance Committee and the Commune of Paris. The latter had seized boxes and portfolios found at the Tuileries during the rising of *August 10,* and it did not wish to give them up, claiming that they contained documents inculpating the members of the Convention's committee who, in turn, demanded that the Commune should hand over the whole lot to them. To persuade the Commune to hand them over, the committee proposed to the Convention that it should order this, but that these boxes and portfolios should first be sealed and that the seals should not be broken except in the presence of two commissioners of the Commune, whom it should instruct to be present at this operation and to sign the inventory.

Nothing seemed more simple than this arrangement, or deal, because that was what it amounted to; but many members objected to it, and a lively discussion was in progress when it was interrupted by a shrill voice asking the president if he could speak. Then, on the benches opposite me, I saw a sickly little man with a pale and hideous visage shaking with convulsive movements; he had a colored handkerchief around his head and was wearing a threadbare greatcoat, which was very dirty and cov-

---

* M. Pache had never seen service; he had been tutor to Marshal Castries's children and his private secretary when he was Minister of the Marine.

ered with stains. This man was *Marat.* It was he who, in his odious paper so impudently entitled *The People's Friend,* demanded every morning that three hundred thousand heads should roll to have done with the enemies of liberty!* So fully conscious was he of the horror he inspired that although he had been regularly elected a deputy and admitted without difficulties at the opening on September 20, he had not yet dared present himself at the Convention and was appearing there for the first time. Therefore, as soon as it was discovered that it was Marat who was asking to speak, a general commotion broke out in all parts of the Assembly, shouts and mutterings rose from all the benches; all eyes were fixed on him, and nearly all the members repeated: "Marat, Marat . . . this is fearful! . . . this is shameful! . . . Down with Marat! . . . Don't let him speak! . . . He is an insult to all of us, a disgrace to the Convention. . . . He is a monster, let his voice not sully these precincts; Monsieur le Président, you cannot let this man speak. . . ." In the midst of this fearful tumult, the president rang his bell and vainly strove to make it understood that as Marat was a member of the Convention, he could not be refused permission to speak. But the clamor redoubled; there was heard: "No, chase him out! . . ." —"You cannot," shouted some members of the Mountain. —"All right," was the reply, "he shan't speak, we won't let him." Then Marat, seeing that they would not hear him, left his place, as the president, Pétion, vainly rang his bell, and advanced toward the rostrum, but it was already besieged by several deputies who blocked his path. When he saw that he would not be able to get there, he stopped at the foot of the steps where, leaning on the bar, he made threatening gestures and roved over the Assembly with a cynical and disdainful look. Then his sour voice was heard asking for a drink of water. "Give him a glass of blood!" shouted one member. "Yes, yes, yes," shouted others, "blood, give him blood!"

Buzot, one of the Girondins, made the formal request that Marat should not be heard because he thought that as Marat had already given abundant warning that he wished to base denunciations and accusation on the papers in the boxes from the Tuileries, it was just and necessary that these boxes should be inventoried and that the Committee of the Convention should make its report on them before Marat was heard. But the majority of the Convention was of another opinion; Lindon exclaimed: "Since the electoral body of Paris has condemned us to the penalty of having Marat as a colleague, our duty is to hear him." Cambon added: "Our duty is to hear the criminal as well as the man of virtue, so let us hear Marat." After this Marat mounted the rostrum, but the shouts and

* Marat's existence was called into question for a fairly long time at the beginning of the Revolution, and many people regarded it as a fiction devised by a Machiavellian calculation of the enemies of the Revolution. However, the existence of Marat, author of *The People's Friend,* was an incontestable fact. He was Swiss, a native of Boudry in the principality of Neufchâteau, and until the Revolution he had been the doctor of M. le Comte d'Artois's Bodyguard.

insults started up again as soon as he appeared, and then he drew a little pistol from his pocket, which he put against his temple and held there for some seconds; but when he saw general laughter caused by this exhibition, he put the little pistol back in his pocket and managed to make himself heard in snatches to say that he had come to denounce Brissot, Guadet, Vergniaud, Gensonné, etc., as being the leaders of a faction that already he called the *Brissotins* and that he accused of having sold themselves to Louis XVI to drag the nation to war, etc. And he added that the proofs of what he advanced were to be found in the boxes and would be removed unless they were printed before they were handed over to the Convention of which those he had just accused were members. At the time, the Convention did not set any store by the declarations and denunciations of Marat; but what must not be forgotten is that as a result of the crescendo of violence and of the ascendancy of the bloodthirsty mentality, it became the instrument of his frenzy and itself sent to the scaffold the unfortunate victims whose blood he had demanded.

Who could have foreseen then that a few months later the same Assembly that had just scourged in this way the unworthy colleague it had had wished on it would confer on him the honor of a Pantheon on whose portico was inscribed:

> To its great men.
> A thankful country.

I returned to the Palais Royal full of disgust at what I had just witnessed, considering as chimerical the hope that people sought to base on the *great stand* that the Convention was going to take, as they said, to preserve France from the bloody anarchy whose ravages it suffered soon afterward.

I did not remain in Paris longer than was necessary for my letters of appointment to be drawn up; every day my brother and I dined with my father, and in the evenings we went with him to the opera or, when there was no opera, to some other theater, because the theater had become an addiction for him, which is easily understood when one considers on the one hand that for him it was the habit of a whole lifetime, and on the other the state of isolation, boredom, and weariness to which he had been reduced by a conjunction of circumstances, political, family, financial, all conspiring to overwhelm him.

I want as far as possible to avoid naming names, but I must begin by saying that with the exception of the Duc de Biron, who, born on the same day as my father, remained loyally and openly his most faithful friend till his death, all the rest, men and women, had in turn withdrawn from my father during the course of the Revolution.* The result was that

* This withdrawal of my father's friends was entirely political and had nothing to do with anything personal to him. It was merely a consequence of the Revolution and of the part my father had played in it. No party wanted to bring him to the throne—and God knows he desired it no more himself—so that all the shades of

313

after the Duc de Biron had left Paris to pursue his military career at the end of the Constituent Assembly, of which he was a member and in which he always voted with my father, the only other friend remaining to my father in Paris was a lady whom I shall not name, although the liaison was unfortunately very public. I shall simply refer to her, as my father did himself, as *la Dame de la Rue Bleue* (where her house was situated). I have had recourse to this designation so that no one can think it is to Mme de Genlis that I am alluding. This exception was not applicable to her, since in 1792 Mme de Genlis, too, had completely broken with my father, as I shall have occasion to say later.

But since I have mentioned *la Dame de la Rue Bleue,* who has been dead a very long time, I owe it to her memory to place on record here that she was always a sincere and disinterested friend to my father, that she never gave him anything but good advice, that her affection for him never failed, and that after the death of my father, she never ceased to give proof of it to my brothers during their captivity at Fort Saint-Jean in Marseille.

I would rather not talk about my father and mother's separation, which has been so painful for us. My filial duty imposes absolute silence on me in this matter; but this separation produced too great a change in my father's social life and habits for me not to say here in what this change consisted. Once this separation had taken place, there could no longer be any reception at the Palais Royal, any social gathering, or even any open table or open house,* reductions that had in any case become inevitable because of my father's financial situation: He lost his right to receive rent, as did all landed proprietors at this period of the Revolution, but still had to satisfy his creditors by making a disastrous *concordat* with them, which caused him the greatest financial embarrassment.

This sorry picture of my father's position in these various respects at the end of September 1792 explains only too well the depression he felt and the state of apathy into which he had fallen. His political position was another source of trouble and continual vexations, and yet no one at this time foresaw the fearful way in which the fatal trial of the King was going to aggravate my unfortunate father's situation two or three months later. He himself—who was naturally disposed to play down the possibility of untoward developments—always replied when I spoke to him of my anxiety at the prospect of the King being put on trial before the Convention that he was persuaded they did not want to make the King a victim, but merely a hostage whom they were happy to have in their hands and

---

opinion concurred in freeing themselves from the suspicion of being his partisans by withdrawing from him. That is why he was sacrificed by the scoundrels who sent him to the scaffold when he was no longer anything but an embarrassment to them and a means for their opponents to attack them.

* Keeping open house was expected of a *grand seigneur* during the Ancien Régime. —ED.

who, because of the uncertainty of the war, was too precious for them to relinquish willingly by sacrificing him. It was all the more natural that he should allow himself to be swept along by this confidence because such arguments were not only in conformity with justice and the public interest but also, in particular, with the personal interest of the governments of the day. For, and I say it with regret, there is no disguising the fact that it was only after the success of our arms in October and November 1792 that a different tone and language were adopted. It was only when we saw the foreign armies expelled from our territory and our victorious armies occupying successively Savoy, Belgium as far as Antwerp and Aix-la-Chapelle, the great fortress of Mainz, and even Frankfurt—it was then, but only then, I saw, that the directors of the Revolution thought themselves sufficiently freed from all fear of external danger to give free rein to their detestable passions, and it was only in the month of December 1792 that they forced or swept along the Convention into seriously undertaking the trial of the King.

But I am breaking into a subject about which I shall have only too much to say later, and suffice it to say that at the end of September, my father was still under the illusion that this trial would not take place and that they would restrict themselves to keeping the King as a hostage until peace had been signed. But if my father did not yet feel the anxiety that was gnawing at him at the time of my last visit to Paris on December 3 or 4, 1792 (the purpose of which I shall explain), he was very preoccupied with his situation in general and in particular with that in the National Convention. He had no more power to leave it than he had to refuse to enter it. He said to me: "How lucky you are, my son, to have escaped these galleys! In the first place it is wearying to have to tone down one's language, and these debates have but little interest, especially for me. You know that I hate public speaking, and even if I didn't, I am too well aware of my situation to be trapped into speaking. It is bad enough to be obliged to vote." —"I can see that only too well," I said, "but, forgive me for saying it, what led you to join the Mountain?" —"Really, it is easy for you to talk when you must know that all the others rejected me and prided themselves on being my enemies like these Girondins, *The Brissotins*,* whom you are always so infatuated with, my poor friend, because they have the gift of the gab and make pretty speeches to fool people like you." —"But do you believe that the Montagnards can really be your

---

* Sobriquet given to the Girondins, to whom Brissot belonged. He had himself called *Brissot de Warville* because he was born at Warville near Chartres in the estates of my father, to whom he had always showed great hostility during the Revolution even though he had been secretary of his chancellery. People even affected to label him the leader of the Girondins, and thanks to this unfounded supposition, he had the grim distinction of being the last of the twenty-one Girondins sent to the scaffold on the same day at the Place de la Revolution, formerly the Place Louis XV and today the Place de la Concorde.

friends?" —"Friends, that is another matter.* After the general defection I have experienced, it is difficult for me to have that confidence, but at least these people wanted to have me, and when all is said and done, they were the only ones who did. Indeed, I sometimes think that unbeknown to me, I must be afflicted with a contagious disease, because certainly there is a general fear of being in contact with or approaching me; and this is no recent observation. I had the first hints of it in the chamber of the nobility in the Estates-General of 1789." —". . . But there you were at the pinnacle, among the minority that determined the union of the Orders. In short, you were one of the forty-seven." —"Yes, I was one of the forty-seven, and that is all well and good. But do you know what those gentlemen said to me when they saw that I was going to leave the nobles' chamber with them to join that of the Third Estate set up as the *National Assembly?* Well, they said to me: 'Monseigneur, don't come with us, or we would seem to be *in your suite,* and that would not be good.' I took no notice; I was with them. But that made them only the more anxious to keep their distance from me and disown me on every occasion." —"The anecdote is striking," I replied, "and seems to me a great lesson." —"All the more striking," he continued, "because that is what I have experienced throughout the whole course of the Revolution. You are well aware that when I was in the Constituent Assembly, I abstained from having myself elected to the Jacobin Club, although I habitually voted with the deputies who were its founding members. Nevertheless, I was constantly the subject of attacks, calumnies, and violent hostility, not only from the whole right wing of the Assembly but quite as much from those of the left wing who, though they had supported the Revolution, founded that hybrid club called the 89 with M. de La Fayette in opposition to the Jacobins." —"I have forgotten none of that," I told him, "and I remember that after agreeing that M. de Sillery† should propose my admission to the Jacobins, you said to me that in your position you were going to abstain from being a member of any club so that your votes could never have any *partisan* coloring." —"Ah, you have not forgotten that," he replied, smiling, "and you are going to ask me, are you not, why I do not act in the National Convention as I did in the Constituent Assembly?" —"Yes indeed, if you will allow me the question." —"Gladly, but here there are subtle differences that are difficult to grasp because they stem from the difference in the state of affairs and the issues that divided the public at the time of the Constituent Assembly and, finally, from the difference there was between the composition of that Assembly and that of the National Convention.

* In fact it was they who caused his downfall a year later! And a few months later, in 1794, the Duc de Biron had the same fate.
† M. de Sillery was the Comte de Genlis, husband of Mme de Genlis. He had taken the title Marquis de Sillery on coming into an inheritance from the wife of Marshal d'Estrées, who had left him the estate of Sillery in 1786.

"During the Constituent Assembly the imprint or the memory of the old order of things, of the Ancien Régime if you like, was much sharper and especially less hateful than it is today. All its members had been elected under the aegis of the old laws and the distinction of Orders and at precisely the time I had just published those *Instructions* that have caused such a stir. I had addressed them to my agents, *grands baillis d'épée,* seneschals, etc., on the occasion of the election of deputies to the Estates-General for the drafting of what were still called *cahiers de doléances.** And even today, who knows what these offices of *grand bailli* and seneschal were or what were *cahiers de doléances, optional or binding mandates,* and, especially, how a Prince had to give instructions for such objects, so rapidly are memories effaced in the midst of political storms and in times of revolution. Nevertheless, you will not have forgotten that one of the points in my *Instructions* that found the most favor with the public at the time was to demand the abolition of all the privileges or pecuniary exemptions of the nobility. Nobody dreamed then of removing its honorific privileges, the conservation of which, on the contrary, seemed desirable for the maintenance of the social hierarchy." —"You did not imagine then" I said interrupting him, "that you would be saddled with the name *Égalité."* "No, indeed, but silence. I was not long in realizing, my dear friend, that it was a mistake and that the progress of democratic opinion demanded the sacrifice of honorific privileges quite as much as that of pecuniary ones; and from that moment I fell in with this with good grace, I consented frankly and without reservation to their entire abolition. People were all the more appreciative because the nobility's resistance caused considerable irritation and increased the antipathy that had existed for a long time in France against the lords and the airs they gave themselves so tactlessly and with such unfortunate consequences for themselves. Moreover, the vast majority, I should say nearly all of the Constituent Assembly, was comprised of people who, in our old ways of thinking, we described as *well brought up,* who retained some respect for their former social superiors. No one was ever lacking in respect toward me, and however unfavorable toward me were the dispositions of a large part of that Assembly, I never experienced any unpleasantness or any difficulty in carrying out my function as a deputy, to which, it is true, I confined myself rigorously and without the slightest affectation.

* *Cahiers de doléances,* or lists of grievances, were drawn up by each village, synthesized at the provincial level, and finally by the Estates-General themselves, who at the end of their deliberations forwarded them to the King, who would then embody them in legislation as he saw fit. *Grands baillis* and seneschals were officers of electoral areas that disappeared with the *Ancien Régime.* The controversy over optional or binding mandates is still with us and relates to the matter of "direct democracy": Is the member of a political assembly a *representative* of the people (and therefore, between elections, a free agent) or a *mandatory* (i.e., bound by an electoral pledge or a party manifesto)?—ED.

"Unfortunately it cannot be the same in the National Convention, for its composition and mentality are very different. As for respect or deference, there can no longer be any question of them, and today they are not even satisfied with having brought us down to the common level; we must expiate our former exalted status by being placed below it and put behind everyone. It was with this in mind that when it was decided to have me as a deputy for Paris, I was carefully put at the bottom of the list as a clear demonstration of disdain for the former category of Prince." —"And yet they wanted to have you?" —"Yes, you or me, it was all one to them, so long as they had a Prince sitting among their party but not exercising any influence over it.

"Weary of everything, abandoned by everyone, I fall into a state of melancholy—especially when I do not have you near me, my dear children—which I would have thought incompatible with my character and my natural disposition."

Such was the substance of my father's conversations with us at the end of September 1792.

I then began to bring up with him again a project we had already discussed previously, that of us all going together to the United States of America. However, I only spoke of it vaguely because, for my part, I was absolutely determined not to leave the army until the foreign armies had evacuated French territory, and at that time I did not at all foresee that their retreat could have been as near as in fact it was. This project suited my father well enough in some respects, but frightened him a lot in others. I said to him: "Europe is barred to us, which you do not regret nor I. But we have no illusions! England, where you would so much like to live, is equally closed to you." —"I know that even better than you," he replied, "and I saw it very well at the time of my last visit there in 1790. But the United States, that's a very hard country, and the descriptions of it Lauzun has given me (that was the name by which, out of long usage, he referred to the Duc de Biron) have inspired me with a kind of dread of it; however, I know that I may have to resign myself to it, but I am in no hurry." After this he repeated to me everything that he had gleaned from the Duc de Biron, who had fought in the American War for two years, commanding the Lauzun Legion; and he told me that unless one worked with one's hands, the only form of enterprise that could be conducted there was running a commercial house, of which he was not capable, or a Negro plantation, like General Washington's, which did not suit him at all; that in the towns, there were neither congenial households, nor society, nor theaters (which was true at the time); that everything was sad and mournful and calculated to make him die of boredom and melancholy. I replied that it was just about the same in Paris, not to mention what was untenable about his position there, and ours; and he replied with a deep sigh: "That is only too true, but in the end there is always the Opéra, and let's go there straightaway to shake off the thought of all this."*

That always ended our conversations, and we went to install ourselves in his box at the Opéra, where he often slept while we were transported by the general enthusiasm always aroused by the magnificent spectacle of the animation of the *Marseillaise*. It was somewhere between opera and ballet, and as soon as the orchestra brought forth the first strains of the *sacred* hymn, the whole house rose with thunderous applause and remained standing till the end. On the stage, the statue of France could be seen with the Phrygian bonnet (though not red), holding in its hand an immense tricolor, further surmounted by a large fleur-de-lis of gold. The statue was surrounded by a host of old men, women, and children, covered in tricolored ribbons, who sang all the verses in succession; and all the public repeated the refrain after each verse, while all the units of the army and the National Guard, in their respective sections, filed past the statue and saluted it with their colors. The penultimate couplet, which was always given to the children—

> We, too, will join the army,
> When our elders are there no more

—was sung exclusively by a troop of children, whose appearance and tiny voices always redoubled the enthusiasm; then everyone on the stage went on bended knees and sang the last couplet in unison—

> Sacred love of the Fatherland,
> Direct, support our avenging arms

—after which the curtain fell in the midst of prolonged applause, and I was still full of the emotions of this scene when, having received my new letters of appointment, I hastily embraced my father and my brother and left immediately to join Dumouriez's army.

I took with me only my new aide-de-camp, César Ducrest, because my father had asked my brother to remain with him in Paris until he had been assigned an appointment in his new rank of adjutant general lieutenant colonel.

* This passion for the opera was one of the rages of the time. I have been told that on May 31, 1793, when the Girondins, the victims of a collective decree of accusation, were leaving the Convention *via the bar* at the end of which they were awaited by policemen, Vergniaud had found a way of disappearing in the crowd and even of leaving Paris by the Clichy gate. Thence, pursuing his journey alone and on foot, he stopped at the crossroads of the *Château* of Saint-Ouen (from this same *château* Louis XVIII dated his *Declaration* twenty-one years later). There, sitting on a milestone, Vergniaud for a long while contemplated his unhappy lot; then, reflecting that each of his colleagues arrested in Paris could go where he liked provided he was accompanied by the policeman assigned to guard him, he said to himself: *And I too, if I were there, could go to the Opéra with my policeman, and what am I going to do here instead?* Then, getting up, he returned to Paris and went to the Opéra in the evening with his policeman and a few months later ascended the scaffold with his colleagues.

319

I was all the more eager to rejoin Dumouriez's army because we had just received the tremendous news that the Prussian army had begun its retreat and that already the *Camp de la Lune* had been struck. This camp, situated opposite the windmill at Valmy on the main road from Châlons to Sainte-Menehould, had taken its name from a little inn called *Au Clair de Lune* where the King of Prussia and the Duke of Brunswick had set up their headquarters.

I felt a deep satisfaction, freely traversing in my post chaise from Notre-Dame-de-l'Épine to the inn whose occupation by the Prussian army had caused so much alarm at Paris. There they saw the enemy intercepting and occupying a position nearer the capital than that of our armies, then concentrated around Sainte-Menehould, and there is no denying that this alarm was not without foundation because the position of the two armies was reversed. But luckily for France, Dumouriez, in his wisdom, had made a better calculation of the odds, and his pertinacity in continuing to occupy the strategic positions in the Argonne settled the retreat of the Prussian army.

Therefore, although I was in a hurry, I would very much have liked to stop for a bit to visit the little inn and the *Camp de la Lune,* now so famous and so glorious for us; but I found there a corps of engineers and officers from the sanitary corps of our armies who prevented me. They were charged with cleansing these sites, which had become pestilent with the mass of badly buried corpses and dead horses strewn on the ground and, above all, by the infected pits that bore witness to the ravages of dysentery in the Prussian army, from which our armies had been completely preserved. These officers had orders to forbid anyone from remaining in or visiting this place of desolation and, indeed, to make those of our troops coming from the south who would have to cross it pass through as quickly as possible.

It was on October 6, 1792 (that is to say, the very day when I became nineteen) that I rejoined Dumouriez's army at Sainte-Menehould just when the General was about to mount his horse; all his columns were already on the move, and he intended to lead in person the one that was to proceed to Autry via la Neuville-au-Pont, Saint-Thomas, and Condé-lez-Autry. Having picked up my horses at Sainte-Menehould, I accompanied him on this march, after presenting him with my letters of appointment. He told me that he would soon assign me a command in his army and that meanwhile, he wanted me to remain with him so that he could put me in the picture and inform me of his further plans.

The roads we passed along on these marches were rutted with the rain and the wagons. They were lined with the carcasses of dead horses, putrefying and with their skin peeling off, and with all kinds of filth. The villages were devastated, provisions were lacking everywhere, and often General Dumouriez had the army's covered wagons opened to succor the unfortunate. All the inhabitants went *en masse* before us, and shouts of joy at seeing our troops again broke out everywhere. They threw themselves on us, they kissed our muddy boots, and the air resounded with applause and prolonged shouts of *"Bravo, bravo, long live France, long live our brave troops, long live the army, long live Dumouriez, long live our liberator!"*

I could not resist depicting such a mixture of emotions as those we felt with each step as we followed the retreat of the Prussian army; but I should be deviating from the aim I set myself in this work if I undertook a detailed account of the military operations. I shall write the history of that campaign elsewhere, and here I shall only say enough about it to make it possible to follow my narrative.

I was struck by the skillful ensemble of the plans that General Dumouriez laid before me as we rode side by side on the march to Autry. I was even more impressed later when I saw these plans executed with complete success and without any changes, at least insofar as it depended on him.

General Dumouriez was bemoaning the fact that when the Prussian army had struck its *Camp de la Lune* and begun its retreat, General Kellermann, his colleague but not his subordinate, had persisted in believing, despite the vain efforts that had been made to disabuse him, that the Prussian army was proceeding to Paris via Rheims and Soissons. As a result of this misconception, General Kellermann had immediately put his whole army on the march in the direction of Somme-Suippes. It was not until he had passed this point that he realized his mistake, on being informed that the Duke of Brunswick's army had taken the opposite direction and that it was leaving Champagne by recrossing the same defiles by which it had arrived, that is to say, via Autry, Grandpré, la Croix-aux-Bois, Buzancy, and le Chêne-Populeux.

This untimely separation of the two French armies without prior consultation paralyzed their operations. While Kellermann was withdrawing from the Prussian army in the belief that he was pursuing it, Dumouriez found himself too weak to undertake anything by himself, and he merely remained in his positions at Sainte-Menehould and the defiles of the southern Argonne, la Chalade, and the Côte de Biesme before les Islettes, which barred the main road. The upshot was that the Prussian army carried out unmolested its difficult and dangerous retreat along the very difficult roads of the plains of Champagne and the defiles of the northern Argonne.

Finally, after wasting four days in his advance to Somme-Suippes, General Kellermann informed General Dumouriez that he was marching back and would arrive at Sainte-Menehould with his army during the evening of October 6. Immediately, General Dumouriez made all his arrangements for leaving Sainte-Menehould that morning, as I have already said above.

321

General Arthur Dillon,* who had defended Côte de Biesme and les Islettes with such perseverance and valor throughout the Prussian occupation, was informed that he and his detachment were being transferred to Kellermann's army and that he was to come out by the main Verdun road so as to occupy Dombasle, which was done immediately.

General Dumouriez considered, and this opinion was amply justified by the event, that the King of Prussia and the Duke of Brunswick, disabused of the illusions that the *émigrés* had spread among foreign Courts about the ease with which Paris could be reached and the Counterrevolution effected, did not intend to take up position behind the Meuse; that on the contrary, the Prussian army was returning to Germany with its numerous auxiliaries, that Verdun and Longwy would be abandoned without our having to lay siege to them, and finally, that all French territory would soon be delivered from the foreign invasion.

General Kellermann, reinforced by the detachments of Leveneur and Chazot—taken, like Dillon's, from Dumouriez's army—was charged with marching immediately to the Meuse to pursue the retreating Prussian army and lay siege, if need be, to Verdun and Longwy.

General Dumouriez was to march north, along the chain of the Argonne, without descending into the basin of the Meuse unless the operations of the Prussian army made this necessary; and when, as he had so rightly and wisely foreseen, this army had gone a sufficient distance from the Meuse for there to be no further fear that it would turn back, he proposed to direct his army toward Flanders, that is to say, to the Department of the Nord, and to have it go by forced marches to the help of Lille, which the Austrians under Duke Albert of Saxe-Teschen had been bombarding for a fortnight.

With this in view, General Dumouriez had chosen le Chêne-Populeux as the central point for his army to assemble. He arrived there, I think, on October 9 and received the good news that the siege of Lille had been lifted on the 7th and that the Austrians had withdrawn to Tournay. He was not, for all that, any less impatient to set his army on the march toward Flanders; he rightly calculated that the corps of thirty thousand Austrians under General Clairfayt, which had joined with the Prussian army, would separate from it as soon as it had left France in order to defend the frontiers of the Austrian Low Countries, which we already called *Belgium,* against us; and in fact, Clairfayt reached Mons almost at the same time as we reached Valenciennes.

All the troops that were to make up Dumouriez's army, after the separation of those who had passed to Kellermann's army, were assembled on October 10 at le Chêne-Populeux and in the neighboring villages.

General Dumouriez immediately formed them into two columns. He gave command of the first to General Beurnonville, and of the second to me. We proceeded at a distance of one day's march apart so that in the

* General Arthur Dillon perished shortly afterward on the revolutionary scaffold!

evening the second column occupied the quarters the first had left in the morning. General Beurnonville left le Chêne-Populeux on October 11 with the first column, and I left the following day, the 12th, with the second.

The first day we were quartered at Poix and at Mazerny; then we continued our march via Mézières, Maubert-Fontaine, Hirson, La Chapelle, Avesnes, Quesnoy, and Valenciennes; and on October 26 we took up quarters between that fortress and Quiévrain, which was occupied by our advance guard.

While we were executing this movement, General Dumouriez proceeded to Paris in order to concert preparations for the invasion of Belgium with the government and to provide for the needs of the army, which was then greatly in want. The clothing was in a deplorable state, and boots were entirely lacking. The soldiers joked about this with the old French wit; they said that the Republic was not content with having made *sans-culottes* of them;* they had to be *va-nu-pieds* as well. All the pieces of cloth from the mills of Sedan were requisitioned, and a truly grotesque costume was made out of them. The result was greatcoats of many colors set off with facings and collars of other shades. So there was no more question of a uniform, nor of any standardization; but the soldiers were at least well covered. As for the boots, the problem was almost insurmountable, and we were never able to procure a sufficient amount, so that our soldiers often left their old shoes behind in place of those belonging to the inhabitants, saying *exchange is no robbery*. The supply of wagons had not been organized in any of our armies, and there was a shortage of horses as well as of wagons for every type of provisions. Everything was done by requisitioning the locality in the most irregular and uncertain manner. The provisioning of bread was carried out fairly well; but for that of meat, recourse was frequently had to requisitioning, which is often fruitless for the troops and always odious to the localities that endure them.

All in all, the administration of this period was chaotic, and it was then that those interminable and shameful wrangles began between the contractors and the speculators at all levels. General Dumouriez wanted his two quartermasters, Malus and Petit-Jean,† to be entrusted with everything; and the Minister, Pache, together with the Executive Council and an important section of the National Convention, on the contrary wanted the Purchasing Committee and the other companies formed around it in Paris to have the exclusive direction of all administrative matters and those relating to provisions.

* The label *sans-culottes* (literally, "without knee-breeches": i.e., wearing trousers) originated as a contemptuous way of referring to the lower orders, who did not wear breeches, but was soon taken up as a proud boast and by 1793 had become a requirement of political orthodoxy. That, of course, is not to say that many, or any, actually changed their mode of dress, still less did they "go barefoot" (*va-nu-pieds*).—ED.
† *Petit-Jean* perished on the revolutionary scaffold, and *Malus* escaped it by a miracle.

General Dumouriez returned to the army very dissatisfied with his visit to Paris and persuaded that the government and many members of the National Convention, jealous of the renown he had just won and fearing the ascendancy that it could give him, were working for the failure of his Belgian enterprise by refusing him the means to assure its success.

The observations he had made on the nature and character of the troops composing his army had pointed to weaknesses in their organization that, so far as this was possible, there was urgent need to rectify. It was neither in the artillery nor the cavalry that these weaknesses were felt. These two arms had never undergone any change in their organization. Our artillery was numerous and superlative: It had retained its superiority over that of foreign armies, and apart from a deficiency of horses, it left nothing to be desired. As for our cavalry, it was good but far too small in number, and among our light cavalry we did not possess a single lancer to oppose the Uhlans, that is to say, the hordes of light troops armed with lances that always flanked the Austrian troops and covered their movements. It is a remark that has been made in every century that France produces fewer horses than other countries and that the French genius is more given to infantry than cavalry. In fact, our infantry marches more quickly than all the others, and none of them possesses that poise that helps a march and that the Italians have so aptly called *desinvoltura francesca,* which, as far as I can judge, is untranslatable.

Our infantry, then, was made up of two very distinct categories: the former regiments of the line and the battalions of National Volunteers; and the latter should be further subdivided into two categories but with fairly pronounced shades of difference, the battalions recruited in 1791 and those recruited in 1792.

The Constituent Assembly had decreed an extraordinary levy of ninety-one thousand men while dominated by the fears generated by Louis XVI's flight to Varennes in June 1791. It would have been more rational and, to my way of thinking, preferable to have incorporated them into the army, whether by increasing the strength and the number of battalions in the existing regiments, or by creating new ones organized along the same lines. The Constituent Assembly thought otherwise. Always distrustful of the army, though not daring to tamper with it openly, the Assembly wanted the new recruits to be distinct and set apart from it by an organization that was different in every respect so as to make them a counterweight to the influence they feared from the old regiments. In a word, it wanted to create a *national army* in opposition to the *army of the line,* without envisaging the disastrous consequences this crazy plan was bound to involve for a France already grievously threatened with a general war against all the Powers of Europe.

I shall give as succinctly as I can a description of this organization in order to give a better understanding of the damage it did to the discipline and to the intrinsic value of our armies, as well as of the confusion or the difficulties to which it gave rise daily for all those who were called upon to exercise any command at all, from the subaltern to the staff officer.

The decree of 1791 ordered the immediate levy of ninety-one thousand *National Volunteers,* who were to be provided by the departments according to a quota fixed for each of them and a new method of recruitment consisting of opening registers in each department where the public-spirited would enroll. These men were then sent to the administrative capital of the department by the civil authority, where they were placed at the disposal of the Administrative Council of the Department,* which alone, without any participation by the Minister of War, was given the task of distributing the men into units of five to six hundred men each and then of forming them into as many different battalions, each separate from the others. As soon as this distribution had been carried out, each unit, still under the care and direction of the departmental authorities, proceeded to the election of all the officers and noncommissioned officers of the battalion without any exception. Once elected, these officers and noncommissioned officers were to remain in possession of their respective rank and emoluments until the battalion was disbanded unless, before this time, they had been cashiered by courts-martial operating military laws, to which alone they were subject. The precedence of officers of the same rank who had been elected on the same day was determined by the number of votes they had obtained in the election and, in the event of a tie, by their age.

When the National Volunteers were serving with troops of the line, with officers of equal rank, the officer of the line took precedence, whatever their respective seniority, but when the officer of the line was of lower rank, the officer from the Volunteers took command. The sedentary and unpaid National Guards alone occupied the right in the army of the line; the battalions of National Volunteers and all paid National Guards took the left.

The officers of the National Volunteers had no right to promotion, and their rank was only temporary. Each vacancy always had to be filled by a new election, and as all the individuals comprising the battalion were equally eligible for all the posts, it followed that a private soldier could be elected a lieutenant colonel, a captain, etc., straight off. These promotions, which were as bizarre as they were damaging to discipline, were repeated quite frequently, especially at the beginning, but later, the good sense of the soldiers from these corps made them realize that they no

---

* This council corresponded to the later *General Councils* but with wider authority; it comprised thirty-six members, of whom eight, specially elected for this purpose, formed the *Directory,* which later became the Council of the Prefecture. They had a president and a public prosecutor, and all were elected by the electors of the department.

longer wished to carry them out.* Once the election has been carried out, it was definitive, without the superior authority having to confirm or being able to annul it. Thus from 1791, the whole organization of these corps of National Volunteers was calculated to abrogate the military hierarchy and paralyze discipline. It was much worse in 1792, as I shall explain later.

The battalions of the same department bore its name, and they were distinguished from each other by a number they drew by lot at the time of their formation: first, second, third, or fourth battalion of such and such a department from the *Aine* to *Yonne.†*

As soon as all these measures relative to their formation had been completed, these battalions were put at the disposal of the Minister of War, who lost no time in sending them a long way from their locality and distributing them among the fortified towns, where they manned the garrisons with the other corps of the army. There they were put in uniform, equipped and armed, then drilled and instructed by the adjutant instructors drawn from the ranks of the army's noncommissioned officers and attached to each battalion. Their task was all the more difficult to perform because it was not only the men whom they had to instruct, but also the officers, most of whom had not the slightest knowledge of the career of

---

* At the battle of Jemappes, after the commander of a battalion of National Guards from Deux-Sèvres had been killed, I assembled the battalion without arms after the combat, and I enjoined it to proceed immediately to the election of a lieutenant colonel to replace the worthy leader who had just fallen on the field of honor fighting for France. Immediately the whole battalion exclaimed with one voice: "No, no, no more elections, we will not conduct them any more, appoint him yourself." —"But I can't, it's against the law." —"So what? We want to be well led like the troops of the line. Choose us a good commander." Finally, feeling that I had to conclude the matter, I said to them: "Very well, take the first captain of your battalion, Captain Pelletier, who has just commanded it so worthily." —"Yes, yes, three cheers for Pelletier and for our General for giving us him." Then I admitted Captain Pelletier as lieutenant colonel commanding the Deux-Sèvres battalion, and this brave officer, later a brigadier general, was killed at the Battle of Marengo.

† These departmental names carried by the battalions of National Volunteers of 1791 were a subject of jealousy for the regiments of the line, who did not consider themselves sufficiently distinguished from each other by the numbers that the laws of the Constituent Assembly had given them instead of their old names with memories of their regimental glory. I remember, at the Battle of Jemappes, at the time of the charge, when Colonel Blanchard of the 5th of the line—a white-haired veteran of the Seven Years' War who had received all his promotions in this same regiment—gave his command *Column advance,* he added in a thunderous voice:

Forever Navarre without fear, march!

Immediately all the soldiers, electrified, raised their right hands and shouted in chorus:

Forever Navarre without fear![a]

At the same time the 17th of the line, which was charging near the 5th, also gave out its old war cry:

"And we, we are Auvergne without blemish!"

[a] The Navarre regiment was the uninterrupted descendant, from the sixteenth century, of the band formed and commanded by Bayard, the Chevalier, *sans peur et sans reproche.*

326

arms and often no other instruction. Nevertheless, these battalions were drilled and instructed much more quickly and much better than could have been expected. Their composition was generally good, as they were drawn from the country population and the upper bourgeoisie of the towns, and their periods in the garrisons, where they were in continuous contact with the troops of the line and mounted guard with them, caused them to acquire the military mentality and fairly good habits of discipline. But only by living, as I did, in the midst of these two kinds of troops, and having them under one's orders, could one get an idea of the mutual irritation caused by the differences in their organization, their way of life, and their pay.

The officers and noncommissioned officers of the National Volunteers had the same pay as those of the line; but the ordinary soldiers had *fifteen sous per day,* while in the line they scarcely had *seven sous a day all in.* It was hard to justify such a large discrepancy, which produced a very bad effect.

All the National Volunteers, recruited at the different periods, wore the same uniform—a blue jacket with white facings, red collar, cuffs, and piping, and yellow buttons—while the infantry of the line kept the white uniform, another subject of discord between the two.

The recruitments of 1792, carried out after the declaration of war and in the midst of great political agitation, produced very different, and unfortunately much worse, results than that of 1791.

After the declaration of war on April 20, 1792, they began with a good measure. An appeal was made to all the departments to raise the number of men in each battalion of National Volunteers to 812 effectives, but this was no longer enough to satisfy the revolutionary leaders, who hindered its execution; and the measure obtained but few results. They claimed that at a time when the invasion of the Duke of Brunswick's great army was imminent, it was necessary to create a new army, independent of those that garrisoned our frontiers and specially assigned to the defense of Paris. That is to say that they were no longer satisfied, as in 1791, with having created a paid army of National Volunteers, alongside the army of the line and better paid, but that they wanted to have at their disposal, whether in Paris or within a narrow radius from it, an entirely *revolutionary* army.

It was at the beginning of June 1792 that the National Legislative Assembly passed a decree ordering that forty-two new battalions with a different organization be raised to form a "mobile camp" at Soissons capable of proceeding rapidly to wherever it was thought best to send it.

At first Louis XVI refused to give the royal assent to this decree, but the too well founded suspicions surrounding him of countenancing the foreign invasion had cost him the nation's confidence. This refusal was merely seen as an attempt to paralyze the defense of France. The Revolutionary movement of June 20 was the consequence. The Tuileries Palace was invaded, and the decree received the assent in the midst of the affronts directed at this unfortunate Prince during this day of unhappy memory.

For the execution of this decree, a different mode was adopted from the one that had been followed the year before for the recruitment and organization of the ninety-one thousand National Volunteers. Instead of charging the departmental authorities with conducting these operations in the administrative capital of their respective departments, it was thought to have them carried out in Paris and to have road maps distributed throughout the kingdom to all those who wanted to come to Paris to enlist in these new battalions; and they were enjoined to be there on July 14 in order to celebrate the anniversary of the fall of the Bastille and of the great Federation of 1790. This circumstance caused the name *fédérés* to be substituted for that of National Volunteers, though the change in name did not produce any in the pay of fifteen sous per day. This new mode of recruiting produced a very different result from that of 1791 and brought to Paris a large number of undesirables, whose lack of discipline and dangerous character were aggravated by the fact of their coming together.

One of the first bands to present itself was that of the *Marseillais,* to which many others rallied, even adopting the name without title to it other than their caprice. The band of the Marseillais entered Paris singing a hymn which became famous and to which, greatly to my regret, they gave their name, although it had not been written for them and its author, Captain Rouget de Lisle, aide-de-camp to General Valence, had composed its words and music two years earlier for a local Federation at Belfort or Huningue.

Once these *fédérés* were in Paris, it became very difficult to get them out. None of them went to Soissons where, indeed, there was not any camp; they remained in Paris to take part in the rising of August 10. Then they abandoned the hymn that bore their name to substitute for it the ignoble song *la Carmagnole,* whose odious words echoed through all the streets and even under the windows of the unfortunate prisoners in the Temple.

This mass of *fédérés* was organized in battalions in the least bad way that was possible; the majority of the officers were drawn by lot;* and this organization was so imperfect that if my memory serves me right, there

* At the siege of Maastricht, in February 1793, I had a battalion in my division whose officers had been drawn by lot. The lieutenant colonel was very limited, and I always noticed a certain embarrassment in him when I had him to dine at my table. One day, when we had to repel a *sortie* from the Dutch garrison, he made such a mess of his command that his whole battalion took flight in confusion. I said to him impatiently: "You are incapable of being a lieutenant colonel and commanding a battalion." —"Alas," he said to me weeping, "I know that only too well, but pity me, General. It is not my fault if I have the misfortune to be a lieutenant

were only seven of these battalions that were judged fit to be sent to Dumouriez's army in Champagne. The rest formed the *camp of Châlons,* command of which was at first given to Marshal Luckner with the empty title of Generalissimo of the French Armies. But he stayed for a very short time, having run the risk of being butchered there.

This camp at Châlons, whose numbers moreover were not considerable, was in fact nothing but a mob completely without discipline. Although those who comprised it had never seen an enemy or fired a shot, several times they started to flee back to Paris, declaring that the generals were all traitors who were going to deliver them to the enemy because they were *patriots.*

However, there was another levy of recruits at this time that produced better results. It was the *levée en masse* of the Parisian National Guard, which in three days turned out forty-eight battalions of National Volunteers, each bearing the name of its respective section. They were animated by a totally different spirit from that of the *fédérés,* and they improved with every day. There were, in addition, battalions, free companies, or companies of light infantry coming from a few other towns, but no National Guard cavalry, though there was a squadron of light cavalry from the Calvados, which was very well mounted.

The details I have just gone into may be overlong, but they seemed to me to be necessary to give an idea of the spirit of the times and to give an understanding of the composition of the army of which General Dumouriez resumed the command at Valenciennes on October 26, 1792.

He realized the necessity of giving his infantry more uniformity by integrating it as completely as circumstances and the diverse categories of troops comprising it permitted. He then had the happy inspiration of substituting for the old infantry formation of regiments, consisting of two or four battalions, that of those half-brigades of three battalions which became so famous and which gave such superiority to French arms in the subsequent wars. The battalion in the center was invariably drawn from

---

colonel, I was a house servant in a furnished lodging house, and as there are no longer any travelers or anyone in Paris, I was dying of hunger and I had myself enrolled in this battalion; but only to be a *private,* nothing else, I assure you. I was led to the Luxembourg Gardens where the battalion was assembled, and there I was presented with a hat full of pieces of paper and told: "Put your hand in there and take out a bit of paper immediately." I did as I was ordered, and there was written in big letters on the paper I had drawn, *Lieutenant Colonel.* Then I was told: "There, you are a lieutenant colonel and our commander. Go and get your epaulets!" —"Citizens," I told them, "that is impossible because I don't have a penny in my pocket!" But they wouldn't listen, and these epaulets you see here were given me against my wages. Everything I have told you is the honest truth, and I beg you, General, not to send me to prison." —"No," I said, "you shall not go to prison, but just try to learn your job and do better another time." —"Oh, I've had enough, please remove these epaulets and put me in the ranks."—"Very well, we shall see later; meanwhile command your battalion as best you can."

329

one of the old regiments of the line, while those on the right and left were one of the battalions of National Volunteers from the levy of 1791 and one of those from the new levies of 1792, and two of three of these half-brigades formed the command of a *maréchal de camp*. By this wise arrangement, troops of the three different categories in our infantry each furnished one of the battalions of the half-brigade and by this association mutually strengthened each other.

Having completed the formation of the half-brigades, General Du-mouriez fixed the order of battle of his army. He had sixteen half-brigades of infantry, or forty-eight battalions, in the line. This force was divided into two wings. Command of the right wing was given to me, with Generals Drouais, Desforêts, and Stetenhof as commanders of my three brigades, and command of the left wing was given to General Miranda, who was a lieutenant general and less senior than I was. As he was in Paris, he was replaced by the most senior *maréchal de camp,* General Ferrand (of the engineers), who commanded the left wing at the Battle of Jemappes, where he had a horse shot from under him.

There was no cavalry of the line in this army, as General Dumouriez had given his heavy cavalry to General Kellermann and kept only the light cavalry. From this he formed three separate detachments, adding to them the battalions of light infantry, and those formed from the companies of grenadiers and light troops from the infantry battalions, and finally the free companies or those of sharpshooters.

These three detachments were (1) the advance guard, commanded by General Beurnonville, with Generals Stengel and Rosière under him; (2) two small separate units, called right flankers and left flankers, which were to cover the flanks of the two wings of our infantry. They were commanded by Colonel Henri de Frégeville (or the Elder) and by General Dampierre, then a *maréchal de camp*.

General d'Harville's division, which was assembled at Maubeuge and was consequently nearer than we were to Mons and the heights of Jemappes, was to operate on our right when the army advanced. The strength of this division was less than six thousand men, and since our army came to twenty-seven thousand at most, it follows that we only had thirty-three thousand men with which to attack the Austrian army that lay before us, even including d'Harville's division, although it did not play any part in the Battle of Jemappes since it did not rejoin us until the fighting had ceased at all points.

General Clairfayt had outstripped us, and he had effected his junction with General Beaulieu at Mons before we had reached Valenciennes. It is true that his army had been weakened by the loss of the strong detachment he had had to send to Luxembourg and by that of a garrison of five thousand men he had left in the fortresses of Namur under General Chasteller.

The total number of Austrian forces then present in the Low Countries under the overall command of Duke Albert of Saxe-Teschen was estimated at around forty thousand men. General Clairfayt occupied the heights of Jemappes with a body of twenty thousand men specially assigned to its defense, which we learned for certain from the assessment we had made of the situation. The advance guard under General Starray, who occupied Boussu, and two or three little detachments around Mons were estimated at five or six thousand men and were not included in our assessment.

Given the respective sizes of the opposing armies, General Dumouriez hesitated and felt all the more anxiety about taking the offensive because, as I have already said, our army was very greatly in want. There was a total lack of money, and we did not know how to comply with the requirements of the law and with previous promises to pay everything in cash as soon as the armies crossed the frontier. We ended up by not keeping this promise, and outside of France as inside, we continued to pay for everything in *assignats*.

However, General Dumouriez saw only too clearly that he could expect nothing from Paris and that he must either give up the invasion of Belgium or make up his mind to undertake it immediately. He therefore profited from an unforeseen incident to justify the course of action he wanted to take.

General Rosière, who commanded a corps of Belgian refugees* like himself in our advance guard, considering that the area of his command was too restricted, had obtained General Beurnonville's permission to extend it as far as Thulin on the banks of the Haine and to have this village occupied by two of his battalions of Belgian light infantry.

On November 2, General Starray left Boussu with a portion of his troops and the artillery and promptly seized the village of Thulin; then he had General Rosière and his Belgian light infantry pursued by Blankenstein's hussars, who slew a large number of them with their sabers on the plain stretching from the Hain to the Quiévrain road. They would have been exterminated if the 2nd Hussars (Chamborant), commanded by Colonel Charles de Frégeville (the Younger),† had not arrived in time to relieve them by a brilliant charge.

On November 3 General Dumouriez, hearing of this misadventure, went to take personal command of his advance guard, to which he sent the artillery and which he reinforced with General Dampierre's detachment. At the same time he ordered me to cover his movement with the brigade to my right, that is to say, the two half-brigades of infantry or six battalions that General Drouais, the *maréchal de camp*, commanded under me.‡ I left Quiévrechain with my little infantry column and half-squadron of the 11th Light Cavalry (Normandy), which Colonel Henri

---

* See Editor's note, page 20, note †.—ED.
† Later a lieutenant general.
‡ General Drouais had rejoined the armly only a few days previously. He presented himself to me as one of my *maréchaux de camp* while I was at dinner at M. de

de Frégeville had given me to act as scouts and cover our march; in addition, there were six four-pounders, in accordance with the old usage still observed in the French army that there should always be four or six pieces of campaign artillery attached to each regiment or half-brigade of infantry.

The Austrians had made the road to Mons impassable from the outskirts of Quiévrain to beyond Quaregnon by removing the paving stones and leaving them scattered along the whole width of the road so that nothing could pass, and we were obliged to take to the fields across ploughed land intersected by ditches, where our sappers lost a lot of time clearing the way for our artillery.

Consequently, we marched in a single column to the right of the road, while General Dumouriez was operating on the left, dislodging the Austrians successively from the villages of Montreuil and Thulin, and attacking Boussu.

My brother, the Duc de Montpensier, who was no longer my aide-de-camp, found himself at my side again as adjutant general. Arriving about four o'clock in the afternoon in front of the hill on which the windmill at Boussu is situated, with its back to the Sars woods, we found the Austrians there, ensconced behind a breastwork and a trench with artillery that began to fire on us at a very long range. I arranged mine in a battery at a good angle to the flank of the breastwork, and I had it supported by my light cavalry while I led my infantry so as to outflank the ridge, as far as the terrain permitted, by climbing the neighboring hill. When we were halfway up, I had the charge beaten, and the Austrians (consisting of O'Donnel's free corps and Leloup's light infantry) did not wait for our arrival. Their artillery, which was in harness, left at a gallop by a road that crossed the woods, and their infantry hastily returned thither, leaving several dead and wounded on the field.*

General Dumouriez was entering Boussu, which the Austrians had

---

Normont's farm at Quiévrain, where I had my headquarters. I had never seen him before, and his manners and dress revealed to me at once a man of the Ancien Régime. He had two very tight and powdered curls in his hair over the eyes, a little three-cornered hat, and a sword with a damask hilt in a shagreen scabbard, which earned him more than one pleasantry. When I invited him to sit at table with me, he went backward bowing before accepting, which astonished my company a little, and when finally he was sitting beside me, I asked him in a very low voice where he had served; and he replied that he had served very little; then, adopting an air of mystery, he added that it was only to me that he dared say that he had been a King's Equerry but under a name he no longer used since he had decided to join up. I did not ask him what that name was and he never told me: My investigations to discover it proved fruitless. He had both feet removed by a cannonball that cut along the ground in the Flénu woods at the Battle of Jemappes. When I saw him pass in the arms of four soldiers who were carrying him to the hospital tent, I came up to him and said: "You'll get better, my dear General, and I shall see you soon." —"No," he said, "I will not see you again." He died the following day at Quesnoy.

* Among the wounded, I found stretched out on the ground an unfortunate young

scarcely defended at all, just when we had overrun the battery by the windmill, and I went down immediately to take his orders. He told me to have my troops bivouac at the windmill, to leave General Drouais there, and to accompany him with my brother.

General Stengel occupied Hornu, outside Boussu, and General Dampierre advanced as far as Saint-Ghislain.

We then went to the Grand-Cerf Inn, in the main square of Boussu, where we found a magnificent supper all laid out that had been prepared there for General Starray and his general staff.

During the supper, General Dumouriez announced that he had decided to give battle to the Austrian army and that he was going to dispatch the necessary orders for all our army to begin its march in the direction of Pâturages and Quaregnon the following day, November 4.

On the night of the 4th my division bivouacked in the Sars wood on the road to Bavay and behind the windmill at Boussu. The heavy artillery greatly retarded our march across the fields and ploughed land, and though we had twenty requisitioned horses on the sixteen-pounders, we were obliged to leave some of them behind. However, it was still broad daylight when we arrived on the 5th at the heights of Pâturages, which are separated from those of Jemappes by a fair expanse of undulating land. In accordance with General Dumouriez's orders, I halted my division there and formed it into a single line, each densely massed battalion having to bivouac in position.

---

man with a charming face who was lieutenant in the O'Donnels. He told me in German that he was Baron von Kleist, the son of a Prussian general whose name was well known to me. I got off my horse, summoned a surgeon, and helped him to dress his wounds while he told me himself that there was nothing to be done for him and that he regretted not having fallen in the ranks of the Prussians. We saw that his hip was shattered by a bullet and that there was no hope of saving him. "Since you are so kind, so *gnädig,*" he said, breaking into tears, "do me the kindness of having me carried to Boussu to the house where I was staying. There is a young lady there who loves me and whom I was going to marry. If I could see her again once more. . . ." Immediately I had a stretcher made for him out of branches, and I sent him to Boussu carried by six soldiers. He was still alive when I went to see him in the evening, and the young lady, in tears, was on her knees beside his bed. He died in the night.

A long time afterward, in 1826, I went to Valenciennes to have my eldest son installed as colonel of the 1st Hussars, formerly the Bercheny, one of those that had most distinguished itself at Jemappes, and I profited from this occasion to revisit our battlefields in Belgium. I went to Boussu, to the *château* of Comte Maurice de Caraman, and having recounted the death of Baron von Kleist to him, I asked whether he knew anything of that young and pretty lady whose tears had so moved me in 1792. He replied that she was still living; that in truth she was no longer either young or pretty, but that she was a good mother of a family and greatly respected at Boussu, and that he begged me to permit him to have her informed that I had asked about her. I readily agreed, and immediately she ran to the *château* to thank me once again for what I had done for the Baron von Kleist all of thirty-four years before.

As soon as the Austrians saw this deployment of twenty-four columns, or rather masses of infantry, all their redoubts opened fire on us, but their artillery was not of a sufficiently large calibre to reach us and no shot got as far as us.

General Dumouriez, with the audacity that characterized him, had carried out this deployment with the intention of letting the Austrians believe that he was showing them only his front line and that he had a second behind it. A lucky chance, which he cleverly exploited, enabled him to persuade them of this even more convincingly.

Count von Reischag,* aide-de-camp to General Clairfayt, no doubt sent to reconnoiter our positions, had imprudently advanced near to the village of Pâturages in the midst of our sharpshooters and was overtaken in his retreat by an old quartermaster from the Chamborant hussars with three stripes who took him prisoner and, holding the bridle of his horse, brought him to General Dumouriez, who greeted him with great politeness while the old hussar asked us: "Anyone want his whip? You can have it for nine francs." General Dumouriez, who had already learned from Count von Reischag who he was, said to him: "Monsieur le Comte, you shall keep your whip and permit me merely to keep your sword and send you back immediately to General Count Clairfayt as a token of my respect and my desire to bring to the conduct of the war that urbanity which the French nation has always displayed toward its enemies." Then, turning to the hussars: "Hussars, take M. de Reischag back immediately at the head of our sharpshooters!" and they set off at a gallop.

However, this position—with my twenty-four masses of infantry, each of a single fairly weak battalion in an open unprotected plain and without any cavalry, though in truth well provided with field guns—gave me considerable anxiety, particularly in the case of an attack by night, in view of the Austrian army's superiority over ours in maneuvering at this period, which its numerous cavalry made me fear even more. I intimated my anxiety to General Dumouriez, and I asked him to withdraw Frégeville and his cavalry from the village of Frameries, where he had no one facing him and was moreover at a considerable distance from our right, so as to form a short line of light cavalry behind my infantry. I reinforced my request with the consideration that since Beurnonville was covering our right with all his advance guard in the plain between Pâturages and Frameries, there could only be advantage, even if a battle on the morrow was envisaged, in Frégeville's cavalry being placed behind my infantry to support it, either when we ascended for the assault of the redoubts or if the Austrians attacked us in the plain during the night.

General Dumouriez at once agreed that he had not sufficiently estimated the size of the plain where my infantry found itself isolated, but that it was dangerous to chop and change, especially in war, and that as

* This is a misspelling of Reischach.—ED.

334

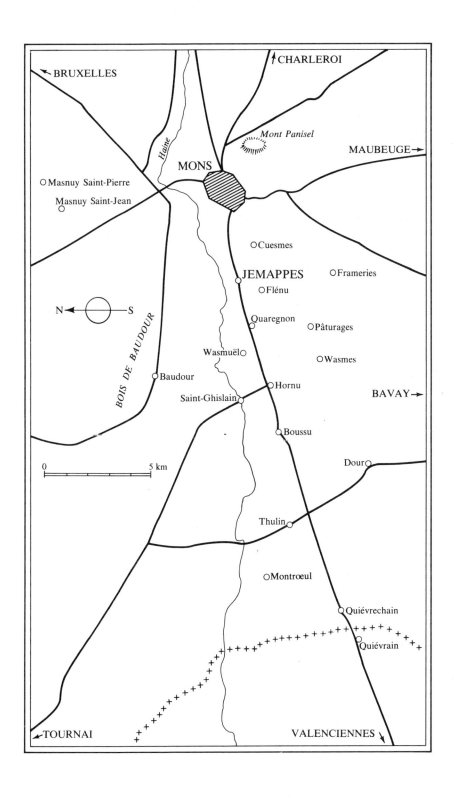

Frégeville's cavalry was tired by a long march, there would be more disadvantages than advantages in withdrawing it from Frameries, making it pack its baggage again and substituting a night of bivouacking behind my infantry for the refreshing rest it was going to enjoy in that fine village. "In short," added General Dumouriez, "all that I can do for you at present is to order Beurnonville to send you a squadron of light cavalry to carry out patrols around your infantry during the night and to reconnoiter the whole front, and especially the enemy's left, so that if he makes a move there will be enough warning for you to form your squares with your artillery in the corners and for me to fall on his flank with my advance guard while he is at grips with your squares." —"We might have a good chance in daylight," I said, "but in the dark, and given the panic that has often overtaken our inexperienced troops, I should greatly fear disorder and confusion." —"And you are only too right," General Dumouriez replied, "but one cannot cater to every eventuality and, as the soldiers say, *When the wine is opened, it must be drunk!* For myself, I don't believe in this night attack. I know the Austrians well, their prudence and their confidence in entrenchments. They have not made all these redoubts just to abandon them, and they will await us there. So have a large fire made in the midst of one of your battalions, bivouac for the night, and I am persuaded that you will spend it peacefully."

After this discussion, General Dumouriez went off to Pâturages, where his headquarters had been set up in the house of the apothecary *Lelièvre;* but such was his preoccupation with the danger of a night attack that at midnight he came and joined me at my watchfire in front of the Deux-Sèvres battalion, the very one whose commander was killed the next day, as I have already said. General Dumouriez remained there with me until daybreak; the Austrians did not stir, and there was no nocturnal attack.

Nevertheless, we later learned that a projected attack had been the subject of deliberation at a war council convened at the Austrian headquarters at the request of General Beaulieu; this general, positioned on the summit of Mount Panisel, had clearly discerned the general layout and even, it is said, all the details of our position; and these observations had led him to recommend to Duke Albert of Saxe-Teschen that he attack us on the plain during the night; but as the war council had not agreed with this advice, the matter went no further, and on November 6 dawn found the two armies in the respective positions they had occupied the preceding evening.

That day was that of the Battle of Jemappes, when victory crowned our arms.

I shall give an account of the principal actions of the battle, as was done in the catalogue of the gallery of the Palais Royal for the fine picture I commissioned from Horace Vernet, whose subject, so glorious for our arms and for the cause of the independence and the liberty of France, has not, any more than the talent of the painter, found favor with the blind rage of the self-styled patriots of February 24, 1848.*

"General Dumouriez had settled the hour of attack for noon in order to give General d'Harville's division time to arrive from Maubeuge to operate on the right of the army; but after a cannonade of three hours' duration, seeing that the Austrian regiment of Coburg Dragoons was coming down at a fast trot and seemed to be making for our artillery, General Dumouriez decided not to wait for General d'Harville and gave the whole army the order to attack immediately. Straightaway the Duc de Chartres, who commanded the center, broke up his division into columns of battalions and marched on the woods at Flénu, which covered the Austrians' center. He placed six of his battalions in reserve, and with the other eighteen he overthrew the Austrian light infantry that was defending the abatis, crossed the woods, and reached the plateau. But the Austrian infantry, supported by the artillery which was firing grapeshot, made such ravages in the front of the columns that it became impossible for them to emerge: They reentered the wood and crossed it rapidly in the greatest disorder. It was there that Colonel Dubouzet of the 104th was struck, killed on the spot, and General Drouais, who had both legs blown off and died a few hours afterward; and Colonels Dupont de Chaumont and Gustave de Montjoye, adjutants general, received bullet wounds. All would have been lost if the Austrians had been able to profit from this momentary advantage; but their infantry remained immobile, and they were satisfied with throwing in a few hussars and light infantry, who did not succeed in crossing the wood; so that while they were being contained by the resistance of the two battalions of the 83rd (Foix), commanded by Colonel Champollon and Lieutenant Colonel Villars, of the 98th (Bouillon) under Colonel Leclerc, the 29th (Dauphin) under Colonel Laroque, and some others, the Duc de Chartres, forming a chain out of light cavalry from the 3rd Regiment to stop those in flight, finally managed to rally them. It was then that, addressing them with a few of those phrases that have such an effect on the soldier's heart, he caused enthusiasm to replace fear. As the battalions were mixed up, he made one column out of them, to which he gave the name of the Mons Battalion, and presented it with the five flags he was holding in his arms belonging to battalions that had been dispersed; then, reinforced by the six battalions he had placed in reserve at the entrance to the woods, he had the charge beaten; and these same soldiers who had just for a moment been driven in fear far from the field of honor intrepidly attacked the Austrian infantry who were filling the gaps in the redoubts, penetrated them with fixed bayonets, and seized a part of the enemy artillery that the Austrian cavalry was vainly trying to bring into Mons. From this moment on victory was no longer in doubt; prodigies of valor were performed everywhere in our ranks. On the left

* The date of the rising that overthrew Louis-Philippe.—ED.

337

wing there was Colonel Thouvenot and General Ferrand, who had a horse shot from under him; on the right wing Beurnonville and Dampierre at the head of the 19th (Flanders), Colonel d'Esponchez and Lieutenant Colonel d'Armenonville; from the 71st (Vivarais) Colonel de Bannes, and from the Parisian battalions Dumouriez, who himself charged at the head of a squadron; everywhere, in short, French soldiers freely spent their blood and their courage. The enemy, driven from all its positions, finally abandoned the field of Jemappes, leaving it covered with its dead and its cannons."

At two o'clock in the afternoon, the battle had ceased at all points. My division occupied the plateau of Jemappes and all the redoubts we had just carried. It was in fairly considerable confusion—all the battalions of National Volunteers having become so intermingled, as I have just explained in my account—that it took me all the following day to sort them out and reconstitute my half-brigades. Nevertheless, we were lining the ridge overlooking Mons and our soldiers were in a manner drunk at the sight of this town at our feet, as it were, the Austrian troops retreating in the best order under the protection of their numerous and fine cavalry and filing off to reenter Mons by the long bridge that crossed the former moats.

While my division, having become the center of the army, occupied the heights of Jemappes, the left wing under General Ferrand occupied its extremity, as well as the villages of Jemappes and Cuesmes, where the Austrians had put up the most vigorous resistance to him. To our right, Beurnonville with his advance guard occupied Berthaimont, and d'Harville's division scaled Mount Panisel, which General Beaulieu had evacuated as soon as he realized that we had won the battle.

On November 7, I accompanied General Dumouriez on his triumphal entry into Mons at the head of his advance guard, the Austrians having evacuated the town during the night. At the head of the bridge over the moats we encountered the Estates of Hainault, the burgomaster and the aldermen in formal dress with the traditional ruffs round their necks, who presented the General with the keys of the town on a silver salver. Dumouriez said, stretching his hand over them:

"I shall not accept these keys, and if I touch them it is only to give you the assurance of the protection of France. The French Republic has abjured conquests, and it wants none other than to give freedom to the peoples among whom its victorious arms pursue their enemies."

After this short address, which was followed by applause, the procession moved off and entered the town. It was very splendid but rather odd because the procession was headed by two long files of monks in the midst of whom a large band of musicians, under the direction of a huge drum-major in a red costume, continuously played the march of the *Patriots of Brabant,* the well-known words of which were scarcely con-

338

sistent with the presence of the monks, since this march was none other than the *Trio of Black Magic:*

> In the heart of a cruel woman,
> Burns secret desire . . .

Behind the monks came the clergy wearing albs, then the Estates of Hainault and the town council.

We traveled the length of the street leading to the great square where the Hôtel de Ville is situated, through an immense crowd and in the midst of the warmest acclamations: *Long live France! Long live the French! Down with the Austrians!* etc.

Our advance guard followed, with the 19th of the line (the former Flanders regiment) at its head under Colonel d'Esponchez, who had been a captain in the Chartres Infantry Regiment and whom I liked a lot. When this brave regiment, which was to one side on the right, took the head of the column the other troops, seeing it arrive, began to shout: *Bravo Flanders* because the day before, at the very beginning of the battle, this regiment had met the charge of the Coburg Dragoons in open country and had continued its march after vigorously repelling them.

General Dumouriez was detained two days at Mons before he was able to procure the necessary supplies to put his army in motion.

Then my division took up quarters to the left and a little way outside Mons in the villages of Masnuy Saint-Jean and Masnuy Saint-Pierre, where I lodged with the parish priest.

Thence I followed what was called the *Brunehaut road,* which was neither paved nor pebbled and which at that time of the year was nothing but a long, straight ribbon, deep in mud, where our poor soldiers suffered a great deal and from which artillery could not be budged, so that I had to have it rejoin the main road with great difficulty.

At the end of the Brunehaut road we arrived at the village of Hornu, where I was lodged in a very pretty *château* belonging to an elderly spinster whom the Comte d'Arschot later told me he knew very well but whose name I have forgotten. When I entered the hall, she came up to me in formal dress, her hair styled in the old manner and completely powdered, and she threw herself at my feet, eyes closed, and exclaimed: "Ah! Monsieur le Général, grant me your protection! Your soldiers are ransacking my orchards and vegetable gardens." —"Madam, I shall rush there immediately and restore order, but I cannot bear to see you in that position, permit me to help you up," I said, helping her, which was rather difficult. As soon as she was on her feet and had opened her eyes, she exclaimed: "Ah, Monsieur le Général, how young you are!" —"Madam, I am only nineteen." And leaving immediately on the double with my officers, I went to chase off the marauders, who fortunately had not had time to do much damage. While I was making this expedition, this good lady learned who I was, and on my return I found her very flustered and she said: "Good heavens, Monseigneur, I little thought I should have the honor of receiving you in my house!" —"And if you had, madam, you could not have acted better; but please call me General, because there are no Monseigneurs in the armies of the Republic." —"Alas, I know that only too well! But what am I to do when I think of all you have done for me and of my profound gratitude for your protection." —"Please don't mention it, I am ashamed that it should have been necessary," Then, when these *politesses* were over, we moved from her drawing room to her dining room, where she had an excellent dinner prepared, and there the *politesses* began all over again, for she wanted to withdraw and I had great difficulty in persuading her to sit at table beside me.

The difficulty in procuring the necessary provisions for the army had led General Dumouriez to have it march in three columns. He led the right-hand column in person, following the main road from Mons to Brussels by Tubize and Braine-le-Comte. This column, comprising his advance guard and flankers, covered the movement of the artillery park. The center column, under my command, followed, as I have already said, the Brunehaut road, while that on the left under General Ferrand followed the other main road through Ath and Enghien.

The three columns were meant to reassemble at Halle whither General Dumouriez had reckoned on sending ahead Colonel Devaux, his aide-de-camp, with a few light troops to requisition food and wagons for him. But Colonel Devaux found Halle occupied in strength by the Austrian rear guard and withdrew to the right-hand column, which General Dumouriez halted until those of the center and of the left had rejoined it. Then he ordered the attack, and we had a first exchange at Halle, a second at Saint-Pieterswoluwe, and a third at Anderlech, which we did not reach until after sunset. We spent the night in the Minim monastery, where General Bender sent someone bearing a flag of truce to ask General Dumouriez that no French troops should enter Brussels before ten o'clock in the morning, which request was granted.

Our entrance into Brussels was not as spectacular as that into Mons, and despite the Belgians' satisfaction at the departure of the Austrians, it was easy to see that they were beginning to be frightened by the cost of their liberation.

General Dumouriez immediately sent some light troops to Kortemberg to reconnoiter the road to Louvain while, after a brilliant action, General Stengel seized Malines, where he found powder magazines, munitions, and a large artillery depot the Austrians had not had time to evacuate. Unfortunately, the different size of the French and the Austrian bores made the value of these resources more apparent than real.

The army was quartered in the villages around Brussels, where General Dumouriez remained a few days to prepare his march on Liège and to give time to the troops proceeding from Lille to Gand to reach Antwerp and invest the citadel before beginning a full-scale siege. General Labourdonnaye, who commanded this column, led it so slowly that General Dumouriez took advantage of his constant complaints about his health to replace him with General Miranda, to whom he had given the title of commander in chief of these troops which were constituted as the Army of the North.

During these operations on our left, General Valence arrived from Longwy, whither he had followed the retreating Prussian army, to come out on our right through Givet with the troops that had been detached from Kellermann's army. These troops formed the Army of the Ardennes, of which General Valence was commander in chief, and this army was entrusted with the siege of the fortresses of Namur.

Although they were commanders in chief, Valence and Miranda were under Dumouriez, whose own army took the name Army of Belgium.

General Henri Stengel replaced General Beurnonville in command of our advance guard: The latter had been called to the command of Kellermann's army, which took the name Army of the Moselle, and General Kellermann passed to the command of the Army of the Alps in place of General Montesquiou, whose arrest had been decreed despite his conquest of Savoy and who had taken refuge in Switzerland.

As a result, a few weeks after the Battle of Valmy, France had seven armies operating outside her frontier and stretching from the Mediterranean to the North Sea, namely:

The Army of the Var in the county of Nice, under General Anselme.

The Army of the Rhine in Mainz, commanded by General Custine.

The Army of the Moselle, marching on Trier, under General Beurnonville.

Finally, there were the three armies of the Ardennes, of Belgium, and of the North lining the left bank of the Meuse from Givet to Ruremonde, which was occupied by General Lamorlière commanding the advance guard of the Army of the North. Maastricht and Stephanswerd were still neutral, and the fortresses of Namur surrendered to General Valence of December 4.

I thought at the time, and indeed I said it with more frankness than prudence when speaking about those advantages in our situation that were only apparent, that this state of affairs would have made peace both more desirable and easier for the two belligerents to conclude had feelings not run so high, generating illusions, causing them to misunderstand their true interests and preventing them from viewing their respective positions more clearly. But each side believed that there was no safety for it but in the destruction or annihilation of the opposing side, and it was this conviction—mistaken, I believe, and fatal—that Edmund Burke so well expressed when he proclaimed in the midst of the English Parliament that it was necessary (according to him) for this war to become a *Bellum internecivum*. What I think is incontestable is that if each side had clear knowledge in advance of the results that the continuation of renewal of the war were going to produce, they would have preferred to suffer any peace whatsoever rather than run such risks, and from this assertion I no more except *Pitt and Coburg** and all the foreign Powers than the National Convention with its Committee of Public Safety, the Directory with its Ancients and Five Hundred, and the Emperor Napoleon with his victories and his absolute power.

I will be pardoned if what I write today, in exile at Claremont, brings me back to the painful reflection I have made so many times in the last six months: that if France had known the results of the rising of February 24, 1848, in advance, it would certainly have been preserved from all that it is now suffering.

But I return to 1792. The Army of Belgium resumed its march to Louvain on November 19. The Austrians had already evacuated the town, but when we entered we found such a large number of their deserters that the way was lined with white uniforms in all the streets and in the square before the Hôtel de Ville, and it seemed that Louvain was still occupied by their troops.†

Lack of supplies and money slowed down our march more than the Austrians' feeble resistance. However, we had two fairly lively combats, not to mention some skirmishes. The first occurred at Kumtich on November 22, and the second on the 27th at Varoux, above Liège, on almost the same ground as that where Marshal de Saxe won the Battle of Rocourt in 1746.

We entered Liège on November 28 amid great applause. The bulk of the army halted on the left bank of the Meuse, but the advance guard, under General Stengel, crossed over to the right bank, and there were two fiercely contested actions, which were concluded to our advantage.

* A phrase often employed in France to designate the enemy Coalition, Pitt being William Pitt, the English Prime Minister, and Coburg, Frederick-Josias, Duke of Saxe-Coburg and Austrian field marshal.—ED.

† The National Convention had passed an absurd decree that granted a state pension of a hundred francs to all the deserters from the foreign armies. Instead of a *hundred francs,* each of them was given, and it was still far too much, one of those little *assignats* for a *hundred sous,* or five francs, which were called *corsets* after the name of the man who signed them, and our soldiers laughed at these poor folk— who were immediately organized into *free companies*—as they danced around them to a round whose words go thus:

> A beneficent law
> Which we will show you
> Gives a hundred francs in bonds
> To every deserter.
> If you like to dance
> Everyone roll up.
> Drink the wine of France
> And dance with us.

My division was quartered at Herstal, the place where Pépin d'Herstal was born in the seventh century and which, as was customary at the time, had given him his name. Pépin d'Herstal, mayor of the palace under our last kings of the first dynasty, was the brother of Saint Arnoul, Bishop of Metz, the father of Charles Martel, and the grandfather of Pépin the Short, the first king of the second dynasty called the *Carolingians* in memory of his son Charlemagne, though he had only been its second king.

Our soldiers, less aware than I of these ancient associations, were not at all content in the villages along the Meuse, where at this time of the year the houses were damp and in general separated from each other by wide paths that had become deep with mud. Consequently, our poor soldiers, who often lacked even boots, demanded the distribution of clogs, which I could obtain only with great difficulty and always in too small quantities.

The army was then in a state of want that increased daily. General Dumouriez had failed in all his negotiations to procure supplies and money. He says in his *Mémoires* that there only remained fourteen thousand francs in the army coffers when he arrived at Brussels and that he had difficulty in scraping together eighty thousand to leave. Arms were lacking to such a degree that he took the dragoons' rifles to arm the free companies formed from Austrian deserters. It was not only the marches and the operations of the army which were hindered by this lack of supplies, but its moral state and discipline, which increasingly deteriorated. Theft and marauding increased with necessity, and we could no longer manage to control them. The army's number of effectives constantly decreased by desertion, not to the enemy, because there was none of this, but back to France whither soldiers from the corps of National Volunteers just went off without leave of absence. Often even their officers thought no more of it, and we had no way of punishing them or even of having them brought back to their units. I believe that given the prevailing climate of opinion, our right to do so would have been contested, but as there was no police force, the question could not arise. So the corps of National Volunteers went to pieces before our very eyes, and in my division I had two battalions of them, of which one was reduced to *forty-two* men and the other to *twenty-six*.

Better discipline was maintained among the troops of the line, and there at least there was little or no desertion. But there was no recruitment either, and the losses incurred were not replaced. It was even worse with our cavalry, too few in number at the best of times, even when the regiments were maintained at full strength in men able to mount a horse and above all in horses. I will give an idea of the reduction it underwent if I say that the 2nd Hussars (Chamborant) had entered the campaign three squadrons strong, each consisting of a hundred and sixty mounted men, and that in the month of March 1793 I saw this same regiment reduced to a showing of *seventy-eight* mounted men, plus I do not know how many on foot, performing, in the absence of horses, the function of light infantry with their little rifles on their belt pistols; and even of these arms there was such a deficiency that scarcely a man had all three.

The administration of the armies was in such confusion, such disorder, that one could say it was nonexistent, and seeing it at close quarters as I did, it would have been impossible to imagine how we managed to achieve the results we did. As there were no regulations defining functions and limiting encroachments, there resulted an internecine war in which each division wanted either to attract everything to itself or to pass the burden on to others, so that while the newspapers were resounding with these administrative conflicts, the poor army was lacking in everything and had no organized means of supply in operation. There were no army wagons—what the Germans call *Führ-wesen*—for baggage, or food, or fodder, or for anything at all apart from twelve or fifteen four-wheeled carts covered in red tarpaulin that served as *ambulances* for the wounded.

The lack of a regular organization for the supply of foodstuffs often exposed us to receiving rations either insufficient or of poor quality. From this resulted at once great discomfort and a great slackening of the discipline and control of the army. When the soldiers lacked everything and were reduced for their nourishment to what they termed the *worst cuts,* it became very difficult, if not impossible, to prevent them from seeking to recoup at the expense of the neighboring farms and villages, where at this time they committed all sorts of thefts and disorderly acts.

Shortly after my arrival at Liège, I received a letter from my father informing me of an occurrence that was very painful for all of us and for which he thought he had need of my presence in Paris. He enjoined me to profit from my division's inactivity in its quarters at Herstal to seek leave of absence and to proceed to Paris as quickly as I could. I left immediately with my brother the Duc de Montpensier.

To explain the nature of this incident, I must take up the story earlier.

For a long time political events, succeeding each other with such rapidity, had caused Mme de Genlis great alarm. She believed her personal safety was in much greater jeopardy than it really was, and each new crisis renewed her desire to withdraw to a foreign country. In the month of October 1791, she profited from the amount of calm that followed Louis XVI's acceptance of the Constitution to tell my father that my sister's health—she was then fourteen years old—required her to take the waters of Bath in England. My father was very reluctant to consent, and he did so only on the express condition that she would bring my sister back at the end of a month.

I was then at Valenciennes with my regiment, and as soon as Mme de Genlis had obtained my father's consent, she hastened her departure so much that I was not informed of her plans until she had already left Paris to take my sister to England. I proceeded immediately with my brother to Calais, and we arrived there just when they were about to board the packet, and we were consequently too late to have any chance of keeping them in France.

My efforts to convince Mme de Genlis of the necessity of a prompt return had no success because instead of a month, she began by spending three in Bath; and despite my father's entreaties and commands, she then proceeded to install herself at Bury Saint-Edmunds in the county of Suffolk, where she rented a small house in the middle of the town without either my father or myself having been able to ascertain the reasons for this bizarre choice, and without her being able to put forward either reasons or pretexts for prolonging her stay in England. Always, she merely announced that she would soon be returning, and these inexplicable delays caused my father the keenest exasperation.

I shall not embark on the details of this unhappy struggle and shall merely say that after putting up with it for *thirteen months* without success, my father decided in the month of November 1792 to take the severe step by which he prevailed upon Mme de Genlis to leave immediately and return to France with my sister.

He sent M. Hugues Maret (later Duc de Bassano), who had been the Duc de Biron's secretary, to England, and he invested him with power of attorney to take legal action to force Mme de Genlis to restore the person of his daughter to him. Immediately upon his arrival, M. Maret notified Mme de Genlis of the nature of his mission, and she departed precipitately with my sister, returning to Paris, where she proceeded, as though nothing had happened, to install herself at Belle-Chasse, in the house where she had lived before her departure for Bath and the one where she had for so long presided over our education.

On their arrival, in accordance with the current regulations, their passports were sent to the Hôtel de Ville, and as soon as the Council of the Commune of Paris had taken cognizance of the matter, it had them arrested and brought before them immediately. They scarcely had time to notify my father, and he rushed to the Hôtel de Ville, where he found that they had been brought into the great chamber of the Commune and were being questioned. There he learned something of which they as well as he were ignorant, namely, that as the result of the length of time that my sister and Mme de Genlis had spent in England without returning to France, they had been placed on the list of *émigrés*. My father was told that they would have to be incarcerated and remain in prison until a decision had been reached on the basis of the reasons he had given for having their names removed from the list. However, my father got them to agree to forego incarceration by promising to get them out of Paris within twenty-four hours and from French territory within five days. He sent them to Raincy immediately to await me there.

My father's intention in having me return from Liège was that I should conduct them to Belgium, where he rightly considered that my sister would be outside French territory without, however, ceasing to be under the protection of our colors, and that there she could conveniently wait till she had been deleted from the list. He was persuaded that this deletion would not meet with any difficulties, and in this he was wrong because it was never obtained, and when I left France, my sister and Mme de Genlis were still included in the list of *émigrés*. The result was that after we had lost the Battle of Neerwinden and Belgium had fallen back into Austrian hands, I was obliged to hand over my sister and Mme de Genlis to their outposts, where they were given passports to retire to Switzerland, which was still a neutral country.

Arriving in Paris on December 2, 1792, I found my father even more distressed by his situation than when I had returned to the army two months previously. He was very angry with Mme de Genlis, whose obstinacy in prolonging her stay in England despite his exhortations and explicit orders had placed my sister in a position that was breaking his heart; and he told me that Mme de Genlis reciprocated his annoyance; that all direct communications between them had ceased and that he had been impatiently waiting for me to arrange my sister's departure and escort her to Belgium. He said that he consented to Mme de Genlis's accompanying her on the journey and remaining in Belgium with her if it suited her, and that if it did not, he would find another lady to accompany my sister to Belgium until she had been crossed off the list of *émigrés,* which would allow him to have her brought back to France and work out with my mother (from whom, as I have already said, he was unfortunately separated) the arrangements to be made as regards my sister.

While I was conversing with my father in his apartments overlooking the gardens of the Palais Royal, we heard the horrible cry *Capet to the guillotine* uttered by the furious bands who were roaming through Paris demanding *the trial* and *the head of the King,* and I said to him that it was only in Paris that these horrible cries were to be heard and that there were no similar demonstrations in any other town in France. He replied that he believed it but that those towns were passive, that it was in Paris that everything was decided, and that the King's trial was inevitable and imminent. He was only too right, because M. Mailhe had already made that terrible report in which he concluded that the National Convention should bring Louis XVI before its bar and try him itself, as Charles I's parliament had done in England, thereby justifying what has been said so many times about the irresistible force of precedent.

I adjured my father anew to take no part in this trial and to abstain from it by disqualifying himself *as a relative.* —"Alas," he replied, "if my kinship were close enough to fall within the limits prescribed by the law for disqualification, the method would be excellent; but I have already

346

consulted the lawyers, and it is only too clear that in terms of the law we are no longer related and that consequently one cannot base a disqualification on a relationship the law does not recognize as such." My father told me that he was all the more troubled to be a member of the National Convention in that deep down he believed that Louis XVI was in league with the enemies of France, that he had carried on communications with them with the intention of overthrowing the Constitution and carrying out the Counterrevolution, and that if he were called upon to pronounce on the question of guilt based on these facts, he could only reply in the affirmative. But he added that if they then passed (as he had no doubt that they would) to calling on him to apply a penalty to that guilt, *there* (and I well recollect his expression) *his difficulties and agonies would begin, and he would no longer know how to extricate himself.*

I replied that to my way of thinking there could be no difficulty in applying the penalty attached to this crime unless the previous legislation defining the acts that constituted it had not determined the penalty applicable to those found guilty of having committed those acts; for only the absolute silence of previous laws on the penalty applicable to these acts could authorize or justify an arbitrary evaluation of that penalty by those called upon to pronounce it.

I added that the National Convention could in no way regard itself as being covered by this last hypothesis in relation to King Louis XVI given that the previous legislation (the Constitution of 1791), which was all that could be invoked to render the King liable to any penalty at all, had explicitly defined the acts that could expose him to it, as well as the nature and extent of the penalty that could be incurred by such acts. To demonstrate that such reasoning was irrefutable, I cited Articles 6 and 7 of the Constitution of 1791,* and I said that I could not comprehend how, either according to law or justice, Louis XVI, who had now forfeited the throne, could have to suffer another penalty in addition to the one he was already paying *by virtue of his forfeiture.*

My father admitted that my reasoning was just and sound, but he considered that the Constitution of 1791 had fallen into such disrepute that nothing could be more impolitic and maladroit than to draw conclusions favorable to Louis XVI from it, particularly when the general opinion was that this Prince had broken his oath by acting in collusion

---

* Article 6. "If the King places himself at the head of an army and leads it against the nation or if he does not explicitly oppose such an enterprise carried out in his name, he will be deemed to have abdicated."

Article 8. "After explicit or presumed abdication, the King will be classed as an ordinary citizen and as such may, for actions subsequent to his abdication, be accused and tried."

I do not cite Article 7 because it relates only to the single case where the King, having left the kingdom and not having returned within a time limit to be fixed by a proclamation of the legislative body, would in that case likewise be deemed to have *abdicated,* that is to say, *forfeited, the Crown.*

with the foreign Powers and the *émigrés* and, he added, that at the opening of the discussion M. Morisson had tried, without the slightest success, to advance at the bar of the Convention the line of argument I had just put forward.*

My father then told me that when he heard me arguing like that on the present situation, it seemed to him I had just fallen from the clouds without having any idea of what was happening on earth; that, nevertheless, I could not be ignorant of the fact that here they were currently prey to the most violent passions, and that to imagine you could calm or repress them by ordinary arguments about justice and legality was unfortunately just an absurd impossibility; that when the Convention had committed itself so deeply to this unhappy trial and declared so many times that it was having it prepared by its Committees, and already the main discussion was about to open, one could no longer say to it that it should abandon the trial and baldly declare that Louis XVI was not liable to any other penalty than that of *forfeiting the throne;* that it was therefore necessary to seek another way of saving the life of that unfortunate Prince (which I can say in conscience he sincerely desired), since any direct and open attempt would merely serve to increase the fury and the power of those who wanted his death at any price and to intimidate those who did not desire it; that things being as they were, the trial had to run its course and that it was only in the sentence, after the inevitable declaration of guilt, that one might manage to substitute *detention* for *capital punishment* on the grounds that it was advantageous to keep Louis XVI as a hostage and, by preserving his life, to prevent the royalist or antirepublican parties from attempting to proclaim another King.

My father added that this was the intention, or rather the wish, of the presumptive majority of the National Convention; but that unfortunately for him, his political affiliations kept him on the opposite side; that there were so many people in the other camp who had openly made themselves his personal enemies that he could not join them; and that in conclusion, he saw no other hope for himself than that of finding a plausible pretext to absent himself from the trial but that he despaired of finding one, since he knew that his disqualification on grounds of kinship was not admissible.

We had a long discussion on this unhappy subject, in the course of which he had the idea (I stress that it was *his* and not *mine* because that is the unadulterated truth) of declaring that he would abstain from voting in the trial because he feared that certain prior disagreements between Louis XVI and himself had put him in the position of being considered not entirely exempt from all personal animosity, and therefore of not

* M. Morisson, deputy for the Department of Gers to the National Convention, was in effect the first to refuse to take any part in the trial of Louis XVI; as soon as the debate opened on M. Mailhe's report, he based his opinion on the Constitution of 1792, as I had myself done in my conversation with my father. . . .

possessing a guarantee of impartiality required in such a case. But he did not want to follow up this happy inspiration unless some other member of the National Convention (whose position *vis-à-vis* the King was in some way analogous to his own) made a similar declaration of his own; then he said to me: "If Pétion, for example, whom the King stripped of his office of mayor of Paris on the grounds that he displayed personal enmity to him, wanted to adopt the same course of action and give the same reasons for it, that could settle the whole matter. However, it is a fact that I cannot approach him on the subject because I am not on speaking terms with him and I belong to the party to which he is politically opposed. But for you this is not a problem. You know him, so go find him and propose to him in a perfectly straightforward manner *on my behalf* that we agree, through your mediation, separately but simultaneously to declare that we will abstain from taking part in the trial for the reasons we have just enumerated. After all," he added, "Pétion is a fairly decent chap, and perhaps he will be as glad as I to seize a good way of getting out of this cruel dilemma."

It was too late to go there that evening, but very early next morning, December 3, I made my way to Pétion's place. He lodged in a house that stood at right angles to the Hôtel de Talleyrand (then the Hôtel de l'Infantado) and that has since been demolished to give access to the little Place de Saint-Florentin for the Rue de Rivoli and the Terrace des Feuillants. I found him in shirtsleeves, a shaving brush in his hand, shaving himself in a square mirror hooked onto his window. If I allow myself to run on with details of such little importance, it is to convey the extent to which the most insignificant circumstances of this mournful period have remained painfully imprinted in my memory.

Pétion seemed very glad to see me, but very surprised; when I told him that I had come on my father's behalf he said: "Is it really he who sends you here? I can't get over it." —"Yes, it is he. I arrived yesterday from the army, summoned in all haste to come and take charge of my sister here and escort her to Belgium, where she can wait till she is removed from the list of *émigrés,* under the protection of our colors." —"There is nothing else to do," he told me, "and I could not give better advice." —"I believe it," I said, "but it is not about that that I have come to speak to you. Last night I had a long conversation with my father in which once more, as I had already done two months ago, and with all the force at my disposal, I expressed the extreme repugnance I would feel at seeing him give any vote at all in the King's trial. . . ." —"Ah! You have done well!" Pétion exclaimed, interrupting me, "this advice is that of a good son and a good citizen, because this unfortunate trial is a cruel complication for all of us, your father above all. Also, he must know that we have done everything either to avoid or at least to delay it; but there is no way out: We are driven to it with a madness and fury you cannot imagine, especially as you have been absent from Paris for some time—luckily for you." —"I can imagine it only too well," I said, sighing, "but what I have come to say to you is that my father shares this repugnance, and having regard for your position and what he knows of your character, he believes that you, too, must feel it." —"As to the repugnance, he is correct; but as to my position, it is very different from his own." —"No doubt, but there is an analogy in this sense at least: that as the King has displayed animosity to you whom he regards as his *personal enemy* and as no more secret was made at the Tuileries of the hatred that was borne my father, there would be grounds there, in these previous quarrels, for a fear to arise, on your part as on his, that neither of you is sufficiently exempt from personal animosity toward the King to be certain of displaying that calm impartiality of which a judge must give the most complete assurance." —"Yes," said Pétion, "I agree there is some truth in what you say; but it is far more true in your father's case than in mine, because the Châtelet's inquiry into the rising of October 5 and all their calumnies against him are an entirely different matter from my dismissal as mayor of Paris for my so-called personal enmity, which caused me very little concern." —"All right, it may only be a pretext as far as you are concerned, but if you want to take advantage of it as a reason for your absence from the trial, I am authorized by my father to tell you that for his part he will make the same declaration and without the slightest appearance of prearrangement with you. Moreover, I think you would be able to find other allies among your friends, who would be delighted to do as much, and that M. Manuel, for example, who is said to be very embarrassed by that very bitter and hostile letter he addressed to the King which has become public, also would be wise to make such a declaration and abstain from being a judge." —"I do not doubt that he ardently desires it," Pétion said, "but at the moment he is fully as unpopular as I, and to that extent I prefer not to meddle in anything he sees fit to do. Our position becomes more and more frightening; every day the Commune of Paris insults the National Convention; it threatens to have it decimated and all of us massacred. Its power increases in proportion as ours diminishes—if indeed we have any left. For my part, I will brave the storm as far as I can; but in such times I can no more say what I will do than what I will not do. Kindly tell your father, from me, that I have no other reply to give his message; that although I deplore seeing him occupy the place where he sits in the Convention, I am not, nor ever shall be, his personal enemy, and of this I do not think I can give him better proof than that of counseling him to abstain from and not to appear at the King's trial; but he must not count on me to do the same. As for you, I advise you to make off as quickly as you can because you are suspected of sharing our beliefs." —"I am proud of it." —"That is very well said, but be off, and lose no time in escorting your sister to Belgium."*

* Manuel did not vote for the death of the King but that he be detained in a fortress as long as the safety of the State did not permit him to be cast on foreign soil

350

When I reported this conversation to my father, he said to me: "I expected it. I should have expected it. You see what sort of people they are. He is not my enemy! I well believe it, poor good-natured chap. But he is surrounded by those who are my relentless enemies. Disqualify myself or abstain alone; they would not let me get away with it!" —"Ah!" I said, "what will not be forgiven you is appearing at the trial. Forgive me for saying so frankly, in the outpouring of my heart, it is those with whom you vote whom you fear will not let you get away with it." —"And how should it be otherwise when they are now the only ones who are not our enemies!" —"Would to God they were your friends! For my part, they do not inspire me with the slightest confidence." —"Ah! there you go again with your infatuation for the Girondins."

I tried anew, but with no more success, to engage him to undertake a trip with all of us to the United States of America since we could now make no other, the whole of Europe being closed to us even before the fatal trial of Louis XVI. I told him that for my part, now that I had had the good fortune of repaying my debt to the Fatherland by helping to free all territory from invasion by foreign armies, I had no further objection to a temporary expatriation, and despite my regret at parting from my comrades in arms, the lack of discipline and state of disorder in our armies, which grew worse each day, was an additional reason for resigning myself to it; also, that I did not want to hide from him the extent to which I was disgusted with everything I saw and, perhaps even more, by everything that I foresaw.

To all this my father objected, first that he could only live in France and that the prospect of any expatriation, especially across the seas and in America, was odious to him; then, that his ruined financial state, the nonpayment of rent due to him, the necessity for him to supervise the operations resulting from the concordat he had reached with his creditors, to whom he had made over the majority of his assets, were reasons enough why this project was absolutely impracticable; and that, moreover, he was sure his party would not quietly let him leave the National Convention. I therefore had to abandon all further insistence on this point.

The time limit for my sister to leave France was about to expire, and I think that it even had already. She was waiting for me at Raincy with Mme de Genlis. On December 3, the day after my arrival in Paris and the same day I had been at Pétion's, I went to dine there with my father, and we both slept there.

---

where he *should be delivered to his remorse!* Manuel perished on the revolutionary scaffold.

Pétion voted for the death penalty. Having escaped arrest, he was *outlawed*. He managed to hide himself in the quarries of Saint-Émilion, near Bordeaux. Some claim that there he died of hunger, others that savage dogs were unleashed there and that they found him, ripped him to pieces, and devoured him . . . !

As my father no longer wished to speak to Mme de Genlis, with whom he was very angry, I had to serve as intermediary between them. I carried the messages, requests, and replies from one room to another, and it was thus that we concerted the arrangements for the journey and for a very modest temporary establishment in Belgium. It was agreed that my sister and I, with Mme de Genlis, should leave early the next morning, and that to avoid reappearing in Paris, we should go straight from Raincy to Le Bourget across country and that there we should take the main Flanders road, sleeping at Mons the same night and the next at Tournay. We had chosen this town to install ourselves as being at once near to the French frontier and removed from the continual coming and going along the direct line of communication between Brussels and Paris.

In accordance with my father's wishes, my brother Montpensier remained behind with him in Paris.

At the moment of our departure from Raincy, Mme de Genlis passed in front of my father and made him a deep bow, which my father returned without speaking; my sister and I bade my father farewell. He took his leave of us tenderly. He was very moved and very sad, and we were all profoundly so. I already had my foot on the first step of the staircase to go down when my father, who remained above, called me back and said (I can still hear his words):

"Adieu, my dear Chartres, if you can think of some way to get me out of this wretched trial, it would be a real comfort to me." Then he commended my sister to me once more, and we left . . . !

It was Tuesday, December 4, 1792. I was not to see my father again . . . !

On our arrival at Tournay, I rented a furnished house in the triangular town square, and having installed my sister and Mme de Genlis and recommended them to the care of the worthy General O'Moran,* who was the commander of this town, I hastened to return to Liège, where my presence was necessary to complete the arrangements for the winter quarters of my division. As soon as they were completed, I returned to Tournay, where I remained until I returned to the army the following February.

Although my father wrote to me fairly frequently, it was not by a letter from him but only by a little evening paper, which gave a compressed and very incomplete account of the sittings of the National Convention, that I learned that in the sitting of December 16 it had pronounced, on Buzot's proposition, that all the Bourbons remaining in France should be ban-

* Having briefly been a commander in chief, General O'Moran suffered the common fate in this terrible period and perished on the revolutionary scaffold in 1794. While he was commander at Tournay, he had as his aide-de-camp M. de Jouey, then a captain, who became a celebrated man of letters and my librarian at the Louvre. M. de Jouey was saved only by a swift flight to Switzerland, where I saw him again when I was at Bremgarten with M. de Montesquiou.

ished or excluded from French territory, while guaranteeing their right to dispose freely of their goods and property. Those who were then detained in the Temple were, notwithstanding, excepted from this measure, the Convention reserving to itself the right to determine their fate later.

The fact of our banishment or exclusion from French territory was therefore certain, though there could have been, and in fact was, some difference between the version in the little paper, which only gave the substance of the order, and the terms in which it was couched.* I

* In the sitting of Wednesday, December 16, 1792, the National Convention, on Thuriot's proposal, passed the following decree unanimously, in a burst of enthusiasm:

"The National Convention decrees that whosoever proposes to destroy the territorial integrity of the French Republic or to detach its constituent parts to join them to a foreign country shall be punished by death."

Immediately Buzot, one of the principal adherents of the Girondin party, said from his seat:

"Citizens, you have done well to promulgate this law against those who would attempt to dismember the Empire; but denunciations of royalists are also being made to you, and this decree does not affect them. With your permission I shall propose a new measure, and one which I believe to be salutary." (Yes, yes! the whole Assembly replied.)

Then Buzot ascended the rostrum and made his proposal at the end of a long speech . . . :

"I demand that Philippe and his sons, etc., should leave the Republic and support elsewhere the misfortune of having been born near to the throne, of having been acquainted with its precepts and imbued with its example; the misfortune of bearing a name that may serve as a rallying point for factious men or emissaries of the neighboring Powers, a name with which it is no longer tolerable that the ears of free men should be affronted!"

The publication of Buzot's speech was called for, as was a decision that his proposal be postponed.

The Girondin party wanted to carry the measure by surprise, while the Mountain wanted to gain time to find ways of annulling it.

Louvet immediately opposed the adjournment and presented Buzot's proposal in the form of a decree, insisting that it immediately be put to the vote.

Saint-Just, the true mouthpiece of the Mountain, vigorously supported the adjournment, while deferring the family's banishment till a later date.

. . . .

[After a lively debate, a two days' adjournment was decreed.]

This two days' adjournment gave the Montagnard party time to activate the Commune of Paris. The forty-eight sections assembled, and they all agreed to demand the total withdrawal of the decree.

The discussion, having been resumed by the Convention in the sitting of Wednesday, December 19, 1792, was interrupted by the arrival of the mayor of Paris followed by a fairly large crowd, which, as usual, promptly filled all the entrances and even the lobbies of the chamber. Then the president (Defermon) caused the following letter to be read:

"Nicholas Chambon, Mayor of Paris, to the President of the National Convention.

"I have the honor of announcing to you that the commissioners of the forty-eight sections, whom I have the honor of accompanying, are awaiting the Convention's orders to present a petition concerning the repeal of the decree passed last Sunday." (Some applause from the galleries.)

understood too well the state of affairs and of the parties to be able to doubt that this measure was adopted in a spirit of hostility toward my father and our family. However, I immediately considered it as *a sheet anchor* in the midst of the fearful storm I saw gathering around our heads. Such I judged it to be, especially for my father, for whom I thought it opened an honorable way of getting out of the National Convention and consequently of the deplorable trial in which it was engaged. The discussions I had had with him recently left me in no doubt concerning the sincerity of his desire to get out of it, but I could no more doubt his extreme reluctance to leave Paris and France and retire to the United

---

The majority party of the Convention, although plainly intimidated by this demonstration, nevertheless wished to give the appearance of adopting what, in the language of the day, was called *a lofty stance,* and it proudly passed to the order of the day. Then it heard the report of Lebrun, the Minister of Foreign Affairs, on the state of diplomatic relations with England. But this report was interrupted by Basire, who, having circulated among the groups around the chamber, wished to make known to the Assembly the state of mind in which he had found them. This request stirred up a new storm. However, the Assembly decided that Basire should be heard, and he was. Afterward Lebrun resumed the reading of his report and finished it in peace.

When it was finished, Pétion ascended the rostrum and in a pretty skillful speech hinted to his own majority party that they must give way and that there was no way of avoiding the repeal of the decree other than that of adopting a half-measure that would in some way save appearances but that would come to the same thing. This half-measure was that the whole matter should be postponed until after the judgment of *the former King.*

This proposal was greeted by repeated cheers. A large part of the Assembly stood up and asked to proceed to the vote. But Kersaint appeared at the rostrum, and it was agreed to hear him; he concluded the few lines he uttered with the following: "You are sensible of the fact that you cannot, without committing an injustice, include all the Capets, women and children, indiscriminately, in this proscription. It is on these grounds that I demand that the execution of the decree be suspended." (*Applause.*)

Then Buzot appeared at the rostrum to propose, as he said, some amendments; but the Assembly did not wish to hear him and closed the discussion. Then, almost unanimously, it voted for adjournment and suspension.

Afterward, the mayor of Paris, Chambon, was brought to the bar and informed by the president that in the course of the debate, Basire and Tallien had accused him of instigating the assembly of the sections, but these two deputies promptly denied it. The mayor of Paris attested that this assembly had been spontaneous, and the Assembly, satisfied with this explanation, offered him *the honors of the sitting.*

After this sitting, the discussion was never resumed, and the desire, although only suspended, became in fact *a dead letter* and there was no longer any question of it. I have gone into such detail in order to give an understanding of the attitude of the various parties toward my father. The Gironde wanted only to remove him from the Mountain, and by banishing all our family and by a great display of republican sentiments, to free themselves of the suspicion of paving the way for the restoration of the monarchy and even to throw it onto their opponents and those who should oppose banishment. The Mountain, on the other hand, wished to keep my father in their midst in order to ruin him by forcing him to compromise himself in the trial of the King and thereby make it impossible for him to come to terms with any

States of America, the sole asylum remaining open to him after the part that he had taken in the Revolution. As he had written nothing to me, had not given me any instructions, and had not even informed me that the Convention had decreed our banishment—though as to this I neither had nor could have had any doubts—I decided to take an immediate step that would put my submission to the decree on record before any injunction on his part supervened, forbidding me to do so and preventing me from carrying out my personal desire to go off to America.

Accordingly, I decided to write directly to the president of the National Convention, and I said in my letter that I had learned from the papers of the decree enjoining us to leave France and withdraw immediately from her armies; that however bitterly I regretted parting from my companions in arms, I requested him to inform the National Convention of my entire submission to what it had thought necessary to prescribe in the interests of France's tranquillity and for the consolidation of that liberty it had so gloriously conquered; that, independent of all the parties and animated by the same devotion to the Fatherland and the sacred cause of liberty as that of which my father had ceaselessly given so many proofs, I would carry with me on foreign soil, together with the hope that more propitious times would reopen the gates of France to me, the remembrance—of such

---

of the parties. A fact that can leave no doubt as to the sad truth of this assertion is that four months afterward, when a decree for the arrest and indefinite detention of all the family in the strongholds of Marseille had replaced that banishment—which was as completely forgotten as if it had never been pronounced—my father and brothers were allowed to languish in the dungeons of Fort Saint-Jean, and it seemed that no more thought was given to them than if they had never existed; and they remained forgotten until the Girondins were sacrificed.

But when six months later, in the sitting of October 3, 1793, the Convention, after hearing Amar's report, passed the horrifying decree by which it sent forty-five of its Girondin colleagues to the Revolutionary Tribunal, that is, to certain death, Billaud-Varennes got up and said:

"The time has come when all the conspirators should be made known and struck down. I demand that we do not pass over in silence a man who has been forgotten, despite the numerous facts that bear witness against him. I demand that d'Orléans be sent to the Revolutionary Tribunal together with the other conspirators." (*Lively applause.*)

"This proposal is decreed."

Thus it was that the name of my father was added to that fatal list without discussion, without reflection, without a single voice being raised against this barbarous addition! . . . And what adds still further to the horror it must inspire is that although it was common knowledge that my father never had dealings whatsoever with the Girondins, and that on the contrary, they had always been his opponents and indeed his political enemies, it was nevertheless under the same indictment and under the same charges that my father was condemned like them and suffered the same fate a few days later . . . and one of the charges being that of attempting to place the Duke of York on the throne of France, my father replied coldly to the president of the Tribunal (the Marquis d'Antonelle, whom he knew and who had dined at his table many times): "Really, Monsieur le Président, this is no more than a bad joke, and you know it better than anyone."

355

consolation to me—that before leaving her I had had the good fortune to fight for her and to help deliver her from the foreign invasion over which she had just triumphed.

When I wrote this letter, I did not know that my father had been temporarily excepted from the decree and that the discussion relative to his status as a representative of the people had been adjourned for two days. Thus, when I wrote to him sending him a copy of my letter to the president of the Convention, I did not question that he would have to leave with us, and I was already asking him which port I should make for with my sister to join him and my brothers, both of whom were in Paris. I commiserated with him on the vexation that I knew only too well he would feel in having to leave France and set sail for America, but added that he must pardon me for saying to him that deep down I regarded this decree of banishment as *a heaven-sent opportunity* for himself and for us. However, as I thought it very important that at all events my letter should safely reach the president and be published in *le Moniteur* (because he would be obliged to communicate it to the Assembly), I thought it prudent not to let it pass through my father's hands and to act in such a way that he would not even know of my letter's existence until after it had been delivered to the president.

Accordingly I sent my personal valet (Gardanne) to Paris entrusted with my two letters, and as I knew my father's habits well enough to know that he did not go to the Convention before eleven o'clock and often not even before noon, I arranged Gardanne's trip in such a way as to be sure he would reach Paris at nine o'clock in the morning. I charged him not to let himself be seen, either at the Palais Royal or at my father's stables, until he had presented himself at the chamber of the National Convention and delivered my letter to the president or deposited it on his desk if he had not yet arrived. All this was worked out to assure the result I desired, but Providence ordained otherwise, to my father's detriment and our own; for I still believe that if my letter had reached the president and had become public before the Convention had voted for the suspension of the decree, it would have ensured its execution and our departure for America.

The decree had been passed during the sitting of Sunday, December 16. I received news of it at Tournay during the evening of Sunday the 17th, and Gardanne left for Paris during the course of Tuesday the 18th. Consequently, he arrived there early on Wednesday the 19th, that is to say, on the morning of the very day when, during the afternoon, the Convention voted to suspend the decree banishing us.

By a wretched twist of fate my father, who quite rightly did not want to attend a sitting devoted to a discussion so directly concerning him, on that day, for reasons unknown to me, went to the chamber of the Convention as early as ten o'clock, and there he found Gardanne, who was asking to be allowed in. "What are you doing here, Gardanne?" he asked as soon as he saw him. "Is my son in Paris?" —"No," Gardanne replied, "he is at Tournay, but he has entrusted me with a letter for you, which I was going to bring you, and with another for the president of the National Convention; and it is to deliver the latter that I have come here." —"Very well, I will take charge of it," said my father, "give me both letters and go and wait for me at the Palais Royal." Gardanne handed them to him and went off. My father proceeded to read them in a private room and he suppressed the one I had addressed to the president of the Convention. The next day, Thursday the 20th—that is to say, after the execution of the decree had been suspended, which he rightly considered as annulling it—he sent Gardanne back to me at Tournay with his reply, which had no trace of pique because he never felt any. He merely told me that this business of banishment was *un coup manqué* of his enemies and that the matter would not arise again; that it would have been very awkward if my letter had been taken as a *resignation* of my commission as a lieutenant general; that above all, he desired that I not come to Paris (which I was not at all tempted to do) and that I wait at Tournay till the resumption of military operations brought me back quite naturally to army duties.

My brother Montpensier, who was in Paris and whose political opinions (much modified since) were then nearer to those of my father than to my own, despite the tender affection that always kept us so sincerely united throughout his life, sent me word that my father had been more pained than angered by the move I had attempted, and it had upset him; he said that if it had run its course the consequences could have been disastrous, that it was impossible to calculate what would have come of it in Paris, where tempers had reached a pitch of which he was persuaded I did not have a clear idea; that, to be sure, justice was still generally accorded to my patriotism and to the sincerity of my attachment to the cause of liberty but that, nevertheless, my political leanings were well known and caused him considerable embarrassment; that I was thought to be hypnotized by the seductive eloquence with which the Girondins masked their real plans, and that my father was assailed with complaints and reproaches from those who were not hostile to us and with threats from those who detested us.

This sorry picture was only too accurate, and shortly afterward I received striking confirmation of it from an incident I shall relate.

One evening, very late, in my sister's house in Tournay where I was staying, I was told that an army doctor wanted to see me immediately and in private. I had never seen him before, but I bade them show him into my apartments. He told me that he had been sent by M. Basire, deputy for the Côte-d'Or, whom I scarcely knew, in order to convey a verbal communication of particular importance to me and mine and that he had made a slight detour so as to pass through Tournay without being noticed; that he had come to speak with me not only on behalf of M. Basire, but also on behalf of some of his political friends who sat like him

357

with the Mountain, including Danton, Camille Desmoulins, Delacroix, etc.—in short, those who perished with him on the revolutionary scaffold in 1794.*

The doctor (whose name I have forgotten) told me that he had been instructed to warn me that a political storm against me was secretly brewing that merited my most serious attention, since unless I managed to disperse it some way or other, I must expect it to break sooner or later with the most fatal consequences, not only for myself but for my father and those close to me. I exclaimed at once that I could not believe such an unfair and barbarous plot was possible. The doctor replied, too rightly, that in the times in which we lived one could believe anything and expect anything; but that he was merely a messenger charged by powerful men who wished me well to warn me of the existence of a source of irritation which it was in our interests to soothe and which, he knew, made my father very anxious; that this source of irritation had two main causes: one was my supposed links with the Girondin party, the other was the efforts I was known to have made to deter my father from taking part in the King's trial.

I replied to him in turn that since he was only a messenger, I would tell him only facts; that the first reason he cited for this source of irritation was an invention of our enemies; that I had no connection whatsoever with the Girondin party nor with any other party, a fact of which those who sent him could scarcely be ignorant; that it was true that I knew two or three of them, just as I knew some from all the other parties, but that having withdrawn to Tournay and living in complete isolation from all society, I did not maintain political relations with anyone; and I confined myself to lamenting everything that seemed to me to distort and drench with blood the cause of our country's liberty, which I served with zeal and loyalty in equal proportion; that as to the second cause of the irritation to which he referred, stemming from what had been picked up concerning what may have passed between my father and myself relative to the King's trial, since it was against me alone that this irritation could be directed and since it was evident that it could not touch my father, I would abstain from saying anything to him on that subject; that I merely begged him to thank M. Basire and his friends for the warning he had just given me on their behalf and asked him whether they had sent me any

---

* I wish to consign here the record of some words M. Basire spoke concerning me in the National Convention at one of the most unhappy periods of my life—the one when the decree ordering that I be arrested and conveyed to the Abbaye prison in Paris left me with no alternative—if I wanted to avoid the fate that inevitably awaited me—other than expatriating myself.

When my flight was announced on April 8, 1793, in the Convention with the words that *I, too, had turned traitor and gone over to the enemy,* Basire exclaimed: "It is possible that he has *deserted,* but it is not possible that he is a *traitor.*"

All my life, I have retained a profound gratitude to Basire for these words, which were very courageous at the time.

advice as to how I could soothe the irritation of which he had come to apprize me. "Without question," he said, "they have confidence in your patriotism, your bravery, and your military ability, and they desire that you should not leave your seclusion at Tournay except to return to the army." —"And do you think," I said, "that if I decide on that, I shall not be hindered?" —"No, and I am charged to tell you so, but at the same time to warn you that this disposition can change at any moment, unless you pay more heed than hitherto to the opinions that are developing and will sooner or later strike down all those who have tried to resist them or stem their course." That said, he got back into his carriage and continued his journey.

This conversation threw me into a state of stupefaction, and I no longer knew where to turn. I knew that I had to return to the army, which was in a deplorable state and daily became more disorganized. And there I anticipated that I would be held responsible for misfortunes it was not in my power to prevent. I could no longer cherish the hope of getting my father and family to retire together to America, and I felt the greatest reluctance to part from them by leaving alone, although it seemed to me, especially after hearing the doctor, that far from being prejudicial to them, my leaving alone might help to allay that irritation of which I was evidently the principal cause. This irritation existed primarily in the party whose fury my father feared the most and which was precisely the one to which he had unfortunately attached himself. However, I was only too conscious that given the almost invariable certainty about the direction human passions will take, it was possible that my leaving alone for America might have the opposite effect for my family to the one I have just indicated. But there was a further circumstance that alone would have made it impossible for me to leave, namely, that I lacked the necessary resources for the undertaking, since all I possessed was three hundred gold louis sewn into a belt I wore on me, which was all I took out of France when I left the following April.

I remained with my sister at Tournay, in the house in which I had installed her with Mme de Genlis, for the whole length of the fatal trial of the King, and I did not leave it till February 1793, when I decided to return to my post in the army, which was about to undertake the siege of Maastricht. Alarmed as I was by our situation, both internal and external, and in particular by the state of disorder and lack of discipline to which our armies were reduced, I saw nothing but difficulties and pitfalls of every kind ahead of me; but the more I was struck by the prospect of such a gloomy future, the more I believed that despite the decree of banishment always suspended over my head, I could no longer be anywhere in France but at my post in the army; and then, without hesitating, I took the decision to return there when active operations were about to recommence.

My brother Montpensier, while not seeing the state of affairs from exactly the same point of view as myself, nevertheless shared my opinion on these last points; in addition, since he had ceased to be my aide-de-camp and consequently always at my side, he had become very disillusioned with his position of adjutant general lieutenant colonel on the general staff of Dumouriez's army, the composition of which was not to his taste—and this, I must admit, was not without cause.

Therefore, he asked for another appointment and got one, with the same rank, in the Army of the Var, which was then the smallest and most remote of all our armies, its headquarters being at Nice. This appointment suited him all the better because our old friend, the Duc de Biron, had just taken command of this army. My brother also thought that it would be best if we were separated and not together at the same spot. I thought so, too, but this was of no avail, for when a decree for my arrest in the Army of Belgium was issued in Paris, a similar one was issued for my brother in the Army of the Var.

My brother did not join this army till February, and up to that time he remained with my father at the Palais Royal in Paris. During the whole length of the trial, my brother never ceased to do all he could to strengthen my father in the resolution he seemed to have taken not to appear at the Convention the day they voted on the sentence. In these pious efforts he was staunchly supported by *la Dame de la Rue Bleue,* whose attitude on this point never wavered, and when they left my father on the eve of the fatal sitting they had both of them left in the conviction that on the morrow he would not go to the Convention. But on the morning of this unlucky day, my father received a very early and unexpected visit from two members of that Assembly whom I am sorry to have to name, however unworthy their action, because I believe they acted out of fear rather than of their own volition. These two members were Merlin (de Douai) and Treilhard, both distinguished barristers and able jurisconsults who had always enjoyed great consideration at the bar. For many years they had been my father's legal counselors in judicial matters, and their honorable reputation naturally added to the confidence that my father was accustomed to place in them. Besides, they belonged to the Mountain and were among the small number of its members whom my father liked to see sitting beside him in the Convention. It is claimed —and I am disposed to believe it—that they hesitated a long time before resigning themselves to giving the fatal vote, but that once they had agreed with their party to do so, they decided to employ all means in their power to drag my father along with them.

It seems that during this discussion whose consequences have been so fatal, they managed to persuade him that his *abstention* from voting either way would be considered an act of cowardice, that as a member of the Convention he owed it to his constituents to vote on a question of such importance, and that consequently, he could not dispense himself from going to the sitting. What is certain is that my father told my brother that in setting off for the Convention, his intention was not to vote for the death penalty but that once seated on his bench, the people around him had so importuned, beset, and threatened him that he had no longer known what he was doing.

My brother, who thought things had remained as they were after his conversation with my father of the day before, went to see him, as was his custom, at the hour when my father usually finished his toilet, and it was there he learned that he had just left with MM. Treilhard and Merlin. My brother at once took in the full significance of this abduction, and he returned in consternation to shut himself in his apartments. There he remained until my father, having returned from the Convention, sent for him. He found him dissolved in tears, sitting before his desk, both his hands over his eyes: "Montpensier," he said, sobbing, "I do not have the courage to look at you." My brother has told me that having himself lost the power of speech, he had wanted to embrace him but that my father had refused him, saying: "No! I am too wretched. I cannot now imagine what could have led me to do what I did!" and they remained for a long time in this attitude without uttering another word.

My heart is broken with writing the foregoing account, and I can conclude this doleful account in no other way than by transcribing the following passage, which my brother Montpensier has consigned to the memory of our unfortunate father in the *Account of his forty-four months' captivity in Fort Saint-Jean in Marseille:*

"Unfortunate and excellent father!
Anyone who was in a position to observe you at close quarters and know you well will be forced to admit (unless he be an unworthy slanderer) that your heart contained not the slightest ambition nor any desire for vengeance; that you possessed the most likable and robust qualities; but that perhaps you lacked the firmness that makes a man act only in accordance with his own impulse; that in addition, you lent your confidence too easily and that scoundrels had found ways of gaining it in order to ruin you and sacrifice you to their atrocious schemes. Such language does no more than pay you the most exacting justice; but it will be stifled by your enemies, and unfortunately they have all too many means. Very well! Let them consummate their work! Let them complete their defamation of the memory of this unfortunate being, this victim! But let it at least be known one day! Let the world know what I know! May I be still alive at that time!"

When I received at Tournay the baleful news of this fatal vote, soon aggravated by that of the catastrophe which followed it so closely, I was prostrated and thrown into a state of agitation that is impossible to describe.

My unfortunate father, doubtless not knowing what to say to me, just referred to what he knew my brother had told me and let me know that since he was writing to me through the post—when all our letters were read by agents of the Convention and of the Paris Commune—he was abstaining from all details about what he himself felt.

I later learned from my brothers that when they were locked up in the dungeons of Marseille, my father often said to them, speaking of me: "I have at times been very annoyed with poor Chartres (this was what he always called me), but after all, I must confess that he knew this lot well and that he has judged affairs and men much better than I have."

It was during February 1793 that I left Tournay to take General Dumouriez's orders at Antwerp, where he was preparing his expedition against Holland. He told me that the declaration of war on England and Holland on February 1 completely altered our position and consequently obliged him to work out a new plan of campaign. Certainly, the one he had had adopted at the end of the preceding year, 1792, was no longer applicable to the state of affairs at the beginning of 1793, since this plan was based on the one hand on the assumption of Holland's neutrality, and on the other on that of the Prussian army's complete withdrawal across the Rhine and to the garrisons in the Prussian Crown lands. Dumouriez was convinced that if Custine had not sent on his advance guard to Frankfurt and rashly marched into the heart of Germany, Prussia's diplomatic system would have led her to adopt a position of neutrality, which would have left the field free for us to conclude the war with Austria.* In accordance with this strategy, General Dumouriez wanted Custine, after taking Mainz, to march along the left bank of the Rhine to besiege Coblenz, while he would himself have made for Cologne, leaving behind him on the one side Jülich—which was neutral and which it would have sufficed to blockade—and on the other Luxembourg—which would have fallen sooner or later, since it could no longer be provisioned. Then, with the French armies extending along the Rhine from Basel to Wesel, France would have offered peace, and Dumouriez thought, though I very much doubted it, that it could be honorably concluded provided we had not demanded too extortionate terms.

"But," General Dumouriez added, "Custine† ruined all that. Instead of following this plan, which he had accepted, he became drunk with the capture of Mainz and his early successes; presently he must establish his independence from me, and seduced by the bait of levying taxes on the rich city of Frankfurt, he took it by surprise, as he had done at Mainz; and after he had ventured as far as Limburg, the Prussian army turned around, defeated him, retook Frankfurt and Königstein, and forced him to fall back on Mainz, where he in turn is going to be besieged.

* Subsequent events fully justified this prediction of General Dumouriez's, since this is exactly what Prussia did in 1795 when it recognized the French Republic, concluded with it the Treaty of Basel, and established the great line of neutrality that, under its protection, covered all the states of North Germany and left France a free hand in the South, and thus against Austria.

† General Custine perished on the revolutionary scaffold in 1793.

"Such was the state of affairs when war was declared on England and Holland. And here," General Dumouriez continued, "is the new plan of campaign I propose to substitute for the old one, and for this one, fortunately, I no longer need the help of Custine or of anyone else, except the generals who are placed under my orders.

"I am assembling a small army corps around Antwerp that I am striving to bring up to twenty thousand men, which will be difficult, but I shall have enough. What hinders me most is our lack of every kind of supplies. Fortunately the Keep of Antwerp and the depot at Malines provide them up to a certain point, but the difference in the French and Austrian bore is a great problem. But I await our great engineer, General d'Arçon, who will organize his arm as well as can be expected, and it will serve. As soon as it's ready, I enter Holland with my army."

"—And I," said I, interrupting him, "will enter with you." —"No," he returned, "you will not enter Holland with me. I have another assignment for you, and the former would not have suited either you or me." —"But how so?" —"How so? For very good reasons I shall reveal to you presently, but just now hear me out.

"When I enter Holland, I shall begin by seizing a few Dutch fortresses —doesn't matter which—and once I am assured of a base for operations and have extracted the artillery and ammunition with which they are well stocked, I shall have the boats from the canals and rivers assembled either at Moerdick or at Lageschwalve, and I shall boldly proceed to install myself on Dort Island or Dordrecht before the Dutch army has had time to reassemble.

"Once I am there, it's all up with the Stadtholder,* who is the only enemy France has in Holland. You will not have forgotten that the office of Stadtholder was abolished in 1785 when the Dutch ousted the House of Nassau." —"But of course I remember it well, since fortunately my regiment, the Chartres Infantry, was to be part of the army that Louis XVI was planning to send to Holland under M. de Maillebois." —"Just so," Dumouriez replied, "but France did not send an army to the help of the Dutch, and its assistance was confined to sending them a few officers and a few odd gunners who were of no use, while in 1787 the King of Prussia sent an army into Holland commanded by the Duke of Brunswick that put the Dutch to flight and restored the Stadtholderate by main force, to the great regret of all Dutchmen, who detest it and like only their old federal government. It is *that* government in its original form, that I am going to strive to restore in Holland. I have acted in concert with the Dutch Patriots who fled to France at that time and were welcomed by Louis XVI. These are no demagogues, but well-to-do and moderate republicans. They will set up a sensible form of government in conformity with the peaceful character of their nation. This government will be the friend of France, and we shall conclude a good treaty with it that will

* See page 18, note †.—ED.

363

detach Holland from England and the Coalition. If I succeed, I doubt very much whether all this will be to the taste of the National Assembly. Therefore—and I make no secret of the fact—in Holland I shall not tolerate its proconsuls, its commissioners, or any other agent of the French government not belonging to our army, which, as long as it is under *my* orders, will protect the liberty of Holland but never oppress it.

"You must understand that for me to be able to carry this out, Belgium must be well-covered and my rear assured. Consequently, the Meuse must play in the new scheme the role I agreed to previously for the Rhine, and for this we must above all seize Maastricht, which is its key. It is for this siege that I have reserved you, not to have overall direction of it." —"Oh! As for *that,* even if you wanted it, I would not, and I have quite made up my mind to refuse any post of commander in chief that you could offer me, and I think that would be unsuitable both as regards my age and my position." —"Ah! how wise and good you are," said Dumouriez, shaking me by the hand, "and what you say on that score makes it much easier for me to tell you all that I intended to tell you, in complete confidence, as regards your situation, mine, and the situation in general.

"Mine toward you is not without difficulties because I must, above all, avert the suspicion that I want to make you into a political pawn in my hands." —"Well, you are perfectly aware that I want that no more than you, and that if you did I should not consent." —"I know, and we have nothing to learn from each other on that score, but we must also let the world know this insofar as we can; and for that we must establish by common consent that you have no part in all the political discussions in which I may find myself engaged and that by your wish as well as mine, you confine yourself exclusively to your military duties and remain, in short, a simple lieutenant general serving in my army." —"That definition suits me in every particular and conforms as much with my intentions as with my sincere wishes." —"Very good, but your difficulty and mine will be to keep you within that definition, because you must realize that if on the one hand your princely birth is an indelible mark that in these times of mania for republican ideas provides your enemies with arms against you, on the other it is to this accident that you owe not merely the fact of being a lieutenant general at your age but also that of being accepted as such without difficulty or reluctance; and this advantage of being born a Prince is, in your case, exempted from that insupportable pride that makes Princes so justly hated and is enhanced by your gift for pleasing and inspiring confidence in the troops, who are always more than willing to see you at their head. If I hung on to you in my little army to associate you with operations in Holland, which will be even more political than military, you would be regarded less as the lieutenant general than as the Prince in my pocket, ready to be pulled out for God knows what—perhaps, if the need arose, to make you my puppet Stadtholder." —"Good God! My dear General, speak no more of it, and pack me off where you will." —"Yes; the appointment I want to give you is in all respects the one that should suit you best. The siege of Maastricht is an important military operation with no political character, in which I am sure you will win yourself much honor. Moreover, you will be there with the armies that we are going to assemble behind the Meuse, if the Convention and its Executive Council don't get in our way, to pit against those the Austrians are now assembling at Cologne and on the Rhine, and therefore you will be in a position to take part in the actions and battles that will necessarily be fought between us." —"Ah! That suits me fine. But tell me, who will be my commander in chief at the siege of Maastricht?" —"I fear I shall make you pull a face, but you must understand that it has to be General Miranda." —"I expected it and I know you cannot do otherwise, but you will also understand if I don't like it. He was appointed a lieutenant general more recently than I was, and when you sent him to me at Mézières to serve under me in the column of your army I was charged to lead from Champagne to Flanders, I saw him only to learn from him that he had jaundice and that he was going to Paris for treatment. He did not return till after the Battle of Jemappes, which, admittedly, he did not believe you would have fought so soon nor won so quickly. But none of this matters. It is General Miranda who commands the Army of the North to which my division belongs at the moment; that is enough for me, and I am completely ready to resume command of my division under him when you think best."

General Dumouriez was delighted with my attitude, and he ordered me to join General Miranda at Liège immediately and resume command of my division.

I left Antwerp the same evening. First of all I went to Tournay to make the minor arrangements that were necessary to ensure that my sister's establishment and that of Mme de Genlis did not suffer through my absence, and from Tournay I proceeded to Liège, arriving on February 14 or 15.

Everything passed off very smoothly between General Miranda and myself. He told me that being a foreigner, he valued me doubly as his second in command, and I felt nothing but satisfaction with the relationship that grew up between us.

General Miranda was born at Caracas in Spanish America. He had reached the rank of lieutenant colonel in the Spanish army and was military secretary to General Cahigal, captain general of the island of Cuba when, at the time of the peace of 1783, political suspicions beset him; and he decided to leave Havana abruptly and take refuge first of all in the United States, then at Saint-Petersburg, and finally in Paris, where, after the rising of August 10, 1792, he had managed to enter our armies with the rank of *maréchal de camp*.

General Miranda was an intelligent and very well informed man. His French was very good, and he spoke it fluently, though with a very strong accent. His appearance and temperament did not go down well with our troops, who are always fairly ready to disparage anything different from their own.

The day the Convention declared war on the King of England and the Stadtholder of the United Provinces, that is to say, Holland, by a decree of February 1, 1793, the neutrality of Maastricht had ended, and consequently we had to set about investing the fortress immediately. General Miranda's army was entrusted with this operation on the left bank of the Meuse on which the town of Maastricht and Fort Saint-Pierre, its citadel, are situated, while on the right bank the suburb of Hyck, also fortified and forming part of the fortress, was to be invested by a division from the Army of the Ardennes under General Leveneur in the absence of General Valence, its commander in chief.

It was from the left bank of the Meuse, that is, from our side, that the siege of Maastricht was to be undertaken, or rather its bombardment, for we lacked the essentials for a regular siege. Our artillery was commanded by old General d'Hangest, who had received his commission as sublieutenant at the siege of the very same fortress, Maastricht, in 1748. His second in command was General Guiscard, a very distinguished officer who was killed a few weeks later at the Battle of Neerwinden. The sappers were commanded by Lieutenant General Dubouchet, who had under him Captains Dembarrère and Marescot* and also the two brothers Lepoitevin, the elder of whom became Lieutenant General de Maureilhan.

I found the troops of my division very discontented and fatigued by the humidity of their winter quarters. I put them on the march to occupy all the villages surrounding Maastricht on the left bank, I had a pontoon bridge thrown across at Visté under the supervision of my staff officer, Captain Régnier—later to be one of the distinguished generals in our armies—and then I set up my headquarters at Lawfeld, famous as the site of Marshal de Saxe's victory in 1747.

As soon as the Dutch garrison at Maastricht noticed that Lawfeld had been occupied by our troops, they made a large-scale sortie, which made me think that they wanted to attack us. In marked contrast to us, they wore splendid uniforms, and at the head of the column was the fine regiment of Brunswick Grenadiers, which still wore pointed copper helmets. The village of Lawfeld is on an eminence and easy to defend, but I had only a battalion of infantry there, the 1st Gironde, and few troops near at hand, which I immediately summoned. However, the Dutch garrison merely formed in a line along the glacis and sent its cavalry in several directions to observe what we were doing. Our dragoons arrived in time to engage in a little combat between the advance guards, in which

* Captain Dembarrère became a lieutenant general, a senator under the Empire, and a peer of France in 1814.

Captain Marescot became a lieutenant general, first inspector of the engineer corps, and a peer of France.

the Dutch cavalry was driven back but only left us a very pretty Frisian horse, which was taken by César Ducrest, my aide-de-camp. The Dutch garrison promptly reentered the fortress.

I then proceeded to the Château of Caster, situated on the banks of the Meuse and to the south of Fort Saint-Pierre on an eminence sloping very steeply down to the river and dominating its course as well as the town of Maastricht and a vast expanse of country. This château, which today belongs to M. Charles de Brouckère, belonged in 1793 to his aunt, who received me most graciously although during the winter she had had a very disagreeable visit from our marauders.

General Miranda, having finally left Liège, came to join me, bringing with him artillery and engineer officers to conduct the operations we were to undertake. If we had had the resources to conduct a regular siege, the unanimous opinion would have been to breach the entrenchment before Fort Saint-Pierre, for once they had been taken, all the defenses of the fortress of Maastricht would have fallen, dominated as they are by the eminence on which this fort is situated. It was from this eminence that the entrenchments had been breached during the preceding sieges, under Louis XIV, and then under Louis XV. But as I have already said, we lacked the essentials for a regular siege, especially since Fort Saint-Pierre had been rebuilt since 1748, enlarged, and put in a state to withstand a long siege. We therefore recognized that since we were forced to limit ourselves to a bombardment, it was toward the town that it should be directed and that we should set up our artillery batteries before the northwest face.

In accordance with this decision, General Miranda set up his head-quarters at Höchten Abbey and I mine at the Château of Petershem, very close to this face of Maastricht. He breached the entrenchment straight-away and called on the governor of the fortress, at the time Prince of Hesse-Philippsthal, to capitulate. Our operations were directed with such accuracy and speed that the fire from the fortress caused us very few losses, while by the evening of February 23 our batteries, fully armed, were installed on the heights of Konventsburg eight hundred yards from the covered way.

General Miranda went there to be present at the firing of the first shell. It was his only appearance in the trench during the whole bombardment. As for me, I spent every night there till that of March 2–3, and I only left with the rear guard, having had no artillery, ammunition, and wagon train file past me, without the slightest loss.

Throughout the siege, the Dutch garrison confined itself to carrying out patrols, and it attempted one sortie.

To the right of our entrenchments there was a wretched sunken road, fairly narrow, leading down to Maastricht. At the bottom of this I had had a breastwork constructed extensive enough to contain four infantry companies. As our battalions were scarcely four hundred strong, I nominated one of them every night to guard this post, with orders to fire a great fusillade to warn me if it saw the enemy approaching and, if it had to, to retreat, firing the whole time, along the sunken road, which, being in a curve, could scarcely be raked by cannon fire.

My foresight was justified, and one dark night a Dutch column came out of Maastricht and tried to surprise us and breach our entrenchments by this sunken road. That night, unfortunately, the battalion guarding this post was the very one commanded by that lieutenant colonel, formerly a house servant in a lodging house in the Rue de Richelieu, of whom I spoke before. When he saw the Dutch advancing on his breastwork, silently and with bayonets fixed, he is said to have asked one of his officers, as was his practice, what order he should give. As the officer seemed to have no more idea and the enemy was coming right up, the commander made his decision and, from what the troops told me, shouted: *"Very well, every man for himself."* What is indisputable is that whether or not it was given, this order was punctually executed, and the whole battalion decamped and scattered in all directions. Some of those in flight reached the entrenchments shouting: *"The enemy is here!"* Luckily, I happened to be at this end of our entrenchments, and I sallied forth at once at the head of an infantry column with all the drums loudly beating the charge, and by the time I reached the bottom of the sunken road, the Dutch were already in retreat. We did the same on our side, climbing back up to our entrenchments after posting another battalion to guard the sunken road.

Next I sent some cavalry from the picket we always had behind the entrenchment to find the commander and reassemble all they could find of his battalion. He was found at daybreak in a barn with most of his men.

I have related above all that he told me then in his defense—how by drawing a lot he had been translated, much against his will, from the position of *house servant* at the China Hotel to the rank of *lieutenant colonel,* and begging me to reduce him to that of a private without sending him before a court-martial.

The day before we raised the siege of Maastricht, or the day before that, I was dining with General Miranda when someone came to report to him that the troops who were to man the entrenchment that day had stopped before its entrance in a state of insubordination and that they had refused to go any further on the grounds that the artillery commanders were *traitors* and that the shot was not of the right caliber. He added that it was the first battalion from the Bouches-du-Rhône, composed of men from Marseille, and at the head of the column that had first disobeyed and fomented the unrest.

It was true that as the prolonged bombardment had used up the shot taken from the French arsenals, they had been supplemented by Austrian shot that we had brought from the arsenal at Malines, where we had found a considerable store of shells with a slightly smaller diameter than that of the French ones. That did not prevent our mortars from firing them, but it is true that the aim was less accurate—a fact of little importance, since it was enough for the bombs to land within such a large area as the town of Maastricht. It was this circumstance that the agitators had exploited to stir up unrest among the troops.

General Miranda took me on one side and confessed the difficulty in which all this placed him: "You know," he said, "that I do not possess the command of the French language I would like, and if you would be good enough to undertake to go there and see that the matter is sorted out, I should take it as a great kindness." —"With the best will in the world," I said, and straightaway mounted my horse and went off to the entrenchment. I found the battalions lined up, standing at ease with their right against the entrance to the long communicating trench that had been constructed to deflect the fire from the fortress. I made as if I believed that the troops were waiting for me, and I said in a perfectly natural voice to the commander of the battalion on the left: "Here I am, Commander, have the drum roll sounded and present arms." This was immediately carried out along the whole line, and I continued my progress along the front. When I reached the rightmost battalion, which was that of the Bouches-du-Rhône, the senior captain who was commanding it, an old soldier who wore the scarlet ribbon with two crossed swords—a long-service badge for noncommissioned officers—advanced toward me, sword lowered, and said:

"General, we have halted here because there is treason somewhere, the shot is not of the right caliber. . . ."

"Be quiet, Captain," I said, interrupting him, "I am placing you under arrest, and you will answer before the appropriate authorities for the act of insubordination you have just committed. Hand over your sword." He handed it to me, blanching and without a word. I continued: "Second Captain: a corporal and four men from the ranks to escort the prisoner to headquarters." They came forward immediately. Then I charged one of my officers to hand the prisoner's sword to the commander in chief and to report to him on my behalf what had taken place.

Then I ordered in a firm voice: "By the right! Column advance, maneuver speed, march!" and the whole column moved off in the most profound silence. I remained on horseback at the entrance to the trench until the whole column had filed past me. Then I got down and followed on behind it as I would have done on any other day.

I relate these anecdotes with the details my memory provides. I have retained a strong impression of them because they seemed one of the best ways of giving some kind of an impression of the general complexion of the period, people's mentality, and my personal situation. I dwell less on the purely military and strategic operations because I had myself only a secondary role in them and because they have already been described several times. I confine myself to saying what I consider necessary to make my own account complete.

The bombardment of Maastricht lasted from the evening of February 23 till that of March 2, 1793, but did not lead to the surrender of the fortress, as on our side we had vainly hoped. The ending of the neutrality of that great fortress on the Meuse was all the more damaging to the position of our armies in Belgium in that the fortress of Jülich on the Roer, which had been neutral in 1792, had likewise ceased to be so in 1793 as a result of the Empire's declaration of war, which involved that of the Elector Palatine, and the Elector of Bavaria, to whom Jülich then belonged.

The fear of seeing Maastricht fall hastened the entry into the field of the great army that Austria had assembled in the Lower Rhine area under Field Marshal the Prince of Saxe-Coburg, whose headquarters were at Cologne.

On our side, despite General Dumouriez's remonstrances, the worst dispositions had been made to prepare for the contingencies of the coming campaign. General Dumouriez, arguing from the example of Marshal de Saxe in 1748, wanted the army corps that was to cover the siege of Maastricht to be placed behind the Gueule instead of on the Roer both because this river, being nearer to Maastricht, gave a less extended front and better defensive positions, and also because with the end of Jülich's neutrality, all positions behind the Roer were absolutely untenable. But the National Convention was implacably opposed to abandoning the Roer and regrouping behind the Gueule because it had made Aix-la-Chapelle into a French Commune and believed it had revolutionized this ancient imperial city and, indeed, all the surrounding countryside, where it had sent commissioners and planted *trees of liberty*. As we could not withdraw behind the Gueule without abandoning the revolutionaries of Aix-la-Chapelle, our unfortunate troops were condemned to remain on the Roer.

It was on March 1, 1793, that the Austrian army, commanded by the Prince of Coburg, emerged from Jülich, crossed the Roer at several points, and attacked our army corps commanded by Generals Lanoue and Stengel at Aldenhoven, completely defeating them. They fell back on Liège in the greatest disorder, while the Austrian army withdrew to their right and made for Maastricht. General Leveneur, who was with his corps before the suburb of Wych, was alerted in time and fell back on Liège before being attacked.

On the morning of March 2 General Miranda was notified of our reverses on the Roer and of the Austrian army's march on Maastricht. He could no longer hesitate to raise the siege, but he rightly decided to continue the bombardment throughout the 2nd and to wait till midnight before beginning the evacuation of our artillery and our retreat.

General Miranda considered it necessary, as commander in chief, to coordinate further operations without delay with his colleague General Valence, like himself a commander in chief, who had just arrived at Liège, and he proceeded there immediately. Before leaving, he handed over command of his army to me with orders to withdraw everything first to Tongres and then to Liège as quickly as possible. I was left, therefore, with the heavy responsibility of evacuating our siege train with the mass of shells and ammunition that we had before Maastricht. There was a paved road from Tongres to Liège, but as far as Tongres there were only mud tracks, very sodden at this time of year, along which I feared our heavy mortars and artillery could not be drawn despite the extra horses I had assembled from the villages as soon as I knew we were going to raise the siege. But I had an even greater anxiety; it was that the Austrian army would pass rapidly through Maastricht and during our march fall on me with its numerous cavalry, which I had no means of opposing. The convoy, in a single column, was so long that it could not be properly supervised and escorted at any point, and General Ruault—chief of staff to General Miranda—who was constantly by my side and for whom I had a very great regard, said to me: "We are supposed to have twelve thousand men, but you can take it as a certainty that you don't even have *nine* thousand and, of these nine, you have more than one battalion that will perform no other service for you if the Austrians attack the convoy than to shout *Every man for himself!*"

The good General Ruault was only too right, but the Austrians were in no hurry, and they proceeded toward Maastricht so slowly that I had already reached the village of Berg, not far from Tongres, when our rear guard, with which I had remained throughout, was attacked quite fiercely by the light troops of their advance guard. This village, situated on a sugar-loaf hill, had a good defensive position, especially to the north, and although their superiority in numbers would have permitted the Austrians to outflank me on my right, I managed to hold out there long enough to cover the entrance of my convoy into Tongres without losing a single vehicle. I was still in the village of Berg after the Tyrolean light troops had entered it, and it would perhaps have been rather difficult for me to escape them had the darkness of the night not prevented them from seeing me clearly and, above all, had their attention not been diverted by tufts of tricolored ribbon with which the *tree of liberty* was decked out. For I saw them at very close quarters wasting their time felling it, and I heard the blows of the axe with which they were hitting it.

I remained at Tongres only long enough to give the troops some rest and carry out the most urgent repairs to my convoy. Then, in accordance with the orders General Miranda had given me, I moved off before daybreak along the Liège road; and during the morning of March 4, with my column and my convoy completely intact, I reached the heights that dominate the city of Liège, amid the remains of its former citadel.

There I found the two commanders in chief, Valence and Miranda, surrounded by the officers of the two armies and the troops who had successively fallen back on the left bank of the Meuse, leaving on the right bank only General Ihler's corps, which still held the excellent position of the Charterhouse of Liège.

I was painfully struck by the spectacle presented by this vast assembly of troops without any order of battle, their arms in heaps, the soldiers in little groups consuming the large ration of victuals with which the town of Liège had been obliged to provide them, all the vehicles unhitched and the horses tethered: In the sunshine we had just then, all this looked more like a fair than an assembly of armies. If the Austrian army had departed from its wonted slow and methodical progress and had crossed Maastricht with the audacious rapidity of a French army and fallen on us unawares, I believe we would not have been able to put up any resistance and that the army, the hope of France, would have been scattered or destroyed with the loss of all its equipment. But not everything that should happen always does, and France escaped this misfortune.

I found all the generals holding an open-air council to decide what to do. All were agreed that it was impossible to remain where we were, but there were divergent opinions on the direction our retreat should take.

Some wanted us to fall back on Namur—there, as they saw, to reorganize and bring our armies up to strength in peace in the delta of the Sambre and the Meuse before resuming the offensive against the Austrian army, if the general situation permitted. This plan entailed abandoning the whole of Belgium to the Austrians, all our garrisons, and, finally, the small army that General Dumouriez was commanding in person in Holland.

The others, on the contrary, wanted us to choose Brussels as the direction for our retreat and, for the moment, to withdraw no further than Saint-Trond, which is eight leagues from Liège on the main road to Brussels.

I was entirely of this opinion, which was that of the majority. It was also, basically, that of the two commanders in chief, but we had great difficulty in getting them to put it into practice, and it was only the impossibility of prolonging our halt at the national Citadel of Liège that forced them to adopt it. Neither of the two was willing to command or be commanded by the other. They would have been well content if we could have cut this mass into two separate armies that the two commanders-in-chief could have commanded independently. This was physically impossible, in the first place for lack of time, and in the second because the troops had so often passed from one command to another, and even from one corps to another, that it was no longer possible to say with any precision to which of the two armies each corps, each regiment, each battalion, should be assigned.

Then we conceived of a middle course that was agreeable to both of them. It was first of all to postpone the solution of all the difficulties till Saint-Trond, and until then neither of them would exercise his command. Then all the troops should be divided, according to where they happened to be, into three columns, each under the command of a lieutenant general; and these columns should then march across the plain, two to the right or north of the main road and one to the south or left, while the main road should be reserved for the artillery train and vehicles of all kinds led by General Stengel with some light troops and, at the back, a rear guard similarly composed to round up the stragglers and get them to move along; finally, MM. the commanders in chief should perambulate in the midst of all this on horseback and could talk over their future plans together without any distractions.

This plan was adopted, and I was designated commander of the right-hand column, General Lanoue of the center, and General Leveneur of the left. We divided the troops into three, just as they were according to the positions they occupied on the ground facing the Meuse. We had them wheel off to the right, each of us placed himself at the head of his column, and we marched off at once without inquiring how our columns were made up, which no one could have told us in any case. I just saw to it that there were no gaps in the column, and the march proceeded very well until some distance from the village of Oreye, which is halfway between Liège and Saint-Trond.

The Austrian corps that had attacked me the day before at Berg had pushed some light troops ahead to Oreye to block the main road. General Stengel forced them to withdraw pretty speedily and even took some of them prisoner. But the sound of a few shots spread alarm in the convoy, cries of *"We are cut off! Every man for himself!"* were heard, the vehicles at the front wished to turn back, and they fell back on those following them; others plunged into the ditches, and there was considerable confusion for a while. However, General Stengel promptly restored order, and the convoy resumed its march through the village of Oreye. Our column continued its march, and General Lanoue, seeing the disorder on the main road, came at a hard gallop to tell me: "Don't you think we ought to halt our column?" —"Far from it!" I replied. "We have battalions here that would instantly disband if we stopped them, if only to see what was going on. To keep our column together we must either have them march nonstop or else deploy them." —"Deploy them!" he said, with a kind of shudder. "By God, I would not take that on," and he hastily returned to his column.

However, he had to decide, as I did, on reaching Saint-Trond, where the infantry should bivouac in three lines and the cavalry should be quartered as best we could. The troops were tired out, and they all just wanted to throw themselves on the ground and sleep.

We were hoping to rest at Saint-Trond the next day, March 5, and to proceed in peace to unravel the chaos presented by the army by sorting out the commands and fixing some kind of order of battle. An unforeseen incident deprived us of that hope.

An ordnance officer sent by General Ihler arrived at Saint-Trond during the night to inform the commanders in chief that this general, seeing himself *forgotten* at the Charterhouse of Liège with the infantry battalion comprising his corps, had waited there all day in vain for orders which had not reached him, and that having ascertained that the whole army had withdrawn to Saint-Trond, he had thought to carry out his duty by passing through the town so as to install himself on the site of the former citadel, whence he planned to depart at daybreak to rejoin the army at Saint-Trond. In addition, since he had reason to fear that the great Austrian army that was advancing slowly but on all sides, would push ahead a sizable detachment to Oreye via Maastricht and Tongres to bar his passage, he requested that Oreye should immediately be occupied in force and that at least a portion of the army should go on ahead during the morning of the 5th to assure the junction of his corps.

Consequently, despite his troops' fatigue, General Valence set off again in the direction of Oreye with what was called *my column* to go before General Ihler. The Austrians did not show up, and it was a sort of *military* excursion; we escorted the General back to Saint-Trond.

We got down immediately to restoring a little order to the army and, hard as it is to believe, our first task was to *count our battalions* and draw up a nominal roll; then we had to try to obtain approximate estimates of their strength, because if there were still some fairly full battalions, others were merely skeletal. The National Volunteers joined such and such a battalion of their fancy for as long as they chose, and the similarity of their uniforms made it more difficult to recognize the one to which they really belonged, to find it, and to return them to it or even to keep them in the one in which we had been obliged to incorporate them temporarily. It had therefore been necessary, in order to emerge from the chaos in the presence of the enemy army before it fell on us, to carry out a partial and makeshift repartition of these shapeless forces between the two commanders in chief. There was no desertion to the enemy in the midst of this disorder, but there was very considerable desertion back to France, which was facilitated, particularly for the National Guards, by the pretext of seeking to rejoin one's battalion.

The lack of unity in the command aggravated difficulties already considerable in themselves. Our two commanders in chief, Valence and Miranda, being independent of each other, never agreed on anything. We were constantly being summoned to councils of war of which one could say with La Fontaine: "I have read many chapters that signify nothing."

And I remember that General Miranda, a very enlightened and informed man but one who was at once indecisive and completely inexperienced either in handling men or troops in the field, always refused to adopt any course of action until General Dumouriez had returned to take over supreme command; and he always ended our long discussions in the councils of war by repeating in his Spanish accent:

"We are the lieutenants of Pompey, *the Petreus and Affraneus.* Pompey is in Holland, and he will decide."

After this learned comparison, uttered in a phlegmatic tone, he went off without associating himself with any decision and leaving M. de Valence in a state of extreme annoyance.

However, with the Austrians controlling the Meuse from below Namur as far as Venlo and all the fortresses commanding it, it was evident that our position at Saint-Trond was far too near that river, especially considering that we were in no state to fight either an offensive or defensive battle there. Therefore, it was at length decided that we should withdraw beyond Louvain to the great defensive position known as the Iron Mountain, with a strong advance guard at Kumtich, between Louvain and Tirlemont, under Lieutenant General Lamarche, and detachments of flankers to the right and left under Generals Stengel and Henri de Frégeville (the elder of the two brothers).

While we were suffering so many reverses on the Meuse, General Dumouriez, at the head of his little army, was boldly pursuing his successful career in Holland, where, having taken Breda, Klundert, and Geertruydenberg in succession, he was laying siege to Willemstad, where the siege works were being conducted by General d'Arçon,* the able engineer

* I shall place in this note a rather curious anecdote whose authenticity seems all the more certain because it has been related to me in the same words by King Charles X on the one hand, and by General Dumouriez, who had it directly from General d'Arçon, on the other.

The political opinions of this staff officer had always been against the Revolution, and after 1789 he had held himself aloof and had not been employed, but equally, he had remained in France and had resisted all the summonses aimed at persuading him to emigrate. However, when he saw war declared in April 1792, he decided to emigrate and made for Coblenz to present himself to the Comte d'Artois, who had always treated him with respect since he had encountered this Prince at the camp at Saint-Roch off Gibraltar. But the firebrands of the Emigration, and they were numerous, claimed that an example had to be made of him for having waited so long to emigrate, and they spoke of nothing less than throwing him into the Rhine. They did nothing of the sort, however, and M. d'Arçon, without letting himself be intimidated by these clamors, betook himself to Charles X's audience, where the room was full of *émigrés.* A general murmur announced his arrival. As soon as he noticed him, Charles X said to him: "To be sure M. d'Arçon, I am sorry to have to say it to you, but time is up and you have arrived too late." —*"Very well, Monseigneur,"* replied M. d'Arçon, bowing low, *"I will perhaps not be too late for the other side,"* and he withdrew.

Back in Paris, where his absence had not been noticed, he presented himself to the Comte de Grave, then Minister of War, to request permission to serve, and he was immediately reintegrated into the Engineering Committee.

When Charles X recounted this anecdote to me, in which he saw merely M. d'Arçon's inconstancy, I evinced some surprise that he had had so bad a reception, and he replied, with his usual naïveté: "What do you expect, my dear, we were mad then and we thought we were so sure of our game that we *played hard to get.*"

who had invented and had constructed those famous *floating batteries,* which became legendary and were destroyed off Gibraltar in 1781.

As soon as General Dumouriez had been informed of our reverses and knew that our armies had entirely withdrawn behind the Meuse, he handed over command of the Army of Holland to General de Flers* and left immediately for Brussels.

Before embarking on this part of my account in which I must necessarily relate the political activity of General Dumouriez, in which I took no part, it is important that I clearly establish the nature of my personal relationship with him in order to free myself from any kind of responsibility for his acts. To this purpose I shall begin by giving the lie to an assertion that, though entirely false, my enemies or political opponents have striven to establish. This they have done with the dual purpose of belittling the possible value of the military services I was fortunate enough to render France and at the same time to give the impression that there was a sort of compact and political understanding between General Dumouriez and myself. This never existed, and he has constantly denied it in all his writings, while I have been no less careful to avoid the appearance as much as the reality.

This assertion is that I was his *aide-de-camp* and that I had served only in this capacity. It is unquestionable that even if I had been his aide-de-camp, it would no more justify any attempt to place responsibility for his actions upon me, but since in fact I never was his aide-de-camp and since it was merely with my rank of lieutenant general that I was employed in his army, I believe that this circumstance, added to all the facts I give, shows the obvious absurdity of the inference people have sought to draw from this so-called political understanding between General Dumouriez and myself.

At this time Belgium was in a state of unrest, which was very alarming for the French army. The French generals had authority only over their troops, and civil authority was exercised exclusively by special commissioners who corresponded directly with the Executive Council in Paris, whose nominees they all were, which led to the Belgians' calling them *the executives.* They had been sent everywhere despite General Dumouriez's vigorous protests and the never-ending complaints of all the French generals, of whom they were independent, their power being unchecked. With only a few exceptions, their selection had been deplorable, and the executives exacted all manner of taxes and perpetrated every sort of harassment. Consequently, partial uprising broke out on all sides; there was one at Wavre, at Halle, and at Alost; the main one was at Grammont, where a large assembly of peasants with arms and even, it was said,

* General de Flers perished on the revolutionary scaffold after becoming commander in chief of the Army of the West Pyrenees.

with artillery had defeated the troops sent to disperse it. We were threat-ened with a general rising of the whole of Belgium.

On his way through Antwerp, General Dumouriez ordered General Marassé, who commanded the troops there, forcibly to release the sixty-seven magistrates and notables whom the "executive" Publicola Chaus-sard had caused to be imprisoned the day before for refusing to sign a request to be incorporated into the French Republic.*

On his arrival at Brussels, General Dumouriez found proof of the accuracy of our reports about the enormous reduction in the strength of our army through desertion back to France; the streets of the city were cluttered with deserters from all the units; and the *commandant de la légion des sans-culottes,* called *Estienne,* was issuing them with sheets of road maps to guide them home just as if they belonged to his own unit. Dumouriez had the gates of Brussels closed, and put the garrison on patrol to apprehend all the deserters and have them conducted to the army under escort. He had Estienne arrested and sent him to the Citadel of Liège, and at the same time, to the great pleasure of the troops and of the whole town, he ordered that the *légion des sans-culottes* be disbanded and disarmed.

It is unquestionable that faced with such a state of affairs, it was the duty of the commander in chief to take the most energetic measures—even if it meant going beyond his terms of reference—to try to remedy the situation somewhat. This duty will be even more evident if we cast our eye rapidly over our military situation at that time, both inside and outside of France.

Our army had retreated as far as Louvain, with its advanceguard at Kumtich under General Lamarche. It was very demoralized as a result of this retreat; and the complete lack of camping equipment, which kept it bivouacking in the mire and rains of March, added to its low spirits and disgruntlement. All the supply services and the army itself being in this disorganized state, there was no question of obtaining regular statements of the number of effectives, but I doubt that the figure amounted even to forty-five thousand men, including the small separate but dependent units. We were not receiving any reinforcements from France, either of men or of horses.

The Austrian army that was marching up on us was said to be sixty to seventy thousand men strong, and this seemed probable.

Our little Army of Holland was put at sixteen or eighteen thousand men, including the garrisons. The English guards had already disem-barked at Moerdick, and they were followed by forty thousand men who arrived in batches and formed the Duke of York's army. The Dutch had

* Publicola Chaussard, furious at their release, went immediately to upbraid Dumouriez for it and told him: "You are no longer a general, you are a *vizier."* —"I am no more a *vizier,* Monsieur Chaussard," replied Dumouriez, "than you are Publicola."

377

also assembled their army, and we were therefore gravely threatened from that direction.

We were equally embattled on the Rhine, where General Custine's dash to Frankfurt as far as Limburg had brought back the Prussians, who were already a long way from the banks of the Rhine and even wished, it was said, to withdraw from the Coalition. The Prussian army, turning on its heel, had defeated Custine, retaken Frankfurt and Königstein, and was preparing to concert operations with another Austrian army, commanded by Marshal Wurmser—not to speak of the Imperial army that lined the right bank of the Rhine before Alsace.

Finally, there were also the Austrian and Piedmontese armies in the Alps, the Spanish army in the Pyrenees, and to complete this unhappy picture, civil war had flared up in the Vendée.

And while Belgium was given over to the disgusting exploitation of the Executive Council's commissioners, what odious and bloody tyranny was France itself a prey to under the deceptive mask of its national sovereignty! It was subject to the most absolute power, to arbitrary government so unlimited that the history of no other century and no other country has yet afforded such a terrifying example. And to what hands was this dread scepter entrusted? To those of a single Assembly, elected without reference to any existing law, not limited by any mandate, without any definition of its competence, with no other limitation on the exercise of its power than that which it was pleased to impose upon itself. Also—not to mention the baleful event my filial pen would doubly wish it could efface from my memory—the National Convention continued to make itself the instrument of the people's frenzy and that of the sanguinary men whom, unhappily for France, it nurtured in its bosom; and it decimated itself several times while its Revolutionary Tribunals and its proconsuls—the so-called *representatives of the people on mission in the departments*— caused the scaffold to run red with the blood of so many innocent victims and of so many men whose talents, virtues, and patriotism were the honor and glory of France.

Countless other evils arose to aggravate still further for our unhappy Fatherland the miseries of this terrifying carnage: the proscription of religion; the confiscation, squandering, and sale for next to nothing of more than a third of the landed property of our vast territory; the ruin of public and private wealth by the *assignats* and the resultant bankruptcy; the destruction of public credit; the cessation of commerce, agriculture, and industry; dearth; the maximum and, in a word, the general ruin of the nation. Such were for France the fatal fruits of arbitrary and absolute government by a single, sovereign assembly that responded with servility to the disgraceful pressure exerted on it by the errors and passions of the populace.

But I return to Belgium and what was going on there in March 1793.

It was on March 11, 1793—exactly seven days before the Battle of Neerwinden, which was joined and lost on Monday, March 18, and ten days after the defeat at Aldenhoven on the Roer—that General Dumouriez began to place himself in an attitude of defiance toward the National Convention by adopting, on his own authority, a series of measures conflicting with the ones it had prescribed. This audacious conduct was bound to lead, as in fact happened, to an open rupture with that Assembly which ruled everything, which decided everything by special decrees, and of which the ministers comprising the *Executive Council* were no more than docile and insignificant instruments.

Dumouriez proclaimed to the provisional assembly of representatives of Belgium, assembled at the town hall of Brussels, and told them* "that it was neither the French nation nor the army he commanded that was responsible for the wrongs of which Belgium had complained; that errors had been made, indeed crimes committed against Belgian people, that he had come to rectify the former and punish the latter, and that he was beginning by reestablishing them in the full extent of their functions."

Then the General notified them of the *Orders of the Day* and the *Proclamation* that he was having read out the same day to the sound of trumpets and posted up everywhere in both French and Flemish at the request of the military commandants.

The Belgian assembly, electrified by this speech and these intimations, rose as one man and escorted General Dumouriez to the main square, which was covered by a vast crowd and where the General was greeted by the most enthusiastic applause.

The measures taken by General Dumouriez consisted in expelling all the "executives," arresting those of them he wanted to be tried for their malfeasances, and dividing their functions between the military commandants and the civil authorities of Belgium, with power to close the clubs or patriotic societies that might give them trouble, to restore the Church's silver and all objects looted from there or anywhere else, etc. Finally, there were other measures relative to the administration of the army, from which he likewise removed a large number of agents sent from Paris.

The immediate result was the spontaneous dissolution of the gathering at Grammont and of those that were beginning to be formed everywhere. General Dumouriez notified the Convention of these measures and of the reasons for his adopting them. These reasons were set out in his famous letter of March 12, 1793, a letter which was not at first placed in *le Moniteur,* as the Convention's Committees had forbidden it to be read out publicly but which is to be found in no. 84 for Monday, March 25, under the heading of The Low Countries, as having been printed and

---

* See *le Moniteur* for Monday, March 18, 1793, no. 77, from which I have taken these words.

distributed throughout Belgium. It is also cited in Cambacérès's Defense of General Security during the sitting of Monday, April 1, 1793.

At this time there were none of the National Convention's representatives-on-mission remaining in Belgium. They had all effected their withdrawal on learning that our army had pulled back; some had gone to Paris, the rest to Lille. The latter speedily returned to Brussels as soon as they learned of the measures General Dumouriez had just taken, in order to discuss them with him. These measures, as one might have expected, were the subject of lively altercations and violent recriminations on all sides.*

I had, and wanted to continue to have, no more part in these discussions than in the measures to which they had given rise, and if I have gone into such details on the subject, it is because it seemed to me essential for a proper understanding of the progressive influence on events of General Dumouriez's position. I was necessarily caught up in these events without having taken any more part in them than that imposed by my military duties, and consequently, I could not have incurred the grievous responsibility with which people have sought to saddle me.

I was then with the army at Louvain and ill enough for Doctor Ménuret, an army doctor, to have ordered me to leave the camp and install myself in the great stronghold of Sainte-Gertrude. General Dumouriez arrived there on March 13, and his presence lifted the spirits of the army somewhat, the soldiers saying: "Now we have the good little chap†️ with us, things will go well."

On March 14 and 15, General Dumouriez was busy with his chief of staff, General Thouvenot, setting up a regular order of battle in place of the lamentable disorder to which so many different things had contributed.

General Dumouriez divided his army into three corps, apart from his advance guard commanded by General Lamarche (who then had as his aide-de-camp Captain, later Marshal, Ney) and other small detachments. The army corps on the right was placed under General Valence, the one on the left under General Miranda, and the one in the center under me, with Lieutenant Dietmann as my second in command and the *maréchaux de camp* Dampierre,‡ Desforêts, Blottefière, and Chancel.

General Dumouriez was informed by General Lamarche on the evening of the 15th that the Austrians had just seized Tirlemont, where we had only a few troops, and that he expected to be attacked at Kumtich at

* It was during this discussion that the representative Camus, the most irascible of the four, said to Dumouriez: "General, you are accused of being Caesar; if I were sure you were, I would become Brutus and stab you." —"My dear Camus," Dumouriez replied, "I am not Caesar and you are not Brutus, and the threat of dying at your hand constitutes for me a guarantee of immortality."
† General Dumouriez was very small.
‡ Dampierre commanded a separate corps almost entirely composed of cavalry, which was placed under my orders only for the day of the Battle of Neerwinden.

daybreak. General Dumouriez decided immediately to advance with his whole army, and it was on the march at eleven in the evening with no other supplies assured than one ration of bread in their packs. This march could not but be very slow because the very broken terrain between Louvain and the heights of Kumtich was at that time so waterlogged that we were obliged to follow the paved road and, consequently, to form a single, extremely long column.

General Valence's division, which was still called the Army of the Ardennes in deference to his title of commander in chief, was at the head of the column.

On March 16, the army halted at Kumtich till daybreak, and there General Dumouriez attacked Tirlemont with General Valence's infantry and that of our advance guard, while General Lamarche's cavalry was clearing the way for my division to turn Tirlemont from the right, and General Miranda was fanning out to the left to occupy the village of Oplinter. However, as the bulk of the Austrian army had not yet arrived, our passage over the streams in our path was not contested, the enemy's light cavalry merely observing our movements and withdrawing in front of our cavalry far enough for there to be no possibility of a combat.

But it was quite otherwise in the town, where the Austrians had concentrated all the infantry at their disposal. Tirlemont is a large, sparsely populated town with wide streets, a large number of gardens, and a very large square in the center. The Austrians defended it street by street with great energy, especially in the square, where the fighting was very fierce but lasted only long enough to cover their retreat and departure from the town. When General Valence reached the gates, he found they were being raked by our artillery battery placed outside on the paved road leading to Saint-Trond and fairly close to the three ancient tombs (or *tumuli*) situated on the right-hand side of this main road. General Valence, with the dashing bravery that characterized him, remained under this gate until, in the interval between discharges, he had brought up one by one, behind the gate to the right and left, enough infantry to form two small columns on each side of the main road, which would certainly have taken the enemy's artillery if they had not retreated as quickly as they did. General Valence was rewarded for his boldness not only by his success, which did not cost him a single man, but by the unanimous shout of *Long live General Valence* with which his infantry greeted him when he left the gate. This did not prevent his being proscribed a few days later. . . . !

When the exit from Tirlemont had been cleared, General Valence's division was deployed before the town, while General Lamarche's vanguard was likewise deployed to his right between the road to Saint-Trond and the village of Goetsenhoven, his light troops being thrown against those of the Austrians who retreated before them.

I directed my division toward Goetsenhoven, which is situated on the rounded summit of a high hill. I had scarcely occupied this village when a column of Austrian infantry moved up to attack us, and it was already entering the village by the main street when a fierce bayonet charge, brilliantly executed by the 17th of the line (Auvergne) under Colonel Dumas de Saint-Marcel and supported by Captain de Rennepont's artillery battery, drove it out of the village and forced it to withdraw.

It was then that I noticed that part of the Austrian army had crossed the little Gette River and was advancing on us. I even saw the Prince of Coburg's *gilded company,* that is to say, this general surrounded by his general staff, perambulating amid the columns. I notified General Dumouriez of this at once while I carried out the troop dispositions necessary for the defense of Goetsenhoven against the general attack which I expected at any moment but which did not materialize. When General Dumouriez arrived, the Austrian columns had withdrawn and recrossed the Gette. Night was drawing near, and General Dumouriez ordered that all the troops should bivouac where they were. On March 17 the army advanced, with its advance posts on the left bank of the little Gette. The Prince of Coburg's headquarters had been reported as being at Landen, and we no longer saw any Austrian troops before us. The enemy army was assembled in the valley behind the great defensive position of Neerwinden, made famous by the two battles that were fought there at an interval of one hundred years. My great-great-grandfather, the Duc d'Orléans, later Regent, played a glorious part in Marshal Luxembourg's victory at Neerwinden on July 28, 1693, over the Allied army commanded by the King of England, William III, whom people in Louis XIV's army persisted in calling merely the *Prince of Orange.* The title borne by the Regent at this battle was that of Duc de Chartres, the same title that still rightfully belonged to me on March 18, 1793. Less fortunate than he, I did not see victory crown French arms on the battlefield of Neerwinden, but I had the consolation that in the sector of my command the battle was not lost.

In the course of March 17 General Dumouriez made all the dispositions for the battle he had decided to give the next day. In the evening all the corps occupied the positions that had been assigned to them, and the commanders of the columns had orders not to cross the Gette before nine o'clock in the morning, in order to give the troops time to eat their soup before beginning the attack.

The army was extended in a single line behind the little Gette and divided into three main divisions, the right under General Valence, the center under myself, and the left under General Miranda. The vanguard, under General Lamarche, was to operate at the head of General Valence's right-hand division, whose flank was covered by General Neuilly's cavalry, just as the left flank of my division was covered by General Dampierre's cavalry.

At this point opened up a stretch of rather difficult terrain that separated my left from General Miranda's division, whose right-hand column, under General Ruault, was to follow the Saint-Trond road as far as the Orsmael bridge. This was quite a way from us in any case, and unfortunately, the extension of our lines did not end there. To the left of General Miranda's division, General Miaczincki's* detachment of outriders was to link it to the division of General Champmorin, who had been charged to occupy the little fortified town of *Léau,* where, to no advantage, he spent the whole day of the battle on March 18 without firing a shot.

This enormous extension formed the basis of General Miranda's defense of his conduct in the controversy that arose between him and General Dumouriez over the reasons for the loss of the Battle of Neerwinden. I shall not attempt to follow it here, and I shall confine my account to the sector of that battle in which I took part personally.

My division crossed the Gette in two columns and by two bridges. I was at the head of the right-hand column, and Lieutenant General Dietmann at the head of the other. We attacked the village of Locer, which was feebly defended by the Austrians. I left General Dietmann there with a few infantry battalions, and in accordance with my orders, I was wheeling to my right with the rest of my infantry and my artillery when an aide-de-camp of General Dumouriez came to inform me on his behalf that as a result of a misunderstanding, General Lamarche had evacuated the village of Neerwinden, the Austrians had promptly entered it, and the General was sending me orders to retake it. I immediately had the column wheel to the left and attacked the village of Neerwinden with five half-brigades of infantry (fifteen battalions) commanded under me by Generals Chancel† and Desforêts.‡ I left the sixth half-brigade at right angles to the entrance on our side. Our troops fell on the village eagerly, and despite the resistance of the Austrian infantry, we were dislodging it street by street and hedge by hedge when, having almost reached the end of the village, we noticed a strong column of infantry in the plain beyond, which, coming from the right wing of the enemy army after defeating General Miranda's division, was advancing on us in silence. Suddenly, as they came up to us, these troops, who had recently served in the war against the Turks and had adopted their war cries, uttered a long howl that affected our young soldiers. The third battalion of Volunteers from the Lot gave ground and gave the signal for flight by shouting *Every man for himself!* The example was contagious, and in a moment the commotion became general. In vain, with all my officers, I struggled to restore order: rifles, cartridge boxes, even knapsacks, all were thrown down in order to cross the hedges more speedily. Seeing I was powerless to prevent this, I made speed to get all the troops who had not yet been

* General Miaczincki perished on the revolutionary scaffold.
† General Nestor Chancel, having withstood for six weeks the siege of Condé, where he was commandant, perished on the revolutionary scaffold.
‡ General Desforêts, the same who had so bravely supported me in the woods of Flénu at the Battle of Jemappes, was grievously wounded in this attack.

affected by the disorder out of the village. I put the 99th of the line, the former Royal Deux-Ponts, in battle array on the village square with orders to hold off the enemy long enough to cover our retreat. Its commander was Colonel *Von der Wisch* who, suffering from gout in one foot, was on horseback. I was expecting that the Austrian column would charge with bayonets fixed: It did nothing of the sort. When it reached the square, the 99th began to fire on it, and without replying to our fire, the Austrian Deutschmeister Regiment,* which was at the head, deployed as calmly as if it had been on parade and then began to fire at such close range that the slaughter was considerable. Despite its great inferiority in numbers, our valiant Deux-Ponts continued its fire until it had spent its ammunition. Then it retreated in good order, and I must say that the Austrians, to their credit, stopped their fire as soon as they saw it in retreat, and they did not pursue it: They were content with occupying the village without venturing out.

To the right of the half-brigade of infantry that I had left to cover the entrance to the village of Neerwinden, in the plain separating Neerwinden from the village of Overwinden, lay our cavalry, belonging to General Valence's division. Overwinden was still occupied by his infantry, and General Neuilly's brigade of dragoons was at right angles to this village. Facing our cavalry, with its back to the tumulus of Middlewinden and behind this tomb, was a second line of Austrian cavalry that was intended to reinforce the first, though this it did not do.†

Just as I was leaving the village of Neerwinden, I noticed our line of cavalry advancing at the trot to charge the Austrian cavalry, which was doing likewise. Immediately I rushed to my half-brigade, assumed overall command of it myself, and, to omit nothing that would make it hold firm, I placed behind it a platoon of light cavalry I had kept with me and ordered them out loud to force back at the point of the sword anyone who tried to break ranks.

I then harangued this half-brigade, whose central battalion was the 38th of the line (the former Dauphiné regiment) commanded by Colonel de la Gardiole with, on its right, the 5th battalion of National Volunteers, called the Battalion of the Commune of Paris, and on its left, the Théâtre-Français section's battalion of National Guards, also from Paris. I told them that although they were operating in open country with neither a ditch nor an embankment in front of them, provided that they maintained discipline and did not let a shot leave their ranks until I had given the order, I would answer for the success of a feat of arms that would bring

* A white uniform with sky-blue facings, collar, and hat brim.

† When a fortnight later I went through the Austrian headquarters on my way to Switzerland, I expressed my surprise that this second line had remained idle. I was told that the reason for this was that its superior officer, General Count Bentheim, had been absent at the time with the Prince of Coburg and that his second in command, General Lilieu, had not considered himself authorized to order the charge without him.

them glory; that I would not give this order until the enemy was thirty paces from us; that then each battalion should begin to fire from the right one after the other at the same time as six cannons placed between them (under Captain de Rennepont) fired grapeshot at the enemy's cavalry. In this they followed my orders and won the success I had promised them.

General Valence's charge was not so fortunate. With his usual audacity he had placed himself alone fifteen to twenty paces in front of the line with two aides-de-camp, Captains Mailly de Château-Renaud and Joubert (from the engineers), and the momentum of their horses catapulted them into the Austrian ranks before the two cavalries met. Valence and Château-Renaud, better horsemen than Joubert, shot through, the General losing his hat and receiving three saber cuts on his head while the other received seven. The unfortunate Joubert fell from his horse, is said to have received forty-two saber blows, and died that night at Neer-Heylissem, to which the ambulance wagon had carried him.

One of the saber thrusts General Valence had received had ripped open the skin of his face from his forehead to his chin, which covered his face with an apron of blood and temporarily deprived him of sight. But despite his seven saber cuts, M. de Château-Renaud took hold of the bridle of his horse, and going behind the fray brought him back within striking distance of our ranks whence I ran to him. He recognized my voice and exclaimed while he was being taken to the ambulance wagon: *"This must be horrible to look at,* but it will be nothing"; and in fact all he was left with were glorious scars.

The Austrian cavalry having scattered ours without losing formation, two squadrons from the Nassau-Usingen regiment charged my half-brigade and were bearing down on it at full gallop when the fire of my infantry and grapeshot cannon, which doubtless they already regarded as their trophies, threw them into complete disorder. Their horses reared in all directions, they lost many men, and in very few seconds these two squadrons disappeared. The same happened to the cavalry that had overthrown General Valence's. It hurled itself too eagerly in pursuit of our cavalry, and General Neuilly, taking advantage of the confusion that had arisen in its ranks, charged it vigorously and succeeded in clearing it from the battlefield of which we remained the masters. While these operations were in progress, I had managed to restore order to my infantry, which had left the village of Neerwinden, despite the fire of a battery that at first somewhat ravaged my right wing. In it I lost a rifleman from the 3rd who had been one of my orderlies since the Battle of Jemappes. He was killed beside me while I was giving him an order and I heard the bullet that hit him in the heart break the blade of his saber. However, the aim of this battery was not sufficiently accurate to hit us after I had wheeled my right wing around in the opposite direction, when all the shot passed over our heads to the great amusement of our soldiers.

My division was drawn up with the Gette to its rear, its left supported by the village of Laar occupied by General Dietmann, and before it lay the village of Neerwinden, occupied by the Austrians without any outposts. To my right was the cavalry of General Valence's division, whose command General Leveneur had assumed, and the village of Overwinden, which was still occupied by our troops. We were therefore in a position to resume the offensive and to join battle again at dawn the next day, March 19.

Such was General Dumouriez's intention and the order he gave me when he left us in the evening to visit the left wing of the army. He was very anxious about this, and with all too good reason, not having received any news from General Miranda and perceiving, as we all had, that since two o'clock in the afternoon no firing at all had been heard from that quarter.

The Austrians did not carry out any operations during the night. I spent it very peacefully in a sunken road, where I set up my bivouac with Generals d'Hangest and Sabrevoix of the artillery and my officers.

It was not until four o'clock in the morning that I saw Captain Rainville, General Dumouriez's aide-de-camp, arrive, though he had been dispatched as early as eleven o'clock at night to bring me and General Leveneur orders to begin the retreat at midnight, beginning by leading all the artillery back across the Gette, and to await further orders on the left bank of that river. Captain Rainville had unfortunately got lost in the dark, and dawn was about to break when we began the operation. A thick mist concealed the fact from the Austrians, which was all the more fortunate in that we had only two very narrow bridges by which to cross the Gette.

General Leveneur was equally successful in carrying out his operations, and our divisions had been reassembled on the left bank of the Gette when General Dumouriez arrived to take over command. He put us on the march in three columns, the artillery, which was intact, forming the central one. General Lamarche with his cavalry and our horse-drawn artillery followed the road from Saint-Trond to Tirlemont in order to cover our right, which was causing General Dumouriez some anxiety: The Austrian army had been in possession of the Orsmael bridge on this road the day before, and he foresaw that it would be from there that they would come out to attack us as we retreated. His fears were well founded and justified by events. But the Austrian army executed its crossing of the Gette so slowly that our artillery park and the majority of our wagons had already entered Tirlemont when our rear guard was attacked by a cannonade, which was without consequence.

I remained at Tirlemont during the night of March 19, and in the morning of the 20th we continued our retreat. General Dumouriez had proposed to reassemble his army at the defensive position of Kumtich and there to face a new battle. He soon realized that this plan was impracticable. The demoralization and faintheartedness of the army was increasing all the time, as was desertion back to France, and with the passing of every moment it was becoming more difficult to persuade the troops to sustain any combat.

The Austrians' slowness in pursuing us gave us time to restore a little order to the formation of our army on the heights of Kumtich, where we bivouacked on the 20th. But General Dumouriez soon lost all hope of our being able to make a stand at Kumtich, especially when he learned that a considerable portion of the Austrian army was slipping past his left wing to cut our communications with France, intercept our convoys, etc.

On March 21, at dawn, we left our positions at Kumtich, not to retreat much further but to avoid a regular engagement, which we could not have been able to sustain; and we fell back on the woods of Bautersem and Lovenjoel in order to take up position in broken and sodden terrain where the odds could be expected to be less unfavorable to us in that the Austrian cavalry could not operate there. Therefore, as soon as I had reconnoitered the defense of these woods and had taken steps to be ready to repel an attack, I ordered soup to be made and set up my headquarters in the bivouac by the side of the main road to Louvain.

I had not even dismounted when I saw a big post chaise roll up. I went up to it and recognized Danton and Delacroix, representatives of the people and commissioners of the National Convention. They told me they were looking for General Dumouriez and that it was very urgent they speak with him. I replied I could not tell them where they would find him, that on leaving me his intention had been to proceed to his left in the direction of Le Pellenberg, where General Champmorin's division was supposed to be; but that even if he were still there, which I doubted, they would still have to return to Louvain, as all other roads were absolutely impassable, especially since I feared that if they ventured forth even on horseback they would be captured by the Austrian detachments that were roaming the country in all directions. They decided to return to Louvain. "But before that," Delacroix said, "we should very much like to see your troops." —"At your orders," I replied. "If you care to mount two of my horses, I will have them present arms and do you the honors." —"All right for the horses," Danton said, "but please, no presenting of arms or honors; we do not wish to disturb or weary the troops."

Then they got out of their carriage, mounted horses, and while their stirrups were being arranged, I went toward the troops and called to them: "Comrades, these are the National Convention's representative-commissioners to our armies who have come to see you. Line up behind the piles of arms." Then we began our progress along the line, the troops in silence and pretty sullen. When we reached the 71st of the line (the former Vivarais regiment) under Colonel Bannes, an excellent regiment that still looked presentable, Delacroix stopped in front of a clearing in the wood through which the heights of Kumtich could be seen and said to me, pointing at them: "But, General, what do I see up there?" —"Up there," I said in a perfectly natural tone, "you see the Austrians." —"What," he replied histrionically, looking at the soldiers to savor his expected effect, "what, the Austrians! So close to us! And we do not *fall* on those b———!" General laughter, breaking the silence hitherto observed, informed the representative that he had failed to achieve the desired effect. I tried to hurry us on so he would not hear the jests that would follow the laughter, of which I was certain neither Danton nor he would have missed a syllable. "Jolly good, yes, why don't you *fall* on them," someone said, "since you know all about it!" —"Go and see for yourselves and *fall* on them," said another, "if that's what you like, and tell us all about it; the rest of us have had enough."

A few steps further on, Danton got out his watch and said to me: "General, I think we have already been too long with you. It's late, and I think we'd do better not to go any further and return to Louvain as soon as possible." Then, on his way back to his carriage, he leaned toward me and said in a low voice: "We are very anxious to speak to Dumouriez about his letter of March 12. He has waged a campaign against us that has had deplorable consequences. He must retract." —"I know nothing about any of that," I replied, "and I am sticking to the advice you gave me. I am concentrating exclusively on my military career without being involved in politics." —"Very well! That is still the best advice you could follow," he replied. Then they got back into their carriage, and I did not see them again.

When I was back among my troops, the unit commanders came and gave me a report of the remarks that the representatives' visit and Delacroix's sally had elicited from the soldiers about them and the National Convention.

I heard one of these jesters myself who said of this Assembly: "In there are seven hundred chatterboxes who make speeches every day and then decrees. Decrees! You lot, you don't know what decrees are or what's the good of them! All right! I don't know either, so I won't tell you. But what I will say, and you know it as well as I, is that we poor soldiers always need people in the army, and someone would be doing us a great service if they sent us the Convention *organized as a battalion of light infantry. . . !*" —"Ah! Well said, that, a good idea," his audience declared. —"Yes," replied a smart aleck, "but if they are as well fed as these two, your infantry will not be light." —"Shut up, you booby, you don't understand a thing about it," the smooth-talker retorted, "we will make sappers out of them, put hooks on them, and they will be splendid under the footboard."

I have always remembered this joke about converting the National Convention into a battalion of light troops because during the period I was with the army, nothing amused the soldiers more than to repeat it and to ring all the changes on it. It stemmed from the French soldiers' dislike of interference from civilians. They wanted no superiors other than stripes, epaulets, stars, and the marshal's *bâton.* They will gladly say with the social levelers:

A man who serves his country well has no need of ancestors.

And not only do they say it, but one has to be very careful to go along with them in this and to realize that they are also imbued with this other notion:

The first King was a successful soldier.

Hence their antipathy toward government by civilian assemblies and, moreover, whatever their *penchant* for republican ideas, the monarchical ideal has always been that of the army, whatever the country's current form of government.

What in all periods has always been the first instinct of the French army, overriding all others, is that of nationalism. But one must not misunderstand the true significance of this word, that is to say, the way it is interpreted or felt. It does not mean the exclusion of foreign soldiers or corps from the ranks of the army fighting with it under the French colors. Quite the contrary—until 1789 the army was glad to see them there because it realized that they increased its moral and physical strength without diminishing its *nationalism* at all, because the nationalism to which it adhered was that of its flag. As long as the white flag, which it called the *unblemished flag,* represented for it France and the King, which at that time seemed inseparable, the army remained fanatically attached to its white flag for centuries. But when by the most deplorable error imaginable, this flag, hitherto *unblemished,* was carried into foreign armies, assigned to those *émigré* corps that formed part of them and were paid by and under orders of foreign governments, and when the Frenchmen who rallied to it thought they could varnish over this absurd fiction by saying to France:

Rome is no longer in Rome,
It is wholly where we are . . .

then the common sense of the army, as well as its sentiments of honor and patriotism, revolted against such a claim. I say sentiments of honor not, indeed, because I wish to lay too heavy a charge at the *émigrés'* door—on the contrary, I acknowledge that in emigrating a great number of them thought they were acting in accordance with the dictates of honor—but I deeply believe that their point of view was erroneous in all respects, and I myself shared the opinion I constantly heard expressed all around me in the army, both by the officers who had not emigrated and the soldiers themselves, and which was summed up by saying that they did not see how an action that for the troops would constitute *the crime of desertion* could be transformed into an honorable and meritorious deed for the officers.

I shall not go into detail about the combats we had to endure during our retreat. The morale of our army got worse and worse; with the sole exception of the action at Pellenberg, where General Champmorin took two cannons, the advantage always lay with the Austrians; but the most disastrous of all was the battle on March 27 to the right—that is to say, to the south—of Louvain, where the efforts of General Dumouriez and of all of us combined could not prevent the army from almost totally disbanding. Luckily for France, night came soon enough to hide from the Austrians the confusion into which we had fallen. The army had become an amorphous mass where all the units were mixed up and wherein it had indeed become impossible to exercise any command. It had to be seen to be believed; and the things that were said had to be heard to appreciate our situation: "Let's go back to our farms," exclaimed the soldiers, "let's return to France; what's the good of battles in which we are crushed and of putting up an impossible resistance to defend this cursed Belgium? Devil take it and all the Belgians with it! Let's be off, comrades, as quickly as possible . . . !"

General Dumouriez then made the decision to assemble all his remaining cavalry—and he had so little left that the 2nd Hussars (Chamborant) could only supply him with seventy-eight mounted men—and to form them into a rear-guard cordon to prevent the Austrian light troops from approaching during the night. He directed the bulk of the troops toward Kortemberg and then returned to Louvain with me. I was still very ill, and I began to be afflicted with scarlet fever, which obliged me to follow the progress of my division from a carriage.

General Dumouriez and I spent the night in the great fortress of Sainte-Gertrude at Louvain, where we had stayed before the battle, and it was there that he had a conversation with me that I shall attempt to reproduce. I have so often gone over it in my mind during the course of my long subsequent career that I can vouch for the accuracy of my recollection of it, and I trust that the account of the events that followed it will suffice to remove all doubts.

General Dumouriez began by assuring me that he did not wish to bring about any changes in the relationship between us that we had both agreed upon all along, and especially in our discussions in Antwerp of which I spoke earlier—that is to say, that he would not ask me for any cooperation in political matters and would indeed leave me out of all his political activities and would only employ me as one of his lieutenants general strictly confined to the limits of his military functions. On the other hand, at a time when the harshness of the times in which we lived had created a situation for France, for the army, and for ourselves such as the one in which we found ourselves—and dangers such as those surrounding us—he thought he owed it to me and to himself to describe them and not in any way to conceal from me the measures he believed this situation required of him.

He said over and over again that he had found no way of preserving us from these dangers except that of an honorable peace with the foreign Powers, combined with the overthrow of the National Convention in order to stop the progress of its misdeeds and to replace it with a government that would represent neither the triumph of the *émigrés* and the Counterrevolution nor that of the instigators of the excesses of the Revolution and the *blood-drinkers** (for that was the horrifying label that had been attached to them and that already they merited only too well, although they were still only at the beginning of their careers of crime!†) . . .

* *Buveur de sang* was one of the stock epithets applied to former terrorists.—ED.

† General Dumouriez came out very strongly on this point, since he advocated, in fact, the same policy as the one I later defined as that of the *juste milieu*. He confided to me that to accomplish it he had secretly resumed the old relations he had had previously with the Baron de Breteuil. I have already in the first part of my memoirs had occasion to reproduce documents proving that this former minister of Louis XVI before the Revolution of 1789 had become at this period his personal representative to the foreign Powers. Louis XVI had, as it were, tacitly accredited him to them to disavow on the one hand his official constitutional ambassadors or representatives, and on the other, up to a certain point, the Princes his brothers and all the representatives of the *émigrés* (by whom he feared he would be dominated after the success of the Counterrevolution, in which that party always had blind confidence). Faithful to these double instructions, the Baron de Breteuil, on leaving France to carry out his mission, had not gone to Coblenz and had installed himself first of all in Switzerland at Soleure, where his great-grandson the present Duc de Montmorency was born, and later at Richmond in England, where I think he was in 1793.

General Dumouriez told me that after the death of Louis XVI he had made use of an agent called *Benoît Tor de la Sonde,* who had the confidence of both of them, to make known to the Baron de Breteuil, under the seal of the most profound secrecy, his plan to restore the throne in France in favor of the Young Prince, Louis XVI's son, by proclaiming him King in conjunction with the reestablishment of the Constitution of 1791. He added that this agent had reported back to him the Baron de Breteuil's complete acceptance of this plan as well as the other conditions that General Dumouriez had decided to impose, of which the principal ones were to be that during the minority of the young King, royal authority should be exercised in his name by a Council of Regency under the presidency of the Baron de Breteuil, as having been the depositary of the personal confidence of the late King, and from which Queen Marie-Antoinette as well as all the Princes without exception would be excluded. The next condition was that a holy veil should be thrown over the past, that there should be neither vengeance nor executions, and that they should scrupulously follow the example Charles II had set in England when, after the Restoration, he had merely banished the judges of Charles I to America. I sympathetically acknowledged this confidence; it lifted a great weight from my mind.

Despite the mistrust that the vindictive intentions of the *émigré* party were bound to inspire, it could be hoped that they would be restrained at this period as in fact they later were. For what was done in this respect in 1814 was precisely what Dumouriez wanted when he required that a holy veil should be thrown over the past. The example given by Charles II was even exceeded under Louis XVII, since no one was prosecuted for his past actions and since the members of the National Convention who had voted for the death of the King were not disturbed in any way during

France found herself at war with all the great Powers, and the only countries remaining in more or less uncertain neutrality were Sweden, Denmark, Turkey, Tuscany, the aristocratic republics of Genoa and Venice, the United States of America, and, finally, Switzerland, whose neutrality—of special value to France, since Switzerland covered one of the most vulnerable parts of her frontiers—had already been compromised by the occupation of Porrentruy and all of the Bishopric of Basel, and by the Genevan revolution that General Montesquiou had vainly tried to oppose. This resistance brought down a decree of accusation on his head, causing him to take refuge in Switzerland.*

Thus, with the solitary exception of the part of its frontiers covered by Swiss neutrality—a neutrality that could have been violated then as it later was—France could expect a general and even simultaneous attack on all fronts from the innumerable armies Europe had fielded. And to these she could only oppose armies far inferior in number that she could neither pay, given the complete collapse of her finances, nor provide with the necessities of war, nor, consequently, raise from the undisciplined and disorganized condition into which they had fallen.†

This general attack would probably become, as it were, one of

---

the first year of the Restoration. It was in fact only in 1815, after the Hundred Days, that advantage was taken of the adhesion of most of them to the *Acte additionnel*— which pronounced the permanent exclusion of the Bourbons—to apply to the signatories alone the penalty of exile. Those, on the other hand, who had not signed remained in peace in France.

It is indeed remarkable that one of these regicides, Fouché, Duke of Otranto, was called to the Council by King Louis XVIII, and he took the oath between his hands as Minister of General Police.

* Such was the general expectation at that time that the Counterrevolution would be successful and such the fear of granting protection to Frenchmen other than the *émigrés* (whose political principles at least, if not their cause, had been espoused by all the Powers) that despite this honorable opposition by General Montesquiou and the feeling of gratitude he should have inspired throughout Switzerland, he was obliged, in order to find asylum there, to lie low in an out-of-the-way place under the assumed name of the *Chevalier de Rionel*.

† To give a proper idea of this deplorable state, I am copying here the following letter from the Minister of War that was read to the National Convention during the sitting of Thursday, March 21, 1793, and which is taken from *le Moniteur*.

Paris, March 21, 1793

Citizen President, a letter, which I received yesterday from General Dumouriez and which I immediately communicated to the Committee of General Defense, informs me that there is large-scale desertion, and this report is unfortunately confirmed by the National Convention's commissioners in Belgium. I immediately took all the measures within my power to stop the rot. The soldiers are abandoning themselves to continual pillaging and theft, which alienates the inhabitants at a time when it is of the utmost importance for us to pursue the fugitives and bring them back. I am enforcing the military code and making full use of courts-martial; but it is not enough. I regard it as a matter of capital importance that the National Convention gets down to drafting a wartime military code. This measure is extremely urgent, every minute makes it necessary, and without it good-bye to the army.

encirclement as a result of the outbreak of war with England, whose naval power would enable her to transport armies by sea and deposit them wherever she wanted on our coasts. This was all the more to be feared as it was in the month of March 1793 that the rebellion in the Vendée broke out and began the civil war that flared up in the western departments.*

This rising was all the more formidable because the National Convention had no troops with which to oppose it, no other means of suppressing it than sanguinary reprisals . . . †

This rebellion was wholly monarchical and religious in character and these features so predominated that it had little chance of securing the cooperation of other parts of France.‡

The primary difficulty, therefore, was to offer the nation a constitutional arrangement near enough to the various shades of opinion to offer hope that they would rally around it. On this point General Dumouriez was explicit, and his plan was well drawn up. He wanted to have the young Prince, Louis XVI's son, abducted from the Temple, proclaim him King in his camp, and march on Paris with his army, adopting as his political banner the restoration of the Constitution of 1791.

In 1790 General Dumouriez had commanded the division from the Vendéen departments of Niort. There had been frequent contacts with

---

* This rebellion, royalist and Catholic in complexion, was most dangerous in the months March-December 1793. In the latter month, the rebels were defeated in the streets of Le Mans; and although the struggle continued, on and off, into the next century, its proportions were reduced to those of guerrilla warfare.—ED.

† The most spectacular of these were, undoubtedly, the *noyades* ordered by Carrier at Nantes, where ships containing royalist prisoners were scuppered in the Loire estuary—ED.

‡ In fact, two or three months later after the rising of May 31 of the same year, 1793, when forty-five departments in the Midi, with Bordeaux, Lyon, and Marseille at their head, banded together against the Convention, whose title and authority they no longer recognized, no contacts or associations were established between the Vendéens and themselves. The Federation of the Midi possessed neither leaders, banners, nor central direction; everything was vague and disjointed, and they did not come out either in favor of the monarchy or against the Republic. Therefore the movement disappeared like a mist, and the city of Lyon was the only place to put up resistance in the glorious siege it endured, after which the Convention decimated its defenders, ordered that it should be razed to the ground and that it should have no other name than that of *Liberated Commune*. The Vendée kept going longer through its royalist and religious fanaticism, but the lack of coordination, understanding, and compromise paralyzed all the resistance movements and assured the triumph of the National Convention, until its execrable rule collapsed under the weight of the contempt into which it had fallen, to be replaced in turn by the Council of Ancients and the Five Hundred with the Directory, the Consulate, and finally, the Napoleonic Empire.

But I have no wish to anticipate events subsequent to the time with which I am concerned, still less to present General Dumouriez as a prophet who could read the future. I merely wish to say that in his wisdom he already foresaw great misfortunes for France and that he regarded the monarchy as the only way of preserving her from them.

those who had become the leaders of the insurrection, and he believed that, provided the Crown was placed on the head of Louis XVI's son, it would be possible to reach agreement with them to act together under the banner of the Constitution of 1791. He had maintained contact with them in concert with the Girondin Gensonné, who, prior to being elected to the Legislative Assembly, had been a government commissioner in these departments at the time when Dumouriez was the military commander there, and they had both of them received assurances from the majority of these leaders that there would be no rising in this region as long as Louis XVI or his son sat on the throne; and in fact there was not, since the insurrection did not break out till March 1793, that is to say, five or six weeks after the death of Louis XVI.

Such were the grounds for General Dumouriez's expectation that he could coordinate the activity of all those who, whatever their shades of political opinion, were agreed in wanting to stay the course of the excesses of the Revolution and to deliver France from the yoke of the factions whose instrument the National Convention had become. And by means of this agreement, he hoped to succeed in coordinating the operations of his army in the north with the risings in the west and in the Midi. Events proved only too well just how chimerical this hope was. But whatever one's assessment of it then, one thing was sure: The army could not take any part in operations within France until, one way or another, he had managed to arrest the progress of the foreign armies that were about to enter France for a second time. There was no longer any hope of attaining this goal through the success of our arms. The loss of the Battle of Neerwinden, with its baleful consequences, had thrown our armies in the north into a disastrous condition. They were so reduced in number, so disorganized, and so demoralized that we were no longer in a position to withstand any large-scale encounter with the Austrian army. Nothing now hindered it from interposing itself between us and our frontier by marching straight for Ath or Mons and Tournay. Not only would this operation cut off our retreat and seem bound to cost us at least the loss of our artillery and equipment, but it would make it impossible for our Army of Holland, with its siege train, to return to France. This army, already threatened by the advance guard of the English and Dutch armies and by twelve thousand Prussians on the march under General Knobelsdorff, would have had no alternative but to shut itself in the fortresses of Breda and Geertruydenberg, where the lack of provisions alone would soon have been enough to force on them an unconditional surrender.

General Dumouriez added that considering the severity of the predicament, he had decided to make highly secret overtures to the Prince of Coburg; that he had communicated to him his plan to have the prisoners in the Temple abducted by a body of light troops when his army was back on French soil; that if this abduction was successful, he would proclaim Louis XVI's son *King* in the midst of his camp, with the title Louis XVII, and that he would escort him to Paris at the head of his army, taking as his political banner the restoration of the Constitution of 1791; that far from requesting assistance from the Austrian army, he had on the contrary emphasized to the Prince of Coburg that such assistance would be fatal and that he had merely requested tacit understanding of a secret armistice or a suspension of hostilities during which he would undertake to withdraw our armies completely to our fortresses and behind our frontiers, to evacuate the Belgian and Dutch fortresses occupied by our troops. Finally, he had asked that the Austrian army abstain from crossing our borders until his plans had either succeeded or failed.

General Dumouriez then informed me that the Prince of Coburg had favorably received all these requests and had declared that he would carry out his side of the bargain without there being any written agreement or any document whatsoever recording the undertakings.

After giving me this exposé, which threw me into the greatest perplexity, General Dumouriez spoke to me of my personal position, which he envisaged as I would have wanted him to. He confessed he would almost have preferred that I had not been in his army in order to remove all suspicion of his wanting to carry me to the throne and of my aiming for it. But since I happened to be in his army before all this blew up, he would not for all the world have me dream of removing myself. Knowing the special position in which I was placed, he had considered that I should not be left in the dark about what he had just confided in me so as to enable me to determine, in full knowledge of the facts, what conduct was most expedient. He regarded it as a piece of luck, however painful for me, that I should have been separated from my father's deplorable stance in the National Convention, but he would never ask anything of me that could ruffle my filial piety, and on the contrary, he promised to do his best to palliate the unpleasantness of what I might experience on this account. For the rest, he was not asking any assistance of me in the political measures he might take, he counted on my discretion, and what he wanted was that I should remain at my post in the army, continuing, as in the past, to devote myself exclusively to carrying out my military duties.

Such were the explanations given to me by General Dumouriez, and such his demands of me.

I replied to General Dumouriez that everything he had just told me had given rise to a confusion in my thinking that I had neither the power nor—I thought it right to acknowledge—the desire to try to sort out immediately. However, my task was made much easier because I only had to reply to him about what concerned me personally. Consequently, I did not have to consider either the measures he had already taken or the plans he had just disclosed to me. He knew that it was to the rule of the National Convention that I attributed both the ills that France was already suffering and the still greater ills that it seemed to me the continuation of this odious tyranny was bound to bring down upon her; but, *disillusioned* as I already was with the theories of government that had previously filled me with enthusiasm, I had decided to confine myself exclusively to carrying out my military duties, as he was asking me to do. I added that there was no longer any tenable position for me in France but with the army, nor any suitable role possible other than that of a soldier devoted to his country. Therefore, I desired to share or endure all the varying fortunes of the army, and I was resolved not to separate myself from it unless constrained by absolute necessity.

I thanked him for confiding in me and promised to keep his secret. There was never any pact other than that between General Dumouriez and myself.

On March 23 the bulk of the army was at Kortemberg, retreating slowly in the greatest disorder amid frightening numbers of deserters who littered the main road, already cluttered with the artillery park, the covered wagons, and the baggages.

On the 25th the army passed through Brussels, making for Halle, where it took the road leading to Tournay via Enghien and Ath.

I followed these operations from my carriage, not being fit to mount a horse. But soon, overwhelmed by a violent fever and the eruption of scarlet fever, I was obliged to go on ahead and take to my bed in the house where my sister was living with Mme de Genlis at Tournay. My sister's drawing room was on the first floor, and I lay in a room on the second.

I relate this detail only to give the lie to the baseless assertion that I was present and took part in a conversation, or rather a scene (which by coincidence took place in my sister's drawing room at Tournay) between General Dumouriez and three emissaries from Paris who had been let loose on him in order to extract imprudent revelations, or at least utterances, that could furnish ammunition against him.

These three emissaries, called *Proly, Pereyra* and *Dubuisson,* were in reality sent by the *Jacobin Society,* but to give their mission a pretext, they had been provided with a letter from Lebrun, then Minister of Foreign Affairs and known to be very closely associated with General Dumouriez, asking him to receive and listen to them.* On arrival at Tournay, they had presented themselves at the Abbey of Saint-Martin, where General Dumouriez's headquarters were situated, but General Dumouriez had sent word to them that he was very busy and would see them later. Scarcely satisfied with this reply, they had kept watch on the General, and on seeing him leave had followed him unobserved; and seeing him enter my sister's house, they had profited from the fact that the

* Lebrun later perished on the revolutionary scaffold. (He also, with considerable phlegm, continued to run the Foreign Office when under house arrest, in particular drafting a set of rules for ambassadors that was adopted by the Committee of Public Safety.—ED.)

door on to the square had been left open to climb the stairs without saying anything and suddenly enter the drawing room, where General Dumouriez was chatting with my sister and Mme de Genlis and perhaps some other people, I do not know.

General Dumouriez had gone into a rage at seeing them enter like this; he had ordered them to withdraw and wait for him at his headquarters. But they insisted on being heard immediately, and it was only after a fairly sharp altercation that they agreed to return to the Abbey of Saint-Martin. I feel certain that it was there that they had their discussion with General Dumouriez.

Nevertheless, they have put on record in what they called the *official* report of this discussion—although this so-called official report was drawn up by *them alone*—that I was *present* at this discussion, which is both false and impossible, since I was ill in bed in the room on the second floor. I also think that my sister's drawing room was too small to have been the site of this discussion, and I have no doubt that as General Dumouriez says in his memoirs, it was really in the Abbey of Saint-Martin that this discussion took place.

It was in the sitting of March 31 that Cambacérès, reporting in the name of the Committees of Defense and General Security on the measures they had taken in the interests of what they termed the *public safety,* read at the rostrum the account of this discussion (termed the *official minutes*) given by Proly, Pereyra, and Dubuisson, and announced that the committees had placed these three citizens under house arrest, not because their trustworthiness was in doubt, but for their personal safety and to preserve such precious witnesses.

This tender solicitude for their *personal safety* and their *preservation* was not long in being replaced by quite other attentions, since these three citizens perished on the revolutionary scaffold on the same day, and here is the note to be found in the reprint of *le Moniteur* at the bottom of their official minutes:

"Proly, Dubuisson, and Pereyra were later condemned to death by the Revolutionary Tribunal as foreign agents. It should cause no surprise [to learn] that these three commissioners had given Dumouriez the hope of bringing about the change in direction he wanted to impart to the Jacobins. But removed from the atmosphere of treason, these three cronies lost their nerve in the presence of the nation and made a virtue of unmasking the projects of Dumouriez."

Such was the result for these wretches of the unworthy mission they had undertaken. They were sacrificed by those very people whose odious instruments they had made themselves, and they were struck down by that very Revolutionary Tribunal whose creation they had taken it upon themselves to defend in their discussion with General Dumouriez; here is this passage that I transcribe from their official minutes:

"He (Dumouriez) became inflamed and went into transports of rage when speaking of the new Revolutionary Tribunal, swore he would not tolerate its existence, which was an abomination. Vainly we tried to demonstrate to him its necessity, given the gravity of the civil war (of which he had spoken with a kind of complaisance); he became more and more carried away and said three or four times that as long as he had *four inches of steel at his side* he would know just how to avert this abomination; that if scenes of carnage were repeated in Paris he would march on it immediately; that, in short, he did not give the Convention three weeks."

And the following year the members of that same Revolutionary Tribunal—created in defiance of all the laws so as to be able to break them and respect none of them, for such is *revolutionary legality**—were sent to their deaths *en masse,* without any exceptions, without any of them being heard or brought before any tribunal and without any judgment but an ordinary† decree of the National Convention outlawing them all.

I shall not go into more detail on Dumouriez's meeting with the three emissaries, and I merely transcribe the conclusions of Cambacérès's report. They constitute fresh proof that the proscription of my entire family had been decided on in advance.‡

On March 31 the army left Tournay to return to French soil, occupying the defensive position of Maulde—made famous by the use General Dumouriez had made of it in the campaign of 1792 to cover our northern frontier from Austrian incursions, despite the reiterated orders he had received to abandon it.

* The question of what constitutes legality in a revolutionary situation is not straightforward, and perhaps the decree of a Constituent Convention—though politically motivated—is not as ordinary as Louis-Philippe implies.—ED.

† Here it should be remembered that the members of the Revolutionary Tribunal were not the only ones included in this decree. The Convention included in it without distinction all the deputies at the Hôtel de Ville, Robespierre and others, as well as all the members of that General Council of the Commune of Paris before whom it still trembled, sending them all to their deaths. Paris, still in ignorance of who had emerged victorious in the struggle of the 9th of Thermidor[a] looked on amazed as a long convoy of tumbrils appeared bearing the *hundred and fifty-seven individuals outlawed en masse* to the scaffold for the occasion at the Throne Gates; it is said that the executions lasted more than two hours. But the amazement turned into thanksgiving as soon as the identity of the victims had been recognized, and it could be hoped that France would be delivered from the most shameful and detestable tyranny that has ever weighed on any people.

‡ ". . . I am instructed to tell you, first, that we have provisionally placed under arrest the three citizens who signed the minutes to which I referred: Not that their truthfulness is in question; this measure has been dictated out of regard for their personal safety and to preserve such precious witnesses.

"Secondly, we thought we should lay hold of all those who, by reason of birth, self-interest, habits, relationships, and circumstances, may be suspected of wanting the restoration of the monarchy. . . ."

[a] Nine Thermidor, year II of the revolutionary calendar, or July 27, 1794.—ED.

Although my sister had not, as my father had vainly expected, been removed from the list of *émigrés* on which she had been so unjustly placed, I had nonetheless decided to bring her back to France if we were forced to evacuate Belgium and to keep her under the protection of our colors as far as it was in my power to guarantee them. Mme de Genlis and Mlle Henriette de Sercey, her niece, who had spent the winter at Tournay with my sister* and like her had been placed on the list of *émigrés,* were equally terrified of facing the consequences in France or incurring permanent expatriation by trying to stay on at Tournay after the Austrian occupation.

I therefore decided to bring my sister with me when I left Tournay, and as it was my first outing after my illness, I placed myself with her, Mme de Genlis, and Mlle de Sercey in a carriage, ordering it to proceed in the center of my division—most of which halted at the camp at Maulde—while I continued my journey in the same carriage as far as the town of Saint-Amand, where we all lodged with a householder called M. Leblanc.

The town of Saint-Amand is about four miles from Maulde and quite close to the thermal baths of Saint-Amand where General Dumouriez set up his headquarters to be nearer the bulk of the army, which occupied the camp of Maulde, and at the same time to be in a central position for this camp, also that of Bruille, our various garrisons, and the artillery park, which was nearer the town of Saint-Amand.

I thought these details necessary for an understanding of the events I am going to relate.

At Lille there was a fairly numerous gathering of the Convention's commissioners, and another at Valenciennes. There was none at Condé, where General Neuilly was in command.

As early as March 29, that is, two days before General Dumouriez had left Tournay with the army, the commissioners at Lille had required him to proceed there, in a letter that was both a summons and the equivalent of a dismissal.† General Dumouriez had refused, and it was then that the

---

* It has been said that Mlle Pamela was there, too. This assertion is false. She had been for some time in Ireland with her husband, Lord Edward Fitzgerald. I only go into these details to give the lie, once and for all, to the absurd inferences people have been pleased to draw from all this.

† Letter of the National Convention's commissioners to General Dumouriez:

Lille, March 29, 1793

The National Convention's commissioners with the Armies of Belgium and in the Nord and Pas-de-Calais departments, jointly require General Dumouriez to proceed today, March 29 in the afternoon, to Citizen Mousquet's house in the Golden Lion Square, Lille, to clarify for them certain grave charges concerning him, which will be intimated.

General Dumouriez will entrust the command of his army, during his absence, to the staff officer under him whom he considers most fitted to replace him.

Lille, March 29, 1793, year II of the Republic.

(Signed) Gossuin, Delacroix, L. Carnot, Merlin de *Douai,* Robert, Treilhard, Lesage-Sénault.

National Convention sent four special commissioners from Paris—Camus, Lamarque, Quinette, and Bancal—with the mission of arresting General Dumouriez and his general staff, escorting them to Paris, and replacing him as commander of the army with General Beurnonville, then Minister of War, who accompanied the commissioners.

They arrived fairly late on the night of April 1 at the thermal muds, or baths, of Saint-Amand, shortly after General Dumouriez had himself arrived there. I shall not undertake a detailed account of what took place there, since I was not present, being as I have already said three miles away in the town of Saint-Amand. It was only the next morning, April 2, that I learned that on the previous night commissioners from the Convention had arrived at headquarters, and after failing in their attempts to have General Dumouriez arrested, had themselves been arrested on his orders and handed over to the Austrian advance posts.

Painfully struck by the event, I proceeded directly to the thermal muds of Saint-Amand to see General Dumouriez and on entering said to him: "Ah! My dear General! What have you done, then, this night?" —"I have done," he replied coldly (and his words have remained engraved on my memory), "I have done what I had to do and what I could not have avoided." —"But to hand them over to the Austrians!" —"They left me with no other alternative. In vain I told them that I was resolved not to allow myself to be dragged before the bar of the Convention alive, that I advised them to go away quietly, and that I would allow them to return freely to Lille and Valenciennes; their pigheadedness and their vehemence were such that they did not listen to me. I even went as far as to warn Camus, who was the most extreme and the ringleader, that he and I were

---

This letter is copied from no. 95 of *le Moniteur,* where it is inserted in a report made by Delacroix *in the name of the commissioners sent to Belgium* after they had announced to the Convention that as they had foreseen, Dumouriez had refused to comply with their request. Delacroix added the following:

"Afterward, being assured that Dumouriez was at Saint-Amand, we resolved on March 31, after arresting some of his accomplices, that we would proceed to Saint-Amand the day following to put to him the questions we had tabled; that after hearing him we would retire to a private room to deliberate, and that meanwhile he should be kept under surveillance, and that if there were occasion to arrest him, this decision would be carried out by the most senior lieutenant general in the army; that we would assume responsibility for replacing him and that we would make known everything to the army by a proclamation.

"We did not conceal from ourselves the dangers of the enterprise, but we were counting on the confidence we had inspired in the army, and I said to my colleagues: 'Since we are going to the camp, Dumouriez must obey and recognize the authority of the Convention. Or if he makes a move, I ask you for authorization to blow his brains out.' All my colleagues had decided to sacrifice their lives, and all were armed. But I solicited the honor of punishing the scoundrel.

"We were about to leave to carry out our resolution when our colleagues arrived (at Lille) bearing your decree, which seemed to leave us under something of a cloud. We informed them of what we had done, and one of us proposed that we should accompany them. This apparently did not suit them, and we did not insist."

in the position of *the earthen pot and the iron pot** but that I was the *iron pot*. He took no notice, and in a paroxysm of rage, forgetting that I possessed main force and that he had none, he notified the officers surrounding me that they were *all under arrest like me* and that they must hand over their portfolios to him on the spot. It was then that I in turn lost patience, and I had them taken away by thirty men. I would have preferred not to include my former friend and companion-in-arms, Beurnonville, in these arrests, and I gave him the chance, but he refused absolutely and declared that he wanted to share the fate of the commissioners." —"All this is very unfortunate," I said to Dumouriez, "and I foresee that it will have a lamentable effect on the army." —"There you are wrong, my young friend; I already know the impression made on the army, and it is not what you think. It has redoubled their indignation with the National Convention, and now that I have crossed the Rubicon, I am drawing up my manifesto against it, and presently I shall go in person to the camp to make it known."

He excused me from accompanying him, and he told me that since the tour of inspection he was going to make of the camps, including the artillery park, would take him near the town of Saint-Amand, he would call on me and ask to stay to dinner before returning to headquarters. This he did.

In order to be kept abreast of what his political opponents had in store for him, he had placed a small detachment of light cavalry at Pont-à-Marcq—the post office between Douai and Lille on the Paris road—under an officer with orders to intercept such couriers as might be sent from Paris to the commissioners of the National Convention at Lille and to bring him their dispatches at Saint-Amand. Faithful to his instructions, this officer stopped one of these couriers, and having consigned him to the custody of his cavalrymen, he came to Saint-Amand immediately with a large bundle of dispatches that he handed to General Dumouriez while he was at dinner with me.

The General, who was sitting opposite me, proceeded to unseal and read them without getting up. Then he tossed me a piece of paper across the table, saying to me nonchalantly: "Here take it, this one's for you!"

This one was nothing less than the original of a signed order from the Committees of Defense and General Security ordering my immediate arrest, that I should be placed in solitary confinement, my papers sealed, and that I should be conveyed under close guard to the Abbaye prison at Paris.†

---

* From the saying *C'est le pot de terre contre le pot de fer,* meaning there should never be a conflict, as the iron pot would always win.—ED.

† I had carefully preserved this original document, through all the vicissitudes of my life, until February 24, 1848, when it disappeared in the looting of the Tuileries. I do not possess a copy, but I have a precise memory of it, and I shall put on record

I had hardly had time to open this document when General Dumouriez said to me again: "And here's one for your brother," tossing me another document, which was an order similar to mine issued against my brother Montpensier, then serving with the Army of the Var as an adjutant general.

Finally, General Dumouriez tossed me a third document, saying again: "Everybody's got one, and here's one for our friend Valence!" Then, flipping through the collection of these warrants* that he held in his hand, he added, with an affectation of gaiety that seemed to me singularly out of place:

"One can't have too much of a good thing."

I was knocked sideways by this long list of proscriptions and above all shaken to see my brother included in it without the slightest pretext, since he was eight hundred miles from us at Nice and consequently had absolutely nothing to do with anything that might be going on in the armies in the north. This gave me a gloomy presentiment of what was in store for us.† However, seeing that no one had comprehended the nature

---

here that it contained two spelling mistakes: One was *selles* instead of *scellés* [seals]; the other was *l'Abéie* instead of *l'abbaye.*

* Maribond-Montaut, one of the members of the Committees of Defense and General Security combined who signed these warrants, attested in the sitting of April 4 that there were thirty of them. See *le Moniteur,* no. 97.

† In my search to collect everything that might shed light on this point, I first of all found in *le Moniteur* for Thursday, April 4, 1793, no. 94, that in the sitting of Tuesday, April 2, Cambacérès had reported, in the name of the Committee of General Security, that one of General Valence's couriers had just been stopped at the gates carrying a box which had been opened in which letters had been found addressed to General Beurnonville, Mme de Montesson, my father, and my mother; that these letters had been handed over to the Committee, which had charged him to ask the Convention what it should do with them.

The Convention answered this question by decreeing that these letters should be opened by commissioners in the presence of the people to whom they were addressed.

Nevertheless, the following numbers of *le Moniteur* contain no report relative to these letters, but I find in the report of the sitting of Thursday, April 4, inserted in no. 97 of *le Moniteur* for Sunday, April 7, 1793, that Buzot had gotten up all of a sudden, and without preface or any kind of explanation, had simply demanded that the Convention order the public reading of the intercepted letter I had written to my father. This proposal having been decreed immediately, it was read out, without a single word being said about my letter to my mother. However, this letter had been seized at the same time as the other, and Cambacérès had likewise announced its existence to the National Convention. The result was that my letter to my mother was not read at a public sitting and that consequently my letter to my father was the only one to be inserted in *le Moniteur* and published in all the gazettes. I have searched for my letter to my mother in vain and found it nowhere. I do not know what determined the ringleaders of the day to make this distinction between my two letters, but I am convinced that the real reason was that only my letter to my father seemed to them susceptible of being used in evidence against me and a pretext for the measures that were immediately taken against my parents, while they possibly feared that the publication of my letter to my mother would have the opposite effect.

of the papers General Dumouriez had tossed me across the table, nor their source, I put a good face on it, and returning to him only the document relating to General Valence, I said: "I am retaining only what concerns us and am returning the rest to you. We'll have a talk about it all after dinner."

He placed all these documents back in their envelopes, and the meal continued as if nothing had happened. After dinner I took him on one side and told him that everything he had just communicated to me—while affecting a lack of concern, which was a good mask to mislead the spies surrounding us but which could not be real—seemed to present my

---

Be that as it may, I shall transcribe here my letter to my father, as I find it in *le Moniteur,* to make possible on the one hand an appreciation of the extent of my so-called guilt, and on the other a comparison between the way I viewed the state of affairs in 1793 with the opinions I have expressed in what goes before.

Tournay, March 30, 1793

I wrote to you from Louvain, dear Papa, on the 24th. It was the first moment I have had to myself since the unfortunate Battle of Neerwinden. I wrote to you again from Brussels and Enghien: So you see it is not I who am to blame. But you have no idea how quickly the postal officials beat their retreat; I have been ten days without letters and newspapers, and in these offices, as in all the rest, there is a fine disarray.

My *rose-color*[a] is now completely gone and has changed to the deepest black; I see liberty finished; I see the National Convention totally ruining France by disregarding all principle; I see civil war aflame; I see countless armies falling on our unfortunate Fatherland from all sides, and I see no army with which to oppose them; our troops of the line are almost wiped out; the fullest battalions have only four hundred men. The brave Deux-Ponts regiment is down to a hundred and fifty men, and they are not being sent any recruits—everything goes to the battalions of Volunteers or the new units. Besides, the decree assimilating the troops of the line with the Volunteers has set them at each other's throats. The Volunteers desert and flee in all directions; it is impossible to stop them; and the Convention believes that in such a state of affairs it can make war on the whole of Europe! I can assure you that if this situation lasts but a moment longer, they will soon be disabused.[b] Into what depths has it plunged France! . . . My sister will not go to Lille, where she may be troubled on account of her emigration; I prefer her to live in a village on the outskirts of Saint-Amand.

According to the same edition of *le Moniteur,* no. 97, in the same sitting of Thursday, April 4, 1793, Châteauneuf-Randon exclaimed:[c] "When a son writes to his father in these terms and when he says that the National Convention has plunged France into an abyss, it behooves us to make sure of the mother. I therefore demand that the wife of Égalité be placed under arrest."

---

[a] It was by saying *that I saw everything through rose-colored spectacles* that my father characterized my illusions about the great advantages I expected France to derive from the implementation of republican theories, in the period when they inspired me with an enthusiasm of which I have since been so cruelly disabused.

[b] The results of the campaign of 1793, so different from those of subsequent campaigns, have but too well justified this sad prophecy.

[c] The Marquis de Châteauneuf-Randon, one of the forty-seven members of the minority of the nobility who, with my father, went over to the Assembly of the Third Estate in 1789. He always sat with the Mountain in the National Convention.

personal position, the fate of my family, and our future in a new light; that it was evident to me that this was the culmination of the long-planned proscription of my family, a process I now thought it impossible to halt; that he knew of my efforts the preceding December to determine my father to take advantage of the decree of banishment that the National Convention had pronounced against us to withdraw to the United States with all his children; that all my life I should regret not having succeeded in making him adopt a course of action that would have constituted an honorable refutation of all the calumnies directed against him and would have forestalled those fatal complications which his continued presence in

---

La Révellière-Lepeaux then proposed the following decree, which was immediately adopted:

"Article 1. The wife and children of General Valence, Citizen Montesson (his aunt), and the wife of Citizen *Égalité* shall be immediately placed under arrest.

"Article 2. Citizens Brûlart-Sillery (his father-in-law) and *Égalité*, members of the National Convention, will be kept under surveillance, with freedom to go where they choose but only within Paris."

This freedom lasted only one day! The day after, by virtue of a new decree, my father was shut up in the Abbaye prison and subsequently in the dungeons of Fort Saint-Jean with my younger brother, then aged thirteen and a half!

Boyer-Fonfrède[d] said:

"As Carrier put it, *we must arrest all the Bourbons and keep them as hostages;* it is the proposal of this republican which I wish to support and of which I shall demonstrate the justice and the necessity." (*Yes, Yes, speak, exclaimed the assembly, rising almost to a man.*)

"People are ceaselessly talking to us about revolutionary laws, about the need to take strong and vigorous measures. Doubtless they may save the Fatherland, but I cannot imagine why the proscription of the former (and always) Royal Family has not been included by you among these laws, this terrible law that the welfare of the people demands and prescribes." (*Yes, yes. . . .*)

. . . .

"Republics only exist through virtue, Princes only plot and live on crimes.

"Corrupted in the Courts, there is for them no honoring of pledges; their ambition hides itself in a thousand guises, and it is by profaning the sacred name of Fatherland that they secretly aspire to become again, one day, your masters."

. . . .

"Citizens, Princes all stick together—at least for crimes. Let us, therefore, keep all these Bourbons as hostages, and if the tyrants to whom our colleagues have been delivered dare, in contempt of the law of nations, strike down the representatives of the French people with the assassin's knife, let all these Bourbons be dragged to the place of execution, let their heads roll to the foot of the scaffolds, let them depart from life as the monarchy has departed from the Republic, and may the land of liberty no longer have to support their miserable existence."

The Assembly rose with applause, shouting *To the vote!* The applause lasted for several minutes, and the proposal was adopted unanimously.

The National Convention decreed that the members of the Bourbon family, apart from those detained in the Temple, should be transferred to Marseille, where they

---

[d] Boyer-Fonfrède was a deputy for the Gironde and belonged to that party. He perished with his colleagues on the revolutionary scaffold on October 31, 1793.

that Assembly had so balefully heaped upon him, to his misfortune and our own. I then recalled to General Dumouriez that at that period he had himself recognized that there was no longer any honorable or even possible post for me in France other than my post with the army (here he interrupted me to say that he thought so more than ever). I added that I was consequently going to continue my military service under him as long as the course of events permitted, having firmly resolved not to be

---

should be held under arrest by the citizens at the responsibility of the municipal authorities.

Thus, in all their severity, were accomplished the sinister predictions and threats that the doctor had been charged to convey to me at Tournay and that my conversation with Danton and so many other signs had made only too clear to me. I am persuaded that anyone who has read the foregoing, that anyone who ponders the fate of Fonfrède—as of so many other victims who had given similar pledges to the party, which in its craving for blood had irrevocably sworn their ruin—will remain convinced that even if I had not escaped a like fate by my flight, no act of mine could have saved my family or averted the fury to which we were prey.

In the same sitting, the following decree was passed on the report of Lasource, in the name of the Committee of General Security.

"Article 1. The fathers and mothers, wives and children of the officers in the army that was commanded by Dumouriez, from the rank of sublieutenant to that of lieutenant general inclusive, will be kept under surveillance as hostages by each municipal authority in the place where they reside until the commissioners sent by the National Convention and also the Minister of War, detained through the perfidy of Dumouriez, have been freed and the Army of Belgium has come under the new general still to be nominated.

"Article 2. Each municipal authority shall be required to send to the District Council, with the shortest possible delay, the minutes containing the names of all the citizens detained as hostages.

"Article 3. The Minister of War will deliver to the National Convention within twenty-four hours the nominal roll of all the officers to be printed and sent to the departments for the execution of the present decree."

During the previous day's sitting (April 3, *le Moniteur*, no. 94) the Convention had passed the following decree:

"The National Convention orders the Provisional Executive Council to nominate a general to replace Dumouriez immediately.

"It declares to the French nation that Dumouriez is a traitor to the Fatherland, that he has sworn to destroy liberty and restore despotism.

"It forbids all generals, all commandants of fortified towns, all soldiers of the Republic, and all the constituted authorities in France to recognize Dumouriez as a general, under pain of being regarded as a traitor to the Fatherland liable for the death penalty and the confiscation of his belongings to the benefit of the Republic.

"It decrees that Dumouriez be outlawed, authorizes all citizens to fall on him, and promises a reward of three hundred thousand francs and civic crowns to anyone who takes him alive or dead or their heirs, and that the three hundred thousand francs shall be kept at the disposal of the Provisional Executive Council by the national treasury.

"It orders that the present decree shall be sent by special couriers to all the departments, to the administrative bodies, and to the generals and commandants of fortresses, and that it shall be immediately read out in the towns and at the head of army corps."

separated from the army until constrained by absolute necessity. Once this had been firmly understood, I requested General Dumouriez's assistance in carrying out two duties that I desired to discharge immediately, and he eagerly gave it.

The first was to warn my brother, the Duc de Montpensier, of the fate with which he was threatened by the decree ordering his arrest. I asked General Dumouriez to give me a parcel of dispatches without a counterseal addressed to *General Biron, Commander in Chief of the Army of the Var at Nice* in order to serve as the pretext for sending the courier I was going to dispatch to my brother. At the same time, thanks to M. Leblanc, the owner of the house where I was lodging (who was, I believe, mayor of Saint-Amand), I obtained a passport for my courier from the town council; and M. Leblanc extended his kindness to me as far as lending me his *cabriolet* for this journey.*

I entrusted my orderly with this mission. He was called *Taupin* and had been very attached to my brother and myself for a long time. He left in the night; near Fréjus, Taupin encountered the faithful Gamache, my brother's valet who acted as his courier. From him he learned that the Duc de Montpensier had already been arrested and was being escorted to prison. Thus, when the two carriages crossed, my brother saw Taupin in the cabriolet, and Taupin raised his hands and his eyes to the sky and continued his journey toward Nice without stopping or saying anything.†

* This loan became permanent, since the *cabriolet* never returned to Saint-Amand. Therefore, on my return to France in 1814, I paid the equivalent to M. Leblanc's heirs, since he died in the interval.

† In this note, I am transcribing the Duc de Montpensier's account of his arrest at Nice from his memoirs, which were published after his death. It is a heartfelt need for me to place on record here this precious testimony of the brotherly love that held us so closely together throughout the course of his life, and equally to place on record the justice he did to the Duc de Biron's conduct toward him in such a cruel situation for this faithful friend of my father and of our family.

Here is this paragraph from his memoirs, to which he gave the title:

My Forty-Three Months' Captivity

This long and harrowing captivity began in the first days of April 1793. The headquarters of the Army of Italy was then at Nice, and I had rejoined it shortly before in the capacity of adjutant general with the rank of lieutenant colonel. The army was commanded by the Duc de Biron, and each day this brave and excellent man gave new proofs of his long-standing attachment to our family and also the uprightness of his intentions. I was going to dine with him on April 8 (a fatal day I shall certainly never be able to forget), and not finding him in his drawing room, I was advancing toward the door of his study when I saw him come out precipitately, displaying the signs of acute agitation. He started when he saw me and then said to me in a whisper that he would have to speak to me in private. I entered his study immediately, and when he had closed the door, he said:

"You see a man in despair: I have frightful news to tell you." Immediately imagining it was about some misfortune that had befallen my brother or my father, I asked him urgently whether my fears were justified. "No," he replied. "It concerns you alone." —"If that is the case I can breathe again, but tell me then, Gen-

The second duty I had to perform concerned my sister. She was under my protection but, after the warrant for my arrest and in the face of the events that surged around us, was now in an impossible situation both from her own point of view and from mine. It was clear that she could no longer remain at Saint-Amand since I was to leave at any moment: and that I could still less undertake to drag her along with me, together with Mme de Genlis and her niece, in the midst of the army. It was also clear that there was no security for her anywhere in France nor even any possibility of procuring a passport for her that would enable her to travel freely there, since it was public knowledge that she was still placed,

---

eral, what personal misfortune threatens me?" —"I have just received orders to arrest you and to have you conveyed, under safe escort, to the Abbaye prison in Paris." —"But does this order concern me alone?" "—You alone. There is no mention of the rest of your family and if it were a general measure I imagine I would have been told. Anyway, here is the order, read it for yourself." I read it: It was signed by the members of the Committee of Public Safety, and it did mention me alone. "Very well, General, I am your prisoner." Tears came to his eyes. "Oh! Do some justice to my attachment to you: It is sincere and unlimited. What can I do? Speak frankly to me, I beg you on bended knee! Is it not possible that either in your letters or in your conversation—in short, in any way whatsoever—you may have committed some indiscretion that has turned the present government against you?" —"No; they can scarcely be ignorant of the feelings they inspire in me, as in all decent men, but they do me the honor of being afraid of me." —"But, after all, do you believe you are in danger?" —"It is impossible to regard oneself as entirely exempt when one falls into such hands." —"My position is appalling. I would a thousand times prefer to receive a bullet in the head than such a commission. But after all, tell me at least if you have any papers that may compromise you so that we can hasten to burn them before they are inventoried and sealed." —"If you care to come to my quarters, we will search together." —"I must escort you to your quarters, place a sentry at your door, and then you will leave for Paris when you like; I shall give you a police escort to accompany you on this sad journey." —"No, I beseech you, do not give me an escort: That would be a sure way of having me butchered on the way by giving the Jacobin Clubs of all the places I go through to believe that I am an aristocrat and a counterrevolutionary." —"Very well, you will not have an escort, but you will have an officer who will take care to cover himself with a gray riding coat." After this conversation, we proceeded to my quarters, and although General Biron had some desire to be alone with me for a moment, he could not prevent the commandant of the town, called *La Barre,* from following us in. However, as we knew him for a decent fellow, and there was not a moment to lose in inspecting my papers before the commissioners arrived, I told him I was going to take this precaution and invited him to take part in this inspection. "Very well," he said, "it is worse than useless to give these people a hold over you. Let's go through your papers and lose no time."

Among some very unimportant letters were found two from my elder brother, in which he strongly expressed his distaste for the way in which the cause we had espoused had developed and his lively desire to separate himself from it. These letters would have been enough to convict me of *culpable correspondence with a counterrevolutionary* and, consequently, to destroy me. La Barre burned them with an eagerness that truly filled me with gratitude, all the more so because I had never had the slightest dealings with him. This same La Barre had been a lieutenant colonel before the Revolution and was then colonel of the regiment of Lorraine

407

though unjustly, on the list of *émigrés*. Consequently, it was my duty to get her back across the frontier by sending her as soon as possible to the country from which I had just brought her so that she could wait there either until events should decide our fate or until our parents' wishes settled the matter for her.

Accordingly, I asked General Dumouriez to give her an escort of cavalry on the morrow, April 3, to accompany her carriage as far as the Austrian outposts, where the French officer in command would have orders to let her pass.

General Dumouriez entrusted the matter to Colonel Montjoye, then an

---

Dragoons and commandant of the town of Nice. He was made a *maréchal de camp* sometime afterward and was killed in an action against the Spanish. I sincerely regretted not being able to show this good man how much I had been touched by his conduct. In time, to return to my account, the municipal officers sent by the Convention's commissioners to seal up my papers arrived a moment after the two letters were burned. They found nothing, but to show that their trouble had not been entirely wasted, they placed their seals on some unimportant letters, some official papers, and some blank paper. After this exploit and the thorough search of all my belongings, they went off in a fair bad temper. The unfortunate Biron, who had been present at this ceremony, then came up to me, shook me firmly by the hand, and rushed out, leaving his hat and his gloves in my room. I sent them back to him, and I profited from this opportunity to write him a note in which I renewed my very sincere assurances of warm friendship and I explained to him how touched I was by the marks of friendship he had just shown me. He sent me a verbal reply to the effect that I had truly consoled him by showing that I did justice to his feelings, but that he was heartbroken and needed to keep repeating to himself that my age (I was then seventeen and a half) and the little to be gained in sacrificing me would keep me from harm. The person to whom I had entrusted this mission informed me that the sentry at my door had no orders and that since he did not really know me or even perhaps that he was guarding me, it would have been very easy for me to have left had I wanted to. It later occurred to me that this circumstance, which seemed the result of absentmindedness, was certainly arranged by M. de Biron to give me the chance to escape, because at the time he was much more upset and worried than I was myself. Be that as it may, I decided, after a little reflection, not to take advantage of this facility. I was quite sure I could escape if I wanted. But what use would my freedom be, and even my life (assuming it was in danger, of which I was not certain), if I had thus sacrificed to possibly trifling fears the peace and safety of the cherished beings whom I would be leaving behind in France and who would not fail to be harassed on my account? This consideration decided me, and I gave up all idea of flight. The circumstances in which my brother found himself were very different. Having had occasion to make his attitude known, at the same time as General Dumouriez, he could have no doubts as to the fate in store for him. He left, and he behaved absolutely correctly. As for me, I was in complete ignorance of what was going on in Dumouriez's army: My brother sent a courier in disguise to inform me, who despite his extreme speed did not arrive until thirty hours after my arrest. He encountered me about a hundred and twenty miles from Nice, under the guard of a police officer. My valet, who was on horseback, recognized the courier, who asked him where I was, and learning that I was being escorted to prison, begged him not to speak of him to anyone, not even to me, and passed himself off as someone merely taking dispatches to General Biron.

adjutant general, and for this purpose he gave him fifty hussars of the 1st Regiment (Bercheny). Montjoye escorted the carriage containing my sister and Mme de Genlis as far as Quiévrain. The Austrian General Quosdanowich, commandant there, made no difficulties about letting her pass and had her escorted to the Prince of Coburg's headquarters at Mons. On arrival, she was obliged to take to her bed with an attack of the measles—a circumstance which greatly increased my difficulties and later forced her to remain there several days after my departure from Mons for Switzerland.

On April 3 I accompanied General Dumouriez on his visit to the troops between Maulde and Saint-Amand to ascertain their mood before ordering the movement he was planning, I think, on Orchies or Marchiennes. This visit passed off better for General Dumouriez than I was expecting. He was well received by the troops of the line, less well by the battalions of National Volunteers, and yet their attitude was not at all pronounced. Rather, they seemed to be saying to General Dumouriez that they were undecided and that they wanted to see what would emerge from all this. My abiding impression of this visit is that their main consideration was not the arrest of the commissioners, which was of little interest to them, but a growing distrust of General Dumouriez's relations with the Austrians; and I believe that the rest of my account will leave no doubt that it was this mistrust, more than anything else, that kept the army loyal to the National Convention; for in the French army the feeling of nationalism has always predominated, and there is no doubt that handing the commissioners over to the Austrians made more of an impression on the troops than their arrest.

On April 4 General Dumouriez, who had slept at Saint-Amand, wanted to continue his inspection of the garrisons by going to Condé, which was under the command of General Neuilly, one of those on whom he most relied. There were none of the Convention's commissioners at Condé, but he knew that those at Valenciennes were working on the garrison through their emissaries, and he hoped to strengthen its resolve by his visit. I was to accompany him on this tour of inspection as I had on that of the previous day. As we were mounting our horses, we realized that we had neglected to order the General's usual escort of cavalry and that there were only ten or twelve orderlies at headquarters. We begged him to wait for the escort, which had just been sent for; but he would have none of it and merely said that as he was carrying out his inspections at walking pace, the escort would easily catch up with him at a trot, and we left with the general staff and the orderlies only.

We should have found, either in the village of Bruille or that of Odomez,* three battalions of National Volunteers under the commander

* I write from memory, and I have had some difficulty in squaring my recollection of the place-names with those on the map I used to check them. If there are errors, their relation to the facts is unimportant. It should be remembered that fifty-six

of the 3rd Oise Battalion, Davout, later Marshal Prince d'Eckmühl. In whichever of these two villages it was that we went through, we found only a small rear guard, which was loading its pack horses. Those whom we asked the whereabouts of the battalion replied that they had received orders to set off at once, and that they were themselves about to follow but that they did not know where they were being sent.

This reply should have given us pause. It did nothing of the sort. We were so accustomed to disorder and generals effecting troop movements on their own initiative and often, indeed, without reporting them, that neither General Dumouriez nor any of his officers suspected what nevertheless had happened—that those orders to march had emanated from the Convention's commissioners who, with the agreement of the commander, Davout, had sent him orders to bring these three battalions to Valenciennes and that he was executing these orders without telling the troops where he was sending them.

So, rather rashly, we continued on our way, and shortly after leaving the village, we caught up with the tail end of the three battalions, who were marching in open order on account of the mud. Then, even more rashly, we mingled with their ranks and asked them where they were going. "Goodness, we haven't a clue," they replied, "they know that at the front." If they had known, as they learned an instant later, we would all have been caught like mice in a trap, because to capture us all they had to do was to lay hold of our horses' bridles and all would have been up with us. Providence ordained otherwise! An adjutant general called Darville, sent from Condé by General Neuilly, reached us just then, having sped the length of the column at a fast trot without asking or being asked any questions by its commanders. Seeing General Dumouriez, he stopped and said to him: "General, please step aside a moment, I must speak with you." We left the ranks at once without difficulty, the soldiers showing no inclination to impede us at all.

General Dumouriez, with Darville beside him, took a path off to the left leading to a farm some distance from the road and situated in low-lying country not far from the left bank of the Scheldt. Darville told him that he was charged by General Neuilly to inform him that the garrison of Condé was in such a state of unrest that he would certainly be arrested if he set foot in the fortesss, but that the cavalry regiment had not yet been contaminated by the unrest among the infantry. General Neuilly believed that if General Dumouriez sent him written and signed orders to that effect, he could still have the cavalry regiment leave the fortress and bring it to him. General Dumouriez at once summoned M. Quantin, his secretary, who leaped off his horse and placed one knee on the ground by General Dumouriez, who remained mounted; but just when Quantin was beginning to write the order at his dictation, we

---

years have elapsed between the period of these events (1793) and that of my account of them (1849).

410

observed a little National Volunteers officer arriving at a gallop, mounted on a little black horse that I still seem to have before my eyes, shouting: "Take flight as quickly as you can or you are lost! The people over there have sworn to deliver you dead or alive to the Convention's commissioners."* At the same time, we saw the three battalions, let loose as sharpshooters, bearing down on us at a run with wild shouts of *"Stop! Stop! Stop!";* they formed a crescent in front of us and already cut us off from the path we had just left. At the same time they fired at us from all sides. We were in the center of this semicircle of rifle shots, which was closing in on us with every minute. We now had only one free side, that to the north, by which to escape through the fields bordering the Scheldt, but we were separated from it by a wide ditch; nearly all of us cleared this very easily with the exception, however, of General Dumouriez, who, always a bad rider, could not persuade his horse to jump it despite the efforts of his luckless groom, who was killed while whipping it to make it cross. Needless to say, none of us left the other side of the ditch until our general had crossed it *on foot*. I at once offered him my spare horse, but as I was presenting it to him it was killed by a bullet between the eye and the ear. Then my groom, named Baudouin, jumped off his horse and said: "General, get on *this quickly, it will bear you well.*" However, all this proceeded very slowly, and the hail of bullets was rapidly increasing; two of our orderlies and two grooms, Colonel Thouvenot's horse, etc., were killed in our midst. Our general, finally mounted on my mare, exclaimed as we led him off at a fast trot: "But I can't reach my stirrups and I shall fall off!" Then, as his legs were very short, I had him put his feet in the stirrup leathers, and he was firmly in the saddle.

We were soon out of range of the bullets, but we found ourselves bogged down in marshy land, where we were obliged to dismount. We were following a long bend of the Scheldt while the Volunteers, who were still following us, were outflanking us to cover our left—on the heights at right angles to us—to cut us off from our camps; it was indeed probable that they would soon have been in a position to descend on us and drive us back on the Scheldt. Such was our situation when we noticed a small boat on the opposite bank, and nearby a girl; we gave her to understand that we would pay her well if she would row us across, and that she did at once. Then we abandoned our horses to those of our grooms who had managed to follow us,† and by backtracking they managed to take them back to the camps by a long detour.

On the right bank of the Scheldt, we began by taking the girl with us to prevent the Volunteers from using the boat in our pursuit.

---

* This little officer, called Saint-Firmin, was the lieutenant colonel commanding the Saint-Denis battalion, which was one of the three Davout was taking to Valenciennes.
† My aide-de-camp, César Ducrest, left with them and managed to salvage those of my horses spared by the shooting. He brought them back to me the next day.

The Jard, or Condé, canal that is marked on the map was not then in existence, so that we met with no obstacle to impede our progress. We were all on foot, following at random the paths leading from the Scheldt toward the north and crossing marshes or meadows much intersected by streams or ditches, which we crossed on planks, taking care to remove them after us.

In this way we arrived at a village—I would not care to say which, and it seems of little importance—where we found a squadron of Austrian dragoons from the La Tour regiment, commanded by an Irishman, Major O'Brien, with Captain de Civalart under him—a Frenchman who died a few years ago with the rank of lieutenant field marshal in the Austrian army. These gentlemen received us most politely, but with some embarrassment. After discussing our case among themselves, they told us that since they had no orders concerning us, they were going to obtain some from the Prince of Coburg, informing him of our arrival—which had taken them quite by surprise—and that meanwhile they must request us to enter a house; here they lost no time in inviting us to dinner.

During the course of the night we spent there, we were joined by several of our officers. Working out the way to find us from the direction that those of our orderlies and grooms who had escaped the fusillade had told them we had taken on foot, they had managed to meet up with us and even to bring us some horses. These officers informed us that the news of our adventure had spread through all the camps and that the fusillade of which we had been the object had aroused general indignation; that the troops did not doubt that we would reappear before the army at daybreak, but that there was not a moment to lose and we must start moving without delay. "Right now!" exclaimed Dumouriez. "My friends, you will follow me and return to the army?" —"We all will," was the unanimous reply. —"Very well! Let us go!" But then the Austrian officers felt they must intervene, and though this scene aroused in our compatriot, M. de Civalart, sentiments he did not seek to hide, we were nevertheless notified once more that we must await orders from the Austrian headquarters and act accordingly.

This delay was not very long. Colonel Mack, the Prince of Coburg's chief of staff, soon arrived, and after conferring with General Dumouriez, gave the order that we should be allowed to leave, which we did at about six o'clock in the morning of April 5.

First we went to a little camp, between Bruille and Château l'Abbaye. There we were well received, especially by the 87th of the line (the former Dillon) where there were shouts of *"Long live Dumouriez! Long live our generals!"*

Thence we passed to the camp at Maulde, which was the main one. The troops were drawn up in lines and without arms. We started with a review of the front line from the right, where the 5th of the line

412

(Navarre) was situated. Our reception was still good, but already it seemed to me colder. As we passed along the line, the battalions broke ranks and the soldiers followed us, either to question us or to hear General Dumouriez's account of what had happened the day before, peppered with his usual declamations against the commissioners and against the Convention itself.

The soldiers' remarks varied. At first it began with: "We are very glad to see you back, but where were you going then, when you were fired on? Because it is not good to fire like that on your generals!" —"No doubt it isn't, but it happened all the same." —"So where *were* you going then when you were fired on?" —"We were going to Condé, where we were expected, and we were already fairly near when these battalions blocked our way on all sides and heaped a hail of bullets on us, obliging us to seek safety on the other side of the Scheldt and to make a wide detour to rejoin you." —"Ah! That is well done, but you came back via the Austrians, and that is a pity." —"It was the fusillade that threw us into their arms." —"Well, here you are back safely with us," friends said, "and that is good!" —"Ah," the others said, "not all of this is clear," and so on.

As we passed along the colors of the different regiments, the crowd around us swelled, the language became increasingly hostile, and by the time we had reached the 45th of the line (the former Crown Regiment), which was the last of all, it had become so tumultuous and the remarks so threatening that we would certainly have been apprehended if this had gone on any longer. But opinions were still divided, and it was clear that a great debate was in progress among the troops. Thus, after we had passed the 45th, the crowd ceased to follow us and remained before the camp, while General Dumouriez continued his progress at walking pace in the direction of Saint-Amand.

In vain those around him pointed out that it was rash and useless to take that direction; he replied coldly that he wanted to go to see the artillery, and he was already a fair distance from the camp at Maulde when he was joined by some officers from his general staff who were looking for him to tell him what had just happened at Saint-Amand, where the debacle was total. They informed him that the artillery had left *en masse* for Valenciennes, taking with it the majority of the troops, to throw in their lot with the Convention's commissioners, while two or three squadrons of dragoons and hussars had returned to Saint-Amand and had forcibly seized hold of his baggage, his horses, mine and General Valence's, etc., and had left by the main road to Orchies.

Dumouriez remained some time in silence with his head lowered, then he said: "Let us go to Rumégies; there we shall decide what's to be done." Then he ordered some of his officers who had just joined him to scout around the camp and bring him at Rumégies continuous reports of what might be going on.

413

We arrived at Rumégies without incident, where we found two squadrons of the 5th Hussars (later the 4th and previously the Colonel General), which maintained absolute neutrality toward us, and I must say that General Dumouriez made no effort to get them to join him.

We were not long in learning that the exchanges in the camp at Maulde had become more and more lively, but that on hearing of the departure of the artillery and the troops from Saint-Amand, all the units had in turn made the same decision; we also learned that the 17th of the line (Auvergne) had been the last to go and that it had only moved off when its commander, Colonel Dumas—not wishing himself to go over to the Convention's commissioners—had bade it farewell, saying that he did not think he should hold it back any longer.

After such news, there could no longer be any doubt about the only course of action open to us, and when General Dumouriez told me this I replied that it was clear; but when he added that his quarrel with the Convention was not over and that we must wait to see how things turned out both inside and outside France, I told him that for me the matter was finished, that once outside France I did not wish to be other than an exile, and that all I would ask of the Austrians would be a permit to withdraw to Switzerland as quietly as I could. He made no objection to this decision.

We left Rumégies during the night of April 5, the parish priest acting as our guide to the Austrian outposts. This poor man said to me: "Ah, Prince, all that I ask of you is to make me your almoner when you return to France, for this won't last forever!" God knows I would gladly have done something for him if I had found him on my return to France, but I never knew what became of him.

We arrived at an Austrian post commanded by an officer who at first spoke of asking for our swords, which threw General Dumouriez into a towering rage. The officer did not insist. He merely caused all our names to be written down and gave us an escort to General Count Clairfayt's headquarters at Tournay; his reception of us was polite but glacial. He occupied the same apartments at Saint-Martin's Abbey as those where I had seen General O'Moran and his family in the winter. Only General Dumouriez and myself were shown into Count Clairfayt's study. He told us he was having carriages prepared to take us to the Prince of Coburg's headquarters at Mons and that he hoped we would not take it amiss if he had us escorted by a superior officer, since such was his duty. He added his regrets that he was too overwhelmed with business to find time to do the honors personally at the dinner we would be served and that General Alvinzy, his second in command, had orders to perform them on his behalf. General Alvinzy did this very courteously, and after dinner we set off in our carriages, *accompanied* by a Hungarian major who preceded us in his.

It was very late at night when we reached Mons. We were lodged in an indifferent inn at the bottom end of the town. Once more I found myself, though this time under proscription, near the gate through which I had entered Mons with our victorious troops after the Battle of Jemappes. It was now April 6 of the following year, five months to the day after our victory! And here I was, approaching the age of nineteen and a half, and visited with the most unjust and odious proscription!

Very early in the morning I received a visit in this inn from Count Clairfayt, who evidently intended to be more courteous than he had been the previous day at Tournay. Then I was visited by the Prince de Lambesc, then called Prince Charles of Lorraine, who was a major general in the service of Austria.

After these two visits, we walked up the long street to the main square to the General Prince of Coburg's headquarters, and at the same time a small corps of French *émigrés,* about two hundred strong, was descending this street to leave the town. They bore the name *Carneville's Light Infantry* after their commanding officer. As they were marching in a square they occupied nearly all the width of the street, and we were obliged to walk in single file between their right and the houses, and while we were observing their crosses of Saint-Louis, they recognized nearly all of us and named us in turn as we passed them, but without the slightest trace of insult. They merely said: "Ah, there is General Dumouriez, and then the Duc de Chartres, and then Thouvenot,* Montjoye, Barrois, Saint-Pardoux, Toreri, Rainville, etc."

When roll call of sorts had been completed and they had passed us, M de Carneville came back by himself, and saluting General Dumouriez's sword, he said: "General, now that we are fighting for the same cause I have come to place myself and my corps under your orders, and you can count on us." —"Sir," General Dumouriez replied, "I am very gratified by your proposal, but I cannot accept it; we are like two separate rivers flowing toward the same point but whose waters cannot mingle."

After this each went off in his own direction, and we soon reached the government offices, where the Prince of Coburg awaited us. He was surrounded by his officers, and Archduke Charles was behind him. As soon as I had been introduced to the Prince of Coburg, Archduke Charles came up to me and embraced me cordially, saying: "Cousin, you are one of my closest relatives, and I am truly glad to see you here. We were very near each other at the Battle of Jemappes, and your conduct that day increased my impatience to know you." I was very moved by this welcome, which was given aloud in front of many onlookers, and I signified as much to him effusively. General Dumouriez was then presented to him, and he received him respectfully. Then he returned to me, and taking me on one side, he said: "Now, my dear cousin, we must have a little chat together, quite freely and as friends—for

---

* The same who, as a divisional general, defended Bayonne in 1814.

415

such I wish you to consider me, and perfectly sincerely, I assure you." —"I am deeply touched." —"No doubt you will remain with us, and, as a good relative, I would be charmed to have you with me." —"If anything could determine me to adopt such a course, it would be what you offer me so sincerely. But I must tell you frankly, I cannot. I cannot turn my arms like that against those with whom I have just been fighting. Considering my position and that in which I leave my family in France, my retirement into obscurity is now the only fitting role outside my country." —"I can only honor such motives," he said, shaking my hand, "but what then is to become of you?" —"I don't know," I said, "at the moment I am thinking no further than to retire to Switzerland, and the only request I have to make of you is that I should be given passports to proceed there as soon as possible." —"Good God," he replied, "it doesn't depend on me. You must apply to the Prince of Coburg, or rather Colonel Mack. But believe me that at every opportunity I will do everything in my power for you, and always count on my friendship." Then, returning to the general conversation, he told me: "We are going to dine together at the Marshal's, and tomorrow it will be my turn to receive you, with General Dumouriez."

It was, therefore, to Baron Mack that I made the formal request for passports to Switzerland, saying that I should like to leave as soon as possible. I advised him that I would be asking him for duplicates, one under my own name, *Duc de Chartres,* and the other under an assumed name that I would give him. I added that I would have to make the same request of him for my sister, who could not leave as soon as I could because she was ill at Mons. Finally, I told him that the people accompanying us would also have to be provided with passports under their real and assumed names.

His first reaction was, quite properly, that he would certainly take immediate orders from the commander in chief, Field Marshal the Prince of Coburg, but that he had not thought I would be in such a hurry and that before deciding on any course, I would at least have waited to see what became of General Dumouriez's affairs and have settled up with him. I replied that on the contrary, what he said was one more reason to hasten my departure, since I was firmly resolved not to associate myself in any way with General Dumouriez's affairs nor any such enterprises as he might formulate; that I was only looking for a temporary shelter from the persecution to which I was being subjected; and consequently that I insisted he hand over to me the passports I requested from him without delay.

The day after, Baron de Mack informed me that this request had been readily granted; he brought me blank passports, signed and sealed in the name of Frederic Josias Prince of Saxe-Coburg, so that they could be entered with the names of my choice. One I made out for myself and my suite; a second one under an assumed name for myself and César

416

Ducrest, who wished to remain my faithful companion; a third for my sister, under her real name, with her suite, and a fourth passport for her, Madame de Genlis and Mlle de Sercey under assumed names; finally a fifth for Colonel Montjoye, who, not caring to form part of the general staff that General Dumouriez seemed to want to keep with him, was anxious to leave for Switzerland to join his sisters and install himself with them at Basel in the house of their relative Viscount Hachslanden. However, this faithful friend who, together with his excellent sisters, has since given me so many marks of affection and loyalty, agreed to wait at Mons until my sister had sufficiently recovered from the measles to be able to undertake the journey and then to accompany her to such a place in Switzerland where she could rejoin me. I did not have sufficient knowledge of the state of Switzerland to designate that spot in advance, but what I did not foresee was that this reunion could not be effected anywhere at all and that the persecution from which I had just escaped would be replaced, outside France, by that animosity which for so long barred all refuge for me in Europe.

As soon as I had made these arrangements I turned my attention to selling the horses and their accouterments (which César Ducrest had salvaged for me) in order to enlarge as far as possible the tiny provision I had for my sister and myself *in my belt with three hundred louis d'or*. All I kept for myself was a pack horse and my carriage drawn by three horses, which I sent direct to Switzerland with three or four servants who had followed my sister and myself and whom I later sent back to France (except for my groom, Baudouin, who only left me in America). My sister kept her Berlin for her journey with Mme de Genlis, her niece, and Montjoye. None of them had a chambermaid, and they traveled with a single *valet de chambre,* on the seat. I also kept a traveling cabriolet for myself, and as soon as these various arrangements had been completed I set off alone in it with César Ducrest and without any domestic servants.

When I left Mons I was still unaware just how far the persecution of my family and all who had been attached to us had gone in France. It was only when I stopped at a little inn near Frankfurt that I learned the awful details from a newspaper.

CONCLUSION

IT WAS at the beginning of April 1793—that terrible year so barbarously bloodstained and sullied by so many crimes—that began the first and perhaps the most painful of the vicissitudes that Providence had in store for me during the long span of life it allotted to me. It was then that my enforced separation from the French army barred the career of arms to me and left me—as my only consolation, in the exile into which I was cast by my own unjust proscription, together with all my family—the memory of having helped deliver France from foreign invasion and the consciousness of having always loyally and faithfully fought under her banner as long as I was permitted to serve her.

Thrown without resource on to foreign soil, I remained faithful to the principle of patriotism that had been my guide in the difficult circumstances I have just described. I no more rallied to the banner of the Emigration in 1793 than to that of Ghent in 1815.* Neither invitations nor threats, nor the inconceivable persecution to which I was subjected outside France once it was known that I would not join the corps of French *émigrés* serving in the armies of the foreign Powers then at war with France, nor anything that could be tried on me ever shook my loyalty to this principle. At this period the influence of the *émigrés,* or rather that of their policies and passions, caused me to be rejected everywhere, and indeed I was able briefly to enjoy the modest refuge provided by a job as schoolmaster at Reichenau only because I was not known there.

If I succeed in my intention of finishing this account of the events of my life, the reader will see that after wandering through Europe for three and a half years, always without assured means and with no refuge save where I was not known, I left for America on September 24, 1796, at my mother's request. She informed me that the Executive Directory then governing France had consented to free my two brothers, imprisoned in Fort Saint-Jean at Marseille, and to send them to America as soon as an agent of the Republic had certified that I had departed. But the delight of my reunion with my brothers at Philadelphia only added their financial difficulties to my own. The three of us were reduced to wandering together over the vast expanse of the United States, always without other resources than the assistance of a few friends.

* Whither Louis XVIII withdrew during Napoleon's Hundred Days.—ED.

It was in the summer of 1797, on our return from a long excursion to the western states where we had camped for seventy nights in forests, that we learned that a decree of the French Legislative Councils had ordained that my mother should be repossessed of her property. This news gave us reason to hope that we should no longer lack the means to establish ourselves in one of the large cities in the East of the United States. This hope was of short duration. The Directory would not allow the decree to be executed, and after the *coup d'état* of *18 Fructidor** that occurred shortly afterward, my mother was deported to Spain, and her property, which had hitherto only been sequestered, was *confiscated* and put up for sale as *biens nationaux*.

We then decided to try to join my mother in Spain. This was very difficult, with conversations then in progress between the French and American governments, from which it emerged that there was no longer any safety or protection for us on board American ships against French corsairs. As a result we saw no other way of reaching Spain than that of descending the Ohio and the Mississippi as far as New Orleans in order to proceed to Havana, where we hoped to obtain passage to Spain on board some Spanish man-of-war. Spain was then at war with England, but since it was allied to France we had nothing to fear in taking this course. We were encouraged in this by the Spanish ambassador to the United States, the Marquis of Casa-Irujo, the father of the present Duke of Sotomayor, who gave us passports. The financial difficulties were likewise alleviated by a generous loan of four thousand dollars from a rich American (Gouverneur Morris) who had been American ambassador to France and remained very attached to my mother.

We reached Havana in the month of March 1798 after a long and difficult voyage. There we found a welcome that exceeded our expectations. A ship of the line (the *San Pedro,* of sixty-four guns) was about to leave for Ferrol; however, despite their good will, the Spanish authorities did not feel authorized to give us a passage on a man-of-war without an order from the King. But they prevailed on us to await this at Havana, where they made great efforts to render this period of waiting agreeable. The very day of our arrival, a very rich old lady (Doña Leonora de Contreras) *put at our disposal* (as the Spanish have it) a fine house, fully furnished, in which she no longer lived, together with carriages, horses, postilions, coaches, etc. Our arrival caused a great sensation. We were the first Princes of the House of Bourbon to appear

* On 18 Fructidor (September 4, 1797) three of the five Directors, with the aid of the army, ousted their more rightwing colleagues (Carnot and Danthélemy) and quashed most of the elections to the legislative bodies that had just taken place and that would have given a royalist majority. The *coup* is a classic instance (another is provided by the situation in Northern Ireland today) of the dilemma: What does a government do when an opposition party aims to overthrow the Constitution by constitutional means? In such a situation, the concept of legality becomes meaningless.—ED.

in America, let alone Havana, and the inhabitants said in their old-fashioned Spanish way, *"Son Borbones, y de la misma Sangre que el Señor Don Felipe Quinto."* ("They are Bourbons of the same blood as Don Philip V"). We soon picked up Spanish, which raised our popularity to the heights.

The *San Pedro* conveyed letters from us to my mother in Spain, in which we informed her of our arrival at Havana and of the obstacles preventing the continuance of the journey we had undertaken, and we asked her: (1) to undertake to make provision for us so that we would not be obliged to accept the generous offers of which there was no shortage and be a burden on the people of Havana; (2) to obtain the King of Spain's permission for us to come to join her and, if he did not consider it opportune to grant us this, to authorize us to stay at Havana until better times.

My mother replied that as to living expenses, she could not give us any unless the hundred-thousand-franc pension assigned to her and her children by the Directory were raised sufficiently to meet this double purpose and, above all, were paid regularly.

As to the two other points, my mother informed us that she was going to make the necessary approaches to the King of Spain at Madrid. Made they were, but my mother got nothing from them—not even, I think, a verbal or indirect reply. Eighteen months passed in this way, and we were under the pleasant illusion, shared by all at Havana, that this silence was the equivalent of a tacit authorization to stay there. But this illusion was dispelled when, in the month of September 1799, we were notified by the captain general of the island of Cuba (the Marquis of Someruelos) of a royal order (*una real Orden*) that had just been sent to him by the Secretary of State (Urquijo) instructing him to cause us to leave immediately. This order was dispatched in all secrecy and without my mother's being informed. It was believed to have been given at the request of or a hint from, the French government. I do not know. This *Real Orden* provided in addition that *Su Majestad attendiendo a las circonstancias de su real Erario* (*that His Majesty taking into consideration the state of his Royal Treasury*) could not give us any financial assistance to leave his dominions.

We knew only too well what it was like staying in the United States to think of returning there in the state of penury to which we had been reduced. We therefore had no alternative other than to return to Europe, and having decided on this course, there was only England we could make for. We considered it very doubtful that we would be received, but we thought that, were it only to alight, we still had to land there to take stock of the state of Europe in order to determine where we should go from there and, in short, to find the means to continue the journey.

The first difficulty to present itself in the execution of this plan was in finding ways of paying for the inevitable expenditure. This difficulty was promptly smoothed out by the people of Havana. The order for our expulsion and the refusal of assistance from the *Real Erario* had roused in them a sort of indignation that we strove to calm. They said: "Since the *Real Erario* is doing nothing, our private *Erarios* will make provision." They got together and soon brought us the sum of fourteen thousand heavy piasters, which we accepted with deep gratitude but with a feeling all the heavier because as it was, it was not the only debt of gratitude we owed some of them.

When this difficulty had been surmounted, we were presented with an obstacle of a different kind. Despite the war, we had to be transported from the Spanish colony of Havana to the English colony of the Bahamas, where we hoped we would be able to embark for England directly. The Spanish authorities, although without orders on this matter, got us out of this difficulty. Don Gabriel de Aristizabal, a naval lieutenant general commanding the Spanish squadron stationed at Havana, put us on board a war schooner, the *Santa Elisabeth,* with sixteen guns and a crew of eighty under Captain Don Angel Crespo. General Aristizabal converted it into an *armed truce ship* by giving its captain orders to fly the Spanish flag at the rear and the English flag from the mainmast. At the same time he ordered him under no circumstances to make use of his cannons except if his neutrality was not respected and there was a possibility of our safety being at risk. At the same time he gave the captain an open letter addressed to the English governor of the Bahamas, Colonel Dowdeswell, in which he told him that three Princes of the same blood as the King his master (*el Rey su amo*) had informed him of their intention to go to the Bahamas and that he had therefore put at their disposal for this purpose one of his Catholic Majesty's warships, which he was dispatching under a flag of truce to his seat of government (the port of Nassau in Providence Island); however, he went on, considering the number of corsairs and pirates infesting the seas, he had been obliged to take extralegal precautions to safeguard the person of the three Princes against any violence and thus avoid *un rubor al trono de su soberano* ("causing his sovereign to blush"). General Aristizabal then explained that his precaution consisted of the order he had given the captain of the *Santa Elisabeth* to keep his cannons in their firing positions while we were on board and to use them against any ship whatsoever that did not respect the flag of truce, but with orders to use them in that eventuality alone and, finally, with special orders to have the cannons stowed away for the return to Havana as soon as we had safely disembarked on Providence Island. The General added that, relying on the English sense of fair play, he trusted that the reasons for this departure from the conventions or from the law of nations regarding truce ships would be duly appreciated by the British authorities and that, placing in turn the same confidence in the word of a Spaniard, they would not molest His Catholic Majesty's ship in any way.

We were not disappointed in this explanation: The Spanish ship was accorded the same reception at the port of Nassau as it would have been if the two Powers had not been at war.

We were perfectly well treated by the British authorities in the Bahamas, and we found them disposed to facilitate our voyage to England, though they informed us that there were scarcely ever any boats going there directly from the islands. They told us that nothing prevented us from remaining at Nassau as long as we liked and that we could probably embark for Halifax (Novia Scotia) on one of their frigates, which they were expecting and which was due to return there after depositing the cargo they had been told to bring to their port.

This frigate arrived at the port of Nassau a few days later. It was a twenty-four gunner, the *Porcupine,* commanded by Captain Andrew Fitz-Roy Evans. This officer came at once to take us aboard his ship and escort us to Halifax.

After a crossing of twenty days we reached Halifax, where the Duke of Kent, fourth son of King George III and father of Queen Victoria, was the military commandant. This Prince received us most cordially, and it was there that a bond of intimate friendship was forged between us that lasted as long as he lived.

As to the desire we experienced to embark on the first warship leaving for England, he told us that since he had no orders concerning us, he found himself, to his deep regret, obliged to refuse his consent; that he was in complete ignorance of his government's intentions toward us and that in our own interests as well as in accordance with his duty, he thought it better that the ministry should be warned in advance of our intentions so as to give them time to send to the port where we were expected such orders concerning us as it judged fit. He added that he would himself write a letter to the Duke of Portland, then Home Secretary, which he would show us and of which he would give us a duplicate in case we arrived before the original. Then he advised us to board a Liverpool ship (the *Lord Duncan*) that was leaving for New York, where we could take the regular English packet that would take us to Falmouth. We could not but follow this advice. We had two long and wearisome crossings, one of twenty-three days from Halifax to New York, the other of twenty-seven from New York to Falmouth, where we arrived about January 1, 1800, having traveled for four months after leaving Havana.

And so we came to England to invoke the generous hospitality that was then bestowed on so many Frenchmen, whether *émigrés* or merely refugees like ourselves. We could be in no doubt that it would have been refused us if we had asked for it earlier; but we hoped that the *émigrés'* influence would no longer be strong enough to maintain the English government's exclusion orders against those not associated with their opinions or activities.* We were not deceived in this expectation, for we were granted the hospitality of England with financial provisions similar to those enjoyed by the other Princes of the Blood who had taken refuge there before us. All this was done without restricting our freedom of action in any way, without imposing any kind of conditions or any demand that might offend our p̕ ₍riotism or run counter to our interpretation of our duty.

It was at the same period, at the beginning of 1800, that our reconciliation was effected with the Princes of the elder branch. King Louis XVIII had two or three times given me to understand, more or less directly, that he desired this, but since it was always added as a *sine qua non* that I should join the *émigré* unit called Condé's Army, I had always refused to follow up these overtures. (See Note 1 at the end of the text.)

On arriving in England I was informed, again indirectly, that this condition would no longer be *insisted upon.* Then, with the agreement of my brothers, who entirely shared my sentiments and political opinions, I wrote a letter to King Louis XVIII, then at Mittau, in which, without disavowing our past conduct, I expressed my brothers' and my own regret that we had been so long separated from him and our desire that he should countenance a reconciliation and let us pledge our loyalty to him as King.

I wrote to *Monsieur* (Comte d'Artois and later King Charles X) who was in London, and I sent him my open letter, asking him to see that it reached the King and to be so kind as to receive me, which he did immediately. His welcome was very cordial; he told me that he would send my letter to the King and that although he regretted it did not contain some references to the past he had hoped to find,† he was nevertheless sure that the King would open his arms to us and welcome us in the same way as he himself had just done. But, still infatuated with the

---

* After a stay of two years in England, Prince Talleyrand was expelled in 1794. General Dumouriez and General Valence had been previously.
† His actual words were—and here my memory is positive: "Some expression *of regret for your errors.* I say that once and for all, and I shall not speak of it to you again." —"You are very kind, sir," I replied, "but in truth I cannot speak of *my errors* in isolation because I believe that everyone has made more than one in the course of the Revolution, and consequently, if I must speak of any errors, I should consider myself bound to say *our errors."* —"Come on," he said with his usual bonhomie, "don't play with words. Surely it is only too true that we are all fairly often mistaken, but you know perfectly well what I mean—namely, that both your brother Montpensier and yourself served under the banner of the Revolution and in the armies of the Republic. What do you want me to say, it is public knowledge." —"Indeed very public," I replied, "but if that is what you mean by my errors, it is possible that those errors will be envied one day." —"Oh," he returned, laughing, "I think that's scarcely likely. But no matter, I am not insisting, and I won't mention it again."

unfortunate misconception that *émigré* thinking represented the real public opinion of France and Europe, he added that in our own interests—having regard to our welfare, which he sincerely had at heart—he thought he must counsel my brothers and myself to betake ourselves to Condé's Army as soon as possible: "Not," he said, rather ingenuously, "to remain there permanently—I can see that that would not be the thing for you, and it would suffice if you were there long enough for it to be duly established that all three of you were ranged under the banner of the Emigration. There, you see, that's all." —"Good God," I said, "that is precisely what all three of us want above all to avoid and why we cannot follow this advice." —"Very well," he replied, "I am sorry for your sake because if you do not make this gesture, I make no secret of it, public opinion will not come around to you, and you will not resume the place in society I would have liked to have seen you occupy; but I shall not insist." (He did, however, a second time, some while afterward and with no more success.) Then he said to us: "But I cannot advise you to stay in England, as I think you would be better placed at Wolfenbüttel, where I know that the Duke of Brunswick would gladly receive you." This choice of Wolfenbüttel seemed to me so odd and illogical that it gave rise to the suspicion that the *émigrés* were giving us this advice so that they could point to us as living under the protection of the man who had given his name to the Manifesto of 1792. But naturally I showed nothing of this and merely replied that I could not imagine what we would do at Wolfenbüttel and that on the contrary, our intention was to establish ourselves in England. "Very well!" he said. "Let us speak of it no more but, I make no secret of it, I fear your stay in England may not be altogether agreeable; because when *one** knows that you do not wish to join Condé's Army, I am sure that the feelings of malice toward you will be revived. Doubtless, when I order the *émigrés* to present themselves to you, the majority will, but there will be recalcitrants, I make no secret of it."† —"We must find consolation in that," I replied, laughing, and the conversation finished there.

Charles X possessed, in a marked degree, *the mentality of a Prince* and a sense of heredity, and he sincerely desired that the Orléans branch should not create a gap in the family circle and that it occupy its place in the order of the succession to the throne. That is what he was thinking about when he said that the aim of his advice to us was to make us *resume the place in society that he would like us to occupy*. For Charles X the word *society* meant, above all, that constituted by the *émigrés*. But here he intended that by resuming our place in *émigré* society, we should by the same token resume the place *in the order of succession to the throne* that he would like to see us occupy. He feared that a hostile

---

* This *one* always signified the Emigration.
† This expression frequently cropped up in his conversation.

attitude on the part of the *émigrés* might succeed in making our title to it lapse (in the legal sense of this old word).* In accordance with his totally monarchical philosophy, Charles X did not accept that Princes could be deprived of their place in the order of succession to the Crown by the voice of the *émigrés*. However, as the fear of alienating them dominated him even more than it did Louis XVIII, he felt that neither he nor the King his brother was in a position to resist them, and he wished to get around the difficulty by preventing the question from arising.

Louis XVIII shared these sentiments, though perhaps to a lesser degree than Charles X, and on this subject I shall cite an anedote, the authenticity of which I do not guarantee, as I did not receive it from his lips, although I believe that he wanted me to know about it and even that it was he who caused it to be related to me.

I was told how there had been a tremendous clamor in Condé's Army when news was received of our reconciliation with the King, how the Prince de Condé had been assailed from all sides to put himself at the head of a *protest in the name of the French nobility* against what was called this *dreadful scandal*. The Prince de Condé had forbidden any protest, but out of weakness had consented to do what was termed *something* to satisfy this clamor, and this *something* had been to send one of the worthies on his general staff to make known to the King the feeling in his army about this incident. The King had given the envoy a very bad reception and had said to him dryly: "Go then, sir, I do not wish to hear such things. People might think that the Prince de Condé wishes to jump the queue in the order of succession, as it would be too insulting to him if by hearing you further, I gave the impression that I thought him capable of that." That is how this anecdote was related to me.

I have been led to prolong this digression beyond my original intention by the desire to shed light on the period, on the actors and the emotions that fired them, and on the various phases of my personal and political situation. At my age of seventy-six, it is only natural to fear that I will not have the time to finish so long a work as that of the history of my life, and it is a real satisfaction to place here, as a foretaste, an accurate sketch of some portions of my political conduct. I can say that this is what I am doing, conscientiously and with scrupulous regard for the truth. So I continue.

The King of England, George III, the Prince of Wales, later George IV, the Duke of York, etc., made a practice of inviting foreign Princes who happened to be in England to take part in their reviews, and the French Princes were invited like the others. From the very first review that my brothers and I attended, *Monsieur* took exception to the difference existing between our dress and his own. As he was, before the Revolution, colonel in chief of the Swiss and Grison Guards in the service

* *Forclore* in legal terminology means that a claim lapsed if it was not brought forward within a specified period of time.—ED.

428

of France, he wore a red uniform with black facings that belonged to one of these regiments. All his entourage, Count François Descars, the Chevalier de Puységur, etc., also wore the old uniforms of the French regiments in which they had served and all, like *Monsieur,* wore the white cockade in their hats.

As for us, my brothers and myself, we never wore either uniforms or cockades. We went to these reviews in morning dress with the Star of the Order of the Holy Ghost on our coat and the blue ribbon underneath. We did not wear the Cross of Saint-Louis because when Louis XVIII had sent the blue ribbon to my brothers after our reconciliation—they, like me, were not old enough to have had it before the Revolution—he had not given us the Cross of Saint-Louis. At the same time it was explained to us that if we had been with Condé's Army or some other *émigré* unit, the King would have given it to us that instant because then we would have had some military service to our credit, but that as we had only served *in France since the Revolution, this service did not qualify for the Cross of Saint-Louis.*

In 1804 King George III invited us to two grand reviews of the London Volunteers, which he was going to review in Hyde Park. My brothers were absent, one in Scotland, the other in Wales. Therefore I proceeded alone, still in the same dress, to the point where I had been informed the King of England would mount his horse. There were no other French Princes there apart from myself. I suppose the King noticed it, but he said nothing. Once he was on horseback, he asked me if I had come from Twickenham just for the sake of saying something to me, and I set off after him. Some distance from there, I noticed *Monsieur,* with the Duc de Berri and the Prince de Condé, who had placed themselves on the route the King of England was to take. All of them were wearing their former French uniforms, as was their retinue, with the white cockade in their hats. *Monsieur* wore his red uniform of the Swiss Guard; the Duc de Berri, that of his regiment in Condé's Army, set off with a white sash; and the Prince de Condé, that of the former Colonel General infantry regiment.

As soon as the King of England had spoken to all three of them, *Monsieur* came up to me and said: "I did not propose that you should come to join us here because I felt sure that you would still be in your morning dress and I wanted to avoid the contrast between your clothing and ours." I merely replied: *"Monsieur* is very kind." —"Yes, I am very kind," he replied rather sharply. "That is all very well, but I must have it out with you about *all this,* and as this is not the place to begin, if it is convenient come and dine with me this evening at South Audley Street and be there at half past five so we shall have time to have our discussion before dinner." —"I'll be there." I proceeded there at the hour arranged and was taken to the second floor, where he was awaiting me in his bedroom. He was pacing up and down and seemed very agitated. As soon as he saw me he said regally: "Monsieur le Duc d'Orléans, you know that I have always been very satisfied with you." —"You are very kind," I said to him once more, adding a smile. —"But," he continued, "on this occasion, I make no secret of it, I am not at all satisfied. All this must stop, and if after what I say to you, you do not decide to wear the uniform of one of your regiments—because after all you have two, one of dragoons, one of infantry—for the review the day after tomorrow, I shall jolly well have to order you to do so." —"What, *Monsieur*," I said, "you will order me to do so! *Monsieur,* excuse me for saying so, with all the respect I bear a Prince who is my senior, but you are only a cadet like me, and you cannot give me orders." —"Very well! If that is not good enough for you, I shall get the King to order you." —"The King is not here; and then, *Monsieur,* I believe the King would think twice before giving me that order, and either way, he has not given it." —"Nevertheless, there can be no difficulty there, and the King can always order you to wear the uniform of one of your regiments." —"But *Monsieur,* to begin with, there is here an incontestable point of fact—namely, that if it is true that I had two regiments in France, it is equally true that I no longer have them." —"That doesn't prevent us from wearing these uniforms, and there is no reason it should prevent you any more than it prevents us." —"I know very well that if it suited me to wear them no one here would stop me, but I think that *Monsieur* has already grasped my difficulty, which is that I don't care to." —"Ah, I understand you very well," *Monsieur* then said in a towering rage, "but I am going to sweep aside all these trifles and get straight to the point, and frankly," he added, raising his voice considerably, "it's the *white cockade* that you don't want to wear." —"Very well! Yes, *Monsieur,* I think that is exactly it; it is the *white cockade* that I don't want to wear; and *I shall not wear it,*" I told him, stressing these last words. —"And yet," he replied, "it is the white plume of Henri IV that you, his descendant, like me, are refusing to wear!" —"Ah! *Monsieur,* I should be proud to put it on my hat if I still saw that glorious quality of patriotism associated with the white cockade that Henri IV knew so well how to impart to his white plumes, especially when he shouted in the fray: *"Spare the French, mow down the foreigners!"* But today the white cockade is nothing more than the *symbol of the Emigration* or of Condé's Army, since that is the name that has been given or permitted it, and it is precisely for that reason that I do not wish to wear the white cockade and never shall."

I knew from what I had learned of the goings on among the *émigré* Princes over the command and formation of the armed units of *émigrés* that this name of *Condé's Army* was a sore point with the senior Princes,* and my vigorously delivered speech was not lost on *Monsieur*. It evidently abated his anger, and he said to me in a gentler tone: "I make no secret of it, I shall report all this to the King. It's my duty." —"Only you can

* See the historical note on the Emigration that is placed at the end of this text.

judge that." —"And am I therefore to understand that you will appear at the review the day after tomorrow in your morning dress without a cockade?" —"Indeed, *Monsieur.*" —"Very well! I am most displeased!"

He continued for a few minutes to pace up and down with me in complete silence; then he suddenly held out his hand and said: "After all, my dear fellow, we must not quarrel nor, above all, must anyone below notice what has just passed between us. So give me your hand and let us go in to dinner as if nothing had happened."

The dinner proceeded as usual, and nobody noticed anything. Two days later I attended the review in my morning dress and he in his uniform. The way he treated me was no different, and it was only indirectly that I later learned that Louis XVIII, without disapproving of what he had done, replied that he would rather the matter were not raised again. And so ten years elapsed without *Monsieur* making a single reference to this conversation, and he only mentioned it again in 1814 when, after the Restoration, I presented myself to him in the Tuileries in my uniform of a French lieutenant general and, as was now fitting, with the white cockade in my hat.

He welcomed me most warmly with open arms, and after he had discussed the great issues of the day with me for a fair while, I saw him fix his gaze on my hat with a malicious smile. Then, taking it in his hands and putting his finger on the cockade, he said: "You have a charming little silver cockade there, and I am all the more pleased to see it in your hat because I seem to recall your having said some years ago that you would *never* wear the white cockade, and yet, my dear cousin, there it is in your hat!" —"Good Lord, yes, *Monsieur,* and when I said it I really did believe that I should never wear it! But I have one consolation," I said, smiling in turn, "and it's to see you in this little National Guard uniform, which I think suits you down to the ground, and yet I think you scarcely expected to be wearing it." —"Upon my word you are right," he said laughing, "and if anyone had predicted it, I would have smartly sent him packing. Well, well! Here we are, both of us, you with the white cockade and me in the uniform of the National Guard." —"That is to say," I said to him, "that to avoid wearing the three colors on your head, you wear them on your chest. Is that not so, *Monsieur?*" —"I don't deny it." —"Very well, *Monsieur,* then permit me to ask you in all sincerity how it is that if I, as you said a descendant like yourself of Henri IV, feel repugnance for the white cockade after it seemed to have become the *symbol of the Emigration,* the King has not realized that its substitution for the tricolored cockade was bound to be painful for the army and consequently for the nation, all of which has passed through its ranks and fought for more than twenty years under the tricolored banner?" —"It would have been regarded," he replied, "as a defeat for the King." —"I fear that it is seen as a victory of the Emigration over the army and the nation," I replied, "and to be sure, I cannot conceive of what possible

431

difference there might be between wearing the three colors on the chest and wearing them on the hat." —"Oh, there is a considerable difference!" he replied. "On the chest, as I have it there, it is only a costume, a uniform that can be changed or left off at will; but a cockade on the hat is the symbol of a party that remains attached. Moreover, mark you well, I am the only one who wears this three-colored uniform, and I only wear it because it belongs to the regiment of which I am colonel in chief, while by adopting the tricolored cockade . . ." —"Say *retaining* it," I said, interrupting him, "because it required force to remove it." —"All right, if we had *retained* it, first of all the King would have had to wear it, and after him the whole army with it also on its colors, and finally the whole nation, and that would have been to perpetuate and cause the triumph of the emblem of the Revolution and the Empire, not to mention how distasteful this would have been to all the royalists in France. That is something the King could never have done." —"I agree," I said, "that these arguments have some force; however, *Monsieur,* you cannot hide from yourself or be oblivious to the fact that it was with deep regret that the majority of the army and the nation saw the tricolored cockade snatched from it, the cockade that it never called by any name other than the *national cockade* and that was associated for it with so many memories of glory and victory; and I thought that by adopting it as his own and placing it in his hat, the King might perhaps have succeeded in appropriating memories so dear to France. Also, it must be kept in view that something to which one submits because one cannot do otherwise daily becomes harder to bear, and it is to be feared that the army and the nation are watching for the opportunity to rid themselves of it at your expense." —"Oh," he replied, "you have too lively an imagination, and you exaggerate all this. This nation is very versatile, and it adjusts to a *fait accompli* faster and more easily than you think."

There the conversation ended. If I had had the gift of prophecy, I would have been able to say to *Monsieur* that six months later, in the month of March 1815, when the King his brother had sent me to join him at Lyon to cooperate under his orders in stopping the triumphal progress of Napoleon, who was bringing back their national colors to France and the army, *I had seen* the soldiers on guard outside his door tearing the white cockade from their shakos and throwing it in the stream, shouting with loud guffaws: "Ah! that's where it belongs!" I did not fail to report this to *Monsieur* when I went in.

I said above that in 1800, at the time of our reconciliation with the Princes of the elder line, Louis XVIII, when sending the Order of the Holy Ghost to my brothers, had not sent us the Cross of Saint-Louis—on the grounds, it was said, that as we had only served in France since the Revolution, this service did not qualify for the Cross of Saint-Louis. The intention of Louis XVIII at that time was that the Cross of Saint-Louis should be exclusively reserved for the *émigrés* or for those who professed their opinions. But after the Restoration had been effected in 1814, he resigned himself to altering not his intention but his tactics, and he realized that to keep the Cross of Saint-Louis alongside that of the Legion of Honor, which he had to promise and guarantee to maintain, it was necessary to disguise its quality of a *Cross of the Emigration,* although he did not want the Cross of Saint-Louis to lose this quality altogether. In pursuance of this design, Louis XVIII began by giving it to all the marshals; then he distributed it in large numbers to the army. At the same time other unlimited distributions were made of what was called the Decoration of the Lily, which was a white ribbon with a little silver fleur-de-lis at the buttonhole. This decoration was at first worn generally as a sort of Order of the Restoration, but it soon became discredited because everyone wore it, and all that remained of it was a white border which, when one had both the Legion of Honor and the Cross of Saint-Louis, separated the two ribbons of those Orders on the same mounting.

It was in the middle of this conflict over Orders and ribbons that I arrived at Paris in the month of May 1814, and no sooner had I been seen once more in my uniform of a French lieutenant general than the old and hitherto completely forgotten memories of my presence in the French ranks at Valmy and Jemappes were reawakened among my former companions-in-arms and among the public—I who *had only served in France* and never with the *émigrés* in the foreign armies.

Louis XVIII had too much tact not to realize how awkward it would be for him if the Duc d'Orléans did not wear the Cross of Saint-Louis and of the Legion of Honor on his lieutenant general's uniform (which no other Prince wanted to wear). Consequently, a few days after my arrival, he came up to me in his closet in the Tuileries and said to me sourly: "Do I perceive that you are not wearing the Cross of Saint-Louis?" —"Good Lord, Sir," I said, "has Your Majesty forgotten that he never gave it to me?" —"That is true, but now I am going to give it to you right away," and immediately putting on his hat and drawing his sword, he told me to go down on one knee and he admitted me as a Knight of the Order of Saint-Louis.

Then he sent the Minister of War (General Dupont) to the Palais Royal to bring the Cross of an officer of the Legion of Honor and with the message that he did not think it appropriate that the Princes should have any other rank in that Order. It was not until 1815, after his second Restoration, that he gave me and the other Princes the Grand Cross of the Order of Saint-Louis and that of the Legion of Honor, with the injunction: "You will only wear the Grand Cross of the Legion of Honor on Saint-Henry's day (July 15) and that of Saint-Louis on his feast-day (August 25), and on those days you will wear no other decoration." This procedure was regularly observed during his reign and that of Charles X.

I shall also place here the account of a conversation I had with Louis XVIII in 1820, shortly after the birth of the Duc de Bordeaux.

After the King's breakfast there was a family gathering in his closet that my wife, my sister, and I attended from time to time. The King was sitting in his revolving armchair at the back of the closet; Mme la Duchesse d'Angoulême* was sitting near the window, and the Princes beside her. The men were standing in the middle of the room and in the embrasure of the window.

The King, seizing the opportunity when *Monsieur* was speaking to the Princesses, raised his finger and said: "Monsieur le Duc d'Orléans," and at once I approached his chair. No one could hear the conversation, and in accordance with the old respectful customs, these fairly frequent asides of the King were never interrupted till the clock struck eleven when, no matter what, Mme la Duchesse d'Angoulême got up, approached the King, and made him a deep curtsy while he kissed her hand. She then retired backward, and everyone bowed to the King and likewise withdrew.

The King (Louis XVIII) began by saying to me: "I have already told you more than once how much justice the King my grandfather (Louis XV) paid to the memory of the late Regent, your great-great-grandfather." —"The King has been so kind." —"I have heard him endlessly praising the Regent's conduct toward him, both in respect of his intentions and of outward appearances. He always spoke of him with real affection, and he displayed the most lively indignation at the calumnies against him, which were as odious as they were absurd. I should like to repeat to you what I heard him say on numerous occasions: *'The best reply to all these calumnies is that I am alive.'* " —"I am deeply sensible of the King's goodness, and it is very precious to me to obtain such a testimony." —"Oh! I give it to you with the greatest of pleasure. All this was the work of that wretched *Grange-Chancel,* who was nevertheless *a great poet.* Have you ever read these calumnies?" —"Indeed no, Sire." —"Well, I have, and indeed I was so ravished with the beauty of the poetry that I have learned several pieces by heart, the prelude among others, which is the most sublime, and I shall recite it to you since you don't know it." Then he declaimed it for me from beginning to end, and he did it admirably. Then he said: "It is execrable, but superb poetry. But I have something else to say to you. I want to ask you to make me a promise, and it is this: that if you become *Regent for my little grand-nephew,* which could be very fortunate, you will be to him what your ancestor was to mine." —"No, Sire, I cannot promise that . . ." —"Why not?" he replied, interrupting me, surprise mingling with irritation. —"No, Sire," I replied in turn, "I cannot pledge myself over a hypothetical situation that may never come to pass." —"Why not? Is it because you are not of the stuff regents are made of?" —"Certainly not, Sire, and

* Louis XVI's daughter, who had married Artois's elder son, the Duc d'Angoulême.—ED.

434

I am not prepared to argue the point. But the King must understand my position; he knows what hostility I would have to face, and if in a much more favorable period than the one we live in my great-great grandfather, the Regent, experienced so many obstacles and difficulties in the way of his faithful and loyal fulfillment of the high mission he had undertaken, it is permissible to regard it as a certainty that all of that would surge around me with ten times the force and make it impossible for me to fulfill this mission with the same success as my great-great-grandfather." —"So you fear, for example, that the Duchesse de Berri might become a *second Duchesse du Maine** for you?" —"Indeed, Sire, that fear may well seem not entirely without foundation; but no matter, I would rather the King permitted me to avoid going into that question. The one that the King desires to discuss with me is, as I see it, exclusively one of duty and conscience." —"Yes," replied the King, "and what is incontestable is that your duty, as a Prince and as a subject, is to come to the aid of your King in his minority in order to exercise for him the high offices that because of his age he cannot exercise himself." —"Without doubt, Sire, and that is not what I would contest—although I could say that no law automatically obliges any Prince to assume the Regency in this hypothesis, and that even the charter Your Majesty has issued contains no provision for the eventuality of regencies or even for the succession to the Crown." —"You don't have to remind me, I know that very well." —"So, Sire, as the Regency is a trust, it is a question not only of duty but also one of conscience to decide whether or not to assume responsibility for such a trust. Very well, Sire, since the King leaves me with no alternative than to explain myself fully, I shall do so without reservation. I will say then that whatever the analogies between the situation of my ancestor the Duc d'Orléans toward Louis XV in 1715 and my possible situation toward the Duc de Bordeaux if he became a minor King, times have changed so much that today I could not expect with the same confidence to have my ancestor's good fortune in being able to hand back this trust to Louis XV when he reached his majority; and Your Majesty will permit me to add that when one has such fears about the fragility of such a trust one does not undertake to look after it when one is heir to it."

After hearing these last words, Louis XVIII lowered his head, and after a few moments of silence he raised it, and fixing on me his bulging eyes whose black pupils filled all the whites, he said to me: "All that I ask of you is not to repeat what you have just told me to anyone." I promised. and in fact I never spoke of this conversation, even to my family, as long as he and Charles X were on the throne. I merely said, to satisfy their curiosity, that the King had once more spoken to me of the justice that Louis XV always paid to the memory of the Regent.

* The Duchesse du Maine, wife of Louis XIV's legitimated son the Duc du Maine, was involved in conspiracies against the Regent Orléans, who had deprived her husband of the considerable powers Louis XIV had intended he should exercise during a regency.—ED.

Note No. 1

I had been completely unknown throughout my travels in Norway and Lapland in 1795, but on my return to Stockholm an incident that I shall relate elsewhere resulted in the Comte de Saint-Priest, who had been a minister of Louis XVI with M. Necker till 1790 and who was then residing in Stockholm with his family, learning that the traveler named Müller was *the Duc d'Orléans.* He sent asking me to receive him, and I went to his house to avoid the bustle of his visiting my modest lodgings. After many expressions of concern and of astonishment at seeing me *fall from the skies on Stockholm,* as he put it, without anyone being able to understand how I had arrived, he came to the point and told me that when he had learned he was so near me, he had wanted to express how impressed he was that, young as I still was, I had managed to get through the Revolution, surrounded by so many reefs, without participating in its actions further than having served in its armies. He said that he knew that the King, Louis XVIII, often expressed the same opinion concerning me and that he had thought to give me pleasure by seeking an opportunity to tell me this; but that he ought to add that though judicious men knew perfectly well that I was untainted by the excesses of the Revolution, those in the grip of party feeling would exploit my services in the armies of the Revolution to keep me under a cloud that only some approach to the King could dissipate. He said that he realized he had no other right to address me in such terms except his attachment to the blood of his Kings, because he should tell me that he was merely a loyal subject of the King; that not only *did* he have no authorization for what he had been so bold as to tell me, but that he evidently *could* not since, assuredly, no one would have imagined that he would have had occasion to see me at Stockholm.

Doubtless what he said to me did not form so coherent a speech as the one I have just reported. It was a conversation intermingled with interruptions on both sides, he rather embarrassed and I very circumspect. However, I can warrant that such was the drift of his words.

437

For my part I told him that the grievous events of which I had been a very passive spectator, but which had deeply grieved me, had shattered the hopes that in my ardent and youthful inexperience I had founded on the Revolution and that my opinion in this respect had undergone profound modification; that I regarded the restoration of the throne as the best way of putting an end to the sufferings of France and the anarchy into which the excesses of the Revolution had plunged her, provided that this restoration took place in such a way as not to offend the feelings and even the prejudices of the nation; that, for example, all thought of a total return to *the Ancien Régime* seemed to me both chimerical and dangerous because, indeed, I considered that the belief—unfortunately only too well founded—that this was the fixed point and the real aim of the King, the Princes, and the *émigrés,* was the main obstacle to the restoration of the throne and the monarchy.

M. de Saint-Priest scarcely replied except by sighing. Then he told me that we must hope that supervening events would lessen these difficulties. He considered that the implementation of the Constitution of the year III, which had just rid France of the detestable government of the National Convention and substituted for it an *Executive Directory* and two *Legislative Councils,* constituted real progress toward a monarchy because, he said, the Directory was clearly a *five-man King;* that although the new arrangement was still very defective and scarcely practicable, he thought that if an understanding could be reached with the two councils, all they needed to do was to *snap their fingers lightly at the Directory,* the office would become empty, and the King could quite simply be put in their place. I asked him if he expected that the King would consent to occupy such an office, and he replied that once this door had opened it would be impossible not to enter, though doubtless this could only be done after considerable modifications.

Then, returning to what concerned me personally, M. de Saint-Priest told me that the moment seemed to him opportune for me to make approaches to the King, since I had only been able to learn that we had lost the young King Louis XVII, who died in the Temple on June 9 of that year (1795), on returning from my journey to Lapland and since it was incontestable that this had completely altered the position of *Monsieur,* now King, and consequently my position toward him. To his way of thinking, I now had an obligation to perform an act of submission to the King. "But," I then said to him, without embarking on a discussion of fundamentals, "before we get involved in that, we must at least have something sure to go on regarding the likely reception of such an initiative and the conditions that are likely to be imposed on me; because you know, my dear Count, that the precedents are not encouraging." —"I cannot deny it," he replied. "Moreover, I have no authority to reply to such questions. I can only speak of what I presume the King's intentions

438

to be. I presume, therefore, that the initiative would be well received and that the King would open his arms to you, but that it would probably be considered necessary, to disperse *that cloud* I mentioned just now, for you to take at the same time the step of *joining Condé's Army."* —"Ah, that is the point that must be definitely clarified, because I must tell you, my dear Count, I have resolved not to do so in any circumstance." —"Perhaps I am wrong," replied M. de Saint-Priest, "I am only speaking for myself; but, although I count for nothing, I must report this conversation to the King, and if you would be so kind as to let me have the honor of writing to you later, I feel sure that I shall be able to let you know the King's intentions."

I accepted this proposal. I gave him the address of my banker in Hamburg, and we parted.

Sometime later, I received a reply from the Comte de Saint-Priest in which he gave me to understand, without explaining himself too precisely, that there would be no chance of an approach from me being well received as long as I persisted in my resolve not to join Condé's Army.

At this time Louis XVIII was at Verona, from which he had dated his proclamation on the occasion of his accession. This circumstance had already alarmed the government of the Republic of Venice, whose neutrality had hitherto been respected by the belligerents but which it feared might be compromised by these publications. But in the spring of 1796 the brilliant successes of the French Army of Italy under General Bonaparte increased this government's alarm, and it requested Louis XVIII to leave Venetian territory. Louis XVIII, deeply stung, betook himself to Venice, had the Golden Book brought to him, and with his own hand crossed out the names of Henri IV and all his descendants, inscribed as *Venetian Nobles.* Then he departed for Germany and made straight for Riegels, on the banks of the Upper Rhine, where the Prince de Condé's headquarters were then situated. This was the period when the *émigrés* flattered themselves they could have secret dealings with the French army stationed on the opposite bank under General Pichegru. It was hoped that the King's presence with Condé's Army would have a big impact. To make his presence known to the French army, Louis XVIII mounted on horseback, accompanied by the Prince de Condé, all the Princes present, and the general staff of that army, all wearing white cockades and sashes, and he proceeded to the edge of the Rhine, onto an elevation from which he could be seen by a French outpost placed on the other bank. There the Princes and the officers formed themselves into two lines at right angles to the river, leaving the King by himself so he could be seen the better; and presently all the hats were waved in the air to shouts of *Long live the King!* while Louis XVIII alone kept his on his head. It is claimed that the French post, which had taken up arms on seeing this troop in front of them, had also uttered shouts, but I have been told that they had not been

439

heard clearly enough to determine if it was *Long live the King!* or *Long live the Republic!* Be that as it may, Louis XVIII returned to Riegels, and this demonstration was without consequences.

However, he wanted to profit from his necessarily brief presence with Condé's Army to add to the effect he hoped it would produce, namely, that which he expected from my arrival; and he judged the moment propitious to make a direct appeal to me and persuade me to join him there immediately. Louis XVIII entrusted this mission to the Baron de Roll, former captain of the Colonel's company of the Swiss Guards. Baron Roll was then commanding a corps of Swiss Guards in Condé's Army that for the most part had served in France and shortly afterward became Roll's Regiment in the service of England. They did not fail to let me know that the King had chosen this staff officer, more particularly attached to *Monsieur* than to himself, to demonstrate to me the perfect accord existing between his brother and himself.

Baron Roll first of all made for Brunswick, where he knew that my faithful companion-in-arms and fellow traveler, Count Gustave de Montjoye, was in permanent residence with his sisters and one of his brothers. I was then in Holstein, completely alone.

Montjoye immediately sent me the communication he had just been given for me, and I arranged a rendezvous with Baron Roll at Itzehohe, a small town in Holstein not far from Hamburg, indicating the day and the inn where he would find me. I had arrived before him, and when he noticed me on entering the room where I awaited him, he exclaimed in his Swiss accent: "Ah, it really is *Monseigneur!*" —"What, Baron," I replied, "did you suspect a trap?" He apologized profusely and then immediately got down to carrying out his mission.

He presented me with an open letter from the King, written entirely in his hand and bearing the heading:

To my cousin the Duc d'Orléans

This letter remained in my hands only for a moment because Baron Roll told me that he was not authorized to leave it in my possession unless I proceeded immediately to Condé's Army, and so I did not have time to memorize its wording. Therefore I shall merely cite the principal point, which was that as the King had put himself at the head of his army, he requested me to come and join him there. There were other phrases (because the letter was fairly long) either about my antecedents, or about his desire to open his arms to me, etc. But the basic point was still the same as that of M. de Saint-Priest's letter: *no reconciliation until you have come over to Condé's Army.*

I had scarcely managed to finish reading the letter before Baron Roll was saying that the King was so anxious to see me again that His Majesty had laid on an excellent traveling carriage in which I should be very comfortable and in which the King had charged him to bring me straight to headquarters at Riegels. He added that this carriage was at the door of the inn and that we could leave directly if I would permit him to travel with me.

I replied that "I was very touched by the King's kindness in concerning himself with such a detail but that I would not be able to avail myself of it at all, as it was impossible for me to join Condé's Army." —"But the King is now with his army." —"I beg you, my dear Baron, not to seek to extract from me explanations that I would rather not go into. I tell you that I will not go to Condé's Army, and that is enough." —"In that case," he rejoined, "I must beg *Monseigneur* to give me back the King's letter, because those are the orders he has given me." —"There you are, my dear Baron." He was then completely at a loss, turning the letter over in his hands; then suddenly he said: "I have only to ask what is *Monseigneur's* reply to the King?" —"What reply?" I said. "One does not reply to a letter one has not received." —"But *Monseigneur* has had a good read of the letter." —"Very good; but since you have taken it back, I have clearly not now received the letter and consequently do not have to reply."

My case was too closely argued for the poor man to get around it. He got back into his fine carriage and I into my modest charabancs, and we left Itzehohe, each going his own way.

Historical Note
on the Emigration,
No. 2

IN this note I record my recollections not only of the formation of the armed units of the Emigration, but of the Emigration in general.

In 1788, when King Louis XVI had resolved to convoke the Estates-General of the kingdom, which had not met since 1614, he summoned to his presence an assembly of important persons drawn from the three Orders in order to inform himself, by their counsels, about the modifications, both in the mode of convocation and the composition of the Estates-General, made necessary by the passage of so long a period of time. This assembly, styled an *Assembly of Notables* as had been the one of the year before, 1787, was divided into seven working committees, each presided over by a Prince of the Blood, namely:

(1) Bureau, *Monsieur* (Comte de Provence, later King Louis XVIII)
(2) The Comte d'Artois (later Charles X)
(3) The Duc d'Orléans (my father)
(4) The Prince de Condé
(5) The Duc de Bourbon
(6) The Duc d'Enghien*
(7) The Prince de Conti

The main question submitted for examination by the Assembly of Notables was this: Should the number of deputies assigned to each Order be the same for the three Orders, or should the Third Estate have as many deputies as the other two combined? This was what was referred to as the *double representation of the Third Estate*. The other questions, though some of them were very important, were of secondary consideration by comparison.

* The Duc d'Enghien was called upon to preside over a committee, while I was not, because being fourteen months older than I, he had already taken his seat in the Parlement as a peer and received the Order of the Holy Ghost, which was not conferred on me until February 1789.

443

The two committees presided over by *Monsieur* and my father* came out in favor of double representation for the Third Estate. The five others decided against this.

Louis XVI in Council adopted the advice of the two committees, and letters patent of convocation for elections in this proportion were dispatched to all the governors of the provinces on December 27, 1788. I can still remember the joy I felt when, as governor of Poitou, I received an enormous packet of these letters patent countersigned by the Comte de Saint-Priest, the minister responsible for this province† and bearing the inscription, in large letters:

General and Free Estates of the Kingdom

It was only then that I believed that the convocation was serious and that the Estates-General really would meet.

The Orders of the clergy and of the nobility were each to elect three hundred deputies, and the Third Estate six hundred. There was only one departure from this rule. It was in favor of Dauphiné, whose provincial estates had requested and obtained that the same proportion should be observed for the election of their deputies to the Estates-General as had served as the basis for the composition of their local estates, that is to say, four deputies for the clergy to seven for the nobility and eleven for the Third Estate.

Shortly after these letters patent had been promulgated and their implementation had begun, the five Princes whose committees had advised against double representation for the Third Estate signed a long protest against this double representation, but they demanded the maintenance of the privileges of the first two Orders and declared their absolute opposition to any modification whatsoever in the legislative process of the kingdom. This document, which was referred to as the Memorandum of the Princes, caused a sensation. It aroused strong indignation against the signatories and increased the popularity of those who had abstained from signing.

I have taken my account of the subject of this note as far back as the drafting and publication of this memorandum because I regard it as having been the *fundamental pact* of the party that a little later became that of the Emigration, when the leaders and then the rank and file, seeing the futility of their efforts to effect the triumph of the system of government defined in this document, decided to seek the means for victory that they lacked in the nation in outside support from the foreign Powers. It was this document that made the Princes who had signed it the real leaders of this party—that is to say, the Comte d'Artois and the Princes

* Louis-Philippe is mistaken here. *Monsieur's* committee alone decided in favor of double representation for the Third Estate.—ED.

† The responsibilities of the ministers during the Ancien Régime were allocated geographically as well as functionally.—ED.

of the Condé branch—to the *perpetual* exclusion of *Monsieur* and, *a fortiori,* the Princes of the Orléans branch.

In order to make this assertion absolutely clear, I shall anticipate the chronological order of events and explain now how *Monsieur* was separated from Louis XVI in June 1791 and drawn into the ranks of the Emigration.

After the departure of the Comte d'Artois and the other Princes who had signed the memorandum, *Monsieur* had remained beside his brother at Versailles. He had accompanied him in his melancholy removal from Versailles to the Tuileries in the month of October 1789, and he had then installed himself in Paris in his palace of the Luxembourg.

It was evident that his secret departure from the Luxembourg on the night of June 21, 1791, was concerted with Louis XVI, who left the Tuileries the same night. Louis XVI did not plan to leave France. It was to Montmédy that he intended to proceed, and it was there that *Monsieur* was to join him by a route that crossed the frontier. But Louis XVI was stopped at Varennes and did not reach Montmédy, while *Monsieur,* traveling by Pont-sur-Sambre, experienced no difficulties, and it was only on leaving France that he learned that the King his brother had been stopped at Varennes and that a horde estimated at more than a hundred thousand men was bringing him back to the Tuileries. Then, realizing that henceforth he was separated from the King his brother by superior forces and no longer being able to return to France, he decided to go to join his younger brother the Comte d'Artois at Coblenz and there make, in a manner, his submission to the Emigration. He was made to feel it, and his reception there was more than cold. Before being admitted, he even had to resign himself to appearing before a sort of general assembly of the Emigration to give an *apologia* for, maybe even a discourse of, his previous acts (although I am sure of the fact and the purpose of this appearance, I have not been informed of his exact words). What I am certain of is that it was only the strength of his position as the first-born and the assurance that his brother the Comte d'Artois hastened to give him that determined the Emigration to *tolerate* him at their head. I stress this word *tolerate* because although he was attached to the *émigré* army in Champagne, although he signed all their papers, and despite the tone of his proclamations—which until his return to France and the grant of the Charter in 1814 were always drawn up in conformity with the policy and political principles of the Emigration, which were, at bottom, also his own—it is nevertheless certain that Louis XVIII was never anything but its *nominal* and in a manner *supernumerary* leader; while in fact at Coblenz, as at the Pavillon de Marsan,* it was Charles X who was always the real leader of this party.

* The Pavillon de Marsan was the portion of the Tuileries occupied by Artois during the reign of Louis XVIII.—ED.

I now return to the month of July 1789.

When the great events of the 14th of this month had removed all hope of subduing by force of arms either the city of Paris or the Estates-General (transformed into the *National Assembly*), Louis XVI decided to send the troops he had assembled around Paris and Versailles back to their respective garrisons and to recall M. Necker to the ministry. On July 17, he left Versailles and entered Paris, where a grand deputation of eighty members of the National Assembly awaited him. They were wearing the dress of their Orders and walked in two files before the King's carriage between two lines of the new National Guard from the Passy Gate to the Hôtel de Ville. Here Louis XVI placed the *national cockade,* that is to say, the tricolor, in his hat as a sign of his adhesion to the Revolution that had just been effected.

While his brother, *Monsieur,* was accompanying Louis XVI in this great act, the five Princes who had signed the Memorandum of the Princes were leaving to go abroad, all on the same day, thereby giving the first signal of the Emigration.

The Comte d'Artois, with his two sons the Duc d'Angoulême and the Duc de Berri, made for Turin, to his father-in-law the King of Sardinia. The Prince de Condé established himself at Brussels with the Duc de Bourbon his son and his grandson the Duc d'Enghien. As for the Prince de Conti, it was at Frankfurt that he made his abode.*

Charles X has told me many a time that at first they had found very little sympathy from the foreign Courts; that the King his father-in-law had received him very badly when he arrived at Turin and had said to him: "Well, there you are! You have only gotten your just deserts because, my God, you were far too *insolent!"* Charles X told this anecdote over and over again with a sort of satisfaction; then he added: "We needed a lot of time and effort to bring them around to our cause, and we would never have managed it if the Revolution had remained within its original limits; and without the excesses that followed, they would never have understood that they had to support us and help us to crush it by force. They realized too late for themselves and for us, but I can say that that was not my fault because I never stopped repeating it to them."

The popular successes of July 14 and the general armament of the population in town and country paralyzed authority throughout the kingdom and guaranteed impunity to all those who fomented disorder. The riots caused by the dearth of grain could no longer be put down. After their storehouses and shops had been pillaged, the so-called hoarders and

---

* The Prince de Conti did not stay there long. He took advantage of Louis XVI's declaration in the National Assembly on February 4, 1790, to dissociate himself from the Emigration. He returned to France, and after taking the civic oath in his electoral district, he retired to his château of La Lande, whence he only emerged three years later to be locked up with my brothers in the dungeons of Fort Saint-Jean at Marseille.

the unfortunate bakers were *mis à la lanterne,* in other words, *hanged,* and their bloody heads were carried around on pikes; and such crimes went unpunished.

The abolition of privileges and the whole feudal system—pronounced by the National Assembly at one fell swoop and without any preliminary discussion on the famous night of August 4—became the signal for pillage, setting fire to manor houses, and the destruction of forests. Alarm spread among the great landowners, who, seeing themselves at the mercy of such excesses, one by one began to seek abroad that personal safety they no longer found in France. These departures, which at first perhaps had no other motive, took on a political complexion in proportion as they increased in number. They soon became a kind of protest against the changes that were being effected in France, a protest the *émigrants* (as they were called at first) intended to place at the disposal of those Princes who were already *émigrés,* together with their offers of help to deliver King Louis XVI from what they termed his captivity and bring about the *Counterrevolution in his name* under the orders of the Princes.

Such was the origin of the *Emigration,* and such its program.

Although the political principles of the King of Sardinia coincided exactly with those of the Emigration, he never allowed them to form even *unarmed* assemblies in his territories. He refused the families of the *émigrants* permission to settle in Turin—they were sent off to Chambéry—and it is even asserted that he considered the Household of the Comte and Comtesse d'Artois, with their children, too large. So the Comte d'Artois did not remain long at Turin, and it was at the beginning of 1790, I think, that, leaving the Comtesse d'Artois with her father the King, he established himself at Coblenz in the palace of the Archbishop-Elector of Trier (Prince Clement of Saxony, the brother of *Madame la Dauphine,* his mother). There he was not subjected to any restrictions whatsoever, and assemblies—armed or not—were formed there without hindrance. Immediately Coblenz became the headquarters of the Emigration, and it was from there that circulars were sent summoning the *French nobility* and warning those who did not obey immediately that they would forfeit their nobility as soon as the Counterrevolution had been effected: Members of this party were not then allowed to doubt that the Counterrevolution would be successful on pain of being condemned *unsound.*

The Prince de Condé did not remain at Brussels for long either. The agitation he found in this part of the Austrian dominions had determined him to leave even before the explosion of the revolutionary movement that briefly drove out the Austrian troops at the end of 1789. The numerous *émigrants* already there left at the same time.

It is remarkable that at this period no part of the Emigration headed for England, which was an object of loathing for the majority of them on account of its political system. Moreover, they were aware that in principle, English opinion was not favorable to their cause. It was only gradu-

447

ally, and especially after the fall of the throne in 1792, that it was modified. In short, it was only the reverses suffered by the Emigration, in common with the armies of the continental Powers, during the campaign of the Champagne that determined the upper echelons of the *émigrés* to take refuge in England and to seek help and protection there.

After leaving Brussels, the Prince de Condé made for the banks of the Rhine with his son and grandson in order to sound out the dispositions of the little Courts of the Germanic Empire and to determine which place would be most advantageous to him and give him most freedom of maneuver in his operations. He decided on Worms, a small Imperial town very near the border with Alsace and Lorraine from which it was easy for him to make contact with the garrisons of our fortresses.

The name of *Condé* had retained great prestige in the French army.* The Prince de Condé had worthily upheld its renown. He had begun his military career at the age of twenty-one with the campaign of 1757 in Germany, and he had participated in all the other campaigns of the Seven Years' War with a distinction all the more appreciated by the army in that he had never left it for a moment to go and enjoy the pleasures of Paris, an object of attraction for so many others. He had brilliantly concluded these seven campaigns by his signal victory in the action at Johannisberg in 1762. In addition, in his capacity as colonel-in-chief of the infantry, he had won great popularity among the officers of this arm, which is always the largest of all.

At this point, to make my account intelligible to present-day readers living in an age so different from the one of which I speak, I must go into some detail about the composition of the officer corps of that period.

I shall just say a word about those who were called *officers of fortune.* They were those who had risen from the ranks. There were very few of them in the period when I began my service, and the further you went back the fewer there were to be found. Until the Revolution of 1789 they never got beyond the rank of lieutenant.†

All the army officers were *nobles* or *deemed to be so,* with very few exceptions. To understand this, one must realize that at the end of the Ancien Régime one acquired nobility by purchasing the office of King's Secretary, which cost, I think, eighty thousand francs.‡ But one will

---

* Because of his ancestor, *le grand Condé,* a brilliant general during the Thirty Years' War who at the Battle of Rocroi in 1643 destroyed the invincibility of the Spanish infantry.—ED.

† I recall that in 1791, after the departure of the officers of my regiment, the senior lieutenant, who was an old *officer of fortune* called Ducastaing, was promoted to the rank of captain. When I handed him his captain's commission, he said in his Midi accent, because he was from Toulouse: "See then, I have been reprieved of that terrible sentence that I repeated to myself every morning: *'Ducastaing, my friend, you will be a lieutenant all your life!'*"

‡ In fact it cost about 200,000 francs to purchase this sinecure, which conferred nobility.—ED.

appreciate that those who had been thus *ennobled,* although exempt from the *taille* and enjoying the pecuniary privileges of the nobility, were regarded as false nobles by those whose nobility had other origins—though this did not prevent the true nobles from seeking their daughter's hand when the girl was rich. They laughed it off by saying with the marquis in Dalainval's *École des Bourgeois:*

Today I keep low company.

But that is not what concerns me here.

There were two categories of nobles that were fairly distinct, *in point of fact* though not *in point of law,* one from the other. The first category comprised the great names—great families whose heads, and even the heads of their cadet branches, were either dukes and peers; or hereditary dukes who, without being peers, were listed in the Parlement; or dukes for life also possessing what was termed the Honors of the Louvre;* and finally a fairly large number of families who, without possessing the same titles, enjoyed fairly considerable prestige on account of the antiquity of their nobility, their riches, and their offices at Court and elsewhere, of which they had a virtual monopoly.

This category of the nobility had fixed its abode in the *hôtels* of Paris, and although the majority of them possessed great feudal estates with fine châteaux in their native provinces, they scarcely ever lived there; and it was always in Paris that they spent their income, to the great discontent of the provincial towns and of their vassals in the country. I believe that this circumstance was one of the main reasons for the nation's antipathy toward the nobility.

The other category of the nobility was the one referred to as the *provincial nobility* when one wanted to be polite, which was by no means a general desire, and on the contrary, the disdainful appellation *petty nobility* was all too often applied to it. However, this petty nobility included in its ranks many families that from a heraldic point of view were in no way inferior to several of those reputed to belong to the *upper nobility.*

Up to the Revolution of 1789, the organization of the army had retained traces of the feudal hierarchy that had regulated the formation of our armies in the remote period when the feudal system was in full vigor. Then the lords of the small fiefs assembled their vassals or their serfs by having their drums *beaten in the fields* to warn them that they were going to take the field. These vassals or serfs assembled under their banners, later called *ensigns* and still later *colors* (because it should be remembered that even in my time, when a fortress capitulated and its garrison was granted the *honors of war,* it was stipulated that it should leave the fortess *drums beating, matches lit,* and *ensigns unfurled*).

Once these assemblies had been effected, the lords of the little fiefs

* I.e., the right to enter the courtyard of the Louvre on horseback or in a carriage.—ED.

organized them into *companies of men-at-arms,* of which they became the *captains* and their sons and their relatives the *lieutenants* or *officers.* Then they led these companies to the lords of the great fiefs upon which their own were dependent, and the latter formed them into *columns* and took command of them with the title of *colonel.* The assemblage of these columns formed the army of the King, their sovereign and feudal superior who, when he did not command it himself, had it commanded by his Constable and his Marshals of France. Later, when the word *column* had fallen into desuetude and had even been almost entirely forgotten, it was replaced by that of *regiment,* and in order to efface even the memory of the feudal lord's right to command, only the *companies* continued to bear the *name of their captain,* and the regiments were given the names of the provinces from which they had originated.

Under Louis XV and Louis XVI, one remaining trace of this original organization was that there were three categories in the army that never overlapped because of the restrictions imposed on promotion from them.

Thus, starting at the bottom, that of the troops, voluntarily recruited and engaged to serve for eight years, this category was confined in its promotion to the lower ranks of corporal and sergeant that were then called the *bas-officiers* (the appellation *sous-officier* not having come into use until after the Revolution).

The second category was that of the officers from the rank of sublieutenant to those of major and lieutenant colonel inclusive. This category consisted of nobles or, as they were then called, *gentlemen from the provincial nobility.* They entered the army as sublieutenants in infantry or cavalry regiments. They never reached the rank of colonel, and in general their promotion stopped at that of *captain* because, as there was only one lieutenant colonel and one major in each regiment to twenty or twenty-five captains, very few captains could reach these two ranks, which were despised in any case by the highest category, who never took them. However, such was then the sense of hierarchy moderating ambitions that after twenty-five or thirty years' service these officers were content to retire to their provincial manors with the Cross of Saint-Louis, the title of captain of infantry or cavalry, and a small retirement pension.

As for the highest category, these gentlemen quite simply began with the rank of colonel, which was distributed with as much prodigality as lack of feeling for the old officers upon whom they were superimposed. To console the latter, it was said that to command a regiment well, you needed to place a young colonel beside an old lieutenant colonel. The stage was even reached under Louis XV when colonels were made so young, and so little past service was required of them, that the army regarded it almost as a blessing when Louis XVI issued two regulations, the first requiring an *age limit of twenty-three* to be appointed a colonel and the other obliging colonels to be with their regiments for *four months of every year,* from June 1 to October 1. During the eight months remaining, the regiments were to be commanded by the lieutenant colonel or by the major, who each year took it in turns to perform this duty.

On top of this again were the privileged units of the King's Household and others where the overcreation of ranks was unlimited. All the captains in the *Gardes-françaises* were colonels, and in the French Grenadiers there were as many colonels as you could wish for. I seem to remember General Montesquiou telling me that he was the eighteenth colonel in this unit at the Battle of Minden in 1759.

One can judge from these details the difference in composition between the two assemblages at Coblenz and at Worms.

As the Comte d'Artois's headquarters were at Coblenz, all the great personages who decided to emigrate proceeded there, together with all those who were attached more or less directly to the King's Household and that of the Princes. But it was around the Prince de Condé on the Upper Rhine that the part of the Emigration gathered which came from the army, and in particular the mass of subaltern, or rather regimental, officers.

However, the resources that the *émigrants* brought out of France with them were insufficient to maintain them for long, and in this respect they, as well as the Princes who summoned and welcomed them, were in the greatest of difficulty.

In the course of 1790 the continental Powers (because England still held herself aloof) came to the conclusion that they should confer as to what contingency plans to adopt in response to possible developments in the French Revolution. They decided to send delegates to Padua to discuss the matter with as little publicity as possible. The Comte d'Artois was secretly invited, but his presence there was no more secret than the gathering itself. I believe they confined their attentions to defining the situation in which the Powers would have to go to war, and in the meantime the Comte d'Artois was tacitly authorized to continue the assemblies of *émigrés* and to organize them in the territory of the Elector of Trier and of the Princes of the Empire adjacent to the Rhine.

The events of the following year, 1791—and in particular the flight to Varennes, with its consequences—determined the same Powers to get together in a Congress at Pillnitz, to which the Comte d'Artois was again invited. I think that war was decided on there, but all that was avowed was a contingent treaty of mutual cooperation if the case arose. This treaty was signed on August 8, 1791.

All that was known, however, was that the proportionate contributions of each Power to the army of invasion had been worked out at Pillnitz and that Gustavus III of Sweden was to have the command. But as this Prince was assassinated in March 1792, the Powers made a new choice, which fell on the Duke of Brunswick.

From that moment the organization of the *émigrés* into armed units was no longer a secret. The Comte d'Artois was obsessed with the notion, prevalent in the Emigration, that it was not the abuses of the Ancien Régime that had brought about the Revolution but that on the contrary, it was the result of the innovations that had been introduced. Therefore, at Coblenz he began by reconstituting all the units of the household troops and of the army, with their superannuated organization, which had been suppressed or modified by Louis XVI's ordinances during the ministry of M. de Saint-Germain.* Some were even created that had never existed, such as that of the Mounted Marines.

This *émigré* army of the Comte d'Artois was at once very unmilitary and very expensive—all the more so as it was almost entirely composed of cavalry. I think there were only a few companies of infantry, which had been called *the men-at-arms,* probably to give themselves the illusion that the feudal régime had been restored. Charles X told me very often that on entering France for the Champagne campaign, he had with him *five thousand of the finest cavalry that has ever existed, capable of breaking through any obstacle whatsoever. . . .*

The Prince de Condé would never consent to merge his assemblies on the banks of the Upper Rhine above Mainz with those at Coblenz. There he created for himself a small, separate army whose organization was more military and less expensive. He had a fairly large proportion of infantry, in which the majority of the *émigré* officers of this arm served as ordinary soldiers. It was this body that was called Condé's Army; but the name *Artois's Army* could not be given to the one at Coblenz because, although it was the Comte d'Artois who commanded it in reality, *Monsieur's* presence in this army rendered this appellation impossible, and to avoid either name, it was called the *Princes' Army,* which probably gave neither of them more than a negative kind of satisfaction.

In 1792, when the foreign armies of which these units were to form part set off on their march into France, there was considerable embarrassment among the *émigrés* over the allocation of roles. The Prince de Condé was determined not to allow his army to be merged with the one at Coblenz, nor himself to be placed under the King's brothers, and it was realized that there was nothing to be gained in trying to overcome a resistance that had the support of the mass of the fighting soldiers of the Emigration. Therefore, by way of a general compromise, an *order of battle* was drawn up for the whole armed force of the Emigration.

This order of battle divided the army into three corps: *the Princes' Army,* forming the center, was to follow the grand Prussian army and march straight on Paris. *Condé's Army,* on the left, was to cooperate with an Austrian army in besieging those of our eastern fortresses that did not open their gates at the first summons in order, as was said, *to bring them back forcibly to their allegiance to the King.*

As these two detachments were the only ones really in existence, and

* The Comte de Saint-Germain, Minister of War.—ED.

452

as neither of them was disposed to allow itself to be weakened to form a third, recourse was had to *a fiction*. The Duc de Bourbon was ostensibly given the command of the corps on the right, charged with assisting the Austrian troops in Belgium to reduce the northern fortresses to their allegiance to the King, as the Prince his father was to do in the east, and he was sent to Liège with some officers to create and organize this body. I do not know whether he managed to gather together a few hundred men or not, but it is a fact that this corps was never more than a fiction, and to my knowledge, when the Austrians besieged and bombarded Lille for eight or ten days in September and October, the Duc de Bourbon was not present, nor was any *émigré* corps.

The Prussian army entered France in the month of August 1792. It began its operations by taking Longwy on August 23 and Verdun on September 2. To its right, Montmédy was besieged at the same time. Because its commander, General Ligneville, rejected all the summonses, this fortress, which is very strong and almost inaccessible, was not regularly besieged. It was quite otherwise with Thionville, on the left.

The Austrian detachment under the Prince of Waldeck, of which Condé's Army formed a part, was entrusted with the siege of this town. The Prince of Waldeck lost an arm there and acted with the greatest of vigor. As a portion of the fortification of Thionville was dominated by a hill—its name escapes me—the enemy was confident that this fortress would be taken as easily as had been Longwy and Verdun. However, it was nothing of the sort. General Félix de Wimpfen, the commandant, put up an energetic resistance: He made daily sorties and constantly engaged the besiegers in battle, and afterward often managed to raze their siege-works. Therefore, after three weeks of open trenches and bombardment, Waldeck's army and Condé's Army were obliged to raise the siege of Thionville and evacuate French territory at the same time as the other invading armies.

This defense of Thionville excited considerable interest in France. It was mounted on the stage in Paris, and henceforth General Wimpfen was always known as the Hero of Thionville—which did not prevent his being outlawed a few months later in 1793, though he had the good fortune not to be captured and thus to avoid the revolutionary scaffold.

Condé's Army suffered fairly considerable losses in the various combats it had to sustain around Thionville.

The Princes' Army sustained none, not through design but because, in accordance with the orders it was given, it did not engage in any action.

Condé's Army left France in good order and proceeded to resume its former quarters on the Upper Rhine, while the Princes' Army, on account of its faulty organization and high cost, was obliged to disband as soon as it had regained foreign soil. A large portion went to join the Prince de Condé. Another, composed of the Bodyguard and some other remains of the household troops, followed the Comte d'Artois to Liège, where it hoped to find reinforcement from the Duc de Bourbon's corps. They found no one, not even the Prince, who had already returned to his father. *Monsieur* installed himself at Hamm in Westphalia, where the Comte d'Artois was not long in joining him, having almost no one about him except the officers of his Household. From then on there was no longer an Army of the Princes, and of the emigration in arms only Condé's Army remained on foot; and that was not finally disbanded until after the preliminaries of the Peace of Amiens had been signed in 1802, such was the great tenacity of the Prince de Condé.

The dissolution of the Princes' Army, combined with the maintenance of Condé's Army—which Austria took into its pay—placed the Princes of the elder line in a very false and difficult position, at least in view of the policies on which they had embarked. For while they were living in complete isolation at Hamm, entirely cut off from those whose emigration they had themselves brought about, the Princes of the junior line of the Condés were the only ones who, by remaining at the head of their troops, kept the promises that had been made to determine them to emigrate.

The Comte d'Artois felt keenly how galling this situation was, and it is fair to say that he did what he could to alter it. Still in pursuit of his policy of seeking support from the foreign Powers to effect the Counter-revolution in France—because he was convinced that it could not otherwise be done—he went to Saint-Petersburg to solicit a Russian corps from the Empress Catherine to throw into the Vendée. He assured her that by this means he would reach Paris without firing a shot. Whether the Empress Catherine did not share his confidence or whether for other reasons, all he obtained from her was a Russian frigate to transport him to England, where he wanted to go to make the same request of the English government. This frigate took him to Hull on the Humber estuary, but there he was informed that if he disembarked he would immediately be arrested for the debts he had contracted with some English financiers to pay and equip the assemblies at Coblenz. Then the Russian frigate brought him to Bremerlehe, at the mouth of the Weser, whence he returned to Hamm.

But from there he entered into negotiations with the English government. The first fruit of these was that an English frigate would take him to Leith in Scotland, which is the port of Edinburgh, where he would be disembarked on a Sunday so that he could proceed from there, without being pursued by his creditors, to Holyrood Palace, which was a sanctuary. The King of England had assigned him a suite of apartments in this residence. The Comte d'Artois remained, I think, three or four years in Edinburgh in this unfortunate situation, unable to leave Holyrood House except on Sundays between sunrise and sunset; and only after this lapse of time did the English government have Parliament pass a bill exempting the French *émigrés* from all prosecutions arising from debts contracted before the date when their goods in France were seized or confiscated.* The Comte d'Artois's debts fell within this category, although contracted after his departure from France to pay the *émigrés* at Coblenz, but it was only after this bill had been passed and received the royal assent that he was able to come to London and circulate freely in England.

About the same time, the English government assembled a small detachment of troops at Southampton under the command of the Earl of Moira (later Marquis of Hastings), which was to make a landing in the Vendée. The Comte d'Artois summoned or sent (because I do not recall whether he was still at Holywood House) his eldest son, the Duc d'Angoulême, to England. He was then very young, and his father entrusted him to Lord Moira to escort him to the Vendéens under the protection of this expedition. As the young Prince was alone and was not to have any command until he had joined the Vendéens in France, Lord Moira installed him at his seat, Donnington Park in Leicestershire, to await the moment when the expedition set sail. This moment never arrived, and when the troops that had been assembled at Southampton for a fairly considerable period of time were sent elsewhere, the Duc d'Angoulême left Donnington Park and returned to Germany.

The Comte d'Artois then sent his two sons to serve in Condé's Army. The Prince de Condé accorded them the honors of procedure due to their rank, but as regards their ranking as officers, he adhered strictly to the military hierarchy. In accordance with the established custom that Princes of the Blood begin their service with the rank of colonel, he gave each of them a cavalry regiment in his army. I imagine that these regiments were not very large, but I do not know what their exact strength was. There were no difficulties here. But then the Prince de Condé put these two regiments together in a brigade and gave the command to his grandson the Duc d'Enghien, who already had several campaigns in his army to his credit and was a staff officer. It was this command, which did not exactly please the young Princes, that gave rise to some wrangling between the senior and junior branches, particularly as the Duc d'Enghien was only three years older than the Duc d'Angoulême and six years older than the Duc de Berri. However, there was no open scene, and both of them remained a fair time with Condé's Army.

After the Peace of Campo Formio in 1797, Condé's Army passed from Austrian into Russian pay. It was shortly afterward, in 1798, that the marriage of the Duc d'Angoulême to the Princess Royal, Louis XVI's daughter, was celebrated at Mittau. Thereafter, the Duc d'Angoulême did not return to Condé's Army.

The Duc de Berri followed it to Russia and was quartered with it at Brescz, in Poland. But he had left it before it was sent to join Souvarov's army in Italy. The same year, 1799, the Duc de Berri had received an

---

* I report all this without giving dates, on which my memory is unsure, although I can answer for the accuracy of the facts.

invitation from King Ferdinand IV of Naples to go to Palermo, where a marriage was being contemplated between himself and Princess Marie-Christine (later Queen of Sardinia). But this projected marriage fell through, and afterward the Duc de Berri did not return to Condé's Army, preferring to rejoin his father in England.

When the Emperor Paul changed his foreign policy and became the ally of France under the Consulate, one of his first acts was to discontinue the pay of Condé's Army. It passed into the pay of England, who put it at Austria's disposal until it was disbanded. The Prince de Condé then established himself in England, and the majority of the *émigrés* returned to France to take advantage of the amnesty that the First Consul had just granted them.

So ended the *armed Emigration*.

Index

Abancourt, M. d', 247 *n.*
Abbaye prison, L', 30 and *n.*, 260, 358 *n.*, 401, 404 *n.*, 407 *n.*
Aboville, General d', 215, 230–32, 239
Affry, Comte d', 247 *n.*
Agoult de Bonneval, Charles-Constance-César d', 128 *n.*
Aigalliers, Brueys d', Baron de, 114 *n.*
Aiguillon, Armand, Duc d', 65
Aire, France, 143, 145
Aix-la-Chapelle, France, 315, 370
Alba-Lasource, Marie-David, 405 *n.*
Albert of Saxe-Teschen, Duke, 228, 295, 322, 331, 336
Albis, M. d' (army officer), 85
Alost, Belgium, 376
Alsace, 168 and *n.*, 244, 378
Alvinzy, General, 414
Alyon, M. (tutor), 12, 144
Amar, Jean-Baptiste-André, 355 *n.*
Ambly, Marquis d', 114 *n.*
Ancien Régime, xvi, xxvi, xxx–xxxi, xxxii, 17, 18 *n.*, 22 *n.*, 78, 108, 153, 170, 178 *n.*, 198, 199, 210, 226, 246, 314 *n.*, 317 and *n.*, 332 *n.*, 438, 444 *n.*, 448, 452
Anderlech, Belgium, 340
Andlaw, Baroness d', 8, 10, 12
Angoulême, Duc d', xxiv, 27, 46, 105, 300 *n.*, 301, 434 *n.*, 446, 455
Angoulême, Duchesse d', 434, 455
Anique, Captain, 283
Anne of Austria, 129 *n.*
Anselme, General Joseph d', 341
Antonelle, Marquis d', 262, 355 *n.*
Antwerp, Belgium, 315, 340, 362, 363, 365, 377, 390
Aoust, Colonel d', 215
apanages, xxx, xxxi, 37–38, 67, 105 *n.*, 182
Arçon, Le Michaud, General, xxxiii, 106 *n.*, 363, 375 and *n.*
Aristizabal, General Gabriel de, 424
Aristocrats (Blacks), 52, 93 *n.*, 103, 109
Armenonville, Le Cousturier, Vicomte d', 338
Armentières, France, 145
army, French, ix, xviii, 6, 77–78, 191, 225–26, 241, 284 and *n.*, 392, 431–32, 433, 439; artillery, 201, 324, 332, 413–14; attitude toward National

Convention of, 387–89, 401, 409; Belgian campaigns, 199–219, 222, 228–34, 237, 315, 323, 330–44, 370–98 *passim*; Belgian Riflemen in, 217 and *n.*, 331; cavalry, 211, 267, 324, 343–44, 410; commissioners sent to, 262, 263, 264–65, 266, 270, 294, 297, 387–88, 399 and *n.*, 400 and *n.*, 401, 405 *n.*, 410–14; desertion from, 343, 374, 377, 387, 392 *n.*, 396, 403 *n.*; discipline in, 281 *n.*, 325–27, 329, 343–44, 351, 359, 367, 368–69, 372–74, 410; Dutch campaign, 362–71, 372, 375–77; emigration by officers of, xii, xxii, xxxiii, 109 and *n.*, 110 and *n.*, 117–18, 124, 125, 134, 139 and *n.*, 140 and *n.*, 147, 148, 166, 201, 203 *n.*, 206, 211, 262, 269, 288 *n.*, 289, 297, 389, 448 *n.*, 451, 452; *fédérés* in, 306, 328–29; and foreign invasion threat, 137, 160, 165–66, 175, 177–78; 14th Dragoons (Chartres Regiment) of, xii, xxii, 19, 21, 79, 84–85, 87, 88 *n.*, 93 *n.*, 94 *n.*, 135–42, 146, 147, 201–02, 205 *n.*, 207, 208–09, 211–12, 297; French campaign, 238–46, 263–87, 292–97, 320–23; in Germany, 362, 378; infantry, 267, 324, 329–30, 332, 410; lack of supplies in, 323, 331, 340, 342–44, 363; of the line, 78, 110, 122, 140, 215, 245, 269, 270, 283 *n.*, 306, 324, 325, 326 *n.*, 327, 330, 343, 384, 387, 403 *n.*, 409, 414; loyalty oaths required in, xiii, 78, 110 and *n.*, 111–13 and *n.*, 114 and *n.*, 115–18, 134–35, 138, 139, 262, 263; mobilization of, 261, 324–29; nationalism in, 108, 109 *n.*, 116, 389, 409, 413; National Volunteers in, xii, 110, 160, 207, 215, 218, 222, 227, 269, 270, 276, 283 *n.*, 297, 324–26 and *n.*, 327–30, 338, 343, 374, 384, 403 *n.*, 409, 411; offensive vs. defensive action in, 197, 199, 200, 202, 211, 212–13, 216, 228–32, 238–39, 292–95; officers of, 78, 89 *n.*, 108–09 and *n.*, 111–13 and *n.*, 114–19, 134–35, 448 and *n.*, 449–51; panic among troops of, 205–06 and *n.*, 207–09, 211, 212, 266, 277–79, 328 *n.*, 373, 383; promotions in, xxii,

457

army, French (*Cont.*)
108–09, 114, 325–26 and *n.*, 328 and *n.*, 450–51; reinforcement volunteers in, 261, 265, 271, 273, and *n.*, 274 and *n.*, 278, 295–96, 297, 304, 306, 308, 326, 403 *n.*; at Versailles, 53, 58–59; *see also* French Revolutionary Wars
Army of Belgium, 341, 342, 360, 405 *n.*
Army of Holland, 376, 377, 394
Army of the Alps, 341
Army of the Ardennes, 341, 366, 381
Army of the Center, 165, 199–201, 202, 214–15
Army of the Moselle, 341
Army of the North, 137, 165, 200–01, 202, 203 *n.*, 212, 213, 214–15, 237, 243 *n.*, 263, 341, 365
Army of the Rhine, 165, 199, 203 *n.*, 215, 240, 243 *n.*, 274, 296, 341
Army of the Var, 341, 360, 402, 406
Arnold, Matthew, xxvii
Arschot, Comte d', 339
Artois, Charles, Comte d', xxiv and *n.*, xxv, xxx, 27, 37–38, 41, 43, 190, 301, 312 *n.*, 434, 443, 445 *n.*; as *émigré*, xxii, xxxiii, 27, 46, 105 and *n.*, 126, 128 *n.*, 129 *n.*, 130 *n.*, 131 *n.*, 149, 152, 153, 161, 171, 190, 243, 375 *n.*, 391 *n.*, 426 and *n.*, 427–32, 440, 444–47, 451–56; *see also* Charles X, King of France
Assembly of Notables, xix, 21 *n.*, 26 and *n.*, 107 *n.*, 133 *n.*, 443
assignats, 133 and *n.*, 169, 331, 342 *n.*, 378
Ath, Belgium, 140 and *n.*, 340, 394, 396
Aumale, Duc d', xvii, xxiv, 304
Aumont, General d' (Duc de Villequiers), 140
Austria, xxii, 62 *n.*, 173, 262, 290 *n.*, 362 *n.*, 378; army deserters from, 342 and *n.*, 343; in Belgian campaigns, xxiii, 197–219, 222, 228–34, 330–43, 362 and *n.*, 365, 370–95 *passim*, 398–99, 400–01, 409, 412–13, 414–16; driven out of Belgium, xxx, 20 *n.*, 447; in Dutch campaign, 363, 370–71; France declared war against, 148, 181–82, 197, 199, 203; in French campaign, 174–76 and *n.*, 177, 179, 181, 240, 243, 244 *n.*, 271–72, 276–77, 285, 289 *n.*, 295, 322, 452–53; supported *émigrés,* 126, 169–71, 172, 454, 456
Austrian Netherlands, *see* Belgium
Autry, France, 277, 320–21
Auvergne, France, 83
Avaray, Comte d', 88, 114 *n.*
Avesnes, France, 323
Avignon, France, 168 and *n.*

Bachmann, General, 252 and *n.*
Bahamas, 424–25
Bailleul, France, 145

Bailly, Jean-Sylvain, 41, 46, 49, 57, 65, 100
Bainville, Jacques, xvii
Baldwin, Mr. (English tutor), 190
Bancal des Issards, Jean-Henri, 400
Bannes, Colonel de, 338, 387
Barère de Vieuzac, Bertrand, 71
Bar-le-Duc, France, 273–75, 279
Barnave, Antoine, 65, 92 *n.*, 96
Barrois, M. (tutor), 12
Barrois, Captain, 283, 415
Basel, Switzerland, 362, 392, 417
Basire, Claude, 220 *n.*, 354 *n.*, 357–58 and *n.*
Bastille: storming of, 43–46, 64 and *n.*, 72, 77, 446
Bath, England, 144, 344–45
Baudouin (groom), 411, 417
Bavaria, Elector of, 370
Bavay, France, 213
Beauharnais, Alexandre, Vicomte de, 65, 90 *n.*, 93 *n.*, 94 *n.*, 96 and *n.*, 203 *n.*, 205, 216, 219, 296
Beaujolais, Louis-Charles d'Orléans, Comte de (brother of Louis-Philippe), xxvi–xxvii, xxxi, 7, 11, 12, 77, 81, 84 *n.*, 214, 216, 239, 252 *n.*, 261 *n.*, 301–02, 353 *n.*, 356, 432; exile of, 421–29; as prisoner, xxiii–xxiv, 314, 355 *n.*, 362, 404 *n.*, 446 *n.*
Beaulieu, General Jean-Pierre, 204 *n.*, 207, 228, 330, 336, 338
Beaurepaire, Colonel Nicolas-Joseph de, 269
Belgium, 61 *n.*, 62 *n.*, 322, 346, 349, 350, 352, 399, 453; Austria driven out of, xxx, 20 *n.*, 447; Convention commissioners in, 370, 376–77, 378, 379–80, 392 *n.*, 400 *n.*; discontent with Austria in, 197, 200, 201, 218–19, 230 *n.*, 231, 233, 338–39, 340, 342; invaded by France, 20 *n.*, 197–219, 222, 228, 315, 323, 330–44, 364, 371–98 *passim*; Riflemen of, 217 and *n.*, 331; unrest in, 376–77, 379
Bélissue, M. de, 25
Belle-Chasse convent, Paris, xxvii, 8–17, 18, 22, 27, 77, 79, 81–84, 136–37, 345
Bellegarde, Antoine Dubois de, 263
Belmont, General de, 242
Bender, Marshal, 169–70, 174, 340
Bentheim, General Count, 384 *n.*
Berg, Belgium, 371, 373
Bergasse, Nicolas, 52
Berlière, France, 272
Berlin, Court of, 62 *n.*, 128 *n.*, 173, 176, 234, 244
Berri, Duc de, xxiv, xxv, xxx, 46, 105, 300 *n.*, 301, 429, 446, 455–56
Berri, Duchesse de, xxiv, 435
Berruyer, General, 242 and *n.*
Berthaimont, Belgium, 338
Berthier, General Alexandre, 203 *n.*, 212, 215, 216, 219, 229–32, 238, 239, 266, 275

Berthier, General César, 216
Bertier de Sauvigny, Louis, 72
Bertois, Colonel, 206
Bertrand de Molleville, Antoine-
    François, 183–85, 189 *n.*; *History of
    the French Revolution during the
    Last Years of the Reign of Louis
    XVI,* 183
Berzieux, France, 278
Besenval (Besenwald), Pierre, Baron
    de, 42
Béthune, France, 139–40, 143, 145
Beurnonville, General Pierre de Riel,
    215, 230–32, 238, 263, 274, 280, 283,
    322–23, 330, 331, 336, 338, 341,
    400–01, 402 *n.*
Beuvron, Duc de, 24
Biaurat, Gauthier de, 26
Bible, the, 16
Bicêtre prison, 260
Billaud de Varennes, Jacques-Nicolas,
    74, 355 *n.*
Biron, Armand-Louis de Gontaut, Duc
    de, xxxi, 23 and *n.*, 29–30, 62 and
    n., 65, 140, 146 and *n.*, 200, 202–03
    and *n.*, 204–10, 213, 215, 230–32,
    238–39, 243, 296, 313–14, 316 *n.*,
    318, 345, 360, 406 and *n.*, 407 *n.*,
    408 *n.*
Bischoffswerder, Johann Rudolf von,
    176 *n.*
Bitche, France, 137, 165, 200, 239
Blanchard, Colonel, 326 *n.*
Blankenstein (Austrian officer), 331
Blottefière, General, 380
Bohemia, 174
Boinville, M. de, 64
Boissy, France, 47
Bombelles, Marc-Marie, Marquis de,
    127 *n.*, 128 *n.*
Bondy, France, 88
Bonnard, Chevalier de, xxvii, 8
Bordeaux, Duc de (Comte de
    Chambord), xxiv and *n.*, 434–35
Bordeaux, France, 198 and *n.*, 393 *n.*
Bossuet, Jacques, xii
Bouchain, France, 145
Bouche, Charles-François, 65
Boucher d'Argis, Alexandre-Jean, 35,
    65, 68
Bouillé, François-Claude, Marquis de,
    89, 91 *n.*, 95, 99 and *n.*, 113, 128 *n.*,
    288 *n.*
Boulainvilliers, M. de, 49
Bourbon, Mme de, 93 *n.*, 94 *n.*
Bourbon, Louis-Henri-Joseph, Duc de,
    46, 105, 243 *n.*, 443, 446, 453–54
Bourbon-Condé, Prince de, xxiv
Bourbon-Penthièvre, Louise-Marie-
    Adélaïde de (mother of Louis-
    Philippe), xxi, xxvi, xxxi, 7–8, 18,
    20, 21, 24, 46–47, 80, 84, 88 *n.*,
    89 *n.*, 93 *n.*, 196, 402 *n.*, 403 *n.*,
    404 *n.*, 421; deported to Spain, 422–
    23; dissatisfaction with Mme de

Genlis, 23, 47, 77, 81–83; marriage
    of, xxxi, 23, 81–83, 314, 346
Bourbons, xxiv, xxv; banishment and
    arrest of, 352–53 and *n.*, 354 and *n.*,
    355 and *n.*, 356–57, 359, 392 *n.*, 404
    and *n.*; Spanish branch, 67 and *n.*,
    422–23
bourgeoisie, xvii, xix, 43 *n.*, 44, 74;
    see also Third Estate
Boussange, France, 242
Boussu, Belgium, 204, 205, 331–33
    and *n.*
Boyer-Fonfrède, Jean-Baptiste, 404 *n.*,
    405 *n.*
Brabant, Belgium, 61, 62 *n.*
Braine-le-Comte, Belgium, 340
Braux Saint-Cohière, France, 279, 285
Breda, Holland, 106 *n.*, 375, 394
Bremgarten, Switzerland, 352 *n.*
Brescz, Poland, 455
Bressac, Marquis de, *see* Brissac
Brest, France, 24, 188
Breteuil, Louis-Auguste, Baron de, 22,
    41, 127 and *n.*, 128 *n.*, 129 *n.*, 130 *n.*,
    131 *n.*, 152, 391 *n.*
Breton Club, 70; *see also* Jacobin Club
Brézé, *see* Dreux-Brézé
Brice de Montigny, Colonel, 217
Brienne, Loménie de, 18 *n.*
Brisgau, Germany, 174–75
Brissac, Duc de, 128 *n.*, 220 *n.*
Brissot de Warville, Jean-Pierre, 98, 99,
    100, 159, 171 and *n.*, 178–79, 257,
    259 *n.*, 292, 313, 315 *n.*
Brissotins, *see* Girondins
Brittany, France, 24, 28, 69–70; *see
    also* Breton Club
Broglie, Prince de, 65
Broglie, Victor-François, 42
Brouckère, Charles de, 367
Bruges, Belgium, 228
Bruille, France, 409
Brulart-Sillery, *see* Genlis, Comte de
Brunswick, Charles William, Duke of,
    243, 244, 265, 269, 270–85 and *n.*
    passim, 287, 290 *n.*, 292, 296, 320–
    22, 327, 363, 451; Manifestoes of,
    244 and *n.*, 245–46 and *n.*, 261,
    291 *n.*, 295, 427
Brussels, Belgium, 20, 125, 129 *n.*, 132,
    200, 204, 215, 340, 343, 352, 372,
    376, 377, 379, 380, 396, 403 *n.*,
    446–47
Bureaux de Pusy, Jean-Xavier, 112 and
    n., 262
Burgot, François, xiv
Burke, Edmund, 341
Bury Saint-Edmunds, England, 144,
    345
Buzancy, France, 276, 321
Buzot, François-Nicolas, 312, 352–53
    and *n.*, 354 *n.*, 402 *n.*

Caen, France, 84, 137
cahiers de doléances, 111 *n.*, 317 and *n.*
Cahigal, General, 365

Calais, France, 142–44, 345
Calonne, Charles-Alexandre de, 165 n.
Cambacérès, Jean de, 380, 397–98,
    402 n.
Cambon, Pierre-Joseph, 312
Cambrai, France, 247 n.
Camus, Armand-Gaston, 65, 380 and
    n., 400–01
Capetian kings, x, xvi, xvii, xix
Caraman, Maurice, Comte de, 333 n.
Carle, General de, 200, 203, 215, 230,
    232, 237
Carle, Raphaël, 250
Carmelite Monastery, 260
Carneville, M. de, 415
Carnot, Lazare-Nicolas, 399 n., 422 n.
Carra, Jean-Louis, 297
Carrier, Jean-Baptiste, 393 n., 404 n.
Casabianca, Colonel, 209 and n., 215
Casa-Irujo, Marquis de, 422
Cassel, France, 145
Castries, Charles, Marquis de, 19 n.,
    129 n., 311 n.
Catherine II, Empress of Russia, 128 n.,
    130 n., 131 n., 150 n., 454
Catherine de Medici, 129 n.
Catholic Church, 4, 5, 393 n.
Catholic League, 70 and n.
Cazalès, Jacques de, 90 n., 96 and n.
Cazenove, General, 204
Cernay, France, 278
Chabot, François, 256
Chabroust, Jean-Baptiste, 65
Chaillot, Paris, 77
Châlons-sur-Marne, France, 89, 96,
    261, 265, 270–71, 274, 277, 280–81
    and n., 286, 292, 297, 320, 329
Chalus, General de, 139–40
Chambon de Montaux, Nicholas,
    353 n., 354 n.
Champagne, France, 105, 118, 271,
    273, 277, 280–81, 287, 292, 295,
    299, 308, 321, 329, 365, 445, 448,
    452
Champmorin, Chesnon de, General,
    383, 387, 390
Champollon, Colonel, 337
Chancel, General, 216, 380, 383 and n.
Charles I, King of England, 5, 7, 16 n.,
    346, 391 n.
Charles II, King of England, 391 n.
Charles IV, King of Spain, 128 n.,
    129 n., 130 n., 131 n., 149 n., 423
Charles X, King of France, xxiv–xxv,
    140 n., 301, 375 n., 433, 435; see
    also Artois, Charles, Comte d'
Charles of Ligne, Prince, 276 and n.
Chartres, Duc de, see Louis-Philippe
Chartres, France, 24, 136
Chasteller, General, 330
Châteaudun, France, 24
Châteaneuf-Randon, Marquis de
    Tournel 403 n.
Château-Renaud, Captain Mailly de,
    385

Châtelet inquiry into October Days, 35,
    55 n., 63–68, 79, 87 n., 350
Châtelet-Lomont d' Haraucourt,
    Duc de, 30
Châtelet prison, Le, 260
Chatellux, Chevalier de, 20, 27
Chatellux, Mme de, 20, 23, 27, 81, 82
Chaumette, Pierre-Gaspard, 74
Chaussard, Publicola, 377 and n.
Chauvelin, François-Bernard, Marquis
    de, 146 n.
Chazot, General, 242, 263, 270, 272,
    276 and n., 277 and n., 278, 283, 322
Cherbourg, France, 24
Chouans, the, 69 and n., 193
Civalart, Captain de, 412
Clairfayt, François de Croix, General
    de, 228, 243, 271–72, 276–77, 285,
    322, 330–31, 334, 414–15
Claremont House, England, xxv, 342
Clavière, Étienne, 180, 198, 216, 221–
    22, 263 n., 305
clergy, 76, 130 n., 152; constitutional,
    85 n., 86; in Estates-General, 26 and
    n., 28, 31–33, 69, 443–44; lands of
    confiscated, 36–37 and n., 83, 133 n.;
    in National Assembly, 39, 41, 48, 52,
    65, 103 and n.; nonjuring, 85 and
    n., 86, 123; refractory, 221 and n.,
    222, 223, 227
Clermont, France, 90–91, 271, 276
Clermont-Tonnerre, Stanislas,
    Comte de, 52, 90 n.
Coblenz, Germany: émigrés in, xi,
    xxxiii, 106 and n., 129 n., 130, 132,
    145, 148, 169, 172, 190, 191, 233,
    244, 297, 307, 362, 375 n., 445, 447,
    451–52, 454–55
Coigny, Mme de, 60
Colloredo-Mansfeld, Count von, 176 n.
Cologne, Germany, 362, 365, 370
Committee of Defense, xxi, 392 n.,
    397, 401, 402 n.
Committee of General Security, xxi,
    380, 397, 401, 402 n., 405 n.
Committee of Public Safety, xv, 253 n.,
    342, 397 n., 407 n.
Compiègne, France, 27
Conade, M., 19
Conciergerie, 211 n., 260
Condé, Louis-Joseph, Prince de, xxvi,
    46, 105 and n., 171, 243 n., 428, 429,
    439, 443, 446–48 and n., 451, 452–
    54, 455–56; see also émigrés, Condé's
    Army of
Condé-lez-Autry, France, 320, 383 n.,
    399, 409–10, 413
Condorcet, Antoine, Marquis de, 71, 99
constitutionalists, 154, 158, 180, 198–
    99, 221, 225–26
Constitution of 1791, xvi, 102–04, 108,
    113 n., 114 n., 115–16, 118, 119,
    120, 124, 143 n., 145, 174, 179, 183,
    198–99, 219, 222, 224, 226, 235–36,
    241, 247 n., 251, 253 n., 268, 290 n.,

460

302–03, 347 and *n.*; enemies of, 104, 105, 108, 118, 120 *n.*, 124, 132, 138, 151–52, 153, 154, 159–60, 161, 165, 167, 168, 170, 171–72, 176, 180, 198, 199, 220 *n.*, 226, 240; hated by foreign powers, 151, 153, 165, 168, 170, 171–72, 176, 240; Louis XVI pretended support of, xxv, xxxiii, 128, 148–49 and *n.*, 150 and *n.*, 151–52, 154–58, 159, 160, 167, 347; overthrow of, 154; planned reestablishment of, 391 *n.*, 393–95; royal authority under, xv, 100, 103, 104, 111, 116, 118, 119, 121 and *n.*, 122–24, 126, 132–33, 149 *n.*, 151, 152, 154, 155–56 and *n.*, 157, 163–65, 166–67 and *n.*, 168, 180 and *n.*, 195, 223, 227, 234–35, 237, 253, 344; suffrage under, 114 *n.*

Constitution of 1792, 348 *n.*

Conti, Louis-François-Joseph, Prince de, xxx–xxxi, 46, 105, 121 *n.*, 186 and *n.*, 187, 443, 446 and *n.*

Contreras, Leonora de, 422

Cordelier Club, 54–55, 74–75, 101, 108, 109, 160

Côte de Biesme, France, 272, 280, 321–22

Council of Ancients, xv, 342, 393 *n.*

Council of Five Hundred, xv, 342, 393 *n.*

Counterrevolution, ix, xxxii, 32, 53–54, 57, 77, 83, 98, 109 and *n.*, 118, 121, 122, 132, 137, 138, 148, 152, 169, 179, 191, 192, 194, 196 *n.*, 232, 248, 258, 259, 270, 307, 322, 347, 391 and *n.*, 392 *n.*, 407 *n.*, 447, 454

County Venaissin, France, 168

Courcy, Colonel, 215

Court of Louis XVI, xi, 27, 28, 39, 80, 98, 101 and *n.*, 180, 197, 219 *n.*, 220 and *n.*, 221–22 and *n.*, 223, 235; attacked Duc d'Orléans, 59–61, 63, 66, 68, 182, 184–86, 187, 188, 191–92, 195; despotism of, xxxi, 30–31, 32, 41–42, 76, 78–79, 158, 191; duplicity in, xi, 158–60, 180, 198, 227, 234; hatred for Constitution of, 151, 154, 159–60, 167, 180, 198, 199, 220 *n.*, 226; inconsistency of, 32–33, 39–40; and National Assembly, 39–42, 46, 52, 53; resisted by Princes of the Blood, xxx, 186–87 and *n.*; supported attack by foreign powers, 159, 170, 198, 199, 210, 226, 246

Courtray, Belgium, 200, 215, 216, 217–19, 228, 230, 231, 232 and *n.*, 233

Crespin, Abbey of, 203, 209

Crespo, Captain Angel, 424

Crillon, General de, 65, 146, 209

Cromwell, Oliver, 16 *n.*

Crusades, 125, 299

Crussol, Alexandre-Charles, 114 *n.*

Cuba, 365, 422–24

Cuesmes, Belgium, 338

Curgies, France, 211

Custine, General Adam-Philippe de, 96, 243 and *n.*, 341, 362 and *n.*, 363, 378

Dambray, Chancellor, 305

Dame de la Rue Bleue, la, 314, 360

Dampierre, General, 203 and *n.*, 330, 331, 333, 338, 380 and *n.*, 382

Dampierre-le-Château, France, 280, 286

Dampierre-sur-Auve, France, 283, 285–86, 288 and *n.*, 292

Dandré, M., 65, 96

Danthélemy, M., 422 *n.*

Danton, Georges-Jacques, 54, 66, 74, 97, 105 *n.*, 160, 263 *n.*, 305–06, 358, 387–88, 405 *n.*; warned Louis-Philippe, xiii, xxiii, 307–09

Darville, M. (army officer), 410

Dauphiné, France, 33, 70, 444

Davout, General Louis, 410, 411 *n.*

Declaration of the Rights of Man, 114 *n.*

Defermon des Chapellières, Comte, 353 *n.*

De Gaulle, Charles, xix

Delacroix, Jean-François, 358, 387–88, 399 *n.*, 400 *n.*

Delage, Colonel, 217–18

Delaporte, M., 96, 222 *n.*

Delessart, Antoine-Nicolas de Waldec, 96, 168, 169–70, 171, 172, 174–75, 177, 178–79 and *n.*, 180, 223

Delmas, Jean-François-Bertrand, 263

Delon, M. (army officer), 91, 94

Dembarrère, Captain, 366 and *n.*

Démeunier, Comte, 65, 71, 96

democracy, 4–7 *passim*, 15, 16, 20 *n.*, 26, 70 *n.*, 73, 98, 125, 133, 317

Denmark, 97 and *n.*, 131 *n.*, 392

Descars, Count François, 429

Desforêts, General, 215, 330, 380, 383 and *n.*

Desmoulins, Camille, 16 *n.*, 43, 74, 358

Desprez de Crassier, General, 242, 265–67, 275, 281–83, 286

Dessain, France, 145

Devaux, Colonel, 340

Deynse, Belgium, 228

Dietmann, General, 270, 380, 383, 386

Dieulouard, France, 274

Dillon, General Arthur, 242 and *n.*, 263, 270, 272–73, 279, 332 and *n.*

Dillon, General Théobald, 139, 140, 143, 200, 202, 206, 210

Directory, xv, xxiii, 192 and *n.*, 325 *n.*, 342, 393 *n.*, 421–22 and *n.*, 423, 438

Dombasle, France, 322

Dommartin-la-Planchette, France, 280–81, 285

Dommartin-sous-Hans, France, 277

Dordrecht, Holland, 363

Dort Island, Holland, 363

Dossion (dancing master), 9

Douai, France, 145, 295, 297, 304–05

461

Dourlens chateau, 22
Dowdeswell, Colonel, 424
Drancy (footman), 144
Dreux-Brézé, Marquis de, 32
Drouais, General, 330, 331 and *n.*, 333, 337
Drouet, Jean-Baptiste, 90
Drouot, General (called Lamarche), 375, 377, 380–83, 386
Dubois, M. (army officer), 85
Dubois de Crancé, Edmond-Louis-Alexis, 109
Dubois-Dubay, Comte, 263
Dubouchet, General, 366
Dubouquet, General, 276, 277, 286, 297
Dubouzet, Colonel, 337
Dubuisson, Paul-Ulric, 396–98 and *n.*
Ducastaing, Captain, 135 *n.*, 448 *n.*
Duchâtelet, Achille, Marquis, 99 and *n.*, 228 and *n.*
Ducos, Pierre-Roger, 159
Ducrest, Marquis, 19–20, 49, 56, 297
Ducrest, César, 11 and *n.*, 12, 297–98, 367, 411 *n.*, 417
Duhoux d'Hauterive, General, 215, 229–30 and *n.*, 231–32
Dumas de Saint-Marcel, Colonel, 382, 414
Dumonceau, Colonel, 217
Dumouriez, General Charles-François, xxii, 24 and *n.*, 97, 106 *n.*, 221, 231, 237–39, 241–42, 243, 263, 269–77 and *n.*, 278–81 and *n.*, 282–85 and *n.*, 286–88 and *n.*, 289 *n.*, 290 *n.*, 291 and *n.*, 292–95, 296, 306, 319–24, 329–43, 360, 362 and *n.*, 363–65, 370, 372, 374, 375 and *n.*, 376–90, 398–417, 426 *n.*; defied National Convention, 364, 377 and *n.*, 379–80 and *n.*, 387–88, 396–98, 399 and *n.*, 400 and *n.*, 401, 405 *n.*, 408 *n.*, 410–14; in ministry, 180, 181, 198, 214, 216, 219, 221–22 and *n.*, 223, 263 *n.*; planned restoration of Constitution, 390–91 and *n.*, 392–93 and *n.*, 394–96
Dun, France, 271
Dunkirk, France, 137, 165, 199–200, 203, 237, 239
Dupont de Chaumont, Colonel, 337
Dupont de l'Étang, General Pierre-Antoine, 433
Duport, Adrien, 65, 101 *n.*, 237
Duportail, Louis le Bègue, 84, 93 *n.*, 136, 141, 165
Duport du Tertre, Marguerite-Louis, 96
Dupuch, Colonel, 203 *n.*, 204, 215
Duranton, Antoine, 180, 198, 216, 221
Duval, General, 203 *n.*, 263, 274, 276, 278, 279
Duveyrier, Honoré, 105 *n.*
Duvigneau, M. (army officer), 206

Edinbugh, Scotland, 454
89 Club, *see* 1789 Club
Eix, France, 267
Elisabeth de France, 59, 84, 88–92 and *n.*, 96, 224, 310
Elizabeth I, Queen of England, 5
émigrés, 72, 104–07, 117 *n.*, 120 *n.*, 123, 138, 144–45, 151, 165 *n.*, 182, 191–92, 233 *n.*, 263, 267, 307–08, 345–46, 348, 349, 375 *n.*, 391, 392 *n.*, 399, 408, 415, 433, 438, 454–55; amnesty for, 155, 456; arming of, xxii, 443, 451–52; army officers as, xii, xxii, xxxiii, 109 and *n.*, 110 and *n.*, 117–18, 124, 125, 134, 139 and *n.*, 140 and *n.*, 147, 148, 166, 201, 203 *n.*, 206, 211, 262, 269, 288 *n.*, 289, 297, 389, 448 *n.*, 451, 452; assemblies of, 113, 117, 125, 127, 161–62, 174, 447, 451; assumption of royal authority by, xi, 126, 128–34; compensation for, xxiv; Condé's Army of, 426–30, 439–41, 452–54, 455–56; deprived Louis XVI of supporters, xxxiii, 106, 124–25, 126, 132, 151, 153, 154; *émigration à l'intérieur, l'*, 140 *n.*; as enemies of Constitution, 105, 118, 132, 152, 154, 165, 199; in England, 425–26 and *n.*, 427–31, 447–48; equality among, xxxiii, 125; and foreign powers, xi, xv, xxiii, 107, 118–19, 126, 137, 152, 153, 163–65, 168–72, 174, 234, 284 *n.*, 287, 293, 322, 389, 421, 433, 444, 446, 451, 454, 455–56; in French campaign, xxii, 243 and *n.*, 247, 271, 276–77, 289 *n.*, 296, 445, 452–53; honorable motives of, 104–07, 117, 119, 122, 125, 162, 166, 389, 447; judiciary as, 124, 125; landed proprietors as, 124–25, 447; and Legislative Assembly, 161, 162, 171; Louis XVI's disapproval of, xi, xxxiii, 107 *n.*, 126–28 and *n.*, 129 *n.*, 130 *n.*, 131 *n.*, 132–34, 149, 152, 153, 161–62; and Louis-Philippe, 426 and *n.*, 427–31, 439–41; nobility as, xxii, 69, 88, 107 and *n.*, 125–26, 191 *n.*, 234 *n.*, 428, 447; planned invasion of France, xxii, 154, 160–66, 168–69, 198, 199, 226; Princes as, xxii, 27, 88, 105 and *n.*, 117, 119, 121 *n.*, 125–26, 128 *n.*, 129 *n.*, 130 and *n.*, 131 and *n.*, 149, 152, 153, 169, 171, 172, 234, 243, 391 *n.*, 430, 438, 445, 446, 447, 451, 454; Princes' Army of, 452–54
Enghien, Louis-Antoine, Duc d', 46, 105, 443 and *n.*, 446, 455
Enghien, Belgium, 340, 396, 403 *n.*
England, xviii, xxxii, xxxiii, 4, 5, 6–7, 16 and *n.*, 18 *n.*, 33, 61 and *n.*, 62 and *n.*, 63 and *n.*, 64, 69, 102, 124, 136, 142, 145, 146 and *n.*, 167, 194, 233, 318, 354 *n.*, 364, 422, 440, 451;

462

French *émigrés* in, 425–26 and *n.*, 427–31, 447–48, 454–55, 456; and French Revolution, 190, 192–93, 194; institutions of admired by French, xiii, 189–90; Louis-Philippe in, xxiii, xxv, xxvi, 423–31; wars with France of, xxx, 187–88, 193, 362, 366, 377, 393, 394, 455

Enlightenment, xi, 4

Esponchez, Colonel d', 338–39

Espréménil, Jean-Jacques Duval d', 103

Estaing, Charles-Hector, Comte d', 58, 183

Estates-General, 5 and *n.*, 21 and *n.*, 69, 70 and *n.*, 111, 191 *n.*; 317 and *n.*; clergy in, 26 and *n.*, 28, 31–33, 69, 443–44; composition of, 26 and *n.*, 443–44; and Louis XVI, xi, 28–29, 30–33, 39–40, 133 *n.*, 317 *n.*, 443; nobility in, xiii, 26 and *n.*, 28, 31–33, 69, 316, 443-44; Third Estate in, xiii, 26 and *n.*, 28, 31–33, 43 *n.*, 69, 443–44 and *n.*; at Versailles, 27, 28, 30–40

Esterhazy, General d', 20, 21

Estienne, M. (army officer), 377

Estrées, Maréchale d', 21 *n.*, 316 *n.*

Étain, France, 267

Eu, France, 82, 83, 84, 93 *n.*

Eure Department, 247 *n.*

European powers, xv, 62 *n.*, 152, 318; Concert of Powers of, 170, 172–77, 179, 181 *n.*, 197–98, 200, 244, 262, 342 *n.*, 364, 378, 392, 403 *n.*); in French campaign, xxii, 244–47, 258, 259, 261, 263, 265–87, 292–97, 315, 320, 448; and French *émigrés*, xi, xv, xxiii, 107, 118–19, 126, 137, 152, 153, 163–65, 168–72, 174, 234, 284 *n.*, 287, 293, 322, 389, 421, 433, 444, 446, 451, 454, 455–56; hatred of Constitution among, 151, 153, 165, 168, 170, 171–72, 176, 240; invasion threats of, xi, 151, 154, 159–66, 168–81, 197–99, 220, 226, 324, 327, 394; and Louis XVI, 149, 163–65, 168–69, 170–77, 236, 246, 290 *n.*, 293, 327, 347–48; secretly asked for aid by Louis XVI, 127 and *n.*, 128 *n.*, 129 *n.*, 130 *n.*, 131 *n.*, 148–49 and *n.*, 150 and *n.*, 151–53, 391 *n.*; *see also* individual countries

Executive Council, xiii, 253 *n.*, 260 *n.*, 261, 303, 311; and French Revolutionary Wars, 263 and *n.*, 264–65, 270, 274, 275, 293, 295, 297, 304 and *n.*, 305–06, 323, 365, 405 *n.*; *see also* National Convention

Fabert, Marshal, 240

Fabre d'Églantine, Philippe-François-Nazaire, 74

Falmouth, England, 425

Famars, France, 211–13, 214–15, 237, 239

Favras, Thomas de Mahy, Marquis de, 35 *n.*

Federation of 1790, 64 and *n.*, 77–78, 110, 121, 221, 239, 248, 328

fédérés, 221, 248 and *n.*, 250, 306, 328–29

Feltre, Duc de, 141

Fénelon, François de Salignac de la Mothe-: *Aventures de Télémaque, Les*, xii, 194 and *n.*

Ferdinand IV, King of Naples, xxiv, 456

Fermont, M., 114 *n.*

Ferrand de la Caussade, General, 330, 338, 340

Fersen, Hans Axel, Comte de, 88, 128 *n.*, 131 *n.*

feudal system, 4, 13, 36, 48, 168, 447, 449

Feuillant Club, 95 *n.*, 100–01, 103, 159, 171 *n.*, 198

Fitzgerald, Lord Edward (Duke of Leinster), 12, 399 *n.*

Fitz-Roy Evans, Captain Andrew, 425

Flanders, 205 *n.*, 239, 243 *n.*, 244 *n.*, 270, 322, 365

Fléchin, General de, 138–39, 140

Flénu, Belgium, 337

Flers, General de, 203 *n.*, 208, 376 and *n.*

Flue, Lieutenant Louis de, 44

Folleville, Marquis de, 114 *n.*

Fonfrède, Jean-Baptiste Boyer, 159

Fontbrune, Abbé de, 128 *n.*

Fontenelle, Bernard de, 22 *n.*

Fontoy, France, 242, 264, 265–66

Force prison, La, 228 *n.*, 260, 261, 310

Forth, Nathaniel Parker, 11

Fort Saint-Jean, Marseille, xxiii–xxiv, 314, 355 *n.*, 361–62, 404 *n.*, 421, 446 *n.*

Fort Saint-Pierre, Holland, 366–67

Fouché, Joseph, 392 *n.*

Foulon, Joseph-François, 72

Frameries, Belgium, 334–36

France, ix, xv–xvi, xviii, xix, 378; aid for America from, 4, 99, 137 and *n.*, 139, 194; aid for Holland from, 4, 18 *n.*, 21, 363; Anglomania in, 189–90; civil war in, 151 *n.*, 378, 393 and *n.*, 394, 403 *n.*; economic crisis in, xi, 378, 392; famine in, 48, 446; history of names and titles in, 299–302; monarchy of, x–xii, xvi, xvi–xvii, xviii–xix, xxx, xxxii, 5–6, 67 and *n.*, 98, 103, 106, 115, 126–30, 152, 192, 393 *n.*; monarchy abolished in, 153, 154, 180 and *n.*, 227, 249, 287, 290 *n.*, 291 *n.*, 310, 448; people of, xvii, xviii, 101 *n.*, 102; Restoration in, xvii, xxv, 392 *n.*, 431–33, 438; Revolution of 1848 in, xvi, xviii, xix, xxv, 337 and *n.*, 342; unrest in, 24, 25 and *n.*, 26, 48, 53–54, 69, 85–87, 105, 151 *n.*, 162, 234, 447; *see*

France (*Cont.*)
also French Revolution; French
Revolutionary Wars; Paris, France;
provinces of France; individual kings
Francis II, Holy Roman Emperor, 181
and *n.*
Frankfurt, Germany, 127, 315, 362,
378, 446
Franklin, Benjamin, 165 *n.*
Fraternal Society, 76
Frederick II, King of Prussia, 7
Frederick William II, King of Prussia,
128 *n.*, 131 *n.*, 243, 276, 284, 288
and *n.*, 289 *n.*, 290 *n.*, 291 *n.*, 320,
322, 363
Frégeville, Colonel Charles de, 286 *n.*,
331
Frégeville, General Henri de, 286 and
n., 297, 330, 333, 334–36, 375
Frémant, M. de, 85–87
French Revolution, ix–xi, xv, xxvi, 4–5,
14, 27, 28, 36, 89 *n.*, 91 *n.*, 151, 258;
and authority seized in crises, 43–44,
55; causes of, 54, 190–94, 452;
decrees of August 4, 4, 48, 52, 447;
fear and violence in, xi, 40, 42, 53,
97, 248; Great Fear of, 47 and *n.*,
48; and inconsistency of Court, 32–
33, 39–40; injustice caused by over-
enthusiasm in, 76–77, 179; lack of
understanding of, 104–05, 106 and
n., 107, 109 *n.*; leaders of influenced
by masses, 71–73, 191, 378; October
Days, xxxiii, 35, 52–60, 63, 63–68,
73, 79, 350, 445; opposition to, 69,
73, 80, 101 *n.*, 106–07, 119, 121,
125, 138, 191–94; participants of
turn against each other, xxxiii, 47,
160, 196, 313, 397–98; public
opinion as cause of, xxxii, 38, 40–41,
68, 71–73, 190–91, 193; storming of
Bastille, 43–46, 64 and *n.*, 72, 77,
446; uprising of August 10, 54, 118,
122, 159, 180 and *n.*, 227, 228, 233
n., 237, 241, 246, 247 *n.*, 248 and *n.*,
249–53, 256, 257, 264, 291 *n.*, 311,
328; uprising of June 20, 123 and *n.*,
223–25, 227, 241, 328; *see also*
Terror, Reign of
French Revolutionary Wars, 392 and
n., 393, 403 *n.*, 439, 455; Belgian
campaigns, xxiii, 20 *n.*, 197–219, 222,
228–34, 237, 315, 323, 330–44, 362
and *n.*, 365, 370–98 *passim*, 453;
Dutch campaign, 362–71, 372, 375–
77, 394–95; and England, xxx, 187–
88, 193, 362–63, 366, 377, 393, 394,
455; French campaign, xxii, 240–46,
258, 259, 261, 263–87, 292–97, 452–
53; and Germany, 240, 243, 362,
365, 378; Manifestoes of Duke of
Brunswick, 244 and *n.*, 245–46 and
n., 261, 291 *n.*, 295, 427; offensive
vs. defensive action in, 197–99, 200,
202, 211, 212–13, 216, 228–32, 238–

39, 292–95; Prussian retreat from
France, 280, 291 *n.*, 293–94, 295,
315, 320–22, 341, 362; threatened
invasions of France, xi, 109 *n.*, 117,
151, 154, 159–66, 168–76 and *n.*,
177–81, 197–99, 220, 226, 324, 327,
394; truce proposed by Prussia, 287–
88 and *n.*, 289 *n.*, 290 *n.*, 291 *n.*, 295;
war declared on Austria, 148, 181–
82, 197, 199, 203; *see also* army,
French; *émigrés*
Fréron, Marie-Louis-Stanislas, 74
Frescaty, France, 266, 268, 274
Fréteau de Saint-Just, Emmanuel, 22,
65
Freytag, Colonel, 204, 207
Frith-Saint-Léger, France, 211
Froissy, Colonel, 203 *n.*, 207
Fronde, the, 6 and *n.*
Furnes, Belgium, 200

Galbaud du Fort, General, 270–72, 279
Gama, Vasco da, 4
Gamache (valet), 406, 408 *n.*
Gand, Belgium, 215, 228, 232 *n.*, 340
Gardanne (valet), 356–57
Gardes-françaises, 22, 27–28, 29–30
and *n.*, 42–43, 49, 119, 250, 451;
defection of, 28, 29, 43, 44
Garnier-Deschènes, Edme-Hilaire, 180
Geertruydenberg, Holland, 375, 394
Geneva, Switzerland, 165
Genlis, Comte de, 21 and *n.*, 46, 49, 80,
83, 297, 316 and *n.*, 404 *n.*
Genlis, Stéphanie-Félicité-Ducrest
de Saint-Aubin, Comtesse de, 18–21
and *n.*, 27, 77, 297; *Adèle et
Théodore*, 88 *n.*; anxieties of, 46–47,
48–49, 55, 56, 79, 83, 136, 143–44,
344; classed as *émigrée*, 345–46, 351–
52, 359, 365, 396–97, 399, 407–09,
417; dissatisfaction with, 23, 47, 77,
81–84; and Duc d'Orléans, xxvi, 7–8,
11, 22–23, 84, 314, 344–46, 352;
and education of Louis-Philippe, ix,
xxii, xxvi–xxix, 7–18 and *n.*, 26,
193 *n.*; letters to Louis-Philippe,
xxvii–xxviii, 87 *n.*, 88 *n.*, 89 *n.*, 90 *n.*,
91 *n.*, 92 *n.*, 93 *n.*, 94 *n.*, 95 *n.*; took
Adélaïde to England, 136, 142–45,
344–45; travels of, 19–21, 24–26
Genoa, 392
Gensonné, Armand, 159, 179, 313, 394
George III, King of England, 61, 425,
428–29, 454
Gérard, Michel, 28
Germany, 4, 215, 262, 322, 439; and
French Revolutionary Wars, 240,
243, 362, 365, 378; Princes of, 4,
129 *n.*, 168 and *n.*, 244, 246, 448
Gertruydenburg, siege of, 106 *n.*
Girardin, Stanislas de, 236
Girey-Dupré, Jean-Marie, 259 *n.*
Girondins, xxiii, xxv, 67–68, 98, 249;
execution of, 160, 196, 315 *n.*, 319

464

n., 355 n., 404 n.; and Jacobins, 160, 225–26; in Legislative Assembly, 159–60, 220, 241, 253 and n.; and ministry, 17 and n., 180, 198 and n., 214, 221, 223; in National Convention, 312–13, 315 and n., 319 n., 351, 353 n., 354 n., 357–58

Givet, France, 19, 21, 165, 200, 203, 341

Gizaucourt, France, 281–83, 285

Goetsenhoven, Belgium, 381–82

Goltz, Bernard Wilhelm, Count von, 173

Gossuin, Louis-Marie, 399 n.

Gouvion, General, 222

Grammont, Belgium, 376–77, 379

Grandchamp, France, 277

Grandpré, France, 240, 271–72 and n., 273, 275, 276–77 and n., 278, 280–81, 287, 292–93, 295, 321

Grange-Chancel (lampoons), 34, 434

Grangeneuve, Jean-Antoine Lafargue de, 159

Grave, Pierre-Marie, Comte de, 145, 147, 178, 180, 185–86, 198, 201–02, 214, 375 n.

Gravelotte, France, 268–69, 274

Greece, ancient, xxxii, 4, 16

Grégoire, Henri, Bishop of Blois, 310

Grouvelle, Philippe-Antoine, 263

Guadet, Marguerite-Élie, 159, 313

Guilhermy, Baron de, 103 n.

Guiraud, M., 260

Guiscard de Bart, General, 366

Guise, France, 239

Gustavus III, King of Sweden, 128 n., 130 n., 131 n., 451

Guyot, Abbé, 8–9, 13, 18

Hachslanden, Viscount, 417

Halifax, Nova Scotia, 425

Halle, Belgium, 340, 376, 396

Hamm, Germany, 454

Hangest, General d', 263, 270, 366, 386

Hans, France, 281, 290 n., 291 n.

Happencourt, General, 228

Harlebeck, Belgium, 232

Harny: Despotisme renversé, xxix

Harville, General d', 214, 239, 242, 330, 337–38

Harville, France, 267

Havana, Cuba, 365, 422–24

Hébert, Jacques-René, 74, 258

Hédouville, General d', 203 n., 216

Heiltz-le-Maurupt, France, 275

Henisdale, M. de (army officer), 143

Henri III, King of France, xxx, 70 n., 179 and n.

Henry IV, King of France, xxx, 5, 70 n., 165 n., 430, 431, 439

Herstal, Belgium, 343–44

Hesse-Philippsthal, Prince of, 367

Heyman, General de, 288 and n., 289 and n., 290–92

Hippocrates, 18

Hirson, France, 323

Hohenlohe, Prince of, 169, 265–66, 276

Holland: independence struggle of, 4, 18 and n., 21, 363; invaded by France, 362–71, 372, 375–77, 394–95

Honfleur, France, 25

Hornu, Belgium, 204, 333, 339

Hôtel de Ville, Paris, 43 and n., 45, 46, 57, 224, 249, 250 and n., 303, 345, 398 n., 446

Hourgues, M., 216, 222

Hua, Eustache-Antoine, 264–65

Hugo, Victor, xvi, xix; Miserables, Les, ix

Huguenin, Sulpice, 259 n.

Hugues Capet, 299–300, 302

Hukange, France, 242

Humanists, 4

Huningue, France, 165, 199

Hyck, Holland, 366

Ihler, General, 215, 372, 374

Invalides, Paris, xvii, 43, 44

Italy, 128 n., 324, 455

Itzehohe, Germany, 440–41

Jacobin Club, 65–68, 70, 74–77, 80 n., 91 n., 92 n., 96, 97–98, 100–01 and n., 102, 109–10, 121, 124, 159, 168, 171, 174, 180, 198 n., 221–22, 298, 316, 396–97, 407 n.; attempted suppression of, 223, 225–27; extremists in, 71, 76, 100; and Girondins, 160, 225–26; as leaders of France, 226–27; and Louis-Philippe, xii, xxii, 80–81, 89 n., 94 n., 95 n., 139; provincial affiliations of, xxxii, 75–77, 89 n., 94 n., 95 n., 101, 139 and n., 225; as tribune of the people, 102, 159–60

Jacquemin, M. (army officer), 135 n.

Jalain, France, 211

Jarry, General, 215, 216–18, 230, 232–33 and n.

Jemappes, Belgium, 204, 338

Jemappes, battle of, xiii, xxii, 326 n., 330, 331, 332 n., 333 n., 336–38, 365, 383 n., 415, 433

Joly, Étienne-Louis-Victor, 251

Josephine, Empress of France, 203 n.

Joseph II, Holy Roman Emperor, 20 n., 62 n.

Joubert, Captain, 385

Jouey, Captain de, 352 n.

judiciary: and criminal tribune of Commune, 255–57, 259; emigration of, 124, 125; nomination of, 107–08

Jülich, Germany, 362, 370

Kaunitz, Wenzel Anton, Count von, 170 and n., 173–74

Kellermann, General François-Christophe de, 243 and n., 264–65, 268–69, 273–76, 279–81, 284 n., 285–86, 288 and n., 291, 295, 296–97, 304–06, 321–22, 330, 341

465

Kent, Duke of, 425
Keraglio, Robert, 74, 298
Kersaint, Simon, Comte de, 234, 262, 354 n.
King's Bodyguard, 49, 53, 58, 59, 64, 89, 93 n., 95, 119, 169, 172, 219 and n., 220 n., 246, 247 n.
King's Council, see ministers of Louis XVI
Kleist, Baron von, 333 n.
Klundert, Holland, 375
Knights of Malta, 94 n.
Knobelsdorff, General, 232 n., 394
Koch, Christian-Guillaume de, 172
Kohler (Prussian officer), 281
Königstein, Germany, 362, 378
Kortemberg, Belgium, 340, 390, 396
Kumtich, Belgium, 342, 375, 377, 380–81, 386–87

Laar, Belgium, 386
Labarolière, General, 279
La Barre, Colonel, 407 n., 408 n.
Labourdonnaye, General, 295, 304, 340–41
La Chalade, France, 271–72, 279–80, 321
La Chapelle, France, 237, 323
La Chapelle-sur-Auve, France, 284
Lacoste, Jean de, 180, 198, 213, 216, 221, 305
La Croix-aux-Bois, France, 271, 273, 276–77 and n., 287, 321
La Fayette, Marie-Joseph du Motier, Marquis de, 64, 136, 165; in army command, 165, 166 n., 170, 177–78, 199–200, 203, 214, 222, 225–27, 228, 229, 230, 233 and n., 237 and n., 239, 241–42, 243, 262, 264, 269, 270; as commander of National Guard, 46, 49, 57, 58, 60, 73, 98, 101 n., 119, 223; in Constituent Assembly, 103, 154, 155; as constitutionalist, 198, 223, 253, 256; imprisonment of, 262–63; in National Assembly, 52, 59–60, 65, 66, 67, 71, 91 n., 96, 97–101 and n., 102, 109 and n., 121, 316
Lafitte-Clavé, Colonel, 203 n.
La Fontaine, Jean de, 374
La Gardiole, Colonel de, 384
La Gaussonnière, M. de, 114 n.
Lageschwalve, Holland, 363
Lagondie, Colonel de, 84, 87, 134
La Grange, Captain, 215 and n., 216–17
Lajard, Pierre-August de, 223, 227, 228–32, 233–34, 238
Lally, Comte de, 52
La Lune, Camp de, 284, 320–21
La Madeleine, France, 201, 214–15, 216
La Marche, Comte de, 187
Lamarche, General, see Drouot

Lamarque, François, 264–65, 400
Lamartine, Alphonse de, xviii; Histoire des Girondins, xi
Lamballe, Prince de, xxi
Lamballe, Marie-Thérèse, Princesse de, 261 and n., 310
Lamberty, Comte de, 114 n.
Lambesc d'Elbeuf, Prince de, 42, 415
Lameth, Alexandre de, 65–66, 96, 100–01 and n., 102, 109, 154, 170, 198, 214, 262
Lameth, Charles de, 65–66, 96, 100–01 and n., 102, 109, 154, 170, 198, 215, 230–32
Lamoignon, Chrétien-François de, 25 n.
Lamorlière, Magallon de, General, 238, 243, 341
Lamotte estate, Normandy, 24
Lamourette, Adrien, Bishop of Lyon, 235 and n.
Landau, Germany, 165, 199, 243, 265
Landen, Belgium, 382
Landrecies, France, 239
Lanjuinais, Jean-Denis, 65
Lanoue, General, 233, 242, 370, 373
Laon, France, 147–48, 201–02
Lapland, xxiii, 437
Laporte, Marie-François-Sébastien, 264–65
La Révellière-Lepeaux, Louis-Marie de, 404 n.
La Roche, M. de (army officer), 139–40
La Rochefoucauld d' Enville, Duc de, 109 n., 224
Laroque, Colonel, 337
Lasource, see Alba-Lasource
La Touche-Fréville, Comte de, 49
La Tour-Foissac, Colonel, 203 n.
Latour-Maubourg, Comte de, 65, 96, 262
Launay, Bernard-René, Marquis de, 45
Lauraguais, Comte de, 189
Lauzun, Armand-Louis, Duc de, 91
La Vauguyon, Paul-François, Duc de, 128 n.
Lavergne, Colonel, 243, 266
Lawfeld, Holland, 366
La Woestine, M. de, 24
La Woestine, Mme de, 10
Léau, Belgium, 383
Leblanc, M., 399, 406 and n.
Le Bourget, France, 352
Lebrun, Auguste, 8–9, 12, 18, 24, 49, 77, 298
Lebrun, Pierre-Henry, 263 n., 305, 354 n., 396 and n.
Le Chapelier, Isaac-René, 65, 71, 96
Le Chêne-Populeux, France, 271, 273, 276–77, 287, 321, 322–23
Leclerc, Colonel, 337
Le Fresne, France, 280, 286, 297
Legion of Honor, 433

466

Legislative Assembly, 167–68, 264, 309 and n., 310; composition of, 143 n., 157; Diplomatic Committee of, 167–68, 171–72, 175, 178, 247 n.; and émigrés, 161, 162, 171; and foreign invasion threats, 159, 162–66, 169–81; and French Revolutionary Wars, 181–82, 197, 212, 219, 222, 228–29, 232–35, 240, 242, 292; left wing of, 158–60, 198, 225–26, 235–36, 241; and Louis XVI, 163–65, 219–20 and n., 222, 236–37, 246, 247 n.; and Manifesto of Duke of Brunswick, 246; national security measures of, 220–23, 227, 235; right wing of, 158–59, 225–26, 235–36; sent commissioners to army, 262, 263, 264–65, 266, 270, 294; submitted to Paris Commune, 254–57, 258, 259 n., 260 n., 261; summoned National Convention, 253 and n.; and uprising of August 10, 159, 248–53; and uprising of June 20, 224–25
Le Havre, France, 24
Le Mans, France, 84, 393 n.
Le Montoir, France, 84
Lenoir, M., 45 n.
Le Nôtre, André, 189 and n.
Lens, France, 145
Leopold II, Holy Roman Emperor, 20 n., 168, 175, 178, 181 and n.; and émigrés, 127 and n., 128 n., 163, 169–70, 172–73, 174–77
Lepeintre, M., 144
Lepeletier de Saint-Fargeau, Louis-Michel, 97, 196 n.
Le Pellenberg, Belgium, 387, 390
Lesage-Sénault, Gaspard-Jean, 399 n.
Les Armoises, France, 272
Les Islettes, France, 271–73, 276, 279–80, 295, 321–22
lettre de cachet, 22 and n., 24–5
Le Vasseur (army officer), 203 n.
Leveneur de Tillières, General, 283, 322, 366, 370, 373, 386
Liancourt, M. de, 247 n.
Liège, Bishop of, 20–21
Liège, Belgium, 200, 340, 342, 344, 346, 352, 365, 367, 370, 371–72, 374, 377, 453
Ligneville, General, 243, 453
Ligny, France, 275
Lilieu, General, 384 n.
Lille, France, 19 and n., 20, 142, 145, 200–01, 202, 206, 210, 211, 214, 216, 230 n., 232, 237, 295, 322, 340, 380, 399 and n., 400 and n., 401, 403 n., 453
Limburg, Germany, 362, 378
Lindon, M., 312
Lion de la Houssaye (father and son), 25
lit de justice, 22 and n.
literature, 7, 8
Locer, Belgium, 383

Logan, M. (army officer), 135 n.
Loménie de Brienne, Étienne-Charles, 26, 107 n., 133 n.
London, England, 144, 426, 455
Longwy, France, 239, 242–43, 265, 266, 269, 271, 280, 322, 341, 453
Lormier, Colonel, 284 n.
Lorraine, 168, and n., 233, 239, 242, 244, 281, 287, 299
Louis IX, King of France, 121 and n.
Louis XIII, King of France, xxx, 5, 129 n.
Louis XIV, King of France, xxi, xxiv, xxx, xxxii, 6 and n., 7, 23 n., 25, 38, 67 n., 129 n., 189 and n., 194 n., 284 n., 300 n., 367, 382, 435 n.
Louis XV, King of France, xxi, xxiv, xxx, 7 and n., 30, 45 n., 67 n., 129 n., 186 n., 187 and n., 189, 194, 301, 367, 434–35, 450
Louis XVI, King of France, xi–xii, xxiv, xxix, 4, 17, 21 and n., 22 and n., 26, 28 n., 32 n., 45 n., 69, 101 n., 107, 119, 130, 136, 148, 179, 180, 187 n., 189, 191 and n., 198–99, 216, 219, 222 and n., 234, 237, 243, 263, 288 n., 301, 363, 434 n., 446–47, 450, 452, 455; arrest and imprisonment of, xxxiii, 106, 122, 254–55, 257, 260–61, 310; authority of suspended, 111, 114, 115–16, 122, 125, 180 and n., 253–54, 262, 263, 264, 287, 347 and n.; constitutional authority of, xv, 100, 103, 104, 111, 116, 118, 119, 121 and n., 122–24, 126, 132–33, 149 n., 151, 152, 154, 155–56 and n., 157, 163–65, 166–67 and n., 168, 180 and n., 195, 223, 227, 234–35, 237, 253, 344; and Declaration of June 23, 32 and n.; disapproved of émigrés, xi, xxxiii, 107 n., 126–28 and n., 129 n., 130 n., 131 n., 132–34, 149, 152, 161–62; and Duc d'Orleans, xiii, xxx–xxxii, 22, 49, 60–62 and n., 63 and n., 182–86, 187–88, 213, 239; and Estates-General, xi, 28–29, 30–33, 39–40, 133 n., 317 n., 443; and European powers, 149, 163–65, 168–69, 170–77, 236, 246, 290 n., 293, 327, 347–48; financial problems of, 31, 120, 133 and n.; flight and capture of, xxvii, 85, 87–90 and n., 91 and n., 92 and n., 93–99, 110, 111–12, 113, 119, 126, 153, 173, 228 n., 237 n., 253, 324, 445, 451; forced to Paris, 55, 59, 119, 445; and foreign invasion threats, xxiii, xxxiii, 149, 154, 159, 160, 162–66, 168, 170, 175, 177–81, 197; and French Revolutionary Wars, 212–13, 240, 244 and n., 245 and n., 246, 313; inconsistency of, 32–33, 39–41, 57, 104, 127; and Legislative Assembly, 163–65, 219–20 and n., 222, 236–37, 246,

467

Louis XVI, King of France (*Cont.*)
247 *n.*; and Louis-Philippe, xxxiii,
24, 30–31, 84, 146–47, 225 and *n.*;
and loyalty oaths, 78, 110 and *n.*,
111–13 and *n.*, 114 *n.*, 115, 121, 155;
movements of restricted, xxxiii, 115,
121–22; and National Assembly, 31,
39–42, 46, 52, 57, 67, 74, 90 *n.*,
92 *n.*, 93 *n.*, 96, 112, 114, 115–16,
119–20 and *n.*, 121, 148, 154–57,
446 *n.*; and nominations for employment, 107 and *n.*, 108, 132; and
October Days, xxxiii, 52–59; people's
suspicion of, 121, 132, 150 *n.*, 151,
161, 167, 168, 180, 225, 226, 247,
327; pretended support of Constitution, xxv, xxxiii, 128, 148–49 and *n.*,
150 and *n.*, 151–52, 154–58, 159,
160, 167, 347; secretly requested aid,
128 *n.*, 129 *n.*, 130 *n.*, 131 *n.*, 148–49
of European powers, 127 and *n.*,
and *n.*, 150 and *n.*, 151–53, 391 *n.*;
and storming of Bastille, 45–46; trial
and execution of, xiii–xiv, xxxii, 7,
132, 150, 154, 185, 192, 195–96 and
n., 197, 298, 302, 309, 314–15, 346–
48 and *n.*, 349–51, 352, 354 and *n.*,
358, 359, 360–61, 391 *n.*, 394; and
troops in Paris, 220–21, 222–23; and
uprising of August 10, 118, 122, 180
and *n.*, 227, 246–54; and uprising of
June 20, 224–25, 227, 328; veto
power of, 72, 123 and *n.*, 124, 161–
62, 164, 221–22, 223–24, 227; *see
also* Court of Louis XVI; ministers
of Louis XVI
Louis XVII, 391 *n.*, 438
Louis XVIII, xxiv and *n.*, xxv, 300 *n.*,
301, 319 *n.*, 392 *n.*, 421 *n.*, 426, 428,
429, 430–35, 437–41; *see also*
Provence, Louis-Stanislas-Xavier,
Comte de
Louis-Charles, Dauphin of France, 59,
84, 88–92 and *n.*, 93 *n.*, 94 *n.*, 96,
125, 130, 224, 250, 254 and *n.*, 310,
391 *n.*, 393–95; *see also* Louis XVII,
King of France
Louis Eugene, Prince of Württemberg,
14
Louis-Joseph, Dauphin of France, 30
Louis-Philippe (Duc de Chartres, Duc
de Valois), 51 *n.*, 301–02; achieved
independence, 79; adventurous deeds
of, 85–87, 92 *n.*, 93 *n.*, 136, 333 *n.*;
in America, xiii, 421–22, 423; as
army colonel, xii, xxii, 19 and *n.*,
20–21, 79, 84–87, 88 *n.*, 89 *n.*, 93 *n.*,
94 *n.*, 134–48, 166 *n.*, 201–11; as
army general, ix, xiii, xxii, xxvi, 211–
19, 228–34, 238–46, 263–99, 304–09,
319–44, 352, 356, 359, 362–403 and
n. passim, 405–16, 421, 426 *n.*, 431,
433, 437; arrest warrant issued
against family and, ix, 355 *n.*, 358 *n.*,
360, 398 and *n.*, 401–02 and *n.*, 403–

07; education of, ix, xii, xxii, xxvi–
xxix, 3, 7–18 and *n.*, 26–27, 47, 79,
193 *n.*; and *émigrés,* 426 and *n.*, 427–
31, 439–41; in England, xxiii, xxv,
xxvi, 423–31; at Estates-General,
28–29; exile of, ix, xiv, xxi, xxiii–
xxiv, xxv, xxvi, 196, 258, 298, 342,
352 and *n.*, 353 and *n.*, 354–58 and
n., 359, 404, 405 *n.*, 408 *n.*, 409,
414–17, 421–31, 437; family of, xxiv
and *n.*, 304, 434; and father's vote on
Louis XVI, xiii–xiv, xxxii, 185, 195–
97, 314–15, 346–51, 354, 358, 360–
62; at Federation of 1790, 77–78;
finances of, xxiii, xxiv, 141, 359, 417,
421–24; in Havana, 422–24; horrified
by Terror, xxiii, 257–58, 307–08,
378, 421; and Jacobins, xii, xxii,
80–81, 89 *n.*, 94 *n.*, 95 *n.*, 139; *juste
milieu* of, xv, xviii, 391 *n.*; as king,
xvi–xix, xxv, xxix, 140 *n.*, 337 and
n.; at Legislative Assembly, 181, 310;
letters from Mme de Genlis to, xxvii–
xxviii, 87 *n.*, 88 *n.*, 89 *n.*, 90 *n.*, 91 *n.*,
92 *n.*, 93 *n.*, 94 *n.*, 95 *n.*; and Louis
XVI, xxxiii, 24, 30–31, 84, 146–47,
225 and *n.*; loyalty to monarchy of,
xiv–xv, xxiii, xxv, xxix, xxxiii, 39–40;
memoirs of, ix, xi, xiv, xvi, xxi, xxiii,
xxvi, xxviii, xxxii–xxxiii, 3, 409 *n.*,
428; at National Assembly, xii, 49,
52, 55, 79, 99, 310; at National Convention, 309–13; offered Regency,
xxiv, 434–35; pacifism of, xv, xviii,
xxv; persecution of, 135, 192, 196–
97, 258, 376, 380, 417, 421; reconciled with Princes, 426–35, 438–41;
sister classed as *émigrée*, 144, 345–
46, 349, 350, 351–52, 359, 365, 396–
97, 399, 403 *n.*, 407–09, 416–17;
supported father, xiii–xiv, xxvi, xxxii,
3, 34–39, 59–68, 182–97, 313–19;
supported Revolution, xii, xiv, xxii,
xxiii, xxvi, xxviii–xxix, 15, 26, 80,
306, 403 *n.*; travels with Mme de
Genlis of, 19–21, 24–26; turned
against Revolution, 358, 378, 395–
96, 403 *n.*, 407 *n.*, 408 *n.*, 438;
warned by Danton, xiii, xxiii, 307–60
Louvain, Belgium, 340, 342, 375, 377,
380–81, 387, 388, 390, 403 *n.*
Louvet, Pierre-Florent, 353 *n.*
Low Countries, xxiii, 18–20, 62 *n.*, 169,
174–75, 177, 231, 233, 262, 322,
330–31; *see also* individual countries
Luckner, Marshal Nicolas, 165–66,
177–78, 199, 212–19, 225, 228–29
and *n.*, 230–33 and *n.*, 234, 237–43,
263–66, 268, 281 *n.*, 329
Lusignan, Colonel de, 53
Luxembourg, Marshal François, 382
Luxembourg, 128 *n.*, 174, 201, 330, 362
Luxembourg Palace, 38, 88, 254, 445
Lynch, General, 215, 230–32, 239, 297
Lyon, France, 83, 84, 393 *n.*, 432

Maastricht, Holland, 341, 366–67, 374
Maastricht, siege of, 328 n., 359, 364–71
Mably, Gabriel Bonnot de, 194
Mack, Colonel, 412, 416
Mailhe, Jean-Baptiste, 346, 348 n.
Maillebois, M. de (army officer), 363
Maine, Duchesse du, 435 and n.
Maintenon, Françoise d'Aubigné, Marquise de, 7
Mainz, Elector of, 162
Mainz, Germany, 199, 315, 341, 362, 452
Maizery, France, 267
Malines, Belgium, 340, 363, 368
Mallet-du-Pan, Jacques, 127, 152
Malouet, Pierre-Victor, 52, 103
Malus de Montarcy, Antoine-Charles, 323 and n.
Mandat, Jean-Antoine, Marquis de, 249–50 and n.
Manstein, Colonel, 288 and n., 289 n., 290 n., 291 n.
Manuel, Louis-Pierre, 249, 350 and n.
Marassé, General, 377
Marat, Jean-Paul, 109 n., 312 n.; Marat, The Friend of the People, 54, 258, 312 and n.; in National Convention, 311–13
Marescot, Captain, 366 and n.
Maret, Hugues, 345
Maribond-Montaut, Louis, 402 n.
Marie-Amélie (wife of Louis-Philippe), xxiv, 434
Marie-Antoinette, Queen of France, 24, 28–29, 31, 41, 56, 57, 58, 59, 84, 85, 88–92 and n., 93, 95–96, 170, 173, 184–85, 222 n., 224, 237 and n., 244 and n., 245, 250, 257, 261, 310, 391 n.; disapproved of émigrés, 126–27, 128n., 130 n., 131 n., 152; secretly requested aid of European powers, 127 n., 128 n., 130 n., 131 n., 149, 150 n.; 152
Marie-Christine, Princess, 456
Marie de Medici, 129 n.
Marie-Thérèse, Princess (Madame), 59, 84, 88–92 and n., 96, 224, 310; see also Angoulême, Duchesse d'
Mariottini, Abbé, 12
Marle, France, 239
Marly, France, 211
Marseillais, Hymne des (Rouget de Lisle), 246 n., 319, 328
Marseille, France, 248, 393 n., 404 n.
Mars-la-Tour, France, 240, 267
Mary Stuart, Queen of Scotland, 6
Masnuy Saint-Jean, Belgium, 339
Masnuy Saint-Pierre, Belgium, 339
Massillon, Jean-Baptiste, 194 and n.
Mastin, Abbé, 46
Mastin, Captain de, 134, 135
Maubert-Fontaine, France, 323
Maubeuge, France, 165, 200, 203, 211, 214–15, 222, 225, 226, 228, 233, 237, 242, 330, 337
Maulde, France, 233, 238, 241–42, 263, 274, 398–99, 409, 412–13, 414
Maupeou, René-Nicolas de, 187 and n.
Maureilhan, General de, 366
Mazerny, France, 323
Meaux, France, 91 n., 292
Menin, Belgium, 215, 216, 217, 219, 228, 231, 232 n., 233, 234, 237
Ménuret, Dr., 380
Mercy, Marie-Charles Isidore de, 114 n., 128 n.
Merlin (de Douai), Philippe-Antoine, 360–61, 399 n.
Metz, France, 54, 166 n., 200, 239, 240, 241–42, 243, 264–65, 266–69, 288 n.
Mézières, France, 323, 365
Miaczincki, General, 272, 383 and n.
ministers of Louis XVI, 41, 46, 54, 57, 96, 98, 114, 126, 157–58, 160, 167, 184, 191, 214, 224, 225, 227, 235, 236, 245, 437, 444 and n.; and foreign invasion threats, 169, 170–71 and n., 177–78 and n., 180; and French Revolutionary Wars, 181, 197–200, 202, 211–12, 216, 219, 220–23, 228–32, 234–35, 241, 242
Mirabeau, Honoré-Gabriel, Comte de, 32, 47 and n., 65–66, 68, 71, 75, 101 and n., 102 and n., 109, 121 n., 178
Miranda, General, 278, 330, 341, 365–75, 380–83, 386
Mirys, M., 19, 141
Mittau, Russia, 426, 455
Moerdick, Holland, 363, 377
Moira, Earl of, 455
Moiremont, France, 279
Monge, Gaspard, Comte de Péluse, 263 n.
Moniteur, le, 113 n., 156 n., 157 n., 161 and n., 162 n., 163 n., 164 n., 165 n., 170 n., 171 n., 172, 173 and n., 175 n., 176 n., 178 n., 181 n., 204 n., 212 n., 224 n., 225, 226 n., 229 n., 232 and n., 235 n., 236, 240 n., 241 n., 244 n., 245 n., 246 n., 247 n., 251, 254 n., 255 n., 256 n., 257 n., 259 n., 260 and n., 264 n., 265 n., 269 n., 274 n., 277 n., 291 n., 310 n., 379 and n., 392 n., 397, 400 n., 402 n., 403 n., 405 n.
Mons, Belgium, 200, 203–04, 207, 215, 222, 228, 322, 330, 331–32, 337–40, 352, 394, 409, 414–17
Montagnard party, see Mountain, the
Montchoisy, Colonel de, 207
Montcornet, France, 239
Montespan, Mme de, xxi
Montesquiou-Fezensac, General François de, 65, 66, 341, 392, and n., 451
Montesson, Mme de, 90 n., 93 n., 402 n., 404 n.

Montjoie: *History of the Orléans's Conspiracy,* 196
Montjoye, Colonel Gustave de, 337, 408–09, 415, 417, 440
Montmédy, France, 126, 128 *n.,* 153, 239, 243, 445, 453
Montmorency, Mathieu, Duc de, 65, 215, 391 *n.*
Montmorin-Saint-Hérem, Comte de, 61 and *n.,* 63
Montpensier, Antoine-Philippe d'Orléans, Duc de (brother of Louis-Philippe), xxvi–xxvii, xxxi, 7–8, 11, 12, 24, 55 and *n.,* 77, 81, 84, 92 *n.,* 93 *n.,* 95 *n.,* 138, 182, 239, 301–02, 313, 319, 344–45, 352, 353 *n.,* 356–57, 360–61, 432; in army, 136–37, 140, 141–46, 202, 203, 208, 210, 212, 213, 217, 239, 267, 295–97, 299, 304, 306, 332–33, 359–60, 426 *n.;* arrest and imprisonment of, xxiii–xxiv, 314, 355 *n.,* 361–62, 402, 406 and *n.,* 407 *n.,* 408 *n.,* 446 *n.;* exile of, 421–29
Montreuil, Belgium, 332
Mont-Saint-Michel, 22, 24–26
Morisson, Charles, 348 and *n.*
Morris, Gouverneur, 422
Mortemart, Duc de, 114 *n.*
Mounier, Jean-Joseph, 52
Mountain, the, xxxii, 298; in Legislative Assembly, 158–59; in National Convention, 160, 249, 298, 312, 315–16, 353 *n.,* 354 *n.,* 358, 360
Mousquet, M., 399 *n.*
Mousseaux, France, 56
Mouzon, France, 272, 273 *n.*
Muratel, General, 274
Murinais, Marquis de, 114 *n.*
Myris, M., 83

Naillac, M., 216, 222
Namur, Belgium, 200, 215, 262, 330, 341, 372
Nantes, France, 24, 393 *n.*
Napoleon I, xv, xvi, xvii, xxiv, xxv, 192 and *n.,* 284 *n.,* 342, 393 *n.,* 421 *n.,* 432, 439
Napoleon III, xviii *n.*
Narbonne-Lara, Louis, Comte de, 145, 146, 147, 165–66 and *n.,* 177–78
Nassau, Princes of, 172
Nassau-Siegen, Prince of, 265
National (Constituent) Assembly, xxxi, 31–32, 35, 54, 70 *n.,* 78, 79, 85 *n.,* 91 *n.,* 97, 102, 103, 104, 110, 118, 124, 130 *n.,* 135, 136, 146 *n.,* 159, 167, 178, 183, 191 and *n.,* 198, 219 *n.,* 228 *n.,* 253 and *n.,* 262, 309 *n.,* 310, 314, 316–17, 446; abolished *parlements,* 22 *n.;* and army, 108, 109 and *n.,* 110 and *n.,* 111, 113 and *n.,* 114 and *n.,* 115–18, 148, 324, 326 *n.,* 327; and Châtelet inquiry, 64–68; clergy in, 39, 41, 48, 52, 65, 103 and *n.;* confiscated Church lands, 36–37 and *n.,* 83; debates of, xii, 50–51, 80, 99–100, 106 *n.;* declared general amnesty, 155; dictated to by extremists, 71–73; dissolved, 143 and *n.,* 157; and *émigrés,* 150 and *n.,* 133, 155; on feudal rights, 36, 48, 168, 447; left wing of, 65–66, 71, 97, 103, 107, 113 *n.,* 121 *n.,* 156, 316; and Louis XVI, 31, 39–42, 46, 52, 57, 67, 74, 90 *n.,* 92 *n.,* 93 *n.,* 96, 112, 114, 115–16, 119–20 and *n.,* 121, 148, 154–57, 446 *n.;* nobility in, 39, 41, 48, 52, 53, 65, 66, 70; and nominations for employment, 107–08; parties (clubs) in, 52, 54, 65–77, 154, 316; responsibility to constituents in, 70 and *n.,* 111 and *n.,* 317 and *n.;* revoked *apanages,* 37–38, 67, 136, 141; right wing of, 65–66, 70 *n.,* 96 *n.,* 97, 103 and *n.,* 107, 109, 114 *n.,* 158, 316; and succession to Crown, 67; suppressed use of titles, 21 *n.,* 299, 301–02, 317, 447; suspended royal authority, 111, 114, 115–16, 122, 125; Third Estate in, 39, 41, 49, 53, 65, 66, 69, 316; at Tuileries, 50 and *n.,* 51, 52, 55, 59, 70, 155, 309 and *n.;* at Versailles, 42, 46, 49–53, 57, 67, 69; and veto for King, 72; *see also* individual parties (clubs)
National Convention, xiii, xiv, xv, xxiii, xxxii, 67–68, 70 *n.,* 74, 98, 110 *n.,* 135, 190, 192 and *n.,* 230 *n.,* 253 and *n.,* 254, 291–92, 293, 302–03, 308–13, 316, 318, 319 *n.,* 362, 393 and *n.,* 403 *n.,* 438; abolished monarchy, 287, 290 *n.,* 310; and banishment and arrest of Bourbons, 352–53 and *n.,* 354 and *n.,* 355 and *n.,* 356–57, 359, 392 *n.,* 404 and *n.;* commissioners of, 265 and *n.,* 297, 364, 370, 376–77, 378, 379–80, 387–88, 392 *n.,* 399 and *n.,* 400 and *n.,* 401, 405 *n.,* 408 *n.,* 409–11, 413–14; Dumouriez defied, 364, 377 and *n.,* 379–80 and *n.,* 387–88, 396–98, 399 and *n.,* 400 and *n.,* 401, 405 *n.,* 408 *n.,* 410–14; Dumouriez planned to overthrow, 390–91 and *n.,* 393–96; and French Revolutionary Wars, 323–24, 342 and *n.,* 365, 366, 370, 392 *n.,* 403 *n.;* issued arrest warrant against Louis-Philippe and family, ix, 355 *n.,* 358 *n.,* 360, 398 and *n.,* 401–02 and *n.,* 403–07; and Paris Commune, 311–13, 350, 353 *n.,* 398 *n.;* parties in, 249, 298, 312, 315, 348–51, 353 *n.,* 354 *n.,* 355 *n.,* 359, 360; and Terror, 378, 398 and *n.;* and trial of Louis XVI, 150, 185 *n.,* 195–96 and *n.,* 298, 302, 309, 314–15, 346–48 and *n.,* 349–51, 354 and *n.,* 358, 359, 360–61, 391 *n.;* *see also* Executive Council

470

National Guard, 56, 78, 110, 123, 245, 325, 326 *n.*, 374, 431; of Paris, 44, 46, 56–57, 59, 73–74, 90 *n.*, 91 *n.*, 92 *n.*, 98, 100, 101 *n.*, 119, 220 and *n.*, 221, 222, 248, 249–50 and *n.*, 251, 254, 261, 298, 319, 329, 384, 446; in provinces, 47–48, 85–86, 88 *n.*, 89 *n.*, 90, 93–95, 136; took loyalty oath, 78, 221; at Versailles, 49, 58

National High Court, 179 and *n.*, 220 *n.*, 260

navy, French, xxx, 19 *n.*, 183, 187–88, 213

Necker, Jacques, 26 and *n.*, 29, 32, 41, 42, 46, 54, 57, 194, and *n.*, 437, 446

Nederbecke, Belgium, 216–17

Neerwinden, battles of, ix, xiii, xxii, xxiii, 346, 366, 379, 380 *n.*, 382–84 and *n.*, 385–86, 394, 403 *n.*

Neufchâteau, François de, 309

Neuilly, General, 382, 384–85, 399, 409–10

Neuville-au-Pont, France, 279, 320

New Orleans, Louisiana, 422

New York, New York, 425

Ney, Captain, 380

Nice, 165, 341, 360, 402, 406 and *n.*

Noailles, Emmanuel-Marie-Louis, Marquis de, 170

Noailles, Louis-Marie, Vicomte de, 48, 207, 208–09

nobility, x, 4, 5–6, 69, 76, 80, 107 *n.*, 130 *n.*, 138 *n.*, 152, 161 *n.*, 448–49; in army, 108, 137 *n.*, 234 *n.*, 448–51; as *émigrés*, xxii, 69, 88, 107 and *n.*, 125–26, 191 *n.*, 234 *n.*, 428, 447; in Estates-General, xiii, 26 and *n.*, 28, 31–33, 69, 316, 443–44; in National Assembly, 39, 41, 48, 52, 53, 65, 66, 70; use of titles suppressed, 21 *n.*, 299, 301–02, 317, 447

Normandy, France, 24

Normont, M. de, 332 *n.*

Norway, 437

Notre-Dame, Paris, 46, 120

Notre-Dame-de-l'Épine, France, 286, 297, 320

O'Brien, Major, 412

Odomez, France, 409

O'Moran, General, 352 and *n.*, 414

Oplinter, Belgium, 381

Orbeval, France, 281

Orchies, France, 145, 215, 237, 409, 413

Order of Saint-Louis, 19, 94 *n.*, 135, 429, 432–33, 450

Order of the Holy Ghost, xxix, 24, 26, 135, 429, 432, 443 *n.*

Orders of Chivalry, 94 *n.*, 135

Oreye, Belgium, 373–74

Orléaniste party, xxxii, 60, 66–68, 138, 196

Orléans, Duc d', xxvi

Orléans, Eugène-Adélaïde-Louise (sister of Louis-Philippe), xxvii, xxviii, 8, 10–11, 12, 17, 27, 77, 81–84, 93 *n.*, 356, 434; classed as *émigrée*, 144, 345–46, 349, 350, 351–52, 359, 365, 396–97, 399, 403 *n.*, 407–09, 416–17; taken to England by Mme de Genlis, 136, 142–45, 344–45

Orléans, Louis-Philippe, Duc d', 79, 138, 186 and *n.*, 187, 189

Orléans, Louis-Philippe-Joseph, Duc d' (Philippe Égalité; father of Louis-Philippe), xxi–xxii, xxiii, xxix, xxx–xxxi, 19, 22 and *n.*, 27, 94 *n.*, 135, 140, 239, 268, 288 *n.*, 289, 301–02, 307, 353 and *n.*, 354 and *n.*, 355 and *n.*, 356, 359; accused of Anglomania, xiii, 189–90; accused of aspiring to throne, 59–60, 63, 66–67, 91 *n.*, 98, 185, 190, 192, 195, 290–91, 313 *n.*; accused of financing Revolution, xiii, xxxi, 34–38, 190, 194; with Army of the North, 213–14, 216, 217, 225, 239; arrest and execution of, xxiv, xxxi, 191, 192, 195–96, 314 *n.*, 316 *n.*, 355 *n.*, 362, 404 *n.*; Châtelet inquiry into, 35, 64–68, 350; and *la Dame de la Rue Bleue*, 314, 360; enemies of, xxxi–xxxii, 23, 34–38, 59–68, 91 *n.*, 98–99, 182–97, 313 and *n.*, 314 and *n.*, 315 and *n.*, 316, 348, 351, 355 *n.*, 357, 361, 404; in Estates-General, xiii, 28, 30, 33, 443–44; exile of, xxxi, xxxii, 22–24, 60; and family, xxvi–xxvii, xxxi, 7, 8, 9, 10, 11, 17, 18, 24, 27, 49, 79–84, 88 *n.*, 89 *n.*, 92 *n.*, 93 *n.*, 95 *n.*, 136–37, 142, 144, 182, 196–97, 214, 296, 304–05, 318, 344–46, 351–52, 399, 402 *n.*, 403 *n.*, 406 *n.*; finances of, xxxi, 36–38, 141, 182, 214, 227, 314, 351; forced to take name of Égalité, xiv, xxxi, 299, 302–04, 317; and Louis XVI, xiii, xxx–xxxii, 22, 49, 60–62 and *n.*, 63 and *n.*, 182–86, 187–88, 213, 239; marriage of, xxxi, 23, 81–83, 314, 346; mission to England of, 61 and *n.*, 62 and *n.*, 63 and *n.*, 64, 77, 79; in National Assembly, 41, 46, 56, 59, 61, 64–68, 91 *n.*, 183, 314, 316–17; in National Convention, xiii, 68, 98, 190, 195, 291–92, 298, 308–09, 311, 316, 318, 347–51, 354, 360–61, 395, 404 *n.*, 405; in the navy, xxx, 183, 187–88, 213; supported by Louis-Philippe, xiii–xiv, xxvi, xxxii, 3, 34–39, 59–68, 182–97, 313–19; voted to find Louis XVI guilty, xiii–xiv, xxiii, xxxii, 185, 195–96 and *n.*, 197, 314–15, 346–51, 352, 354 *n.*, 358, 360–61

Orléans, Philippe, Duc d' (Regent of France), xxxii, 7, 67 *n.*, 129 *n.*, 186 *n.*, 300 *n.*, 382, 434–35 and *n.*

471

Orléans, House of, xxiv, xxx, xxxi, 22 and *n.*, 30, 38, 43, 56, 267, 301, 427–28
Orléans, France, 27, 179, 220, 260 and *n.*
Orvilliers, Comte d', 188
Ouessant, battle of, xxx, 187–88
Overwinden, Belgium, 384, 386

Pache, Jean-Nicolas, 311 and *n.*, 323
Padua, 451
Palais Royal, Paris, xxiv, xxxi, 8–9, 10, 12, 18, 22, 23, 30, 38, 43, 45, 56, 61, 77, 79, 81–82, 88 *n.*, 135, 138, 189, 252 *n.*, 261 *n.*, 299, 303, 313, 314, 336, 346, 356–57, 360, 433; as a meeting place, 33, 72
Palatine, Elector of, 370
Palermo, 456
Pamela, Mlle, 10, 11–12, 17, 83, 144, 399 *n.*
Panis, Étienne-Jean, 74
Paris, Comte de Juigné, Archbishop of, 45–46
Paris, France, 6, 27, 29, 34, 43 and *n.*, 44, 50, 53, 91 *n.*, 136, 145–46, 190, 274 *n.*, 352, 433, 446, 448, 449; atrocities in, 45, 58–59, 72, 252, 257, 259–61, 307–08; defense of, 220–21, 222–23, 227, 259, 270, 274, 292–93, 320, 327; district assemblies of, xxxii, 43 and *n.*, 44, 46, 54–55, 56, 73–74, 254; extremism in, 54–55, 71–74, 346, 349, 357; Federation of 1790 in, 64, 77–78; lower classes of, 55, 73, 76; and Manifesto of Duke of Brunswick, 244 *n.*, 245; National Guard of, 44, 46, 56–57, 59, 73–74, 90 *n.*, 91 *n.*, 92 *n.*, 98, 100, 101 *n.*, 119, 220 and *n.*, 221, 248, 249–50 and *n.*, 251, 254, 261, 298, 319, 329, 384, 446; Parlement of, xxxi, 6, 21 and *n.*, 22 and *n.*, 25 *n.*, 26 *n.*, 28 *n.*, 124 *n.*, 187 *n.*; sections of, xxxii, 74, 248, 254, 255–57, 258, 259; troops in, 29, 41–45 and *n.*, 46, 446; unrest and rioting in, xxiii, xxv, 21, 27–28, 30, 33–34, 42–46, 53–59 *passim*, 96, 100, 101 *n.*, 179, 219 *n.*, 223–27, 234, 248–52; *see also* French Revolution
Paris Commune, 74, 224, 249–50, 258–59, 362; Committee of Surveillance of, 258–59 and *n.*; Councils of, 302, 303, 345, 398 *n.*; criminal tribunal of, 255–57, 259; established Reign of Terror, 258; forced Duc d'Orléans to become Égalité, xiv, xxxi, 302–04; Legislative Assembly submitted to, 254–57, 258, 259 *n.*, 260 *n.*, 261; and National Convention, 311–13, 350, 353 *n.*, 398 *n.*; and September massacres, 257, 259–60 and *n.*, 261
Paris Opéra, 319 and *n.*
Parlement of Paris, xxxi, 6, 21 and *n.*, 22 and *n.*, 25 *n.*, 26 *n.*, 28 *n.*, 124 *n.*, 187 *n.*

parlements, 21 and *n.*, 22 *n.*, 25 *n.*, 39, 63, 124 *n.*, 186–87 and *n.*; abolished by National Assembly, 22 *n.*
Passavant, France, 279
Passy, France, 49, 55–56, 57, 59, 77
Patriote-Français, le, 259 *n.*
Pâturages, Belgium, 204, 333–36
Paul I, Emperor of Russia, 456
Pelletier, Captain, 326 *n.*
Penthièvre, Duc de, 304
Penthièvre, Louis de Bourbon, Duc de, xxi, xxii, xxx, 23 and *n.*, 82, 84, 119, 188
Péraldi, Marius, 262
Pereyra, Jacob, 396–98 and *n.*
Perrin, M. (army officer), 135 *n.*
Petier, Claude-Louis, 271
Pétion de Villeneuve, Jérôme, 65, 92 *n.*, 96, 100, 144, 248–49, 254, 312, 349–51 and *n.*, 354 *n.*
Pétion de Villeneuve, Jérôme, 65, 92 *n.*,
Philadelphia, Pennsylvania, xxiii, 421
Philip V, King of Spain, 67 *n.*
Philippeville, France, 165, 200
Pichegru, General Jean-Charles, 439
Pieyre, Pierre-Alexandre, 84, 85, 88 *n.*, 89 *n.*, 90 *n.*, 92 *n.*, 93 *n.*, 141
Pillnitz, Treaty of, 126, 164, 234, 451
Pitt, William, 342 and *n.*
Plain, the, 158
Pognon, Edmond: *De Gaulle et l'histoire de France,* xvi
Poitou, France, 26, 444
Poix, France, 323
political clubs, *see* individual clubs
Pont-à-Marcq, France, 401
Pont-à-Mousson, France, 274
Pontavice, M. de (army officer), 203 *n.*
Pont-sur-Sambre, France, 242, 263, 274, 276, 445
Porrentruy, Switzerland, 392
Portland, Duke of, 425
Pozzo di Borgo, Count Carlo Andrea, 240 and *n.*
press: freedom of, 4, 53
Pressac, M. de (army officer), 203 *n.*
Prieur (*valet de chambre*), 9
Prieur (de la Marne), Pierre-Louis, 297
Prilly, Colonel, 211
Princes of the Blood, xiii, xxi, xxii, xxiv, xxvi, xxvii, xxix–xxx, 6, 7, 9, 15, 19 and *n.*, 23, 24, 26, 29, 192, 201, 426, 443–44, 455; resisted the Court, xxx, 186–87 and *n.*
printing press, xxxii, 4
Proly, Pierre-Jean, 396–98 and *n.*
Protestants, 4, 5, 16 and *n.*
Provence, Louis-Stanislas-Xavier, Comte de, 26, 29, 37–38, 84, 301, 443–44 and *n.*, 445, 446; as an *émigré,* 88, 125–26, 129 *n.*, 130 and *n.*, 131 and *n.*, 149, 152, 153, 161, 171, 243, 391 *n.*, 445, 452, 454; *see also* Louis XVIII, King of France
provinces of France, xxv, xxx, 85 and *n.*, 137, 165 *n.*, 449; affiliations with

472

Jacobins in, xxxii, 75–77, 89 n., 94 n., 95 n., 101, 139 and n., 225; delegates from, in Paris, 64 n., 78; intendants in, 107 and n.; National Guard in, 47–48, 85–86, 88 n., 89 n., 90, 93–95, 136; Revolutionary Committees in, 77 and n.; unrest and rioting in, 48, 69, 85–87, 105, 151 n.
Prussia, 18 n., 119, 126, 173, 232 n., 233, 333 n., 362 n., 378; in French campaign, 176 and n., 177, 181, 240, 243, 267, 270–87, 292–97, 394, 452–53; proposed truce, 287–88 and n., 289 n., 290 n., 291 n., 295; retreated from France, 280, 291 n., 293–94, 295, 315, 320–22, 341, 362
public opinion, 70 and n., 111 and n., 129 n., 151, 154, 158, 160, 225; as cause of Revolution, xxxii, 38, 40–41, 68, 71–73, 190–91, 193; and French Revolutionary Wars, 198, 211
Puységur, Chevalier de, 429

Quantin, M., 410
Quaregnon, Belgium, 204, 332–33
Quesnoy, France, 141, 323, 332 n.
Quiévrain, Belgium, 140, 203–04, 207–09, 238, 323, 331–32 and n., 409
Quiévrechain, Belgium, 203, 331
Quinette, Nicolas-Marie, 400
Quosdanowich, General, 409

Raincy, France, xxxi, 22, 23, 46, 47, 345, 351–52
Rainville, Captain, 386, 415
Rancennes, France, 203
Raynal, Guillaume, 14 and n., 194
Reformation, 4
Regnaud de Saint-Jean d'Angély, Comte de, 96
Régnier, Captain, 366
Reichenau, Switzerland, 421
Reischag (Reischach), Count von, 334 and n.
Rémaucourt, France, 240
Rennepont, Captain de, 382, 385
Rennes, France, 24, 25
Republic, the, xiv, xvi, xxiii, 54, 69, 99, 132, 154, 196 n., 246, 290 n., 291 n., 323, 353 n., 362 n., 404 n.
republicans, xv, 98–100, 103–04, 115, 150 and n., 154, 167, 195, 228 n., 236, 254, 364
Restoration, xvii, xxv, 391 n., 392 n., 431–33, 438
Rethel-Mazarin, France, 240, 277
Réveillon factory riot, 27 and n., 28 and n., 29
Révigny-aux-Vaches, France, 273–74
Revolutionary Tribunal, 211 n., 228 n., 243, 355 n., 378, 397–98 and n.
Rewbell, Colonel, 284 n.
Rheims, France, 273 n., 274, 277, 281, 321
Rhineland, 162, 172

Richardot, Colonel, 211 and n.
Richardson, Samuel: Pamela, 11 and n.
Richelieu, Armand-Jean du Plessis, Cardinal de, 5 and n.
Richemont, France, 242, 263–64, 266
Richmond, England, 391 n.
Riegels, Germany, 439–40
Rime, Mlle (subgoverness), 10 n., 12
Robecq, Prince de, 19
Robert, Pierre-François-Joseph, 74, 399 n.
Robespiéristes, 67–68, 74
Robespierre, Maximilien de, xiii, xv, xvii, xxix, 16 n., 66, 100, 160, 171, 243, 249, 256, 298, 398 n.
Rochambeau, General de, 203 and n., 206, 208 and n.
Rochambeau, Marquise de, 138
Rochambeau, Jean-Baptiste-Donatien, Marshal de, 137–43, 145–47, 165–66 and n., 177–78, 199–203, 206–13, 238
Rochefort, Luxembourg, 262
Rodemack, France, 265
Roederer, Pierre-Louis, 65, 71, 224, 250–51
Roland de la Platière, Jean-Marie, 98, 180, 198, 216, 221 and n., 222, 263 n., 305
Roland de la Platière, Manon-Philipon, 180
Roll, Baron de, 440–41
Rome, ancient, xxxii, 4, 16, 27
Rosière, General, 217, 330, 331
Rothenbourg, Colonel, 284 n.
Rouen, France, 24, 42, 247 n.
Rousseau, Jean-Jacques, xxviii, 14–15, 27, 194; Discourse on Inequality, 26; Émile, xxvii, 17 and n.; Institutions of Poland, The, 88 n.; Social Contract, The, 26, 88 n., 193 n.
Roussel, M. (army officer), 135 n.
royalists, 126–27, 132, 150, 151 n., 152–53, 154, 184, 193, 248, 348, 353 n., 393 and n., 422 n., 432; see also émigrés; nobility
Ruault, General, 371, 383
Rumégies, France, 413–14
Russia, 455–56

Sabatier, Abbé, 22, 24
Sabrevoix, General, 386
Sahuguet d'Espagnac, Colonel de, 141, 212, 268
Saint-Amand, France, xxviii, 145, 215, 237, 238, 399, 400 and n., 401, 403 n., 406, 407, 409, 413–14
Saint-Brice, Mme de, 261
Saint-Cloud, Château de, 8, 121, 189
Saint-Dizier, France, 275
Sainte-Menehould, France, 90, 270–72, 276, 277 n., 279–81, 285–86, 289 n., 291 n., 292–93, 295, 296, 297, 320
Sainte-Pélagie prison, 260
Saint-Firmin, Colonel, 411 and n.

473

Saint-Germain, Claude-Louis, Comte de, 452 and *n*.
Saint-Ghislain, Belgium, 333
Saint-Just, Antoine-Louis de, 265, 353 *n*.
Saint-Leu, France, 9, 18, 29, 30, 46–48, 77, 79
Saint-Malo, France, 24
Saint-Mihiel, France, 273 *n*., 275
Saint-Omer, France, 143, 145
Saint-Pardoux, M. (army officer), 415
Saint-Petersburg, Russia, 454
Saint-Pierremont, France, 272
Saint-Pieterswoluwe, Belgium, 340
Saint-Priest, Comte de, 437–40, 444
Saint-Sauve, France, 207–09
Saint-Simon, Louis de Rouvroy, Duc de, 67 *n*.
Saint-Thomas, France, 279, 320
Saint-Trond, Belgium, 372–75, 381, 386
Santerre, Antoine, 250
Santo Domingo, 25
Sardinia, King of, 289 *n*., 446–47
Sarre-la-Brousse, M. de (army officer), 139
Saultain, France, 211
Sausse, Jean-Baptiste, 90–94
Savonnières, M. de, 58
Savoy, 315, 341
Saxe, Maurice, Marshal de, 294 and *n*., 342, 366, 370
Saxe-Coburg, Frederick-Josias, Duke of, 342 and *n*., 370, 382, 384 *n*., 394–95, 409, 412, 414–16
Schauenbourg, General, 275, 285, 288
Schérer, Captain Barthélemy-Louis, 267 and *n*.
séance royale, 22 and *n*., 33, 39, 157
Sedan, France, 237, 243, 262, 263, 269–72, 323
Ségur, Philippe-Henri, Marquis de, 18 *n*.
Senarmont, General, 284 *n*.
Senuc, France, 277
Seraincourt, France, 239
Sercey, Henriette de, 10, 11, 12, 17, 25, 83, 144, 399, 407, 417
Sergeant (Sergent-Marceau), 74
Servan de Gerbey, Joseph, 123, 214, 216, 220–22, 263 *n*., 304–05, 311
1789 Club, 65-66, 71, 75, 79–80, 91 *n*., 97, 100, 198, 316
Shakespeare, William, 3, 123
Sierck, France, 265
Siéyès, Abbé Emmanuel-Joseph, 26, 31, 65, 71, 72, 111 *n*., 253 *n*.
Sillery, Marquis de, *see* Genlis, Comte de
Siret, M., 136 and *n*.
Society for the Friends of the Constitution, *see* Jacobin Club
Soissons, France, 27, 223, 227, 321, 327–28

Soleure, Switzerland, 391 *n*.
Someruelos, Marquis of, 423
Somme-Bionne, France, 284
Somme-Suippes, France, 321
Somme-Yèvre, France, 286
Southampton, England, 455
Souvarov, M. (army officer), 455
Spa, Belgium, xxviii, 17–21
Spain, 4, 378, 422–25; Bourbon branch of, 67 and *n*., 422–23
Sparre, General de, 281, 286
Speyer, Bishop of, 162
Stadtholder of the Netherlands, *see* William V
Starray, General, 331, 333
Stenay, France, 271–72
Stendhal: *Rouge et le noir, Le,* xxv *n*.
Stengel, General Henri, 272, 278, 281–83, 285, 330, 333, 340–41, 342, 370, 373, 375
Stetenhof, General, 330
Stockholm, Sweden, 437
Strasbourg, France, 215, 238, 243, 265, 275, 296–97
Stuarts (royal family), 5
Suleau, François-Louis, 248 *n*.
Sweden, 97 and *n*., 392
Swiss Guards, 22, 27, 29, 42, 46, 49, 53, 119 and *n*., 122, 219 *n*., 220 and *n*., 246–47 and *n*., 250, 251–52, 255, 440
Switzerland, 298, 341, 346, 352 *n*., 392 and *n*., 409, 414, 416–17

Talleyrand-Périgord, Charles-Maurice de, 65, 71, 78, 146 *n*., 426 *n*.
Tallien, Jean-Lambert, 249, 260, 354 *n*.
Tannay, France, 272
Taupin (orderly), 406
Temple, the, Paris, xxxiii, 38, 122, 186 *n*., 254 and *n*., 261, 310, 328, 353, 393, 404 *n*., 438
Tennis Court Oath, 31
Terror, Reign of, xv, 257–58, 313, 391, 393 *n*., 394, 421, 438, 446; Indulgents try to reduce, 105 *n*.; murder without trial in, 307, 398; and National Convention, 378, 398 and *n*.; Revolutionary Committees of, 77 and *n*.; Revolutionary Tribunal of, 211 *n*., 228 *n*., 243, 355 *n*., 378, 397–98 and *n*.; September massacres of, xxiii, 257, 259–61, 307–08, 310; suspicion of crime equal to guilt in, 161 and *n*., 199, 378
Thermidor, xv, 398 *n*.
Thévenard, Comte, 183
Thionville, France, 242, 243 and *n*., 265, 266, 269, 453
Third Estate, xi, 43 and *n*., 97 *n*.; in Estates-General, xiii, 26 and *n*., 28, 31–33, 43 *n*., 69, 443–44 and *n*.; in National Assembly, 39, 41, 49, 53, 65, 66, 69, 316

474

Thouret, Jacques-Guillaume, 65, 157
Thouvenot, General, 270–71, 285, 288, 290 *n.*, 338, 380, 411, 415 and *n.*
Thulin, Belgium, 331–32
Thuriot de la Rosière, Jacques-Alexis, 44, 353 *n.*
Tirlemont, Belgium, 375, 380–81, 386
Tolozan, Colonel, 281
Tongres, Belgium, 371, 374
Topin, Mme, 83
Tor de la Sonde, Benoît, 391 *n.*
Toreri, M. (army officer), 415
Toul, France, 274–75
Tournay, Belgium, 200, 206, 228, 322, 352 and *n.*, 356–59, 361–62, 365, 394, 396, 398–99, 405 *n.*, 414–15
Tours, France, 24
Tourville, Colonel, 207
Tourzel, Louise-Elizabeth, Duchesse de, 88, 261
Tourzel, Marie-Charlotte de, 261
Tousch, M. (army officer), 135 *n.*
Tracy, Antoine-Louis Destutt de, 65
Treilhard, Jean-Baptiste, 360–61, 399 *n.*
Trier, Elector of, 162–63 and *n.,* 169–70, 171, 172, 174, 177, 241, 447, 451
Trier, Germany, 340
Troyes, France, 21
Truchot, M., 260
Tubize, Belgium, 340
Tuileries palace, Paris, 42, 257, 309, 311, 401, 431, 433, 445 *n.*; Louis XVI in, 84, 88, 101 *n.*, 115, 119, 120, 123 and *n.*, 125, 155, 185, 224, 227, 237 *n.*, 244 *n.*, 246–52, 328, 445; National Assembly in, 50 and *n.*, 51, 52, 55, 59, 70, 155, 309 and *n.*
Turin, 446–47
Turkey, 392
Tuscany, 392
Twickenham, England, xxiii, 429

Uckange, France, 266
Uhlans, 203–04, 207, 324
United States, 4, 365, 391 *n.*, 392; Constitution of, 27, 194, 253 *n.*; emigration to, 318, 351, 354–56, 359, 404, 417; independence struggle of, 4, 99, 137 and *n.*, 139, 194, 228 *n.*, 318; Louis-Philippe in, xxiii, 421–22, 423
Urquijo (Spanish official), 423

Valabris, Colonel de, 141
Valence, Comtesse de, 10, 90 *n.*, 93 *n.*, 404 *n.*
Valence, General de, 21, 79, 90 *n.*, 215, 216–18, 228, 230–32, 242, 275, 281–83, 285, 288, 328, 341, 366, 371–75, 380–82, 384–86, 402 and *n.*, 403, 404 *n.*, 413, 426 *n.*
Valenciennes, France, 20, 136–43, 145–46, 147, 166 *n.*, 200, 201–03, 210, 211, 213, 214–15, 233, 238, 241–42,

322–23, 329, 330, 333 *n.*, 344, 399–400, 409–10, 411 *n.*, 413
Valmy, France, ix, xiii, xxii, xxxiii, 281–87, 292, 295, 296, 306, 320, 433
Valois Kings, 5
Varennes, France, xii, 85, 87, 90 and *n.*, 91–95, 119, 173, 228 *n.*, 237 *n.*, 240, 253, 271–72, 324, 445, 451
Varoux, Belgium, 342
Vau, France, 243
Vaublanc, Comte de, 162
Vaux, France, 267, 270–72, 277–78
Vendée, France, 454, 455; uprising in, 151 *n.*, 193, 378, 393 and *n.*, 394
Vendôme, France, xii, xxii, 84–87, 88 *n.*, 94 *n.*, 95 *n.*, 134–36, 137
Venice, 392, 439
Venlo, Belgium, 375
Verdun, France, 240, 243, 259, 267, 269–71, 273, 276, 280, 322, 453
Vergniaud, Pierre-Victurnien, 159, 178–79, 234–35 and *n.*, 237, 313, 319 *n.*
Vernet, Horace, 336
Vernon, Simon-François, Colonel de, 21
Versailles, xvii, 29, 46, 49, 119, 189 and *n.*, 220 *n.*, 260 and *n.*; Estates-General at, 27, 28, 30–40; National Assembly at, 42, 46, 49–53, 57, 67, 69; troops at, 41, 42, 49, 52–53, 58, 446; uprising of October 5 at, 55–59, 445
Vestris (dancing master), 9
Vevelghem, Belgium, 216–17
Victoria, Queen of England, xxv, 425
Vienna, Court of, 169–70, 172–73, 175–76, 181, 234, 244
Vienne, M. Lefranc de Pompignan, Archbishop of, 41
Vienne-le-Château, France, 279
Villars, Colonel, 337
Villers-Cotterêts chateau, xxxi, 22–23
Vilmet, M. (army officer), 135 *n.*
Vincennes, France, 190
Vioménil, Baron de, 127, 129 *n.*
Vitry-le-François, France, 275, 280, 281, 296
Void, France, 275
Voidel, Jean-Georges-Charles, 144
Voilemont, France, 285–86
Volney, Constantin-François, 71
Voltaire, 7, 194
Vouziers, France, 240, 276–77, 280

Wagram, Prince de, 203 *n.*
Waldeck, Prince of, 453
Washington, George, 318
Wasmes, Belgium, 204
Wasnielles, Belgium, 204
Wavre, Belgium, 376
Weissembourg, France, 243
Werwicke, Belgium, 216
Wesel, Germany, 362
Willemstad, Holland, 375

475

William III, King of England, 382
William V, Stadtholder of the Netherlands, 18 *n*., 363
Wimpfen, General Félix de, 103, 242 and *n*., 453
Wisch, Colonel Von der, 384
Wittgenstein, M. de (army officer), 165
Wolfenbüttel, Germany, 427

Worms, Germany, 132, 448, 451
Wurmser, Marshal, 378

Yonck, France, 272
York, Duke of, 377
Yypres, Belgium, 200

Zinzendorf, Count von, 207